The Rise and Decline of England's Watchmaking Industry, 1550–1930

This survey of the rise and decline of English watchmaking fills a gap in the historiography of British industry. Clerkenwell in London was supplied with 'rough movements' from Prescot, 200 miles away in Lancashire. Smaller watchmaking hubs later emerged in Coventry, Liverpool, and Birmingham. The English industry led European watch-making in the late eighteenth century in output, and its lucrative export markets extended to the Ottoman Empire and China. It also made marine chronometers, the most complex of hand-crafted pre-industrial mechanisms, crucially important to the later hegemony of Britain's navy and merchant marine. Although Britain was the 'workshop of the world', its watchmaking industry declined. Why? First, because cheap Swiss watches were smuggled into British markets. Later, in the era of Free Trade, they were joined by machine-made watches from factories in America, enabled by the successful application to watch production of the 'American system' in Waltham, Massachusetts after 1858. The Swiss watch industry adapted itself appropriately, expanded, and reasserted its lead in the world's markets. English watchmaking did not: its trajectory foreshadowed and was later followed by other once-prominent British industries. Clerkenwell retained its pre-industrial production methods. Other modernization attempts in Britain had limited success or failed.

Dr Alun C. Davies, was educated at the universities of Aberystwyth and Princeton and retired in 1999 after thirty-three years at The Queen's University of Belfast as Reader (and sometime Head of Department) in the Department of Economic and Social History.

Routledge Studies in Modern British History

Provincial Police Reform in Early Victorian England
Cambridge, 1835–1856
Roger Swift

Diplomatic Identity in Postwar Britain
The Deconstruction of the Foreign Office 'Type', 1945–1997
James Southern

The Development of British Naval Aviation, 1914–1918
Alexander Howlett

Britain and the Puzzle of European Union
Andrew Duff

The British Aircraft Industry and American-led Globalisation
1943–1982
Takeshi Sakade

British Responses to Genocide
The British Foreign Office and Humanitarianism in the Ottoman Empire, 1918–1923
Amy E. Grubb and Elisabeth Hope Murray

The British Jesus, 1850–1970
Meredith Veldman

The Rise and Decline of England's Watchmaking Industry, 1550–1930
Alun C. Davies

For more information about this series, please visit: https://www.routledge.com/history/series/RSMBH

The Rise and Decline of England's Watchmaking Industry, 1550–1930

Alun C. Davies

Routledge
Taylor & Francis Group
NEW YORK AND LONDON

First published 2022
by Routledge
605 Third Avenue, New York, NY 10158

and by Routledge
4 Park Square, Milton Park, Abingdon, Oxon, OX14 4RN

Routledge is an imprint of the Taylor & Francis Group, an informa business

Library of Congress Cataloging-in-Publication Data
Names: Davies, Alun C., 1938- author.
Title: The rise and decline of England's watchmaking industry, 1550-1930 / Alun C. Davies.
Description: New York, NY : Routledge, 2022. |
Series: Routledge studies in modern British history | Includes bibliographical references and index.
Identifiers: LCCN 2021052664 (print) | LCCN 2021052665 (ebook) | ISBN 9781032131344 (hardback) | ISBN 9781032131351 (paperback) | ISBN 9781003227823 (ebook) | ISBN 9781000571875 (adobe pdf) | ISBN 9781000571905 (epub)
Subjects: LCSH: Clock and watch making—Great Britain—History. | Clock and watch industry—Great Britain—History.
Classification: LCC HD9999.C583 G733 2022 (print) | LCC HD9999.C583 (ebook) | DDC 338.4/76811140942—dc23/eng/20211108
LC record available at https://lccn.loc.gov/2021052664
LC ebook record available at https://lccn.loc.gov/2021052665

ISBN: 978-1-032-13134-4 (hbk)
ISBN: 978-1-032-13135-1 (pbk)
ISBN: 978-1-003-22782-3 (ebk)

DOI: 10.4324/9781003227823

Typeset in Sabon
by codeMantra

For

Carolyn

Kim and Kate

And to the memory of my parents and Menna

Ten Quotations That Help to Tell the Story

'In the making of a Watch, If one man shall make the Wheels, another the Spring, another shall engrave the Dial-plate, and another shall make the Cases, then the watch will be better and cheaper, than if the whole Work be put upon any one Man. And we also see that in Towns, and in the Streets of a great town, where all the Inhabitants are almost of one trade, the Commodity peculiar to those places is made better and cheaper than elsewhere.'

Sir William Petty, '*Another Essay on Political Arithmetic Concerning the Growth of the City of London,* 1682'

'They have invented that Curious Engine for the Cutting the Teeth of a Wheel, whereby that part of the Work is done with an exactness which farr exceeds that which can be performed by hand: then there is an engine for equalling the Ballance Wheel; Likewise the Engine for cutting the turnes of the Fusie; and lastly the Instrument for drawing of the steel pinion wier: All which ingenious Inventions were first conceived and made at *Leverpool* in *Lancashire* in *England.*'

John Carte, *Horology and Cosmology: A Transcription ... of Bodleian Library Ms Carte,* 1703

'I think I may make bold to say that there is neither any other Mechanical or Mathematical thing in the world that is more beautiful or curious in texture than this my watch or Timekeeper for the Longitude... and I heartily thank Almighty God that I have lived so long, as in some measure to complete it.'

John Harrison, *An Explanation of my Watch or Timekeeper for the Longitude...* (7 Apr 1763).

'[in the 1860s] I commenced work in my father's movement making shop in which were a few hands for assembling the parts as they came in from outside workers. These workers were scattered over an area of some six or seven miles, without any public means of conveyance. We had no recognised gauges in the trade, each movement maker having his own arbitrary standards. Therefore, after the frames were made, we had to carry them about from workshop to workshop in order to have all the other parts made to each individual frame. On going to Liverpool to finish my apprenticeship, I found this same system in vogue among the watch manufacturers; indeed the wastefulness was intensified as, instead of carrying about in dozens, as in Prescot, we carried them one by one.'

T.P. Hewitt, Speech on 12 Jan. 1893, in Alan Smith, *The Lancashire Watch Company (1973)*

'The losses of the *Minotaur, St George, Defence, Hero,* and *Grasshopper* to the want of timekeepers to ascertain their longitude ... Can it be believed ... that if there had been only one good chronometer on board the *Hero* or the *Grasshopper*, that they could have made a mistake of near two degrees and a half, or ten minutes of time, in their longitude?'

'A naval Captain', letter on chronometers, *The Naval Chronicle* (1812).

'[On factory production] 'I am persuaded that there is no more possibility of competition between the two than there is between the power loom and the old spinning wheel; ... we might as well try to restore the packhorse as a substitute for the railway or the canal. Other nations will adopt new discoveries if we do not; and your own case, my fear, I confess, would be not the disturbance of existing interests at Coventry or Clerkenwell, but the utter extinction of their trade, by the transfer, to Paris or Geneva, of Mr Ingold's machines.'

H.G. Ward, letter in *The Times,* 13 April 1843

'It must be obvious to anyone that such a system [applied in Waltham] directed by Yankee skill and ingenuity, must very nearly approach perfection, and greatly excel handicraft production ... Ordinary workers with a little training could supervise the machines: not one... need be a watchmaker.'

Horological Journal, vol.1 no. 1 (September 1858)

'My own settled conviction is that the failure of English horological art, our finest mechanical trade, would foreshadow the decay of all out mechanical industries.'

Henry Ganney, 'Report of Watch and Clock Making', *Artisan Reports on the Paris Universal Exhibition of 1878* (London: Society of Arts, 1879)

'[The] practical question is not how good a watch it is possible to make, as how cheaply can you make a watch of the first class. One has long been able to get as good as watch as can be made from Frodsham or Jurgensen by paying from $300 to $500 for it. What the world has gained from [Waltham's watchmaking] revolution is the ability to command a watch equal, or but little inferior, to the best, but at less than half the old price.'

['S.N.'], 'The Watchmaking Industry in Switzerland', *Science: The American Association for the Advancement of Science*, 1/11 (April 1883)

'The wages paid, and the prices obtained for the work of our trade, do not bear comparison with those of any other whatsoever. Here you have a really skilled man doing, in many cases, beautiful work for prices that a bicycle repairer would have a good laugh at.'

Horological Journal 24/2 (October 1891), 23

Contents

Figures

Tables

Preface

The French historian Emmanuel Le Roy Ladurie observed that some historians are either truffle hunters or parachutists. The noses of the former are buried in the tiniest details revealed by artefacts or preserved in archival documents. They dig deeply to uncover hitherto unseen treasures and know a lot about a little. Parachutists, on the other hand, see the broad lie of the land and the major landmarks; they hang high in the air, looking for general patterns in the landscape of the past, far below them. They know a little about a lot, but are often hazy about detail. Sometimes the comparisons are about those who use microscopes or telescopes. In this overview of the rise and fall of England's traditional watchmaking industry I have tried to use a microscope for some chapters (Chapter 9), for others a telescope (Chapter 15), but mostly a bit of both.

England's watchmaking industry is a topic largely neglected in the historiography of British industry. Its trajectory foreshadowed and was later followed by other once-prominent British industries. This monograph advances David Landes's findings about English horology in his *Revolution in Time: Clocks and the Making of the Modern World* (1983). The present book is not about horological technology, but about a consumer durable that people wanted, about why they wanted it, and how it was supplied. My approach is not that of an horologist, for the achievements of English clock and watchmakers are well recorded by antiquarian horologists in books and articles on leading makers and their products. My perspective is that of an historian, using basic and easily understood economics concepts such as demand, supply, productivity, markets, tariffs, free trade, and so on.

The industry emerged in the sixteenth century, matured in the seventeenth, reached its golden age in the eighteenth, declined in the nineteenth, and died in the twentieth. The book's three parts have a chronological sequence. Part 1 surveys the emergence of the industry's four English hubs and the features of its golden age. Part 2 addresses smuggling, protective tariffs, and the French wars – the challenges that triggered the industry's initial decline. Part 3 describes how after Free Trade in 1860 the decline accelerated. Swiss watches were joined in British markets by American machine-made watches, following the successful application in Waltham, Massachusetts in 1858 of the 'American system of manufacture'. The Swiss watch industry adapted itself appropriately and gradually and, by 1914, regained its leadership in the world's markets. But watchmakers in Clerkenwell ignored the mass market growing around them. Its firms persisted with hand-craft methods to supply a small, luxury market with traditional, expensive watches. The industry's new institution, the BHI, resisted machine-tool instruction in its training for apprentices until it was too late. Apart from Alan Smith's work on the *Liverpool Watch Company* (1973), there is little on the efforts by the other watchmaking hubs in Birmingham, Coventry, and Liverpool to modernise by adapting features of the American system. Their attempts achieved limited but mostly unsuccessful consequences. Britain's domestic, foreign, and imperial markets were left to the Swiss and Americans. Despite English watchmaking's decline, its firms still dominated the world's small market for chronometers. The Great War temporarily revived the industry but thereafter Britain's traditional mechanical watchmaking industry entered its terminal phase.

The title, *The Rise and Decline of England's Watchmaking Industry, 1550–1930,* is what the book is about. It was an 'English' watchmaking industry – but a 'British' market. As a Welshman I know about the old *Encyclopaedia* entry 'For Wales, see England'. The short-lived making of watches in Wales in the late nineteenth century was not manifestation of a 'Welsh watchmaking industry', any more than earlier the finishing of watches in Edinburgh and Dublin indicated 'Scottish' or 'Irish' watchmaking industries with clear-cut national characteristics. 'English watches' – with or without fusees – were the products of an industry distinct from their equivalents made in Switzerland (often in imitation) and later in the United States. It was an English industry, but the markets were British.

Acknowledgements

Over the last forty years I published papers that became building blocks for the present monograph. When writing those I incurred many obligations. Those who kindly replied to emails from an horological 'outsider', a 'non-techie', included many from the *Antiquarian Horological Society*, namely Jonathan Betts, Ian Greaves, John Griffiths, Pierantonio Maragna, Günther Oestmann, David Penney, Alan Treherne, and Anthony J. Turner. I hasten to add that none were involved in constructing the present monograph. Three scholars whose own horological publications are seminal also gave encouragement: they were the late Alan Smith (Manchester), the late Theo Barker (LSE), and the late David Landes (Harvard). When I started putting together this monograph a few years ago, Julian Holland, Roger Smith, and David Thompson read drafts of some early chapters. Bill Linnard also read most. Later, James Nye (Chairman of the AHS), John Griffiths, and David Penney helped me to assemble illustrations, as did Peter de Clercq (editor of *Antiquarian Horology*). He, like his predecessors, had long encouraged an 'horological outsider' to publish papers on the industry's ups and downs. I am very grateful to all for their help. The conventional disclaimer applies: any remaining errors of fact or interpretation are mine.

My research was supported by the Queen's University of Belfast. Its Library conveniently contained a complete set of British Parliamentary Papers, and its Inter Library Loan desk made available a stream of sometimes obscure publications, long before the days of DOIs. At Queen's, I owe a great debt to friends and colleagues in the former Economic & Social History Department. Ken Brown read early drafts, and three colleagues (alas, no longer with us), namely Cyril Ehrlich, David Johnston, and Jim McAllister, plied me with helpful references. Liam Kennedy was enthusiastically supportive and a former colleague, Eddie Hunt, offered valuable suggestions. Above all, with enormous patience, Leslie Clarkson, long after our retirements, offered constructive suggestions and helpful comments. I am grateful to all. My penultimate thanks go to Steve Mayer of Poole, who rescued me from my computer on innumerable occasions. My greatest thanks go to Carolyn, for her benign tolerance and support of my preoccupation.

Aberystwyth
and
The Queen's University of Belfast (1966–1999)

Part 1

Rise

1 Origins

From Craft to Industry

Time consciousness and effective demand

Watches are portable personal devices that tell the time. The emergence and growth of the craft that became England's watchmaking industry entailed two necessary conditions. The first was an awareness and acceptance of 'mean time', an understanding of 'equal hours', or what we call 'clock time', shown by pointers on a dial that display numbers from 1 to 12, for hours that, today, start at midnight or noon.[1] Clock time is different from 'solar time', in different places indicated by a sundial; it reflects the passage of time based on the Sun's position in the sky.[2] The first clocks appeared in Europe in the late thirteenth century, and 'Mean Time' (another phrase for 'mean solar time') followed in the fourteenth century.[3] It gradually became accepted as public clocks increased in numbers. By the sixteenth century clockmaking was well established in England, France, the Low Countries, the Germanic States, and especially in cities like Genoa, where trade and commerce were well advanced.[4] But mean time was not ubiquitous and came late to some remote areas.[5]

The second necessary condition was an effective demand. ('Effective demand' is the economic principle that suggests consumer needs and desires must be accompanied by adequate purchasing power to be considered *effective*.) The first watches were expensive luxuries. A sufficient level of demand was present in the Tudor royal court, and it spread to prosperous London. The seeds of the industry were probably first sown by Henry VIII. His 'inquiring mind' was interested in astronomy, and he purchased 'clokkes and dialles' from France and the Low Countries, although there was no evidence yet of watches.[6] But watches appeared in royal and noble inventories during the latter part of the reign of Henry's daughter, Queen Elizabeth I. They were imported. An account of the jewellery of Elizabeth revealed twenty-four watches including one made in the shape of the ensign of the Order of the Garter. Dozens more were owned by her courtiers.[7] One of the Queen's watches cost £12, but although 'it looked pretty, [it] did not keep time'. Others were 'shaped like walnute and pomegranate'.[8] They required frequent cleaning, adjustment, and repair, which explained the presence after 1554 in the royal

DOI: 10.4324/9781003227823-2

court of immigrant Huguenot clockmakers. Three prominent foreign clockmakers who were listed among the 'strangers' in 1571 in London were also 'heads of households'. Their number rose to eight in 1593.[9] Thereafter, London's small horological trade in clocks and watches grew.

The nascent craft acquired respectability when Nicolas Kratzer became Henry VIII's royal clockmaker. Elizabeth appointed Bartholomew Newsam as her royal clockmaker in 1590; he was succeeded by Randolph Bull. Newsam and Bull were prominent amongst the growing number of horological craftsmen attracted to London by a demand for watches greater than that initially stimulated by the patronage of the royal court.[10] As the economist Alfred Marshall observed, the emergence of an industry and its location were often the result of 'the rich folk there assembled [who] made a demand for goods of an especially high quality and this attracts skilled workmen from a distance and educates those on the spot'.[11] For any new industry to evolve commercially, like clock and watchmaking, an initial minimum level of demand was needed to cover the costs of development and construction. The sheer expense and difficulties involved in making and then maintaining a complicated mechanical timekeeper, of whatever size, limited the market to individuals and institutions that could afford them, like wealthy members of royal courts, the church, and the rich.

European origins of mechanical horology

Mechanical clocks had been invented in Europe in the thirteenth century and are among the most important technological inventions in the history of the world. They initially spread in response to demands from the Church to indicate the time for those at prayer.[12] Then they were used in commerce as devices for measuring the passing of time. Joel Mokyr concluded that 'here was a "macro invention" if ever there was one': it was a clear break from existing technology.[13] By the end of the fourteenth century, at least seven devices described as 'horologia' had been installed in England, including elaborate examples at cathedrals in Salisbury (1386), and Wells (1392–93).[14] The number of cathedrals with clocks increased, and parish church clocks followed: apparently ninety-eight were built between 1336 and 1400, and another sixty-five in the fifteenth century with seventy-five more in the sixteenth century. Glennie and Thrift concluded that most documented parishes possessed working clocks 'at some stage between 1400 and 1700' and that by the beginning of the eighteenth century 'most English parishes had clocks'.[15] The next phase in the growing acceptance of clock time came when prosperous individuals commissioned 'household clocks' for daily timekeeping. For their owners, a clock combined function and prestige; it impressed visitors and regulated daily routine.[16] In England, the most popular domestic version was the lantern clocks that appeared at the beginning of the seventeenth century; with parish church clocks, they reinforced the awareness and acceptance of 'mean time' and equal hours.[17] This helped the demand for further miniaturisation, in the form of watches.

A public clock gives time to a community, a domestic clock gives time to the household, but a watch is personal. Watches had first appeared in Europe in about 1510 or possibly earlier and surviving examples date from about the middle of the sixteenth century. They were hung on straps or chains around the neck or waist. The first watches seem crude and inaccurate little timekeepers, compared to later examples, but they were the most sophisticated of contemporary machines. Some sixteenth-century wheel work was finely made and often had striking mechanisms, alarms, and calendar indications. Some watches were cylindrical; later ones were drum-shaped and then oval. Those with fusees (see below) ran for maybe sixteen hours, whilst German stackfreed watches commonly ran for thirty hours or more. Gradually, brass and steel were substituted for iron, and movements were reduced in size. Watchmakers were distinguished from clockmakers by the far higher level of skills that they developed. Both kinds of skills coexisted in some workshops but, as demand for watches grew, distinctions between watchmakers and clockmakers widened because small, intricate mechanisms were more difficult to make than large clocks. Difficulties of manufacture and assembly increase in inverse proportion to the desired size. Watches were expensive possessions whose construction, assembly, and repair were complicated. Initially, only a few metalworkers were sufficiently adept at making the miniaturised mechanisms; after each windup, watches needed re-setting, for which some in France were guided by the inclusion of sundials inside their cases.[18] Portability carried a price. A clock or watch driven by a spring was less accurate than a stationary clock powered by falling weights. The inherent difficulty with an unwinding spring was its uneven driving force: a spring exerted a greater power at the beginning of its 'unwind' than at its end, unless its 'escape' could be well controlled. In the fifteenth century, two innovations successfully addressed the problem of regulating the uneven torque of an unwinding spring.

First was the fusee, invented by an unknown craftsman sometime in the early fifteenth century, perhaps inspired by a similar contrivance used to operate crossbows.[19] It was a cone-shaped barrel inserted between the spring and the gearing, with a spiral groove whose diameter varied sufficiently to offer a nearly perfect adjustment to an unevenly unwinding spring (Figure 1.1). The fusee's technical elegance led G.H. Baillie to say, 'Perhaps no problem in mechanics has ever been solved so simply and so perfectly'.[20]

Fusees were noticeably better at controlling 'an unwinding spring than its near contemporary, the stackfreed was an eccentric cam … engaged by [a] long spring-loaded roller arm … to compensate for the decline in the mainspring's force as it unwound'. The stackfreed was devised specifically for watches and was used for about a century, mostly by German watchmakers. Clutton and Daniels described it as 'a most brutal arrangement.[21]

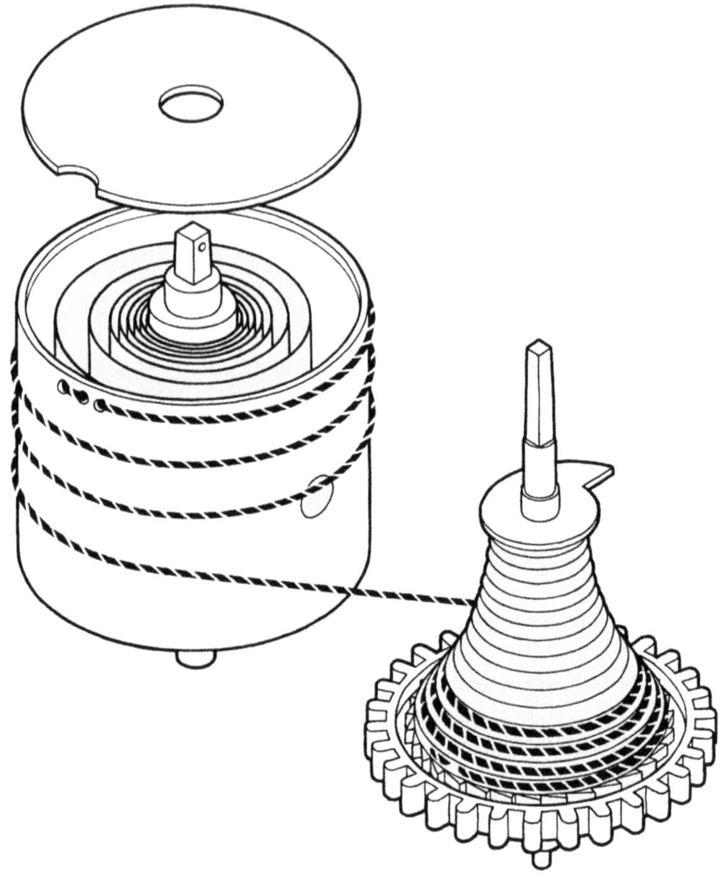

Figure 1.1 Fusee and barrel. Copyright: David Penney. http://www.antiquewatchstore.com/.

Demand widens from court to metropolis

The level of demand for clocks and watches throughout Europe depended on local economic conditions. Gradually, between the extremes of very rich and very poor, there emerged a *bourgeoisie*, a middling class of merchants and traders, lawyers, and doctors. They grew into a category of (mostly) urban dwellers sufficiently large and prosperous to 'afford decent houses, good clothes, and a few amenities of life' that included clocks and watches.[22] As this group enlarged, so did the numbers of skilled craftsmen to make and repair those commodities. In clocks, a division of labour emerged between specialists who made different parts. In England, the division in watchmaking also acquired geographical dimensions, when 'rough movements' were made 200 miles away from London, in Prescot, Lancashire. They were assembled and 'finished' in the district that later became known as Clerkenwell, not too distant from the royal court and near the centre of London's flourishing market (Chapter 2). Unsurprisingly, the earliest London-made watches that have survived resembled those made and bought in Flanders and the Southern Netherlands, largely because that is from where the horological immigrants to England came.[23] Similar clusters of watchmakers prospered in European cities, notably Augsburg, Munich, and Nuremberg, in towns in the Low Countries, and in Paris and Blois (where the French court often resided).

London's expanding market

Royal and aristocratic patronage was not the only explanation for the emergence of London's market for watches. Demands exerted by the city's economic and commercial expansion were felt in every area. Professor Wrigley observed that 'access to the London market was the making of many a manufacturer and a forcing house of change in methods of manufacture'.[24] London's population in 1550 was about 75,000; it rose rapidly to 'at least 200,000 by 1600' and had become the biggest and wealthiest city in Europe.[25] By 1650, it had doubled again, to approximately 400,000. By 1700 London was nineteen times the size of Norwich, and twenty-five times that of Bristol. Ten per cent of England's population lived there. Levels of effective demand from the court, government, and private purchasers for luxuries like watches grew there at a rate unmatched elsewhere in Britain. London was the seat of the royal court, parliament, and judiciary and its port the hub of internal and overseas trade. Its proximity to these institutions offered a comparatively immense marketplace for specialist, luxury, and semi-luxury consumer goods, and especially of luxury trades. The magnet of the metropolis favoured cultural innovations and business enterprises and attracted artisans, craftsmen, designers, and inventors who constructed buildings, machines, and instruments. The city became the centre for the production and consumption of an extraordinarily wide range of products. They included commodities, like clocks and watches, that needed regular servicing and repairs that, as Professor Fisher pointed out, 'were best carried on in the capital that formed their largest market… in close proximity to the consumer'.[26]

Immigrant horologists

As London's horological market grew, it attracted immigrants including Huguenots who migrated from France to escape its religious wars. They set up business in the 'Liberties', the area around the edge of the city, extending about three miles from the Tower of London to Fleet Street. It was 'an ambiguous geopolitical domain' over which the jurisdiction of the Lord Mayor, sheriffs, and Common Council had theoretical authority but little real control.[27] The immigrants were unpopular amongst native-born artisans and in 1622 over eighty 'native' horological craftsmen (including sixteen watchmakers) had tried to prevent the importation of foreign timepieces.[28] They complained that twenty-four overseas rivals (nearly all Huguenots) competed unfairly because their businesses were established without permission.[29] They claimed that the newcomers' poor quality of work defrauded the public because 'inferior' movements were put into good cases. For self-protection, they attempted to establish a guild.[30] Their first petition was unsuccessful, but five years later another was submitted. It asked that French clockmakers be denied the *letters patent* needed to set up shop in the city. Finally, in August 1631, a royal charter was granted that incorporated the Worshipful Company of Clockmakers.[31] It became the fifty-eighth craft guild in London.[32]

Worshipful Company of Clockmakers

Guilds had been established in several European cities in the Middle Ages by craftsmen who wanted to restrict competition and control apprenticeship before admitting new members ('freemen') to their trade.[33] By the seventeenth century, the new trades of makers of spectacles, guns, tobacco pipes, and framework knitters had their own guilds in London. These crafts all had a division of labour in their workshops that combined with a putting-out system which employed independent outworkers. A similar pattern of production evolved among London's clock and watchmakers.[34] Parts of the new horological guild's constitution were borrowed from earlier European clockmakers guilds. That in Paris, established in 1544, had about twenty master clockmakers; Blois, created in 1597 had about forty-five by 1639.[35] One of the largest was in Augsburg, with about forty-three master clockmakers in 1615 and as many journeymen. The charter for London's new guild in 1631 had sixty-three statutes that authorised the election of a Master, three Wardens, and ten Assistants to oversee the 'Fellowship of the Art and Mysterie of Clockmaking in the City of London'. It gave the guild theoretical control over those who made clocks and watches in the city within a radius of ten miles (about 300 square miles). Clockmakers in towns distant from London were comfortably outside the reach of the new guild. For example, in Grantham, ninety miles from London, that town's trade was controlled by a body of Freemen to which local clockmakers had to belong.[36] It was similar in other towns for tradesmen who wanted to practice on their own account. In Scotland, clockmakers fell under the jurisdiction of the Incorporation of Hammermen, the most powerful of Scottish trade organisations (established in Edinburgh in

1646 and Glasgow in 1649). The Hammermen included workers in any metals – blacksmiths, gunsmiths and armourers, cutlers, tinsmiths, locksmiths (who knew how to temper springs) and, of course, clockmakers. [In Scottish jargon, the word for clock was 'knock', a term used until the 1670s.[37]] The most eminent of contemporary Scottish clockmakers had already moved to the best market – London and its court. David Ramsay from Dundee was chief clockmaker to the king and became the first Master of the Clockmakers' Company in 1631.[38] Those who were members ('freedmen') of the new Worshipful Company of Clockmakers were eligible to become journeymen after their apprenticeships and helped to make clocks and watches for other people to name and sell. The Company was funded by a fee collected each quarter ('quarterage') and by 'fines' that its officials might levy if they discovered faulty workmanship, forgeries, or smuggled goods. One difference from other European horological guilds was that masterpieces from those admitted to freedoms were not obligatory. In Germany, for example, apprentices were trained to replicate elaborate clockwork 'toys'; in London young clockmakers 'could apply themselves to learning newer technology, whenever it became available'.[39] At first, this brought beneficial consequences because the Company welcomed horological innovations and believed patents might protect them. Later, it was hostile to patents.[40]

The objectives of the new guild were to control entry into the industry and to regulate the making and sale of its products. They were intentions not easy to achieve. In practice many formal regulations remained unenforced in the city and, of course, were unenforceable outside its boundaries. For example, it was intended that an apprentice's father would pay a premium to a watchmaker to train the youth for seven years, usually between age fourteen and twenty-one. The length of the term arose from the Statute of Monopolies of 1623/24, and the average cost was about £20, although premiums were not rigorously or uniformly enforced. Some fees were as low as a penny; others up to £300 or more. Apprenticeships arranged by some charities and workhouses were exempt.[41] In theory, someone who had not served an apprenticeship of seven years was not allowed to practice, and thus liable to have their clocks or watches seized. In practice, as Brian Loomes observed, 'in most provincial towns the testimony that the lad had finished his apprenticeship was usually taken as adequate proof of his ability, and he was normally allowed the freedom of the town ...' (that is, freedom to *trade* in the town).[42] In provincial towns, customs and practices varied. We will see that the watch finishing centres that emerged in Coventry and Liverpool differed from that in Clerkenwell because they reacted more to market forces than to the guild's special horological by-laws.

Adam Smith's celebrated dictum about 'the division of labour being limited by the extent of the market' explains why specialisation in the horological industry appeared – and went furthest – in London.[43] The prosperous metropolis offered a huge local market for clocks and watches and Clerkenwell's makers supplied watches to the rest of the country and abroad. In the early period, there were few provincial watchmakers. Sizable provincial towns – like Norwich or Bristol – of course had 'watchmakers' who retailed and repaired watches and, perhaps, also had acquired the skills to 'finish' a few watches whose rough movement and parts had been bought-in. All evaded interference by London's Clockmakers' Company. Like other craft guilds, the clockmakers' attempted to control the market's prices by regulating the supply of labour. Restricting the recruitment of apprentices would leave the existing horological workforce with plenty of piecework at fixed rates. If demand continued to be buoyant, it was reasoned, incomes of existing horological workers would be protected. Control over apprentices was important but difficult. Apprentices were prohibited from marrying whilst they 'served their time', and the Company asserted its right to 'turn over' apprentices to new masters if the old one died, for the remainder of their terms, but such occasions happened rarely, perhaps only three or four times a year.[44] Even when apprentices were 'out of their time' (i.e., had served the full period) they were still required, in the city of London and its Liberties, to give two more years' service, as journeymen before they could themselves become masters. It was unsurprising that some immigrants established themselves where the Company had no jurisdiction.

The theory that only two apprenticeships at a time could be attached to each master was impossible to enforce. By the end of the seventeenth century even the great Thomas Tompion, sometime Master of the Company, flouted this: during his career, he retained at least twenty-four apprentices. Some may have been journeymen and he may have circumvented the restrictions by paying 'fines' to employ others.[45] Tompion's example showed that the Company's regulations might be bypassed. Some saw the guild's customs and regulations as obstacles to innovation and growth and resented restrictions that impeded the expansion of their own workshops.[46] Again, the intention to eliminate frauds and forgeries was admirable, and the clockmakers' charter authorised it to impose fines on miscreants.[47] In practice, it proved difficult to prevent imports of cheap watches with forged signatures of London makers, even after 1682 when new by-laws were passed to reinforce these penalties.[48]

The Goldsmiths' and Blacksmiths' guilds

The Clockmakers' Company had frequent contact with two other guilds. The new guild was obliged to conform to the ancient prerogatives of the Goldsmiths' Company because all items made from precious metals – including watch cases – had to be hallmarked after 1697 at an assaying office once an appropriate 'fine' had been paid. Like clockmakers, goldsmiths were also irritated by the steady influx of foreign craftsmen.[49]

But contact with the Blacksmiths' Company was less straightforward. The founding fathers of the Clockmakers' themselves had once belonged to the Blacksmiths' guild of metal workers because iron movements of the first clocks were constructed by clock smiths who belonged to that Company. The Blacksmiths' saw the Clockmakers' as a child breaking away from a parent. There were frequent disputes and squabbles.[50] Before 1675 the Blacksmiths' Company repeatedly – and successfully – opposed the requirement that all clock and watchmakers should join the Clockmakers', and 'double allegiance' became a problem for both companies.[51] Eventually, as we shall see, it became too late to matter.

While watchmaking was still a craft, the guild's meetings were held in local taverns because the Company had no hall. At first, the Company exercised its authority effectively, and unqualified watchmakers were easily frightened off.[52] But, as demand for watches grew and the number of makers increased, the enforcement of guild regulations became difficult, especially when divisions of labour developed, and the craft became a small industry. In 1698 to try to protect the specialism of 'finishing' watch movements, the Company promoted an Act of Parliament (9 & 10 William III, c.28) 'to protect the high reputation' of its members. It wanted to prevent the export of parts (like cases and dials) unless the finished movement was also 'made up and fit to run, with the makers' name engraved thereon'. It was one of many attempts by guilds to control workmen and their products. It was an unattainable goal. If Britain's society, economy, and the population had remained static, it might have been possible. But the economy and society were changing, and the population was increasing. Rising demand for clocks and watches prompted radical technological innovations (Chapter 4) that eventually further loosened the Company's uncertain grip over its industry.

Growth of watchmaking in the seventeenth century

We do not know the value of the infant industry's output for most years after the Company's charter. But it is indisputable that it grew, despite disruption during the years of the Civil War and Commonwealth. London's horological workshops numbered about eighty in 1632 (just after the Company's founding). They had doubled by 1662, just before the Plague and the Great Fire (Table 1.1).

Almost half of London's 167 clockmakers were in Loathbury (Lothbury: the area now around the Bank of England). Sir George White has suggested that the locations were probably either workshops of lantern-clockmakers or small brass founders who supplied cast brass clock parts, finials, dial plates, and frets. Dial engravers also settled there. Special sub-divisions of labour had already emerged in making lantern clocks, the most popular and fashionable model of house clock.[53]

Table 1.1 Tuet's table. 'A list of all the clockmakers, both freemen and farreners, alians, and outliers' (sic): 26 June 1662

Blackfriars	6
Fleet Street	18
Whitefriars	2
Fleet Lane	2
Temple Bar	3
Shoreditch	4
Cannon Street	2
Chancery Lane	18
Westminster	20
Cornhill	11
Loathbury	81
Total	167

Source: LMA/CLC/L/CD/B/004/MS02732: Compiled from a list (by Edward Tuet), Court Minutes, 1632–1804, relating to the Company's authority and jurisdiction, with list of members of the Company, 26 June 1662 (arranged topographically).

A year or so after Edward Tuet compiled his table, the Plague and the Great Fire affected many horologists and their workshops. The consequences for London's people and their city were cataclysmic, but fortunately were not disastrous for the industry. The Plague left about 100,000 deaths in London in spring 1665 (three or four times higher than in non-Plague years, according to Bills of Mortality). The Great Fire caused only a handful of deaths, but property destruction was vast. Four hundred acres of the city were destroyed, and 13,000 houses were burned. They included about eighty horological workshops. Of 167 members of the Clockmakers' Company listed in 1662 'at least half worked in areas destroyed by flames ... [although] ... the progress of the flames was relatively slow and many clockmakers must have had time to carry their tools and stock from its path'.[54] The following year, 1667, saw a different kind of disruption because of war with the Netherlands. The Dutch fleet invaded Chatham and people fled. The cumulative disruptive effects of events in the 1670s caused output in all trades to fall. Despite these setbacks, the city's population growth quickly resumed, principally from internal immigration. By about 1680 the horological industry had also recovered, notably in the production of lantern clocks which 'once more became a flood': they were the 'bread-and-butter line of the average clockmaker in seventeenth century'.[55]

The high-spending Restoration court revived luxury and semi-luxury crafts, like clock and watchmaking.[56] London's economy flourished when it benefitted from a building boom propelled by expanding trade with the East Indies, and the horological industry shared in the recovery. Nearly 2,200 youths were apprenticed to the Company between 1631 and 1700. Enrolments per decade rose from under 100 in the 1630s to 600 in the 1690s.[57] Half (about 1,200) eventually became Freemen, but only about 60 per cent were bound to the Company itself. This suggests it was the industry in general that had grown faster than the Company's membership. Horological craftsmen approximately doubled in number but the Company's influence on – and power over – new recruits was weak. This was perhaps because after the Great Fire, those who made pendulum clocks in premises that were 'almost certainly unaffected by the blaze [and] their owners never bothered to obtain their Freedom'. Half of the horological workshops rebuilt after the Fire was outside the effective range of the guild's notional reach.[58]

Waning influence of the guild

The guild's influence weakened for other reasons. First, it failed to prevent the continued immigration of skilled craftsmen from abroad. In 1681 despite opposition from London's guilds, Charles II promised potential immigrants that they might set up businesses. Subsequently, over ninety Huguenot watchmakers settled in England, and opened shops in Soho and the City, from where many later migrated to Clerkenwell.[59] Second, since 1598 the Edict of Nantes had theoretically protected France's Protestant workmen from discrimination after the religious wars of the sixteenth century, but its revocation in 1685 prompted an exodus. Some 13,500 Huguenots left France for England in that year, later joined by thousands of others. London's expanding horological industry ultimately benefitted from their skills (as did those in Calvinist Geneva who made and decorated watch cases).[60] The haemorrhage of French clock and watchmakers coincided with – and perhaps helps to explain – the rise of the watch-making industry in England and its temporary relative decline in France.

An indication of the Clockmakers' weakening influence appeared when only 355 of its 594 members of the Company signed the 'Association Oath Roll', an affidavit of loyalty to the new king, William III. Possibly Catholic horologists refused to sign the oath, and Quakers refused to take oaths anyhow, because they were afraid that 'restrictions of such a nature and magnitude would [be] imposed upon them [and they would be] pushed out of the London trade'.[61] By 1700 membership of the Clockmakers' Company had fallen abruptly, from about 600 to about 400, indicating that a third of its members had been lost in a few years. The decline in membership appeared not to affect the Company's healthy financial assets, for it invested £500 in the stock of the newly founded Bank of England in 1693 (the only corporate body to do so) to which they added another £125 in 1697. Yet they had lost craftsmen members 'at a rate faster than [could be] expected from natural death causes', accounted for 'neither [by] war, epidemic, nor catastrophic event'.[62] Why?

One possibility is that the Company's 'missing' members were still there but, taking advantage of transferrable skills, perhaps had shifted to separate – but related – trades for which they provided parts, and never bothered to join the relevant Company. Another possibility is that supply of horological craftsmen in London temporarily exceeded effective demand, because of labour-saving innovations (Chapter 4).[63] If so, for some displaced craftsmen, attractive prospects beckoned outside the metropolis, because of the widespread diffusion of the relatively simple clockwork technology embodied in thirty-hour longcase clocks. We know that a diaspora of clockmakers left the metropolis for provincial towns and villages and, by the mid-eighteenth century, that 'country clock makers' were well entrenched in provincial towns and villages. Their main prerequisite was knowledge of what to do and the skills with which to do it. Capital costs were not great. Tools were mostly simple hand tools. Raw materials – iron, copper, and brass – were available in market towns, and there was abundant wood locally for carpenters. The most expensive item after about 1700 was a wheel-cutting engine, not prohibitively priced at £5 or so (Chapter 4). It cannot be a coincidence that the rise of rural clock making, so distinctive a feature of provincial life in eighteenth-century Britain, dates from this time. Hitherto, relatively few clockmakers had operated outside London. Afterwards, many towns had one or two; in some counties like Somerset 'by 1730 virtually everyone lived within ten miles of a clockmaker'.[64]

Watchmaking was different. There was no possibility of making a portable miniaturised watch equivalent of a thirty-hour longcase country clock. The guild in London may have declined in its numbers, but outside its 300 square-mile jurisdiction, a new market for clocks was opening in the rest of Britain. Time awareness was spreading.[65] Although London's great workshops, like Tompion's and Quare's, long retained the capacity to make both clocks and watches, concurrently a geographical division of labour emerged that distinguished the watchmaking industry. It is not quite clear when that geographical division stabilised. Eventually, Prescot in Lancashire specialised in making 'rough movements' for watches ('movements in the grey', or *ébauches*, in French speaking Europe) that were mostly finished in and around Clerkenwell's parish in London. There are examples of some watches being started in London and finished in Prescot, but, as we will see, the flow was mostly in the opposite direction (Chapter 2). Two other watchmaking hubs emerged, in Liverpool and Coventry (Chapter 3).

Notes

1 Bohemian and Italian hours began and ended at sunset and Nuremberg hours began at mid-night.
2 For an explanation of the equation of time see David Thompson, *Watches* (London: British Museum, 2008), 169, showing illustrations of such watches by Ferdinand Berthoud and David Pons on 76 and 82. For an account of

how clock time, evolution of the modern calendar, and biorhythms and timekeeping, see Anthony Aveni, *Empires of Time: Calendars, Clocks, and Cultures* (New York: Basic Books/Harper Collins, 1989), esp. Chapter 3, 'The Western Calendar', 85–118.

3 Lynn Thorndike, 'Invention of the Mechanical Clock about 1271 AD', *Speculum: A Journal of Medieval Studies*, 16 (April 1941), at https://doi.org/10.2307/2853618; also Derek J. de Solla Price, 'On the Origin of Clockwork, Perpetual Motion Devices, and the Compass', *United States National Museum Bulletin, No. 218* (1959), 81–112. There is valuable background in Gerhard Dohrn Van Rossum. 'Regulating Working Hours and Timekeeping Devices in the Middle Ages: An Addendum to Gian Carlo del Vecchio's Contribution', *Antiquarian Horology*, 16/2 (June 1986), 145–47; and id., 'The Diffusion of the Public Clock in the Cities of Late Medieval Europe, 1300–1500', in B. Lepetit and J. Hoock (eds.), *La Ville est l'innovation en Europe* (Paris: Ecole des Hautes Etudes en Sciences Sociales, 1987).

4 Stephen A. Epstein, *Wills and Wealth in Medieval Genoa, 1150–1250* (Cambridge, MA: Harvard UP, 1984); and id., 'Business Cycles and the Sense of Time in Medieval Genoa', *Business History Review,* 62 (Summer 1988), 238–60, at https://doi.org/10.2307/3116000

5 Alun C. Davies, 'Time-consciousness in the Aran Isles', *Antiquarian Horology*, 34/3 (Dec. 2013), 539–40. See the opening anecdote in David S. Landes, 'Clocks and the Wealth of Nations', *Daedalus*, 132/2 (Spring 2003), 20–26, at https://www.jstor.org/stable/20027836; also William Linnard, 'Shaping the Day in Wales: Indications of Awareness of Clock Time in Wales before 1800', *Antiquarian Horology*, 34/3 (December 2013), 526–38.

6 Cedric Jagger, *Royal Clocks: The British Monarchy and Its Timekeepers, 1300–1900* (London: Robert Hale,1983), 8–14; also Christina Juliet Faraday, 'Tudor Time Machines: Clocks and Watches in English Portraits c.1530–c.1630', *Renaissance Studies*, 33/2 (April 2019), 239–66, at DOI: 10.1111/rest.12517

7 Cedric Jagger, *The Artistry of the English Watch* (Newton Abbott: David and Charles, 1988), 14; Catherine Cardinal, *The Watch, From Its Origins to the Nineteenth Century,* trans. Jacques Pages (Secaucus, NJ: Wellfleet Press, 1988), 18. For the 'Order of the Garter' watch, see J.H. Leopold and Clare Vincent, 'An Extravagant Jewel: the George Watch', *Metropolitan Museum Journal*, 35 (2000), 137–38, at https://doi.org/10.2307/1513030 and https://www.jstor.org/stable/1513030.

8 Lisa Picard, *Restoration London: Everyday Life in the 1660s* (London: Weidenfeld & Nicolson, 1997), 115: some survive in the Ashmolean Museum, Oxford.

9 Lien Bich Luu, *Immigrants and* the Industries of London, 1500–1700 (Aldershot: Ashgate, 2005), 316, at DOI: S0020859007013260: Appendix 3, 'Number of Strangers Engaged in Luxury and New Trades in London, 1571–1593'.

10 Adrian Finch, 'Bartholomew Newsam (c.1530–1587)', *ODNB*; Cedric Jagger and Eric Bunt, 'A Chronological Directory of Royal Clockmakers: 1369–1900', *Clocks*, 8/6–9 (Dec. 1985–March 1986), 16–18, 39–41, 39–42, 47–48.

11 Alfred Marshall, *Principles of Economics* (London: Macmillan, 1890; reprinted1964), 221, at https://doi.org/10.1177/000271629000100217

12 Gervase Rosser, 'Urban Culture and the Church, 1300–1540', in D.M. Palliser (ed.), *The Cambridge Urban History of Britain: Vol. 1, c.600–c1540* (Cambridge: Cambridge UP, 2000); also Nina Gockerell. 'Telling Time without a Clock', in Klaus Maurice and Otto Mayr (Eds., translated

by H. Bartlett Wells,) *Clockwork Universe: German Clocks and Automata, 1550–1650* (Washington, DC: Smithsonian, 1981).

13 Joel Mokyr, *The Lever of Riches: Technological Creativity and Economic Progress* (Oxford: Oxford UP, 1990), 49; see also Donald S.L. Cardwell, *Turning Points in Western Technology: A Study in Technology, Science and History* (Cambridge: Science History Publications, 1972), 14.

14 For Salisbury, see William G.C. Backinsell, *The Medieval Clock in Salisbury Cathedral* (Trowbridge: South Wiltshire Industrial Archaeology Society, Historical Monograph 2, 1977); For a general survey, see Pierre Mesnage (translated by Eileen B. Hennessy), Chapter 13: 'The Building of Clocks', in Daumas, *History of Technology*, Vol, II, *The First Stages of Mechanisation, 1450–1725* (London: John Murray, 1980).

15 Paul Glennie and Nigel Thrift, *Shaping the Day, A History of Timekeeping in England and Wales, 1300–1800* (Oxford: Oxford UP, 2009), 153ff. The scope of Glennie and Thrift's book has been valuably extended in Linnard's, 'Shaping the Day in Wales', 526–38. Also David Webster Herring, *The Lure of Clocks: An Account of the James Arthur Collection of Clocks and Watches at New York University* (Oxford: Oxford UP, 1932), 10.

16 Frances and Joseph Gies, *Cathedral, Forge, and Waterwheel: Technology and Invention in the Middle Ages* (New York: Harper Collins, 1994), 273.

17 Sir George White, '"Not a bad timekeeper": The English Lantern Clock in the Seventeenth Century', *Antiquarian Horology*, 31/5 (Sept 2009), 621–36.

18 Cardinal, *The Watch*, 69–70.

19 Annie Launtink-Ferguson, 'The Origin of the Clockwork-Escapement', *Nature*, 330 (17 December 1987), 615; Lynn White, Jr., 'The Act of Invention: Causes, Contexts, Continuities and Consequences', *Technology and Culture*, 3/4 (Autumn, 1962), 'Proceedings of the Encyclopaedia Britannica Conference on the Technological Order', 486–500 (esp. 497), at https://www.jstor.org/stable/i355984; also H. Allen Lloyd, 'The Origin of the Fusee', *The Antiquaries Journal*, 31 (July–Oct. 1951), at https://doi.org/10.1017/S000358150007637X

20 Granville H. Baillie, *Watches: Their History, Decoration and Mechanism* (London: Methuen, 1929; reprinted Christchurch, NZ: NAG Press, 1979), 85; Mike Cowham, 'Portable Sundial Making in Nuremberg', *Antiquarian Horology*, 29/1 (Sept. 2005).

21 Cecil Clutton and George Daniels, *Watches* (London: Batsford, 1971), 3–7; Harry L. Nelthropp, *A Treatise on Watchwork, Past and Present* (London: Spon, 1863), 60; Peter Honig, 'History and Mathematical Analyses of the Fusee', in Klaus Maurice and Otto Mayr (eds.), *Clockwork Universe: German Clocks and Automata* (Washington, DC: Smithsonian Institution, 1980), 114–20.

22 Carlo Cipolla, *Clocks and Culture* (London: Collins, 1967); also part of his *European Culture and Overseas Expansion* (Harmondsworth: Penguin, 1970), 124–25.

23 Terence Camerer Cuss, *The English Watch, 1585–1970: A Unique Alliance of Art, Design, and Inventive Genius* (Woodbridge: Antique Collectors' Club, 2009), 14.

24 E.A. Wrigley, 'A Simple Model of London's Importance in Changing English Society and Economy, 1650–1750', in Philip Abrams and E. A. Wrigley (eds.), *Towns in Societies: Essays in Economic History and Historical Sociology* (Cambridge: Cambridge UP, 1978), 232.

25 Lien Bich Luu, *Immigrants and the Industries of London, 1500–1700* (Aldershot: Ashgate, 2005), Chapter 2 for the population of London; C.G.A. Clay, *Economic Expansion and Social Change: England 1500–1700*: Vol. 1, *People, Land and Towns* (Cambridge: Cambridge UP, 1984), 20.

26 F.J. Fisher, 'London as an 'Engine of Economic Growth', in J.S. Bromley and E.H. Kossmann, *Britain and the Netherlands*: Vol. 4, *Metropolis, Dominion and Province* (The Hague: Martinus Nijhoff, 1971), 15; also id. 'The Development of London as a Centre of Conspicuous Consumption in the Sixteenth and Seventeenth Centuries', *Transactions of the Royal Historical Society*, 4th ser., 30 (1948), 37–50, at DOI: https://doi.org/10.2307/3678697
27 Sir George White, *Lantern Clocks* (London: ACC Art Books, 1989), 51.
28 The estimate is Cipolla's: see *Clocks and Culture*, 142; Brian Loomes, *Early Clockmakers* (London: NAG Press, 1981), 20.
29 Elizabeth Randall, 'A Special Case? London's French Protestants', in Debra Kelly and Martyn Cornick (eds.) *A History of the French in London: Liberty, Equality, Opportunity* (London: University of London Press (2013), 13–42, at www.jstor.org/stable/j.ctv512xmz.2; also Cardinal, *The Watch*, 35. For an account of the regulations and laws governing apprenticeship after the Statute of Apprenticeship, 1563, see Dennis Moore, *British Clockmakers and Watchmakers Apprenticeship Records: 1710–1810* (Ashbourne: Mayfield Books, 2003), 3–5; also LMA/CLC/L/CD/C/001/MS03939/1: Alphabetical list of Apprentices, 1632–96.
30 LMA/CLC/L/CD/A/012/MS03969: List of undated petitions of the Company and orders of the Court of Aldermen, with copies of reports and orders 1629–32, relating to the obtaining of the Company's charter; and tables of the principal points contained in the charter of 1631 and the ordinances of 1631/2 [Table compiled c.1808.]; S.E. Atkins and W.H. Overall, *Some Account of the Worshipful Company of Clockmakers* (London: Privately Printed, 1881), 1–7; William C. Hazlitt, *The Livery Companies of the City of London: Their Origin, Character, Development and Social and Economic Importance* (London: Sonnenschein, 1892, reprinted London: Andesite, 2015), 417–26; George Unwin, *The Guilds and Companies of London* (London: Methuen,1908).
31 Sir George S.J. White, *The Clockmakers of London* (London: Worshipful Company of Clockmakers, 1998) is the best brief introduction. Also see Cecil Clutton and George Daniels, *The Clocks and Watches of the Collection of the Worshipful Company of Clockmakers* (London: Sotheby, 1975); John Robey, *Longcase Clock Reference Book* (2 vols., Ashbourne: Mayfield, 2001), 1/34–35; and Loomes, *Early Clockmakers*, 19–31.
32 Sir George White, 'Don't mention the war!' The Chequered Early Years of the Worshipful Company of Clockmakers', *Antiquarian Horology*, 38/2 (June 2017), 175–90. For a transcript of the charter, see *BPP*, 1817, 6, 'Report from the Committee on the Petitions of Watchmakers of Coventry ... and an Appendix'. Also Valerie J. Finch, Adrian A. Finch, and Anthony W. Finch, 'Edward East (1602–c. 1695): Part 1 – Early Stuart Period and Commonwealth', *Antiquarian Horology*, 38/3 (Sept. 2017), 342–64; 348–54 for the genesis and early years of the Clockmakers' Company.
33 Sheelagh Ogilvie, *The European Guilds: An Economic Analysis* (Princeton: Princeton UP, 2019), at https://doi.org/10.2307/j.ctv3s8sm9; id., 'The Economics of Guilds', *Journal of Economic Perspectives*, 28/4 (2014) 169–92, at DOI: 10.1257/jep.28.4.169.
34 L.A. Clarkson, *The Pre-industrial Economy in England, 1500–1700* (London: Batsford, 1971), 103–05; T.P. Camerer-Cuss, *Early Watches* (London: Country Life Collectors' Guide, 1971), 13; Leonard Schwarz, 'London Apprentices in the Seventeenth Century: Some Problems', *Local Population Studies*, 38 (1987), 18–22.
35 For the Paris guild, see Catherine Cardinal (trans. Anthony J. Turner), 'The Earliest Masters of the Paris Clockmakers Corporation: A New Account based on Archival Sources and Surviving Works', *Antiquarian Horology*, 41/3 (Sept. 2020), 341–56.

36 Hugh F. Watson, *Keeping Time: A History of Clocks, Watches and Barometers in a Provincial Town from 1700 until 1900* (Grantham: privately published, 2008), 7.
37 Donald Whyte, *Clockmakers and Watchmakers of Scotland, 1453–1900* (Ashbourne: Mayfield Books, 2005); Aaron M. Allen, *The Locksmith Craft in Early Modern Edinburgh* (Edinburgh: Society of Antiquaries of Scotland, 2007), 74. Also, Trevor Waddington, 'Archibald Miller: Clockmaker and the Hammermen of Glasgow', *Antiquarian Horology*, 24/3 (Autumn 1998), 229–33.
38 Anita McConnell, 'David Ramsay (c.1575–1660)', *ODNB*; David Thompson, 'David Ramsay', *Watches*, 32–33; also Adrian A. Finch, Valerie J. Finch and Anthony W. Finch, 'David Ramsay, c. 1590–1659', *Antiquarian Horology*, 40/2 (June 2109), 177–99.
39 White, *Clockmakers of London*, 12.
40 Alun C. Davies, 'Horological Patents, 1662–c.1800: Restraining Trade, Stifling Innovation or Rewarding Invention?' *Antiquarian Horology*, 37/1 (March 2016), 82–100.
41 Moore, *Apprentice Records*, 4–5.
42 Loomes, *Early Clockmakers*, 14.
43 George J. Stigler, 'The Division of Labor Is Limited by the Extent of the Market', *Journal of Political Economy*, 59/3 (June 1951), 185–93.
44 LMA/CLC/L/CD/C/015/MS02722: Register of turnover of Apprentices.
45 Jeremy Evans, *Thomas Tompion at the Dial and Three Crowns, with a Concise Checklist of the Clocks, Watches and Instruments from His Workshop* (Ticehurst: Antiquarian Horological Society, 1993), 18, 49.
46 Davies, 'Horological Patents', passim.
47 LMA/CLC/L/CD/G/003/MS03941/40: Order of the Recorder of London to compel persons carrying on the trade of watch and clock makers to become free of the Clockmakers' Company: 4 August 1641. LMA/CLC/L/CD/G/003/MS03941/41: Information against persons using the art of watch and clock making without having served their apprenticeship, 1654.
48 Atkins and Overall, *Clockmakers*, 78–81; see LMA/CLC/L/CD/A/013/MS03942/5, for Ahasuerus Fromanteel's refutation that he kept an unlawful number of apprentices. 3 March 1656; LMA/CLC/L/CD/A/013/MS03942/9: Order of the Lord Mayor directing that Thomas Loomes should keep only two apprentices instead of five: 25 Feb. 1656.
49 Loomes, *Early Clockmakers*, 32–41; Atkins and Overall, *Clockmakers*, 7–19. Also John Forbes, 'Search, Immigration and the Goldsmiths' Company: A Study in the Decline of Its Powers', Ch. 8 (115–25) in Ian Anders Gadd and Patrick Wallis (eds.), *Guilds, Society and Economy in London, 1450–1800* (London: Centre for Metropolitan History, Institute for Historical Research, 2002), 120–23.
50 Arthur Adams, *The History of the Worshipful Company of Blacksmiths, from Early Times until the year 1785: Being Selected Reproductions from the Original Books of the Company, An Historical Introduction, and Many Notes...* (London: Blacksmiths Company, 1939; 2nd ed., Sylvan Press, 1951), 133–41.
51 LMA/CLC/L/CD/G/003/MS03941/61 and other copies in LMA/CLC/L/CD/A/013/MS03942: 'Printed Abstract of an Act of Common Council for regulating the Company of Clockmakers passed 5 October 1765'.
52 Loomes, *Early Clockmakers*, 21.
53 White, *English Lantern Clocks*, 127; R.W. Symonds, 'Medieval Clocks and the English Lantern Clock', *Antiquarian Horology* (Supplement no.

1, March 1953); W.F.J. Hana (Translated by E.J. Tyler), *English Lantern Clocks* (Poole: Blandford Press, 1977), illustrates the large variety of models.

54 White, *English Lantern Clocks,* 163–71.

55 Hugh Tait, *Clocks and Watches* (London: British Museum, 1983), 19.

56 White, *Clockmakers of London:* 13, and id., *English Lantern Clocks*, 126. The affairs of the Clockmakers' Company were disrupted between 1643 and 1645, and the Court Minute Books were not written up.

57 Maria P. Fernandez and Pedro C. Fernandez, 'David Mells, Musician and Clockmaker and an Analysis of the Clockmaking Trade in 17th Century', *Antiquarian Horology*, 16/6 (June 1987), 602–17. (Mells was a violinist and bandmaster to Charles II.) Their analysis draws on Loomes, *Early Clockmakers*; and LMA/CLC/L/CD/C/001/MS03939/1: Alphabetical list of Apprentices, 1632–96.

58 White, *Clockmakers of London:* 18–19.

59 Randall, 'London's French Protestants', 29–30; Fernandez, 'Clockmaking Trade', 607–09. Also P.J. Shears, 'Huguenot Connections with the Clockmaking Trade in England', *Proceedings of the Huguenot Society of London:* 20 (1961), 158–76, esp.166–67; Maritella Botticini, 'Huguenots, Diaspora', *Oxford Encyclopaedia of Economic History*, Vol 1, 478–80; David J. Boullin, 'Historical Clerkenwell', *Horological Journal*, 130/1 (Sept 1988), 13; E.J. Tyler, 'Horology in Soho', *Clocks*, 8/10 (April 1986), 13–15; Cardinal, *The Watch*, 38–40.

60 David Thompson, *Watches in the Ashmolean Museum* (Oxford: Ashmolean Museum Handbook, 2007), xvii.

61 Fernandez, 'Clockmaking Trade', 611, and subsequent quote. Richard R. C. Barder, *English Country Grandfather Clocks: The Brass Dial Long Case* (Newton Abbott: David & Charles, 1983), 19 suggests 363 signatories; Fernandez and Fernandez, 'Clockmaking Trade', 611, suggest 355.

62 Sir John Clapham, *The Bank of England: A History* (2 vols; 1944, Cambridge: Cambridge UP, 1970), 1/280.

63 Fernandez, 'Clockmaking Trade', 615; Michael Grange, 'English Provincial Clockmaking 1605–1840. The Role of the Thirty-Hour Longcase Clock', *Antiquarian Horology*, Part 1, 36/3 (Sept. 2015), 361–77, Part 2, 36/4 (Dec 2015), 481–501; Brian Loomes, *Country Clockmakers and their Origins* (Newton Abbott: David and Charles, 1976), 57.

64 Robey, *Longcase Clock Reference Book*, 1/19; also Jeff Darken (ed.), *Time and Place: English Country Clocks 1600–1840* (London: Antiquarian Horological Society and the Museum for the History of Science, 2006).

65 For a discussion of its impact on literature, see Michelle Wright, 'Time, Consciousness, and narrative play in late medieval secular dream poetry', (unpublished PhD thesis, University of Glamorgan, 2007), at https://core.ac.uk/download/pdf/388411.pdf).

2 Supply

Clerkenwell and Prescot: A Geographical Division of Labour

Emergence of watchmaking centres

After about 1700 watchmaking and clockmaking became essentially separate industries. The transition was not overnight and did not happen for every workshop that made clocks and watches. Leading firms in London and a few provincial cities continued to make and sell a range of timekeepers. But differences became more distinct between the two main branches of the horological industry. London's clockmaking firms continued to make long-case, and table clocks (and in the eighteenth-century 'mantel' clocks), many of high quality for a luxury market. 'Lantern' clocks, initially the most popular model, declined but continued to be made in provincial centres into the eighteenth century. They were largely superseded by thirty-hour longcase clockmaking, which became ubiquitous: there were clockmakers in small self-contained production units in most towns and many villages, where they made most of the parts, except perhaps dials and the cases themselves. Many, like Samuel Roberts of Llanfair Caereinion in rural Wales, made longcase clocks – with occasional family help: in Roberts' case whilst simultaneously running a smallholding.[1] Comparable clockmakers supplied hundreds of mostly local markets with thirty-hour or eight-day longcase clocks. At first, they constructed almost every part themselves (except dials and cases). In London, in the second half of the seventeenth century, it is possible that whole movements may have been made by 'a single manufactory'.[2] Gradually, prefabricated parts were bought-in for assembling and fitting and, by the second half of the eighteenth century, entire 'suites' of clock parts could be bought ready for assembling. In the 1750s – and especially from the 1790s – Britain's market for clocks was supplemented with small wall clocks imported from Germany's Black Forest.[3] They were cheaper than longcases. In the 1840s clocks from New England began to be imported and, later, other clocks from France and Germany. Faced with competition from cheaper, imported clocks, demand for Britain's country longcase makers withered away.

Watchmaking was different. Four main centres emerged. By the late eighteenth century, the location of the industry's 'heart' in Clerkenwell

DOI: 10.4324/9781003227823-3

was influenced by the pull of the metropolitan market. It specialised in 'finishing' rough movements made 200 miles away in the village of Prescot, then near (but today within) urban Liverpool. In Liverpool itself a small watch finishing centre developed and, in Coventry, watchmaking's fourth location emerged, with an idiosyncratic system of manufacturing that included independent outworkers and proto factories that employed apprentices (Chapter 3).

Clerkenwell's attraction for the horological industry

The magnetism of London's market for watchmakers and other skilled craftsmen created an effective demand for the sales and services necessary to cover the costs of tools and renting or buying a workshop. The 'finishing' end of the industry in the parish of Clerkenwell lent its name to 'London watchmaking'. It was never the only location in the city of the industry and its agents, for some horological workshops were elsewhere, mostly in the neighbouring parish of St Luke's. Nevertheless, 'Clerkenwell' will henceforth be used in this monograph as a synonym for 'London watchmaking'. It broadly included the area 'from the eastern fringe of Holborn, through Clerkenwell and St Luke's, Old Street, to the western part of Shoreditch and [which] extended south to Smithfield, Cripplegate, Moorfields and north to Islington'.[4] Like watchmaking in Clerkenwell, other parts of London had their own specialisms, such as silk weaving in the Spitalfields and brewing in Southwark (Figure 2.1).[5]

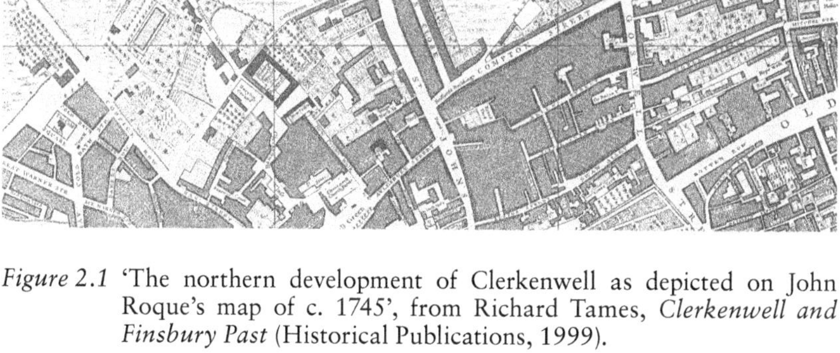

Figure 2.1 'The northern development of Clerkenwell as depicted on John Roque's map of c. 1745', from Richard Tames, *Clerkenwell and Finsbury Past* (Historical Publications, 1999).

Watchmakers were attracted to the district because of the prior existence of small workshops of metalworkers, blacksmiths, braziers, and pewter workers. They were joined by horological workshops. Chris Elmers observed that there were 'no great psychological, social, economic or physical barriers to the ... watch working trade' moving there because all other workshops were similarly organised.[6] Related specialist trades like dial makers were also attracted to the district. After the Great Fire, metal workers – members of the old brass foundry industry – moved to the Moorfields area north of the old city walls: during the eighteenth century, over seventy firms connected with horology had addresses there. Other metal workers, including wire drawers, were nearby in St Giles, Cripplegate. In terms of the numbers of people employed in different categories of London's industries, 'metalworkers' were ranked in second or third place.[7] An 'agglomeration momentum' occurred that enabled such industries to enjoy the advantages of readily available skilled labour. The economist Alfred Marshall has explained its notional, benign, theoretical benefits:

> When an industry has thus chosen a locality for itself, it is likely to stay there long: so great are the advantages which people following the skilled trade get from near neighbourhood to one another. The mysteries of the trade become no mysteries; but are as it were in the air, and children learn many of them unconsciously. Good work is rightly appreciated, inventions and improvements in machinery, in processes and the general organisation of the business have their merits promptly discussed ... And presently subsidiary trades grow up in the neighbourhood, supplying it with implements and materials, organising its traffic, and in many ways conducing to the economy of its material ... a localised industry gains a great advantage from the fact that it offers a constant market for skill.[8]

A parish census in 1677 recorded only one clockmaker's name. After 1685 numbers grew when they were joined by skilled French Huguenots, refugees from the Revocation of the Edict of Nantes (Chapter 6), most of whom settled in Covent Garden and Soho in the 1690s. By 1695, the list of *London Inhabitants within the Walls* accounted for ten watchmakers and one 'clockturner', even though Clerkenwell was 'without the walls'.[9] However, an 'Association Oath Roll' (an oath of loyalty to the Crown and Church of England) of the members of the Clockmakers' Company in 1697 shows the signatures of more than a hundred members involved in the business of clock and watchmaking.[10] Many in the luxury industries were immigrant Huguenots – jewellers, silversmiths, goldsmiths, silk-weavers, tailors, wigmakers, hairdressers; they included those who made and sold perfume, wine, fans, fur, boots and shoes, food, drink, guns, and clocks and watches. Over several generations, they transformed London's luxury industries. Later they were reinforced by Swiss economic migrants who strengthened London's reputation for horological excellence.[11] Some set up workshops in Soho, well away from Clerkenwell.[12] Leading horological retailers gravitated to the main shopping districts of Cheapside, the Strand, and Fleet Street.[13]

Growth of the industry in the eighteenth century

By 1720, many of London's watchmaking community lived and worked around Red Lion Street and Red Lion Square in Clerkenwell – an area of about one and a half square miles that included shopping districts.[14] Eventually, those on the periphery were no more than five- or ten-minutes' walk from an array of specialist craftsmen and suppliers of parts and materials. A kind of horological ecosystem evolved in Clerkenwell and its district. The records of Vulliamy of Pall Mall include addresses of about 400 outworkers in 1760 that covered scores of different specialisms, although only a minority of their workers lived within the Clerkenwell parish itself. Specialisation was not completely rigid: and workers could move from one category to another.[15] When masters and independent outworkers lived near each other, relatively small watch and clock-making workshops could take advantage of economies of scale when organising production and acquiring supplies.[16] There were serious inefficiencies and disadvantages, as we will note later. But over time a community was created which led to powerful expressions of solidarity in times of crisis (Part II: Chapters 7 and 9).

The district's topography and many buildings were well developed by about 1750. A description (made almost a century later, in 1843) noted how the industry had expanded by the mid-nineteenth century. It comprised scores of small units where hundreds of self-employed men worked in their own homes, in 'well-ventilated streets, containing exclusively small, private houses which look neat and comfortable'.[17] A similar contemporary account notes

> ...the making of pocket watches has centred in a most remarkable way in the parish of Clerkenwell in London: to so great a degree, indeed, that there is scarcely a street in that district which does not contain some artificers employed in this way; while in some of the streets almost every house contains inmates so employed.[18]

The industry's structure inhibited the organisation of trade unions. Clerkenwell was home to small traders and artisans in scores of specialist branches. Its industry did not depend on waterpower or coal. Motive power was human. Production was labour intensive, mostly with simple hand tools that needed no external power – pedalled treadles and 'engines' (lathes) turned with a bow. Professor Mathias well captures the flavour of their working lives:

> It was a world ... which had induced all sorts of specialist tools, slide-rests, screw-cutting lathes, pre-set lathes ... a world in miniature and for the luxury market in many cases. All these tools fitted into a vice on a bench. The material used was mostly brass, an easily worked metal (which could be worked cold) ... The maximum motive power ... was clockwork, the steel spring. Human muscle power worked all the watch-making tools. There was no mass production of parts by automatic machinery. Each unit produced was therefore expensive, and the market was a luxury market only. Productivity per head was low, even though production was rationalised by division of labour.[19]

[Nevertheless, the division of labour sufficed to enable relatively large numbers of watches to be made in Clerkenwell and Liverpool. Productivity was low only relative to machine tool technology (Chapter 11).] In 1801, the census recorded Clerkenwell's population as 23,396, with an average of seven persons in its 3,320 households.[20] Seven thousand are estimated to be 'artisan watchmakers', with another thousand in the neighbouring parish of St Luke's. If workers' families are included, then perhaps about a half of the district's population was primarily dependant in some way or another on the horological industry. Clerkenwell had many properties classified as 'shops' but most were 'petty shops' that catered for the daily needs of the inhabitants, not workshops. The ratio of 'persons to shop' was high, numbering thirty-one in Clerkenwell and thirty-five in St Luke's, suggesting they included adjacent buildings, as shopkeepers often covered overhead expenses by letting lodgings 'most probably to journeymen watchmakers'.[21]

Above all, watchmakers required good light. The upper stories of houses with workshops had extra-large windows and long workbenches. The district was unlike other British industrial centres. It had few of the distinctive features – such as large factory buildings, smokestacks or steam engines – commonly found in other contemporary industrial or manufacturing centres as, for example, in textile districts in Lancashire, in Yorkshire's West Riding, or the iron districts of South Wales. Apart from firms that made movements for turret clocks, horological workshops did not need large buildings or use non-human power sources. Three large firms that made turret clocks were established in the late eighteenth century, namely Thwaites & Reed of Bowling Green, Smith & Sons of Clerkenwell (both established in 1780), and John Moore & Sons (set up in Clerkenwell in 1798 by apprentices who broke away from Thwaites).[22]

Clockmaking had given rise to small, self-contained independent units, usually led by one man, perhaps helped by an apprentice. Watchmaking in Clerkenwell developed differently. Craftsmen in hundreds of small workshops made diverse watch parts that were assembled by firms (including retailers) that specialised in commissioning watches (Chapter 14). It was an industry whose products were distributed by wholesale traders who had been commissioned by the large retail houses whose names appeared on the dials. Professor Mathias's generalisation that 'the market was a luxury market only' needs qualification. By the 1790s, the market for Clerkenwell's best horological products was still large and important. But the whole national watch market was no longer as exclusive as it had been for the Tudor royal courts or even the prosperous metropolis. It had been widened by the demand for different kinds of horological products that included public clocks for shops, churches, and large buildings. Demand for watches had also spread to members of the growing middle classes (Chapter 5) not just for watches made in Clerkenwell but also for cheaper watches made in Coventry and Liverpool (Chapter 3) and, ominously for Clerkenwell, for Swiss watches made in the Jura (Chapter 6).

Growth of the horological workforce

The demand for clocks and watches increased as Britain's population grew in numbers and prosperity. Between 1700 and 1800 population doubled from about 5–10 million. That in London increased from 575,000 in 1700 to 900,000 in 1801. As the market widened, so watchmaking in Clerkenwell flourished. Snapshots that indicate the numbers 'carrying on the trade of clock and watchmaker' in 1782 can be seen in Benjamin Vulliamy's survey for the Clockmakers' Company. He counted 286 such 'persons' ('production units' might be a more apposite description?).[23] But his list excluded an unknown number of non-members of the Company who worked in some or other branch of watchmaking elsewhere in the metropolis. Nor did his survey consider those watchmakers outside the reach of the guild. Eight years later in 1790 Peter Barfoot and John Wilkes offered another glimpse of watchmaking in *The Universal British Directory of Trade and Commerce*.[24] Such directories were not comprehensive surveys for, at best, they offered minimum estimates. Barfoot and Wilkes listed 388 'firms' connected with clock and watchmaking, a hundred more than Vulliamy had found. Neither survey says how many employees there were in each workshop, nor how many were independent outworkers. Their list accounted for about 3 per cent of entries for all businesses in London. Even at the cusp of the industry's importance, watchmaking was a minor activity in London. Yet, small though it was, the industry had grown.

It has been noted that in 1662 Edward Tuet counted 167 'clockmaking' units in London (Table 1.1). Another indication of the growth of London's horological industry may be derived from the numbers of apprentices recruited by the Clockmakers' Company between 1630 and 1789. Over those 160 years, there were 5,981 apprentices. Unsurprisingly, employment was overwhelmingly male: only seventy (just over 1 per cent) were female. We know that female workers predominated in some horological trades whose employees were *not* represented by the Clockmakers' Company: they included polishers and piercers and, later, young girls making fusee-chains in Christchurch (Chapter 10).[25] Nor did apprenticeship enrolments indicate how many lived 'outside the walls' of the City and evaded – or simply didn't bother with – the Company. Recruitment as apprentices, and subsequent enrolment as Freemen declined during the Civil War years, and then revived. These statistics reveal a partial picture, for some apprentices joined other companies and not all apprentices to the Clockmakers' Company's worked as clock or watchmakers.[26]

The old Elizabethan apprenticeship system weakened between 1720 and 1780 and the influence of the Clockmakers' Company over its industry declined, as did the authority of other guilds over their industries.[27] Until 1735 the Company's members had paid four pence a quarter for 'searches'; thereafter they gave that up. Watchmaking had grown beyond the strict control of its guild. By the time it reached its peak of production in the 1790s, it had been transformed from the small handcraft trade of its founders. In 1800, Clerkenwell still had about 400 mostly small 'firms' of outworkers, dominated by a dozen or more large finishing houses that each organised the commission of up to 3,000 or 4,000 watches annually. As the industry had grown, the production sequences outlined by Sir William Petty in 1682 and Robert Campbell in 1747 (Chapter 4) had acquired inefficiencies that sharply contrasted with Alfred Marshall's benign assessment, quoted earlier. The visiting American, Aaron Lufkin Dennison (1812–95) described the chaotic characteristics which had arisen by the nineteenth century. It helps to explain Clerkenwell's gradual and eventually terminal decline:

> The party setting up as a manufacturer of watches bought his Lancashire movements – a conglomeration of rough materials – and gave them out to A, B, and C and D to have them finished; ... A, B, C, and D gave out the different jobs of pivoting certain wheels of the train to E, certain other parts to F, and the fusee cutting to G. Dial making, jewelling, guilding, motioning etc, to others, down almost the entire length of the alphabet; and how that taking these various pieces of work to outside workpeople – who, if sober enough to be at their places, were likely to be engaged on someone else's work who had been ahead of them, and how under such circumstances, he would take the occasion to drop into a pub, and drink and gossip, and, perhaps, unfit himself for work the remainder of the day.[28]

Dennison was an acute observer: watchmakers, like those in other remaining unmechanised small workshops, were often absent on 'Saint Mondays', recovering from an alcoholic hangover.[29]

Estimates of Clerkenwell's output of watches

If estimating the number of London's watchmakers is difficult, an accurate measurement of their output – either in numbers of watches or in their value – is impossible. Unknown numbers of watches were finished by unknown numbers of independent craftsmen from bought-in parts. At best, rough estimates – guesses of minimum output – can be made, extrapolated from the number of gold and silver watch cases assayed in London in the 1790s (Table 2.1).[30]

Assay numbers indicate that about one and a half million watch movements were cased in precious metal cases which passed through the city's Goldsmiths' Hall in the 1790s. Their annual rate was about 150,000, with a high of over 191,000 in 1796. The number of watch *movements* (mechanisms) finished in Clerkenwell – let alone in Liverpool or by independent finishers elsewhere – is simply unknown. Complications arise when guessing output from assaying statistics because unspecified numbers of 'pair watchcases' (that is, a cased movement placed inside a protective outer case) were counted twice. Possibly the double counting of paired gold and silver watch cases offset the non-counting of movements in base metal cases? Carlo Cipolla's conservative guess probably underestimated real output: he suggested that, at the end of the eighteenth century, London produced a yearly average of 'about eighty thousand timepieces for export and about fifty thousand time pieces for the home trade'.[31] A French estimate for 1794 put the world's annual production of

Table 2.1 Gold and Silver watches assayed in the Goldsmith's Hall, London, 1791–1801

Year	*Gold*	*Silver*	*Total*
1791	6,768	123,288	130,057
1792	7,766	138,160	145,826
1793	5,630	126,044	131,674
1794	4,668	135,845	140,513
1795	5,714	152,928	158,642
1796	6,576	185,102	191,678
1797	3,355	140,393	143,748
1798	3,523	125,275	128,798
1799	7,597	160,074	167,671
1800	9,396	154,144	163,540
1801	10,006	136,569	146,575

Source: *BPP*, 1818; vol. 9, 'Report from the Select Committee appointed to consider the laws relating to watchmakers', 12–13.

watches as between 350,000 and 400,000.[32] David Landes has pointed out that the trouble with watch statistics 'is that not every case was destined to hold a British-made movement, while on the other hand, a large number of British movements went into brass cases'.[33] There are no reliable measurements of the numbers of movements set in single or pair cases or in cases made of enamel or base metals, such as those cased in the alloy of zinc and copper invented by – and named after – Christopher Pinchbeck. Such watch cases looked like gold but did not need to be stamped in an assay hall.[34] And unknown numbers of gold and silver cases were not assayed at all.

Notwithstanding the lack of exact measures of output it is generally accepted that, in the 1790s, Clerkenwell (finishing Prescot's rough movements) was the largest single watchmaking centre in Europe. England's annual output (led by Clerkenwell, with lesser numbers from Coventry and Liverpool) supplied its domestic market with perhaps 100,000 watches; possibly another 70,000 were exported. Europe's next biggest watchmaking centre was Geneva. Japy's production records at Beaucourt of *ébauches* by all Neuchâtel makers suggest that 40,000 watches were produced there annually in the early 1790s, rising to about 100,000 in 1801 (Chapter 6). Based on these estimates, Clerkenwell's watchmakers in the 1790s finished about half Europe's watches. When Clerkenwell's output reached its peak in the middle 1790s, it marked the end of the golden era for England's watchmaking industry. Thereafter, watchmaking in Britain declined. A rough indication of its consequences may be seen in the census returns for the second half of the nineteenth century. Population in Clerkenwell and St Luke (two of five boroughs that eventually comprised the single parish and metropolitan borough of Finsbury) peaked in 1851 (125,000) and 1861 (129,000) but then steadily fell. By 1911, it was down to 88,000. It offers a crude but relevant indication of the shrinking size of the community surrounding its traditional finishing industry, in a period when the population of other London boroughs grew steadily.

Lancashire's cottage industries: tool making

Clerkenwell's watchmakers were not self-sufficient. They were like one side of a coin. The other side lay 200 miles away in Lancashire's villages and especially in Prescot, a village then seven miles from Liverpool (but today within the city). Clerkenwell's watches would not – could not – have been 'finished' without two parallel but separate developments in Lancashire. One was the making of horological tools in cottage industries in the county's villages. The other development, Prescot's speciality, was making the 'rough movements' of watches or 'movements in the grey' (*ébauches*).[35] Both developments gave rise to rural industries, where anonymous independent outworkers supplemented their subsistence from agriculture.[36] They appeared where grazing enabled part-time work, or because small farms on poor soil were not productive after repeated subdivision. Similar places in Europe where tools and parts were made in comparable ways were at Couvet, in Neuchâtel, Switzerland, and Montbélliard in France. In Lancashire, watch parts were made in small workshops in – or attached to – dwellings. Most were independent of local raw materials and fuel, except for some with a forge.[37] At first, earnings from making tool and parts were irregular – perhaps from ten shillings to a guinea a week. Gradually, it became more attractive to work full-time, and farming was contracted as the main source of livelihood.[38]

Lancashire's cottage industries had their origins (like Clerkenwell's) in the region's early metal working trades. A local legend relates that a chain armoury and weapon-making industry was 'settled at Warrington by Hugo de Lupus in William the Conqueror's time'. In the late medieval period, smithies worked brass, pewter, iron, and steel and, by the seventeenth century, different districts had specialist craftsmen who worked in wood and metal to make tools for carpenters, gunsmiths, and locksmiths. Others made small tools for those who worked in silver or copper to make jewellery and, crucially, parts for the infant horological industry.[39] Helped by wives and children, men worked at home in the winter months and may have moved in and out of agriculture and tool making in response to changes in weather, family circumstances, or the volume of demand. Some of Lancashire's villages made small horological bench implements like pliers, nippers, files, vices, and lathes. Eventually, barrel and wheel-cutting engines and fusee tools were added. Workshops in the village of Prescot became the centre for making 'rough movements' of watches.[40]

Prescot: rough movements

Why did this happen in Prescot, rather than in villages nearer London? The apparently unplanned production of rough watch movements in Prescot may have started when Clerkenwell makers contracted out making of basic parts, perhaps because outside London, labour costs were lower and free of guild restrictions. A nineteenth-century account of the origin of Prescot's specialism suggests, vaguely, that making watch movements was 'introduced about 1730 by Mr John Miller from Yorkshire ... the district has long been celebrated as the centre of the manufacture of watch tools and movements'.[41] Another account awarded credit to French Huguenot refugees.[42] The simplest and most plausible explanation is that offered by Professor Theo Barker and F.A. Bailey, a local historian, who concluded that Prescot's specialism, like those in other Lancashire villages, simply grew from an earlier tradition of metalworking.[43]

Thus a geographical division of labour evolved in the watchmaking industry between making the rough movements and assembling them for finishing. There are parallels with other industries, such as shoemaking in Northampton, glove-making in Ludlow, straw hat-making in Luton, and small-arms in Birmingham (Chapter 4). It underlines the broad economic point that, if the final product had a high value relative to labour and transport costs, then location might well be a matter of chance.[44] Once such developments started, they gained momentum. In the case of Prescot, it became a flourishing village with many small workshops. In 1795 Jonathan Aikin, in his survey of the industry in and around Liverpool in 1795, described Prescot as follows:

> [Prescot is] the centre of the manufacture of watch tools and movements ... the watch-tools made here have been excellent beyond the memory of the oldest watchmakers; and the manufacture has been much extended by improvements in making new tools of all sorts, and inventions for first cutting teeth in wheels, and afterwards for finishing them with exactness and expedition.... They [also] make here small files, the best in the world, at a superior price, indeed, but well worth the money, from the goodness of the steel ... They make watch-movements most excellent in kind, which is greatly owing to the superior quality of their files and tools ... they likewise excel in what is called motion work, such as dial wheels, locking springs, hour, minute, and second hands ... All these branches extend from Prescot to the surrounding villages, and all along the road to Liverpool, in which town the business seems finally to have centred ... All Europe is more or less supplied with the articles above mentioned made in this neighbourhood.[45]

A few years later the traveller Thomas Pennant confirmed that Prescot 'abounds in manufactures of certain branches of hard-ware, particularly the best and almost all the watch-movements used in *England*, and the best files in *Europe*'.[46]

As the national market for watches grew in the nineteenth century so did the size of communities surrounding the industry that supplied them. Prescot's population, busy making rough movements for watch finishing centres in Clerkenwell, Liverpool and Coventry, nearly doubled between 1800 and 1850.[47] The 1861 census recorded that Prescot's 'watchmakers' included 182 workers and fifty-four apprentices. Another 177 workers and thirty apprentices were toolmakers (including file cutters); seventy-two workers and nine apprentices made pinions, and thirty-five workers and seven apprentices made rough movements. In all, twenty branches of the industry employed 848 workers including 112 apprentices.[48] Another account in 1864 (using a different taxonomy) identified forty distinct branches. About half of the work was done in outworkers' homes and the other half in a master's workshop. Each master's workshop had one or two journeymen and one or two apprentices who worked in rooms of about twenty to thirty feet long by about eight feet wide; two or three walls consisted mostly of windows, along which ran workbenches.[49] Figure 2.2 shows the workshop of Harry Pybus, who succeeded his grandfather Joseph Preston, and spent the entire sixty years of his working life in the rather dilapidated old shop of the family firm.[50] 'Pybus could literally turn his hand to anything', Professor Torrens wrote, 'from frames, fusees and barrels to wheels, pinions, keyless work, and a dozen other branches, any one of which was at one time almost a trade in itself'.

The working day was relentless. For six days, it stretched from 6.00 a.m. to 8.00 p.m. with two hours off for meals. The only holiday was three days at the beginning of August.[51] Each workshop specialised in one component, with the predictable result that narrow skills were acquired and apprentices in one branch learned little about another. There was no standardisation. Each movement maker had his own – or his customer's – different sizes, 'and in consequence of this variety in everything, dials and cases had to be made to each movement separately'.[52] Nevertheless, the best workshops, like Joseph Preston's, proved remarkably flexible and supplied parts for whatever idiosyncratic measurements

Figure 2.2 David Torrens in Pybus's Prescot workshop (1953). Copyright: Prescot Museum, Knowsley Council.

were demanded by Clerkenwell's or Coventry and Liverpool's different finishers. Some masters took no apprentices, but Prescot's largest workshop employed up to twenty journeymen and ten apprentices.[53] The tools used were turned by bow or treadle; in only two workshops were steam engines eventually introduced (although it is not clear how or why they were used). What is astonishing is that Prescot's system survived into the late nineteenth century, as T.P. Hewitt described in 1893.

> I commenced work in my father's movement making shop in which were a few hands for assembling the parts as they came in from outside workers. These workers were scattered over an area of some six or seven miles, without any public means of conveyance. We had no recognised gauges in the trade, each movement maker having his own arbitrary standards. Therefore, after the frames were made, we had to carry them about from workshop to workshop in order to have all the other parts made to each individual frame. On going to Liverpool to finish my apprenticeship, I found this same system in vogue among the watch manufacturers; indeed the wastefulness was intensified as, instead of carrying about in dozens, as in Prescot, we carried them one by one.[54]

These characteristics of the organisation of production were still alive in the 1860s when Hewitt was apprenticed.[55] This ponderous experience prompted him to establish the Lancashire Watch Factory, a last-minute attempt to create in Britain a factory to make watches applying the 'American system of manufacturing' (Chapter 15).

Lancashire-London trade axis

By the end of the eighteenth century the commission, collection, and distribution of rough watch movements and tools from Lancashire's villages were in the hands of middlemen. Making rough movements in Prescot for finishing in London or elsewhere was viable only because of the development of a reliable national transport network. From the early eighteenth century, improved roads offered Prescot's movement makers a dependably routine means to supply finishers in Clerkenwell and Coventry. The small finishing centre in Liverpool was, of course, only a few miles away, reached by a toll road, maintained in good condition that smoothly transported goods to the finishing centre and from Liverpool's port for export.[56] Compared with their weight and size, transport costs of watches and their parts – in packages on stagecoaches – were trifling, amounting to only a tiny percentage of a watch's final price. Stagecoaches were reliable and frequent. In the 1750s over thirty, a week ran between Liverpool and London; it took two days in the summer and three in the winter to cover the 200 miles.[57] By 1790 roads had improved, timetables were synchronised, and the Royal Mail's coach system had shortened the journey to twenty-seven hours. The itinerary from Prescot included, significantly, Liverpool, Coventry, and London. At each end of the axis were two of Britain's great seaports, enabling exports west to Ireland and the Americas and east to Europe. It was easy for Clerkenwell to order and for Prescot to dispatch parcels of movements.[58] When, after about 1770, a marine chronometer-manufacturing sector emerged in London, Prescot workshops that already supplied rough movements to watchmakers extended their range to include rough movements for chronometer makers. Possibly Thomas Earnshaw, a Lancastrian, initiated the supply of 'standard rough movements' for chronometers from his home county, and it is known that John Arnold used several Lancashire craftsmen.[59] In the nineteenth-century superior transport connections – canals and railways – were used. (Later, railways were certainly used by Clerkenwell's outworkers.) But the essential connections that linked watchmaking in Lancashire and finishing in London were initially facilitated by its reliable coach system.

The middlemen: Wyke, Stubs, and Ford & Co

By the end of the eighteenth-century tools of all kinds made in Lancashire's villages supplied a nationwide market. Their distribution was dominated by three firms of wholesalers that systematically organised the industry whose products they distributed through a national road network. Their intermediaries controlled the work done by Lancashire's cottagers and gave out orders, raw materials, and tools.[60] Usually, piece work for the week was distributed on a Monday and collected and paid for on the following Saturday. The putting-out, decentralised production system formed an horological example of 'proto-industrialisation' – industrialisation carried on in small workshops in rural areas – that preceded large factories.[61] These firms acted as middlemen through their agents: they were entrepreneurs between the makers and their customers. Each of the three leading firms of distributors started in the 1770s – Wyke & Green of Liverpool, Stubs of Warrington, and Ford, Whitmore & Brunton of Birmingham. All were well-established by the turn of the century.

Wyke & Green initiated and gave impetus to the systematic collection and distribution of watchmakers' and repairers' tools from Liverpool's hinterland. The enterprise began when John Wyke supplied capital to underpin a partnership with Thomas Green, his foreman. Wyke was born in Prescot, the son of a part-time farmer and watch springer and grew up among the movement makers in the village.[62] He moved to Liverpool in 1771 where he became a celebrated civic figure, a friend of Josiah Wedgwood, and a supplier of 'engine counters' to Boulton and Watt.[63] Wyke was Liverpool's first merchant banker. Less is known about Green, who handled sub-contracts with the individual cottagers who made the tools. He continued the business after Wyke's death in 1787. The firm commissioned complicated and expensive tools like wheel-cutting and fusee engines that were illustrated in catalogues of watch tools and parts.[64] The catalogues had full-size or scaled engravings and price lists. Like the earlier clockmaker's books by John Smith and William Derham, they must have helped to disseminate horological technology 'for those with enquiring minds'.[65] The wheel-cutting engines were probably made at Wyke's Court in Liverpool, an enclave with workshops and seven houses, where forty-eight workers, wives, and children lived.[66] There is no evidence that Wyke himself designed the 'engines' that were sold to Coventry's and London's watchmaking establishments, although some became known as 'Wyke engines' (Chapter 4, Figure 4.1: engine by Thomas Green, his foremen and partner). Other firms made similar engines after plagiarising illustrations from his catalogues.

An enterprise of comparable importance to Wyke's was that of Peter Stubs, an independent file maker from Warrington. Like Wyke he, too, became a supplier of horological tools and parts in the 1770s. Stubs first contracted with several other outworkers, small 'firms' in themselves, to handle supplies and sales. Some made clock and watch tools and parts but kept their independence and enjoyed Stubs's special trade discounts.[67] When his file-making enterprise expanded in 1802, Stubs built a three-story red-brick 'factory' building in Warrington; it measured seventy-five by fifty feet and was lined with windows. The various traditional processes – forging, grinding, cutting, and hardening – were allocated separate workshops in the factory. Stubs added an inspection shop to examine products made by both his in-workers and those outworkers he continued to employ in their scattered cottages. Stubs' 'factory' was initially intended to organise the different tools, rather than make them. It recruited eleven workers and then added ten file journeymen from outside the district. New apprentices were attracted by two-year contracts. By 1841, the enterprise had almost two hundred employees – some in the factory, others still outworkers. The 'factory' was an immediate success. Stubs' main product was 'saw' files, essential for those who constructed anything out of metal (or who wanted to sharpen teeth on a saw for cutting wood). Output in 1800 reached 15,000 dozen made by outworkers: by 1803 the factory nearly doubled output, to 28,000 dozen. So, too, making special files for clock and watchmakers increased from 1,400 to 3,000. As well as files, the firm made and sold an assortment of other horological tools, including pliers, nippers, vices, and pinion wire. Eventually, Stubs supplied more complicated labour-saving devices, for making watch fusees, lathes, and wheel cutting engines. They were collected, inspected by Stubs, given the imprimatur of his trade name, and sold as 'Stubs' products.[68] The firm even handled brass castings, bells, and forgings. Its network of seventy outlets increased after Stubs's death.[69]

The firm's success was based not on anything new that Stubs himself invented or made but on the better organisation he imposed on those products. His efficiency enabled him to control quantity, quality, and sales. Stubs and Wyke became the major wholesale distributors of parts and tools to watchmakers, clockmakers, and jewellers. With a third firm, Ford, Whitmore & Brunton, of Birmingham, they dominated the national market for craftsmen's tools and parts.[70]

Ford, Whitmore & Brunton, like its counterparts, also bought-in from Lancashire's outworkers as well as from the products of small craftsmen in Birmingham. Theodore Crom has analysed the firm's catalogue for 1777 and compared its wares with those of Stubs and Wyke. He concluded that 'many of the tools, wheel-cutting engines and lathes were duplicated in the three catalogues'. This suggests that much of what Wyke, Stubs, and Ford offered for sale was made and bought-in from the same pool of craftsmen, who probably worked to comparable specifications.[71] Thus, cottage industries in Liverpool's hinterland mainly supplied England's watchmakers through Stubs and Wyke, whilst the nation's clockmakers were supplied with parts made by small firms in Birmingham and distributed by Ford, Whitmore & Brunton. Clock and watch components were made in embryo 'factories', small workshops, perhaps with two men and a boy, who made watch-dials, pinion wire, spandrels and wheels. By 1800, comprehensive pre-fabricated 'suites' of all parts of clock movements might be bought. They included finished sets of plates, pillars, brass castings, and forgings, ready for assembly by a country clockmaker, and then to be housed in a longcase made by a local carpenter.[72] Hereafter country craftsmen – like the successors of Samuel Roberts of Llanfair Caereinion – were no longer obliged to master the several different skills needed to make parts before assembling them.

Similar developments for the production of watches in quantity were impossible. The tolerances needed for the tiny parts of watches were too fine, the range of skills needed to assemble them was almost too complicated for a single watchmaker to master (although some of the pioneers must have done so, before the division of labour evolved).[73] Thus, the watchmaking industry emerged with a geographical division of labour as well the elaborate specialisation within and between workshops. Three features are striking. First, the distances involved – 200 miles between rough movement makers in Prescot and assemblers and finishers in Clerkenwell. Next was the remarkable extent of specialisation and in the division of labour in Prescot's and Lancashire's cottage industries and amongst Clerkenwell's outworkers, although some manufacturers initially carried out the whole process in London. The distinction between the two was only clarified after a time. Third, watchmaking was an industry that did not require extensive investment in fixed plants. The economics of the early production system is explained by cheap labour and low rents in Lancashire and a rapidly growing market in London.

Notes

1 W.R.T. Pryce and T.A. Davies, *Samuel Roberts, Clockmaker: An Eighteenth-Century Craftsman in a Welsh Rural Community* (Cardiff: National Museum of Wales, 1985); Alun C. Davies, 'Rural Clockmaking in Eighteenth Century Wales: Samuel Roberts of Llanfair Caereinion, 1755–1774', *Business History Review*, 59 (1985), 49–75, at https://doi.org/10.2307/3114855
2 Jon Parker, 'Was there High-Quality, Wholesale Movement Manufacture in Seventeenth-Century London', *Antiquarian Horology*, 40/4 (Dec. 2019), 469–86.
3 Paul Buck, 'Black Forest Clockmakers, Carriers and Retailers with United Kingdom Connections', *Antiquarian Horology*, 26/4 (Dec. 2001), 389–406.
4 'C.E.' (Chris Elmers), 'Watch and Clockmaking', in Celina Fox (ed.), *London: World City, 1800–1840* (London: Yale UP and the Museum of London, 1992), 524.
5 Charles Harvey, Edmund M. Green and Penelope J. Corfield, 'Continuity, Change, and Specialization within Metropolitan London: The Economy of Westminster, 1750–1820', *The Economic History Review*, 52/3 (Aug. 1999), 472, at www.jstor.org/stable/2599141
6 Report of a lecture on Clerkenwell by Chris Elmers, *Antiquarian Horology*, 12 (Spring 1981), 549–50.
7 Peter Earle, *A City Full of People: Men and Women of London, 1650–1750* (London: Methuen, 1994), 8–9, 15; id., *The Making of the English Middle-Class: Business, Society and Family Life in London, 1660–1730* (London: Methuen, 1989), 22–23; John A. Robey, 'Moorfields and Clock-Brass Founders: Part 1: The London Horological Trades in Moorfields', *Antiquarian Horology*, 33/4 (June 2012), 479–86.
8 Alfred Marshall, *Principles of Economics* (1890; Reprinted London: Macmillan, 1964), 225.
9 David Glass, ed., *London Inhabitants within the Walls (1695)*, (2 vols., London: London Record Society, 1966, 1968); information from vol. 2. The list is not comprehensive because only a small proportion of assessments mentioned trades. For the 1677 census, see the letter by C.A. Osborne in *Antiquarian Horology*, 4 (1964), 183.
10 R.W. Symonds, *Thomas Tompion: His Life and Work* (London: Batsford, 1951); I owe this reference to David Thompson.
11 For the Vulliamys see Roger Smith, 'Justin Vulliamy (1712–97) and the Protestant Swiss Community: Networks, Institutions and National Identity in 18th Century London', *Huguenot Society Journal*, 30/3 (2015), 327–45; also id., 'Benjamin Vulliamy's Library: A Collection of Neo-Classical Design Sources', *The Burlington Magazine*, 141/1155 (June 1999), 328–37, at www.jstor.org/stable/888303; also Robin D. Gwynn, *Huguenot Heritage: The History and Contribution of the Huguenots in Britain* (London: Routledge, 1985), 70–74.
12 David J. Boullin, 'Historical Clerkenwell', *Horological Journal*, 130/1 (Aug. 1987), 12–17; E. J. Tyler, 'Horology in Soho', *Clocks*, 8 (April 1986), 13.
13 Earle, *A City Full of People*, Appendix, 263 ff. draws on the evidence of witnesses appearing before the Church Courts between 1695 and 1725.
14 On his eighty-third birthday, in 1776, John Harrison died in 12 Red Lion Square. For an account of other eminent residents, see Theo Barker, *Three Hundred Years of Red Lion Square, 1684–1984* (London: Borough of Camden, 12pp pamphlet, 1987). The *Old Red Lion* public-house was at one time the residence of Thomas Paine: see T. Cromwell, *History and Description of the Parish of Clerkenwell: The Historical Department* (London: Longman &

Green, 1828; reprint, London: British Library, Historical Print Editions, 2011), 388.

15 Roger Smith, 'Some mid-Eighteenth-Century Craftsmen: Gray and Vulliamy Outworkers and Suppliers, c.1760', *Antiquarian Horology*, 29/3 (March 2006), 348–58; Francis Wadsworth, 'Some Early Nineteenth Century Workmen', *Antiquarian Horology*, 19/4 (Summer 1991), 401–12.

16 Paul M. Hohenberg and Lynn Hollen Lees, *The Making of Urban Europe, 1000–1950* (London and Cambridge, MA, Harvard U.P., 1985), 202. A classic theoretical discussion is Allyn Young, 'Increasing Returns and Economic Progress', *The Economic Journal*, 38 (Dec. 1928), 527–42, at https://www.jstor.org/stable/2224097

17 For Clerkenwell in 1843, see 'Report on the Education Committee', *Journal of the Statistical Society of London*, 6 (1843), 28–29, at https://www.jstor.org/stable/2338010

18 Carol Hayter, 'Instruments for Measuring Time', *Antiquarian Horology* (March 1973), 187 quoting *The Picture Gallery of Arts* (London: Charles Knight, 1847), 382.

19 Peter Mathias, *The First Industrial Revolution: The Economic History of Britain, 1700–1914* (1969; London: Methuen, 2nd ed., 1983), 139–40.

20 Hoh-Cheung Mui and Lorna H Mui, *Shops and Shopkeeping in the Eighteenth Century* (Kingston, Ont., and London: McGill UP, 1989), 119–20; T. Cromwell, *History and Description of the Parish of Clerkenwell*, 23, suggests that about 5,000 were described as 'persons chiefly employed in trade, manufactures, or handicraft'. This seems an underestimation.

21 Mui and Mui, *Shops and Shopkeeping*, 118–20.

22 Geoffrey T.E. Buggins and F.B.M. Devereux, 'John Thwaites', *Antiquarian Horology*, 1 (June 1956), 161–63; T.P. Camerer Cuss, 'John Moore & Sons', *Antiquarian Horology*, 6 (Dec. 1968), 32–33; Anon., 'A Visit to a Clerkenwell Clock Factory' (Smith's), *Illustrated London News Supplement*, 20 September 1851; Rita Shenton, 'Clerkenwell', *Clocks*, 1 (Feb. 1979), 14.

23 LMA/CLC/L/CD/E/031/MS03961: 'A list of 286 persons carrying on the trade of clock and watch makers in the year 1782, formed by Mr Benjamin Vulliamy'; also LMA/CLC/L/CD/E/033/MS03962: 'List of names and addresses of clock and watchmakers in London, arranged topographically'.

24 Peter Barfoot and John Wilkes (eds.), *The Universal British Directory of Trade and Commerce* (London: published by and printed for the patentees, 1790).

25 Guildhall: Clockmakers' Company, Pamphlet 306: 'Female Apprentices of the London Clockmakers' Company'.

26 Compiled from LMA/CLC/L/CD/C/015/MS02722: Register of turnover of apprentices, 1771–1808; with, at front, examples of the different summonses sent out by the Clerk to members of the Company. 1770, and LMA/CLC/L/CD/C/015/MS02722: Register of turnover of apprentices, 1771–1808; with, at front, examples of the different summonses sent out by the Clerk to members of the Company, 1770.

27 M.A. Crawforth, 'Instrument Makers in the London Guilds', *Annals of Science*, 44 (1987), 327, at https://doi.org/10.1080/00033798700200261; L.D. Schwarz, *London in the Age of Industrialisation: Entrepreneurs, Labour Force and Living Conditions, 1750–1850* (Cambridge: Cambridge UP, 1992), 215: https://doi.org/10.1080/00033798700200261. Also J.R. Kellett, 'The Breakdown of Guild and Corporate Control over the Handicraft and Retail Trade in London', *Economic History Review* (2nd Ser.), 10 (1958), 381–94, at https://doi.org/10.1111/j.1468-0289.1958.tb00013.x.; Also LMA/CLC/L/CD/A/013/MS03942/17: Report of a Committee appointed by the [Clockmakers']

Company to examine the Charter and Bye-laws of the Company... November 1795; Anthony J. Turner, *Early Scientific Instruments: Europe, 1400–1780* (London: Sotheby, 1987), 21, suggests that for those who made scientific instruments the decline in influence was probably to their benefit.

28 Aaron L. Dennison quoted in Henry G. Abbott, *The Watch Factories of America, Past and Present* (Chicago, IL: Hazlitt & Co, 1888), 12–13. For Dennison's later success, see Chapter 15.

29 Douglas A. Reid, 'The Decline of St Monday, 1766–1876', *Past and Present*, no. 71 (May 1976), 70–101 (esp. 91), at https://www.jstor.org/stable/650355

30 *BPP*, 1818, 9, 'Report from the Select Committee Appointed to Consider the Laws Relating to Watchmakers', 12–13.

31 Carlo Cipolla, *Clocks and Culture* (London: Collins, 1967), 75, at DOI: 10.1086/ahr/73.5.1473 (drawing evidence from Atkins and Overall, *Company of Clockmakers*, 263).

32 J.A. Neale's report of a lecture by John Leopold on 'The Wholesale Trade in Watches in the Eighteenth Century', *Antiquarian Horology*, 19/4 (Summer 1991), 392.

33 David S. Landes, *Revolution in Time: Clocks and the Making of the Modern World* (Cambridge, MA: Harvard UP), 442, n.18; the estimate for Geneva is on p. 254.

34 Rita Shenton, 'Pinchbeck Family (*per. c.* 1720–1783)', *ODNB*; Alan Smith, *Clocks and Watches* (London: Ebury Press, 1975), 50.

35 John Griffiths, 'The Rise and Fall of Toolmaking in Lancashire', *Journal of the North West Society for Industrial Archaeology and History* (1994), 3–8; Alan Treherne, 'The Contribution of South-west Lancashire to Horology: Part 1: Watch and Chronometer Movement Making and Finishing', *Antiquarian Horology*, 31/4 (June 2009), 457–76.

36 Denis Moore recorded names for the Prescot Museum of between 1,600 and 2,000 toolmakers before 1870, and about 1,500 file makers.

37 John R. Harris, *Essays in Industry and Technology in the Eighteenth Century: England and France* (Ashgate: Variorum, 1992), 12.

38 F.A. Bailey, 'An Old Watchmaker s Workshop', *Transactions of the Ancient Monuments Society* (1953), 3–8.

39 G.H. Tupling, 'The Early Metal Trades and the Beginnings of Engineering in Lancashire', *Transactions of the Lancashire and Cheshire Antiquarian Society*, LXI (1949), 11–25; suggests that it sprang up in the second half of the eighteenth century in and around Prescot; also Bailey, 'An Old Watchmaker's Workshop', 3–8. (quotation, 3).

40 Swiss rough movements (*ébauches*) were made to a different stage of completion: email from John Griffiths, July 1997; also Alan Treherne, 'Unfinished or Raw Movements "In the Grey"', *Your Time* (Ticehurst: Antiquarian Horological Society Northern Section, 2008), 59–64; Leonard Weiss, *Watchmaking in England, 1760–1820* (London: Robert Hale, 1982), 56–60; Terence Camerer-Cuss, *The English Watch, 1585 to1970* (Woodbridge: ACC Art Books, 2009), 83.

41 Edward Baines, *The History of the County Palatine, and Duchy of Lancaster*, rev. ed. by John Harland, continued and completed by Brooke Harford, 2 vols. (London: John Heywood, 1885), 2/245.

42 James Hoult, 'Prescot Watchmaking in the XVIII Century', *Transactions of the Historical Society of Lancashire and Cheshire* (New ser.), XLI, (1925), 39–53; id, 'Old Prescot Chronometer Makers', *Horological Journal*, 68/5 (Jan. 1926), 100–04; and *Victoria County History, Lancashire* (London: Victoria County History, 1907), vol. 3, 353, 358.

43 F.A. Bailey and T.C. Barker, The Seventeenth-Century Origins of Watchmaking in South-west Lancashire, in John R. Harris, *Essays in Industry and Technology in the Eighteenth Century: England and France* (Ashgate: Variorum, 1992); John R. Harris (ed.), *Liverpool and Merseyside* (1969); Theodore C. Barker, and John R. Harris, *A Merseyside Town in the Industrial Revolution: St Helens, 1750–1900* (London: Routledge, 1954).

44 Curiously, this serendipitous explanation was prophesied by a Clerkenwell watchmaker who visited the district in 1877. He concluded that 'the location of movement making is most probably an accident'. [Report of excursion], *Horological Journal*, 29/11 (Aug. 1877), 158.

45 John Aikin, *Description of the Country from Thirty to Forty Miles Round Manchester* (London: John Stockdale, 1795), 310–12,

46 Thomas Pennant, *A Tour from Downing to Alston Moore* (London: Harding, 1801), 21. Files were exported to France and Switzerland: see John Griffiths, 'Rise and Fall of Toolmaking in Lancashire', 5.

47 Barker and Harris, *A Merseyside Town*, 127.

48 Robert Kemp, 'Watch Movement Making in Prescot', *Antiquarian Horology*, 13/1 (Sept. 1981), 78–79.

49 Charles K. Aked, 'Joseph Preston and Sons', *Antiquarian Horology*, 18/3 (Autumn 1989), 298–306 describes the demise of one of the most famous firms that made rough movements. See also David S. Torrens, 'Obituary: Harry Pybus; Last of the Prescot Watchmakers', 515–16; also David Thompson, 'Joseph Preston: Movement Maker', *Watches* (London: British Museum, 2008), 126–27. The cash books of Preston & Sons from 1893 to 1904 are in the London Metropolitan Archives, as LMA/CLC/B/141/MS14545; also LMA/CLC/B/MS138 for volumes describing parts, c.1890–95 and 1892–1914.

50 Torrens, 'Obituary: Harry Pybus: Last of the Prescot Watchmakers', 515–16.

51 Bailey, 'An Old Watchmaker's Workshop', 3–8.

52 David Glasgow, 'Watchmaking by Machinery', *The New Technical Educator* (London: Cassell, 1890).

53 The skills of watchmakers and watch tool makers and their links to apprenticeship have been analysed by Neil Cummins and Cormac Ó Gráda, 'Artisanal Skills, Watchmaking, and the Industrial Revolution: Prescot and Beyond', *UCD Centre for Economic Research: Working Paper Series*, WP19/24, October 2019, at https://econpapers.repec.org/paper/ucnwpaper/201924.htm. They note the relatively high literacy levels of both watch and tool makers, especially during the heyday of the industry.

54 Alan Smith, *The Lancashire Watch Company: Prescot, Lancashire, England 1889–1910* (Fitzwilliam, NH, Ken Roberts, 1973), 11–12, quoting T. P. Hewitt s speech on 12 Jan. 1893.

55 Alun C. Davies, 'Hewitt, Thomas Peter (1848–1933), Watchmaker and Businessman', *ODNB*. Hewitt was apprenticed to his father from 1863 to 1866 and then to Thomas Lowe, of Messrs Roskell & Sons, Church Street, Liverpool (1866–9). He took over his family business in Prescot in1869–70.

56 Amy Glasmeier, *Manufacturing Time: Global Competition in the Watch Industry, 1795–2000* (New York: Guilford Press, 2000), 76.

57 Theodore C. Barker and Dorian Gerhold, *The Rise and Rise of Road Transport, 1700–1900* (Cambridge: Cambridge UP, 1993, new ed., 1995), 5, 15.

58 Kemp, 'Watch Movement Making in Prescot', 78; Alun C. Davies, 'Greenwich and Standard Time', *History Today*, 38/3 (March 1978), 194–99; Howard Robinson, *Britain s Post Office: A History of its Development from the Beginning to the Present Day* (Oxford: Oxford UP, 1953), 102–18;

Alan Bates (compiler), *Directory of Stage Coach Services* (Newton Abbott: David & Charles, 1969).

59 Jonathan Betts, 'Arnold and Earnshaw: The Practicable Solution', in William J. H. Andrewes (ed.), *The Quest for Longitude: Proceedings of the Longitude Symposium, Harvard University, 1993* (Cambridge, MA: Harvard UP, 1996). 325.

60 Theodore Crom, *Horological Wheel Cutting Engines, 1700 to 1900* (Gainesville, FL: Crom, 1970), 101–02; also id., 'A Few Eighteenth-Century Liverpool/Prescot Area Toolmakers', *Antiquarian Horology*, 19(4), (Summer 1991), 419–30; P.H.J. Baker, 'Early Lancashire Watch Fusee Engines', *Antiquarian Horology*, Parts 1 and 2, Vol. 21/3 and 4 (Spring and Summer 1994), 215–28, 315–21. W.J. Roberts and H.C. Pidgeon, 'Biographical Sketch of Mr John Wyke, with Some Remarks on the Arts and Manufactures of Liverpool from 1760–1780', *Transactions of the Lancashire and Cheshire Antiquarian Society*, 6 (1853–54), 66–76, and James Hoult, 'Prescot Watchmaking in the 18th Century', *Transactions of the Historical Society of Lancashire and Cheshire* (New Series), 61 (1925), 44–47.

61 Leslie A. Clarkson, *Proto-Industrialization: The First Phase of Industrialization?* (London: Macmillan Studies in Economic & Social History, 1985).

62 Alan Smith, 'Introduction and Technical Commentary: The Lancashire Watch and Watch Tool Trade', *A Catalogue of Tools for Watch and Clock Makers by John Wyke of Liverpool* (Charlottesville, VA: Virginia UP, 1978). Also, summary of lecture on Wyke by Alan Smith, *Antiquarian Horology*, 10 (1978), 736. Only four originals of this document survived into the twentieth century; two were owned by Torrens. See Alun C. Davies, and Sir Peter Froggatt. 'David Smyth Torrens: Physiologist and Horologist, 1897–1967', *Hermathena, Journal of Trinity College, Dublin.* (1986), 20, at https://www.jstor.org/stable/23041095.

63 An 'engine counter' was a device installed in steam engines that enabled royalty payments to be worked out.

64 Griffiths, 'The Rise and Fall of Toolmaking in Lancashire', 5. The first catalogue was issued in 1760 followed shortly after by Daniell Mather s catalogue, and subsequently by Mather & Lassels of Toxteth Park.

65 Anita McConnell, 'John Smith (1647/8–1727)', *ODNB*. Smith's *Horological Dialogues* (1675) and *Horological Disquisitions* (1694) have been reprinted in facsimile (Reading: Thames Facsimile Co., 1962); also Charles K. Aked, 'William Derham and *The Artificial Clockmaker*', 3 parts: *Antiquarian Horology,* 6 (March, June and Sept. 1970), 367–72, 416–27, and 495–505; Marja Smolenaars, 'William Derham (1657–1735)', *ODNB*; William Derham, *The Artificial Clockmaker* (London: printed for James Knapton, 1696; Reprinted Reading, Thames Facsimile, 1962); also, David Barker, 'Thomas Lister s *Artificial Clockmaker*', *Antiquarian Horology*, 24/4 (1998), 353–56.

66 Smith, Introduction to *Wyke s Catalogue*, 2. Also, summary of a lecture on Wyke by Alan Smith, *Antiquarian Horology*, 10 (1978), 736.

67 T.S. Ashton, 'The Domestic System in the Early Lancashire Tool Trade', *The Economic Journal*, 36, Issue Supplement_1 (Jan. 1926), 131–40, at https://doi-org.eres.qnl.qa/10.1093/ej/36.Supplement_1.131; id., *An Eighteenth-Century Industrialist: Peter Stubs of Warrington, 1756–1806* (Manchester: Manchester UP, 1939), 21; Report of a lecture on Stubs by Alan Treherne, 25/5 (Sept. 2000), 565–69; Weiss, *Watchmaking in England, 1760–1820*, 70; Tupling, 'Early Metal Trades and the Beginnings of Engineering', 23–25, and Theodore Crom, 'A Few Eighteenth Century Liverpool/Prescot Area Toolmakers', 424–29.

68 E. Surrey Dane, *Peter Stubs and the Lancashire Hand Tool Industry* (Altrincham: Sherratt, 1975), Ch. 5, 'The New Workshop', 57–82.
69 Names of the firms are in John A. Robey, *The Longcase Clock Reference Book* (2 vols. Ashbourne: Mayfield, 2001), vol. 1, 94–97.
70 Weiss, *Watchmaking in England, 1760–1820*, 72.
71 Theodore Crom, *Horological Wheel Cutting Engines,* 101–02; also id., 'A Few Eighteenth Century Liverpool/Prescot Area Toolmakers', 419–30; Baker, 'Early Lancashire Watch Fusee Engines', 215–28, 315–21; Roberts and Pidgeon, 'Biographical Sketch of Mr John Wyke', 66–76, and Holt, 'Prescot Watchmaking in the 18th Century', 44–47; Kemp, 'Watch Movement Making in Prescot', 77–81, 83.
72 Robey, *Longcase Clock Reference Book*, 1/64, 68–70, 89.
73 Too great, at least until the present day: the late George Daniels (1926–2011) and a few others have designed and made exquisite watches from scratch with the aid of modern machine tools. Tiny output meant high prices.

3 Supply

Two Other Hubs: Liverpool and Coventry

Introduction

The emergence of a watch-finishing centre in Clerkenwell is explained by its proximity to London's prosperous market. Its location in a metal-working district was similar to the advent of rough movement making in Prescot and toolmaking in Lancashire's other villages. The origins of the watchmaking hubs that began in Liverpool and Coventry were different. Their origins are less easy to explain because they did not start where earlier metal-working trades had been. Other cities of roughly the same size and importance at the beginning of the century might also have developed watch-finishing centres but did not. Cork, Birmingham, Manchester, Glasgow and Bristol, for example, all had domestic long-case clockmakers and a few individual 'watchmakers' who retailed and repaired. Yet no watchmaking hubs emerged in any of those cities. This chapter reviews how and why watchmaking began, first in Liverpool and then in Coventry.

Aspinwall of Toxteth Park, Liverpool

The city of Liverpool grew around its port's trade in cotton and slaves. The development of nearby Prescot's rough watch movement trade may have helped to explain the rise of a small watch-finishing centre between 1607 and 1624 in Toxteth Park (about eight miles from Prescot; today a part of Liverpool's inner city). 'Finishing' watches appear to have been done by Thomas Aspinwall, described as a 'gentleman watchmaker' (more accurately, perhaps, 'yeoman farmer and part-time watchmaker'?).[1] A surviving watch with his signature is dated 1607. An inventory of his goods testifies to his evident technical ability, and he completed watches until he died in 1624. His entrepreneurial talents may be implied from his trade in the 1620s with three other Lancastrians known to be watchmakers in London, two of whom were relatives.[2] Amongst evidence that reinforces connections between the watch-making Thomas Aspinwall in Liverpool and his tradesmen relatives in London is an order from London for a brass watch 'of the best sort'

DOI: 10.4324/9781003227823-4

made in Toxteth Park.[3] From these London connections, his business expanded. He 'had customers of his own and dealt in finished watches' and did piecework for another maker. Jeffrey Tang believes that Aspinwall bought parts – springs, cases, and possibly pinion wire – from other local specialists for his workshop and its sales outlet in London. Quite how many watches were finished at Toxteth Park is unknown.[4] His success may have been based on taking advantage of cheaper labour costs in Lancashire's villages compared with London.

Tang suggested that Aspinwall's trade with London resulted from a surplus of watches in Liverpool that exceeded effective local demand. Even if Toxteth's watch-making temporarily waned after Thomas Aspinwall's death, it was revived by his son, Samuel.[5] When Samuel died in 1672 the family's watchmaking business had clearly prospered, for he left an estate of £2,268 that included watch-making materials valued at £797.[6] It was an amount that simply 'could not have [been] amassed', John Griffiths concluded, 'by selling [only] a few watches to his neighbours'.[7] Aspinwall seems to have sown and watered the crucial seed from which Liverpool's watch-finishing took root. It may be that his enterprise was the only early example of watch-finishing in the Liverpool area, for if there were similar enterprises neither artefacts nor records have survived. It is not clear if the connection between this early episode and later developments is unbroken. A parish register for the 1670s contained names of a dozen described as 'watchmakers', who included spring and case makers. By 1675, there were in Liverpool 'almost fifty watchmakers', and perhaps more.[8]

Richard Wright's notebook: early eighteenth century

More substantial evidence about watch-finishing in Liverpool in the early eighteenth century is in a rare surviving business record, the *Notebook* of Richard Wright. Professor Alan Smith's analysis described details of 129 rough movements 'finished' between 1713 and 1732 and shows that Wright (like Aspinwall, a century earlier) *received* some watches to *finish* for London makers.[9] Wright, scion of a well-established land-owning family of Cronton, Lancashire (about ten miles east of Liverpool), evidently augmented his income by employing local craftsmen to finish watches – a reversal of what became the normal flow in the Prescot–Liverpool–London horological axis in which Prescot's rough movements were sent to London to be finished and cased in Clerkenwell.[10] Wright's clients were well-known London makers; they included Daniel Quare and John Ellicott. Again, it may be that some London makers used cheaper labour in south-west Lancashire not only to make parts and rough movements but sometimes to finish watches. The numbers of watches involved were not great: Richard Wright's annual average was about six or seven finished watches over twenty years. Although this confirms the existence of some 'finishing' in Liverpool in the early eighteenth century, its output was tiny compared with that of Clerkenwell. Nevertheless, Liverpool's small hub gradually grew. Information about half-a-dozen watchmaker specialists has been uncovered by Oliver Fairclough in his research into the city's local clock-making industry; by the 1750s, they numbered about a hundred and by 1800 over 430. Their connection with watchmaking was explicitly identified by Fairclough as 'watch case makers, engravers, spring-makers, gilders, chain makers, hand makers, enamellers and one watch wheel maker'.[11] The Liverpool Museum's horology database (formerly in the Prescot Museum) compiled by Denis Moore, identified twenty-three specialist watchmaking occupations in Prescot.[12]

Fairclough's tables summarise fragmentary information and must be viewed with caution because of uncertainties about the boundaries of 'Liverpool and District' and ambiguities in entries allocated to 'watchmaking' or 'allied trades'. Nor is it clear if a single entry represented one craftsman, plus an apprentice or two, or referred to an 'establishment' – a workshop unit that may have employed several. There were probably larger numbers in various branches of watchmaking after the 1720s than those revealed in Fairclough's survey.[13] Nevertheless, it offers evidence that, after an erratic and uneven start, watch-finishing in Liverpool was established by 1750. Later, it enjoyed substantial growth, probably five-fold over the next forty years.[14]

The Plate Act, 1784

Because so few business records have survived, historians are uncertain about the size and output of Liverpool's early watch-finishing sector. H.R. Fox-Bourne, who wrote in the 1880s, cited a contemporary source that claimed in 1753 Liverpool was 'well-known' for finished watches, 'which are not to be excelled in Europe... all the different branches are manufactured in and about the town, to supply London and foreign markets'.[15] Plausible assumptions may be deduced from evidence of the local consequences of applying the Plate Act of 1784. The Act was intended to raise money to pay for Britain's involvement in the War of Independence in America, and it imposed serious penalties for non-compliance of hallmarking (£50 fine, forfeiture of goods, even death). The threat worked. In 1784–85, eight Liverpool case makers registered for the first time at Chester. One suggestion is that workers in gold and silver watch cases had hitherto evaded hallmarking duties and boxes of finished but allegedly uncased movements had been shipped directly to the Americas.[16] Another glimpse of the city's small watch-finishing businesses comes from sixteen watch case makers, in business between 1785 and 1798. Their combined weekly output increased from sixteen 'pair cases' in 1785, to forty-three in 1792, then fell to thirty-three in

1797 (perhaps a consequence of Pitt's tax? see Chapter 7). Between 1785 and 1797 some 18,026 silver and eighty-four gold cases were assayed – an annual average of 1,386 'pair cases'.[17] Unknown numbers of Liverpool's movements may also have been set in base metal cases. If an individual finisher might 'finish' two watches a week, these figures suggest that fourteen or fifteen of Liverpool's finishers were employed finishing movements to be set in precious metal cases. It is possible that an unknown number of movements intended for base metal cases were exported, uncased. In 1790, Barfoot and Wilkes in their *Universal Directory* listed fifty-three 'horological' firms in Liverpool; it included twenty-nine 'watchmakers'.[18] Although the city's population of about 20,000 in 1750 had grown to about 80,000 by 1800, nevertheless the potential home market (including Liverpool's hinterland) was still small. Other fragments of evidence show growth in the city's small watch-finishing centre. Of the twenty-nine 'watchmakers' who voted in the 1806 parliamentary election possibly some were proprietors of a dozen to twenty small 'finishing' units in the city.[19] By 1824, Liverpool had over a hundred specialist spring-makers, finishers and case makers in a population of 118,972 in 23,309 families.[20] Watchmaking in Liverpool had grown from delicate but deep roots.

Growth after 1800 can be explained by two elements – location and serendipity. Liverpool was only eight miles from Prescot that by then was well established as the supplier of rough movements to London's watch finishers. Prescot's proximity helped Liverpool's finishing hub. But it was not essential, because distances from components were not crucial: short-distance transport costs formed only a fraction of a watch's price. Prescot's rough movement making was an advantageous but not a crucial feature for the growth of Liverpool's watch-finishing. More important were the external trade links of Liverpool's port. It connected watchmakers – and others – to Ireland and especially to lucrative markets in the Americas.[21] Serendipity – chance – was the second factor in the growth of the city's watch industry. It enjoyed important supporting specialisms, thanks to the inventive and entrepreneurial skills of three individuals – Peter Litherland (1756–1804), Edward Massey (1768–1852), and Mayer Isaac Tobias (1762–1838) and his family.

Litherland, Massey, and Tobias

Peter Litherland was born in 1756 in Warrington, where he worked as a watchmaker before moving twenty miles west to Liverpool in 1790, enticed by the port's connections with profitable markets. Just at a time when chronometer manufacturing in London was growing (Chapter 10), Litherland took out two patents for escapements in 1791 and 1792. He hoped they might enable ordinary watches to perform with the precision of the chronometers currently being made by Arnold, Earnshaw, and others. He invented (more accurately, re-invented) the rack lever escapement, enabling watches to be smaller, lighter, and thinner. He saw the potential for

> an entire escapement to be applied to watches or clocks for the use on sea or land which acting upon an entire new principle producing greater certainty of time than any hitherto invented being more simple and less likely to be out of repair and repaired with less danger to the mechanical principles on which it is constructed than former watches and which he conceives will be of great public utility especially for ascertaining the longitude at sea at much less expense than those now used.[22]

At the end of the eighteenth century, Clerkenwell's finest watches were fitted with a chronometer escapement to enable better precision. They needed a full plate layout with a fusee, which resulted in a one-inch-thick watch weighing between five and eight ounces. Navigators, who wanted accuracy above all, did not mind the size and weight of the movement in a box chronometer. But size and weight were important to watch buyers. Litherland's hope that his escapement might lead to cheap chronometers proved over-optimistic, although his second patent, for watch number 306 in 1792, emulated contemporary trends in Europe because it incorporated a going barrel instead of a fusee. Vaudrey Mercer observed that Litherland's invention was essentially a re-invention of a type of escapement first made in 1722 by the Abbe de Hautefeuille. He 'simplified the movement greatly, and [it was] no longer in trouble with broken [fusee] chains'.[23] His improvements boosted the output of Liverpool's finished watches. Had Clerkenwell's makers followed Liverpool's lead (or that of the Swiss in the Jura?) and adopted the going barrel earlier than they did, then the subsequent fortunes of England's watchmaking industry might have been different.

The technical advantages of Litherland's rack lever were modified and improved in 1812 by Edward Massey – the inventor of a successful 'sounding machine' (a device to measure the depth of water under a ship), and the 'detached lever' escapement.[24] He had moved from Newcastle-under-Lyme not to Liverpool but to Coventry, where many of his early lever watches were produced by that city's firms (see below). By the 1820s, lever movements dominated English manufacture and they took over gradually from the cylinder escapement, hitherto typical of eighteenth-century English watches. The lever was a reliable escapement for 'ordinary' watches and, technical descriptions suggest, it kept time to within ten to fifteen seconds a day. Because it was unusually resistant to sharp movements, it almost never 'stopped' and thus, David Landes noted, 'found ever wider acceptance'.[25] It became a staple of Liverpool's watch production in the first half of the nineteenth century, boosting its watch trade in both home and export markets.[26] But although two of Massey's sons – escapement makers – represented the family firm in London, his detached lever was rarely used by Clerkenwell's firms. Its diffusion to the continent was also slow until the Swiss took up their production on a large scale in the 1840s. Those Swiss watches were intended as much for sale in British markets as in other parts of Europe. 'Liverpool watches', as they became known, were more expensive than Swiss equivalents, but cheaper than Clerkenwell's. This was perhaps because some hand work was eliminated in their assembly. George Daniels explained that special jigs and tools were devised to make pallets on 'a semi-mass-production basis', so that there was uniformity 'in the rough', and some parts were interchangeable within the broad limits (at that time) set by the condition and wear of the tools. The volume of production was not increased but the use of semi-skilled workers lowered labour costs.[27]

Litherland died in 1804. The firm relocated in Liverpool several times in subsequent partnerships: the most durable were 'Litherland, Whiteside & Co., Patent Lever Watchmakers' and, in the 1830s, 'Litherland, Davies & Co., Chronometer and Watch Manufacturers'. Estimates of the firm's output using the serial numbering system (started in 1791 and continued until 1865) reveal that in its first phase the firm made about 4,000 watches at an average of 285 a year. Between 1805 and 1814 annual output grew to an average of 440 a year. Output fell by half over the next few years, but then rose to about 500 annually. Between 1825 and 1865 (when the firm closed), it made another 30,000 watches at an overall average annual output of about 750. Robert Roskell bought Litherland's patent rights for his rack lever escapement and made more than 100,000 serially numbered watches – an annual average of about 1,000 a year for the rest of the century.[28] It was an output greater than that of another leading Liverpool firm, Richard Hornby, which made 280 watches a year between 1830 and 1850.[29]

The technical innovations of Litherland and Massey that enhanced Liverpool's watch industry were further stimulated by the entrepreneurial activities of the Tobias family. Morris Tobias (1762/3–1846) had a workshop in Wapping, London, between 1797 and 1814. From 1805 to about 1812, it had a branch in Liverpool run by his adopted relative Meyer Isaac Tobias (1763–1838). Morris Tobias refurbished chronometers in Wapping for the British Admiralty and supplied Bond of Boston. Michael Edidin's analyses of his output indicate that his workshop finished annually a maximum of a thousand watches between 1801 and 1806 and about 700 between 1806 and 1809. He thinks that surviving examples of his watches show the 'train and escapement of the rack levers reflect[ed] Liverpool; their casing, some of their details and their finishing reflect[ed] London ... [and that the] ... jewelling and engraving of the watches are very much Liverpool'.[30]

The Liverpool industry's trade with America was led by Morris's nephew, Meyer Isaac, who ran the Liverpool branch of the Tobias network at 5 Pool Lane on his own account. He established connections between rough movement makers in Prescot, finishers in Liverpool and Clerkenwell, and merchants and traders in the United States. His American agents included other Tobias relatives in New York and Philadelphia, from where there were further links to other retailers. Tobias watches were reputed to be of 'good, though not outstanding' quality, but were so well regarded in America as good value for money that they were later widely 'forged with impunity' by both Coventry and Swiss makers (Chapter 12).[31] Thanks to the efforts of Litherland, Massey, and M.I. Tobias, watchmaking in Liverpool reached its high point by the mid-nineteenth century.[32] It declined thereafter when it lost its home markets to even cheaper watches made in Coventry and Switzerland. Its export markets were lost because of the success of the revolution in American watchmaking led by Waltham and Elgin (Chapter 11).

Coventry: origins of watchmaking

Coventry became an important provincial business hub in the early modern period from an economy built on trade in wool and textiles. By the nineteenth century, its industrial base had widened to include ribbon making and watchmaking. Information about the city's early watchmaking industry is sparse and not much can be gleaned from standard histories. The traveller and writer Thomas Pennant thought no significant watchmaking industry existed in the city before 1760.[33] John Prest's *The Industrial Revolution in Coventry* cited Samuel Timmins' 1866 account of the region's hardware industries, with only its brief reference to watchmaking.[34] Neither G.C. Allen's survey of Coventry's industrial development, nor the *Victoria County Histories* add much.[35] Two university theses by local historians offer more, although one is concerned mostly with developments after 1820. The other deals only briefly with watchmaking as its primary focus lies with the ribbon trade. Other accounts of Coventry's watchmakers concern the late nineteenth century and do not discuss the industry's origins.[36]

Why such paucity of information about the origins of Coventry's watchmaking industry? Robert Kemp implied it reflected the view that it was because the poor quality of Coventry's watches never generated the kind of veneration paid to Clerkenwell's great makers or Liverpool's entrepreneurs. The vagueness of the industry's origins, he writes, 'was largely self-imposed as an almost conscious policy. In an era when other cities stamped their products boldly as '*Made in…*' Coventry never got closer than an occasional tentative '*warranted English*'.[37] Perhaps it is also explained by the destruction of the city's early historical records in the Second World War; bombing destroyed the business records of Coventry's best-known watchmaking firm, Rotherham.

The little that *is* known records the good reputation of individual watchmakers from Coventry in the late seventeenth century. One was Samuel Watson, a sheriff in 1682 who later moved to London and made an astronomic clock bought by Charles II. Another was his Coventry watchmaking apprentice, John Carte, who established a business in London in 1695.[38] It is reasonable to infer that George Porter, a watchmaker who became the city's mayor in 1727, had started in the trade some years earlier and had become sufficiently successful and wealthy enough to occupy that position. The city's most notable watchmaking firm, Rotherham, was founded in 1747 by Samuel Vale. It became 'Vale, Howlett and Carr', and later still 'Vale, Carr and Rotherham'.[39] Vale was four times elected mayor. Joan Lane has suggested that his personal prosperity indicated the growth and success of the city's watchmaking industry.[40] Kemp noted that during the third quarter of the eighteenth century some Coventry firms made rough movements that they then fitted and finished; other firms supplied London with 'partially finished movements and to a lesser extent met the needs of Liverpool [finishers]'.[41] But even as late as 1890 the largest Coventry firms still bought wheels and pinions from Prescot.[42]

Coventry's apprenticeship system

It was the apprentice system that differentiated Coventry's watch industry from those in Clerkenwell and Liverpool.[43] The use of apprentice labour in a watch 'factory' had apparently been attempted earlier in Birmingham but failed, for obscure reasons. The proprietor concerned (unnamed, but possibly the Rotherham who joined Samuel Vale's firm?) then moved to Coventry and set up a finishing 'factory' that employed apprentices. Other firms were founded at about the same time, possibly in emulation, and in the 1770s an elementary division of labour separated production between 'first halfers' and 'second halfers'.[44] After 1781 an indication of the industry's growth was the steady flow of boys into watchmaking recorded in the city's apprenticeship registers. Over 900 were indentured and another 360 were bound to various branches. From 1780 to 1820, some 1,550 apprentice watchmakers were admitted as Coventry Freemen, and 1119 between 1841 and 1860.[45] Masters retained a firm grip on recruitment, and it seems that few poor boys were indentured, and parish paupers were excluded.[46]

At that time, the practice of 'long apprenticeships' – of seven years – was under threat. Adam Smith thought them 'altogether unnecessary ... making clocks and watches contain no such mystery as to require a long course in instruction'. He wrote that the trade might be explained 'to any young man... in the lessons of a few weeks; perhaps those of a few days might be sufficient'.[47] Smith did not mean, of course, that the skills and ingenuity needed for one man to design and construct an entire watch single-handedly might be taught quickly. The division of labour in Clerkenwell had already separated those skills. Consequently, hardly any apprentices were, or could be, trained in all – or even most – aspects of the trade. It was simply more advantageous to use them as cheap labour, trained to perform one or two narrowly defined tasks. Essentially, Coventry's watchmakers exploited cheap apprentice labour because their 'wage costs' were low compared with those for equivalent work done by adults in Clerkenwell. Such exploitation was not confined to watchmaking but could also be seen in Coventry's silk-weaving trade, its ribbon making industry, in calico printing to the north, and in the printing trades in London.[48]

Coventry's biggest firms brought apprentices together in large workshops or factory buildings where, crucially, some were taught to *finish* watches.[49] Hitherto, 'finishing' had traditionally been the preserve of master craftsmen, who opposed the idea that this feature of the 'art and mysterie' of their craft should become routine. Yet in Coventry it did. Apprentices finished watches that were mostly intended for the bottom end of the market and were usually inferior in quality compared with standard Clerkenwell and Liverpool products. The 1817 parliamentary *Inquiry* and its *Report* in 1818 (Chapters 7 and 8) showed that there were about thirty watch-making 'factories' in Coventry that took advantage of the 'ingenuity' of adolescent lads, contrary to the spirit as well as the laws behind apprenticeships. The number of apprentices taken on was 'far beyond the probability of employment when they become journeymen... [and] the Coventry system... produces more than can be maintained in the profession and depreciates the value of labour... the increased number of hands makes a surplus of watches'.[50]

Coventry's two largest firms each employed between twenty-five and forty apprentices in their factories; a dozen smaller houses between them employed another 160. Independent journeymen – or masters with one or two apprentices – also assembled watches in their own homes. On a piece work basis in prosperous times they earned between 25s and 30s a week. Normally, this was an adequate wage, but in a depression – like that in the years before and after Waterloo – incomes fell or disappeared (Chapter 7).[51] By the 1840s numbers of journeymen had grown to about 800, many of whom surely signed the petition to parliament to protest the possible setting up of Ingold's watch factory in London in 1842 (Chapter 9).[52]

Rotherham

Most of Coventry's watches were made, like those in Clerkenwell, in scores of small units; but the city was also home to Rotherham, then the largest watchmaking firm in the country. Its annual output of about 6,000 watches in the 1840s rose to about 9,000 in the 1850s. The writer Harriet Martineau visited the works in 1852 and left a long, rambling account in Charles Dickens' *Household Words*.[53] She reported that Rotherham employed 'the higher order of workmen [who] average twenty-eight shillings, or thirty shillings' a week. Boys of fourteen were apprenticed for seven or eight years at a cost of £8 for the first year, 'advancing £1 a year every year until they are out of their time, which is about 4s 3d per week on average'.[54] In such a system, every boy made his employer a notional 'profit' of 18s–24s per week. The wholesale price to retailers of Rotherham's best watches was £20, 'which mounts up to a good deal more in London shops'; their most expensive cost £35. Coventry's masters claimed the best watches they made were 'as good as any produced at London or Liverpool'. Outsiders were unpersuaded – indeed contemptuous – of this view. They believed Coventry watches were generally poor because the factories that made them were set up by people who were 'not themselves brought up in the business, and they, to teach their apprentices, employ men who are... ill qualified for the purpose'. Miss Martineau described the clumsy and old-fashioned characteristics of Rotherham's cheapest watches, sold to agricultural labourers at £3. Such watches were, she explained, because

> They are of wondrous size; about two inches thick. There is silver to the value of two pounds in a watch which costs four pounds. The thing looks as if it could never be lost – hardly broken; and it is inconceivable that damp or soil could get in. On its face is painted a gay picture – Speed the Plough, or the Foresters' or the Odd Fellows' Arms. Next in bulk to these are the watches for the Scotch market. The Scotch seem to like to feel that they have a watch in their pocket.

But only about eight or nine were still being made from a weekly output of about 150. Demand was declining because the cheapest Coventry watches were more expensive and less attractive than those imported or smuggled from Switzerland (Chapters 7 and 8).

****

Watchmaking outside the four main hubs

Clerkenwell, Prescot, Liverpool, and Coventry constituted the four bases of England's watchmaking industry in the eighteenth century; in the nineteenth century they were joined by a hub in Birmingham. Between them, they made the overwhelming majority of 'English watches'. Other 'watchmakers' may have flitted in and out of watchmaking in other cities in the British Isles, assembling and finishing unknown numbers of watches. Most 'watchmakers' listed in town and regional trade *Directories* were self-employed retailers and repairers ('jobbers'). Although their titles normally included the appellation 'clock and/or watch maker', their main business was retailing and repairing, usually in small workshops on their premises. Some may have also looked after neighbourhood public clocks. They may have had an apprentice or, if the business was in a good commercial area, a shop assistant. Many retailers stocked and sold a range of jewellery and silverware as well as clocks and watches, like James Ritchie of Edinburgh (below) and perhaps finished a watch on which they put their name. In practice, they might have done not much more than assemble and case the movement. Of the watchmakers outside the industry's four main centres, brief case studies from Scotland, Ireland and Wales illustrate aspects of what happened elsewhere. Donovan in Ireland and Hughes in Wales seem quite distinctive examples, as there is no evidence so far of others like them. But Ritchie of Edinburgh may be more typical of similar experiences of independent 'watchmakers' in other large cities.[55]

Three case studies: Edinburgh, Dublin, and Llangollen

James Ritchie had served an apprenticeship to an Edinburgh watchmaker and subsequently opened his own shop as a watch repairer in 1809. His archive shows that of his first 2,500 business transactions about 80 percent were for cleaning and repairing watches, and he evidently learned much from dismantling and reassembling their movements. Occasionally, he sold completed watches he bought-in from Clerkenwell. Sometimes he 'finished' a few rough movements for sale. Of the eighty-two new silver watches assembled and sold between 1809 and 1812, thirty-two were top-grade, signed as 'made' (finished) by him and inscribed 'Ritchie, Edinburgh'. Those of lesser quality were signed with his inverted name, 'R. James, Edinburgh'.[56] Customers chose the case and thereby determined how much they spent. Ritchie's experience may have been typical of other 'watchmakers' in cities such as Bath, York or Manchester. For example, Bath and Bristol respectively professed five and fourteen 'watchmakers' in the *Universal British Directory* of 1790.[57] It is not known if they just sold and repaired or, like Ritchie, also finished some and added their own name. If records have survived, they have not yet been analysed. Similar firms named as 'watchmakers' in provincial towns and cities also retailed luxury and semi-luxury goods.

Quite different, and on a much larger scale, was John Donovan of Dublin, reputed to be 'the sole remaining Irish watchmaker' in the mid-nineteenth century. He imported rough movements 'at comparatively little cost' (probably from Prescot) that were then 'finished' in a workshop that employed between forty and sixty workers. Productivity was low and output was modest.[58] Between 1843 and 1852 Donovan's firm finished about 4,000 watches – an average of around 400 a year, or fewer than ten movements per worker. The little watch factory was an interesting example in Ireland of an enterprise which used inexpensive labour and an elementary factory organisation applied to a complex technology that made a product for which there was potentially a huge market. A contemporary decried Donovan's watches because they allegedly had 'inferior movements such as are [also] made by the gross in Scotland and are turned out in a hasty manner...'.[59] Unfortunately for Ireland, watchmaking did not develop as it did in Switzerland, and Donovan's enterprise followed an earlier unsuccessful attempt to establish watchmaking in Ireland by Genevans, in the 1780s.[60]

Another unusual example of watchmaking outside the four main centres was Robert Hughes of Llangollen. Between 1872 and 1905, he launched and sustained in North Wales a watchmaking unit that assembled and finished 10,000–11,000 watches. He bought rough movements from Prescot, imported twenty 'finishers' from Coventry, and travelled around rural Wales to sell them. He was especially successful in Welsh-speaking areas where his bilingualism enabled him to assemble a network of loyal retailers. His largest annual output was about 500 'Llangollen' watches, a miniscule number in comparison with the massive contemporary production of 'dollar' watches in America.[61] He also acted as an agent for large firms, like Williamson of Coventry, the Lancashire Watch Company, and even Waltham.

The four main hubs of England's watchmaking industry were well established by the end of the eighteenth century. They were joined in the nineteenth century by firms in Birmingham (Chapter 15). Neither of the short-lived regional markets catered for by Donovan and Hughes nor the urban markets by individuals like James Ritchie, added much to the aggregate output of watchmaking in the United Kingdom. Among the original four hubs, Clerkenwell and Prescot complemented each other, and Prescot's proximity to Liverpool must have helped the latter to survive for as long as it did. Coventry was distinctive, with its mixture of proto-factories and outworkers. Led by Clerkenwell, new technologies were developed that increased output, as we shall see next, in Chapter 4.

Notes

1 R. John Griffiths, 'The Early Watchmakers of Toxteth Park Near Liverpool, and the Origins of the Industry, the Aspinwalls, with Some Notes on their Successors', *Antiquarian Horology*, 27/2 (December 2002), 163–78; also Ted Crom, 'A Few Eighteenth Century Liverpool/Prescot area Toolmakers', *Antiquarian Horology*, 19/4 (Summer 1991), 419–30.

2 F.A. Bailey and T.C. Barker, 'The Seventeenth-Century Origins of Watchmaking in South-west Lancashire', in J.R. Harris (ed.), *Liverpool and Merseyside: Essays in the Economic and Social History of the Port and Its Hinterland* (London: Cass, 1969), 1–15; T.C. Barker and J.R. Harris, *A*

Merseyside Town in the Industrial Revolution: St Helens, 1750–1900 (London: Routledge, 1954); also F.A. Bailey, 'An Old Watchmaker s Workshop', *Transactions of the Ancient Monuments Society* (1953), 3–8.

3 Jeffrey D. Tang, 'Timely Success: The Role of Locational Lock-in and Path-dependence in the Rise of the Southwest Lancashire Watchmaking Industry' (unpublished MPhil thesis, Oxford University 1996), 69, cites evidence culled from F.A. Bailey's unpublished 1955 MS on Lancashire watchmaking, then held in Prescot Museum's archive (now in Liverpool Museum). For a discussion of 'path-dependence', see S.J. Liebowitz and Stephen E. Margolis, 'Path Dependence, Lock-in, and History', *Journal of Law, Economics, & Organization*, 11/1 (April 1995), 205–26, at https://doi.org/10.1093/oxfordjournals.jleo.a036867, and Chapter 9 below.

4 Tang, 'Timely Success', 35ff, 56–68, 235.

5 Bailey and Barker's general conclusions are reinforced in R.A.H. Ward, 'Watchmaking in the Liverpool Area before 1730' (Unpublished B.Phil. dissertation, Department of History, Liverpool University, 1970), 1–8, who suggests that after Thomas Aspinwall s early start, watchmaking in the district might have temporarily died away, and then revived.

6 For Samuel's wealth at death see Geoffrey Timmins, *Made in Lancashire: A History of Regional Industrialisation* (Manchester: Manchester UP, 1998), 25.

7 John Griffiths, 'The Rise and Fall of Toolmaking in Lancashire ',*Journal of the North West Society for Industrial Archaeology and History* (1994), 3. On the acquisition by Prescot Museum of two watches (one each by Thomas Aspinwall and his son Samuel), Charles Allix wrote 'they show progressive refinement in both execution and elegance': *Antiquarian Horology*, 23/3 (Autumn 1997), 213–14.

8 Bailey and Barker, 'Seventeenth Century Origins', 5–6; Bailey, 'Old Watchmaker's Workshop', 3–6.

9 My italics. Alan Smith, 'An Eighteenth-Century Watchmaker's Notebook: The Lancaster-London Connection', *Antique Collecting* (March 1985), 37–43. The notebook is reprinted, with an expanded commentary, in *Antiquarian Horology*, 15 (Dec. 1985), 605–25. Also R.A.H. Ward, 'A Watchmaker's Pocket Book', *Transactions of the Lancashire and Cheshire Historic Society*, 122 (1971), 153–57.

10 Smith, 'Watchmaker's Notebook', 38–39.

11 Oliver Fairclough, 'Joseph Finney and the Clock and Watchmakers of Eighteenth Century Liverpool.' (Unpublished MA Thesis, Keele University, 1975), 11, 304–05 for tables on 'Growth of the Main branches of the trade'. Fairclough's evidence is drawn from local parish registers and directories, and summarised in his Appendix VII, 'Biographical Index of Liverpool Clockmakers, Watchmakers, Instrument Makers, and Workers in Allied Trades,' 331–418.

12 Neil Cummins and Cormac Ó Gráda, 'Artisanal Skills, Watchmaking, and the Industrial Revolution: Prescot and Beyond', *UCD Centre for Economic Research: Working Paper Series* (WP19/24, October 2019), 4–5, at https://econpapers.repec.org/paper/ucnwpaper/201924.htm

13 John Griffiths (Prescot Museum; email, July 1997).

14 Alan Smith, 'Introduction', in Alan Smith (ed.) *A Catalogue of Tools for Watch and Clock Makers by John Wyke of Liverpool* (Charlottesville, VA: Henry Francis du Pont Winterthur Museum and Virginia UP, 1978), 2.

15 H.R. Fox-Bourne, *England Merchants: Memoirs in Illustration of the Progress of British Commerce* (2 vols., London: Chatto, 1886), 2/75, citing Williamson's *Liverpool Memorandum Book* (n.p., n.d.) Other background

material is in F.H. Cheetham, 'Notes on some Ormskirk Watch and Clock Makers', *Transactions of the Antiquarian Society of Lancashire and Cheshire*, 51 (1936), 1–10.

16 Dennis S. Moore and P.T. Priestley, 'Some Account of Liverpool Watch Case Makers, 1785–1798', *Antiquarian Horology*, 23 (Summer 1997), 342.

17 Moore and Priestley, 'Liverpool Watch Case Makers', 341–53; 'Odd boxes and cases have been matched and counted as pair cases [which] as hunters were then a characteristic of English watches'.

18 Peter Barfoot and John Wilkes, *The Universal British Directory of Trade and Commerce* (5 vols., London: printed for the Patentees, 1794), Vol. 3, sub 'Liverpool', 680–730.

19 Godfrey W. Mathews, 'Some Notes on the Liverpool Election of 1806', *Transactions of the Historical Society of Lancashire and Cheshire*, 79 (1927), 81.

20 ['F.G.'], 'Liverpool Horologists of 1824', *Horological Journal*, 81/4 (Dec. 1939), 438–39.

21 Bailey and Barker, 'Seventeenth Century Origins', 5–6; Bailey, 'Old Watchmaker's Workshop', 3–6.

22 For an account of Litherland, and the source of the quotation, see R. Vaudrey Mercer, 'Peter Litherland and Co.', *Antiquarian Horology*, 3 (June 1962), 316–24.

23 Vaudrey Mercer, 'Litherland', *Antiquarian Horology*, 4 (1962), 319–20; Report of a lecture by Alan Treherne on 'Litherland Lever Watches', *Antiquarian Horology*, 33/3 (March 2012), 406.

24 For Massey's 'sounding machine, see James Poskett, 'Sounding in Silence: Men, Machines and the Changing Environment of Naval Discipline, 1796–1815', *The British Journal for the History of Science*, 48/2 (no. 177) (June 2015), 213–32, at https://www.jstor.org/stable/26898183; for his 'detached lever' escapement, a technical explanation was offered by Alan Smith (letter, 1986): 'The rack lever is not good in principle, but it had certain advantages. It led to improvements by Massey and others, leading to the English lever and subsequently the straight-line lever employed by Swiss and American makers.' For Massey, see Alan Treherne, *The Massey Family: Clock, Watch, Chronometer and Nautical Instrument Makers* (Newcastle under Lyme: Borough Museum, 1977); also lecture report in *Antiquarian Horology*, 36/2 (June 2015), 278; David Thompson, 'Edward Massey', *Watches* (London: British Museum, 2008), 108–09.

25 David S. Landes, *Revolution in Time: Clocks and the Making of the Modern World* (Cambridge, MA: Belknap, Harvard UP, 1983). 142–43.

26 Michael W. Piece, 'Moncas of Liverpool. A Short History of a Nineteenth-Century Watch-Making Family', *Antiquarian Horology*, 36/1 (March 2015), 40–52 identifies 139 recorded Moncas watches, many with Massey-type escapements. Their number amounts to over 17,000 but it is not possible to indicate the firm's precise output.

27 George Daniels, *English and American Watches* (London: Abelard Schuman, 1967), 41; Landes, *Revolution in Time*, 267; R.T. Gould, *The Marine Chronometer; Its History and Development* (1923: London: Holland Press, 1960). 152.

28 David M.W. Evans, 'Liverpool Watchmakers', *Antiquarian Horology*, 9/6 (March 1976), 705; id., 'Peter Litherland, Liverpool, and the Rack Lever', *Antiquarian Horology*, 32/1 (March 2010), 93–96, that concluded 'no two watches by the firm are ever the same. All sorts of variations were tried ...'. Serial numbers suggest an output of up to 22,000 of the several different types of watch (and some two-day chronometers).

29 Alan Treherne (email, 8 October 2014) notes that as well as Massey, other Liverpool firms used detached lever escapements including George Savage and Hornby & Son.
30 Michael Edidin, *English Watches for the American Market: A History of Watchmaking by the Tobias Families of London and Liverpool* (NAWCC *Bulletin*), 1992 (Part 1: Oct.), 515–44; (Part 2: Dec.), 659–93.
31 Edidin, *Tobias*, 679ff. Tobias forgeries ('*Lepines*') cost 13 shillings to make but could be sold for as little as one tenth of the cost of a Clerkenwell watch. For a note on forgeries for the Swedish market made 'either in Switzerland ... or the French Jura', see Jan Kraminer, 'Swedish Forgeries', *Antiquarian Horology*, 29/3 (March 2006), 330–34.
32 For the growth of exports from Liverpool between 1825 and 1832 see Chapter 8, Table 8.1.
33 Thomas Pennant, *Tour from Downing to Alston Moor* (London: Harding, 1801).
34 John Prest, *The Industrial Revolution in Coventry* (Oxford: Oxford UP, 1960), 81; Samuel Timmins (ed.), *The Resources, Products, and Industrial History of Birmingham and the Midland Hardware District* (London: Hardwicke, 1866), 194–95; C. H. d'E. Leppington, 'The Evolution of an Industrial Town,' *The Economic Journal*, 17/67 (Sept. 1907), 345–57, at www.jstor.org/stable/2220473, adds little.
35 G. C. Allen, *The Industrial Development of Birmingham and the Black Country, 1860–1927* (London: Routledge, 1929); *Victoria County Histories, Warwickshire*, vols. II (London: Archibald Constable, 1908) and III (Oxford: Institute of Historical Research and Oxford UP, 1945).
36 For early watchmaking in Coventry see Prest, *Industrial Revolution in Coventry*; Peter Searby, 'Weavers and Freemen in Coventry, 1820–1861: Social and Political Traditionalism in an early Victorian town' (unpublished Ph.D. thesis, Warwick University, 1972), at http://webcat.warwick.ac.uk/record=b1735976~S15; also id., 'Watchmaking in Coventry', *Warwickshire History*, 3 (1976), 106–14. [Reprinted in *Antiquarian Horology*, 10/4 (Sept. 1977), 465–68]. Robert F. Prosser, 'Coventry: A study in Urban Continuity', [unpublished MA thesis, Birmingham University, 1955], Chapter 5 (60–67) contains a brief survey of watchmaking developments there in the nineteenth century; J.R. Bailey, 'The Struggle for Survival in the Coventry Ribbon and Watch Trades, 1865–1914', *Midland History*, 7 (1982), 132–52. My own paper is concerned with the late nineteenth century: Alun C. Davies, 'Old and New Technology in Watchmaking in Coventry, 1850–1920', *Antiquarian Horology*, 18/4 (Winter 1989), 397–410.
37 Robert Kemp, 'The Coventry Watch Trade', *Horological Journal* (March 1984), 17–20; quotation, 17.
38 Anthony J. Turner (ed.), *John Carte on Horology and Cosmology: A Transcription, with Introduction and Notes, of Bodleian Library Ms Carte 264ff. 18r–57r*, Turner & Devereux Occasional Paper No.5 (Ticehurst & Le Mesnil-le-Roi: Antiquarian Horological Society & Rogers Turner Books, 2014), 17, 23, 48.
39 Kevit Rotherham, 'Watches and Clocks', *Horological Journal* (Jan. 1924), 86–88. Much of this is repeated in Hugh Rotherham, 'The Watch Trade Past and Present', *Horological Journal*, 70 (May 1928), 62–64, and again in id., 'The Rise and Wane of English Watchmaking', *The Practical Watch and Clock Maker* (15 May 1928), 170–72; the two last items are based on a lecture given by Hugh Rotherham to the British Horological Institute; also John Woodward, 'Rotherham and Sons, Ltd., The Firm and the Family' (Coventry Public Library, 1975: Typescript MS, courtesy of Mr A.J. Mealey, sometime principal librarian at CPL).

40 Joan Lane, *Apprenticeship in England,* 1600–1914. (London: University College Press, 1996), 157–59.
41 Kemp, 'Coventry Watch Trade', 17.
42 'James Berry Notebook/Sales Ledger', in Liverpool National Museum, formerly in Prescot Museum archives. Information from John Griffiths, Prescot Museum.
43 Alan Treherne, 'The Contribution of South-west Lancashire to Horology: Part 1: Watch and Chronometer Movement Making and Finishing', *Antiquarian Horology*, 31/4 (June 2009), 457–76, esp. 461ff 'The Coventry Apprenticeship System'.
44 Mary Montes, *Brown Boots in Earlsdon: A Study of a Watchmaking Community, Its Rise and Fall* (Coventry: Historical Association Pamphlet no. 15, 1989), 18; also D.H. Bacon, *Watchmaking in Llangollen by Robert Hughes: a Genuine Late Nineteenth Century Welsh Watch Manufacturer* (Ticehurst: Antiquarian Horological Society New Series, no. 5, 2000), 19–20.
45 Peter Searby, 'Weavers and Freemen in Coventry, 1820–1861', 12: Table 1 summarises his analysis, by trades, of apprenticeships served by men admitted as Coventry Freemen from 1781 to 1860. Not included in the table in the text are 30 out of 520 of Searby's 'Group 1: professionals', who were also described as watchmakers; Also id., 'Chartists and Freemen in Coventry, 1838–1860', *Social History*, 2/6 (Oct. 1977), 767–68, at www.jstor.org/stable/4284734. See also *BPP* 1840, 24: 'Report from Assistant Commissioners, Hand-loom Weavers' (on watchmakers' wages in Coventry, 1838).
46 Lane, *Apprenticeship in England, 1600–1914*, 157–59. Two large firms were established by 1750, namely Bradshaw & Ryley, with seventy-nine apprentices and Vale & Howlett with 170 apprentices by the 1780s.
47 Adam Smith, *The Wealth of Nations* (1776: Harmondsworth: Penguin, 1970), 226; Morgan Kelly and Cormac Ó Gráda, 'Adam Smith, Watch Prices, and the Industrial Revolution', *Quarterly Journal of Economics*, 131[4] (2016), 1727–52, at https://doi.org/10.1093/qje/qjw026
48 John Rule, *The Experience of Labour in Eighteenth Century Industry* (New York: St Martin's Press, 1981), 99–100.
49 Prescot Museum had photos of about twenty of these, taken c.1984.
50 *BPP*, 1817 Minutes, 84–85.
51 *BPP, 1817 Minutes,* 74.
52 See Chapter 10 below. *BPP, 1817 Minutes,* 76; LMA/CLC/L/CD/E/006/MS03943/12, 13, 14.
53 Harriet Martineau, 'Time and the Hour', *Household Words*, 6 March 1852, and for subsequent quotations.
54 *BPP, 1817 Minutes*, 82, and for subsequent quotes.
55 Alun C. Davies, 'Starting up a Watchmaking Business: James Ritchie of Edinburgh, 1809–1812', *Antiquarian Horology*, 20/3 (Autumn 1992), 260–72.
56 David Alexander, *Retailing in England during the Industrial Revolution* (London: Athlone Press, 1970), 149; the practice of 'naming' had also spread to the cutlery trade.
57 Barfoot and Wilkes (compilers), *The Universal British Directory* (1793), vol. 2, 97–110 for Bath, 129–200 for Bristol.
58 Alun C. Davies, 'Ireland's Crystal Palace, 1853', in J.M. Goldstrom and L.A. Clarkson (eds.), *Irish Population, Economy and Society: Essays in Honour of the Late K.H. Connell* (Oxford: Clarendon, 1981), 249–70; id., 'The Society of Arts and the Dublin Exhibition of 1853', *Journal of the Royal Society for the Encouragement of Arts, Manufactures and Commerce* (June 1975), 433–36, at https://www.jstor.org/stable/41372165
59 J.F. Maguire, *The Industrial Movement in Ireland, as Illustrated by the National Exhibition of 1852* (Cork, John O'Brien, 1852), 143–46; Alun

C. Davies, 'Horology at International Industrial Exhibitions, 1851–1900', *Antiquarian Horology*, 33/5 (Sept. 2012), 594–95; id., "The First Irish Industrial Exhibition: Cork 1852', *Irish Social and Economic History* (1975), 2:46–59, at https://www.jstor.org/stable/24337058

60 Isadore Ryan, 'Republicans Seeking Asylum', *History Ireland*, 26/2 (2018), 22–25, at www.jstor.org/stable/90019384; also McNutt, Jenifer P, and Richard Whatmore. 'The Attempts to Transfer the Genevan Academy to Ireland and to America, 1782–1795', *The Historical Journal*, 56/2 (June 2013), 345–68 (esp. 353–55), at www.jstor.org/stable/24528840

61 Bacon, *Watchmaking in Llangollen by Robert Hughes*, 24; Rita Shenton, 'The Coventry Watch Trade', *Clocks*, 7 (Nov. 1984), 17–21.

4 Towards English Horology's Golden Age

Technology, Organisation, Rewards

A new horological era

From the mid-seventeenth to the late eighteenth century, a sequence of inventions and innovations transformed horological mechanisms. Collectively they signified the onset of horology's second epoch and paved the way for English horology's golden age. As the quality, accuracy, and reliability of clocks and watches improved, their cost of production fell. So did prices to consumers. The first major innovation was the application of pendulums to clocks, developed in 1656–57 by the Dutch scientist and horologist Christiaan Huygens after Galileo's experiments with a pendulum a decade or so earlier. Huygens had arranged for Salomon Coster, a clockmaker in The Hague, to make a prototype pendulum clock. One of Huygens' apprentices, Johannes Fromanteel, worked in Coster's workshop and brought details of the pendulum back to the London workshop of his father, Ahasuerus Fromanteel (1607–93).[1] Within a year the Fromanteels made and sold pendulum clocks from their houses 'on the Bankside in Mosses Alley, Southwark', and 'at the sign of the Mermaid in Loathbury, near Bartholomew Lane end, London'. An advertisement in the Commonwealth newspaper *Mercurius Politicus* famously set out the qualities of the new clocks.

> There is lately a way found for making of clocks that go exact and keep equaller time than any now made without this Regulator:... and this is very excellent for all House clocks that go either with Springs or Waights. And also Steeple Clocks that are most subject to differ by change of weather. Made by Ahasuerus Fromanteel that made the first that were in England.[2]

The time-keeping improvements arising from the introduction of pendulums were impressive: they were relatively simple to make and, when added to an existing clock, dramatically improved its performance. What the Fromanteels could do, others could copy, and they were rapidly adopted in the workshops of Anglo-Dutch clockmaking families in the

DOI: 10.4324/9781003227823-5

Dutch Republic and England.[3] Daily errors of longcase clocks were reduced to about a minute and even less for those of best quality. Demand grew. In the annals of technology, the application of so important a development has rarely been more speedily diffused. It is recognised as 'the greatest advance in the quest for accurate timekeeping in hundreds of years'.[4]

Watchmaking improvements: balance spring, and wheel-cutting engine

Improving the accuracy of watches followed. The invention of the spiral balance spring (sometimes termed a hairspring) also enabled remarkable advances in timekeeping.[5] That innovation was also rapidly diffused, partly because it could be applied at existing workbenches without the need for expensive extras, such as new power sources or larger buildings. Stocks of otherwise technically obsolete watches could be – and were – converted and fitted with a balance spring. As with many technical innovations, old and new technologies temporarily overlapped. Watchmakers introduced a minute wheel to control a minute hand that, David Landes thought, 'revolutionised time discipline'.[6] What previously had been little more than a rich man's ornamental toy became a serious timekeeper and, in its finest examples, a scientific instrument. It was another three centuries before there were improvements analogous to the dramatic impact of the balance spring, namely the shift from mechanical clockwork to quartz in the mid-twentieth century (Postscript). By about 1710, according to Terence Camerer Cuss, 'the accuracy of the well-made watch ... controlled by a balance spring had become an assumed condition of the watchmaker's art'.[7] More watches of better quality were made when London's clockmakers adopted anchor escapements and balance springs.[8]

The greatest labour-saving devices that cut wheels for both watches and clocks were 'engines'. They first appeared in the early 1670s when the scientist Robert Hooke helped introduce them in London's workshops. His diary for August 1672 and March 1673 mentions 'wheel-cutting engines' and, in one entry, Hooke referred to his meeting with 'a Lancashire watchmaker's son working in London at that date.[9] Another entry in May 1674 reads: 'told [Tompion] the way of making an engine for finishing wheels, and a way how to make a dividing plate'. [Jeremy Evans has suggested that 'it is far more likely that Hooke was receiving information rather than imparting it, as has been supposed'.[10]] By 1680, Thomas Tompion had wheel and pinion-making engines which either he made himself or had made for him. He recommended ready-made wheel-cutting engines 'made by [a] Mr Smith' which could be bought for £7.[11] The engines were relatively inexpensive; eventually, they cost about £4 or £5 each.[12] Writing in about 1708 John Carte recorded

Lancashire's connection with the adoption of machines and tools used by watchmakers. He noted

> the peculiar improvement the English have made in their Engines & Tooles for the working-part whereby their works are performed with more quickness and exactness. They have invented that Curious Engine for the Cutting the Teeth of a Wheel, whereby that part of the Work is done with an exactness which farr exceeds that which can be performed by hand: then there is an engine for equalling the Ballance Wheel; Likewise the Engine for cutting the turnes of the Fusie; and lastly the Instrument for drawing of the steel pinion wier: All which ingenious Inventions were first conceived and made at *Leverpool* in *Lancashire* in *England*.[13]

Carte's observations were correct. Lancashire wheel-cutting engines became the model, the kind that Crom explained was the 'most favoured by all English clock and watchmakers', and widely distributed by Wyke and Green (Chapter 2). By 1800, its characteristic features were well-established: 'two bowed legs at the back and a heavy spike at the front... solid brass wheel...very heavy, extremely sturdy'.[14] The image depicted in Figure 4.1 is described by John Griffiths as

> a late eighteenth-century brass framed wheel cutting engine signed by Thomas Green, Liverpool with the early form of gallows arm for securing the wheel being cut to the axis of the division plate, the circles of holes in the plate representing the number of teeth to be cut.[15]

The impact on labour productivity was profound. Previously, hand-cut wheels were made by marking out blanks with 'dividers and punch' using a division plate and then taken to a vice for the teeth to be cut and filed. It was laborious work that invariably involved mistakes, as 'small errors in setting the compasses would accumulate as the marking progressed'.[16] That bottleneck was eased by the wheel cutting 'engine' which reduced the time spent on dividing blank wheels by hand. An added benefit of the 'engine' was that it enabled the period of timekeeping of clock mechanisms, hitherto of about twelve or fifteen hours, to be increased to either thirty hours or even to eight days.[17] Before the late eighteenth century, although wheels still had to be 'finished' by filing, the 'engines' increased productivity more than any other contemporary innovation. It enabled relatively rapid manufacture in batches of twenty or more of *almost* standardised parts.

Other innovations: pinion wire and jewelling

The production of pinion wire mentioned by Carte was the outcome of another important labour-saving device. Pinions are tiny gears, usually

Figure 4.1 Wheel-cutting engine. Courtesy: Private collection.

made of steel, driven by larger wheels. They were made by drawing wire through a template which offered different sizes of holes shaped to the desired pattern. Its first development has been ascribed to William Houghton of Hale Bank, near Prescot, in the late seventeenth century: it was another example of the maturity of the tool-making industry in Lancashire's villages.[18] Wheel-cutting engines cut large brass wheels, but small steel pinions were 'much more difficult to cut'. Expert examination by John Griffiths of surviving work by leading makers has revealed that machine-cut pinions were in use by 1700.[19] Other specialist tools were later added to the watchmaker's repertoire, notably including the mandrel, 'one of the largest, most expensive and spectacular of the traditional watchmaking tools'. The earliest English mandrels were developed by the Liverpool toolmaker John Barker and his son Robert in around 1765.[20]

Innovations in the working of raw materials further improved the quality of clocks and watches. The use of jewels as bearings reduced friction at the ends of pivots; the time-keeping quality of watches was augmented not because of the intrinsic value of the jewels but because they improved accuracy. The innovation arose from a collaboration between Nicholas Facio (or Fatio), a Swiss mathematician and two brothers, Peter and Jacob Debaufre (another example of the debt English horology owed to Europe). The Debaufres were French Huguenot refugee watchmakers who migrated in the 1680s, settled in Soho, and were among Isaac Newton's circle of scientific friends.[21] In 1704, Facio and Peter Debaufre perfected a method of cutting and piercing precious jewels such as rubies, diamonds and sapphires that reduced wear in watch movements and thus improved accuracy and durability. Their virtue was not their inherent worth but their hardness.[22]

Despite opposition from jewellers and lapidaries, a patent in 1704 was granted for fourteen years (the period spanning two apprentices' terms).[23] Although the Goldsmiths' and Clockmakers' Companies disapproved of patents on the grounds that all mechanical improvements should be open and free, the technique of jewelling was somehow retained as a trade secret in England. It was adopted with great benefit by London's leading watchmakers for their highest-grade movements.[24] Continental makers used a hard steel plate, called a '*conqueret*', to act as an endstone for pivots. Not until much later in the century were jewels pierced as settings for pivots. It was an important attribute of the best English watches. Anthony Turner thinks 'the inability of French workmen to learn how to make jewels for watches' revealed a major failure in the contemporary French watch industry. Turner cites the evidence of John Gregson, a witness to parliament's inquiry into watchmaking in 1798, who averred that

> watch jewelling could not be done outside of England. During the thirty years, I resided at Paris as a watchmaker, I had always recourse to London for those works, the workmen in other countries not being able to make them.[25]

Other advancements

As with jeweling, improvements in the use of two crucial metals became a feature of horology's new era. In 1738, William Champion improved the quality of the brass used to make components for clocks and scientific instruments by enabling brass to be rolled rather than hammered: this reduced thickness and made it uniform.[26] Then, in the mid-eighteenth century, another important advantage for London's clock and watchmakers came with the development of a superior quality of steel for springs. Before 1740, the 'imperfect homogeneity' of even the best steel 'posed problems for trades that needed a consistent quality, such as the watch or clock spring maker'.[27] Benjamin Huntsman, a Quaker clockmaker and repairer in Doncaster, had tried to improve quality by using imported German steel, but with unsatisfactory results.[28] After several trials, Huntsman eventually made 'crucible steel', suitable for watch springs and a range of high-quality small metal goods (like swords, cutlery, pen-knife blades, scissors, pen-nibs, needles, and even axes). Although he exported to Paris and Geneva, it was England's best watchmakers and instrument makers who most benefitted from Huntsman's crucible steel. They made watch mainsprings of 'infinitely better quality than hitherto – springs which throughout their length were of even height, thickness and temper'.[29] Jewelling, better brass, and superior steel all contributed to Clerkenwell's horological ascendancy during the eighteenth century.[30]

The division of labour

A division of labour had emerged in clock and watchmaking the seventeenth century when specialised branches made different parts. Similar divisions appeared in other metalworking trades, like small arms, and in fashionable and semi-luxury crafts that made shoes, furniture, and coaches. Locational divisions of labour were also a feature of some new industries: parts were made in one place and assembled and 'finished' elsewhere. Subcontracting to outworkers became the standard way of organising production for many of London's trades.[31] Parts of small arms (hand guns) made in Birmingham were sent to London where gun 'makers' assembled the weapons. It was similar to the system in which rough movements of watches made in Prescot were sent to Clerkenwell to be assembled and 'finished'.[32] As George Stigler noted about the nature of Birmingham's small-arms industry by 1860: 'the division of labour ...is a fundamental principal of economic organization'.[33]

Indeed, watchmaking's complex sequences of production could have provided a more elaborate alternative contemporary example for Adam Smith than that of the pin factory in his *Wealth of Nations*. Smith's choice reflected the essential importance of pins for making clothing; watches were 'desirable' and much more complicated, but at that time not quite so vital as pins.[34] David Landes identified three basic categories in the division of labour. First, were those between distinct crafts (e.g. case makers and dial makers). Next were those arising from separation within a craft (e.g. spring-makers and pinion makers). The third was a division of labour within each specialist workshop.[35]

Petty, Campbell, and Pearson

Two classic descriptions of early and more mature stages of the division of labour in horological workshops are from the seventeenth and eighteenth centuries. First, Sir William Petty noted the extent of specialisation in London in 1682 when he described the preliminary divisions that had already emerged during the overlap between horology's first and second eras.

> For in so vast a City Manufactures will beget one another, and each manufacture will be divided into as many parts as possible, whereby the Work of each artisan will be simple and easie; As for Example. In the making of a Watch, If one man shall make the Wheels, another the Spring, another shall engrave the Dial-plate, and another shall make the Cases, then the watch will be better and cheaper, than if the whole Work be put upon any one Man. And we also see that in Towns, and in the Streets of a great town, where all the Inhabitants are almost of one trade, the Commodity peculiar to those places is made better and cheaper than elsewhere. [36]

Over the next half-century, the main branches noted by Petty continued to evolve and gave rise to numerous offshoots. Their features were explained in Robert Campbell's *The London Tradesman* (1747). His description, like Petty's, deserves a full account.

> At the first Appearance of Watches they were but rude to what they are now: they were began and ended by one Man, who was called a Watch-maker; but of late years the Watch-Maker, properly so called, scarce makes anything belonging to a Watch; he only employs the different Tradesmen among whom the Art is divided, and puts the several pieces of the Movement together, and adjusts and finishes it... The Movement-Maker forges his Wheels of Brass and turns them to the just Dimensions; sends them to the Cutter and has them cut at a trifling Expence; ... the Cutter [has] but to finish them and turn the Corners of the Teeth. The Pinions made of Steel are drawn at the Mill, so that the Watch-Maker has only to file down the Pivots and fix them to their proper wheels. The Springs are made by a Tradesman who does nothing else ... but the Caps and Studs for Watches, and Silver-Smiths who only make Cases, and Workmen who cut the Dial-Plates, or enamel them... When the Watchmaker has got home all the Movements of the Watch, and the other different parts of which it consists, he gives the whole to a Finisher, who puts the whole Machine together, having first had the Brass Wheels gilded by the Gilder, and adjusts it to proper Time. The Watchmaker puts his Name upon the Plate and is esteemed the Maker, though he has not made in his Shop the smallest Wheel belonging to it. It is supposed, however, that he can make all the Movements, and Apprentices are learned still to cut them by Hand: He must be a Judge of the Goodness of Work at first Sight, and put his Name to nothing but what will stand the severest Trial; for the Price of a Watch depends upon the Reputation of the Maker only.[37]

These categories were well established by the middle of the eighteenth century. They remained with few changes in Clerkenwell until the demise of traditional watchmaking after the Great War. Divisions within each broad category are not clear, for much depended upon how the subdivisions were labelled. In 1808, Dr William Pearson (who compiled the horological entries for Abraham Rees's *Cyclopaedia*) counted seventeen distinct branches in clockmaking and twenty-one in watch finishing in Clerkenwell. Each branch had its own sub-divisions.[38] Pearson identified fourteen branches making rough movements in Prescot. Two other distinct sectors of the horological industry – turret clockmakers and chronometer manufacturers – developed their own separate specialisms during the eighteenth century. In Parliament's commission of inquiry into watchmaking in 1817, one witness estimated an aggregate of 102 separate branches in horology. The following schematic diagram outlines the main structure of the industry but does not include every possible subdivision (Figure 4.2).

The broad categories of the extensive division of labour in the schematic diagram revealed that each worker performed one function on the finished product or made one of its small parts. The system tied up the making of various parts for many months, as T.P. Hewitt's memoir explained (Chapter 2). Even in the late nineteenth century, it took up to two years before some of Victor Kullberg's top-of-the-range products were returned to the master's workshop (Chapter 16). Subdivision of skills also meant that many were relatively easily learned. The irony of seven-year apprenticeships was that it left most workers unable to perform the full range of skills needed to make a whole watch. In Coventry, as noted, apprentices were used as cheap labour for 'finishing'. When trade was poor, wages fell. Workmen had no control over production decisions made by assemblers (masters), who could quickly reduce commissions when demand declined. Independent subcontracted craftsmen often waited a long time to be paid and during depressions, like that in 1797, pawned tools (Chapter 7).[39]

Thomas Tompion: organisation of production

To increase output and lower costs of production London's horological workshops needed suitable organisation to implement even the basic divisions of labour described by Petty. The transition from Petty's broad outlines in 1682 to Campbell's more clearly identified subdivisions a half-century later can be seen in the system of production developed by Thomas Tompion and other makers in the late seventeenth century. The developments were not Tompion's own, but were present in several workshops at the time: masters learned from each other, and the descriptions that follow owe much to Tompion's fortune in having excellent modern biographers.[40] The workshop evolutions became distinctive

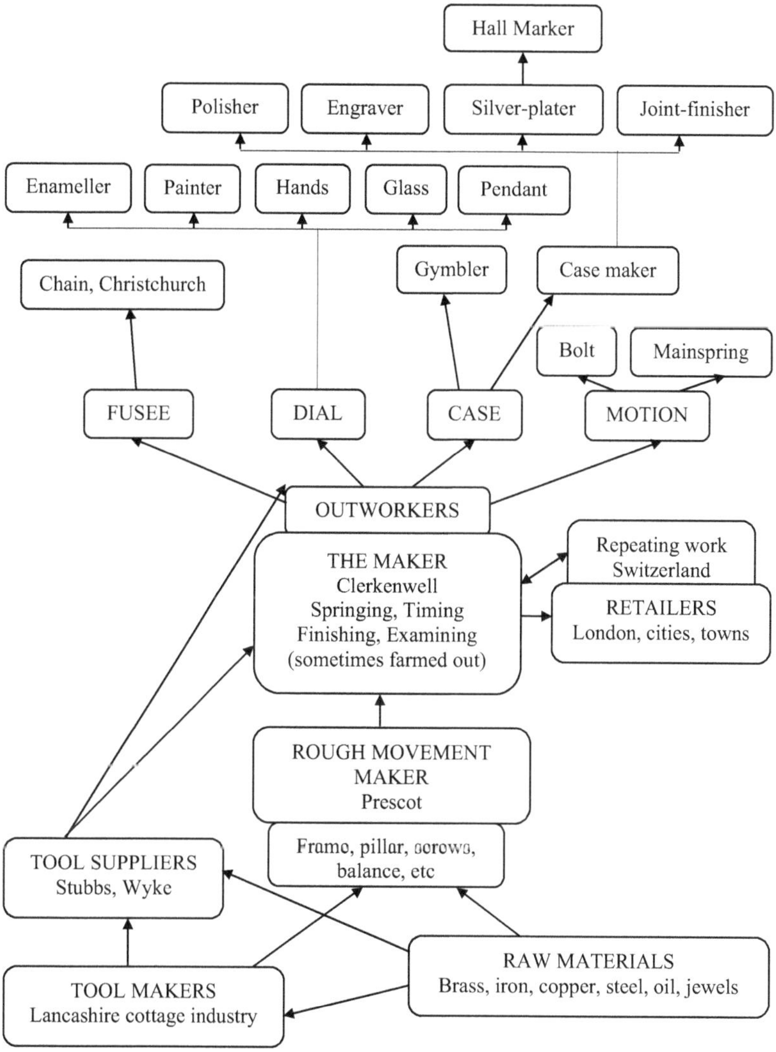

Figure 4.2 Schematic diagram showing the main sequence of the traditional method of making watches and chronometers. Courtesy: Mrs. Kim Bradick.

features of Clerkenwell's 'golden era'. The methods of Tompion – and others – of organising their workshops and the independent out-workers (to whom they subcontracted) must have improved productivity. Tompion himself did not *invent* horology's new technologies, but he grasped and exploited the advantages of pendulums, balance springs, better escapements, and wheel and pinion cutting engines. He and his peers applied and carried forward developments that were already under way. Tompion's reputation as the 'father of English horology' owes as much to the way production was organised as to the superb quality of the best of his clocks and watches.

Tompion was the son and grandson of blacksmiths in rural Bedfordshire.[41] As his recent biographer Jeremy Evans explained, he had acquired 'experience with non-ferrous metals, brass, copper, and lead'.[42] He moved to London in 1671 when the city was recovering from the Plague and Great Fire, and occupied one of the first post-fire houses rebuilt in Water Lane, where he opened a workshop and took on four apprentices. Thereafter as Symonds, his first biographer, described, 'his business was in a state of continual expansion'.[43] In 1680, his household had two lodgers, craftsmen who worked on piecework. Over the next fifteen years, it grew to nineteen or twenty people, including his widowed sister (who perhaps acted as housekeeper, and her children). Eleven men listed in his house were probably living-in apprentices and journeymen. This was many more than was allowed according to the letter and spirit of the Clockmakers' Company's regulations which specified one apprentice at a time, or two in the case of a Master, Warden, or Assistant. During his working life, an aggregate of over a hundred employees made separate parts of items that carried the name 'Tompion'.

Tompion's reaction to the guild's rules revealed how ineffectual they were becoming, not least in the eyes of leaders of the guild itself. Brian Loomes has explained that rules might easily be broken

> so long as a fine was paid – you could do almost anything with official approval if you agreed to pay a big enough fine... a work master with perhaps five journeymen could soon build up as large a workforce as wanted.[44]

Although Tompion was admitted to the Court of Assistants in 1691 and later served as Senior Warden and Master, between 1673 and 1699 his venture provided work for up to two dozen apprentices.[45] His workshop system must have been similar to other contemporary leading watchmakers, given their roughly comparable outputs. A century later, when large watchmaking houses in London contracted for 3,000 or 4,000 watches a year, the production practices developed in Tompion's time were still used. His workshop, Symonds observed, 'was the embryo of the late eighteenth century clockmaking manufactory'.[46]

Tompion's clocks and watches

Tompion's system was developed during the 1680s. He improved his premises, created distinctive 'house-styles' for his products, and devised a recording procedure that involved stamping serial numbers with a punch on back plates, clock cases, and keys. These numbers were then recorded in a ledger to keep track of each clock component, facilitating control of production and stock. Although orders for clocks normally came singly, his workshops made parts in batches of four.[47] Only 'bespoken' orders were finished. Incomplete mechanisms and their parts were stored for later completion and eventually finished to the specific wishes of other customers. His workshops therefore accumulated running stocks of unfinished wheels, back plates, longcase dials and other parts in anticipation of future demand. He did not advance from 'batch production' to the next stage, namely, to complete a large stock of entire clocks, ahead of demand, in readiness for potential customers. That was the crucial advance made by Eli Terry, over a century later in New England. Terry completed batches of 200 clocks at a time, because the size of the market for his kind of clocks, at their low prices, was much larger than Tompion's. Most of Tompion's customers (like those of other leading makers) were drawn from the small pool of wealthy (some very wealthy) persons who wanted – and could afford – expensive, complicated, masterpieces. Many were designed 'with impeccable taste', such as the famous 'Mostyn' Tompion (now in the British Museum) made for William III: it was a remarkable example of a spring-driven clock that struck the hours and went for a year between windings. The 'Medici' Tompion (William III's gift to Cosimo de Medici) was another aptly named masterpiece.[48] But a few were cheap thirty-hour movements of ordinary quality. His workshop possibly made or bought-in a few simple one-handed lantern clocks and some turret clocks.

Once owners of domestic clocks had become accustomed to knowing the time, they stimulated a demand for watches. The benefit of a clock was shared by the household. But watches were personal. They wore out faster than clocks because they were far more susceptible to damage, loss, theft, accident, and even changes in fashion. This helps to explain the number of about seven or eight watches relative to one clock that was made by Tompion (and many other makers).[49] Over almost thirty years, between 1685 and 1713, his workshop's aggregate output was nearly 5,000 timepieces (non-striking watches) and 500 striking watches. His workshops were busy, with a weekly average of three or four watches and the construction of various other instruments. They made about 700 clocks (roughly, one a fortnight).[50] Given the constraints of contemporary technology, they were remarkable achievements. They could not have been made by one person, helped by only a journeyman and a few apprentices. Like his contemporaries, he depended not only on his well-organised workshop but also the efficient employment of anonymous independent outworkers. They included 'unknown numbers of gilders, engravers, spring makers, and case makers', who worked similarly for other masters.[51]

Tompion classified his watches into three main categories (timepieces, clockwork, and repeaters) that were 'probably made in different workshops by different teams of craftsmen'.[52] The time taken to make a single watch was considerable. Typically, the 'maker' received rough brass movements from Prescot. These might comprise a pair of plates with some, though not necessarily all, of the holes drilled, and some other parts. They were then sent to assorted specialised outworkers for further work and refinement before being returned for finishing and adjustment. 'Finishing' was slow and delicate work; estimates suggest most finishers normally completed only two watches a week – an individual output of about a hundred a year. Consequently, a 'large' manufacturer might employ ten or more finishers to produce a thousand watches a year.[53] Some parts of Tompion's watches, including rough movements, were sufficiently standard so that parts of one were *almost* interchangeable with equivalent parts from the same batch, but adequate interchangeability was not achieved until the late nineteenth century in the United States (Chapter 11). Each of Tompion's watches, therefore, was empirical. Careful individual fitting and finishing – not just 'assembly' – was still needed. Given the difficulty of precisely replicating parts with the aid only of hand files, tools and treadle-powered bench machinery, the best clocks and watches of Tompion and others in the 'golden era' represented prodigious technical and creative achievements. Tompion himself was so busy that he employed a clerk to handle accounts and serve in the shop. His workshop, like others, sometimes bought items started and finished elsewhere, including some complete clocks. But they were 'signed' by Tompion. So great and widespread was his reputation that his name on watches, like those of a handful of other leading English makers, later became regularly counterfeited by foreign forgers.

Tompion's workshop did not make clock or watch cases. In his early years in London a co-tenant at his first location, 67 Fleet Street, was Jasper Braem, a cabinet maker who made several of the longcases that housed Tompion's movements. Clock and watch case making had already evolved into separate crafts. Watch case-makers, closely connected with silversmiths, goldsmiths, and jewellers, were also specialists – like Nathanial Delander who, from his workshop in Old Bailey, supplied Tompion with over a thousand watch cases between 1676 and 1691.[54] During his career, Tompion may have employed up to a dozen different watch case makers, probably from those who set up their own workshops near their customers, the movement makers. They made either standard cases or special ones to order. They had transferable skills. If business became slack, watch case makers could make other kinds of jewellery or ornaments and clock case makers could make other furniture.[55] Carpenters and joiners did the construction and rough work whilst cabinet makers (most of whom belonged to the Joiners' Company) did fine work. Initially, clock case makers were independent outworkers but, by the 1740s, the Lancaster furniture firm of Gillow made clock cases as part of its general output. By the 1780s, its factory employed thirty-two workers; it had a workshop in London and a retail branch in Oxford Road (now Oxford Street) to cater for the London market.[56] It was not for another century that an equivalent development for watches saw the establishment of a large-scale case-making enterprise in Birmingham, led by the American, Aaron Lufkin Dennison (Chapter 15).

Output of the great makers

Tompion's example was matched by other contemporaries during the golden era, who must have adopted roughly similar arrangements in their workshops to have achieved their large outputs. George Graham inherited Tompion's workshop, but after he took over the production rate of clocks and watches – if sales are a true reflection – fell sharply, to 'about fifty timepiece watches a year compared to Tompion's 140, and twelve repeating watches to Tompion's seventeen'.[57] It was Tompion's near contemporary, Daniel Quare (1648/9–1724), who 'made and retailed most types of clocks and watches' including 5,000 timepieces, 1,150 repeating watches and 300 clocks and alarm watches. It is thought probable that 'the business sold twice that number' including some bought-in from Tompion.[58] The Ellicott family's business was also prolific: John Ellicott, Senior, and his successors (John Junior, and others in the family) 'sold about 11,000 watches and numerous clocks' between 1696 and 1840. Ellicott's production rates were at first low: six per month, then fourteen. The firm became a leading retailer of high-quality watches and, like many production houses, bought-in from other workshops. John Ellicott Senior's routine personal involvement in daily production was probably minimal; he paid most attention to the organisation of his business and cultivated aristocratic and wealthy customers.[59] The entrepreneurs and merchants, Joseph and Thomas Windmills, augmented their own production by buying-in parts and assembled rough movements from other makers. A cautious estimate of their personal output suggests 272 clocks and 167 watches, but their firm's overall production serial numbers reached almost 10,000. The leaps in their numbering series perhaps indicated different suppliers.[60]

Even smaller enterprises in the late eighteenth century, like those of Josiah Emery and Thomas Mudge, delegated work to apprentices, outworkers, and other specialists. Emery, an immigrant from Switzerland, produced clocks, regulators, and sold about 1,400 watches, including the one Nelson had at Trafalgar (Chapter 10). His workshop's watch production was about forty a year – 'a typical output for a small quality concern' and he probably 'imported movements from Switzerland, to finish and sell in London'.[61] Thomas Mudge, Snr., had been one of George Graham's apprentices and was probably the greatest innovator of the time. The annual output of Mudge and his partner Mathew Dutton over the long period 1736–94 was also about forty, although in sub-periods it fluctuated between nine and thirty-six.[62] Perhaps dips in production reflected Mudge's preoccupation with his quest for technical excellence rather than with maximising output and profit. His absorption produced the escapement that became used in most mechanical watches, 'the most significant advance since the application of the balance spring'. His detached lever escapement in a watch he made in 1770 for George III (a present for Queen Charlotte) has remained 'in use as the best that can be fitted to mechanical watches'.[63]

The search for technical excellence

It was the search for technical excellence by Mudge and others that lent extra lustre to London's horological golden age. Tompion himself helped to introduce the balance spring and was involved in improving watch design by using jewelling (Facio's and Debaufres' innovation) of diamond 'end stones' to reduce friction and wear on his best watches. Caps were developed to protect against dust. Tompion's successor, George Graham, was acknowledged as 'the finest English instrument-maker of his generation'.[64] They included temperature-compensated mercury pendulums, dead-beat clock escapements and notably, in 1726, cylinder escapements for watches (subsequently widely adopted). Because it enabled thinner movements and thinner cases it indirectly influenced fashion. Above all, John Harrison's 'persevering and inventive mind' not only made his prize-winning marine chronometer (Chapter 5) but innovated the grid-iron temperature-compensated pendulum (with four brass and five steel rods) and the grass-hopper escapement. All these technical improvements led to better timekeeping.[65] These innovations, and the exquisite quality of the best clocks and watches, were impressive features of the second horological era and help explain the rise to pre-eminence of London's watchmaking industry.

Status and rewards: wealth at death

Not all eminent horologists had acquired wealth and assets by the time they died. David Ramsey, Clockmaker to James 1, and first Master of the Clockmakers, Company, died in 1660, having 'fallen into poverty' probably because of unsuccessful investments.[66] But after him most of those who achieved high distinction in London's golden era were prosperous. The watchmaking industry was profitable for most of those at its top. Artisans in workshops were not wealthy but were probably better off than most contemporaries, who were still mainly employed in agriculture. The best clocks and watches were expensive, mostly confined to a luxury market. Leading watchmakers commanded high prices and became rich. Estimates of their wealth at death show how some – though not all – of the best-known makers were well off. The Lancashire-London pioneer, Samuel Aspinwall (1609–72), left watches and tools worth almost £800 and an estate worth over £2,000.[67] Thomas Tompion was not quite as wealthy. His biographer, Jeremey Evans, writes that when he died in 1713 he left £1,000 and that

> ... in June 1694 he bought £1,000 worth of Bank of England stock (he was one of the first subscribers), and the 1695 assessment on marriages, etc., classed him as an individual with personal estate worth not less than £600 or real estate worth not less than £50 per year. He also invested money in the Million Bank, to the tune of £1,500 by 1704.[68]

Among Tompion's contemporaries, Daniel Quare (1648/9–1724) seems even wealthier. He had refused an invitation, at £300 per annum, to become the King's watchmaker; his excuse was that as a Quaker 'he could not swear an oath but begged the king not to appoint anyone else'. At his death in 1724 he left to his wife £2,800 with all his household goods – including two gold watches – and two houses. His son Jeremiah inherited £2,000 and the residue of his estate. Six grandchildren each had £400. In twenty-first century terms, he would comfortably have been a millionaire.[69] Estimates of Thomas Windmills' wealth at his death in 1737 were even more impressive. His assets were about '£18,000, excluding real and other personal estate'.[70] Nearly forty years later, John Ellicott and his son Edward ran a flourishing business selling to wealthy aristocratic customers: when John died in 1772 he left 'one copyhold and nine freehold houses, a minimum of £3,365 in assets, plus £500 worth of annuities and the 'goodwill' value of his business'.[71] Christopher Pinchbeck (d.1773) and Larcum Kendall (d.1790) had assets at their deaths of about £1,500 each, approximately the same as 'Honest' George Graham (d.1751), who was perhaps less interested in money than in his absorption with technical improvements. Probably the most famous name from horology's golden era was John Harrison (whose achievements are noted next, in Chapter 5). He left at death '£6,500 plus clocks, watches, scientific instruments, and contents of studio workshop'.[72]

The substantial wealth accrued during the lifetimes of these, and other leading horologists comfortably lifted them into the ranks of the affluent upper-middle classes. They enjoyed incomes and assets far above the levels of most of the population. By the end of the eighteenth century, their products supplied the growing market for timepieces that marked the rise of England's watchmaking industry. Innovations in production methods enabled output to be boosted. Britain's emerging middle-classes in the eighteenth century underwent a retailing and consumer revolution. We will next examine (Chapter 5) the features of the different demands on the industry that contributed to its growth and ascendency.

Notes

1 Brian Loomes, 'The Fromanteel Story', *Antiquarian Horology*, 9 (March 1975), 175–85; Percy Dawson, 'The later Fromanteels', *Antiquarian Horology*, 17 (Winter 1987), 175–78; Anita McConnell, 'Ahasuerus Fromanteel (bapt. 1607, d.1693)', *ODNB*, 2004.

2 For the advertisement, see David Penney, 'The Earliest Pendulum Clocks: A Re-evaluation', *Antiquarian Horology*, 31/5 (Sept. 2009), 619–20; Richard R.C. Barder, *English Country Grandfather Clocks* (Newton Abbott: David and Charles, 1983), 10; R.W. Symonds, *Thomas Tompion: His Life and Work* (London: Batsford, 1951), 9, n. 2.

3 J.H. Leopold, 'Clockmaking in Britain and the Netherlands', *Notes and Records of the Royal Society of London*, 43 (1989), 155–65, at https://doi.org/10.1098/rsnr.1989.0012

4 Sir George White, *Clockmakers of London* (London: Worshipful Company of Clockmakers, 1998), 4 for quote; Enrico Morpurgo, 'The Clock and the Pendulum', *Antiquarian Horology*, 2 (1958), 138–42, 151; Seth G. Attwood, 'The Development of the Pendulum as a Device for Regulating Clocks Prior to the Eighteenth Century', 416–50 of J.T. Fraser and N. Lawrence (eds.), *The Study of Time: Proceedings of the Second Conference of the International Society for the Study of Time* (New York: Springer-Verlag, 1975); J.H. Leopold, 'Christiaan Huygens, The Royal Society and Horology', in Denys Vaughan (ed.), *The Royal Society and the Fourth Dimension: The History of Timekeeping* (Ticehurst: Antiquarian Horological Society Monograph No. 27, 1993), 19–24.

5 Martin Ball, 'The Early English Balance Spring Watch: A Brief History', *Antiquarian Horology*, 29/6 (Dec. 2006), 760–74.

6 David S. Landes, *Revolution in Time: Clocks and the Making of the Modern World* (Cambridge, MA: Belknap, Harvard UP, 1983), 128; Cecil Clutton and George Daniels, *Watches* (London: Batsford, 1971), 11.

7 Terence Camerer Cuss, *Early Watches* (Littlehampton, Country Life, 1971), 30–39.

8 For the emergence of specialist makers of balance springs, see Jeremy Evans, 'Mainspring Makers of London and Liverpool: Some Observations and Lists', *Antiquarian Horology*, 27/1 (Sept. 2002), 63–89.

9 F.A. Bailey and T.C. Barker, 'Seventeenth Century Origins of Watchmaking in South-West Lancashire', in John R. Harris (ed.), *Liverpool and Merseyside: Essays in the Economic and Social History of the Port and Its Hinterland* (London: Cass, 1969), 1–15 (quote, 7); also Charles K. Aked, 'Doctor Robert Hooke, FRS', *Horological Journal*, 120/9 (May 1978), 11–15.

10 Jeremy L. Evans, 'Horological Wheel-Cutting by Mechanical Means: An Early Reference and Some Further Notes', *Antiquarian Horology*, 24/6 (Summer 1999), 551–55 (quote, 553).

11 Jeremy L. Evans, *Tompion at the Dial and Three Crowns* (Ticehurst: Antiquarian Horological Society, 2006), 25; Theodore Crom, *Horological Wheel Cutting Engines, 1700–1900* (Gainesville, FL: Crom, 1970), 84, 99, 116–17; J. Malcolm Wild, *Wheel and Pinion Cutting in Horology: A Historical and Practical Guide* (Marlborough: Crowood, 2001), 11–22; also Anthony J. Turner, 'Dividing Plates and Wheel-Cutting Machines: Some Seventeenth-Century Evidence', *Antiquarian Horology*, 40/4 (Dec. 2019), 514–24 discusses the diffusion of wheel-cutting engines revealed in correspondence between John Locke and Nicholas Toinard.

12 Aked, 'Doctor Robert Hooke, FRS', 11–15; Patri J. Puglese, 'Robert Hooke (1635–1703)', *ODNB*.

13 Anthony J. Turner (ed), *John Carte on Horology and Cosmology: A Transcription, with Introduction and Notes, of Bodleian Library Ms Carte 264ff. 18r–57r*, Turner & Devereux Occasional Paper No.5 (Ticehurst & Le Mesnil-le-Roi: Antiquarian Horological Society & Rogers Turner Books, 2014), 56; Bailey and Barker, 'Origins of Watchmaking', 7–8.
14 Crom, *Wheel Cutting Engines*, 99 and 116–17, notes that it remained unchanged until challenged by the importation of Swiss machine tools in the early twentieth century.
15 Email, August 2021.
16 R. John Griffiths, 'Methods of Cutting Wheels and Pinions in Horology: An Historical Review, Part 1', *Horological Journal*, 136/7 (March 1992), 296–99; Part 2, 136/8 (April 1992), 344–49. For a contemporary account of the tediousness and empirical nature of wheel-cutting before the engine, see Joseph Moxon, *Mechanick Exercises*, 1, 37–58 (1677; New York: Praegar, reprint 1970).
17 John Robey, *The Longcase Clock Reference Book* (2 Vols., Ashbourne: Mayfield, 2001), 1/11.
18 Bailey and Barker, 'Origins of Watchmaking', 7–8.
19 R. John Griffiths, 'Methods of Cutting Wheels and Pinions', 296–99.
20 P.H.J. Baker and R.J. Law, 'The English Watchmaker's Mandrel: Its Origins and Development: Part 1, Some Early Examples', *Antiquarian Horology*, 24/5 (Spring 1999), 415–26, 'Part 2: Part 2: Later examples', *Antiquarian Horology*, 24/6 (Summer 1999), 5389–50.
21 David Bodley-Scott, 'Watch Jewelling', *Horological Journal*, 132/11 (Aug. 1990), 57–58; Scott Mandelbrote, 'Nicolas Fatio, of Duillier (1664–1753)', *ODNB*.
22 For a technical note, see David S. Torrens, 'Early Jewel Bearings', *Horological Journal*, 87/5 (Jan. 1945), 21; and Ian Greaves, 'A Study of English Watch Jewelling', *Antiquarian Horology*, 35/4 (Dec. 2014), 1085–1106.
23 Alun C. Davies, 'Horological Patents, 1662–c.1800: Restraining Trade, Stifling Innovation or Rewarding Invention?', *Antiquarian Horology*, 37/1 (March 2016), 82; Steven Van Dulken, *British Patents of Invention, 1617–1977: A Guide for Researchers* (London: British Library, 1999), 2; see also Mario Biagioli, 'From Prints to Patents: Living on Instruments in Early Modern Europe', *History of Science*, 44 (2006), at https://doi.org/10.1177%2F007327530604400202
24 Eric Bruton, *The History of Clocks and Watches* (New York: Rizzoli, 1979), 118–19.
25 Anthony J. Turner, 'Berthoud in England, Harrison in France: The Transmission of Horological Knowledge in Eighteenth Century Europe', *Antiquarian Horology*, 20/3 (Autumn 1992), 224–25, and note 28, citing *House of Commons*, 'Report on the Clock and Watchmakers Petitions, 27 February 1798', 25.
26 Maurice Daumas, 'Precision Mechanics', Ch. 13 of Singer, et al., eds., *A History of Technology: Volume IV, The Industrial Revolution, c.1750–1850* (Oxford: Clarendon, 1957), 130, 404ff. Joan Day, 'Champion Family (per. c.1670–1794), William Champion (1710–1789)', *ODNB*.
27 John R. Harris, *The British Iron Industry, 1700–1850* (London: Macmillan and Economic History Society, 1988), 45–46. Also, J.H. Leopold and M.L. Wayman, 'General Introduction and Analytical Methods', in M.L. Wayman (ed.), *The Ferrous Metallurgy of Early Clocks and Watches: Studies in Post Medieval Steel* (London: British Museum Occasional Paper, no. 136, 2000), 4 notes that '... it was the materials demanded for these applications [better steel for clock springs] which were the driving force behind Huntsman's development of the crucible steel making process'.

28 David Hey, 'Benjamin Huntsman (1704–1776)', *ODNB*; Eric N. Simmons, 'Benjamin Huntsman: Clockmaker Pioneer in Casting Steel', *Metallurgica*, 51 (1955), 181–84; Chris Evans and Alun Withey, 'An Enlightenment in Steel? Innovation in the Steel Trades of Eighteenth-Century Britain.' *Technology and Culture*, 53/3 (July 2012), 533–60, at www.jstor.org/stable/41682700; Landes, *Revolution in Time*,138; id., *The Unbound Prometheus: Technological Change and Industrial Development in Western Europe from 1750 to the Present* (Cambridge: Cambridge UP, 1969) 253; Samuel Smiles, *Industrial Biography: Iron Workers and Tool Makers* (1863; reprint, Newton Abbott: David & Charles, 1967), Ch. VI: 'Invention of cast steel: Benjamin Huntsman', 99–113, especially 102–03; Leslie Paton, 'The Iron and Steel Available to the Horological Masters of the Past', *Antiquarian Horology*, 15 (Sept. 1984), 47–51; Charles K. Aked, 'A Clockmaker's Steel', *Horological Journal*, 129/7 (May 1987), 10–13.

29 The quotation is from the British Horological Institute's *Correspondence Course in Technical Horology: Preliminary Grade; Lesson*, 3 (Newark: British Horological Institute, 2011), 6; Landes, *Revolution in Time*, 135–38; Anthony G. Randall and Richard Good, *Catalogue of Watches in the British Museum, VI, Pocket Chronometers, Marine Chronometers, and other Portable Precision Timekeepers* (London: British Museum, 1990), 13, stress that 'Huntsman's work was crucial to the development of English chronometer making'.

30 Camerer Cuss, *Early Watches*, 39.

31 Giorgia Riello, 'Strategies and Boundaries: Subcontracting and the London Trades in the Long Eighteenth Century', *Enterprise & Society*, 9/2 (June 2008), 243–80, at https://doi.org/10.1017/S1467222700006959' also Anita McConnell, 'From Craft Workshop to Big Business – The London Scientific Instrument Trade's Response to Increasing Demand, 1750–1820', *London Journal*, 19/1 (May 1994), 36–53, at https://doi.org/10.1179/ldn.1994.19.1.36

32 For horology and small arms see David J. Williams, 'The Birmingham Gun Trade and the American System of Manufactures', *Transactions of the Newcomen Society* 75 (2005), 85–106, at https://doi.org/10.1179/tns.2005.004; id., *The Birmingham Gun Trade* (Stroud: The History Press, 2009); and Alun C. Davies, 'British Watchmaking and the American System', *Business History*, 35 (1993), 40–54. Also Peter Earle, *The Making of the English Middle Class: Business, Society, and Family Life in London, 1660–1730* (London: Methuen, 1989), 23; Maxine Berg, *The Age of Manufactures: Industry, Innovation and Work in Britain, 1700–1820* (Cambridge: Cambridge UP, 1985), 272.

33 George J. Stigler, 'The Division of Labor Is Limited by the Extent of the Market', *Journal of Political Economy*, 59/3 (June 1951), 185–93, at www.jstor.org/stable/1826433 (quote, 193).

34 Adam Smith, *The Wealth of Nations*, ed. Andrew Skinner (1776; Harmondsworth, Penguin; 1976), 109; Morgan Kelly and Cormac Ó Gráda, 'Adam Smith, Watch Prices, and the Industrial Revolution', *Quarterly Journal of Economics*, 131[4] (2016), 1727–52 at https://doi.org/10.1093/qje/qjw026

35 Landes, *Revolution in Time*, 201–08.

36 Sir William Petty, 'Another Essay on Political Arithmetic Concerning the Growth of the City of London, 1682', in Charles Henry Hall (ed.), *The Economic Writings of Sir William Petty*, 2 vols. (Cambridge: Cambridge UP. 1899); vol. II, 451–77; quotation, 473.

37 Robert Campbell, *The London Tradesman, Being a Compendious View of All the Trades, Professions, Arts* (London: Gardner, 1747), 250–52; M.

Dorothy George, *London Life in the Eighteenth Century* (London and New York: Kegan Paul, 1925), 176–77; Peter Earle, *The Making of the English Middle Class; Business, Society and Family Life in London* (London: Methuen, 1989), 23.
38 Abraham Rees, Clocks, *Watches and Chronometers (1819–20)* (Newton Abbott: David & Charles, 1970), 281–82; A. Woolrich, 'Abraham Rees (1743–1825)', *ODNB*; A.M. Clerke, rev. David Philip Miller, 'William Pearson (1767–1847), ODNB. For Pearson's sixty-three articles in Rees's *Cyclopaedia*, see S.J. Gurman and S.R. Harratt, 'Revd Dr William Pearson (1767–1847): A Founder of the Royal Astronomical Society', *Quarterly Journal of the Royal Astronomical Society*, 35/3 (1994), 271–92.
39 Peter Earle, *A City Full of People*, 74.
40 R.W. Symonds led the way, with *Thomas Tompion: His Life and Work* (London: Batsford, 1951); more recently, Jeremy L. Evans has added to our knowledge with 'The Numbering of Tompion's Watches: Series and System', *Antiquarian Horology*, 14 (June 1984), 585–97; id., 'Horological Wheel-Cutting by Mechanical Means: An Early Reference and Some Further Notes', *Antiquarian Horology*, 24/6 (Summer 1999), 551–55; id., 'Thomas Tompion (Bapt. 1639–1713)', *ODNB* (2004); and especially id., *Thomas Tompion at the Dial and Three Crowns*,(Ticehurst: Antiquarian Horological Society, 2006).
41 Adrian A Finch, Valerie J. Finch and Anthony W. Finch, 'What's in a Name? The Family and Early Years of Thomas Tompion', *Antiquarian Horology*, 42/2 (June 2021), 187–98 explored the genealogy and early life of Tompion.
42 Evans, *Thomas Tompion at the Dial and Three Crowns*, 13.
43 Symonds, *Tompion*, 38–39.
44 Brian Loomes, *The Early Clockmakers of Great Britain* (London: NAG Press, 1981), 17.
45 Charles Edward Atkins (compiler), *Register of Apprentices of the Worshipful Company of Clockmakers of the City of London from its Incorporation in 1631 to its Tercentenary in 1931* (London: Worshipful Company of Clockmakers, 1931), 338.
46 Symonds, *Tompion*, 40.
47 Evans, *Tompion at the Dial and Three Crowns*, 38, 62.
48 Evans, *Tompion at the Dial and Three Crowns*, 41–43; David Thompson, 'Thomas Tompion', *Clocks* (London: British Museum, 2004), 54–55.
49 William C. Bopp, 'Some Early English Table Clocks', *Antiquarian Horology*, 8/8 (September 1974), 838–53.
50 Symonds, *Tompion*, 114, 134–35; David Thompson, 'Thomas Tompion', *Watches*, 50–51, 54–55.
51 Evans, *Tompion at the Dial and Three Crowns*, 45–47.
52 Evans, *Tompion at the Dial and Three Crowns*, 53. A comprehensive check list of his known output of numbered and unnumbered clocks and watches in their various categories is on 65ff; id., 'The Numbering of Tompion's Watches: Series and System', *Antiquarian Horology*, 14 (June 1984), 585–97.
53 Michael Edidin, *English Watches for the American Market: A History of Watchmaking by the Tobias Families of London and Liverpool* (NAWCC *Bulletin* (Part 1: Oct. 1992), 539.
54 Jeremy L. Evans, 'Thomas Tompion (bap. 1639, d.1713', *ODNB*.
55 B.W.E. Alford and T.C. Barker, *A History of the Carpenters Company* (London: Allen and Unwin, 1968), 78–80.
56 Susan E. Stuart, 'Gillow Family (per. c.1730 – c.1830)', *ODNB* (2004); id., 'The First White Dial Long case Clocks and their Cases', *Antiquarian Horology*, 13 (Dec. 1982), 534–49; and id., 'A Neat Long Case Ornamentation: A

1760 Gillows Drawing Discovered,' *Antiquarian Horology*, 15 (Dec. 1984), 125–43; Nicholas Goodison, 'Gillows' Clock Cases', *Antiquarian Horology*, 5 (March 1968), 348–61.

57 David Thompson, *Watches*, 70–71; Jeremy Lancelotte Evans, 'George Graham (*c.* 1673–1751)', *ODNB*.

58 Craig Spence, *London in the 1690s: A Social Atlas* (London: Institute of Historical Studies, 2000), 136. Among the table clocks were movements probably made by Tompion's workmen, and equation clocks by Joseph Williamson; Thomas Grignion worked as a finisher for Quare, as did Richard Wright of Warrington; E.L. Radford, rev. by Jeremy Lancelotte Evans, 'Daniel Quare, 1648/9 – 1724', *ODNB* (2004); David Thompson, 'Daniel Quare', *Watches*, 56–57.

59 David Thompson, 'John Ellicott, 1702/3–1772', *ODNB*; id., *Watches*), 100–01; id., 'The Watches of Ellicotts of London: Part 1', *Antiquarian Horology*, 23/4 (Summer 1997), 306–21, and graph on 311.

60 J.A. Neale, *Joseph and Thomas Windmills: Clock and Watchmakers, 1671–1737* (Ticehurst, Antiquarian Horological Society, 1999), 103, 286–87.

61 Jonathan Betts, 'Josiah Emery: Watchmaker of Charing Cross: Part 1', *Antiquarian Horology*, 22/5 (Spring 1996), 394–401.

62 Charles Allix, 'Mudge Milestones: Watch Dates', *Antiquarian Horology*, 12/6 (Jan 1981), 627; David Thompson, *Watches*, 74–75; George Daniels, 'Thomas Mudge: The Complete Horologist', *Antiquarian Horology*, 13 (Dec. 1981), 150–73, contains many illustrations and much technical detail.

63 Thomas Seccombe, rev. David Penney, 'Thomas Mudge (1715/16–1794)', *ODNB*.

64 Richard Sorrenson, 'George Graham, Visible Technician', *The British Journal for the History of Science*, 32/2 (June 1999), 203–21, at https://www.jstor.org/stable/4028084; also, for the collaboration between two remarkable contemporaries, see Ann McBroom, 'George Graham and John Theophilus Desaguiliers: Mixed Mathematicians', *Antiquarian Horology*, 42/2 (June 2021), 219–42.

65 Andrew King, 'John Harrison (b. 1693, d. 1776)', *ODNB*.

66 Anita McConnell, 'Ramsay, David (c.1575–1660)', *ODNB*.

67 See Chapter 3, above; and Jeffrey D. Tang, 'Timely Success: The Role of Locational Lock-in and Path-Dependence in the Rise of the South-west Lancashire Watchmaking Industry' (Unpublished M.Phil. thesis, Oxford University, 1996), 46–51.

68 Jeremey Lancelot Evans, 'Tompion, Thomas (bap. 1639, d. 1713)', *ODNB*.

69 E. L. Radford, *rev.* Jeremy Lancelotte Evans, 'Daniel Quare (1648/9–1724)', *ODNB*.

70 J.A. Neale, 'Joseph and Thomas Windmills', *Antiquarian Horology*, 16/6 (June 1987), 573–84 (wills, 581–83).

71 David Thompson, 'John Ellicott (1702/3–1772)', *ODNB*.

72 Andrew King, 'John Harrison (bap. 1693, d. 1776)', *ODNB*.

5 Demand

Domestic, Government, and Foreign

Demand: three categories

The first four chapters have focussed mostly on the supply side of England's watchmaking industry, at how it developed in four hubs, and how productivity in Clerkenwell was improved by labour-saving innovations and better organisation. This chapter looks at changes in demand in the eighteenth century. Demand for the first watches had come from the royal court and London's prosperous metropolis. During the eighteenth century, it widened and deepened. Britain's population doubled from about 5 million to about 10 million and, as its economy grew, so watchmaking – initially a small craft – enlarged into an industry. It responded to three distinct kinds of demand. The first arose from the private sector, from the growing real incomes of Britain's emerging 'middling classes'. Some individuals may have been wealthy compared with Elizabeth's courtiers, but a new level of prosperity had created a *bourgeoisie,* of legal and medical professionals, small and medium-size landowners, farmers, businessmen, and even some skilled artisans. They generated a greater demand for watches than that of the Tudor courts and contributed to what may be called a 'consumer revolution'. David Landes claimed it was the high wage economy in eighteenth-century Britain – half as high again as in Europe – that created an expanding market that included clocks and watches.[1] In themselves, 'clocks and watches were peripheral to the industrial revolution', but, it has been argued, 'their large-scale production had important indirect 'spin-offs' in the form of the 'clockwork' inherent in textile machinery.[2]

The second category of demand was more specialised. It came from the public sector, from the government on behalf of the nation's maritime interests. The nature of this demand was not for personal watches, but for stimulating the development of a clock or watch, carried on a ship, that would be sufficiently accurate to aid in determining longitude. The strategy succeeded. The marine chronometer was the most complex product of a pre-industrial handcraft technology and was watchmaking's greatest contribution to Britain's industrial revolution. The establishment of a small chronometer-manufacturing sector by the end of the

DOI: 10.4324/9781003227823-6

eighteenth century provided a vital navigational instrument for Britain's Royal Navy and merchant marine in the nineteenth century. It was the one sector of England's watchmaking industry that flourished, despite its parent's relative and absolute decline.

The third category of demand was foreign. It flourished in the late eighteenth century but, for England's horological industry, was not permanent. It came from new, exotic, and profitable export markets to the Ottoman Empire and China. It deserves attention because it was different from the routine export of watches to Britain's imperial, European and American markets. It faded in the early nineteenth century following the wars with France.

A consumer revolution

The growing demand for necessities and semi-luxuries that appeared in Britain in the late seventeenth and early eighteenth centuries was a phase of a newly evolving consumer market. It first emerged in the 1540s, when Tudor governments had encouraged national 'projects' to manufacture goods that were otherwise imported.[3] Clocks and watches were initially not among those commodities. But by the end of the seventeenth century, after the disruptions of Civil War, Plague and Great Fire, the presence first of clocks and then watches became noticeable amongst manufactured goods. Evidence can be seen in the probate inventories (lists of moveable goods made after a person's death) of the lower gentry, professionals and tradesmen who owned what was once classified as luxuries. Clocks, porcelain, and mirrors are among early examples, along with household items and a variety of small wares, such as buttons, ribbons, buckles, and fancy goods – things that were bought, rather than made at home. Tradesmen in luxury and semi-luxury wares in towns and cities in the mid-eighteenth century sold what Maxine Berg has described as 'items worth saving for, [commodities] ... within the means of the middling class'. These 'household decencies' were somewhere on the spectrum between luxuries, semi-luxuries, and necessities': they included house clocks and were soon followed by watches.[4] They were among the key elements in the changing patterns of consumption in Britain's domestic mass market between 1750 and 1780. The desire to know the time was spreading.

Examples of the early demand for the products of the infant horological industry can be seen in Chris Williams' case study of probate records in the village of Charing, Kent from 1600 to 1750.[5] The 150 instances of clocks in the records reflected both the prosperous economic condition of their owners and the spread of time-awareness as indicated by the twelve-hour dials. Unsurprisingly, until the late seventeenth century, 'clock ownership was almost exclusively confined to the wealthiest one-third in [Williams'] sample of Charing's households – about half of whom owned a clock'.[6] Williams constructed an ownership graph that traced a 'classic *S*-shaped take-up: slow in the adoption phase; rapid during 'take-off'; slow again as the market saturate[d]'. It was a portent of the later demand for watches. Lorna Wetherill's study of nearly 3,000 probate inventories over a wider area reinforced the veracity of Williams' picture. It revealed a substantial increase in the ownership of all domestic goods between 1675 and 1725 among men and women of different social statuses. Wetherill's study established that, for London, domestic clocks were found three times more often at the end of the period compared with the beginning, again a predictable finding. But there were interesting regional variations. Over 78 per cent of farmers in Kent owned clocks by the 1740s, whilst only 12 per cent of Cornishmen did. The decade between 1705 and 1715 was crucial; '... it stands out as the one in which most change took place', and that previously 'known' things, such as clocks and watches, pictures, and looking glasses, became much more common everywhere.[7] The growth of clock and watch ownership spread and reinforced an understanding of 'equal hours' among much of the population.[8] The Purefoy family of Shalstone, Buckinghamshire, was probably typical of many of the 'small gentry' of the 1730s and 1740s. Their manor house had several clocks and Henry Purefoy and his mother Elizabeth both had gold repeating watches. Their household and estate were run according to local mean time: awareness of time in their village was indicated by the sundial at the church and reinforced by the sound of the bell of the manor house's Great Clock.[9] Time-consciousness was spreading beyond the gentry for, in 1747, the *Universal Magazine* reported (perhaps with some exaggeration?) that 'the clock has become the genteelest piece of furniture in almost every cottage'.[10] By the end of the eighteenth century, the consumer revolution was driven also by 'social emulation', where each social class aspired to the patterns of consumption and habits of their superiors.

Specialist retailers: Benjamin Gray

To cater for growing demand, major horological houses established links with retailers in London and leading provincial towns. Their shops offered customers a selection of clocks and a choice of watches of different qualities and prices. For owners of watches, they most importantly offered a repair service. Benjamin Gray exemplified the exactitude of Robert Campbell's comment in 1747 that 'The Watchmaker puts his Name upon the Plate and is esteemed the Maker, though he has not made in his Shop the smallest Wheel belonging to it' (Chapter 4).[11] Gray's business records from 1704 to 1726 have survived, revealing he occupied several premises in London, first in Drury Lane, then St. James's Street

West and later in Pall Mall.[12] His records show he occasionally sold clocks – although only seventeen in over two decades. More extensive was his watch repairing trade, especially cleaning and mending watches for other watchmakers. They included leading makers like Daniel Quare and Joseph Windmills.[13] Gray's even more profitable line was selling watches. Over twenty-two years, he bought some 160 watches from various manufacturing houses that he then re-sold. Of these, thirty-eight were cased in gold and twenty-eight in silver. Eighty-eight were movements he sold on to other watchmakers in the trade. He specialised in supplying intricate and expensive watches, including high-quality repeating movements (thirty-eight repeated the previous hour, forty the proximate quarter, two were 'half-quarter' and eight were five-minute repeaters). His clientele were wealthy aristocrats and some prosperous tradesmen – like periwig makers and glaziers. Their presence showed how the market was widening, revealing the validity of E.P. Thompson's comment that 'when any group of workers passed into a phase of improving living standards, the acquisition of timepieces was one of the first things noted by observers'.[14] His records demonstrated the distinction growing between those who made and those who sold. Retailing expensive watches was becoming a speciality.

Innovations in newspaper advertisements helped the growth in demand for clocks and watches. Some claimed to refute the supposed unreliability of cheap watches and promised that faults in the watches would be 'rectified free during the course of a whole year'.[15] The biggest changes came in the shops that sold watches. In the seventeenth century, 'shops' had been the workshop part of a craftsman's home, with boards let out onto the street to display goods for sale. After the retailing part of the business prevailed, a small workshop was sometimes kept carrying out repairs and cleaning. Developments in glassmaking in the eighteenth century enabled shops to have bow windows where goods were laid out for display. Ornate window displays were important for customers who wanted to examine stock – and prices – before entering to make a purchase. The first such specialist clock and watch shop appeared in London in 1760; by 1770 there were six more.[16] Sophisticated marketing techniques helped to secure custom: in Oxford Street, some bow windows were brilliantly lit by oil lamps to attract the attention of window-shoppers until late evening. For those who could afford it, shopping had become a pastime.[17] Even modestly sized market towns like Shrewsbury (with a population of about 5,000–7,000 in 1700) had some specialist shops that sold clocks and watches. Shrewsbury's 'frankpledge' lists for 1668 and 1709 include one 'watchmaker' on each occasion; by 1731 there were four 'watchmakers' and one 'clockmaker' out of 913 tradesmen practising 111 different trades. Between 1750 and 1775 of the 355 tradesmen practising eighty-four different trades, five were watchmakers.[18]

Extent of watch ownership

Maxine Berg has observed that 'time was kept for a whole range of purposes apart from the world of work; equally, watches and clocks were kept for an even greater range of reasons'.[19] By the late eighteenth century, demand for luxury watches was affected by changes in clothing fashions; watches communicated strong symbols of status when they were visible. Changes in dress styles stimulated accessories for a fashion market. Ladies wore watches with other jewellery on a girdle and, occasionally, as a wristwatch disguised as a bracelet. Possessions were important ways of communicating one's position in society, and gold watches were visual indications of status, especially conspicuous marks of wealth and class distinction.[20] Daniel Defoe in 1722 described the symbolic importance of Moll Flanders' possession of a gold watch: 'on these Adventures we always went very well Dress'd, and I had very good Cloaths on, and a Gold Watch by my Side, as like a Lady'. Moll felt, when she was wearing one, that it was her badge as a gentlewoman.[21] When a man took a watch out of his pocket to tell the time his companions could see it and might be impressed by its expensive appearance. Pockets made carrying watches more convenient than on a ribbon or chain around the neck. Gentlemen usually kept watches in pockets at the top of breeches or trousers. After about 1780 fashion and horological technology became more harmonised following the availability of thinner watches (Chapter 6). The custom spread of wearing shorter waistcoats with convenient pocket space to display, prominently, jewelled watches and chains; sometimes 'two watches, or one watch and a miniature, suspended from ribbons or watch chains, were the prevailing mode'.[22] From the middle of the nineteenth century, men's watches were almost invariably worn in waistcoat pockets attached to a watch chain, often with trinkets fastened, especially seals. Some had a heraldic emblem, for stamping into heated sealing wax on documents or letters.

Watches were easily transported and gradually became more widely available. They were sold in rural areas by peddlers supplied by middlemen from the watch finishing centres in Clerkenwell, Liverpool and Coventry.[23] The extent of watch ownership is difficult to estimate. Amongst one-third of the 'better-off' of Bristol's population, about a quarter had watches. Chris Williams speculated that the level of watch ownership in households in Charing, Kent, might have been of the order of 10 per cent in 1710, 20 per cent in 1750 and 40 per cent in 1780.[24] The level of ownership of watches was higher in London and Lancashire than elsewhere, perhaps because of their proximity to watchmaking centres. By the 1790s, John Rule claimed, a watch had become 'the marginal purchase of the working man… [There was] presumed to have been one in every Lancashire handloom weaver's pocket during their golden age … as there were in the mule spinners' pockets in Manchester fifty years later'.[25] Working-class demand for watches was small but not negligible. It is estimated that in the 1790s the annual income of a country labourer was about eighteen guineas.[26] E.P. Thompson observed that when labourers occasionally received an unexpected windfall, perhaps from a militia bounty, harvest savings or a yearly lump payment, then they 'might blow it on a watch'.[27] Kelly and Ó Gráda have calculated from an analysis of stolen watches that 'watch ownership among working men rose steadily through the eighteenth century and had become extensive by 1800'.[28] Even if expensive watches were beyond the reach of most working men, nevertheless cheap and second-hand watches were increasingly available. Ownership conferred prestige, and a watch served a purpose in emergencies. When it was difficult to find other sources or places to keep savings, a watch held some value and, if pawned, could be converted back into cash.

By the early nineteenth century, ordinary working men and tradesmen had joined the market for watches. Entries in the *Shop Book* (1809–12) of James Ritchie of Edinburgh note the occupations of his customers. A few from the upper classes sent their servants with watches for repair. Two of his first customers were indeed famous – namely Madame Tussaud (who brought her wax works to Edinburgh in 1810) and Walter Scott, the novelist. Customers from the lower professional classes included teachers, printers, and clerks. Other customers were also important. Some evidently worked near the shop, and Ritchie may have known them personally. They included at least one each with the following occupations: grocer, butcher, baker, confectioner, candle maker, smith, coach maker, bootmaker, shoemaker, comb maker, haberdasher, upholsterer, and tailor. James Ritchie's father-in-law was a builder involved in the contemporary building boom in Edinburgh's New Town, and the occupations of James's customers included several described as builders, masons, painters, plasterers, and glaziers.[29] Their patronage helped ensure the success of his business venture and their ownership of watches is evidence of the broadening demand for personal goods created by rising real incomes.

Twenty per cent of Ritchie's transactions included selling a few clocks and a selection of miscellaneous merchandise, such as silver thimbles at 2s each, earrings at 7s 6d and toothpicks at ls 6d. His basic stock included watch keys, for which there was always a steady replacement demand because they were often lost, and watch chains, which cost from 3s for a gilt chain to 9s 6d, 14s, and even £3 for gold chains. Watch glass, which broke easily, cost 6d. Seals for hanging on a watch chain to impress wax cost from 2s 6d each. Sometimes, perhaps as a discount for an expansive purchase, Ritchie occasionally threw in a 'chain and seal' free of charge. One of his most profitable side lines proved to be silverware which he 'made and engraved' (or perhaps arranged for it to be done). He stocked silver snuff boxes and milk pots, and, in November 1811, he started buying and selling 'old silver' spoons and other tableware. All these side lines were no doubt profitable. Nevertheless, 80 per cent of the transactions in Ritchie's shop comprised of cleaning and selling watches. Ritchie's repair service was important, for watches were exposed to movement and shock and broke far more frequently than static clocks which needed relatively little maintenance. Most watches needed regular cleaning from a skilled repairman (a 'jobber') at least every other year.[30]

Generalisations and estimates about the extent of watch ownership have been prompted by Professor Landes's 'guesstimate' that England produced about half of Europe's total output between 1750 and 1800 (between 150,000 and 200,000 pieces annually in the 1790s). From this, Hans-Joachim Voth estimated the size of the stock of watches in England between 1750 and 1830 and included assumptions about the average useful life of a watch. He guessed the number of watches in circulation as a percentage of the population over the age of fourteen and deduced that 'even moderately conservative conjectures lead to the conclusion that up to one third could have owned a watch'. Perhaps over-optimistically, he suggested that watches were owned by 40 per cent of the population in 1750, over 60 per cent in 1800, and close to 100 per cent in 1830'.[31] Clearly, the short life expectancy of many watches must have created a replacement demand. Even the most cautious of Voth's estimates reveal how deeply an awareness of mean time – and the need to know it – had permeated British life. The market had expanded greatly since the times of Henry VIII and Elizabeth I.

During the Puritan era, those who wanted to know the time had watches that were unembellished and unadorned, usually with a rounded oval case. By the eighteenth century, they had become potent status symbols, and the best watches reflected an element of conspicuous consumption and cost many times the annual income of ordinary artisans. The high prices of the finest watches were partly because of the quality of the movement but mostly because of the craftsmanship and expense of their cases. The prices of Tompion's and George Graham's watches ranged from those cased in plain silver for £11 to gold-cased repeaters from about £60 to £70. Even more expensive were the thirty-five watches by Josiah Emery, sold at between 100 and 150 guineas.[32] Nelson had an 'Emery' watch at Trafalgar (Chapter 10). Horace Walpole bought watches by John Ellicott and Benjamin Gray in 1759, one for 134 guineas: its seals (hanging from the watch chain) cost another sixteen guineas, making 150 guineas in all.[33] Such purchases of high-grade movements set in expensive jewel-embellished cases were exceptional. Nevertheless, during the era of the classic 'turnip' shape watch, decorative cases flourished; hunters, half-hunters, and pair cases offered creative opportunities for artistic enhancement, as did pendants, dials and hands, watch cocks and other features of the movements.[34]

The supply of watches spanned a wide range of qualities. At the bottom end, those made of modest bits of metal, accurate to half an hour or so a day, gave way to watches – still of low quality and price – which nevertheless showed improvements in timekeeping accuracy. One estimate suggests that the retail price of good quality London pair-case silver watches fell from about £8 10s to £2 10s in the period 1710–1810'.[35] Adam Smith thought, perhaps optimistically, that better watches were being produced for twenty shillings in 1776 than for £20 a century earlier.[36] The rhetorical licence of Smith's claim has been examined by Kelly and Ó Gráda through an ingenious analysis of changes in the value of over 3,200 stolen watches reported in trials in London's Old Bailey. They found that the real prices of nearly all watches had fallen by 1.3 per cent a year, 'equivalent to a fall of 75 per cent over a century', and concluded that 'sustained innovation in the production of a highly complex artefact had already appeared in one important sector of the British economy by the early eighteenth century'.[37] At the top end of the market were gold and silver-cased items, bejewelled and decorated, accurate daily to a minute or less. By the end of the eighteenth century, various refinements were available for luxury watches including a variety of 'repeaters'. Some chimed the minute or the quarter; others were 'dumb' repeaters, which pulsed (used by visually impaired, and to tell time, unostentatiously, in sermons, meetings, or concerts). Such innovations had the effect of creating fresh categories from old products that, when developed, created new market niches, especially amongst those who were 'neither very poor nor very rich, but still wielded effective purchasing power'.[38] Prosperous 'middling classes' were able to afford watches and clocks. It was a demand fuelled by the growing acceptance across most of the nation that the passing of time was best measured by the equal hours in mean time. Such was the nature of the domestic demand for watches in eighteenth-century Britain that helps to explain the rise of its watchmaking industry.

Maritime demand

A demand quite different from that generated by ordinary customers also emerged in the early eighteenth century and helped create a feature of English watchmaking that added to its distinction. It resulted from the resolution of 'the Greatest Scientific Problem of the Time', namely the creation of a sea-going clock sufficiently accurate to enable longitudes to be calculated. Its solution enabled Clerkenwell to make the marine chronometers that became one of its greatest attainments. The chronometer-manufacturing sector that resulted flourished over the next century and a half and survived until after the Great War, in contrast to its parent industry's decline.

Marine chronometers were the response to the call for safer sea navigation following a spectacular disaster in 1707, when seven out of twelve Royal Naval ships commanded by Sir Clowdesley Shovell were lost because of navigational error. Two thousand sailors drowned off the Scilly Islands (ironically, from mistaken latitude, not longitude). It prompted a public outcry. In response, the government established the Board of Longitude in 1714 and offered £20,000 to anyone who invented a practical method of determining longitude at sea.[39] It was a massive sum of money, and it presented an enormous challenge and potential award to England's horologists.

The project was inspired by several motives. It combined humanitarian intentions (saving lives) with economic benefits (reducing expensive sea wrecks and delays) and national security (improving the maritime and Royal Navy's navigational efficiency). Commercial reasons were among the most pressing. By the early eighteenth century, the high cost of transoceanic trade had been lowered. Productivity had improved and profitability increased because piracy had been diminished or nearly eliminated. Larger ships carried heavier payloads and turn-around-times in ports were more efficient.[40] But even greater efficiency was impeded because imprecise navigation caused ships to be delayed or disappear because of inaccurate navigation.[41] The accurate determination of longitude had two putative solutions.[42] One was the 'lunar method' that used the night sky as a clock. But it was ponderous and needed difficult and complicated astronomical calculations. The other solution was to navigate using a sea-going timekeeper sufficiently robust and accurate to carry time from a base meridian (such as Plymouth, Portsmouth, or Greenwich). This might then be compared with 'local' time at the destination, hence enabling longitude to be calculated. Such a timepiece required the maintenance of a timekeeper with precision on board a rolling ship, well beyond anything yet achieved by the best watches.

Accounting for the solution to the problem proved expensive.[43] Eventually, it cost far more than the capital resources of any private individual whose purchases fuelled the contemporary 'consumer revolution'. The putative market for sea-clocks was important, but it was limited. The largest potential private 'customer' was the East India Company, a trading company whose captains were extensively involved in transoceanic trade. In the long run, the most important customers would be the rest of the merchant marine and especially the Admiralty, on behalf of the Royal Navy. Thus the British government, through the Longitude Act of 1714, offered its Longitude prize to anyone who devised a practical method to determine longitude at sea to within half a degree (equivalent to about two minutes of time).[44]

Harrison's chronometer: developmental costs

The horologist who triumphed was John Harrison, a carpenter and clockmaker from Barrow-in-Humber, 180 miles from London. Starting in 1728 he experimented for over forty years with several prototypes (the great Sea Clocks now known as H1, H2, and H3) before he developed his marine chronometer (H4) that won the Longitude Award.[45] He famously commented

> I think I may make bold to say that there is neither any other Mechanical or Mathematical thing in the world that is more beautiful or curious in texture than this my watch or Timekeeper for the Longitude... and I heartily thank Almighty God that I have lived so long, as in some measure to complete it.[46]

His story is probably the best known episode in the history of horology, thanks first to Samuel Smiles' heroic portrait of Harrison in the 1880s and, more recently, to the published proceedings of Harvard University's 1994 Longitude Symposium that led to Dava Sobel's colourful best-selling account, its illustrated version, and a television adaptation of the odyssey.[47] Harrison's triumph was one of the great technical achievements in English horology's golden period. It was a product of his perseverance, and of the exceptional horological and scientific instrument-making community from whose skills he drew. In Clerkenwell, he had settled within easy reach of a group of expert horological craftsmen, including a well-developed mathematical- and scientific-instrument trade.[48] Leading scientists included several members of the recently formed Royal Society and Greenwich Observatory. Many lived in the community near St Paul's Cathedral, rebuilt after the Great Fire, and 'belonged to the same coffee-houses'.[49] A short walk from the cathedral was Tompion's workshop in Water Lane, just off Fleet Street. It had become a favourite haunt of Hooke and other Fellows of the Royal Society. Among them was George Graham, initially Tompion's apprentice, then partner and, after 1613, his successor. Graham sometimes met with the Royal Society Club (a discussion group for Fellows) and helped John Harrison in his work on marine timekeepers. His own network of outstanding watchmakers included Thomas Mudge, John Jeffreys and Larcum Kendall. They formed, in Jonathan Betts' words, 'part of the finest watchmaking team of the day'. They contributed to the environment from which Harrison's successful chronometer emerged.[50]

The aggregated developmental costs were huge. Between 1737 and 1764 as Harrison tested his prototypes he was supported by assorted grants from the public purse.[51] In all, his rewards included immortality as 'the first artisan recipient' of the Royal Society's Copley Gold Medal.[52] Ultimately, in various portions, he received an aggregate of over £23,065 from the government, a vast sum at that time. During some of his 'barren years' between 1741 and 1760 private support came from friends in the Royal Society amounting to £2,750.[53] Grants from the Board of Longitude that came to £12,747 were also given to eight other individuals who significantly participated in resolving the longitude problem by amassing and contributing essential background information.[54] In all, this early example of government funding for research and development cost the state over £35,000; it succeeded because it induced into existence watchmaking's chronometer-manufacturing branch. The only other comparable contemporary awards from the public purse were those of £5,000 to Samuel Crompton (1753–1827) inventor of the widely copied spinning mule (5 million made by 1812); of £10,000 in 1809 to Edmund Cartwright (1743–1823) inventor of the power loom; and of £30,000 (almost as large as all the Longitude awards) to Edward Jenner in 1815 for discovering the smallpox vaccination process. Each of those payments reflected appropriate perceptions of the importance of their contribution to the nation's social and economic well-being.

Emergence of a chronometer manufacturing sector

Harrison's award-winning fourth timekeeper (H4) was a great mechanical accomplishment.[55] Ironically, it was not in itself the end of the story, but the end of its beginning. After such expense, the Board resolved that knowledge of how to construct a chronometer should henceforth be made more widely available, to stimulate chronometer manufacturing. The first stages were slow. Harrison's complex design was minutely examined and copied ('reverse engineering') in 1769 by Larcum Kendall, one of Clerkenwell's most skilled horological craftsmen. The intention was that a stock of machines might be built up by further replication, improvement, and modification (an example of the 'design recovery' stage of reverse engineering). Kendall made a twin, now known as K1, of John Harrison's prize-winning H4.[56] It took over two and a half years to make and cost £450, plus £50 bonus. Compared with the many tens of thousands of pounds it cost to build and fit out large ships (and several thousand pounds more when adapting one for major expeditions), £500 was a relatively modest amount for a crucial navigational instrument. It was taken by James Cook on his second voyage. Kendall's second, simpler, copy known as K2 ('the *Bounty* watch') cost £200. His third (K3) cost half that: it assisted in the great cartographic surveys conducted by Captains Cook and Vancouver.[57] Knowledge of their success with it gave impetus to the growth of chronometer manufacturing (Chapter 10).

After Kendal, further experiments modified the chronometer's layout and escapements, and the subsequent chronometers owed more, perhaps, to other pioneers than to the prize-winner Harrison. Thomas Mudge, Senior, designed three prototypes and his son, Thomas Junior, copied his father's models – the first attempt to supply significant numbers of chronometers on a commercial basis.[58] For the watchmaking industry it was an unlikely but faintly possible 'might-have-been' for, a little later, Mudge's American contemporary Eli Whitney secured from the United States' war department in 1798 a contract to produce muskets with standardised parts in a factory. Demand for muskets was large. The tolerances of parts for muskets and watches were obviously different, but the production concepts were similar. The concept of bulk – if not mass – production was in the air.[59] Mudge Junior's attempt was unsuccessful. Contemporary machine tools were not sufficiently sophisticated, chronometers were much more complex than muskets and, above all, the market for chronometers was tiny, compared with that for guns in America. But the concept of large-scale production was being envisaged during these years and was successfully applied in 1802 by Marc Brunel to mass produce naval pulley blocks in Portsmouth. Whitney's attempts came to fruition more slowly.[60]

Ironically, by the turn of the century elements of Harrison's original model became obsolete. Henceforth the chronometer's essential features included a French component, the detent escapement, invented by Pierre LeRoy shortly after he had examined Harrison's masterpiece in 1766. 'Harrison', Commander Gould declared, 'built a wonderful construction on the sand, but LeRoy dug down to the rock'; and he gave generous credit (perhaps over-generous in the eyes of some?) to LeRoy for developing the crucial element in the modern mechanical chronometer, namely the first detached escapement.[61]

Referring to Harrison, David Landes observed 'Invention may follow genius, but production follows demand'.[62] Harrison and Kendall's successors were the real pioneers of English watchmaking's chronometer-manufacturing sector. Growth in the demand for chronometers was fostered by the work of John Arnold and a handful of others. Between 1772 and 1775, Arnold continually experimented with layout and made thirty-five pocket timekeepers.[63] His and Earnshaw's resort to patent protection perhaps hindered competitors and helped Arnold's lead in England's early chronometer production.[64] In economists' jargon, the House of Arnold was a 'gorilla' – that is, a firm that dominated chronometer manufacturing without having a monopoly. When Arnold's second patent's fourteen-year term expired, it has been estimated that Arnold's workshop between 1783 and 1796 made at least 500 pocket and box chronometers – many more than were made by Thomas Earnshaw during this period.[65] It reflected the larger scale of Arnold's enterprise. As demand grew, supplies increased and costs fell. Their acquisition became a priority for the chronometer's biggest single customer, the East India Company. By the early 1790s, several of the Company's ships had already acquired chronometers, mostly from John Arnold, thanks to his connection with Alexander Dalrymple, first the Company's hydrographer in 1779 (and then, after 1795, the Admiralty's).[66] George Margetts, who had already been involved in supplying the Company with longitude tables also made 220 chronometers between the mid-1790s and 1804, many for officers of that Company. After half a century of research and trials the government's strategy of offering an enormous carrot as an award had indeed proved successful. It had induced the desired outcome – namely, an effective and reliable mechanical solution to the problem of how to determine longitude. It was the supreme achievement of any pre-industrial handcraft technology and the industry's greatest contribution to the British economy during the era of the Industrial Revolution: it helped make possible Britain's worldwide trading network in the nineteenth century. The chronometer market at first was small, but after the outbreak of war with France in 1793 it grew (Chapter 10).

Foreign markets

Exports formed the third category of demand for the products of England's watchmaking industry. Although there are few reliable trade statistics, English-made watches had long been sold in Europe and the Americas. The old colonial and early national market for traditional 'English' watches in the United States survived until about the mid-nineteenth century, largely thanks to Liverpool's makers led by Mayer Isaac Tobias and his family's trading network (Chapter 3). Trade with South America's nations was evidently substantial enough for some London firms to customise their products by translating their names on the dials. For example, dials of clocks exported to Spain and then on to Spanish colonies in South America by Peter Higgs and David Evans of Sweeting's Alley, Royal Exchange, were proudly translated to 'Pedro Higgs y Diego Evans, Junto Ala, Bolsa Real, Londres'.[67]

Exports to Europe were not easy because of the substantial domestic watchmaking industries in France and especially Switzerland.[68] Nevertheless, the high reputation of London's best clocks and watches attracted customers from Europe and beyond. London became a magnet for leading European dealers in clocks and watches. Amongst several emigrant Swiss makers and dealers drawn to the metropolis was Louis Recordon (c.1750–1824). He sold his own commissioned watches and was also the London agent who retailed the fine, expensive watches made by two of the most prominent Swiss and French houses – Jaquet-Droz of Geneva and Abraham-Louis Breguet of Paris. Those who wanted English watches but were unable to travel to London used specialist agents as middlemen, such as the Portuguese J.H. de Magellan. Although not a maker himself, Magellan undertook to arrange the purchase of all kinds of clocks, watches, and scientific instruments and their delivery to private individuals or institutions like universities.[69] The great Trade Fairs of Frankfurt, Leipzig and Lyon became locations for the distribution of English and European horological products and, from those places, to a web of other markets.[70] Some English watches even penetrated Frances's difficult domestic market: Julien LeRoy complained that English 'Ship's Captains bring Watches to every port in Brittany, doing all this the more handily since Watches are easy to hide...'[71] The flow, however, was mostly the other way (as we will see in Part 2, 'Challenge'). But international demand for English clocks and watches was not confined to Europe and the Americas. Of great importance in the late eighteenth century were the markets that London's dealers established through the Levant Company to the Turkish Empire and through the East India Company to China.[72]

The Ottoman Empire

The origins of this trade lay in the late sixteenth century when Elizabeth I's ambassadors (like those of other European monarchs) presented clocks and gifts to the Sultan of Turkey, ruler of the immense Ottoman Empire.[73] Subsequently, royalty, courtiers, emissaries, and merchants gave clocks and watches as presents or bribes to well-off and influential individuals across Western Europe, Russia, North Africa, Persia, even Nepal and the Far East. Their gifts were followed up by commercial exports from London's horological firms, including some that even established agents abroad. Inevitably presents and sales needed maintenance, and repairers followed agents.

London suppliers dominated but did not monopolise the export trade to the Orient in the eighteenth century; it was shared with Swiss and French makers, notably Julien Le Roy, whose firm developed a flourishing trade with Turkey in the 1770s.[74] Eventually, the top end of the trade was dominated by Breguet's London agent, Louis Recordon and, after 1811, especially through Breguet's Istanbul agent, a member of the Le Roy family.[75] Recordon's trade with the Turkish Empire and Persia attracted attention at Thwaites & Reed's newly established London clock factory. It made 'musical clocks' especially for the Turkish market and arranged not just the movements and musical barrels but the complete clocks, in decorated cases, ready for dispatch.[76] Other export houses included those of George Clarke of Leadenhall Street, Isaac Rogers of Bell-Alley ('near the Bank'), and George Prior.[77] As with the earlier example of 'Tompion', the name 'Prior' became well known after it was forged on dials of inferior movements made by Swiss firms. Demand for 'Prior' watches was so large that many movements bearing that name were bought-in wholesale by export houses. The precise value of the watch market is not known but, Otto Kurz estimated, George Prior's firm exported 'between forty and fifty thousand watches to Turkey' during his lifetime. After his son Edward took over, the number rose to over 78,000 watches.[78]

Timepieces intended for the Ottoman Empire displayed distinguishing characteristics. The biggest demand was for watches that typically had luxurious ornamental decorations, dials with distinctive Islamic (not Roman) numerals for hours and minutes and several protective cases – two of silver or gold, richly engraved and decorated sometimes with diamonds or other jewels and a third case of leather or tortoiseshell (more accurately the latter were from 'the belly of the hawksbill turtle'.)[79] The trade included elaborate large organ clocks and some with complicated musical automata.[80] There was also a market for relatively ordinary long-case pendulum clocks, prompted by mosques where Islamic worshippers wanted routine reminders of times for prayers (just as in late medieval Christian churches and monasteries). Religious sensibilities were respected by shaping finials as crescents and avoiding the depiction of female figures.[81]

Trade with China

The export trade to China had also grown from initial tributes, presents and business gifts.[82] Western mechanical horology had been introduced into China by the Jesuits in the late sixteenth century and an Imperial 'watch and clock factory' (a warehouse rather than a 'manufactory') was established within the palace precincts in the late seventeenth century. In 1715, the East India Company had set up a trading house in Canton and much of that trade was carried out privately by officers of the Company (to their personal profit).[83] By mid-century a growing volume of England's exports to Asia, in return for imported silks and spices, consisted of a wide range of luxury articles that included clocks and watches. Compared with European markets there was not much demand in the Far East for the woollen cloth that had long been England's staple export.[84] Both main eastern markets wanted heavily decorated clocks and watches, preferably with complex automata 'powered by clockwork... highly ornamental... and often musical'. Basic mechanisms for the automata were usually made in Switzerland and finished and cased in London. The Chinese called the items 'toys' or 'sing-songs' (from the Chinese '*zimingzhong*', meaning 'bells that ring by themselves'). In some complicated automata, mechanical animals moved parts of their bodies; others were set in elaborate *objects*, including carriages and chariots studded with jewels. They were more important as status symbols and decorative personal adornments than as timepieces. Their appeal lay in their relative rarity, expense, and in the performances of animated figures with music and bells.[85] One report in 1735 described the Imperial Palace as 'stuffed with them. Watches, carillons, repeaters, automatic organs, mechanised globes of every conceivable system – there must be more than four thousand from the best masters of Paris and London'.[86] Not all horological movements were from elite workshops; some were relatively unsophisticated and took second place to the decorated paraphernalia surrounding them. The clocks and watch movements embedded in these contraptions were unlike the best products of English horology, in which precision was paramount.

After 1757 trade in Canton was confined by an imperial order to three months in the year. Some European traders relocated to Macao (a trading post leased to the Portuguese). Despite these impediments, the value of exports was thought to be enormous. Britain was no longer preoccupied with the global conflict of the Seven Years War after 1763 and trade picked up, funded from Canton's customs revenues. Estimates suggest that horological items exceeded £17,000 by 1773, a value that doubled by the end of the century. By the end of his reign in 1796, the collection of the Emperor of China (Qianlong, who reigned from 1735) is thought to have been worth at least £2m.[87]

The extensive China trade comprised a range of traditional clocks, watches, and chronometers, including musical coach watches.[88] The best-known figure at the London end of the trade was the jeweller and entrepreneur, James Cox, of Shoe Lane (near Fleet Street).[89] Although he personally made no horological movements, he and his technician, John Joseph Merlin from Liege, were at the centre of a network of London's independent suppliers and specialist craftsmen. Cox employed 'a small army of them' and, in evidence to a House of Commons committee in 1773, he claimed that for the last seven years he had employed '800 to 1000 workmen' (meaning he had contracted for that number of outworkers).[90] Amongst those who sold musical clocks to Asian markets in the 1780s was George Margetts; with Thomas Earnshaw, he made 'pseudo-scientific instruments that were primarily intended to display mathematically correct astronomical indications'.[91] From the middle 1760s, James Cox exported, not only to China but to India, a variety of lavishly ornamented articles including luxury clocks and watches made in London and Geneva. Commissions from China to Cox were truly sumptuous and expensive: one included 'three pairs of mechanical clocks valued at £3,000'.[92] He employed outworkers, designers, and craftsmen based in London and Switzerland to supply his export trade to the Far East. Cox became bankrupt in the 1780s but managed to re-establish his business. Some clocks and watches he sold from the Jaquet-Droz workshops in la Chaux-de-Fonds included 'London' in 'signatures' on their dials that sparked complaints from the Clockmakers' Company. In the late eighteenth century, London's makers stopped competing with the Swiss for the Far Eastern market. Instead, it was easier to use Swiss movements, cases, and even complete watches, sold under their own names as London-made products, as Cox's partner and successor, Jean Frederic Leschot, admitted to a potential German trade buyer:

> We have always had the name engraved as though [made] in England, because it is the general opinion that everything of this kind made in that country is of better workmanship, more *recherché* and stronger than elsewhere; nevertheless, they are assembled in my workshop [i.e. in Switzerland], with the difference that, if you obtain them from me, they will cost you less than if you buy them from anyone else.[93]

Demand from eastern markets was quite distinct from other exports. It was a feature of its time, an important component of Britain's export trade to the east. But it did not last. It was affected by the French wars and never recovered its former importance. The industry's once-buoyant trade with the Ottoman Empire slipped away, replaced in the nineteenth century by musical boxes and watches with automata from Switzerland, and cheap and popular musical clocks from the Black Forest. After 1815, the English industry's horological trade with China also fell off. That too was a consequence of Clerkenwell's stagnation and decline in the face of competition from Switzerland, the Black Forest and, during the 1840s, by clocks from the United States. American penetration of Britain's former Eastern horological markets dated from 1844, when American consular agents reported on potential sales in Hong Kong.[94] Chauncey Jerome claimed that by 1860 'millions' of his clocks had been sold in 'Asia, Europe, South America, Australia, Palestine and, in fact, to every part of the world'.[95] This foreshadowed the later world-wide exports of American watches (Chapter 11). Unsurprisingly, when Japan opened to trade during the Meiji era, British horological exports were negligible. The first clocks had been brought to Japan by Portuguese and Spanish in the sixteenth century and became the first western consumer durable there in the later 'westernisation' during the Meiji era.[96] Watches were imported from America and, overwhelmingly, from Switzerland. Of eighteen trading houses in Yokohama handling time pieces, three were American, one was German, and fourteen were Swiss. The British and French pocket watchmakers were nowhere, Hoshimi Uchida concluded, because 'they had already thrown in the towel'.[97]

These were the three categories of demand that underpinned the rise of England's watchmaking industry – a consumer revolution at home, specific maritime demand that induced the creation of a chronometer-manufacturing sector, and exports to exotic markets in the Ottoman Empire and China. Thanks to the stimulus of these markets, England's watchmaking industry was preeminent by the end of the eighteenth century in both output and quality. Thereafter, for internal and external reasons, the industry slowly declined, as we shall see in Part 2, 'Challenge'.

Notes

1 David S. Landes, *Revolution in Time: Clocks and the Making of the Modern World* (Cambridge, MA: Belknap, Harvard UP, 1983), 227.
2 R.C. Allen, 'Why the Industrial Revolution Was British: Commerce, Induced Invention, and the Scientific Revolution', *Economic History Review*, 64/2 (May 2011), 357–84, at www.jstor.org/stable/41262428. Allen points

to the example of Arkwright's Quarry Bank Mill that, over time, employed half-a-dozen clock and watch makers. (376).

3 Joan Thirsk, *Economic Policy and Projects: The Development of a Consumer Society in Early Modern England*, [Ford Lectures, Oxford] (Oxford: Clarendon, 1978).

4 Maxine Berg, 'New Commodities, Luxuries and Their Consumers in Eighteenth Century England', in Maxine Berg (ed.), *Consumers and Luxury, ...Consumer Culture in Europe, 1650–1850* (Manchester: Manchester UP, 1999), 65, 69; T.H. Breen, '"Baubles of Britain": The American and Consumer Revolutions of the Eighteenth century', *Past and Present*, 119 (May 1988), 73–104, esp. 75–77: https://doi.org/10.1093/past/119.1.73

5 Its church is said to contain the stone on which John the Baptist was beheaded.

6 Chris H.K. Williams, 'Seventeenth- and Eighteenth-Century Clock Demand, Production and Survival: An Economic and Statistical Analysis', *Antiquarian Horology*, 28/5 (March 2005), 571–72.

7 Lorna Wetherill, *Consumer Behaviour and Material Culture in Britain, 1660–1760* (London: Routledge, 1988; 2nd ed., 1996), 25, 41.

8 Paul Glennie and Nigel Thrift, *Shaping the Day: A History of Timekeeping in England and Wales, 1300–1800* (Oxford: Oxford UP, 2009), esp. Chapters 4–6.

9 Alun C. Davies, 'Keeping time at Shalstone: the Horological Tribulations of the Purefoys, 1735 to 1752', *Antiquarian Horology*, 36/1 (March 2015), 71–83; George E. Eland (ed.), *Purefoy Letters, 1735–1753* (London: Sidgwick and Jackson, Ltd, 1931; reprinted, ed., L.G. Mitchell, 1973).

10 Quoted in Brian Loomes, *Country Clockmakers and their London Origins* (Newton Abbot: David & Charles, 1976).

11 Robert Campbell, *The London Tradesman, Being a Compendious View of All the Trades, Professions, Arts* (London: Gardner, 1747), 250–52. (See Chapter 4).

12 E.F. Bunt, 'An Eighteenth-Century Watchmaker and his Day-book', *Antiquarian Horology*, 8 (1973), 175–82; S. Benson-Beevers, 'Benjamin Gray: Short Biography', *Antiquarian Horology*, 1 (March 1955), 76–77; Vaudrey Mercer, 'Benjamin Gray and the Vulliamys: An Attempt to Decipher the Cryptic Code Which they Used on Their Watches', *Antiquarian Horology*, 14/3 (Sept. 1983), 266–71; David G. Vulliamy, *The Vulliamy Clockmakers* (Ticehurst: Antiquarian Horological Society, 2002).

13 J.A. Neale, 'Joseph and Thomas Windmills', *Antiquarian Horology*, 15/6 (June 1987), 573–75; E.L. Radford, rev. Jeremy Lancelotte Evans, 'Daniel Quare (1648/9–1724)', *ODNB*.

14 E.P. Thompson, 'Time, Work-Discipline, and Industrial Capitalism', *Past and Present*, 38 (1967), 70.

15 Neil McKendrick, John Brewer, J.H. Plumb, *The Birth of a Consumer Society; Commercialization of Eighteenth Century England* (London: Harper Collins, 1984); for a broad study, see Nancy Cox, *The Complete Tradesman: A Study of Retailing, 1550–1820* (Aldershot: Ashgate, 2000).

16 Hoh-Cheung Mui, and Lorna H. Mui, *Shops and Shop Keeping in Eighteenth Century England* (London and Kingston ONT: McGill UP,1989), 62–63, 119–20; Kathryn Morrison, *English Shops and Shopping: an architectural History* (New Haven, CT and London: Yale UP, 2003), 68–69.

17 Charles Harvey et al., quote a 'German visitor in 1786, 'dazzled by the luxurious goods displayed in 'lovely Oxford Street. . . . First, one passes a watchmaker's ...', in 'Continuity, Change, and Specialization within Metropolitan London: The Economy of Westminster, 1750–1820', *The Economic History Review*, 52/3 (Aug. 1999), 469–70, at www.jstor.org/stable/2599141

18 Angus McInnes, 'The Emergence of a Leisure Town: Shrewsbury, 1660–1760', *Past and Present*, No. 120 (August 1988), 53–87, at https://doi.org/10.1093/past/120.1.53. 'Frankpledge' is derived from the ancient legal system in which units or 'tithings' of ten households were formed; in each, members were held responsible for one another's conduct.
19 Maxine Berg, *Luxury and Pleasure in Eighteenth Century Britain* (Oxford: Oxford UP, 2007), 227.
20 For differences in the ways with which men and women wore watches, see Marcus Tomalin, 'The Intriguing Complications of Pocket Watches un the Literature of the Long Eighteenth-Century', *The Review of English Studies*, New Series, 66/274 (April 2015), 316, at https://www.jstor.org/stable/24541234
21 Daniel Defoe (with an introduction by G.A. Starr), *Moll Flanders* (1722: Oxford: Oxford UP, 1971), 211.
22 McKendrick, Brewer and Plumb, *Birth of a Consumer Society*, 75; Genevieve Cummings, *How the Watch Was Worn: A Fashion for 500 Years* (Woodbridge: Antique Collectors Club, 2010), 9–10, and especially Chapter Two: 'Watch Wearing: Eighteenth Century: Waist-Hung Chains and Chatelaines', 19ff.
23 Walter Minchington, 'Patterns and Structure of Demand, 1500–1750', Ch. 2 of Carlo Cipolla (ed.,) *The Fontana Economic History of Europe*: vol. 2, *The Sixteenth and Seventeenth Centuries* (Glasgow: Collins, 1974), 101.
24 Williams, 'Seventeenth- and Eighteenth-Century Clock Demand', 574.
25 John Rule, *The Labouring Classes in Early Industrial England, 1750–1850* (Harlow: Longmans, 1986), 70–71.
26 Sir Frederick Morton Eden (A.G.L. Rogers. ed.), *The State of the Poor* (1797; Cambridge: Cambridge UP, 1928), 166–67.
27 Thompson, 'Time, Work-Discipline, and Industrial Capitalism', 69.
28 Morgan Kelly and Cormac Ó Gráda, 'Adam Smith, Watch Prices, and the Industrial Revolution', *Quarterly Journal of Economics*, 131[4] (2016), 1733, at https://doi.org/10.1093/qje/qjw026; for the strong association between watches and theft, see Marcus Tomalin, 'The Intriguing Complications of Pocket Watches un the Literature of the Long Eighteenth-Century', *The Review of English Studies*, New Series, 66/274 (April 2015), 305–06, at https://www.jstor.org/stable/24541234; also Sara Horrell, Jane Humphries and Ken Sneath, 'Consumption Conundrums Unravelled', *The Economic History Review*, 68/3 (August 2015), 147, at www.jstor.org/stable/43910109.
29 Alun C Davies, 'Starting up a Watchmaking Business: James Ritchie of Edinburgh, 1809–1812', *Antiquarian Horology*, 20/3 (Autumn 1992), 260–72.
30 Alexis McCrossen, 'The "Very Delicate Construction" of Pocket Watches and Time Consciousness in the Nineteenth-Century United States', *Winterthur Portfolio*, 44/1 (Spring 2010), 1–30, at https://doi.org/10.1086/651538. She analyses the incidence of watch ownership, and the sorts of repairs most watches needed. For a regional case study see Martin Bruegel, '"Time That Can Be Relied upon." The Evolution of Time Consciousness in the Mid-Hudson Valley, 1790–1860', *Journal of Social History*, 28/3 (Spring1995), 547–64, at www.jstor.org/stable/3788464
31 Hans-Joachim Voth, *Time and Work in England, 1750–1830* (Oxford: Clarendon, 2000), 47–50; also id., 'Time and Work in Eighteenth-Century London', *The Journal of Economic History*, 58/1 (March 1998), 29–58, at www.jstor.org/stable/2566252.
32 Anthony Turner, 'The Tribulations of Jean Helot', *Antiquarian Horology*, 32/6 (June 2011), 782; Jonathan Betts, 'Josiah Emery: Part 3, The Lever Escapement', *Antiquarian Horology*, 23/1 (Autumn 1996), 30.
33 *Horological Journal*, 28 (Dec. 1885), 54.

34 Cedric Jagger, *The Artistry of the English Watch* (Newton Abbott, David and Charles, 1988).
35 'C.E.' (Chris Elmers), 'Watch and Clockmaking', in Celina Fox (ed.), *London: World City, 1800–1840* (London: Yale UP and the Museum of London, 1992), p.524.
36 Adam Smith, *The Wealth of Nations* (1776; Harmondsworth: Penguin Classics, 1976), 351.
37 Morgan Kelly and Cormac Ó Gráda, 'Adam Smith, Watch Prices, and the Industrial Revolution', 1727–1752. Proceedings of the Old Bailey (1674–1913) are searchable online at http://www.oldbaileyonline.org.
38 D.E.C. Eversley, 'The Home Market and Economic Growth in England, 1750–80', in E.L. Jones and G.E. Mingay (eds.), *Land, Labour and Population in the Industrial Revolution: Essays presented to J.D. Chambers* (London: Edward Arnold, 1967), 259.
39 Humphrey Quill, *John Harrison: The Man Who Found Longitude* (London: John Baker, 1966), Ch. 1, 'Longitude and the Act of 12 Queen Anne'. Two good introductions, one based on a Greenwich exhibition, are both by Richard Dunn and Rebekah Higgitt, *Ships, Clocks and Stars: The Quest for Longitude* (London: Collins and Royal Museums Greenwich, 2014), and id., *Finding Longitude* (London: Collins, 2914).
40 Douglass C. North, 'Sources of Productivity Change in Ocean Shipping, 1600–1850', *Journal of Political Economy*, 76 (Sept/Oct. 1968), at https://doi.org/10.1086/259462.
41 J.H. Parry. *Trade and Dominion: The European Overseas Empires in the Eighteenth Century*. Praeger History of Civilization (New York: Praeger, 1971), 220–34; Mrs G.W. Nockolds, 'Early Timekeepers at Sea', *Antiquarian Horology*, 4 (Sept. 1967), 112.
42 D.W. Waters, 'The Instrumental and Astronomical Solutions to the problem of Longitude at Sea in the Eighteenth Century', in Sorbom (ed.), *Transport Technology and Social Change* (1980); also Michael S. Mahoney, 'Christiaan Huygens: The Measurement of Time and of Longitude at Sea', in H.J.M. Bos et al. (eds.) *Studies on Christiaan Huygens* (London: Routledge, 1980).
43 For the costs of inefficient navigation – and a guide to salaries, costs and 'rewards'- see Eric G. Forbes, 'Index to the Board of Longitude Papers at the Royal Greenwich Observatory' (in 3 parts), *Journal of the History of Astronomy*, 1 (1970) 169–79, and 2 (1971), 58–70 and 135–45, at DOI:https://ui.adsabs.harvard.edu/link_gateway/1970JHA.....1..169F/doi:10.1177/002182867000100215; and id., 'The Foundation and Early Development of the Nautical Almanac', *Journal of the Institute of Navigation*, 18/4 (Oct. 1965), 301–401, at DOI: https://doi.org/10.1017/S0373463300046324; and id., 'The origin and development of the marine chronometer', *Annals of Science*, 22 (March 1966), 1–25, at https://doi.org/10.1080/00033796600203005; also D.H. Sadler, *Man Is Not Lost: A Record of 200 Years of Astronomical Navigation With the Nautical Almanac, 1767–1967* (London: National Maritime lMuseum, 1968).
44 Quill, *John Harrison*, Ch. 1, 'Longitude and the Act of 12 Queen Anne'; Andrew King, 'Winner or Loser: Did John Harrison Win the Longitude Prize?', *Antiquarian Horology*, 37/1 (March 2016), 73–81. £20,000 in 1714 would be worth about £4 million in 2020; also Charles K. Aked. 'Longitude and the Marine Chronometer', Part 1, *Antiquarian Horology*, 8/7 (June 1974), 732–44; Part 2, *Antiquarian Horology*, 8/8 (Sept. 1974), 854–65.
On the question of prizes or patents, see B. Zorina Khan, 'Inventing Prizes: A Historical Perspective on Innovation Awards and Technology Policy',

The Business History Review, 89/4 (Winter 2015), 631–60, at www.jstor.org/stable/43896955. An unconvincing analysis is in M. Diane Burton and Tom Nickols, 'Prizes, Patents and the Search for Longitude', *Explorations in Economic History*, 64 (April 2017). 21–36, at https://doi.org/10.1016/j.eeh.2016.09.001

45 Andrew King, 'John Harrison, Clockmaker at Barrow, Near Barton upon Humber, Lincolnshire', in William J.H. Andrewes (ed.), *The Quest for Longitude* (Cambridge, MA, Harvard UP, 1996). 170; also id., 'Winner or Loser: Did John Harrison Win the Longitude Prize?', *Antiquarian Horology*, 37/1 (March 2016), 73–81; also Daniel A. Baugh, 'The Sea-Trial of John Harrison's Chronometer, 1736', *Mariners' Mirror*, 64 (1978), 235–40.

46 John Harrison, 'An Explanation of My Watch ...' (1763), quoted in Rupert T. Gould, *The Marine Chronometer: its History and Development* (1923; London: Holland Press, 1960), 65.

47 Samuel Smiles, 'John Harrison: Inventor of the Marine Chronometer', *Longman's Magazine*, 1/2 (December 1882), 156ff. It was re-written and enlarged for his *Men of Invention and Industry* (London: John Murray, 1884) Vol. 2, Ch. 3; at http://gerald-assey.org.uk/smiles/c_industry_2.htm. For the Longitude symposium, see Alun C. Davies, 'The Art of Time at Harvard: Museum Exhibitions at the Longitude Symposium, 1993, *Antiquarian Horology*, 21/4 (Summer 1994), 352–58; Dava Sobel, *Longitude: The True Story of a Lone Genius Who Solved the Greatest Scientific Problem of His Time* (London: Fourth Estate, 1995); and Dava Sobel and William J.H. Andrewes, *The Illustrated Longitude* (London: Fourth Estate, 1998); Jonathan Betts, *Marine Chronometers at Greenwich: A Catalogue of Marine Chronometers at the National Maritime Museum, Greenwich* (Oxford: Oxford UP and Greenwich Maritime Museum, 2017), ch1, 'A History of the Chronometer'.

48 D.J. Bryden, 'Evidence from Advertising for Mathematical Instrument Making in London, 1556–1714', *Annals of Science*, 49/4 (1982), 301–36, at https://doi.org/10.1080/00033799200200281; and id, 'Bankrupt and Insolvent Scientific Instrument Makers: The London Gazette as a Source for the History of the English Instrument Trade: 1720–1849', *Bulletin of the Scientific Instrument Society* no.123 (2014), 28–44 and no.124 (2014), 31–38; and Gerard L'E. Turner, 'The London Trade in Scientific Instrument-Making in the 18th Century', *Vistas in Astronomy*, 20 (1976). 173–82, at https://doi.org/10.1016/0083-6656(76)90029-5

49 Randall C. Brooks, 'Nautical Instrument Makers in Atlantic Canada', *Nova Scotia Historical Review*, 6 (Jan.1986), 36–54 (quote, 38); Allan Chapman, 'The New London and the Heavenly Jerusalem: Science and Craftsmen in Sir Christopher Wren's London', online at http://www.gresham.ac.uk.

50 Betts, *Marine Chronometers at Greenwich*, 20.

51 William J.H. Andrewes, 'Even Newton Could Be Wrong', in Andrewes (ed.) *Quest*. (1996), 224, n.130 and Appendix 2, pp. 234ff for details of the payments.

52 M. Yakup Bektas and Maurice Crosland, 'The Copley Medal: The Establishment of a Reward System in the Royal Society, 1731–1839', *Notes and Records of the Royal Society of London*, 46/1 (1992), 51, at www.jstor.org/stable/531440; J.C. Taylor, and A.W Wolfendale, 'John Harrison: Clockmaker and Copley Medallist: A Public Memorial at Last', *Royal Society Journal of the History of Science: Notes and Records*, 61/1 (January 2007), at https://doi.org/10.1098/rsnr.2006.0164. For a gentle challenge of heroic explanations, see Rebekah Higgitt, 'Challenging Tropes: Genius, Heroic Invention, and the Longitude Problem in the Museum', *Isis*, 108/2 (June 2017), 371–80, at https://doi.org/10.1086/692691

53 Quill, *John Harrison*, 12. For an overview of the Society's interest, see Sir Alan Cook, 'Time and the Royal Society', *Notes and Records of the Royal Society of London*, 55/1 (Jan. 2001), 9–27, at www.jstor.org/stable/532142

54 Jonathan Betts, 'Arnold and Earnshaw: The Practicable Solution', in Andrewes (ed.), *Quest*, 311–28.

55 Anthony G. Randall, 'The Timekeeper that Won the Longitude Prize', in Andrewes (ed.) *Quest*, 235–54; Andrew King, 'John Harrison, Copley Medallist', in Robert Vaughan (ed.), *Royal Society and The Fourth Dimension: History of Timekeeping* (Ticehurst: Antiquarian Horological Society, 1993), 34–41.

56 Gerard L'E. Turner, 'The Auction Sale of Larcum Kendall's Workshop, 1790', *Antiquarian Horology*, 5 (1967), 269–75; Jonathan Betts, 'Larcum Kendall (1719–1790)', *ODNB*; Rupert T. Gould, *The Marine Chronometer: Its History and Development* (1923; London: Holland Press, 1960), 71–74.

57 Eva G.R. Taylor, *Navigation in the Days of Captain Cook* (London: National Maritime Museum, 1974); also Johnathan Betts, 'The Eighteenth Century Transits of Venus, the Voyages of Captain James Cook, and the Early Development of the Marine Chronometer', *Antiquarian Horology*, 21/1 (Autumn 1993), 60–69.

58 Beresford Hutchinson, 'Some Observations on the Timekeepers of Thomas Mudge', *Antiquarian Horology*, 10 (1978), 714–19; Gould, *Marine Chronometer*, 74–82; Charles Allix, 'Mudge Milestones, Watch Dates', *Antiquarian Horology*, 13 (Summer 1981), 627–34; Thomas Seccombe, rev. David Penney, 'Mudge, Thomas (1715/16–1794)', *ODNB*.

59 Although Whitney failed to deliver what he promised (parts of the first generation of his muskets were far from interchangeable) the American government was patient. The episode is regarded as a milestone in the development of the 'American system' of manufacturing and Whitney is regarded as a promoter rather than pioneer of interchangeable parts. See Brooke Hindle and Steven Lubar, *Engines of Change: The American Industrial Revolution, 1790–1860* (Washington, DC: Smithsonian Institution, 1986), 218–26; Merritt Roe Smith, 'Eli Whitney and the American System of Manufacturing', in Carroll W. Pursell, Jr. (ed.) *Technology in America: A History of Individuals and Ideas* (Washington DC: Voice of America, 1979), 49–65.

60 Carolyn C. Cooper, 'The Portsmouth System of Manufacture', *Technology and Culture*, 25/2 (April 1984), 182–225, at https://doi.org/10.2307/3104712; id., *Shaping Invention: Thomas Blanchard's Machinery and Patent Management in Nineteenth Century America* (New York: Columbia UP, 1991), 134–43

61 See Paul Ditisheim's elegant tribute in 'Pierre Le Roy, 1717–1785', *Horological Journal*, 83 (Jan. 1940), 20–23, reprinted from *Revue Chronometrique*; Rupert T, Gould, 'The History of the Chronometer', *The Geographical Journal*, 57/4 (Apr. 1921), 263–64, at http://www.jstor.com/stable/1780557; also Jonathan Betts, *Time Restored: The Harrison Timekeepers, and R.T. Gould the Man Who Knew (Almost) Everything* (Oxford: Oxford UP and National Maritime Museum, 2006), who thinks Gould 'much too heavily overemphasised Le Roy's influence'. For a technical assessment of Le Roy's contribution see Charles Allix and Guiseppe Brusa, 'The Eminent Pierre Le Roy in the Art of Timekeeping: Part 2, 'Marine Timekeepers and Watches', *Antiquarian Horology*, 29/6 (Dec 2006), 775–89.

62 David S. Landes, 'The Creation of Knowledge and Technique: Today's Task and Yesterday's Experience', *Daedalus*, 109/1 (Winter 1980), 111–20 (quote, 115), at www.jstor.org/stable/20024651

63 Only about ten survive, though none in their original form as Arnold constantly upgraded them. See also David Thompson, 'John Arnold', *Watches* (London: British Museum, 2008), 96–97.

64 For dispute about Earnshaw's patent, see A.D. Stewart, 'John and Miles Brockbank: Their Life and Works', *Antiquarian Horology*, 26/4 (Dec. 2015), 511–13; also Betts, *Marine Chronometers at Greenwich*, 234–35.

65 Anthony G. Randall, 'Thomas Earnshaw's Numbering Sequence', *Antiquarian Horology*, 17/4 (Summer 1988), 368–71, lists over 220 of the Earnshaw firm's box and pocket chronometers between 1783 and 1841.

66 Howard T. Fry, *Alexander Dalrymple (1727–1808) and the Expansion of British Trade* (London: Cass for the Royal Commonwealth Society, 1970); Simon C. Davidson, 'Marine Chronometers: The Rapid Adoption of New Technology by East India Captains in the Period 1770–92 on Over 500 Voyages', *Antiquarian Horology*, 40/1 (March 2019), 76–91; also id., 'The Use of Chronometers to Determine Longitude on East India Company Voyages', *Mariner's Mirror*, 102/3 (July 2016). 344–48. https://doi.org/10.1080/00253359.2016.1210326

67 C.R. Richard Barder, *The Georgian Bracket Clock, 1714–1830* (Antique Collectors Club, Woodbridge, 1993). 154, 158.

68 For Swiss exports, see Eugene Jaquet and Alfred Chapuis, *Technique and History of the Swiss Watch* (London: Spring Books, 1953; reprinted Littlehampton: Hamlyn, 1970), Chapter 5, 113ff.

69 Gerard L'Estrange Turner, 'The Portuguese Agent: J.H. de Magellan', *Antiquarian Horology*, 9/1 (Dec. 1974), 74–76; also Jonathan Betts, 'John Hyacinth de Magellan, 1722–1790: Horological and Scientific Agent: Part 1', *Antiquarian Horology*, 27/5 (Sept. 2003), 509–17.

70 Jaquet and Chapuis, *Swiss Watches*, 114 for the Fairs, and 155 for Jaquet-Droz.

71 Catherine Cardinal (trans., Jacques Pages), *The Watch: From its Origins to the Nineteenth Century* (Secaucus, NJ: Wellfleet Press, 1988). 81.

72 Ralph Davis, *The Industrial Revolution and British Overseas Trade* (Leicester: Leicester UP, 1979), 14; Cardinal, *The Watch*, 57–58, 63–64.

73 Otto Kurz, *European Clocks and Watches in the Near East* (Studies of the Warburg Institute, ed. E.H. Gombrich, vol. 34) (London: Phaidon, 1975), 43–44; Gottfried Mraz, 'The Role of Clocks in the Imperial Hororaria for the Turks', in Maurice and Mayr, *The Clockwork Universe: German Clocks and Automata, 1550–1650* (Washington, DC: Smithsonian, 1980), 37–48.

74 Guiseppe Brusa and Charles Allix, 'Julien and Pierre Le Roy; their Business, their Relatives, and their Namesakes', *Antiquarian Horology*, 7/7 (June 1972), 598–606.

75 Kurz, *European clocks and watches in the Near East*, 94; Also Roger Smith, 'The Swiss Connection: International Networks in Some Eighteenth-Century Luxury Trades', *Journal of Design History*, 17/2, 132–35.

76 E. M. Barraud, *Barraud, The Story of a Family* (London: Research Publishing Company, 1967), 53–57 for the firm's dealings with Thwaites & Reed, including some 'for the China market'; Kurz, *European clocks and watches in the Near East*, 73, 86.

77 Barder, *Georgian Bracket Clock*, 155, 162.

78 Kurz, *European clocks and watches in the Near East*, 78–79, 97.

79 Terence Camerer Cuss, *The English Watch, 1585 to1970* (Woodbridge: Antique Collectors Club, 2009), 81.

80 Roger Smith and David Thompson, 'Vulliamy Musical Clocks for the Turkish Market: The Benhacock Clocks', *Antiquarian Horology*, 21/2 (Winter 1993), 118–31. The clocks that are discussed and illustrated in the article date from 1802 to 1804 and were exported by the Benhacock firm, founded in 1788.

81 Barder, *Georgian Bracket Clock*, 162,

82 For a history of indigenous Chinese clockwork, see Joseph Needham et al., *Heavenly Clockwork. The Great Astronomical Clocks of Medieval China* (Cambridge: Cambridge UP, 1960); for later developments, see Georges Bonnant, 'The Introduction of Western Horology in China', *La Suisse Horlogère* (International Edition) 1 (1960), 31. For a review of the origins and nature of the trade with China see Allen H. Weaving, 'Clocks for the Emperor', *Antiquarian Horology*, 19/4 (Summer 1991), 367–89, especially an Appendix listing London makers of clocks in Peking's Palace Museum; and Anon., 'London Makers Who Opened Up China', *Clocks*, 3 (July 1980), 39–40.

83 Roger Smith, 'Penduliers neuchâtelois et connexions londoniennes', *La neuchâteloise: Histoire et technique de la pendula neuchâteloise*, xviiie-xxie siècle (Le Locle: Musee international de l'horologerie, 2017), 175–92. I am grateful to Roger Smith for this reference.

84 Roger Smith, 'The Sing Song Trade: Exporting Clocks to China in the Eighteenth Century', *Antiquarian Horology*, 30/5 (March 2008), 629–58: (quote, 630–31); Heather Hobden, 'The Sing-Song Trade', *Antique Clocks*, 11/7 (December 1988), 41–42. Also, Klaus Maurice, 'Propagatio fidei per scientias; Jesuit gifts to the Chinese Court', in Klaus Maurice and Otto Mayr, *The Clockwork Universe: German Clocks and Automata, 1550–1650* (Washington, DC: Smithsonian, 1980), 27–36.

85 For a review of the connection between imperial patronages, artistic style and technical expertise in the seventeenth and eighteenth centuries, especially in connection with the demand for elaborate clocks see Catherine Pagani, 'Clockmaking in China under the Kangxi and Qianlong Emperors', *Arts Asiatiques*, 50 (1995), 76–84, at https://www.jstor.org/stable/i4013820.

86 Barder, *Georgian Bracket Clock*, 171; also Pagani, 'Clockmaking in China', 76–84, at www.jstor.org/stable/43485475

87 Roger Smith, 'The Sing Song Trade', 636–37. The clocks are still on display in the Beijing Palace Museum.

88 Alexander D. Stewart, 'John and Miles Brockbank, Their Life and Work', *Antiquarian Horology*, 36/4 (Dec. 2015), 502–29, esp. 510, 516–18.

89 Clare Vincent and J.H. Leopold, 'James Cox (c.1723–1800): Goldsmith and Entrepreneur', http://www.metmuseum.org/to *Antiquarian Horology*/hd/jcox/hd_jcox.htm

90 Roger Smith, 'James Cox (c. 1723–1800); A Revised Biography', *The Burlington Magazine*, CXLII (No. 1167) (June 2000), 353–61, at https://www.jstor.org/stable/888937, citing *Commons Journals*, 34, 19 March 1773; id., 'The Swiss Connection', 123–39; Clare Le Corbeiller, 'James Cox and His Curious Toys'. *The Metropolitan Museum of Art Bulletin*, New Series, 18/10 (Jun. 1960), 318–24, at https://www.metmuseum.org/toah/hd/jcox/hd_jcox.htm; also Ian White, *English Clocks for the Eastern Markets: English clockmakers trading in China and the Ottoman Empire, 1580–1815* (Ticehurst: Antiquarian Horological Society, 2012), Chapters 5 and 6.

91 Jonathan Betts, *Marine Chronometers at Greenwich: A Catalogue of Marine Chronometers at the National Maritime Museum, Greenwich* (Oxford: Oxford UP and National Maritime Museum, 2017), 233.

92 Smith, 'James Cox: revised biography', 356–57.

93 Jaquet and Chapuis, *Swiss Watch*, 155; also cited in Smith, 'The Swiss Connection: International Networks', 132

94 John Joseph Murphy, 'The Establishment of the American Clock Industry: A Study in Entrepreneurial History', [Unpublished PhD thesis, Yale University, 1961), 219.

95 The sales gave rise to a painful horological pun when the American showman, P.T. Barnum, observed that in China 'the innards [of Jerome's clocks] were removed so that the cases could be used as temples for the gods, proving that faith was possible without "works"'; Irving Wallace, *The Fabulous Showman: A biography of P.T. Barnum* (New York: Knopf, 1959), 164–66.

96 For distinctive Japanese developments in clocks, see, Maria P. and Pedro C. Fernandez. 'Precision Timekeepers of Tokugawa Japan and the Evolution of the Japanese Domestic Clock', *Technology and Culture*, 37/2 (April 1996), 221–48, at www.jstor.org/stable/3106815

97 Hoshimi Uchida, 'The Spread of Timepieces in the Meiji Period', *Japan Review*, 14 (2002), 175, 181–82, 187, at www.jstor.org/stable/25791261

Part 2

Challenge

6 Clouds on the Horizon

Switzerland's Challenge

Origins of the European challenge

By the 1790s, Clerkenwell, at the heart of England's watchmaking industry, led other European watch centres in the number of watches it made. Evidence supporting this assertion comes from the records of between 150,000 and 200,000 precious metal watchcases assayed annually in London's Goldsmith's Hall. This estimate did not include the unknown number of watch movements cased in base metal, or of the uncounted (but fewer) numbers of watches finished in smaller watchmaking centres, in Liverpool and Coventry. In all, it seems that at the peak of its industry's golden era, Britain accounted for about half of Europe's output. Although great European Houses, notably that of Breguet, made clocks and watches of superlative quality, in the matter of the fine precision of their chronometers, Clerkenwell led. They were the most sophisticated of contemporary mechanisms, and those by Arnold, Earnshaw, and Barraud were as advanced as any others and were made in greater numbers. By 1800, their use in the East India Company's merchant ships was extensive. Yet from this pinnacle, England's watchmaking industry started a decline that continued through the nineteenth century. By 1914, although Britain was still a major industrial power, its watchmakers' share of their home market was small and, in the watch markets of the world, almost negligible. There is no monocausal explanation for this decline, or for the waning of other once-dominant British industries – radios, televisions, and motor cars – in the century that followed. Watchmaking's decline was caused by a mixture of reasons. They included the complacency of its retailers (responsible for commissioning watches) who were happy to make comfortable profits from a small luxury market. Also culpable were masters and outworkers, who resisted new methods of production. In the long run, the industry's two institutions, the Clockmakers' Company and the British Horological Institute, were also accountable. Neither was successful in dealing with the industry's internal and external challenges. The Clockmakers' Company blamed the success of the Swiss in penetrating Britain's home market on the inability – unwillingness – of British governments to enforce

DOI: 10.4324/9781003227823-8

protective tariffs. In the 1860s, more Swiss watches were sold in Britain than were made by England's watchmaking firms. When horological tariffs disappeared after free trade in 1860 Britain's market was wide open, and within a decade the Swiss were joined by American firms that 'revolutionised' the method of making watches. Ultimately, England's watchmaking firms lost Britain's home and former export markets. At first the Swiss watch industry, too, suffered from the successful revolution in American watchmaking, but – unlike English watchmaking – it appropriately adapted itself and recovered. By1914, Swiss exports dominated in the world's watch markets (Chapter 11).

The present chapter examines how and why Switzerland's watch industry was able to invade Britain's home market in the first half of the nineteenth century. How was Switzerland, a country with few obvious initial advantages, able to prosper and exploit foreign watch markets, despite many seeming disadvantages? It was landlocked. Its centres of trade were far from Europe's main ports. Its population was small (under 2 million in the early nineteenth century). Compared with Britain, for example, it had few natural resources (no coal, little iron ore). It was mountainous, with poor roads and severe winters. Given their earlier starts in mechanical clockwork, the availability of skilled craftsmen, and with goodish home markets, other countries as well as Britain – Italy, France, Germany, the Netherlands – were much more likely candidates for their existing watchmaking industries to expand and dominate world markets. Yet watchmaking in Switzerland, along with its textile industry, became of major importance to its national economy. Its people were thrifty and hardworking, proficient linguists (with German, French, and Italian neighbours), who concentrated on manufacturing products requiring a high degree of skill (watchmaking, machine making, precision engineering, and chemicals).[1] These features help to explain why Switzerland became successful, despite its few natural resources. Watchmaking in England was of minor importance to Britain's economy, whereas in Switzerland it was central. The triumph of its watchmaking industry by the mid-nineteenth century offers one explanation for the English watch industry's problems.

****

The revocation of the Edict of Nantes, 1685

The roots of the Swiss watch industry lay in sixteenth-century Geneva. Surrounded by the Alps and the Jura region bordering France and Switzerland, the city had become a centre for finishing watches.[2] The industry's initial growth and later prosperity were an indirect consequence of the French wars of religion. Those had ended in 1598 with the Edict of Nantes, which inaugurated a policy of tolerance to end discrimination against France's protestant Huguenot population.

When Louis XIV revoked the Edict in 1685, protection ceased. It prompted a haemorrhage of skilled craftsmen from France's metallurgical industries. About 200,000 Huguenots sought asylum in tolerant neighbouring countries. Of the 50,000 who emigrated to Britain, many were watchmakers who gravitated to Clerkenwell.[3] Similarly, the exodus eventually helped the infant horological industry of Switzerland, although the ultimate benefits were delayed until the consequences of the Revocation were played out in France.[4] The initial damage done by the Revocation to France's horological industry was grave but not fatal. In 1715, attempts were made to revive and repair the harm to its textile and metal manufactures by enticing immigrants to those industries. One such project was led by the itinerant Scottish banker, John Law, who became Controller General of French Finances. He set up a watch factory in Versailles. It was directed by Henry Sully, a talented English-born watchmaker who, after an apprenticeship in London, lived in France. The scheme lured about sixty immigrant English watchmakers and their families but, after two years, it floundered, and Sully was dismissed as its director. He then led an attempt to establish another watchmaking factory at St Germain, Paris. It, too, failed after a year when it ran out of money. Most of the English craftsmen were repatriated after the British parliament passed an Act in 1719 that encouraged the return of emigrant workers.[5]

Both of Sully's short-lived projects were unsuccessful. Nevertheless, their legacy proved invaluable because they contributed unanticipated long-term benefits to French and especially Swiss watchmaking. The use of English watch tools, notably Lancashire-made wheel-cutting engines, had much impressed France's most eminent contemporary watchmaker, Julien Le Roy (1686–1751).[6] He thought Sully's English craftsmen introduced 'a standard of workmanship superior to anything they had [hitherto] known, [which ultimately] led to great advances in French horology'.[7] The Sully episodes were ephemeral. But they imported the best practices of English watchmaking. ultimately to the benefit of the Swiss industry. They were an important inheritance during the revival of watchmaking in the Jura in the late eighteenth century.[8]

Watchmaking in the Jura: the *établissage* system

That revival, as Pierre-Yves Donzé explains, came in the last quarter of the eighteenth century.[9] It arose from different but nearly contemporaneous innovations in making watches that changed the design of watches from antecedent and prevailing kinds. They resulted in a watch distinctive from traditional models, especially those made in Clerkenwell. Amongst its most important features was the abandonment of bulky fusees in favour of 'going barrels' that made watches slimmer. Although it was generally agreed that fusees were mechanically superior, they *were* an additional complication and therefore an extra cost; fusee chains could and often did break down, requiring an irritating need for expensive repairs. The alternative that the Swiss adopted was a 'going-barrel', with a long, thin, spring. If power was taken from only around the middle of the spring, its torque was *almost* uniform along the limited length used for its running period of twenty-four hours. That it ran slower at the end was offset by running a little faster at the beginning. Such small errors were tolerable and adequate for most customers, except for those who wanted the nearly exact precision of chronometers and the finest carriage clocks. Using a simpler escapement (developed by George Graham), watches with going barrels kept good time, again well within the normal needs of laymen. Above all, going barrels avoided a fusee's potential trouble if they broke down. An incidental benefit of the slimmer watch was that because a going barrel took less room inside the movement it needed a 'thinner' case (thus less expensive gold or silver). The consequence was a distinctively slimmer watch that was desirable when wearing waistcoats became fashionable in the 1780s. As David Landes observed, 'fashion abhors bulges'.[10] The new thinner watches were successful in Europe's two largest national watch markets. Their successful penetration of France's domestic market was recognised in 1817 when, it was claimed, 'ninety-nine out of a hundred of the watches sold in Paris as French watches are not made in France'.[11] In the late eighteenth century, Swiss watches cut into sales of Clerkenwell's traditional bulky watches in Britain, to the perpetual annoyance of the Clockmakers' Company.

The new watches gave a great boost to the growth of Switzerland's watchmakers. Indications of the size of the finishing industry in Geneva can be seen in its growth from the late seventeenth century. Then, approximately a hundred masters employed about 300 outworkers to make 5,000 pieces annually; after 1760 perhaps 800 masters and 4,000 outworkers made 85,000 pieces. But by 1800 Geneva had about a 1,000 masters who finished proportionately more watches. They were supplied by the cottage industry which made parts for watches and clocks in the hinterland of the Jura region.[12]

The emergence of watchmaking's characteristics in the Jura was similar – but not identical – to the organisation of Lancashire's cottage industries (Chapter 2). In the Jura, the division of labour took the form of the *établissage* system. Watches were assembled from parts made in different places before being brought together by the *établisseur* – the trader, entrepreneur, or intermediary.[13] He collected *ébauches* (the rough movements) and cases, dials, and small parts for final assembly from a network of specialist sub-contractors in small independent units. Each production unit made one out of dozens of different components. Their workshops were autonomous, but greatly interdependent on each other. The organisational network that developed for watchmaking was like that which already existed for Switzerland's textile and metallurgical industries. They, too, converted imported raw materials into highly finished goods for export to markets far larger than that offered by the country's small population (about 1½ million in 1800). Watchmaking, a part-time activity in summer, became the main occupation during snow-bound winter months when villages were isolated for lengthy periods. The industry flourished, helped by 'the wonderful light reflected from the snow [that] contributed greatly to the success of horology in these regions'.[14]

Lépine and Japy

Serendipity – happenstance – contributed to these developments. It can be seen in the careers and contributions of Jean-Antoine Lépine (1720–1810) and Georges Frédéric Japy (1749–1812). In about 1770, Lépine re-arranged the design of the movement by introducing what became known as 'Lépine bars'. They enabled watches to be thinner. He used a 'virgule' escapement, yet 'timekeeping remained reasonably good [even] without the costly fusee'. He favoured other technical refinements such as keyless winding, new calendar mechanisms, and various devices including rear-winding (already in English watches), hand-setting, and a cuvette (cap) in gilt-brass, hinged to the movement. Lépine's layout (*calibre*) became a feature of the new-style watches produced by his workshop in Ferney (a small village in France, but close to Geneva) between 1775 and 1778.[15] There was a time lag before many of these innovations were adopted by others but in the nineteenth century several became standard features.[16] Lépine was, David Penney concluded, 'years ahead of his time and had a great influence on watch design … [and he helped to] lay the foundation of the modern mechanical watch'.[17]

Lépine's own output was substantial. Between about 1770 and retirement in 1792, his workshop made about 6,500 watches annually, much more than was made by comparably sized units in London. His construction methods were adopted and modified by his contemporary Abraham-Louis Breguet. Breguet was, arguably, the greatest of all watchmakers because he 'combined mechanical ingenuity, inventiveness, [and] splendid execution with an elegance which has never been surpassed and seldom equalled'.[18] His innovations made it easier and acceptable for lesser makers to assemble going-barrel watches in slim cases. Perhaps inspired by his lead, other watchmakers adopted Lépine's *calibre*. French and Swiss watch industries were both greatly stimulated – including those firms that specialised in 'the watch as a jewelled ornament'.[19] Several contemporary refinements served the niche luxury market in which some Jura watchmakers specialised. In the late nineteenth century, elite Clerkenwell firms still fulfilled special orders for complicated and expensive repeater work by subcontracting to specialists in the Jura.[20] More importantly for the wider market, Lépine's thin *calibre* was especially suitable for the cheap Swiss watches that ended in the pockets of first-time buyers in Europe and. increasingly, in Britain.

Less expensive watches were also a consequence of the career of Lépine's contemporary, Georges Frédéric Japy. Born in Beaucourt in the *Franche Comté*, Japy was the son of a wheelwright and blacksmith who made and repaired locks and agricultural tools.[21] After his apprenticeship, he returned to Beaucourt in the early 1770s and, by 1777, he had designed machine tools for a simple production line that made *ébauches*. Sir John Bowring, in his influential report on Swiss watchmaking in the 1830s, explained it was operated by semi-skilled apprentices, not by trained watchmakers.[22] Annual output rose steadily from 43,000 pieces in 1780 to 70,000 pieces in the 1790s and 100,000 by 1805. As demand grew, prices fell and quality improved. Production was not completely rationalised by the firm, as uniformity was never imposed (by 1870 it had made about a 1,000 different *calibres* for its customers).[23] Japy's prototype machine tools made *ébauches* for the traditional French watches of the time, but they still needed finishing and adjustment. Parts were similar and their tolerances were adequate, but not uniform or perfectly interchangeable. Japy's later machines were modified so that at Beaucourt *ébauches* were produced for the new-style, slimmer, Lépine *calibre* movements. Another plant at Fontainmelon was started in 1793.[24] In 1809, Japy turned his attention to providing *blancs roulants* (rough movements for clocks) that were made in a separate factory in Badevel (in France, near Beaucourt and the Swiss border).[25] They were assembled and finished by Paris firms. A formula successful for watches was equally successful for clocks – an interesting reversal of the usual sequence, in that these improvements in making clock parts with broad tolerances were adapted from the earlier example of watches with much finer tolerances. By 1805, Japy employed 300 workers to make *ébauches* and *blancs roulants* and had successfully industrialised a key part of watch and clock making. The consequence for English watchmaking was that the price of Jura watches undercut those made in Clerkenwell. The employment of women and children meant that labour costs there were cheaper than in Clerkenwell, an element of the economies of scale that arose from a more efficient organisation of production. On this point David Landes quotes the Swiss historian Adolf Pfleghart:

> For every kind of work they use the ever fully identical rough movements of Japy... the various parts and accessories are easy to match... at the cheapest price;... everything is planned out in advance, every piece is made the same and costs proportionally less... They make there an endless series of cases to fit one and the same plate size, knowing full well that any and all watches of the appropriate calibre will fit. The same holds for dials, hands, springs, and so on.[26]

Britain: imported and smuggled watches

Even before Japy's and Lépine's innovations fully developed into the thinner, cheaper Swiss watches, London's watchmakers had complained about the appearance of smuggled 'Geneva' watches in London's shops. The Clockmakers Company's members regularly fulminated about them, but there seemed little that their officials could do. In the first half of the eighteenth century, foreign-made watches and clocks had entered Britain in an irregular, unsystematic, inflow: little is known of the number or value of these casual imports. At first, it was not smuggling as such (that is, the deliberate avoidance of tariff duties). Unknown numbers of individuals brought in unknown numbers of foreign (mostly Swiss) watches for personal use or gifts. Wealthy individuals simply brought them back as souvenirs, especially expensive pieces. A small customs presence at scattered ports on an extensive coastline could not methodically examine every person entering and leaving the country. Watches were easy to carry on the body or in luggage and those who travelled to and from the continent were not accustomed to having their persons and possessions searched. Indeed, smuggling was occasionally a two-way process, when ship's captains brought English watches to France.[27] Such trade was difficult to prevent and impossible to measure. Smuggling of all kinds of goods from Europe, not just watches, lent 'an air of unreality to the official statistics on English foreign trade during the eighteenth century'.[28] Customs officials were unable to search everything, and London's shopkeepers were happy to stock Swiss watches.

In the second half of the century, the pattern of smuggling changed, and its volume increased. Individuals continued to bring in foreign-made watches, but systematic large-scale smuggling now developed to supply retailers. Shopkeepers were pleased to have a range of attractively priced watches and cared not who had made them or from where they came. In the late 1780s, the market was growing. As real incomes of some of Britain's middle class began to rise, so did the demand for inexpensive watches and clocks.[29] For a first-time buyer of modest means the best value for money was not a watch from Clerkenwell or even Coventry, but a foreign model. The Swiss watch industry was able to satisfy the demand for watches, and London's shops were willing to sell them. For those in Britain who had never owned a watch before, a Geneva model was 'good enough'. Swiss watchmakers fully understood that because Switzerland's domestic market was small, its watch industry depended on exports for growth. Consequently, they expertly cultivated Britain's home market.

The Clockmakers' Company repeatedly complained about smuggled timepieces, especially those made to look like 'English watches' that carried on their dials forged names of English makers and places. Indeed, Britain's market became so lucrative and important to the Swiss that they developed a special production line of pseudo-London timepieces in which highly decorated Geneva watches of mediocre quality, with painted enamel cases, were about a half or a third of the cost of an authentic English equivalent.[30] In 1784, a special court was convened by the Clockmakers' Company to explore this 'growing threat'. It concluded, rather lamely, that the best and most expensive English watches were superior as timekeepers, because Swiss and French watchmakers 'trust only to appearance, the English to performance'.[31] It was an early example of the many later assertions by English watchmakers that of course their fusee-watches *were* superior; it was the customers who were wrong, when they chose 'inferior' foreign-made models.

The 'Devil Taverners' and the 1784 Plate Act

Leading watchmakers such as Arnold, Emery, Vulliamy, and Brockbank were so annoyed at the continued inflow of foreign watches that they supported a short-lived trade association that met at – and took its name from – the *Devil Tavern* in Fleet Street.[32] It even gained support from those outside the City Walls who were not members of the Clockmakers' Company, and who otherwise had ignored the guild. An alliance of 101 assorted *Devil Tavern* supporters signed a memorial placed by the Company in advertisements in three London newspapers. It promised a reward of ten guineas (later increased to twenty guineas) for information leading to the conviction of anyone involved in illegal imports.[33] Nothing much seems to have happened.

Perhaps this was because complaints by the *Devil Taverner*s about smuggling converged with protests about the malignant consequences for the watchmaking industry of the Plate Act of 1784. That Act was an attempt to raise revenue to pay for Britain's recent unsuccessful involvement in the war with its former American colonies, the newly independent United States. It targeted the two precious metals used to make quality watch cases, with levies of 8s per ounce on wrought gold and 6d per ounce on wrought silver. All watch case makers had to submit their wares to Assay Offices for the mark of the sovereign's head to be added to show that duty had been paid. The penalties for non-compliance were a £50 fine and a forfeiture of goods. The penalty for counterfeiting hallmarks was even more draconian: death, as a felon, without 'benefit of clergy' (the ritual through which first-time offenders might receive a more lenient sentence if found guilty). It caused a flurry of activity that led to eight Liverpool case makers registering for the first time at Chester.[34]

The forceful objections from the Clockmakers' Company prompted by the Plate Act stressed how much it had increased the cost of English compared with French and Swiss watches. English cases of 22 carat gold had to compete with lower qualities from France (20 carat) and Switzerland (18 carat). The protests were ignored by the government and the duties remained. From 1786, the Company complained again and reiterated its objections about the lower quality of gold in foreign cases. This time the Company's pleas were successful. The changes could be seen in William Eden's Anglo-French commercial treaty of 1786 (an attempt to bring to an end the economic war with France that had followed the Seven Years' War).[35] Although the treaty aimed to reduce tariffs on goods from either country, it retained a duty of 27½ per cent on imported watches.[36] The Company thought this was a justified reaction to French and Swiss watchmakers who, they argued, unfairly benefitted by exploiting the cheaper labour of women and children to undercut Clerkenwell's prices. At first, the Treaty seemed to satisfy the Clockmakers' Company because it maintained horological tariffs at 27½ per cent. But the effect on the continued official influx of foreign watches was negligible because although many foreign gold watches were imported, only a 'few... paid the duties'.[37] It was the first taste of the problem that would afflict English watchmaking for the next sixty-odd years – smuggling watches was easy, but preventing it was difficult. In 1789, the Company again protested that the Eden Treaty offered ineffective protection for the industry; 'frauds and counterfeit names threaten[ed] the excellent reputation of the good watchmakers' of London.[38]

After 14 July 1789, the treaty became irrelevant, following the Revolution in France. Trade with Europe was disrupted by the Terror and, after 1793 trade was interrupted by the war with France. The brief period of peace during the Treaty of Amiens was followed by the Napoleonic war. The retention of high duties made smuggling profitable; and, when tariffs were increased, even more so. 'For the next thirty years', Roger Prouty correctly concluded, 'protection and smuggling remained the order of the day'.[39]

****

What explains the Swiss success? First, they enjoyed comparative advantages in metal working and the manufacture of what in the eighteenth century used to be called 'toys'. This category was expanded to include watches. Second, they used cheap family labour with plenty of time on their hands during the long snowy winter months. Last, and most importantly, they adopted going barrels instead of fusees and made watches that were cheaper than (and sometimes as good as) all but the best English time pieces. Above all, they were successful because they offered good value for money. The flowering of Switzerland's watchmaking industry at the end of the eighteenth century coincided with and marked the end of English horology's golden era. In retrospect, there can be little doubt that the Swiss played a significant role in the English industry's decline. The creations of the titans of the golden age – Tompion, Graham, Mudge, Harrison, Arnold, and Earnshaw – had been sustained by a buoyant domestic market, and exports notably to Turkey and China. Clerkenwell's watchmaking had reached a level of extraordinary technical achievement with the marine chronometer, thanks to the government's stimulus through the Longitude prize. Then the wars with France intervened. Thereafter, through the nineteenth century, the English economy flourished – especially its textile, engineering, and commerce sectors. But England's watchmaking industry didn't: it stagnated and then slid into decline (Chapter 7). It never recovered its former importance, although its chronometer makers defied decline and retained their primacy. Clerkenwell remained dedicated – long into the nineteenth century – to making watches with fusees, in the enduring conviction of their technical superiority. The best clocks and watches with fusees were, indisputably, technically superior. But it was a poor economic and commercial choice for its industry, in the face of the enormous widening of the watch market, in Britain and the rest of the world. A more flexible industry might have satisfied the markets for both expensive and affordable watches. The first phases of the industry's decline set in during the French wars, unmistakably a direct consequence of competition from lighter, simpler, cheaper Swiss watches – either legally imported or smuggled (Chapters 8 and 9). We shall see how, during the wars, smuggling became extensive. But only four years after the outbreak of war an urgent problem for English watchmaking arose when the Prime Minister, William Pitt the Younger, attempted to raise money by levying a tax on horological goods (Chapter 7).

Notes

1 W.O. Henderson, 'J.C. Fischer: A Swiss Industrial Pioneer', *Zeitschrift Für Die Gesamte Staatswissenschaft: Journal of Institutional and Theoretical Economics*, 119/2 (April 1963), 361–76, at www.jstor.org/stable/40748679; also id., 'Introduction: Industrial Switzerland', in *J.C. Fischer and His Diary of Industrial England, 1814–51* (London: Cass, 1966), xiii–xvi.

2 On the origins of watch making in Geneva, its introduction into the Jura and its rapid growth in the eighteenth century, see Chapters 1–3 of Eugene Jacquet and Alfred Chapuis, *Technique and History of the Swiss Watch* (1953; London: Littlehampton Book Services, 1970 ed.), esp. 73–76; also David S. Landes, *Revolution in Time: Clocks and the making of the modern World* (Cambridge, MA: Harvard UP, 1983), Chapter 14, 'The Ups and Downs of International Competition' (esp. 224ff), and Chapter 15 'Multum in Parvo', 237ff.

3 P.J. Shears, 'Huguenot Connections with the Clock-making Trade in England', *Proceedings of the Huguenot Society of London*, 20 (1966), 158–76; Warren Scoville, 'The Huguenots and the Diffusion of Technology', *Journal of Political Economy*, LX (1952), 294–311, at DOI: 10.1086/257238 and https://www.jstor.org/stable/1828923

4 Roger Smith, 'The Swiss Connection: International Networks in Some Eighteenth-century Trades', *Journal of Design History*, 17/2 (2004), 125, at https://www.jstor.org/stable/3527171; Bruno Fritzsche, 'Switzerland', in Joel Mokyr (ed.), *Oxford Encyclopaedia of Economic History* (Oxford:

Oxford UP, 2003), Vol. 5, 42–49; Carlo M. Cipolla, 'The Diffusion of Innovations in Early Modern Europe', *Comparative Studies in Society and History*, 14/1 (Jan. 1972), 49, at http://www.jstor.com/stable/178059

5 For legislation against the export of machinery and the emigration of skilled workers see John R. Harris, *Industrial Espionage and Technology Transfer* (Aldershot: Ashgate, 1998) 7–28; id., 'French Industrial Policy under the Ancien Regime and the Pursuit of the British Example', *Histoire, Économie et Société*, 12/1 (1993), 93–100 at *https://www.jstor.org/stable/23611290*; and for the broad context, id., 'French Industrial Espionage in Britain in the Late Eighteenth Century', *Journal of the Royal Society of Arts*, 137/5398 (Sept. 1989), 629–34, at https://www.jstor.org/stable/413750033

6 For an analysis of the relationship between Sully and Le Roy that touches on the two projects, see Robert St-Louis, '1716: "A Watch of New Construction" – A Meeting of Two Great Horological Minds', *Antiquarian Horology*, 2/2 (June 2021), 199–218.

7 F.J. Britten, *Britten's Old Clocks and Watches and their Makers* (9th ed., revised by Cecil Clutton, G.H. Baillie, and Courtney Ilbert (London: Spon, 1956; reprinted Woodbridge: Antique Collectors' Club, 1978); Rupert T. Gould, The *Marine Chronometer: Its History and Development* (1923: London: Holland Press, 1960 edn.), 35–39.

8 Anthony J. Turner, 'Berthoud in England, Harrison in France: The Transmission of Horological Knowledge in Eighteenth Century Europe', *Antiquarian Horology*, 20/3 (Autumn 1992), 219–39, esp. 221–25.

9 Pierre-Yves Donzé, *History of the Swiss Watch Industry: From Jacques David to Nicolas Hayek* (Switzerland: Peter Lang AG, 3rd ed., 2014), 5–7; Landes, Revolution in Time, 257ff; B.M. Biuchi, 'The Industrial Revolution in Switzerland' (1969), in Carlo M. Cipolla (ed.) *The Fontana Economic History of Europe*, vol. 4, book 2, *The Emergence of Industrial Societies* (London: Collins, 1973), 628–85.

10 David S. Landes, 'Watchmaking: A Case-study in Enterprise and Change,' *Business History Review*, 53 (1979), 264, at https://doi.org/10.2307/3114685.

11 LMA/CLC/L/CD/E/002/MS03951: 'On the Distress of the Trade'.

12 Landes, *Revolution in Time*, 254–55, and especially Chapter 16, 'Notwithstanding the Barrenness of the Soil', 257ff.

13 Donzé, *Swiss Watch Industry*, 7ff, 29 ff. The *établissage* system flourished until the 1870s (Chapter 11).

14 Charles Allix, *Carriage Clocks: Their Historical Development* (Woodbridge: Antique Collectors Club, 1974), 130, fn. 2.

15 Lépine worked in Ferney for the great philosopher Voltaire, before opening his workshop in Paris.

16 Donzé, *Swiss Watch Industry,* 15. Also David Thompson, 'Jean-Antoine Lépine', *Watches* (London: British Museum, 2008), 100–01; Adolph Chapiro, 'Jean-Antoine Lépine, 1720–1814: An 'unknown' Maker', *Antiquarian Horology,* 9/4 (Sept. 1975), 443–54.

17 David Penney, 'Review of Adolphe Chapiro', *Jean-Antoine Lépine, horloger (1720–1814)*, (Paris, 1988), in *Antiquarian Horology*, 18/4 (Winter 1989), 427–28.

18 For the relationship between Lépine and Breguet, see Adolphe Chapiro, 'Lépine, Breguet, and the Origins of the Lever Escapement in France', *Antiquarian Horology*, 14/4 (Dec. 1983), 369–96; and id., 'Addendum', *Antiquarian Horology*, 14/6 (Jan. 1984), 616–17. For illustrations, see Andrew Crisford, *Masterpieces from the Asprey Collection: Vol. 1, Abraham-Louis Breguet* (London: Quartet Books, 1994), and Anthony J. Turner, Herve Chayette, and Jean-Claude Sabrier, *Mr. Breguet chez*

Cheyette (London and Paris, Rogers Turner Books, 2010); Sir David Lionel Salomans, *Breguet, 1747–1823* (London: privately printed, 1923; Classic Reprint, 2017), and George Daniels, *The Art of Breguet* (London: Sotheby's, 1975). David Thompson, 'Abraham Louis Breguet', *Watches*, 102–03.

19 Landes, 'Watchmaking: A Case-study', 226.

20 For Lépine's repeating watches see Chapiro, 'Lépine, an 'unknown' Maker', 443. The mechanism was designed in 1763 and published in *Memoires de L'Academie des Sciences*, in 1766; id., 'Lépine, Breguet, and ... the Lever Escapement', 369–70. For a survey of the development of repeating watches, see Francis Wadsworth, 'A History of Repeating Watches', *Antiquarian Horology*, 4/12 (1965), 364–67, and 5 (1, 2, and 3) (1966), 24–26, 48–52, and 90–92.

21 Allix, *Carriage Clocks*, 133–37; Maxwell Cutmore, *Watches: 1850–1980* (Newton Abbott: David and Charles, 1989), 19–20,

22 *BPP*, 1836/14: 'Report on the Commerce and Manufactures of Switzerland' by Sir John Bowring, 36, suggests that the machines were invented by Jeanneret of Locle, who sold the discovery to Japy. Bowring's report stressed the importance for Switzerland of its cheaper prices that helped it in foreign markets protected by tariffs.

23 Donzé, *Swiss Watch Industry*, 18.

24 Catherine Cardinal (trans. Jacques Pages), *The Watch, from Its Origins to the Nineteenth Century* (Secaucus, NJ: Wellfleet Press, 1988), 54–58.

25 Allix, *Carriage Clocks*, 137, 148. By 1868 the firm had made almost 22 million *ébauches* for watches; it employed over 5,500 persons, and the Badevel factory had produced almost 2 million movements.

26 Landes, 'Watchmaking: A Case-study'; id., *Revolution in Time*, 262–63, citing Adolf Pfleghart, *Die Schweizerischen Uhrenindustrie* (1908).

27 Cardinale, *The Watch*, 61.

28 Hoh-Cheung and Lorna H. Mui, 'Trends in Eighteenth Century Smuggling Reconsidered', *Economic History Review*, 28/1 (Feb. 1975), 28–42 (quote, 28), at https://www.jstor.org/stable/2594370

29 Average real earnings of some clerks doubled between 1780 and 1840: see H.M. Boot, 'Real Incomes of the British Middle Class, 1760–1850: The Experience of Clerks at the East India Company', *Economic History Review*, 52/4 (Nov. 1999), 638–68, at https://www.jstor.org/stable/2599322.

30 Landes, 'Watchmaking: A Case-study', 234.

31 UofL MS 755, folios 8–9, Dec. 1784: Material Relating to the Clockmakers' Company.

32 It was the inn where Samuel Pepys and Dr Samuel Johnson drank.

33 Roger Smith, 'The Devil Tavern Group: An Eighteenth-Century Horological Trade Association', *Antiquarian Horology*, 24/5 (Spring 1999), 427–31.

34 Dennis S. Moore and Philip T. Priestley, 'Some Account of Liverpool Watch Case Makers, 1785–1798', *Antiquarian Horology*, 23/4 (Summer 1997), 341–53.

35 Named after William Eden, Lord Auckland (1744–1814).

36 LMA/CLC/L/CD/B/001/MS02710/005: Court Minute Book Covering 1778–1804, 11 Dec. 1786; Landes, *Revolution in Time*, 235–6.

37 UofL MS 755, folios 39–40, 44, 46–47: 'Memorial to the Treasury from the Committee of London's Workmen: 7 June 1790', and subsequent correspondence.

38 UofL MS 755, folios 10–11 (1789).

39 Roger Prouty, *The Transformation of the Board of Trade, 1830–1855* (London: Heinemann, 1957), 5.

7 War and Peace, 1793–1817

Crisis, Recovery, and Crisis Again

1797–98: Pitt's horological taxes

Swiss watches had first entered Britain in substantial numbers in the 1780s. Thereafter they were a constant challenge to England's watch industry, to the annoyance of the Clockmakers' Company. Initially, the French Revolution seemed not to affect Clerkenwell, which achieved its highest ever annual output, of 191,000 watches in 1796, as measured by watch cases assayed at London's Goldsmith's Hall. Then, Pitt's taxes on clocks and watches in 1797–98 coincided with a slump in watch production. Protests followed. The taxes were revoked and by 1808 the industry recovered. But Clerkenwell and Coventry experienced a second, more severe, depression that lasted for about eight years, until after Waterloo. This chapter examines both of the depressions and surveys the industry's fortunes during the interim years. The consequences for the industry's chronometer-manufacturing sector during the two decades of the war will be examined separately (Chapter 10).

****

Four years after the outbreak of the first phase of the wars with France, Prime Minister William Pitt the Younger introduced new taxes.[1] They were intended to raise revenue to pay for Britain's army and navy in the war and to help him subsidise the armies of his European allies.[2] First, in June 1797, Pitt increased the duty on wrought silver to 16s per ounce: it doubled the cost of silver watch cases. He had deduced from the assaying statistics at London's Goldsmith's Hall (notably those for the preceding year) that Clerkenwell and its watchmaking community were busy and prosperous.[3] This led him in his next budget to levy explicit taxes on watch and clock ownership.[4] Households were required to complete a form, listing the timepieces owned by its inhabitants: the amounts to be levied were 10s for a gold watch, 5s for a clock, and 2s 6d

DOI: 10.4324/9781003227823-9

for every silver or metal watch. There were a few general concessions. They included

> Persons occupying Houses, together with Offices, not rated at more than Ten Windows [were to be] exempted from the Duty on one Clock, provided the Movements are made of Wood, and the Price or Value of which is not more than Twenty Shillings.

Clocks costing less than twenty shillings would also be exempt. [No doubt this relieved Black Forest clockmakers, who had long exported their wooden clocks to Britain.] Nor was a tax to be imposed on clock and watchmakers' and dealers' stocks, although they had to pay a levy for employees amounting to 2s 6d each in London and 1s elsewhere.[5]

Pitt was unfortunate. What had seemed a good idea for raising money coincided with the onset of an unforeseen general economic recession caused by four successive poor harvests. Bread prices rose and triggered a spate of protest riots in the south of England that were only partially ameliorated by the 'Speenhamland System' (a scheme of outdoor relief intended to mitigate rural poverty). The winter of 1797–98 that followed has been described as 'the third most severe in the entire eighteenth century'.[6] General discontent about bread prices coincided with the threat of a French invasion: it was also feared that English workers might emulate their French counterparts and rise in revolution. Pitt urgently needed money for his war chest, but when investors panicked and withdrew gold deposits, the Bank of England suspended payments in specie (gold) and adopted paper money. Financial panic combined with poor harvests converted a recession into depression. It caused severe distress in Clerkenwell and Coventry because sales of clocks and watches fell by 'more than one Half'. Pitt's new taxes were blamed. They were an obvious scapegoat.[7]

Consequences of the taxes

The taxes prompted an unusual degree of unity among Clerkenwell's three 'horological' constituencies, namely the Clockmakers' Company, independent outworkers (not necessarily members of the Company), and shopkeepers. They set aside their often-conflicting differences and, at a meeting on 6 July 1797, asked the guild to co-ordinate opposition to the tax. The consequences were petitions that claimed to represent the interests of perhaps 7,000 horological workers and about 15,000 dependants in Clerkenwell, several thousand others in Coventry and Prescot, and innumerable 'watchmakers' ('jobbers' and retailers) in other towns and cities.[8] They claimed that the recent doubling of duties on precious metal cases meant English watches cost from 50 to 100 per cent more than 'equivalent' Swiss products. British law required the use of 22-carat gold, a standard higher than that applied in France (20 carat) or Switzerland (18 carat). But, the complainants contended, if the minimum quality required in Britain might be lowered to 18 carat (better still, to 14 carat) then the prices of English watches would be competitive.[9] It seemed an attractive argument. But it addressed only one facet of the problem. Pitt promised to consult the Goldsmiths' Company about the matter. In the meantime, the new taxes for clocks and watches remained in place. Discontent and protests continued.[10]

About a third of Clerkenwell's population of about 21,000 made parts for clocks and watches. When demand for watches fell, workmen were laid off and the community's income experienced a downward, or negative, 'multiplier effect'. Aggregate weekly earnings of workers, once estimated at about £1,500, dwindled to £400. Part of the shortfall was raised by pawning tools (they raised £1,500). Even so, up to 150 watchmakers depended on parish poor relief and in December 1797 parish vestries in Clerkenwell and St Luke's set up committees to organise help. A separate soup society was formed, known as the 'General Committee for the relief of the distressed watch and clock makers' to which Lloyds Bank's donated £150, fifty tons of potatoes and several cauldrons of coals. The soup fed 1,101 'distressed workmen', 301 apprentices, 886 wives and 1,945 dependent children.[11] The vestry clerk for St. James, Clerkenwell, later explained that had it not been for the soup society even more would have fallen on parish relief.[12] The depression worsened in January and February 1798 and more outworkers were laid off. Between March and May another 12,300 portions of 'good, nutritious meat soup' were supplied, at a penny a quart.[13] Similar conditions affected England's other main watchmaking community. In Coventry, poor rates were 'collected with extreme Difficulty [and] already amount to Eleven shillings in the pound'. On 21 February 1798, petitions to the Commons were submitted from 'watchmakers' (mostly retailers and jobbers) in Bristol, Coventry, Newcastle-upon-Tyne, Liverpool, Edinburgh, Carlisle, and Derby. They stressed the importance of the horological industry to the national economy and succeeded in bringing about a parliamentary inquiry.[14]

Parliament's inquiry: the committee's hearings and report

At the inquiry, a committee of the House of Commons listened to twenty witnesses who represented a variety of special horological interests – finishers, distributors, movement makers, provincial jobbers, and retailers. They submitted graphic accounts stressing the depth of distress, illustrated by examples from their sales books. Richard Bayly, one of Clerkenwell's largest 'manufacturers' (that is, a middleman who commissioned watches to be made and arranged for their sale) employed a network of outworkers. He gave details of his annual sales of finished movements that showed a fall from 3,000 to 4,000 watches intended for silver cases to a third of their previous level. Trade in gold watches had simply disappeared. Consequently, the number of outworkers Bayly commissioned fell from over a hundred to fewer than twenty. His weekly wage bill – once in the region of £100 to £150 – had fallen to under £20. Indeed, he claimed, 'in endeavouring to employ some few of my best workmen rather than turn them away' his stock of unsold watches kept growing. Bayly denied that he and other manufacturers overstated their case to justify wage reductions. He believed there would be no improvement until Pitt's 'infamous' tax was removed.[15] Similar complaints came from other Clerkenwell masters who commissioned watches. Like Bayly, Peter Upjohn (of Smith and Upjohn), and Benjamin Webb (later of Red Lion Square, who became Clockmaker to the King,) asserted that the collapse of trade to about a third or less of earlier levels was a direct result of the increased cost of buying a watch because of Pitt's tax.[16] An imposing witness at the inquiry was John Grant of Fleet Street, watchmaker for the aristocracy: 'The Clocks and Watches I make are of the best Quality – none of the Common sort'. Grant claimed Pitt's tax had ruined his trade. His watches were expensive, he explained, because of the value added by the cost of the labour that made them (and profit accruing to him as the 'maker'). Sometimes, he confessed

> a watch [that] sold for 150 guineas is intrinsically, with respect to the materials, not worth 20s. The materials are increased in value, in many instances, by Labour, a Thousand Times. We thought, before the passing of the Act, that the higher Watches and Time Pieces which I make would not be affected by the Tax; but we find it otherwise.[17]

No one challenged Grant's assertion that a 10s tax on a single watch was enough to kill demand for watches costing up to 150 guineas. Neither Grant nor any other witness pointed out that when incomes fell so did demand for luxuries.[18] For most people, timepieces were not essential. They were a desirable but deferrable purchase. No one on the committee queried these opinions and explanations. Everyone assumed – took it for granted – that the industry's problems arose solely from Pitt's new taxes. No one considered that in a recession many customers might postpone buying a watch, or that first-time buyers might afford only cheap Swiss watches. No one pointed out that the reason for Bayly's remark that 'trade in gold watches had disappeared' was because gold itself had virtually disappeared. When Pitt had subsidised his European allies in February 1797 the Bank of England's gold reserves were drained and paper banknotes were introduced in lieu of payments in gold.

In depressions like that of 1797–98, even a small fall in demand for watches resulted in a rapid accumulation of surplus stocks: new commissions to Clerkenwell's hundreds of outworkers dried up from large manufacturing houses (such as those of Upjohn, Webb, or Grant). It illustrated the advantage enjoyed by employers in any craft industry, like watchmaking, that relied on a putting-out system of production. When demand fell, less work was given out. For entrepreneurs like Grant, the size of their workforce could be easily adjusted – contracted – to match a fall in demand. The pains were felt mostly by outworkers. By 15 March, the House of Commons' committee had heard enough. The complainers and their petitions were successful. The committee unanimously agreed that the cause of the crisis was Pitt's new tax, which ought to be repealed. Eight days later, after a brisk second reading, parliament decided that 'the Duties on Clocks, Watches and Timekeepers... do cease'.[19] After only eight months on the statute book, the tax was lifted. Pitt looked elsewhere to raise revenue and, in 1798, he inaugurated the first tax on incomes.

Pitt's miscalculation

Pitt has a great reputation as an astute financier, but of all his assessed taxes the horological ones were probably 'the most unpopular and unsuccessful'.[20] What had Pitt hoped to obtain from them? No one was sure what their potential yield might be. Estimates varied widely. One projection surmised they would raise at least £200,000 per annum from about 700,000 households if each household had one watch owner and that there were three watches in gold cases for every four in silver or base metal cases. Initially, Pitt himself was optimistic. He thought the tax would raise £600,000 from estimates that 800,000 silver or metal watches might raise revenues of £100,000 and 400,000 gold watches another £200,000. The tax on about 1.4 million clocks might yield another £300,000 or £400,000. Pitt thought that about a fifth of the population already owned watches or had clocks in their house and that a third of households owned more than one timepiece. He assumed that in Britain's population of about 10 million some 2½ million owned timepieces.

Pitt was widely out in his assumptions, especially about the ratio of gold to silver watches. Between 1791 and 1796, an annual average of about 150,000 of Clerkenwell's watches went to the Goldsmiths Hall to be assayed. Ninety-six per cent were Clerkenwell's staple production – watches cased in silver. Less than 4 per cent were in gold cases.[21] Although Pitt's assumptions about the extent of watch and clock ownership show how widespread he believed personal time-keepers had become, his guesstimates about likely revenues were too optimistic. For the eight months the tax was in force it produced a mere £50,000, less than 10 per cent of the amount he had hoped.[22] Even that yield was surprisingly high, for it was a tax easy to evade, indeed 'almost impossible to collect'.[23] Pitt had seriously miscalculated. In theory, most owners of clocks and watches, each costing several pounds, might be presumed well able to afford a few extra shillings for what today might be called a 'sales tax', equivalent to about 5 or 10 per cent of the purchase price and in most instances much less. But in practice, it depended upon voluntary quarterly returns from households and individuals. It could be enforced only by a government willing and able to search persons and houses. There was neither a national police force to carry it out nor a bureaucracy able to keep records. Collection expenses would have been greater than potential yields. Pitt rapidly became aware of its inadequacies and, after eight months on the Statute Book, the tax was repealed in March 1798. Pitt had made an unrealistic calculation and levied a cost-ineffective tax. He recognised his mistake, quickly reversed his decision, and thereby helped save his reputation as a great financier.

Explanations

The suffering in Clerkenwell and Coventry's communities is indisputable. But the link between Pitt's taxes as their direct cause is less clear. There was indeed a fall in the number of Clerkenwell's watches whose gold cases were assayed in London's Goldsmith's Hall, but it was a fall by under a half, not the 'two thirds' claimed by some witnesses. Paired gold watch cases with hallmarks had averaged 2,917 annually over the six years from 1791 to 1796. After the 1797 tax, that number fell by about 40 per cent, to 1,692. For single cased gold watches, the numbers assayed fell by just over a half, from 6,500 in 1796 to about 3,400 in 1797 and 1798.[24] The numbers of assays quickly recovered, and soon approached their previous highest recorded level. In Birmingham's assays, too, there was a dip in the number of gold and silver watch cases made for Coventry's watchmakers between 1796 and 1798. That fall was also followed by a quick recovery.[25] Evidence supporting Clerkenwell's blame on the tax for the community's distress is reflected in Dr Bryden's analysis of bankruptcies among London's horological firms. Between 1795 and 1799 they more than doubled compared with the previous quinquennial.[26]

But there are alternative explanations for the crisis. They suggest that the distress arose less because of Pitt's taxes and more from a shortage of specie caused by fluctuations in the price of gold and silver with which the cases were made. Precious metal cases amounted to a substantial portion (often the largest) of the final purchase price of a watch. Adrian Burchall has pointed to the damage done to business confidence when bullion reserves at the Bank of England fell from a high of £8m in 1795 to just £1¼m by February 1797.[27] This resulted in the suspension of specie payments and a shortage in the supply of gold for 'ordinary' purposes, such as making jewellery or watchcases.[28] It was the shortage of precious metals, Burchall concluded, that depressed demand more than Pitt's tax and offered a better explanation of the crisis in watchmaking's communities.

This explanation is supported by indirect evidence, but about clocks, not watches. Thwaites & Reed, clockmakers of Bowling Green Lane, showed no fall in their output that might have been expected if Pitt's tax was alone responsible for the crisis.[29] Clocks did not need to be assayed, and the tax seems to have had no discernible impact on the demand for them. [30] Unlike John Grant's expensive watches, no gold was wanted for clock cases. Tax or no tax, Thwaites & Reed comfortably survived short-term fluctuations in demand. Their *Day Books* show that output of domestic clocks doubled in the 'crisis years' that spanned 1793–1799.[31] Sales of their clocks may well have been enhanced by an increased demand for the public timepieces that they specialised in making. Pitt's tax, then, may have been a persuasive explanation of the distress for the watchmaking communities, but not its only cause. Watches were products sensitive to economic fluctuations beyond the control of their makers.

Pitt's short-lived but mostly uncollected taxes lingered in the collective memories of England's horological communities. Later, it became identified as the crucial episode that triggered the industry's long decline after its prosperous golden age.[32] The temporary revival of the industry's fortunes in the early 1800s was ascribed to the successful lobbying that had abolished Pitt's tax. In 1817, when the Commons' Select Committee investigated the watchmaking communities' much harsher second depression (below), it started with the widely accepted conviction that the industry's problems could be blamed on the government's ineptitude, exemplified by Pitt's tax.[33] A similar perception was reiterated in 1824 in the popular *Book of English Trades*.[34] Even in 1887, Clerkenwell still alleged that 'the first real check to [the industry's] prosperity was caused by the imposition of a duty, levied in 1797 [that had] a paralysing effect on trade'.[35] Pitt's tax had painful short term consequences. Hindsight suggests that it was a minor but short-lived episode that marked the beginning of the prolonged decline of English watchmaking. But it was not the sole cause.

****

The French and Napoleonic Wars

War with France lasted between 1793 and 1815, interrupted briefly by the Treaty of Amiens from March 1802 to May 1803. The overall effects on English watchmaking were uneven. Although the crisis of 1797–98 was painful, it was brief. We shall see later that during the war the industry's small chronometer-manufacturing sector did better than its watchmaking parent (Chapter 10). Watchmaking recovered rapidly from the painful episode prompted by Pitt's tax when, for almost a decade, it shared in a war-induced boom. The war created a demand for war *materiel* and brought work to those crafts that supplied small and large arms, uniforms, boots and shoes for the army and navy. It also stimulated demand for desirable but not necessarily essential 'discretionary purchases', such as watches. If it could be afforded, soldiers and sailors – especially officers – wanted to go to war with a watch in their pockets.

War often has the effect of accelerating a variety of demands. Assaying statistics reveal that the demand for watches during the war was, initially, substantial. It cannot be precisely measured, but its potential size can be gleaned from the enlargement of Britain's armed forces. In 1793, the army comprised about 40,000 soldiers; by its peak, it had grown to 250,000. Naval personnel increased from 36,000 sailors and 9,000 marines in 1793 to over 113,000 and 31,000 by the war's final years. Army officers needed private means to buy commissions and their own uniforms. If they did not already have a watch, many could afford one of modest quality for a relatively small portion of their total outlay. Ordinary recruits needed uniforms and shoes, and probably few had watches. Demand for watches was not confined to one side: Napoleon's land armies eventually numbered almost 600,000 men and included officers with watches to help synchronise troop movements. Such watches were almost certainly made in France or Switzerland and were unlikely to have been made in England.

War and smuggling

Revolution in Paris in 1789 was followed by the Terror and, from 1793 to 1802, the first phase of the war between France and Britain. The outbreak of war caused ordinary trade and travel across the Channel to be interrupted. Few tourists ventured to France before the brief treaty of Amiens in 1802–03. Nevertheless, some horological trade continued as before, for a list of horological exports to Hamburg in 1802 included 'one chest of watch springs from London ... three chests from Havre de Grace and Rouen' and 110 chests and ninety-five pieces of watches and pendulums between Dieppe, Havre, London, Newcastle, New York and Stockholm'.[36] The size of the chests is not known; neither is their value, nor the numbers of springs and glasses, nor how regular were shipments. Evidently, some business continued. Other notable effects were the continued trade with Britain of the great Abraham-Louis Breguet. He had fled from Paris to his native Switzerland to escape the Terror, but returned in 1795.[37] Yet through his agent, Louis Recordon, his regular trade with London continued; an account book shows that by 1807 he had dispatched at least twenty-eight consignments of watches to Recordon.[38] Despite the war, he apparently visited London 'two or three times' between 1791 and 1795 (probably from Switzerland?) and enjoyed a close friendship with his most eminent English contemporary, John Arnold. In return, Arnold sent his son, John Roger, to train with Breguet.[39] These exchanges seem exceptional.

During the eighteen-month interlude of the Treaty of Amiens, 'normal' tourism resumed. According to one report, when the peace preliminaries were announced, 16,000 English people flocked to Paris to celebrate Napoleon's coronation.[40] The Clockmakers' Company was annoyed, because of a reported increase in souvenir watches brought back from France. When, in May 1803, war restarted, tariffs on imported watches were raised from 27½ per cent (set in the Eden Treaty of 1786) to 50 per cent *ad valorem*. It was a policy intended to be both protective and revenue-raising but had the opposite effect. The smuggling of watches simply became even more lucrative, and revenue fell. Although customs officers occasionally caught smugglers and levied tariffs, Britain was not a police state and total prevention was difficult if not impossible. The Clockmakers' Company had for decades repeatedly complained about smuggled watches but during the war smuggling reached new levels as it was 'undertaken on a huge scale'.[41] This was because ordinary trade that continued from neutral countries facilitated smuggling: it was impossible to search everyone on each boat docking in Dover or London, let alone in smaller ports.[42]

Smuggling watches *out* of Switzerland and the mountainous Jura region was not difficult. Customs officials were foiled by watches sewn into waistcoats: one bizarre method included the use of dogs as carriers.[43] The evasion of tariffs proved lucrative for Swiss watchmakers who already had – or were establishing – new markets. French tariffs (10 per cent on silver watches and 6 per cent on gold) were low compared with Britain's, but France's hallmarking laws required that all gold and silver articles should be stamped by an assay officer. These costs on top of tariffs were sufficient to make smuggling profitable, firstly from Switzerland to France and, ultimately, from there to other markets. To get Swiss watches *into* Britain, goods first crossed at least one other country (usually France) and sometimes more (Belgium, Holland, and Germany) through well-established trade routes.

Despite naval blockades, smuggling watches into Britain was not difficult. The Royal Navy's cordon of major European ports was not meant to protect minor industries like watchmaking. It was primarily intended to corral France's navy, prevent Napoleon's proposed invasion of Britain, and dislocate trade that threatened major British industries, notably textiles. Attempts to prevent smuggled luxury goods from small continental ports were left to the customs and revenue service. Their resources were limited. In 1809, there were only nine revenue cutters and sixty-three boats to patrol the entire British coastline and in 1811 only 120 officers to patrol coastal lines on land. The channel was porous. Smuggling was especially profitable for luxury products with a high value in relation to weight, such as lace and silk (shawls, bonnets, and ribbons), leather products (gloves) and alcohol (French brandy, Dutch, and French gin). These commodities accounted for the greatest share of the value of smuggled goods. Profit from smuggled watches (and perfumes and playing cards) was less, but still sufficient to make it worthwhile.[44]

After 1805 the organised smuggling of watches into Britain increased, encouraged by an elaborate arrangement that lessened risks and made it more secure and lucrative. Well-organised insurance agencies in London and Antwerp were set up by enterprising 'importers' with depots in Brussels and Paris. They guaranteed safe deliveries of foreign clocks and watches in Britain ('without payment of duty and free from seizure') after adding a small surcharge of 10 per cent as insurance to guard against discovery.[45] The strategy worked. Thereafter, hardly any imported foreign watches and clocks or other merchandise – like lace, silk, leather products, French brandies, and perfumes – were 'regularly entered at the Customs House' as legal imports.[46] Evasion of duty for watches, and much else, became normal.

Smuggling temporarily became a little more difficult after 1806 when the Royal Navy stepped up its blockade of French harbours. Napoleon responded in kind, through the 'Berlin Decrees' and tried to block Britain's trade. But both blockades were permeable because ships with neutral flags were able to trade with Britain through Spain. By sailing to and from small ports, smugglers and neutral merchants created loopholes through which Swiss watches could enter Britain.[47] The Clockmakers' Company in its quarterly meetings and midsummer courts grumbled endlessly that customs officials did not perform their duties 'strictly enough'. Worse, after 1808, was the arrival of smuggled Geneva-made watches that replicated the typical appearance of Clerkenwell's products, with the names of well-known London makers forged on the dials. When the Royal Navy did briefly tighten its blockade to deter cheap watches being smuggled from the Jura, the Company's protests seemed successful. But the respite was short-lived. The navy was preoccupied with its military priority, to prevent invasion. Stopping smuggled watches was relatively unimportant, and difficult to thwart. Customs officials were under-resourced and mostly powerless.

The Clockmakers' Company's repeated complaints came to a head in December 1808 when Isaac Rogers drafted An Act *for the better prevention of Frauds and Abuses in the Importation, Manufacture and Exportation of Sundry Wares and Manufactures*.[48] It suggested that in future all trade in watches and clocks should be exclusively channelled through the port of London. If so, might not imported watches and clocks be then monitored, marked, and charged excise duty? The suggestion came to nothing, partly because it was deemed impractical, and partly because the Company declined to pass Rodgers' proposal on to Parliament.

Why? Although to Clerkenwell and Coventry's watch manufacturers smuggling was a serious nuisance, shop keepers were quite happy to sell cheap smuggled foreign watches. Dealers, retailers, and their networks of travelling salesmen all profited.[49] It was an early instance of the times when makers of watches learned that shop keepers did not really care from whence watches came, or who had made them.

Silver linings: 1800–1810

Despite their irritation about smuggled watches, Clerkenwell watchmakers remained busy, as numbers of watches assayed in London's Goldsmiths' Hall indicated. Between 1805 and 1808, as can be seen in Table 7.1, they showed that output had nearly recovered to the 1790s levels of production. Several caveats apply to statistics of assayed watchcases. Some gold and silver cases may have been fitted with unknown numbers of smuggled foreign movements, and some movements might have been placed into base metal or enamelled cases and not needed to be assayed. Nevertheless, if it is assumed that most cased movements were made in Clerkenwell, then by 1808 Clerkenwell had nearly matched its highest level of production. Coventry's watchmakers were also busy. Output of movements, normally with cases assayed in Birmingham, increased from approximately 9,000 in 1802 to over 28,000 by 1810.[50] Thus, despite annoyance about smuggling, England's watchmaking industry in its two largest hubs seems to have recovered from the depression associated with Pitt's tax. First-time buyers from among enlisted soldiers and sailors were surely among customers who bought either English-made watches (perhaps second-hand) or their smuggled equivalents – including those forged to be in the 'English style'.

Table 7.1 Gold and Silver watches marked at the Goldsmith's Hall, London, 1796 and 1800–1808

Year	*Gold*	*Silver*	*Total*
1796	6,576	185,102	191,678
1800	9,396	154,144	163,540
1801	10,006	136,569	146,575
1802	10,618	161,334	171,952
1803	8,806	163,239	172,045
1804	1,912	149,570	157,482
1805	9,952	163,047	172,999
1806	11,845	164,503	176,348
1807	15,264	150,972	166,236
1808	15,049	165,340	180,389

Source: BPP, 1818, vol. 9; Appendix 2, p.12. The 1796 total was the highest.

From recession to depression

These optimistic – even benign – circumstances for English watchmakers ceased after 1810. There were two reasons. First, smuggling continued: Swiss watches became even cheaper following Japy's improved production methods at Beaucourt (Chapter 6), and well-organised, professional smugglers now began to target English watchmaking's traditional export markets. In 1810, some 140 Geneva-made watches with fictitious English names were seized; they had been intended for Charleston, South Carolina.[51] Smuggling was not confined to horological items. One ingenious entrepreneur made his town and country residences part of a network for smuggled watches, chains, and snuff boxes ('some of which were grossly obscene'). The extent and profitability of selling forged 'English' watches were exemplified by the scam perpetrated on the Foreign Secretary George Canning (later briefly Prime Minister). He was sold a Swiss watch with a forged English name for 80 guineas 'that was not intrinsically worth £30'.[52]

The second reason was that a poor harvest in 1810 initiated a depression that evolved into one of unprecedented severity and length. A meagre harvest in 1810 was followed by three consecutive failures. Shortages could not be relieved by imports from Europe, because crops there also failed.[53] Once again, just as in 1787–98, demand for English-made watches fell off. Dr Bryden's research shows that about a hundred watchmaking firms in Clerkenwell became bankrupt or otherwise went out of business.[54] The Clockmakers' Company was unable to help because its influence had waned. A *Census* of the industry, conducted in 1813 by its clerk, Henry Clarke, revealed that many small watchmakers were simply indifferent to the Company. Its apprenticeship laws were circumvented or ignored. Clarke found that although 1,068 persons described themselves as 'clock or watch makers' only about a half (563) were free of either the Clockmakers' or other guilds. Of those whose main activity was something other than watchmaking, over fifty had other principal occupations – such as 'fisherman', 'potato merchant', 'musician' and 'attorney'.[55] The guild found it impossible to control a fluid labour force in times of economic uncertainty. By January 1814, the crisis had become so severe that the Clockmakers' tried to gain the support of anyone – everyone – involved in making and selling watches, whether free or not of the Company. Resolutions were passed that urged more tariff protection.[56] They were to no avail. Soup kitchens, like those in 1798, reappeared in Clerkenwell. In despair, the Clockmakers' Company asked all watchmakers, including those not free of their Company, to support the *Statement of Inconveniences* 'to remedy the bad state of the trade' that they submitted to parliament on 23 May 1814.[57] The *Statement* prompted a debate in the Commons on 6 June 1814. Spokesmen for the Company stressed the national importance of an industry that, it claimed, made annually about 100,000 watches from raw materials worth 'at least £500,000'. Their industry was threatened, they argued, because governments had failed to enforce tariff laws explicitly intended to protect it from foreign competition.[58] But the debate also uncovered the growing appeal of free trade sentiments, inimical to mercantilism. Sir William Curtis, Tory member since 1790 for the City of London, rather awkwardly exemplified this when he mentioned the views of Clerkenwell's makers who suffered from smuggling, and those of the retailers who had profited from it. He thought parliament ought to do something about the problem – but was not quite sure what.[59] When some suggested that the tariff on imported watches should be raised to the unprecedented level of 75 per cent, the Clockmakers' Company seemed to triumph. [60]

The watchmaking industry's predicament in the years between 1808 and 1817 can be seen in the fall of about two-thirds in the numbers of watch cases annually assayed in London's Goldsmith's Hall. Seemingly modest recoveries in 1814 and 1815 were followed by another fall in 1816 and a calamitous drop in 1817. Assayed watchcases had plunged to a third of their former peak.

There was a similar decline in Birmingham's assays of cases for Coventry's movements (Table 7.2). Their busiest year had been 1815 when more than 29,000 gold and silver cases were assayed; then assays plummeted to 18,000 in 1816 and 12,000 in 1817.[61] Watchmaking communities were not alone in their misery. Thousands of workers in other industries sought parish relief especially in places (like watchmaking communities) that depended on old handicraft industries that had initially benefitted by supplying war *materiel.* The House of Commons was inundated with petitions for relief not only from watchmakers, but

Table 7.2 Gold and Silver Watchcases, Marked at the Goldsmith's Hall, London, 1808–1817

Year	*Gold*	*Silver*	*Total*
1808	15,049	165,340	180,389
1809	17,566	143,274	160,840
1810	17,257	152,587	169,844
1811	12,579	130,246	142,825
1812	12,921	124,088	137,009
1813	13,073	113,177	126,250
1814	13,974	133,766	147,740
1815	12,544	121,725	134,269
1816	10,766	91,346	102,112
1817	9,638	52,149	61,787

Source: *B.P.P., 1818, vol. 9;* Report from the Select Committee to Consider of the Laws relating to Watchmakers *Appendix 2, p. 12.*

from tanners, shoemakers, silk spinners, frame-knitters from Leicester, Nottingham and Manchester, and handloom weavers from Bolton and Scotland.[62]

Watchmaking in peacetime

Waterloo marked the end of the war with France, but it brought no instant domestic improvement. On the contrary, the depression deepened. The years from 1815 to 1820 were, in Sir John Clapham's judgement, 'economically and politically, probably the most wretched, difficult and dangerous in modern English history'.[63] Unemployment swelled when 300,000 soldiers and sailors were demobilised from the army and navy. Civil unrest followed. It was exemplified 'on a frightening scale [by the Peterloo massacre; and to] the feeling of insecurity amongst those in employment was added ... the blank frustration of the many ... in all industries [that] were without jobs'.[64] Before Waterloo, the prevention of smuggling was not a high priority for the Royal Navy, even when it controlled the seas. After 1815, it became still less of a concern for a smaller navy. So, smuggling of watches continued, especially that of forged 'English' watches, about which the Company had long complained.[65] Exports of English-made watches and clocks virtually ceased, except for modest numbers to India. Stocks of unsold watches cumulated in Clerkenwell. Outworkers who were lucky to find work had to accept lower rates. Relief funds helped some to maintain a bare subsistence, but reserves trickled away.

In desperation, the Company convened yet another special committee. Its chairman was Paul Philip Barraud, and its deliberations were given extra weight by Benjamin Lewis Vulliamy, John Thwaites, and John Roger Arnold, titans of London's four leading horological houses.[66] In December 1815, they drafted a bill 'for the prevention of the illicit introduction of Foreign Clocks and Watches into the Realm'. It was sent to the Treasury, but nothing happened. [67] More pamphlets were circulated in 1816. They included appeals from parish authorities, from small clockmaking workshops, and from jobbing watchmakers in provincial towns.[68] Coventry sent three petitions, one each from its different watchmaking groups. In the first, merchants and retailers blamed the industry's crisis on the recent doubling of duties on plate licences. In the second, masters of small, struggling firms, and unemployed journeymen blamed the abuse of the apprenticeship system. The third, from Coventry's largest firms, refuted this.[69] Each protected their own vested interests and blamed others, but all blamed smuggling. In a letter of 21 April 1817, the Company warned the Home Secretary, Lord Sidmouth, that unless something was done the entire industry would go the same way as it had in France. As the Company reminded the Home Secretary, Swiss watches had so penetrated [France's] domestic market that 'at present 99 out of 100 of the watches sold in Paris as French watches are not made in France'.[70] Finally, Parliament acted. A Select Committee was convened to meet in July 1817 to examine the state of watchmaking.[71] The *Minutes* of its proceedings and *Report*, as we shall see in Chapter 8, reveal much about England's traditional watchmaking industry just after the start of its long decline.

Notes

1 Act of Parliament, 1797: Duties on Clocks and Watches Act. (38 Geo. III, c. 108).

2 W.R. Ward, 'The Administration of the Window and Assessed Taxes, 1696–1798', *English Historical Review*, 67 (Oct 1952), 522–42, at https://www.jstor.org/stable/556134; *Commons Journals*, 53 (1797–98), 326–36; Pitt's taxes included those 'assessed' on male and female servants, horses, carriages and houses.

3 LMA/CLC/L/CD/E/008/MS03940/87: 'Abstract of the numbers of gold and silver watch-cases marked in the Guild Hall, 1791–97'; for single cases, see *BPP, 1818*, Vol. 9, 'Report from the Select Committee Appointed to Consider the Laws Relating to Watchmakers, 1796–1802', 12. This records Clerkenwell's peak in 1796 at just over 191,000.

4 LMA/CLC/L/CD/B/005/MS03975/5: Clockmakers' Company Court Minute Books, vol. 5, 11 Dec. 1796. The tax form is reprinted in *Antiquarian Horology*, 23/2 (Winter 1996), 170–71.

5 LMA/CLC/L/CD/E/028/MS03945/9: 'Bill for Granting to George III Certain Duties on Clocks and Watches: 5 July 1797. The penalty for failing to make a return was £10.

6 Roger A.E. Wells, *Wretched Faces: Famine in wartime England, 1793–1801* (Gloucester: Sutton, 1988), 36 and 184ff.

7 For these and the following quotations, see Chris Ellmers, 'The Impact of the 1797 Tax on Clocks and Watches on the London trade', in Joanna Bird, Joanna, Hugh Chapman, and John Clark (eds.), *Collecteana Londoniensia: Studies in London Archaeology and History Presented to Ralph Merrifield* (London: London and Middlesex Archaeological Society,1978), 388–400, esp. 392–93, citing Clerkenwell's Vestry Minute Books at Finsbury Library; also *Commons Journal*, 53 (1797–98),158–59.

8 Donald Whyte, 'Petition of Edinburgh Watchmakers to Parliament, 1797–98', *Antiquarian Horology*, 18/4 (Winter 1989), 417–22; also LMA/CLC/L/CD/E/028/MS03945/11-32: Correspondence presenting memorials; and UofL MS 755, folios 88–89, 91, 93–101 draft memorials to Pitt, reports of meetings and committees; LMA/CLC/L/CD/E/028/MS03945/25: Letter 5 July 1797; LMA/CLC/L/CD/B/001/MS02710//5, WCC Court Minute Books (1778–1804) for 6 July 1797.

9 LMA/CLC/L/CD/B/005/MS03975: Petition, 8 July 1797.

10 Ellmers, '1797 Tax', 391–92.

11 Paul Sutton, 'Soup and Supervision: the Metropolitan Watch and Clock Making Trade 1797–1817', *Journal of Historical Sociology*, 9/3 (Sept. 1996), 315–34. Sutton employs Michel Foucault's 'post-structuralism' approach to expound the theory that, prompted by the war with France, explains the philanthropy of Clerkenwell's soup kitchens in 1797 (and again in 1817: see Chapter 8). Sutton thinks they were 'channels of power through which artisanal culture was transformed'. He argues that 'soup kitchens dispossessed

Clerkenwell's outworkers of their property and undermined their independence and respectability' and concluded 'never before were so many of these tradesmen reduced to the dishonourable position of applying for charity'.

12 *Commons Journal,* 53 (1797–98), 333, 335.

13 *The Case of the distressed Watch and Clockmakers* (1798: Pamphlet; copies in the Guildhall Library and in UofL MS 755: folios 106–07; W. Pinks, *The History of Clerkenwell* (London: Charles Herbert, 2nd. ed., 1881), 117; and Ellmers, '1797 Tax', 394.

14 *Commons Journal*, 53 (1797–98), 167–68, 174, 178–79, 232–33, 239, 247, 250–51 and 316.

15 UofL MS 755, folio 129.

16 UofL MS 755: folios 147, 149; *Commons Journal*, 53 (1797–98), 329–31.

17 *Commons Journal*, 53 (1797–98), 334.

18 LMA/CLC/L/CD/B/001/MS02710/005: Court Meetings on 16, 21, and 27 Nov., 1797; Arthur Gayer, W.W. Rostow and Anna J. Schwartz, *Growth and Fluctuations in the British Economy, 1790–1850: An Historical, Statistical, and Theoretical Study of Britain's Economic Development* (2 vols. 1953, Oxford, Clarendon, repr.1975), 1/31.

19 *Commons Journal*, 53 (1797–98), 373, 401, 405.

20 E.P. Thompson, 'Time, Work-discipline, and Industrial Capitalism', *Past and Present*, No. 38 (Dec. 1967), 56–97; quotation, 66, at http://www.jstor.org/page/info/about/policies/terms.jsp

21 Calculated from *BPP*, 1818, IX, 'Report from the Select Committee Appointed to Consider the Laws Relating to Watchmakers', 12: Abstract of the numbers of gold and silver watchcases marked in the Guild Hall.

22 *BPP* 1799–1800, vol. 109, Accounts and Papers, LI, 1009 (2) and 1,013 (2). A total of about £50,000 was received, mostly in arrears, namely £300 in year ending Jan. 1798; £35,420 in year ending Jan. 1799; and £14,966 in year ending Jan. 1800.

23 Thompson, 'Time, Work-discipline', 68.

24 LMA/CLC/L/CD/E/008/MS03940/00/87: for paired gold watchcases, see 'Abstract of the numbers of gold and silver watch-cases marked in the Guild Hall'. For single gold cases, 1796–1802, see *BPP 1818*, IX, 'Report from the Select Committee Appointed to Consider the Laws Relating to Watchmakers', 12.

25 *BPP 1818*, vol. 9, Appendix 2, p. 13: Birmingham assays 1796–1817.

26 D.J. Bryden, 'The London Gazette as a Source for the History of the English Horological Trade, 1720–1849', *Antiquarian Horology*, 37/4 (Dec. 2016), 477–95 (graph, 479).

27 Adrian Burchall, 'Pitt's Clock and Watch Tax: A Reassessment', *Antiquarian Horology*, 13/5 (Sept. 1982), 454–61.

28 John Ehrman, *The Younger Pitt*: vol. 3, *The Consuming Struggle* (London: Constable, 1996), 7–12.

29 Burchall, 'Pitt's Tax', 457.

30 LMA/CLC/B/215/MS06788/002: Thwaites and Reed archives, Daybooks, vol. 2, 1788–1798 and LMA/CLC/B/215/MS06788/003: vol. 3, 1799–1804, for sales of clocks during Pitt's tax.

31 Burchall, 'Pitt's Tax', 458, table 3; his estimates differ from those in G.T.E. Buggins and Anthony J. Turner, 'The Context of Production, Identification, and Dating of Clocks by A. and J. Thwaites', *Antiquarian Horology,* 8 (1973), 372–81.

32 T. Cromwell, *History and Description of the Parish of Clerkenwell* (1828; London: British Library Historical Print Editions, 2011), 258–59; H.A. Lloyd, *The Collector's Dictionary of Clocks* (London: Country Life, 1964),

14–15; Muriel Goaman, *English Clocks* (London: Michael Joseph, 1967), 108–09.

33 *BPP*, 1818, vol. IX, Report of the Select Committee appointed to consider the laws relating to watchmakers, 135.

34 *The Book of English Trades and Library of the Useful Arts* (London: Society for Promoting Christian Knowledge, 1824) sub 'The Watchmaker', 423.

35 Richard Wood, 'The Hall-Marking agitation, with a Glance at former Periods of Depression in the Watch Trades', *Horological Journal*, 29/7 (March 1887), 98.

36 J. Jepson Oddy, *European Commerce: Shewing New and Several Channels of Trade with the Continent of Europe* (London: Richardson, 1805), 438.

37 Peter Toot, 'Should Breguet's Box Chronometer No 2741 Be Run? The Potential Decision-making Protocols in Horological Conservation', *Antiquarian Horology*, 41/3 (Sept. 2020), 373–82 (374, on Breguet and French chronometer making).

38 Oliver Fairclough, 'Louis Recordon, King George III and Richard Simmon', *Antiquarian Horology*, 9/5 (Dec. 1975), 551–55.

39 David Thompson, 'John Arnold and Abraham Louis Breguet', *Watches* (London: British Museum, 2008), 84–85.

40 Tsai-Yeh Wang, 'British Women's Travel Writings in the Era of the French Revolution' (Unpublished PhD thesis, Birmingham University, 2010), 257, at https://etheses.bham.ac.uk/id/eprint/1029/1/Wang10PhD.pdf.

41 David Syrett, 'The Role of the Royal Navy in the Napoleonic Wars after Trafalgar, 1805–14', *Naval War College Review*, 32/5 (Sept.-Oct. 1979), 75–76, at https://www.jstor.org/stable/44641939

42 LMA/CLC/L/CD/E/028/14537/27-33: (1 April 1808 to 11 Feb. 1809).

43 Alun C. Davies, 'Swiss Watches, Tariffs and Smuggling with Dogs', *Antiquarian Horology*, 37/3 (Sept. 2016), 377–83. For an account of smuggling from Switzerland (including watches and watch parts) during wartime, over a century later, see Neville Wylie, 'British Smuggling Operations from Switzerland, 1940–1944', *The Historical Journal*, 48/4 (Dec. 2005), 1077–102 at www.jstor.org/stable/4091649

44 Gavin Daly, 'English Smugglers, the Channel, and the Napoleonic Wars, 1800–1814', *Journal of British Studies*, 46/1 (Jan.2007), 30–46, at https://www.jstor.org/stable/10.1086/508397; id., 'Napoleon and the "City of Smugglers", 1810–1814', *The Historical Journal*, 50/2 (2007), 333–52, at https://doi.org/10.1017/S0018246X07006097; also Jeffrey A. Frankel, 'The 1807–1809 Embargo against Great Britain', *Journal of Economic History*, 42/2 (June 1982), 291–308, at https://doi.org/10.1017/S0022050700027443

45 For the continued complaints of the Company see LMA/CLC/L/CD/E/028/14537/27-33: (1 April 1808 to 11 Feb. 1809). For smuggling in general, see Judith Blow Williams, *British Commercial Policy and Trade Expansion, 1750–1850* (Oxford: Clarendon, 1972), 345 ff.

46 Daly, 'English Smugglers', 30–46.

47 Daly, 'Napoleon and the "City of Smugglers"', 333–52.

48 LMA/CLC/L/CD/E/008/MS03940/82 and 83 are drafts; also *1817 Minutes*, 42–46.

49 LMA/CLC/L/CD/B/005/MS03975/6: Clockmakers' Company Court Minute Books (1804–1815).

50 BPP. 1818, vol. 9, Report from the Select Committee to Consider of the Laws relating to Watchmakers *Appendix 2, p.1.*

51 LMA/CLC/L/CD/B/005/MS03975/6: Clockmakers' Company, Court Minute Books, 16 August and 3 September 1810.

52 LMA/CLC/L/CD/E/002/MS03951/55: Printed copy of the resolution passed at a meeting of the master manufacturers and tradesmen of London and Westminster; LMA/CLC/L/CD/E/002/MS03951/68: Resolutions of a meeting of practical artisans interested in the British Manufactory of clocks and watches, held 2 June 1814; also LMA/CLC/L/CD/E/002/MS03951/69: Copy of a circular letter transmitting the 'Petition of the Master, Warden, and Court of Artisans of the Clockmakers' Company', 6 June 1814.
53 Frank O. Darvall, *Popular Disturbances and Public Order in Regency England* (Oxford: Oxford UP, 1970), 21.
54 Bryden, 'The *London Gazette* as a Source', *Antiquarian Horology*, 37/4 (Dec. 2016), Appendix 4.
55 LMA/CLC/L/CD/A/013/MS03942/34 and 35: 'Report and Order of the Court of Aldermen for increasing the livery of the Company' to 200 (1810) and to 250 (1826); and LMA/CLC/L/CD/E/032/MS03977 and LMA/CLC/L/CD/E/033/MS03962: Henry Clarke's Census of 1813.
56 LMA/CLC/L/CD/E/028/14537/55: Resolution ... to consider the best means to preserve and promote the propriety of their Trade, 14 Jan. 1814; LMA/CLC/L/CD/G/003/MS03941/54: Petition to Parliament in favour of retaining the system of Apprenticeships.
57 *BPP*, 1813–14, Vol. 69: 'Statement of Inconveniences'; also LMA/CLC/L/CD/E/028/14537/43–45, 49, 53a, 56, 58, 59, 60, 61, 62, 63, 65, 66 for protest meetings. For the *Statement of Inconveniences* formed part of Paul Phillip Barraud's testimony to the Commons Committee in 1817, in *BPP, 1817*, vol. 6, 59–60, with subsequent correspondence; LMA/CLC/L/CD/E/001/MS02727/2: 'Minutes of the Proceedings of the Committee for Correspondence and Laws for the more effectual suppression of malpractices in the trade, 1808–1815', 14 Dec. 1813 to 29 Dec. 1815.
58 LMA/CLC/L/CD/E/028/14537/68: 'Resolutions of a meeting of practical artisans interested in the British Manufactory of clocks and watches, held 2 June 1814'; *Commons Journal*, 69 (1813–14), 329–30; also UofL MS 755, folios 159–174 for other background material.
59 *Hansard*, 1st ser., vol. 27, 1073–74, 6 June 1814. For Curtis, see Norman Gash, 'Sir William Curtis, first baronet (1752–1829)', *ODNB*.
60 *Hansard*, 1st ser., vol. 27, 1078, June 1814.
61 *BPP*, 1818, vol. 9, Appendix II, p. 13.
62 Clive Emsley, *British Society and the French Wars, 1793–1815* (Totowa NJ: Rowman and Littlefield, 1979), 154.
63 Sir John H. Clapham, 'Europe after the Great Wars, 1816 and 1920', *Economic Journal*, 30 (Dec. 1920), 423–35 (quotation 427), at www.jstor.org/stable/2222868.
64 Sydney Checkland, *The Rise of Industrial Society in England* (London: Longmans, 1966), 10–11.
65 See LMA/CLC/L/CD/E/029/MS02728: Minute Book of the 'Committee appointed relative to the illicit introduction of foreign clocks and watches', 10 October 1814.
66 LMA/CLC/L/CD/E/029/MS02728: Minute Book of Committee appointed to examine the illicit introduction of foreign clocks and watches; 10 October 1814 to 25 June 1819.
67 Barraud's testimony, *1817 Minutes*, 59; the putative Bill is on 60–61.
68 LMA/CLC/L/CD/E/006/MS03943/54–55: Dec. 1816 and Jan. 1817; 'Addresses on behalf of ... the poor clock and watchmakers of the parish of St Luke's, Middlesex'; LMA/CLC/L/CD/E/028/14537/74a: 'A Report on the Destitution of the Working Classes and a List of Donations Received'. The

Clockmakers' advertisements of 19 Jan. 1817 appeared in *The Times* and *The Morning Advertiser*, LMA/CLC/L/CD/E/002/MS03951/73.

69 *Commons Journals*, 72 (1817), 31 (5 Feb. 1817), 364–67 (17 June 1817), and 435 (1 July 1817); and *The Times*, 2 July 1817. Protest meetings were held in February and March 1819; see LMA/CLC/L/CD/E/028/MS03944/15, 16, and 17.

70 LMA/CLC/L/CD/E/028/14537/81: Letter to Viscount Sidmouth, Secretary of state, on the distress of the trade; also LMA/CLC/L/CD/E/028/14537/74: Circular of the Clockmakers' Company complaining about the 'immense illicit Importation of Foreign clocks and watches'.

71 *Commons Journals*, 72 (1817), 452–53, 4 July 1817; also LMA/CLC/L/CD/E/001/MS02727/001-002: Minutes of the Proceedings of the Committee for … the more effectual suppression of malpractices in the trade, 1808–1815' (2 vols: vol. 1, 1808–13. Vol. 2, 1813 to 1815).

8 The 1817 Inquiry

Tariffs and Smuggling: 1818–42

The committee of inquiry

The stream of petitions to Parliament from watchmaking's different hubs resulted in a House of Commons committee to investigate the state of the industry. It met in July 1817 and its *Minutes* and *Report* constitute the fullest published accounts of the state of English watchmaking as it began its long decline. Two Coventry MPs took turns as chairmen: Peter Moore (1753–1828), described as 'the last wearer of a pigtail in London society', officiated on Monday, Tuesday, and Thursday; Joseph Butterworth (1779–1826, a well-known philanthropist) took the chair on Wednesday and Friday.[1] Thirty-five witnesses described what they believed caused the industry's distress and offered possible remedies. Copies of correspondence between government departments and the Clockmakers' Company, including valuable historical and statistical information, were submitted.[2] The *Minutes* and *Report* have the formal titles *On the Petitions of Watchmakers of Coventry* although only five of the witnesses came from that city. Most were from Clerkenwell. They included three independent craftsmen (a watch wheel finisher, a wheel cutter, and a hand maker). Others voiced the interests of large manufacturers, distributors, and sellers (including some in 'the country trade'). Several were horological veterans. Of the twenty-four asked 'how long they had been in the business?' only three reported fewer than ten years and a half claimed over twenty. Four had over fifty years' experience and were well able to remember Clerkenwell's golden era. Their titles indicated their social status: twenty 'in the watch trade' or 'manufacturers' of substantial enterprises were designated 'Mr'.[3] They included three representatives of 'relieving' institutions in the parishes of Clerkenwell and St Luke. Clerkenwell's main charitable organisation was 'The General Philanthropic Society for the Relief of the Temporary Distress of the Labouring Poor who do not receive Parochial Relief'.[4] There was a similar society in neighbouring St Luke's. William Grimshaw, secretary of the 'Committee for Distressed Watchmakers' admitted his own horological interests as founder of Grimshaw and Baxter (a company selling watch materials and tools that occasionally commissioned watches).

DOI: 10.4324/9781003227823-10

He claimed he was there mainly because of his philanthropic activities, to which his business was only indirectly connected.[5] The Clockmakers' Company was represented by its eponymously named clerk, Henry Clarke, conductor of its 1813 *Census*, expert in the Company's history, laws and customs, and by Paul Philip Barraud, Master of the Company in 1810 and 1811 and much involved in its past committees of inquiry and complaint.[6]

Witnesses stressed the effects of the long depression on watchmakers. John Bartholomew, administrator of Clerkenwell's relief society, described the community's suffering as 'beyond imagination', for which normal parish poor relief funds were inadequate. His society had dealt with more than 700 cases from over 1,200 applications. The downward spiral had accelerated when workmen pawned tools for pittances to pawnbrokers who were already overstocked with unsold and irredeemable pledges.[7] Another witness claimed that conditions in Clerkenwell in 1817 were worse than they had been in 1797–98.[8] Coventry's watchmaking community fared no better. It had two watchmakers' friendly societies; one with ninety members who subscribed a shilling a week to a fund that paid out 14s a week when members were sick, ten guineas when one died, and five guineas if a member's wife died. Initially, it had £100 'in the box as a bond of compact' to be shared at Christmas'. But that £100 reserve had already gone, and the Society was on the verge of extinction. The other society's benefits had been reduced by a half.[9]

All witnesses stressed the depths of the depression into which the industry had sunk and offered personal supporting evidence. F.B. Adams, of St. John's Square, had contracted between 1812 and 1814 annual commissions for 2,500 watches; this fell to 821 watches in 1816 and in the first six months of 1817 to just 403. Another 'manufacturer' (perhaps better labelled as a 'middleman in the wholesale and export trade'?) claimed that 'in good times' he sold about 2,000 watches a year but in 1816 his sales fell to 1,200.[10] Watchmaking's subsidiary trades also experienced a downward multiplier effect. William Grimshaw – wearing his hat as a horological tool manufacturer – reported that compared with 'prosperous' times his weekly sales had fallen by a third, to only £60 or £70.[11]

These affirmations were all from witnesses with substantial previous businesses that had now diminished, but nonetheless somehow survived. No independent outworker, without any work at all, was questioned. But their plight can be inferred from those lucky enough still to have a little work. In Clerkenwell's halcyon days, outworkers had been well-paid: weekly earnings of a highly skilled craftsman ranged from 30s to 4 guineas. By 1817, incomes of those still able to work had fallen by about two-thirds. A watch fusee maker who once earned 30s 'could now earn only 9s per week'. 'Finishing' was now paid at 'piece rates' (a fixed rate of pay for each unit produced, regardless of the time it took). Good workmen could 'finish' in a week 'on average...two or three (watches) ... some exceptional workmen could do four'. Those who once had comfortably earned between 20s and 36s a week now, in the depressed circumstances of 1817, had to work 'extremely hard' to obtain 12s.[12] Those who once earned between 10s 6d and 12s 'for the regular manufacturer', now worked 'for the Jews' at 3s 6d a piece.

As that gibe hinted, the muddied waters of anti-Semitism were stirred. London's Jewish community had long sold timepieces and jewellery and some members were prominent pawnbrokers. Witnesses repeatedly were asked leading questions: 'was the trade ... very much injured by the Jews and other persons of low description?' Or were watches that had passed through the hands of Jewish traders 'things that were never intended to perform, (many of them never went an hour)'? Were Jews responsible for scams and mock auctions in which 'inferior watches' were unloaded onto a gullible public?[13] Anti-Semitic coat-trailing failed. Mathew Wood, Lord Mayor of London, had issued a proclamation, warning people to guard against swindlers and impostors who worked 'a scam' in which someone would *personate* a Jew as part of the fraud.[14] Even persistently hostile anti-Semitic questions induced responses that manufacturers who offered low wages were not exclusively Jewish. 'The reduction in the price (of labour)', reported Grimshaw, 'is not wholly confined to Jews, but some under the denomination of Christians are falling into the practice'. The industry's crisis could not be attributed to Jews.[15] Witnesses struggled to explain why the depression had happened. Among the culprits they identified were Coventry's apprenticeship system, hall-marking charges, and the plate laws. Above all, the extent of smuggling was blamed.

Explanations: apprenticeships

Coventry's apprenticeship system was criticised because it ignored the Elizabethan apprenticeship laws endorsed by the Clockmakers' Company. Those laws originally were intended to limit recruitment, safeguard scarce skills, protect expert knowledge, and thus control prices. Ideally, entrants to the magic circle would be drawn from the offspring of existing practitioners or from a select few for whom substantial premiums might be demanded for the privilege of instruction. The system was intended to produce self-sufficient, rounded craftsmen. But outside London those apprenticeship laws did not apply, the use of children to make fusee chains in Christchurch (Chapter 10) exemplified how intention and practice had already diverged in watchmaking (as it had in other craft industries).[16] Apprentices learned only a small part of the craft and, at the end of their term, were discharged 'untaught and unskilled' and swelled the ranks of semi- or un-skilled workers. They had become specialists only in isolated stages of the production process.

By 1817, the Clockmakers' Company's influence was weak, even in Clerkenwell. In Coventry it was non-existent, and the intent of the apprenticeship laws was ignored. Some firms took up to thirty or forty apprentices as cheap labour in their 'factories'.[17] They enabled Coventry annually to make about 20,000 watches 'in good times', and even 14,000 'in bad times'.[18] The consequences 'in bad times' were that apprentices and outworkers could easily be laid off and, if and when circumstances improved, then rehired or replaced by newcomers.[19] Indeed, of the 150 watchmakers of Coventry whose petition had prompted the committee's hearing, eighty-two were reputed to have already left the over-manned industry. Their narrow competencies had made them unemployable, except as unskilled hawkers, labourers, or road repairers.

Licence fees and hallmarking

Other grievances were subsequently added to complaints about apprentices.[20] Clerkenwell's watchmakers protested about plate licence fees and hallmarking practices because, at Chester's assay office (where Liverpool and some Coventry watches were sent), only the bottom of gold cases was scraped, assayed, and marked. Unscrupulous case makers used 'inferior' gold (lower carat) for sides and pendants, thus undercutting Clerkenwell's prices.[21] Further irritation was caused when in 1817 the annual licence fee was doubled to £4 12s. License fees had to be paid by five different categories. For gold and silver watchcases, the first category started with refiners. They sold silver or gold ingots on to the second group, the case makers, and the third, the pendant makers. Movement makers were fourth. The fifth category, retailers, included shopkeepers, traders, and pedlars. The first four typically sold precious metals used in scores or hundreds (some, perhaps, thousands) of watchcases a year. For some, a single plate licence was a minor irritant amounting to a tiny portion of the price of a watch that might cost several pounds. Such fees were not problems for others, such as large retailers in London or in expanding businesses, like James Ritchie's in Edinburgh. Ritchie, and those like him in other cities, could bear the annual cost of a single plate licence because. as well as repairing and selling watches, they sold silver in jewellery and silver plate, thimbles, snuff boxes, milk jugs and spoons.[22] But small rural retailers suffered from the doubled licence fee. In the 'country trade', a clock or watch repairer in towns and villages might also buy a handful of watches a year from a travelling salesman to sell on. A licence fee of £4 12s could devour much of his annual profit in that line. Country dealers, it was submitted, were reluctant to take out a licence: in depressed times it was simpler to stop selling watches. Selling a gold or silver watch without a licence was risky: if caught they were liable to conviction by magistrates. It gave a shrinking market another downward twist. One witness reported a substantial decline to his 'country trade': annual sales of watches fell from 800 or 1,100 to about 200; another claimed sales were down from four or five thousand to ten or twelve hundred.[23] A third affirmed that he had once sub-contracted thirty to forty outworkers to make the six or seven dozen watches he used to sell in South Wales's iron districts but, he complained, 'in one day, on my last journey I did not sell one'.[24] From his perspective, the plate licence seemed a more obvious culprit than the current depression in South Wales iron industry.

Smuggling

Above all, the main reason cited to explain the industry's depression was the extent of smuggling. Large manufacturers, notably those who had been substantial exporters, protested that markets were swamped by cheap watches made in the Jura, especially by those with forged English names intended for re-export. Boxes of movements were cased in Switzerland with punch marks forged to appear English.[25] Two categories of smuggling were blamed. First were 'individual purchases made by gentlemen when abroad, which are very considerable'. George Clerke, a 'watch manufacturer', complained that 'many of my private customers who have visited the continent have brought home one or two watches'. As a result, Clerke claimed, by 1817 his outworkers' wages had halved.[26] Even worse, he thought, were the second group, namely traders who systematically smuggled watches in 'great numbers, and in every stage of manufacture'. In one shop window, he had seen 'nearly ninety foreign watches at one time'. He believed that 'vast numbers of watches [are] smuggled into the country and sold by the dress makers at the west end of the town'. Some were 'locket watches ... worn around ladies' necks [that] yielded great profit because they were sold for seven, eight or even ten guineas: nevertheless, they were 'little better than toys; they are elegant in their appearance, but as to their performance they are worth nothing'.[27]

Few foreign watches and clocks passed legally through customs. Smuggling was a full-time career for one importer, Frederick Louis Faton (later of Bond Street, self-described as another *élève de Breguet*). When he arrived from Neuchatel via Paris with goods worth £700–£800 (including six watches each worth between 50 and 100 guineas) they were seized by customs.[28] Faton's watches were expensive, aimed at the top of the market for wealthy customers who might otherwise patronise leading London makers (like John Grant of Fleet Street (Chapter 7) now succeeded by his son). Because customs officers were not horological experts, they could not tell who made the movements and the seized goods were restored to Faton without duty being paid (perhaps after a bribe?). Most smuggled watches were much cheaper than Faton's and were aimed at first-time buyers who had few scruples about buying foreign-made timepieces. Barraud contemptuously described the latter as 'watches to last two years. They are made without names, so that no responsibility attaches to the maker; he, of course, has no interest whether they turn out good or bad'.[29]

Swiss watches – like silk, lace, gloves, and jewellery – were profitably smuggled across the Channel. They were small, light in weight, high in value and easily carried.[30] When the Clockmakers' Company had investigated the problem in 1814, it concluded that the exact extent of smuggling was unknown.[31] The motive was easy profit for both smugglers and shopkeepers if tariffs were avoided. When the original duty of 27½ per cent (fixed by the Eden treaty in 1786) had been increased to 50 per cent (after the Treaty of Amiens broke down in 1803), smuggling became even more lucrative, especially when insurance arrangements guaranteed delivery in London for a small fee (Chapter 7). The mark-up on most silver watches was about 25 per cent, yielding about 10s–15s profit for a watch that sold for two to three guineas. Profit was about a pound from the sale of a four-guinea watch. Most profitable were watches bought for 40s and sold on for £3 10s.[32] Unscrupulous London watchmakers even signed Swiss watches as their own. Equally annoying were fake English movements in authentic English cases with genuine English dials. Hundreds, perhaps thousands, of Swiss watches were re-exported to the United States, notably from Liverpool, many bearing the forged name 'Tobias'.[33] Only persons 'who have long been in the watch trade can at once discover the differences between British and foreign manufacture', it was explained, 'but of course not persons who are not familiar with them'.[34]

How might smuggling be prevented? One solution suggested that sellers should have permits, and watches have labels – certificates – attached. But hallmarks might also be forged and, to prevent this, an elaborate bureaucracy with cooperation by retailers would be needed.[35] To raise tariffs to 75 per cent would be counterproductive; it would simply increase the incentive to smuggle. The Clockmakers' Company was perplexed. Its charter gave it the right to regulate trade in London and seize 'such contraband articles as they could discover', and then apply to customs officers to have them destroyed. But that right had lapsed in practice long before 1817. Customs officers routinely dealt independently with the goods they seized.[36] They found it easy to close one eye to imported foreign watches (perhaps helped by a bribe?) and were equally adept at closing the other to the re-export of watches with either foreign or forged English names. Besides, laws relating to the export of horological items and materials were muddled. An Act of Parliament in 1697 had allowed watches to be exported but prohibited the export of certain kinds of horological materials.[37] The intention had been to retain for the mother country the business of assembling watches. By the early nineteenth century, such mercantilist notions resulted in absurdities because the export of parts essential for repairing English watches already sold abroad was legally prohibited. In practice they were simply smuggled, without duty being paid. Grimshaw, who sold tools to Quebec, could export 'all kinds of tools, and one or two articles of materials, but the general materials I could not send ... that were necessary for repairing watches'. Either he lost that trade entirely, 'or some friends of the purchaser would come and take them [the repair materials] away in their pockets, by which the duty is evaded'.[38]

Retailers, exporters, and foreign watches

Trade regulations were annoying and petty, but in themselves were not the main reason for the increase of smuggled watches seen in London's shops. Shop keepers who sold watches were not always members of the Clockmakers' Company, and some dealt extensively in foreign watches. Like brokers of other foreign-made commodities, they wanted trade restrictions lifted at a time when much of the watch industry's former export trade was declining. No one knew what the putative value of exports from Clerkenwell and Coventry might have been. No one disputed that Geneva- and Jura-made watches were conquering British and European markets and were also re-exported to Britain's former foreign markets. One witness estimated that in 1798 exports had accounted for 70,000 watches out of an aggregate of 120,000 made in England.[39] By now even favoured imperial exports to India and Canada was being challenged. The profitable Turkish and Chinese horological markets of the late eighteenth century (Chapter 5) were falling away rapidly, spoiled – it was thought – because unscrupulous dealers ruined the market by off-loading watches of inferior quality. 'Regular' Anglo-American trade (mostly from Liverpool) was also seeping away, in difficulty anyway after the War of 1812.[40] In North America, short term profits had been made by some firms that exploited native-born American Indians with jewellery, trinkets, and 'very low priced watches... all they had to do was (sic) merely to make the watch go'. Examples included watches with second hands but without gearing mechanisms: 'the hand went round, but it was not regular'. In a scramble for quick profits, old and potentially lucrative new markets in North America were spoiled.

Only one witness at the inquiry recognised the connection between the national economy's well-being and the watchmaking industry's prosperity. John Powell of Coventry grasped the notion of 'income elasticity of demand' – that, when incomes fell, so did demand for non-essentials. He observed that 'when our agricultural interest flourished, almost every farmer's man set up a watch ... a watch being in general the first article put off in times of distress, and the last put on again when distress is removing'.[41] In 1816 and 1817, harvests had been poor and, as about a third of the population was primarily employed in agriculture, demand for watches slumped.

The committee's conclusions and report

The Commons' committee listened to the different diagnoses of – and putative solutions for – the industry's problems. There was general agreement that the government must do something, but uncertainty about what. The industry's importance was conceded. It created employment and earned export revenues. Its skills were deemed especially important because it was believed watch and clockmakers had helped build machines for textile and other industries: the structure of machines generally was contained in a clockwork mechanism, and those who knew how to make such mechanical things had a skill that was, conceptually, transferrable. [This was the first iteration of a connection that became an accepted wisdom that has resonated to the present day.[42]] In the national interest, it was argued, the industry deserved protection, or watchmakers might emigrate.[43] The dangers of that threat were well understood. Since the 1690s, manufacturers' pressure groups had supported laws that prohibited the emigration of skilled workers, including horological workers. Agents who enticed skilled workers to emigrate were liable to a £200 fine and a year's imprisonment.[44] The committee heard of rumours that two Dutchmen had tried to recruit ten or twelve English watchmakers to set up 'An English Movement Factory' in Rotterdam. But the reports were vague. There had been inquiries, but 'no one had gone'.[45] Nevertheless, potential emigration was a plausible danger because of a general belief in the transferable – marketable – skills of some watchmakers. Likely attractive destinations were the United States, because of opportunity and language, and Holland, because of proximity and its great horological tradition. Although the Admiralty had not yet formally recognised that chronometers were essential for Britain's future mercantile prosperity and national security, the unspoken underlying implication was that chronometer-manufacturing was the ace in English watchmaking's pack. Witnesses would have remembered the Sully episode a century earlier (Chapter 6) and known of the Spanish government's unsuccessful attempt in 1793 to set up a rival chronometer-manufactory.[46] The danger of foreign recruitment of skilled watchmakers was credible, especially during an economic depression. It reinforced support for government intervention.

The inquiry's *Minutes of Evidence* was published in autumn 1817. Another petition (this time from the Clockmakers of Aberdeen) in February 1818 prompted the committee to be reconvened just before its final *Report* was published. When it met it recommended, rather vaguely, that 'some parliamentary regulation ... in the preservation of the art, manufacture and trade of clock and watchmakers... should be adopted'. [47] A bill followed 'for the more effectual prevention of frauds and abuses, and for the Relief of distressed workmen brought up to practice the manufacture of clocks and watches'.[48] It was an anodyne proposition.

The bill got nowhere because other views were sought before its first reading in May. They must have swung the balance. Ominously for watchmakers, the new opinions were unsympathetic to tariff protection: they came from manufacturers who favoured free trade in their own industries. Consequently, on its second reading, the bill was deferred.[49] Free traders now swung into action, with petitions that 'prayed it [the bill] might not pass into law'.[50] In June the watchmakers tried again. Again the bill failed to get a second reading. After another free trade petition, a third attempt never came about.[51] Dealers and shopkeepers in favour of lower tariffs and freer trade had triumphed. It was no longer feasible or desirable to block imported cheap foreign watches after 1818: a growing general sentiment was moving to the diminution or elimination of tariffs on all goods, including watches.

****

The 1820s: Huskisson and tariff reform

Led by its iron and textile industries, Britain's national economy recovered in the 1820s from the long depression. The market for clocks and watches gradually resumed its familiar pattern.[52] Its top end was still dominated by Clerkenwell's best clocks, watches and chronometers. Coventry and Liverpool shared the rest, with large but unmeasured numbers of smuggled Swiss watches. Despite some 'distress' during the war years in the Jura's watchmaking regions, François Crouzet has concluded that 'no irreparable damage was done to Swiss watchmaking by the blockades'.[53] After the war, the Swiss industry began to assemble an ever-larger market. Smuggling to France and Russia was unnecessary because tariffs were low until another border was reached. Although Austrian and Swedish governments tried to hinder Swiss watches with tariffs, exports still grew, as they did to Spain and most Italian states. The Swiss watch industry was well organised. Its importance to its national economy meant that it had to be.

In Britain, the Clockmakers' Company on behalf of its industry continued to battle with the government for another two decades. After the interruption of the wars with France, the pressure for freer trade that had begun began in the late eighteenth century resumed in the 1820s. Those who argued for higher protective tariffs were especially vexed by the policies of William Huskisson, President of the Board of Trade between 1823 and 1827 in Lord Liverpool's Tory government.[54] Huskisson, an advocate of freer trade, introduced a tariff reform programme intended to stimulate British industries and their exports. It included the proposal that imported clocks, watches and watch-glasses should be 'warehoused' before paying duties.[55] The Company welcomed the idea at first because it hoped that foreign watches, parked in a warehouse, might then be stamped with a distinguishing mark until a tariff was paid before being released for sale.[56] The Company's optimism seemed justified when two ships were seized that carried 846 gold, silver, and metal watches. Following another similar seizure, customs officers acted with such 'enthusiasm' that the smuggled watches were thereafter regarded as valueless. From the Clockmakers' perspective, the new Act seemed to be working to their advantage. [57] But they were mistaken. The Treasury concluded that such interventions were not worth the cost and trouble.

These episodes were the first of many miscalculations by the guild. Worse followed when, in 1825, Huskisson revised his Warehousing Act but omitted the precise clause that had initially pleased the Clockmakers'. Instead, new regulations permitted timepieces intended 'for home consumption' to be released immediately.[58] The next seizure of Swiss watches became known as the 'Stiffnose incident'. It involved the attempt to smuggle watches made 'in the English style' and engraved as by 'Charles Stiffnose, Regent Street, London'. They were restored to their importer after payment of duty but were still able to be sold at prices lower than authentic English equivalents. They also became eligible for re-export to Britain's traditional markets abroad. This prompted the first of more than a dozen *Memorials* that the Company sent to the Board of Trade, over several years.[59] All reiterated the old complaints and added further examples of smuggling. All were ignored. The 'Stiffnose incident' was followed by the 'Eardley Norton' episode, when twenty-three silver-cased watches 'of the very worst quality' but engraved 'Eardley Norton, London', with forged goldsmiths' hallmarks, were seized by customs in May 1828. Eardley Norton had been a well-known Clerkenwell watchmaker between 1760 and 1794.[60] The forged 'Norton's' were valued by customs officers for duty at five shillings each and, at a routine custom auction, they were sold off for nine shillings each. The Company complained they 'suppl[ied] the place of so many English watches' and added that if the watches had been made in England, their makers would have broken both criminal law (for applying false marks to the case) and civil law (for using the name of another maker). Because they were foreign made, neither ruling applied. [61] To the embattled Company, it seemed another example of flagrant injustices that favoured forgers and smugglers but penalised domestic watchmakers.

The Company's protests appeared to have succeeded in 1828 when a revised Customs Act specified that foreign imitations of English watches with faked assay marks would be prohibited.[62] Elatedly, the Company sent multilingual translations of the crucial clauses to Swiss and French embassies in London. Henceforth, they hoped, foreign makers and their agents would be aware of the new regulations and warned away.[63] In 1830, the Company was again briefly euphoric when more 'Eardley Norton' Geneva fakes were seized. Customs officers destroyed their movements and melted the cases. It led the Clockmakers' again to think that they had at last triumphed.[64] Once more, they were too optimistic. In reality, random seizures and destruction of some smuggled watches were unable to protect Britain's watchmaking industry. Political will to supply the extensive resources necessary to enforce rigorous tariff laws was lacking. Unknown numbers of Swiss watches with forged names and hallmarks continued to enter Britain, to be sold as 'English' watches.[65] In 1832, yet another *Memorial* complained that even when occasional parcels of clocks and watches *were* declared at customs, they were deliberately undervalued to minimise tariff liability. The memorial alleged that the volume of 'illicitly imported' watches had grown 'twenty fold in the last two years, without the smallest benefit to the Revenue'.[66] Low-risk variations of the 'very lucrative' insurance strategy established during the Napoleonic War continued: tourists or their agents could order a watch, to be paid for only when smuggled and safely collected in London. In the unlikely event of smuggled watches being seized, the customer paid nothing.

Exports and imports, 1825–32; reaction and response

In 1833, an attempt was made to pacify and reassure the watchmaking industry. The government published official statistics of recent imports and exports in 1833 through Britain's two largest ports, London and Liverpool.[67] They showed the industry that its still-substantial watch exports were greater in number and value than imports (Tables 8.1 and 8.2).

The government's statistics claimed that 85,816 English watches had been exported since 1825, and only 14,996 imported. They indicated a

Table 8.1 Exports of English watches 1825–32, via London and Liverpool

Year			*Port of Export*			*Type of watch*		
	Total No	*London*	*Lond %*	*L'pool*	*L'pool %*	*% Gold*	*% silver*	*% metal*
1825	7,908	2,668	33.7	5,137	64.9	10.7	81.5	7.7
1826	6,697	2,429	36.2	4,105	61.3	8	81.2	10.6
1827	9,258	2,985	32.2	6,088	65.8	4.5	82.7	12.8
1828	8,603	2,759	32.1	5,711	66.4	2.5	79.7	17.8
1829	8,633	3,692	42.8	4,773	55.3	4	60.2	35.7
1830	10,943	4,599	42.0	6,109	55.8	3.8	60.3	35.7
1831	15,096	4,122	27.3	10,694	70.7	3.3	63.3	33.4
1832	18,678	3,967	21.2	14,281	75.6	2.3	71.6	22.4

Source: BPP, 1833, vol.33, 191–97: 'Clocks and watches: An account of the Number of Metal Clocks and Watches exported in each year since 1825 showing the several Ports of Exportation; also an account of the number of metal clocks and watches imported since 1825'.

Table 8.2 Foreign watches imported and re-exported, 1825–32

Year	*Imports £*	*Re-exports £*
1825	833	442
1826	795	576
1827	594	249
1828	2,346	1,750
1829	3,043	2,838
1830	2,399	2,278
1831	2,688	2,509
1832	2,298	2,088

Source: as for Table 8.1, above.

balance of trade heavily in favour of England's watchmaking industry. The publication incensed the Clockmakers' Company because the figures showed – could only show – legally imported watches, ones that had been declared to customs officials. The returns ignored the unknown numbers of smuggled Swiss watches. Publication of the tables prompted a radical change in the guild's strategy. Hitherto, its *Memorials* of complaint had stressed the *immorality* of smuggling: laws that should have been upheld were being flouted.[68] Henceforth, the Company emphasised the alleged 'opportunity costs' to the nation, the negative *economic* consequences of smuggling.[69] It claimed that the ease with which watches were smuggled, so openly boasted about by dealers, left the Exchequer 'enormously defrauded'. The few watches that had been declared were simply 'a cover for the others'.[70]

In their response to the government's tables, the Company offered its own alternative estimates of the numbers of smuggled clocks and watches and calculated – guessed at – the supposed tariff revenues that had been lost. Between 1825 and 1832 government figures indicated 'clocks' had raised £99,600 and 'watches' £2,937. But because imports had been deliberately undervalued to avoid duty, the guild claimed, the true loss of revenue on clocks was 'no less than £200,000' and that on watches was 'at least £700,000'. It was an assertion impossible to prove or refute. It was extrapolated from an assumption that over each of four years 25,000 gold watches and 10,000 silver watches had been smuggled into Britain, at prices averaging £7 for gold and 15s for silver. From these conjectures, the supposed values of imported timepieces were £930,000, which should have yielded duties of £232,500, thus leaving a notional deficit of about £200,000.[71] Linked to these conjectures were more rumours that English watchmakers might migrate to the United States to join other skilled migrants, such as 'bookbinders, engravers, carpenters, millwrights and wheelwrights'.[72] Again, the assertions were unsubstantiated anecdotes.

The Company's putative statistics and reports of rumours were to no avail. When the government replied to the Company's May 1833 *Memorial*, its final sentence was crushing: 'it does not appear to my Lords that any attempt to relieve you from Foreign competition, by rigid Customs-house regulations, would have a beneficial effect in protecting your Trade'.[73] Despite Sir Robert Peel's creation of a metropolitan police force in 1829, there were simply insufficient police or customs officers available to search incoming passengers on every arriving ship for something easily concealed on a person or in luggage. Moreover, as the Clockmakers' Company conceded, 'this power of search and seizure, it is obvious, never could be granted': it was impracticable and undesirable.[74] Henceforth, views in the relevant government departments hardened further. The Board of Customs stated, curtly, that it was simply not prepared to recommend 'any further measures for adoption in respect of the importation of clocks and watches'. The Treasury informed the Clockmakers' that although they had instructed customs officers 'to keep alert to prevent smuggling', they would not approve of any increase in protection 'in the way of Augmented Duty' by raising tariffs. It would only add an inducement to smuggle, for to 'bring an entire branch of trade under the supervision of the Excise, appears... very objectionable... and not likely, with respect to the sale of watches and clocks, to attain the object sought for'. The impasse continued. The Company complained that evidence of 'the extreme negligence of the [Customs] officers' could be seen in the large numbers of smuggled watches in shop windows in every town and city. Worse, ministers in the Foreign Office were themselves guilty of smuggling, for an 'immense bag [was] brought over twice a week by the Messenger in his bag with Despatches and Papers'. The Treasury did not deign to reply for four months. Then a letter bluntly asserted that 'it does not appear to my Lords that any further measures can be adopted for the prevention of smuggling in Clocks and Watches'.[75]

Hostilities in the long conflict between government and the watchmaking industry deteriorated further when the requirement that imported foreign watches needed a name and place *engraved* on them was amended. Henceforth, compliant sellers of smuggled watches found business easier, for names and places might just be *painted* on. Then, once safely through customs, it was possible to remove the foreign name 'without difficulty or injury to the work by Alcohol' and a real or forged English place or name could then be substituted. In some cases, names on watches were fixed to 'little metal straps dovetailed into the work which could easily be removed' and replaced by other slips bearing different names. In its quarterly meetings, the Company's Court of Assistants railed about forgeries and smuggling and sent more complaints to the Board of Trade.[76] Eventually, their secretary conceded, ruefully, 'for upwards of half a century [the Company] has been in correspondence with Her Majesty's Government' but had failed to resolve the conflict.[77]

The inquiry into tariffs, 1840

In 1840, a Commons select committee met to *Inquire into Abuses of the Revenue.* It took evidence on every item of foreign trade, what the duties were, and how much they produced for the Exchequer. Clocks and watches, still at Huskisson's 25 per cent tariff, raised just £9,628.[78] Following the *Inquiry*, tariffs on horological goods fell to 10 per cent, a large step towards their abolition.[79] By then London had become 'the headquarters of all the principal Foreign Watch Manufacturers: and there is no description of Foreign Watch that, if wanted, cannot be immediately procured in this City'.[80] Further *Memorials*, in 1841 and 1842, reiterated the Company's complaints. Notional lost revenue since 1815 was now claimed to be £1½ million. The Clockmakers' bitterly concluded that 'the experience of upwards of fifty years sufficiently proves the total uselessness of all Customs House regulations'.[81]

As always, the Company voiced the protectionist views of Clerkenwell's movement makers. They were supported by case makers because although foreign gold watches sold in Britain purported to be of 18-carat gold, many were of only 16 or 14 carats. Genuine English-made cases *had* to be 18 carats to obtain an assay mark. English watches were thus at a price disadvantage. The guild pleaded that foreign watches should be stamped (as they were in France) and enclosed as an example a French-stamped watch. The Treasury formally acknowledged receipt of the *Memorial* but rejected its suggestion. It returned the French watch without comment.[82]

In 1842, a new problem for Clerkenwell's watchmakers appeared. A Swiss watchmaker, Pierre Frederic Ingold, and his supporters proposed establishing a factory in London to make Swiss-type watches. If successful it would obviate smuggling because 'Swiss' watches might henceforth be made in England. Worse, it would pose a great threat to English watchmaking because it intended to use unskilled or semi-skilled labour, to make parts with machine tools in a factory. It became the decisive battle in the Clockmakers' Company's long war with the government. We shall see in Chapter 9 that although the guild won that battle, it proved to be a pyrrhic victory.

Notes

1 Leslie Howsam, 'Joseph Butterworth (1770–1826), publisher and politician'; and E.A. Smith, 'Peter Moore (1753–1828), Politician', both in *ODNB*.

2 *1818 Report*, Appendix 1: 'A list of laws...which ...bear upon the manufacture of Clock and Watchwork'; also Leonard Weiss, *Watchmaking, 1760–1820* (London: Robert Hale, 1982), 232–45. The armoury of records from which the Company's representatives could draw included much of LMA/CLC/L/CD/B/005/MS03975, namely 'Abstracts of and index to the journals of the ordinances, orders and public acts; precedents (1632–1816) in the journals of the Clockmakers' Company concerning the exercise by that company of 'the rule and diverse branches, arts and trades'.

3 In the nineteenth century and earlier, two gradations of 'gentleman' were recognised; the higher were 'esquires', the lower employed 'Mr' before the name.
4 For a record of donations, etc., see [Watch and Clock Makers' Benevolent Institution]. *Watch and Clock Makers' Benevolent Institution, for the Relief of Aged Necessitous Workmen of Good Character Belonging to the Several Branches in the Manufacture of Clocks and Watches, and of the Widows of Such Workmen: Instituted March 6th, 1815* (Clerkenwell: Berry, 1825), at jstor.org/stable/10.2307/60212945
5 *1817 Minutes*, 15.
6 David S. Landes, *Revolution in Time: Clocks and the Making of the Modern World* (Cambridge, MA: Belknap, Harvard UP, 1983), 281.
7 LMA/CLC/125/MS21339/001-006, namely
Watch and Clock Makers' Benevolent Institution: annual report and accounts. 6 volumes covering 1849–1910, for the relief of aged necessitous workmen ... in the manufacture of chronometers, watches, and clocks, and of widows of such workmen, instituted 6 March 1815.
Also *1817 Minutes*, 5.
8 *1817 Minutes*, 20, 27.
9 *1817 Minutes*, 87.
10 *1817 Minutes*, 35–36.
11 *1817 Minutes*, 16.
12 *1817 Minutes*, 14, 28, 36.
13 *1817 Minutes*, 14, 16, 20, 28, 31–32, 52–55, 68.
14 *1817 Minutes*, 31–32.
15 *1817 Minutes*, 14.
16 See Sir John Clapham, *An Economic History of Modern Britain* (3 Vols, Cambridge: Cambridge UP, 1926–38), Vol. 1, 370–74.
17 *1817 Minutes*, 74–84.
18 *1817 Minutes*, 77.
19 *1817 Minutes*, 84–85.
20 *BPP*, Vol. 72 (1817–18), Vol. 73 (1818), and Vol. 74 (1819), 'Petitions of Grievances'.
21 *1817 Minutes*, 66–67.
22 Alun C. Davies, 'Starting up a Watchmaking Business: James Ritchie of Edinburgh, 1809–1812', *Antiquarian Horology*, 20/3 (Autumn 1992), 265.
23 *1817 Minutes*, 7–8, 19, 30.
24 *1817 Minutes*, 71.
25 Jan Kraminer, 'Swedish Forgeries', *Antiquarian Horology*, 29/3 (March 2006), 330–34.
26 *1817 Minutes*, 26, 36.
27 *1817 Minutes*, 36.
28 *1817 Minutes*, 41.
29 *1817 Minutes*, 59.
30 *1817 Minutes*, 18.
31 LMA/CLC/L/CD/E/029/MS02728, namely 'Clockmakers' Company Minute Book of Committee ... on illicit introduction of foreign clocks and watches, 1814–1819'; and LMA/CLC/L/CD/E/029/MS02728: Documents relating to patents, imports, and hall marks.
32 *1817 Minutes*, 28, 34.
33 Michael Ededin, *English Watches for the American Market* (NAWCC *Bulletin*, Dec. 1992, 659–91), 687ff.
34 *1817 Minutes*, 58.
35 *1817 Minutes*, 8–9, 23, 25.

36 *1817 Minutes*, 69.
37 *1817 Minutes*, 10.
38 *1817 Minutes*, 15–16.
39 *1817 Minutes*, 38.
40 *1817 Minutes*, 26.
41 *1817 Minutes*, 90; E.P. Thompson, 'Time, Work-discipline and Industrial Capitalism', *Past and Present*, 38 (1967), 70, cites the example of a workman (in the 1820s) who bought a watch for £5, and 'popped it more than twenty times ... it's a garjian haingel to a fellar, is a good watch, ven you're hard up', [quoting Charles Manby Smith, *The Working Man's Way in the World* (London: Cash, 1853), 67–68].
42 The standard modern view of horology's contribution to mechanisation during the Industrial Revolution derives from Albert E. Musson and Eric Robinson's influential study, *Science and Technology in the Industrial Revolution* (Manchester: Manchester University Press. 1969), 60–61, 132; and id., 'The Origins of Engineering in Lancashire', *Journal of Economic History* (June 1960), 209–33, at https://doi.org/10.1017/S0022050700110435. They stress the link between scientific instrument makers and clockmakers. Contrary evidence that de-emphasises the role of horology is in Gillian Cookson, 'The West Yorkshire Textile and Engineering Industry, 1780–18950' (unpublished D.Phil. thesis, York University, 1994), 57–64 at ID uk.bl.ethos.387169; and id., 'Millwrights, Clockmakers, and the Origin of Textile Machines', *Textile History*, 27/1 (1966), 43–59, at https://doi.org/10.1179/004049696793711680; and id., 'Innovation, Diffusion and Mechanical Engineers in Britain, 1780–1850', *Economic History Review*, 47/4 (1994), 749–53, at https://doi.org/10.2307/2597715. For more of the debate, see Christine MacLeod, 'The Peculiarities of Yorkshire Inventors: A Reply', *Economic History Review*, 47/4 (Nov. 1994), 754–59, at https://doi.org/10.1111/j.1468-0289.1994.tb01401.x; see also Cormac Ó. Gráda, 'Did Science Cause the Industrial Revolution?', *Journal of Economic Literature*, 54/1 (2016), 224–39 (esp. 235) at www.jstor.org/stable/43932447
43 *1817 Minutes*, 47.
44 David J. Jeremy, 'Damming the flood: British Government Efforts to Check the Outflow of Technicians and Machinery, 1780–1843', *Business History Review*, 51 (April 1977), 1–34: https://doi.org/10.2307/3112919
45 *BPP*, 1871, *vol.* 36: 19, 52–53.
46 For the Spanish attempt, see Rupert T. Gould, *The Marine Chronometer: Its History and Development* (1923: London: Holland Press, 1960), 101–03.
47 *The Times*, 26 Feb. 1818; *Journal of the House of Commons,* 73 (1818), 30–31, 100–11, 39–40.
48 *Journal of the House of Commons,* 73 (1818), 195; *BPP, 1818,* 1/581: 'Bill for the relief of watchmakers and for preventing Frauds in their Trade; also *BPP, 1819*, 887: 'Bill to regulate the manufacture of clocks and watches'; see also LMA/CLC/L/CD/E/028/MS03944/19.
49 *The Times*, 8 and 9 May 1818; *Journal of the House of Commons*, 73 (1818), 340, 15 May 1818.
50 *Journal of the House of Commons*, 73 (1818), 373, 392, May 1818.
51 *Journal of the House of Commons*, 74 (1819), 535, 553, 561, 563, and 571, 14, 21, 23 and 25 June 1819; LC/L/CD/E/028/MS03944/15-21: also *BPP*, 1818, vol. 1 (282), 581.
52 Donald McCloskey, '1780–1860: A Survey', in Roderick Floud and Donald McCloskey (eds.), *The Economic History of Britain since 1700, Vol 1, 1700–1860* (Cambridge: Cambridge UP, 1994), 243ff.

53 François Crouzet, 'Wars, Blockade, and Economic Change in Europe, 1792–1815', *Journal of Economic History,* 24/ 4 (Dec. 1964), 567–88; quotes, 569, 584, at https://EconPapers.repec.org/RePEc:cup:jechis:v:24:y:1964:i:04:p:567-588_06.

54 Martin J. Daunton, *Progress and Poverty* (Oxford: Oxford UP, 1995), 534–35; A.C. Howe, 'Huskisson, William (1770– 1830)', *ODNB*. [Huskisson became the first railway fatality when he fell into the path of the *Rocket*.]

55 *BPP*, 1824: 3 [Warehousing of Goods Act, 4 George IV, Cap 24, sec. 81]. Act for regulating duties on imports and exports of clocks and watches to make more effectual provision for imported goods to be imported to "be secured in warehouses, or other places, without payment of duty on the first entry thereof". Also BPP, 1824, vol. 17, Excise licences: Dealers in watches.

56 LMA/CLC/L/CD/E/028/MS03945/41-44: Warehousing Bill letters, June to Oct. 1822; LMA/LC/L/CD/E/006/MS03943/45: 'Petition of ... Masters and Workmen, 7 June 1822'; S.E. Atkins and W.H. Overall, *Some Account of the Worshipful Company of Clockmakers* (London: Privately printed, 1881), 285–89; William Smart, *Economic Annals of the Nineteenth Century* (London: Macmillan, 1917), Vol. 2/158–59.

57 LMA/CLC/L/CD/E/028/MS03944/45: Newspaper clippings (1823, 1828, and 1839) warning the public against buying foreign watches with forged English makers' names on them.

58 *BPP* 1825, vol. 3: 6 George IV, Ch. 107: An Act for the Regulation of the Customs; 5 July 1825.

59 Atkins and Overall, *Clockmakers*, 291–92, Memorial, to the Board of Trade: 8 January 1827; LMA/CLC/L/CD/E/002/MS03951/ 43–45, 53a, 60, 61, 62, 63, 65, 66. Correspondence presenting memorials and arranging for the reception of various deputations lobbying on behalf of the Clockmakers' Company and other factions in the horological industry; also LMA/CLC/L/CD/E/002/MS03951/27–33/49, 56, 58 and 59. Continued complaints of the Company and its correspondence with the Treasury.

60 F.J. Britten, *Old Clocks and Watches and Their Makers* (London: Spon, 1956; reprinted Woodbridge: Antique Collectors' Club, 1978), 555; also John A. Robey, 'Eardley Norton's 1771 Patent for Striking Clocks and Repeating Watches', *Antiquarian Horology*, 30/1 (March 2007), 88–95, who notes that 'his name was sometimes faked on Swiss watches'.

61 Atkins and Overall, *Clockmakers,* 292–93; Memorial to the Board of Trade, May 1828.

62 *BPP* 1828, 1: [9 George IV. Ch 76: 25 July 1828.] "An act to amend Laws relating to the Customs": included a special clause, added to the bill "at the express solicitation of the Clockmakers' Company".

63 9 George IV, Ch. 76: An Act to amend laws relating to the Customs. The Clockmakers' Company translated its fourth clause for the Swiss and French Consuls General; Atkins and Overall, *Clockmakers,* 292–93.

64 LMA/CLC/L/CD/E/008/MS03940/001/135: Letter, Goldsmith's Company to Board of Trade about Hall Marks on watch cases, 19 June 1830; LMA/CLC/L/CD/E/008/MS03940/001/138; LMA/CLC/L/CD/E/028/MS03944/22: Memorial to the Treasury; March 1830; Atkins and Overall, *Clockmakers,* 293–94.

65 See *BPP* 1832–3 [3 & 4 William IV, Cap 52, sec 58] for regulating the duties on imports and exports as relates to the importation of Clocks and Watches: these articles are now allowed to be entered for the payment of duty with the name of the maker and the place printed on them.

66 LMA/CLC/L/CD/G/003/MS03941 3941: Memorial, to the Treasury: January 1832; Atkins and Overall, *Clockmakers,* 294–300.

67 London's statistics were drawn from BPP, 1830, vol. 25: An account of the number of Gold and Silver watch cases annually stamped at Goldsmith's Hall, London: for the year 1814 to the year 1829, both inclusive.
68 LMA/CLC/L/CD/E/008/MS03940/001 3,940/140: 'The Importation of Foreign Clocks and Watches'.
69 LMA/CLC/L/CD/E/028/MS03944/28: (Seventh) Memorial, to the Treasury, 6 May 1833. Quotations are from this; Atkins and Overall, *Clockmakers*, 300–04.
70 Atkins and Overall, *Clockmakers*, 304 (Thomas Lack to Atkins, 24 May 1833).
71 Atkins and Overall, *Clockmakers*, 301–03.
72 Daunton, *Progress and Poverty*, 414.
73 LMA/CLC/L/CD/E/008/MS03940/001: Letters, 2 March 1832, 7 June 1833; 13 June 1833; 21 June 1833 and reply, 29 June 1833; LMA/CLC/L/CD/E/028/MS03944/35-43: Letters, August to October 1832. (Reprinted in Atkins and Overall, *Clockmakers*, esp. 305–310, and 313–14 for *Report on Smuggled Clocks and Watches*.
74 Atkins and Overall, *Clockmakers*, 309–10, letters 21 and 29 June 1833; 11 July 1833.
75 Atkins and Overall, *Clockmakers*, 319, letter 7 March 1834.
76 PRO, BT: 334/2531, and LMA/CLC/L/CD/B/001/MS02710/001/8; October 1841.
77 LMA/CLC/L/CD/E/028/MS03944/56 and 59: Petition of Clock and Watch Manufacturers, Dec. 1841; Atkins and Overall, *Clockmakers*, 322–28.
78 *BPP*, 1840, vol.5: Report from the Select Committee on Import Duties, together with minutes of evidence.
79 John R. McCulloch, *A Dictionary, Practical, Theoretical, and Historical of Commerce and Commercial Navigation* (Philadelphia, PA: Hart, 1859), 291 and 1,276 for tariffs on clocks, and 1,284 for tariffs on watches.
80 LMA/CLC/L/CD/E/028/MS03944/46-55, 63–65: Jan. 1841 to July 1842.
81 LMA/CLC/L/CD/E/008/MS03940/001/154; Atkins and Overall, *Clockmakers*, 328–30; also LMA/CLC/L/CD/E/002/MS03951/27-33/49, 56, 58 and 59: Continued complaints of the Company and its correspondence with the Treasury.
82 LMA/CLC/L/CD/E/008/MS03940/001/155 and LMA/CLC/L/CD/E/006/MS03943/1-5 and LC/L/CD/E/028/MS03944/60; 29 Jan. 1842, correspondence, April to July1842; also, *BPP*, 1843, vol. 1, 816: A Bill to amend the laws relating to the Customs'. Clause 10 proposed to repeal the prohibition of importing 'Clocks and Watches not having foreign makers' names on the frame and face, or in an incomplete state.'

9 The Ingold Episode and After, 1842–60

The significance of the episode

The long struggle between the Clockmakers' Company and the government over smuggling and tariffs came to a head during the 'Ingold episode' of 1842–43. It did not quite end the conflict but, in retrospect, it was a crucial landmark in the long decline of England's watchmaking industry. The episode revolved around a scheme to make Swiss-type watches in London. It was a battle between conservatives and innovators. Clerkenwell's traditionalists won because the Clockmakers' Company successfully mobilised opposition, firstly from masters and outworkers in Clerkenwell and Coventry, and then in parliament. Parliament's rejection of Ingold and his supporters marked the guild's only real success in its long struggle with government. But the victory was Pyrrhic. Swiss-type watches were indeed prevented from being made in London, but Clerkenwell was still unable to block them from being smuggled. Almost two decades later a comparably radical new method of making watches did succeed, in Waltham, Massachusetts. It instigated changes in watchmaking methods in Switzerland, but not in Clerkenwell. After Ingold, England's watch industry resumed its decline, with ultimately fatal consequences for Clerkenwell (Chapter 14).

Pierre Frédéric Ingold and the BWCC

The background to the Ingold episode was the unknown number of Swiss watches smuggled into Britain during the previous half-century. Ingold and his supporters proposed setting up a factory to make them in London. Earlier attempts in Paris in 1835–36 and Versailles in 1838 were unsuccessful. Four years later they tried again when they formed a *National Metropolitan Watch and Chronometer Company*, subsequently renamed as the *British Watch and Clock Making Company* (BWCC). It envisaged a new level of watchmaking technology, beyond that in the independent workshops of Prescot and Clerkenwell or in Switzerland's *établissage* system. It proposed that watch parts, hitherto made by hand, would instead be made by machine tools and assembled in a factory.

DOI: 10.4324/9781003227823-11

Another break from Clerkenwell's tradition would be to make watches with going barrels, not with the fusees that then differentiated Clerkenwell's products. The proposed factory would employ women (at lower wages) as in England's textile factories. The watches would be cheaper than those from Coventry and sold at prices lower even than those from Switzerland (thus presumably obviating smuggling). News of the project horrified Clerkenwell's and Coventry's watchmakers. The introduction of machine production in a handcraft industry was seen by its opponents as 'an enemy force ... which, if left to continue unchecked would make every class of worker redundant'.[1]

Pierre-Frédéric Ingold was born in 1787 in Bienne (Figure 9.1). He had been apprenticed with Abraham Louis Breguet's House in Paris between 1816 and 1822 and thereafter proudly signed himself '*Ingold, élève de Breguet*'.[2] Fundamental to the project were the machine tools he designed. They were depicted in each of the four printed editions of the BWCC's *Prospectus*. One made top and bottom plates, with holes bored 'with such accuracy as greatly to improve the article manufactured; and with

Figure 9.1 Pierre-Frédéric Ingold (1787–1878) Portrait. Copyright: David Penney. http://www.antiquewatchstore.com/

such rapidity and [using] such an inferior class of workman as greatly to diminish the cost'.[3] Modern experts have explained that 'to us it would look something like a turret lathe'. It included an eccentric chuck (a feature borrowed from contemporary ornamental lathe makers) which Ingold modified, so that

> by its various movements... [it] presented the centres of each hole and countersink... the various operations were true and could be repeated to produce innumerable plates exactly alike... to produce at one chucking a completed plate requiring no further machining. Anyone familiar with modern precision chucks will appreciate the importance of this.[4]

Another was a 'stamping and polishing machine' to punch wheel blanks from a strip of metal, simultaneously polishing the edges and removing 'a very fine sliver of metal'.[5] In this and claims about the other devices, the *Prospectus* inferred impressive productivity increases:

> The barrel could be turned in one minute by machinery while it now took two hours. The lower plate, a principal part of the watch, could be finished in twenty minutes, [whereas] it took two days by hand... the wheel and balance could be made by hundreds, where by hand they can only be made by dozens. The pivots, which now took a week, could be made by machinery in a quarter of an hour, with the most beautiful accuracy... one set of machines could perform as much work per day as 300 men.

What could *not* be speeded up was the highly skilled final assembling and 'springing' of the watch. Its parts would still need 'fitting' and, on Ingold's proposed scale of production, would require an estimated 300 'finishers' to fit them. Even so, the *Prospectus* claimed, 'a first-rate watch may be completed in one week, which at present cannot possibly be accomplished under six'. The promoters claimed that each full 'set' of machines [Ingold's prototypes, and about twenty replicas] if worked by 'numerous artificers' might produce daily between 200 and 300 watches. This would amount to an estimated annual production of 70,000–100,000 watches, almost equivalent to Clerkenwell's current yearly output.[6] By contemporary yardsticks this was prodigious. Masters and apprentices in Clerkenwell and Coventry were understandably alarmed. The phrase in the *Prospectus*, 'inferior class of workmen', must have rankled in the minds of Clerkenwell's and Coventry's outworkers. But two formidable hurdles faced Ingold and his supporters. Substantial capital needed to be raised, and patent approval to be authorised. Both would be indispensable if the project was to succeed.

Financial implications

How much capital was envisaged, and how might it be raised? A production line in a factory with twenty sets of machine tools would likely require an investment of about £40,000, an amount unprecedented in the history of English watchmaking. The first edition of the *Prospectus* offered 10,000 public subscription shares at £25 each. It stated that Ingold would hold 2,400 shares (face value £60,000), plus a fifth of net profits and an unspecified salary as Managing Director for ceding his patent rights to the Company. The three later editions of the *Prospectus* tactfully left out Ingold's proposed generous remuneration and inferred substantial future financial rewards for subscribers. Indeed, if two-thirds of shareholders agreed, the projected £250,000 capital might be doubled. Initial claims about likely profits of 90 per cent were hastily amended to read 'at least 30 per cent'. Another sanguine assurance was that there would be 'a very large additional profit to the [retail] trade'. But, to bring all this to fruition, the Company first needed Parliament to approve a Charter that limited the liability of the BWCC's shareholders. At that time, laws on patent protection and limited liability were unclear; they did not then extend to commercial undertakings or become a general right until 1855.[7] To raise capital for the BWCC, an Act of Parliament was needed to lend propriety and remove uncertainty.

Factory precedents

The BWCC's intention to achieve large volume production had precedents. As noted earlier (Chapter 5) they included Eli Whitney's attempt to make muskets for the United States' war department in 1798; that did not do well at first, but later was successful. In 1802 Marc Brunel mass produced pulley blocks for Britain's navy in Portsmouth, but blocks needed tolerances broader than musket parts and, especially, watch parts.[8] Following inventions of the spinning jenny, water frame, the power and Jacquard looms, factories mass-producing textiles were already features of contemporary England. There were even some horological precedents: Peter Stubs had a 'factory' – admittedly not to make, but to organise, inspect, and endorse tools collected from his outworkers. Elsewhere, at Japy's production line in Beaucourt semi-skilled workers made standardised *ébauches*. In America, Eli Terry's production innovations marked the end of America's traditional clock making, when he provided the first example of 'interchangeable parts in any mechanical product [with] … 3,000 identical longcase clock movements made from wood'.[9] Seth Thomas's machine tools made standardised clock parts that had broad tolerances, but they were interchangeable only in their first stages of construction and assembly.[10] By 1827, Vacheron and Constantin in Geneva improved layouts and their workman, Georges-Auguste

Leschot, went a step further when factory-made watch parts were created to be similar though not interchangeable.[11] Ingold's unsuccessful attempts in Paris were almost contemporaneous with those of the Pitkin brothers in America, who set up a production line that made about 800 watches between 1835 and 1841. The Pitkin project failed, for a mixture of entrepreneurial and technical reasons: it had been based on miniaturised brass clock movements fitted out with imported English dials, hands, jewels, and springs. The ideas of interchangeability and mass production were already in the air; Ingold's intentions had illustrious horological precedents.

The production and assembly of watch parts in a factory was considerably more difficult than for clocks. There are two imperatives for the successful mass production of parts by machine tools for any product. First, there must be a large market for the end product. For watches, the putative market was already there, and its further growth was likely. Second, technical obstacles must be overcome. Machine tools with especially great precision were needed. Watch parts required accuracy to 1/1,000 of an inch or better. In the long run, interchangeability of parts might be expected when subsequent generations of machine tools were improved. The making of very high-quality watch movements before the 1840s was hindered by the technical limitations of contemporary machines. Ingold's project promised to improve on those.

Ingold's prototype watches

Ingold's first watches were made from parts assembled in a garden shed at 75 Dean Street, Soho. Probably a handful of workers were employed, for only a few score watches – maybe a hundred or so – were made, of which eighteen are known to have survived (Figure 9.2).[12] For a short time, Ingold did as well as – or better than – his predecessors. By comparison with what has been described as the 'the poorly made and amateurish attempts by the Pitkin Brothers', Ingold had designed tools that created, David Penney concluded, 'a well-made watch of sophisticated design, one [that was] far ahead of its time' ... the quality of Ingold's limited 1843 production was much superior to Pitkin's because they were 'produced by trained and skilful watchmakers who knew they had to compete with their peers'.[13] The evidence of these watches and the intention to make more was sufficient to galvanise Clerkenwell. After a protest meeting in the *Crown and Anchor* tavern on Clerkenwell Green, angry outworkers marched on the little proto-factory.[14] According to a later account,

> workmen engaged in the factory were attacked by the workmen of Clerkenwell. Their windows were broken, and great injury and cruelty inflicted... there is reason to believe it was done at the instigation of those by whom they were employed.[15]

Figure 9.2 An Ingold Watch: dial. Copyright: David Penney. http://www.antiquewatchstore.com/

Another anecdote, also chronicled long after the event, claimed that 'Ingold went in fear of his life' because of the hostility of the trade.[16] These intimidations must be seen in the context of violent contemporary resentment to the introduction of machines in other British industries. In the minds of some who attacked 75 Dean Street would have been the 'Swing Riots' in 1830, when agricultural labourers in the south of England protested against the introduction of threshing machines. More recently, papermakers in Buckinghamshire and sawyers in Southampton damaged machines that threatened their jobs.[17] Although not about machines, other widely known contemporary examples of populist violence were the 'Rebecca riots' in west Wales, against taxes and tolls, and John Frost's Chartist riots in Newport concerning political and economic reform.[18]

Supporters and opponents

Ingold's prototypes especially worried the Clockmakers' Company. They set up a committee to organise opposition to the scheme and sent letters to *The Times*, *The Morning Herald*, *The Standard*, and *John Bull* that denounced the project. Pamphlets appeared, for and against.[19] Reaction in Coventry was equally hostile; 800 watchmakers signed a petition to Parliament pleading for the scheme to be rejected.[20] The Clockmakers' committee also sought support from leading watchmakers and tried to recruit Benjamin Lewis Vulliamy (1780–1854) and William James Frodsham (1778–1850), but these two titans arrived at different conclusions (Figures 9.3 and 9.4).

Both Vulliamy and W.J. Frodsham belonged to illustrious and much respected horological families. Freed of the Clockmakers' Company in 1809, Vulliamy had five times been its Master and was the Royal Clockmaker – first to George IV, then to William IV, and currently to Queen Victoria. He had long argued on behalf of the Company in favour of protective tariffs in their unsuccessful struggles with the Board of Trade and the Treasury.[21] His eminent contemporary was William John Frodsham, Fellow of the Royal Society (FRS), of 4 Change Alley, Cornhill [where, with William Parkinson, he had established the firm of Parkinson & Frodsham]. He too was a former Master of the Clockmakers' Company. Like London's other leading watch and chronometer makers, Vulliamy and W.J. Frodsham had received letters soliciting support for the BWCC's project.[22] But the reactions of the two horological titans were different. Vulliamy was sceptical about Ingold's

Figure 9.3 William John Frodsham, FRS (1778–1850). Copyright: Worshipful Company of Clockmakers. Photo by Keeper Emeritus Sir George White, Bt.

Figure 9.4 Benjamin Lewis Vulliamy (1780–1854). Copyright: Worshipful Company of Clockmakers. Photo by Clarissa Bruce.

scheme. He was well aware of the consequences for Clerkenwell of imported or smuggled Swiss watches, and he grasped the implications for traditional watchmakers if a Swiss watch factory might be established in London itself. But, he pleaded, at sixty-two years he was too old to be involved. For two decades, he had struggled on behalf of the guild with the government over tariffs and smuggling. He was not willing to expend further energy to oppose the project but would not take sides. He would remain neutral.[23] However, his friend, W.J. Frodsham, was not impartial. He was indeed willing to help the opposition to Ingold's project by rallying support from London's larger manufacturing houses and from Clerkenwell's independent outworkers and masters (hitherto more used to competition between themselves than cooperation).[24]

Thus, the BWCC's recruitment drive successfully recruited W.J. Frodsham, but failed with Vulliamy. Other horological notables, like Vulliamy, also cautiously sat on the fence. William Connell of 22 Myddleton Street, Cheapside, initially condemned Ingold's proposal but changed his mind when he saw successful demonstrations of Ingold's machines in the workshop in Dean Street, Soho. He was impressed by them and was, briefly, tempted to become a Director. But as a cautious businessman, he wished to offend as few people as possible. In the end, he, like Vulliamy, remained neutral.[25] The BWCC had more success with other distinguished horologists. Thomas Earnshaw, Junior, succeeded to the family's business at 119 High Holborn after his illustrious father retired in 1815. Earnshaw Junior agreed to become one of the two 'Managing Directors' proposed by the BWCC. [26] The other Director would have been John Barwise, owner of an important horological shop in St Martin's Lane. He died suddenly in 1843 but was immediately succeeded by his son of the same name who energetically picked up his father's involvement.[27] A less desirable supporter was Anthony Vieyres of 40 Pall Mall. Vieyres was attracted to the idea of making Swiss-type watches in London on a potentially large scale, but eventually withdrew 'on personal grounds'. This was perhaps to avoid embarrassing the project because he was currently under investigation by Mr Gladstone's Board of Trade, about profiting from the sale of smuggled Swiss watches.[28]

However, another Frodsham became a prominent supporter. John Frodsham (1785–1849) of the firm Frodsham & Baker of Gracechurch Street was the younger brother of William James Frodsham (who opposed the project).[29] John Frodsham supported the BWCC because he thought it might be profitable. He did not worry about where watches were made or who made them. Indeed, if the project had succeeded then John Frodsham would have been its designated chief 'agent' in London, responsible for supplying its large market. The most bizarre of Ingold's supporters was Alexander Douglas, the tenth Duke of Hamilton.

Although named as a 'trustee', there is no evidence that he had any connection with horology. His name and imposing title on the first edition of the *Prospectuses* suggest he was a front figure, no doubt one who hoped to profit from the scheme (although he was, by any measure, already exceptionally wealthy).[30] Other speculators with no previously known horological connections included a Lombard Street bank, a firm of lawyers (who supplied a Company Secretary), a city merchant and a civil engineer.[31] The BWCC's plans to market the proposed watches were ambitious. Eighty-eight 'agents' were enrolled to support the scheme. They included retailers in seventy-nine provincial towns; most were traders with experience in Britain's once-lucrative watch exports to markets in the United States, South America, Portugal, Spain, Italy, India, China, Australia, the West Indies, Turkey, and Germany. Unsurprisingly, no agents were allocated to sell watches in France or Switzerland.

Debate in Parliament

The bill was debated in the House of Commons on 31 March 1843 proposed that limited liability be granted to Ingold and the Watch Company (that is, shareholders would be liable only for the amounts they had invested).[32] Prominent supporters included John Lewis Ricardo, free trader nephew of the great economist David, and Dr (later Sir) John Bowring, expert on tariffs and author of a recent parliamentary report on the Swiss watch trade.[33] A third was Edmund Beckett Denison (later Lord Grimthorpe), fond of mechanical invention, future designer of Big Ben's escapement, future President of the British Horological Institute and, in his later years, scourge of the anti-machinery faction there (see Chapter 13). Of these, only Bowring spoke in the debate. The Prime Minister, Sir Robert Peel, was not present. The bill was proposed by the member for Sheffield, H.G. Ward. His argument – with variations – touched on the Inevitability of Progress (and, implicitly, its Desirability). He compared the prospect and potential of factory production with the reality of traditional ways of watchmaking and, presciently, admitted he was

> persuaded that there is no more possibility of competition between the two than there is between the power loom and the old spinning wheel; ... we might as well try to restore the packhorse as a substitute for the railway or the canal. Other nations will adopt new discoveries if we do not; and your own case, my fear, I confess, would be not the disturbance of existing interests at Coventry or Clerkenwell, but the utter extinction of their trade, by the transfer, to Paris or Geneva, of Mr Ingold's machines.[34]

A noteworthy contribution on behalf of the government came from a rising star in British politics, the thirty-three-year-old William Ewart Gladstone, a member of Sir Robert Peel's cabinet. He was cautiously sympathetic and suggested that the bill might be referred to a Committee of the House for further investigation. From his vantage point as Vice-President of the Board of Trade he saw Ingold's scheme as being favourable to the nation's broader economic interests because the project promised better and cheaper watches and the possibility of recapturing domestic and foreign markets being lost to the Swiss. The current stagnation of English watchmaking was regrettable: perhaps Ingold's scheme might resuscitate an entire industry? If the price of innovation was the dislocation of existing handcraft methods of production and short-term unemployment, then so be it.

Parliamentary opposition to the bill was led by members who sat for the two main watchmaking constituencies, Clerkenwell and Coventry. Thomas Duncombe, radical politician, and Chartist supporter, might have been thought a likely enthusiast for innovation. But he chose to reflect the interests of his constituents in Clerkenwell, as did William Williams, MP for Coventry, conscious of the importance of watchmaking in that city.[35] Viscount Sandon, member for Liverpool, England's third watchmaking centre, also voted against the motion but otherwise played no part. Prominent opponents of the bill included the radical politician Joseph Hume, Lord John Russell (leader of the opposition to Peel's government), Henry Labouchere, later president of the Board of Trade under Russell, and the eccentric Colonel Sibthorpe, who opposed Catholic emancipation, free trade, and just about everything. *Hansard* records that ten members spoke. A comfortable majority rejected the bill by two to one: seventy-seven voted for and 154 against. Because it was a private member's – not the government's – bill, voting was not on party lines. Both sides included 'reformers' and 'conservatives'. Broadly, however, it was generally supported by those in favour of free trade and sympathetic to industrial innovation, although some prominent industrialists, like Sir John Guest the Merthyr ironmaster, opposed the bill. The defeat of the bill in parliament proved decisive. The BWCC's attempt to obtain patent protection failed. Without it, not one share was bought.[36]

Aftermath

Ingold's supporters made belated attempts to reverse the outcome. In April 1843, just *after* the bill was defeated, the BWCC published affidavits from a group of eminent technical experts. It testified that they had, indeed, seen Ingold's machinery demonstrated at 75 Dean Street and, moreover, they believed the machines *were* well capable of doing what their promoters promised.[37] The group included the Attorney General, the Secretary to the Royal Institution, and three distinguished scientists, namely Augustus de Morgan (Professor of Mathematics at University College, London from 1831 and later the first president of the Mathematical Society), Henry Moseley, FRS (Professor of Mechanics, Kings College London), and Edward Bell (Professor of Mechanics, College for Civil Engineers). Had their expert endorsements come earlier, they might perhaps have lent Ingold's proposal the imprimatur of respectability and authority that the bill needed to pass. If so, the public might have subscribed. The scientists' belated endorsement was interesting, but futile.

Shortly afterwards two further attempts were made to re-open the project, in the hope of inducing Gladstone and the government to support a new Bill. The first suggested that on each watch manufactured, a shilling tax might be levied. The high-minded Gladstone may have resented it and seen it as a clumsy attempt to bribe the government and was unconvinced. Perhaps it was because he also knew of Pitt's failure to tax clocks and watches half a century earlier? (Chapter 7). In a second attempt, John Barwise wrote to Gladstone to say that Ingold had 'had an offer that morning from Paris to establish the company there under favourable terms'. He vaguely implied that unless the Bill was reintroduced, the impetus for the project would return to France and a great opportunity would be lost. Gladstone remained unimpressed. The affair may have contributed to his – and Peel's – hardening belief in the cost-ineffectiveness of tariff protection, and the merits of free trade.[38]

Thus the Ingold episode ended. One reason for its failure was because the contemporary commercial climate was unpropitious.[39] Since the onset of a downswing in the economy in 1837, fifteen major projects had started up and then collapsed. They led to the comment that 'The world has been at the mercy of anyone who chose to publish an advertisement, call himself a company, and receive money for assurances and annuities'.[40] Newspapers were full of reports of failed enterprises, bankruptcies, burst 'bubbles' and hypothetical ventures, like the proposal for a patent for an 'Aeriel (sic) Steam Carriage' – a flying steam-engine to carry passengers – discussed in the same week Ingold's Watch Factory Bill came to Parliament.[41] A speculative frenzy – the 'railway mania' – currently surrounded the expansion of the railway network. The public was suspicious of grandiose schemes they believed were promoted by unscrupulous opportunists. Promises of effortless, large profits made it easy for opponents to depict Ingold's scheme as a scam. It was not the best time to launch a new enterprise.

Consequences

After the bill's rejection, the opportunity and momentum for technological change in the watchmaking industry moved decisively away from

Britain. Ingold left for America: although there seems to be no direct connection between Ingold's machine tools and those later pioneered by Waltham. David Penney's expert conclusion is that Ingold's ideas were nevertheless significant.[42] It was time for a change in the watchmaking industry, but after the failure of Ingold's project, Clerkenwell persevered with its craft-based methods for more than half a century.[43] Its pre-industrial means of production were 'locked-in', self-inflicted by the perseverance of its prevailing technology. The rejection of Ingold's project limited any putative decisions about changing methods of production, and it continued even when past circumstances were no longer relevant.[44] Productivity in other contemporary industries, notably textiles, was being revolutionised by factory production and the application of steam power. English industries produced half of the world's manufactured goods and, as Disraeli observed in 1838, Britain had become 'the workshop of the world'. For English watchmaking, the Ingold episode was the decisive turning point. Had Ingold's project succeeded it would surely have changed England's watchmaking industry. Different labour skills would have been needed to use machine tools compared with those in traditional handcraft watchmaking. Hindsight suggests that later generations of Ingold's prototype tools would have been better: the manufacture in a factory of watches with machine-made parts would have speeded-up output through 'learning by doing', as happened in Waltham, Massachusetts, in the late 1850s and 1860s (Chapter 11).

The Clockmakers' Company's victory over Ingold extended the life of Clerkenwell's handcraft technology and prolonged the culture of its community until the Great War. But not even the Clockmakers' Company could buy the future and save England's watchmaking industry. Although factory production of watches never took root in Clerkenwell, it was later attempted in Birmingham and Coventry with limited successes, and failed completely in Prescot (Chapters 14 and 15). English watchmaking never regained its former ascendancy in its own or world markets.[45] Some Clerkenwell firms survived and continued profitably to make traditional watches for a small luxury market. Small numbers of superb chronometers were also made as their firms successfully supplied the numerically limited demand for them. But during the decades when Britain was a leading industrial and economic power, it was the products of Swiss cantons and huge American factories that supplied its domestic and former export watch markets.

****

After Ingold: the Great Exhibition

Sporadic skirmishes between the Clockmakers' Company and successive governments continued during the decade following the Ingold episode.

Great strides towards free trade were made, with the belief that cheap imports would benefit consumers as well help to maintain Britain's industrial supremacy. At the Board of Trade Gladstone concluded that to protect England's small watchmaking industry by imposing tariffs on foreign watches was a hopeless tax, cost-ineffective to collect. Tariffs on something as easily concealed as watches simply lent a great incentive to smuggle.[46] After the repeal of the Corn Laws in 1846, popular sentiment and political will converged and domestic markets were further opened to foreign competition. If a consequence was that a minor industry – watchmaking – continued its decline, then that price would be paid.

Problems for the Clockmakers' Company that caused additional worries for its industry came with the Great Exhibition held in Hyde Park in 1851, the impressive display that demonstrated Britain's latest achievements in its material progress. Although the Exhibition marked a high point in Britain's international economic presence, the Clockmakers' Company warned in advance that the exhibition would 'prove extremely prejudicial to British [horological] manufacturing, which is and has been for a long time past in a very depressed state'.[47] The guild was right. The exhibition's 6 million visitors saw attractive displays of the products (and attractive prices) of foreign clock and watchmakers.[48] The 'immense importation' of French and American clocks continued, just as the Company had correctly forecast, and 'completely destroyed the manufacture of [British] clocks of any but the most superior description'. A significant foreign horological triumph at the exhibition included that by Japy of Paris whose prize medal was for 'movements of watches and small clocks [that] are made by machinery on a very large scale'.[49] Ironically, Yankee mantel clocks failed to win any exhibition medals, although they had enjoyed remarkably high sales in Britain from the early 1840s.[50] More importantly, the implications of the revolutionary means by which American clocks (and small arms) were manufactured were recognised by the government. It sent a committee of experts in 1853 to New England to visit the New York's own Crystal Palace exhibition, with the explicit remit to examine the 'American system of manufacture'. Its report confirmed that the parts of small arms and clocks were made to be interchangeable to a fair degree of accuracy and were assembled by unskilled labour.[51] Because the government was by far the largest customer in Britain for small arms, the Report helped to induce changes on that industry. But there was no equivalent single large customer for clocks and watches able to impose its will and force change in Clerkenwell's method of production.[52]

The Swiss invasion resumes

Clerkenwell's watchmakers were distraught by the aftermath of the Great Exhibition, with good reason. Swiss watchmaking had been temporarily paralysed during the 'year of revolutions' in 1848, when political upheavals in Italy, France, Germany and Austria hindered trade. The Exhibition gave the Swiss an incentive to resuscitate its industry. The Crystal Palace offered an unprecedented shop window, and Swiss watchmakers seized the opportunity. Their workshops reopened in 1850 and, by 1851, some 60,000 watches were finished in Geneva. All the Swiss watches sent for display at the Great Exhibition were sold.[53] Indeed, the exhibition revitalised Switzerland's watch exports. Those to Britain rose from 42,000 in 1852, to 70,000 in 1854, to 90,000 in 1855 and reached 160,000 in 1861. Over the decade after the exhibition the annual values of Swiss watch sales in the UK climbed from £174,000 to £565,000; it indicated the putative annual 'opportunity-cost' lost by England's watch industry.[54] In the 1860s, Britain imported more watches from Switzerland than were made in Clerkenwell.

Statistics of imports and exports must be viewed with caution. It is unclear how many precious metal cases were assayed for foreign watch movements, or how many movements went into base metal or other cases. Statistics of watch imports before 1853 were, Sir John Clapham thought, 'worthless', because they were unable to take account of smuggling. Officials only began to record numbers in 1853 when Gladstone finally modified tariffs before their complete removal. Thereafter records improved, and long-term trends can be discerned. In 1854, the UK imported 228,000 clocks and 79,500 watches. 'As these are the figures for home consumption', Clapham continued, 'it would seem that English mantelpieces were filling up rather rapidly with French clocks and Swiss watches'.[55] Not only Clerkenwell and London's Goldsmith's Hall felt the consequences, for Birmingham's assays of precious metal cases for Coventry-made watches fell, from 40,000 silver ounces in 1850, to 24,000 in 1860 to less than 12,000 ounces by 1866. In the same period, the number of gold cases assayed in Birmingham fell from about 750 to zero.[56] It may of course have reflected an increase in casing watches in base, not precious, metals. There is no way of knowing. But production in Britain's watchmaking centres was undoubtedly in decline.

Another blow for English watchmaking had come in 1852, when the Treasury removed from the statute book prohibitions on re-exporting watches made abroad 'in the English style bearing English – or British – names and places on the dial'. They had been exported in British ships in the hope that this conveyed the impression that the watches, like the ships, were also British. The Company reiterated its objections in another Petition to the House on 30 January 1852 and in a further *Memorial* to the Treasury. From there, in the dying days of Lord John Russell's Whig ministry, George Cornwall Lewis replied to the Clockmakers' that the Treasury was 'not prepared to revoke or make any alteration' in the new regulations.[57]

The triumph of free trade

The new Tory government proved just as unsympathetic to the watchmaking industry and its guild as the Whigs had been. Indeed, Benjamin Disraeli, the incoming Chancellor of the Exchequer, brusquely ended the government's formal communications with the Clockmakers' Company; the guild learned of the new government's proposals to deregulate watch exports only from reading about it in *The Times* newspaper.[58] Disraeli's officials explained that 'it had always been within the power of the Foreign maker to export watches bearing any mark from one foreign port to another, without the British government having any ground for interference'. They indicated that to seize and examine such watches would 'interfere materially' with the carrying trade of ship owners without offering effective protection to watch manufacturers'.[59] In other words, ship owners – and especially the trade they conducted – were more important to the nation than watchmakers. It simply reflected how much Britain's commerce with the rest of the world had increased since Waterloo and was still growing. In 1815, the value of Britain's annual exports was then about £55m; by the mid-1850s exports had more than doubled, to over £123m. The share of clocks and watches in that trade shrank from 1.23 per cent to 0.55 per cent.[60] In the era of free trade the well-being of England's watchmaking industry did not rank highly in government concerns or policies.

Disraeli's budget of 1852 lowered tariffs further, on a range of fancy articles that comprised musical harmoniums, hats, bonnets, umbrellas, and toys.[61] The list also included clocks and watches, as McCulloch's crisp summary of a complicated menu revealed:

> **Clocks:** clocks 'of and from foreign countries' enjoyed similar rates as clocks 'of and from British possessions'. The duty charged on clocks 'not exceeding the value of 5 shillings each per dozen' was 4 shillings; for those between 5 shillings and 12s 6d each, per dozen, the duty was 8 shillings. Individual clocks of value between 12s 6d and £3 carried a duty of 2s each; on individual clocks worth between £3 and £10, a duty of 4s.; and of individual clocks of value greater than £10, a duty of 10s.
>
> **Watches:** on watches of gold, silver, or other metal, exceeding the value of £10, a duty of £1 was applied. For gold watches with 'open faces', a tariff of 5s was applied to each; on gold hunters, a tariff of 7s 6d; and on repeaters, a tariff of 15s each; for silver and other metal watches, the respective categories were 2s 6d, 3s 6d, and 8s.[62]

The dozen different rates for watches and clocks were difficult for customs officers to enforce and brought in only about £16,000 annually. They were more expensive to collect than the sum they produced. In

1853, in Gladstone's first budget, tariffs on over 200 items were either reduced or abolished. The essential features of free trade were nearly completed by the vast tidying-up tariff exercise of Gladstone's 1860 budget. He removed import duties on 400 items and retained tariffs for revenue purposes only on fewer than twenty imported 'luxury' goods. It made possible the 'Cobden-Chevalier' free trade treaty with France by lowering the duties on French wines in return for cuts in French tariffs on British manufactured goods. The Anglo-French treaty inspired reciprocity treaties with other countries in the following decade.[63] For English watchmaking, its lucrative home market henceforth lay wide open to unfettered competition. It was another nail in the English watchmaking industry's coffin.

For over half a century watchmaking in Britain had stagnated or shrunk, as the Swiss overwhelmed British competition with their low prices and varied designs. Free trade triumphed, and its golden era began, and watches were imported in ever-growing numbers.[64] English watchmaking firms had to accept the inexorable consequences. In 1858, the Clockmakers' Company finally abandoned its long campaign to urge successive governments to prevent foreign watches and clocks from entering Britain: it ceased playing an active role in the day-to-day affairs of its declining industry. The Company remained – and remains – in existence. But after 1860 it became preoccupied with charities and annual dinners that honoured benefactors but, later in the century, it re-connected more closely with watchmaking. In the meantime, the leadership of the industry passed to the British Horological Institute, a new organisation established in 1858 (Chapter 13).

Yet, not all sectors of Britain's horological industry were as weak as watchmaking. The erection of Big Ben in the great clock tower at Westminster encouraged the widespread construction of public clocks when civic authorities wanted smaller local equivalents: public clocks were not merely useful devices, but symbols of civic status and progress. Department stores and railway stations, too, acquired clocks placed to show the time. The large sizes of turret clocks and the need for local involvement in their construction gave British makers an advantage over foreign competitors. Time-awareness and acceptance of Greenwich Mean Time became almost ubiquitous, encouraged by the need to synchronise railway timetables.

But the small horological sector that did best in meeting and beating foreign challenges by mid-century was chronometer manufacturing (Chapter 10).

Notes

1 Raphael Samuel, 'Workshop of the World: Steam Power and Hand Technology in Mid-Victorian Britain', *History Workshop*, 3/1 (Spring 1977), 6–72 (quotation, 11), at https://www.jstor.org/stable/4288092.

2 Alun C. Davies, 'The Ingold Episode Revisited: English Watchmaking's Pyrrhic victory', *Antiquarian Horology*, 31/5. (Sept. 2009), 637–54; id., 'British Watchmaking, 1842–43: Technical Expertise and Public Decisions', *Proceedings of the International Symposium on Technology and Society* (Princeton: Princeton Univ., 1996), 438–47; David Penney, 'Pierre Frederick Ingold (1787–1878): His Impact on Watchmaking Both in Europe and America', in *Boston: Cradle of Industrial Watchmaking, NAWCC Supplement* No. 5 (2005); Leonard Waldo, 'The Mechanical Art of American Watchmaking', *Journal of the Society of Arts*, 34/1 (21 May 1886) 740–51, at http://www.jstor.org/stable/23852799. An account of Ingold's earlier and later life is in G.A. Berner and E. Audétat (translated by Richard Watkins, 2008), 'Pierre Frédéric Ingold 1787–1878', *Schweizer Pioniere der Wirtschaft und Technik*, 13, 1962, at http://www.watkinsr.id.au/Ingold2.pdf

3 LMA/CLC/L/CD/E/006/MS03943/10-11: There were four versions. Subsequent quotes are from that of 28 October 1842.

4 R.F. and R.W. Carrington, 'Pierre Frederic Ingold and the British Watch and Clockmaking Company', *Antiquarian Horology*, 10/6 (1978), 98–714 (quote, 704).

5 Carrington, 'Ingold', 713.

6 H.G. Ward, letter to *The Times*, 13 April 1843 reported the national output of watches was less than 100,000 in 1841. It had approximately halved in fifty years.

7 E.L. Woodward, *The Age of Reform, 1815–70* (1939: Oxford: Clarendon, 1962 ed.), 604–05; Bishop C. Hunt, *The Development of the Business Corporation in England, 1800–1867* (1936; Cambridge, MA: Harvard UP, reprinted 1969), 89.

8 For Whitney see David A. Hounshell, *From the American System to Mass Production: the Development of Manufacturing Technology in the United States* (Baltimore, MD and London: Johns Hopkins UP, 1984), 30–34; Carroll W. Pursell, *The Machine in America: A Social History of Technology* (Baltimore, MD and London: Johns Hopkins UP, 1995), 87–90. For Brunel, see Carolyn C. Cooper, 'The Portsmouth System of Manufacture', *Technology and Culture* (1984), 25, 182–225. https://doi.org/10.2307/3104712. Marc Brunel had at one time been apprenticed to Abraham-Louis Breguet: see Derek Portman, 'Henry Marc Brunel: Civil Engineer', *Construction History*, 20 (2004), 71–83, at www.jstor.org/stable/41613878.

9 John Joseph Murphy, 'Entrepreneurship in the Establishment of the American Clock Industry', *Journal of Economic History*, 26 (June 1966), 169–86, at https://www.jstor.org/stable/2116226; also Fortunat F. Mueller-Maerki, 'Review of the Proceedings of a Colloquium on 'The American Challenge in Watchmaking', *Antiquarian Horology*, 33/3 (March 2012), 365–66.

10 Alun C. Davies, 'An Invasion in Time: American Horology and the British Market', *Antiquarian Horology* (2008), 30, 829–44.

11 David S. Landes, *Revolution in Time: Clocks and the Making of the Modern World* (Cambridge, MA., Belknap, Harvard UP, 1983), 293–94.

12 The Horological Students' Room in the British Museum houses the Ilbert Collection. It has watches, printed books, pamphlets, and photocopies of Swiss and French material relating to the Ingold episode.

13 David Penney, paper at the 23rd Annual NAWCC Seminar (October 2002), *NAWCC Supplement* No 5 (2005), and email, January 2009.

14 The *Crown and Anchor* tavern was reputedly where Lenin and Stalin met when in London in 1905.

15 *Watchmaker, Jeweller and Silversmith*, 10 (1884), 58–60.

16 Waldo, 'Mechanical Art of American Watchmaking', 740–51; remarks of William Frodsham in the discussion, 749.
17 Jill Chambers, *Buckinghamshire Machine Breakers– The Story of the 1830 Riots* (Letchworth: Jill Chambers, 1991); Adrian J. Randall, 'The "lessons" of Luddism', *Endeavour*, 22/4 (1998), 152–55, at https://doi.org/10.1016/S0160-9327(98)01145-4.
18 Adrian J. Randall, 'Reinterpreting "Luddism": Resistance to New Technology in the British Industrial Revolution', in Martin Bauer (ed.), *Resistance to New Technology: Nuclear Power, Information Technology, and Biotechnology* (Cambridge: Cambridge UP, 1995), 60–61; David Williams, *John Frost: A Study in Chartism* (Cardiff: University of Wales Press, 1939); id., *The Rebecca Riots, A Study in Agrarian Discontent* (Cardiff: University of Wales Press, 1955).
19 LMA/CLC/L/CD/E/006/MS03943/12, 13, 14, being 'Statement of the Origin and Progress of the BWCC presented to a Meeting convened for the purpose of inquiring into its Character and Pretensions'; 'Statement in support of the Bill for establishing the BWCC'; and 'Watch and Clock Manufacturers: Objections to "A Bill for forming and regulating a Company to be called the BWCC"'.
20 *The Times*, 24 October 5, 10, and 24 November 1842; 1 and 13 April 1853; *The Morning Herald*, 29 October and 4 November 1842. *The Standard* and *John Bull* reprinted earlier correspondence and comments.
21 Roger Smith, 'Vulliamy family (*per. c.* 1730–1886)', *ODNB*.
22 LMA/CLC/L/CD/E/006/MS03943/9: letter from Richard Paddington, Secretary of BWCC.
23 LMA/CLC/L/CD/E/006/MS03943/7, B.L. Vulliamy to W.J. Frodsham, October 31, 1842; and LMA/CLC/L/CD/E/006/MS03943/9: Richard Paddington to B.L. Vulliamy.
24 LMA/CLC/L/CD/E/006/MS03943/8: clipping from *Morning Herald*, 4 November 1842: letter opposing the scheme from nine leading chronometer houses, namely Parkinson & Frodsham; Barraud & Lund; McCabe & Co.; James Murray; Brockbank, Atkins & Son; Clement Harris; John Carter; John French; Hunter & Edwards. Also, *The Times*, 5 November 1842.
25 *The Times*, 13 April 1843, from H.G. Ward's letter.
26 On the reputational significance of the name 'Earnshaw' see Jonathan Betts, 'Thomas Earnshaw, 1749–1829', in *ODNB*. Thomas Earnshaw Junior died in 1854.
27 John Barwise, senior, 1790–1843; Clutton, et al., eds., *Britten's Old Clocks & Watches and their Makers* (London: Methuen, 9th ed., 1982), 363; also A.D. Stewart, 'Barwise & Sons: Watchmakers to the King. A Brief History of Family and Firm', *Antiquarian Horology*, 35/1 (March 2014), 621–34 (esp. 626–31).
28 PRO, BT: 334/2531 and LMA/CLC/L/CD/B/001/MS02710/001/8: WCC Court Minute Books, Vol. 8: 11 October 1841; also H.G. Ward's letter in *The Times*, 13 April 1843.
29 The firm was originally established by John Arnold and his son, John Roger.
30 L.C. Sanders rev. K.D. Reynolds, 'Alexander Douglas-Hamilton, tenth duke of Hamilton and Seventh Duke of Brandon and Chatelherault (1767–1852)', ODNB (2004); he was the premier peer in Scotland and claimed to be heir to its throne. His name as Patron disappeared from the last edition of the *Prospectus*.
31 LMA/CLC/L/CD/E/006/MS03943/11: List of intended agents for the BWCC.

32 *Hansard* (3rd ser.), LXVII: 31 March 1843 for subsequent quotations and paraphrases.
33 *BPP,* 1836/14: 'Report on the Commerce and Manufactures of Switzerland' by Sir John Bowring.
34 *The Times*, 13 April 1843, H.G. Ward's letter.
35 Matthew Lee, 'Thomas Slingsby Duncombe (1796–1861)'; D.T.W. Price, 'William Williams (1788– 1865)', both in *ODNB*. Williams was a radical Welsh politician, later famous in Wales for his role in the 1846 inquiry into Welsh education that gave rise to *'Brad y Llyfrau Gleision'* (the 'Treason of the Blue Books').
36 Bennett Woodcroft (ed.), *Alphabetical Index of Patentees of Inventions* (1854; London: Evelyn, Adams and Mackay, 1969 edn.): See applications for Patents Nos. 9511, 9752, 9993.
37 Linked with this was an unsuccessful attempt to enlist the support of George Biddle Airy, the Astronomer Royal. See Roger F. Carrington, 'The British Watch and Clock Making Company: Some Further Notes', *Antiquarian Horology*, 19 (1990), 44–46.
38 PRO, Board of Trade Papers, 1/407/44: Barwise to Gladstone, 6 April 1843 and 5/51/595, 8 April 1843; M.R.D. Foot and H.C.G Mathew (eds.) *The Gladstone Diaries, with Cabinet Minutes and Prime Ministerial Correspondence* (14 vols; 1968–94, Oxford: Clarendon), vol.3, 1840–47 (1974), 267, 269, 272, for meetings with the Clock Making Company, the Commons' debate, and letters.
39 G. Kitson Clark, 'Hunger and Politics in 1842', *Journal of Modern History*, 25 (1953), 355–74, at https://www.jstor.org/stable/i332166
40 Quoted in Bishop C. Hunt, *The Development of the Business Corporations in England, 1800–1867* (1936: Cambridge, MA: Harvard UP, reprinted 1969), 102.
41 *The Times*, 31 March 1843.
42 David Thompson, report of a lecture by David Penney, *Antiquarian Horology*, 29/1 (Sept. 2005), 98–99.
43 Alun C. Davies, 'Time for a Change? Technological Persistence in the British Watchmaking Industry', *Material History Review: Revue d'histoire de la culture materielle* (1992), 36/57–64, at https://journals.lib.unb.ca/index.php/MCR/article/view/17529
44 See S.J. Liebowitz and Stephen E. Margolis, 'Path Dependence, Lock-in, and History', *Journal of Law, Economics, & Organization,* 11/1 (April 1995), 205–26, at ttps://doi.org/10.1093/oxfordjournals.jleo.a036867.
Relevant theoretical discussions about modern technologies are in W. Brian Arthur, 'Competing Technologies, Increasing Returns, and Lock-In by Historical Events', *The Economic Journal*, 99 (394),1989, 116–31, at www.jstor.org/stable/2234208; and Robin Cowan, 'Tortoises and Hares: Choice Among Technologies of Unknown Merit', *The Economic Journal*, 101 (1991, 801–14, at www.jstor.org/stable/2233856
45 Alun C. Davies, 'British Watchmaking and the American system', *Business History*, 35 (1993), 40–54, at https://doi.org/10.1080/00076799300000003
46 BPP 1846–47 [8 & 9 Victoria: cap 86, section 68]: 'Foreign Clocks and Watches, made in imitation of the British, forbidden to be imported and warehoused and afterwards exported'. Smuggling as an issue faded as free trade triumphed.
47 LMA/CLC/L/CD/E/028/MS03944/92: Memorial from the Clockmakers Company, dated 5 August 1850.

48 BPP 1852, vol. 1: 'Second Report for the Commissioners for the Exhibition of 1851 and Appendix'. Also Christopher Hobhouse, *1851 and the Crystal Palace* (London: John Murray, 1851); K. Luckhurst, *The Story of Exhibitions* (London: Studio Publications, 1951).
49 [Great Exhibition, 1851], *Reports of the Juries*, II, Class Xb, 'Report on Horological Instruments', 731–45; also, Robert Hunt (ed.), *Hunt's Handbook to the Official Catalogues* (Clowes & Sons, 1851), Vol. 1, 314–35.
50 Edward Riddle, 'Report of the World's Exposition', in *Report of the Commissioner of Patents, 1851* (32 Congress: 1st Session: House Doc no. 102), 485; also Marcus Cunliffe, 'America at the Great Exhibition of 1851', *American Quarterly*, 3 (1951), 115–26, at http://www.jstor.org/stable/27557689; Merle Curti, 'America at the World's Fairs, 1851–1893', *American Historical Review*, 55 (1950), 833–56, at http://dx.doi.org/10.2307/1841163.
51 BPP 1854–55 50: 'Report of the Committee on the Machinery of the United States'. Nathan Rosenberg (ed.), *The American System of Manufactures: Report of the Committee on the Machinery of the United States, 1854–55* (Edinburgh: Edinburgh UP, 1969). Also *BPP*, 1854, vol. 36: New York Industrial Exhibition. Reports (a) of British Commissioners; (b) of Wallis on manufacturing; (c) of Whitworth on machinery) on, inter alia, the extent of standardisation and interchangeability in making American small arms and clocks.
52 Marcus Cunliffe, 'America at the Great Exhibition', 115–26; also Peter Temin, 'Labor Scarcity and the Problem of American Industrial Efficiency in the 1850's', *The Journal of Economic History*, 26/3 (Sep. 1966), 277–98, at https://www.jstor.org/stable/2115648; and Davies, 'British Watchmaking and the American System', 40–54.
53 Ann G. Imlah, *Britain and Switzerland 1845–60: A Study of Anglo-Swiss Relations During Some Critical Years for Swiss Neutrality* (London: Longmans, 1966), 107–08; *Horological Journal*, 6 (1864), 57–58; and *Horological Journal*, 7 (1865), 103.
54 *Horological Journal*, 4 (May 1862), 101.
55 Sir John Harold Clapham, *An Economic History of Modern Britain* (3 Vols, Cambridge: Cambridge UP, 1926–38), Vol. 3, 15–16.
56 'Fourteen Years Statistics of the English Clock and Watch Trade', *Horological Journal*, 23 (April 1881), 102–07. These carry statistics for 1850–63 and 1864–67; original returns are in *BPP*, 1864, 58: Return of the number and value of watch cases (gold and silver) assayed and marked ... from 1850 to 1863; and 1867, 64: Return of the number of gold and silver watch cases marked ... also the computed number of watches imported since the last return made .... (1864–66).
57 LMA/CLC/L/CD/E/028/MS03944/93: Memorial, to the Treasury, on foreign clocks and watches, 1 April 1852; Atkins and Overall, *Clockmakers*, 337–38.
58 *The Times*, 9 June 1852.
59 Atkins & Overall, *Clockmakers*, 338–39, George A. Hamilton to the Clockmakers' Company, 16 Nov. 1852.
60 Extrapolated from Ralph Davis, *The Industrial Revolution and British Overseas Trade* (Leicester: Leicester UP, 1979), 14, 27: Table: 'Value of Exports'.
61 Disraeli's December 1852 budget is discussed in H.C.G. Matthew, 'Disraeli, Gladstone, and the Politics of Mid-Victorian Budgets', *The Historical Journal*, 22/3 (Sep. 1979), 615–43 (esp. 621–25), at https://www.jstor.org/stable/i324990

62 John R. McCulloch, *A Dictionary, Practical, Theoretical and Historical of Commerce and Commercial Navigation* (London: Longmans, 2nd ed., 1859). Tariffs on clocks, 291 and 1276; on watches, 1284.

63 For an overview, see Peter J. Cain, 'British Free Trade: Economics and Policy, 1850–1914', *Refresh: Recent Findings of Research in Economic & Social History* (1999), at https://files.ehs.org.uk/wp-content/uploads/2020/07/29061005/Cain29a.pdf

64 Peter Temin. 'Two Views of the British Industrial Revolution', *The Journal of Economic History*, 57/1 (March 1997), 79, at www.jstor.org/stable/2951107

10 Meeting the Challenge

Chronometers in War and Peace, 1793–1860

Chronometers during wartime: demand and supply, 1793–1815

Watchmaking's chronometer manufacturing sector was emerging from its first phase of development when war with France broke out in 1793. Following Harrison's success with H4 and Kendall's copies in the 1760s, a few watchmaking firms with well-established workshops had begun to supply what was at first a small market. Demand was limited because of the expense of the first instruments, uncertainty about how reliable they were, and the continuation of the old ways of navigation. The few firms that made the new instruments were led by Arnold, Earnshaw, Brockbank, Barraud, and Pennington.[1] Much of the initial demand for the instruments came from captains and officers of Britain's East India Company (EIC). It was the largest trading company in the world and then carried about half of Britain's overseas trade. On over 500 voyages between 1770 and 1792, it pioneered the instrument's use, and its printed logbooks had special spaces for entries of 'longitudes determined by chronometer'. Its captains could afford the high price of chronometers because of the profits they made from private trading.[2] Few other merchant marines followed the EIC's practice until much later. Even officers in the EIC's rival, the Dutch East India Company, regarded chronometers as of secondary importance, as a back-up to supplement traditional 'rule of thumb' navigation methods. National navies, too, were slow to enter the market: the Dutch Admiralty, for example, included chronometers as part of their standard issue to navigators only when its flotillas sailed to the East and West Indies.[3] Although some navigators gradually accepted chronometers, most continued using lunar distances to help determine longitude. In the Royal Navy, chronometers were not part of the standard provision when the Admiralty fitted out ships until 1822 (below). Even when a privately owned instrument was on board, 'dead reckoning' (estimating speed, direction, and time) and lunar observations were continued as checks on chronometer readings. The time-consuming deduction of longitudinal position by lunar observation remained as an important part of a British naval officer's

DOI: 10.4324/9781003227823-12

training; exclusive reliance on chronometers was deemed risky, because of possible mechanical failure. Until then, demand for the instruments came from individuals who could afford them and had learned how to use them. During the wars with France many officers, but not all (as we shall see later) bought chronometers privately.[4]

Nevertheless, we can presume that, during the wars, demand for chronometers from naval officers grew. This proposition is supported by rough estimations of production during the war years which indicate that, between them, Arnold and Earnshaw made over 2,000 box and pocket chronometers. Paul Philip Barraud's firm made probably about 1,000 'chronometers and clocks' between 1796 and 1820, and approximately 10,000 'pocket watches' (not all would necessarily have had a chronometer escapement).[5] Brockbank's firm accounted for about 280 chronometers per annum (and about 2,200 watches, at an annual rate of about 150). A.D. Stewart's estimate of the approximate number of chronometers made between 1800 and 1820 (most years which spanned the wars with France) suggests that the four leading makers (Brockbank, Barraud, Arnold, and Earnshaw) made about 1,410 marine (box) chronometers and almost 2,500 pocket chronometers.[6] Although chronometers were a tiny fraction (under 1 per cent of the estimated aggregate output of 2 million watches made in Europe between 1790 and 1815) deck or ordinary watches were probably used by officers in the Royal Navy.[7] The possible extent of such demand may be gleaned from the growth in the numbers of ships and personnel. Britain's warships increased from about 125 in 1793 to over 400 by 1815. Recruits increased from 45,000 sailors and marines in 1793 to over 144,000 by 1815. To pay for this, the navy's annual budget rose from just over £4 million in 1793 to about £20 million by Waterloo. By then, the Royal Navy had become by far the largest navy in the world.[8] By contrast, France's navy at the start of the war had 152 warships but ended with only ninety-two in 1815. About 150 captured French vessels were added to the Royal Navy. If chronometers had been lost on board a sunken ship, a demand for replacements followed.

Fusee chains

Details of the use of chronometers during the war remain unclear. But the first instance of problems concerning the instruments came within a few years of the outbreak of war, when the handful of English chronometer makers faced a predicament. It was caused by uncertainty about the supply of fusee chains to make new instruments. It was a problem quite different from that caused by Pitt's taxes. Its context was the growing demand for more navigational instruments. As the war proceeded, firms that made sextants, telescopes, and compasses naturally became busier.[9]

But for the few firms that made chronometers, an unusual problem arose because of uncertainty about the supply of fusee chains, a crucial component. Fusee chains for watches, clocks, and chronometers are like miniscule versions of bicycle chains: they varied in length from five to ten inches and contained 14.9 links per inch. The *Horological Journal* later explained that they were 'not thicker than a horse's hair and the separate links can just be perceived by the naked eye. Modern invention has yet discovered no substitute for the chain equal to it in slenderness, strength and flexibility'.[10] Simple tools -files, punches, dies, miniature hammers, and anvils – made the links. It was an intricate craft process that needed good eyesight and special patience.

Although there was reputedly a supplier in Clerkenwell, most fusee chains had been made in Switzerland. War made reliance on such sources uncertain.[11] A potential crisis was averted when a watchmaker, Robert Harvey Cox, organised a reliable supply. He established an extraordinary cottage industry that specialised in making the single component – fusee chains – in Christchurch (then in Hampshire, now in Dorset). Christchurch was a village with a population of about 300 in 1801; thereafter, it supplied fusee chains to English makers until the Great War.[12] Cox's enterprise obviated a crisis for England's chronometer firms, but it had unsavoury consequences. Because the skills involved in their construction were limited, children could be trained for the task. Young girls with small fingers and a 'delicate touch' proved ideal recruits. Cox employed forty to fifty pauper children from parish poorhouses in Christchurch and neighbouring Wimborne (ten miles to the north-west, in Dorset). It was claimed they 'would otherwise have been a burden not only to their families but perhaps to the parish'. Cox maintained that they might earn 'on average four to five shillings a week'.[13] In reality, evidence from his workhouse contracts between 1801 and 1804 showed that only about 1s 6d per week was paid and in 1805 and 1806 the rate of 'pay' dropped to 9d per week. Even then, payments did not go directly to the girls – aged nine years and upwards – but into a general workhouse fund. It constituted a ruthless exploitation of child labour. An indication of the continuation and extent of the abuse can be seen in the growth of the chronometer sector during the war: by 1807 over a hundred children were so employed. The growing recognition of the importance of chronometers led their makers in 1808 to argue that laws must be introduced explicitly to protect the instruments.[14] There can be little doubt that the fusee chain enterprise – an unforeseen side-effect of the war – constituted an example of pauper child labour – a feature of Britain's early industrial revolution that spread well beyond mills and mines.[15] Nevertheless, Christchurch remained an astonishing anachronism as English chronometer makers' supplier of fusee chains.[16] It remained so until the Great War (Chapter 17).

Publicity helps demand

During the war years, the supply of chronometers and knowledge of how to use them was advanced by favourable publicity about the instrument's merits. An early example was Captain George Vancouver's account of Britain's fourth great expedition in his *Voyage of Discovery to the North Pacific Ocean, and Round the World in the Years 1791–95* (completed in six volumes by his brother John in 1798).[17] Vancouver's odyssey was longer than Cooke's three earlier voyages, and it offered convincing evidence of the reliability of chronometers in determining longitudes on lengthy transoceanic expeditions.[18] Other books and pamphlets augmented this publicity. Expert instruction on how to use chronometers for navigation classes was in Joseph Whidbey's *Remarks on Timekeepers* (1799). A year later William Wales, veteran navigator of Cook's second voyage, re-edited his 1794 handbook *The Method of Finding Longitude at Sea.*[19] Both accounts guided navigators in the day-to-day use and care of the instrument. Pamphlets by leading chronometer makers also promoted the instruments' merits, notably Thomas Earnshaw's *Longitude: an appeal to the public* in 1808 with its section on 'Their Superior Going in Numerous Voyages'.[20] In the following year, James Horsborough's enormous *Directions for Sailing the Oriental Seas* stressed that chronometers 'would be highly useful for the improvement of geography' with the argument that navigators should adopt [like the EIC] 'a uniform method in marking in their journals the longitude obtained by these excellent machines'.[21] All these publications made navigators better informed and, indirectly, invigorated suppliers of chronometers.

Because the Admiralty did not issue chronometers to its officers during the war; their ownership remained a private matter. It is not known how many officers used them, but many could afford to buy them, especially if they had once been with the EIC before joining the Royal Navy. Annual salaries of between £100 and £300 allowed the Royal Navy's officer class of Masters, Lieutenants, and Commanders to afford a good watch. Salaries of leading captains ranged from £300 to £800 annually, depending upon their ship's rate. This enabled some to buy more expensive box chronometers, especially if they topped up their pay with prize money.[22] If not an essential accessory, they must have been desirable. Chronometers were evidently not issued to the fleets that blockaded the Bay of Biscay between 1794 and 1813, but some officers carried their own.[23] Nelson bought good quality watches with prize money earned from his victories. After he secured promotion from Commodore to Rear Admiral at Cape St Vincent, he gave his watch to Joseph Haydn, the composer. [In return, Haydn composed his *Missa in Angustiis*, the 'Nelson Mass'.[24]] At Trafalgar, Nelson carried a better one, by Josiah Emery.[25] Before hostilities, he ordered that officers who had watches

Figure 10.1 Nelson's watch at Trafalgar. Copyright: © National Maritime Museum, Greenwich, London.

should synchronise them with his own (Figure 10.1). The inscription on the case now reads:

> The chronometer of Horatio Viscount Nelson worn by him at the bottle of Trafalgar, placed in this case by his niece Charlotte Mary Lady Bridport, to be preserved for any one of her descendants who may enter the navy.

French and British strategies to stimulate supply

Both major protagonists took initiatives explicitly to stimulate their own chronometer production. The French led the way during the fourteen-month interval of peace in 1802–03 of the Treaty of Amiens. France's chronometer manufacturing sector had developed from the pioneering contributions of Pierre Le Roy and Ferdinand Berthoud. In 1780, Berthoud's apprentice Jacques Vincent Martin had been given a post at Brest as *Horloger de la Marine* to oversee chronometers issued to the navy. But the numbers of available instruments were few and output was low. Berthoud's workshop made about eighty chronometers, including thirty-one for the government.[26] Although Napoleon was mostly preoccupied with land wars (his army grew to over 600,000), nevertheless, to improve his maritime resources in 1804, he centralised the supply of chronometers (like much else) in an *École d'Horlogerie,* established as part of the *École des Arts et Métiers.* It fostered horological talent with an annual grant of 10,000 francs by stipulating that five pupils were to be instructed in chronometer making. It was part of a broad effort to strengthen France's watchmaking industry that led to the Paris industrial exhibition in 1806.[27] But output remained low, until Ferdinand Berthoud was succeeded by his nephew Louis as Horologist to the Observatory and to the Board of Longitude in Paris. Louis Berthoud made about another 160 instruments and, of the forty-two known to have survived, most were constructed during the war years and, it may be presumed, some were used by the French navy.[28]

France's strategy to increase output was to concentrate production in the *École.* The British approach was different. It opted for open competition between existing and putative chronometer makers. The Admiralty announced in March 1805 that it wanted 'to purchase Timekeepers for the use of His Majesty's ships' following two trials. One, onshore, would last three months to establish the instrument's 'rate of going' (a known daily rate of losing or gaining that could be factored into subsequent readings). Then a sea trial would follow, lasting between four and six months on a ship sailing to somewhere with an 'already ascertained' longitude. If trial chronometers did not err by more than four, six, or eight minutes (an error of 1, 1½, or 2 degrees of longitude) the three best instruments might then be bought by the Admiralty at the attractive prices of 100, 80, and 60 guineas.[29] To encourage competition and entice new makers the Board published *Explanations of Time-Keepers constructed by Mr Thomas Earnshaw and the late Mr John Arnold* in 1806. It described the methods of construction followed by the instrument's two illustrious pioneers.[30] Thus blueprints were in effect available to watchmakers who bought a copy and possessed or acquired the appropriate skills. It helped to lift the veil of uncertainty about their construction that hitherto might have deterred potential makers. *Explanations of Time-Keepers* became a crucial reference source for aspiring makers of chronometers and the navigators who used them. The strategy of financial inducement and open competition was like – but less expensive than – that which had successfully encouraged Harrison's H4.

How effective were the rival approaches? The war's most crucial naval battle occurred off Cape Trafalgar, a headland in Spain, in October 1805. The battle happened before either of the protagonists' new production strategies could be implemented. For France, the *École d'Horlogerie* did not offer a quick resolution – it did not become a magic policy that changed the outcome of war at sea. The French lost the sea war because their fleets were outmanoeuvred and outgunned in close encounters, and not because of the presence or absence of chronometers. Napoleon later claimed he had always believed in the importance of chronometers in naval warfare as he, famously, revealed to a surgeon who saw him in St Helena. When he asked if the visiting British ship had a government chronometer, the surgeon replied in the negative. Napoleon thought the vessel might have missed the island for the want of one.

> How shameful it is ... for your government to put three or four hundred men on board of a ship for this place without a chronometer ... for the sake of saving three or four hundred francs [then about £12 to £16] for a watch. I ordered every ship employed in the French service should be supplied with one. [31]

His apparent enthusiasm had made no difference to the outcomes of his navy's battles. After Trafalgar, the Royal Navy 'controlled the seas of the world with an iron hand'.[32] But, for the rest of the war, chronometers were not conspicuously crucial to the resolution of sea battles. The decisive clashes at Cape St. Vincent, the Nile, Cadiz, Copenhagen, and Trafalgar all took place between the Baltic and the Mediterranean, in relatively familiar European and Mediterranean waters, whether their navigators had – or had not – used chronometers to get there. But chronometers may have helped ships to arrive at distant theatres of war, in the East Indies and the western Atlantic. The war of 1812 with the United States was played out across immense distances from Britain's home waters. It ranged across many thousands of miles, from the Great Lakes and the St Lawrence River down the eastern seaboard to the Gulf of Mexico. Although all navigators were trained in lunar navigation, it is possible that captains availed themselves of the latest navigational instruments, even if they had had to pay for them.[33]

Because it was left to individuals to buy chronometers, the precise consequences of the British Admiralty's production strategy remain unclear. Annual increases of chronometer output are not known but Henry Clarke's *Census* for the Clockmakers' Company in 1813 revealed that, among over a thousand persons connected with London's watch trade, nine were explicitly described as 'chronometer-manufacturers'. They were the firms of Arnold, Barraud, Robert Cooke, J.M. French, Frodsham & Baker, Thomas Grignon, Grimaldi & Johnson, James Hutton, and Richard Price. Clarke's list was not comprehensive, for it did not include the Brockbanks, Pennington, Earnshaw, and others.[34] Some independent craftsmen like William Howells, induced by high prices and profits, bought instruments from major firms, 'finished' them, put their name on the dial and thereafter designated themselves 'chronometer-makers'. Howells was not on Clarke's list, but he evidently made a few chronometers for others to 'name' and sell.[35] His activities indicate the complexity of chronometer manufacturing. But not all Royal Navy officers had a chronometer in the war years, or knew how they could be used, as became evident in Britain's greatest maritime catastrophe.

Disaster in the Baltic, 1811

The biggest losses of British ships and lives during the war with France happened in 1811. It was the worst naval catastrophe since Sir Clowdesley Shovel's ships had sunk off the Scillies a century earlier. It occurred not because of a naval battle but was an unforeseen, indirect, consequence of Napoleon's attempts to block Britain's trade with the Baltic. To protect that trade the Royal Navy routinely provided convoy escorts, for timber and tar were vital for building and repairing British ships. In winter 1811, a merchant fleet of 129 vessels was escorted by eight Royal Navy ships of the line. Seas around the Baltic coast were hazardous, with hidden reefs. Five vessels, including two major warships with almost their entire companies of 2,000 sailors, foundered in gale-force storms on Haak Sandbank, off Jutland. The loss accounted for twice the number of sailors that died at the battles of Cape St. Vincent, Nile, Copenhagen, and Trafalgar.[36] The calamity was ascribed to a navigational error. It prompted a letter to *The Naval Chronicle* from 'A Captain in the Royal Navy' who attributed the losses of the *Minotaur, St George, Defence, Hero,* and *Grasshopper* to 'the want of timekeepers to ascertain their longitude ... Can it be believed', he lamented, 'that if there had been only one good chronometer on board the *Hero* or the *Grasshopper*, that they could have made a mistake of near two degrees and a half, or ten minutes of time, in their longitude?' He calculated that ships of the entire fleet of the line could be supplied each with two chronometers (at an estimated cost, then, of about £100 an instrument), good sextants, and marine barometers for the next ten years, all at a cost less than 'the value of these two ships alone, to say nothing of the [rest of the] convoy, or men's lives'.[37] The Baltic catastrophe resulted in greater damage to national security than any sea battles. Yet its consequences were not acted upon by the Admiralty for another decade.

Peace and the Greenwich trials

The catastrophe of 1811 was not forgotten, but it took more than a decade for the Admiralty to change its policy and issue chronometers to all its ships. To encourage the continued supply of chronometers the Astronomer Royal, John Pond, instituted annual competitive trials in 1822. Chronometer trials had been held intermittently at Greenwich since the 1760s, to test H4 and other instruments.[38] The new trials enabled Pond to 'purchase, annually, chronometers that kept the best time' [measured for their accuracy by a regulator] for £300 and the second best for £200.[39] In 1828 the terms were modified, adjusting awards for the best three at £200, £170, and £130, respectively. In the lists of annual entrants after 1823, some crossed-out entries suggest that occasionally instruments were 'withdrawn', maybe because they were performing poorly in the early stages before the Trials were completed. A poor performance might damage a maker's reputation: better, perhaps, that an instrument was removed for fine-tuning and re-entered in the next year.

The Admiralty's initiative succeeded. It offered makers an incentive to encourage improvements in quality and enabled the Royal Navy to have the first choice of the best instruments. Potential purchasers – the Admiralty or independent merchant navigators – now had a seemingly objective measure of an instrument's quality. The number of makers who competed every year increased, and at least eighty-two different 'makers' (mostly with London addresses) participated between 1822 and 1835. This exaggerated the number of firms capable of assembling and 'finishing' instruments from Prescot's rough movements because several 'makers' acquired basic models from a few specialist firms' that they then 'finished' and then engraved their own names on the dials. Parkinson & Frodsham, for example, claimed that they had supplied twenty basic instruments to 'different watchmakers' for finishing and that four of the best ten chronometers in 1833 were made by them but entered under other names.[40] Indeed, Robert and Henry Molyneux protested that Richard Webster of Cornhill took third place with a chronometer made by Parkinson & Frodsham. The complaint succeeded. Pond held an enquiry, found the inscription 'Frodsham' on Webster's movement, and disqualified him. He then promoted the Molyneux brothers from their fourth position to take the £100 third prize.[41]

Although the Webster-Molyneux episode temporarily halted the annual Trials, nevertheless the prizes had encouraged production. By 1835, the Admiralty's stock amounted to 356 instruments made by more than fifty different 'makers'. Pond thought that they had also stimulated an improvement in quality and commented that 'the six first on the list would have obtained the first prize in former years'.[42] [A century later Commander Gould queried Pond's endorsement and observed that by then 'no marked improvement [was] shown, nor any new invention or discovery brought to light'.[43]] However, competition had indeed stimulated output and lowered prices. After 1828 the Trials attracted a record number of seventy-eight instruments, several priced between 60 and 75 guineas. Pond explained to the Admiralty why he thought these prices were too high and could fall further:

> Chronometer makers, in affixing a price for their chronometers, are governed by their own discretion. On some former occasions I have been directed by their Lordships to offer lower prices ... I have reason to believe that some of the makers of the chronometers in question will take less than the sums announced.[44]

Pond's enthusiasm for the Trials was not shared by his successor as Astronomer Royal, George Biddell Airy, who suspended them in 1836. This was, Airy complained, because the 'chronometer business' at Greenwich had 'developed excessively'. Up to a third of the valuable time of his staff was devoted to the 'tedious business of 'rating' the chronometers. Meanwhile, the Observatory's stockpile grew. Moreover, finding that the Trial prizes cost £500, Airy deemed it a recurring budgetary expense that no longer offered good value. For the same outlay perhaps ten good chronometers might be bought? His prudence proved correct.[45]

Thanks to Pond, Airy, and the Greenwich Trials, England's chronometer manufacturing sector continued to prosper, in contrast to its parent, watchmaking. (When similar trials for watches were eventually inaugurated at Kew it was too late to prevent English watchmaking's decline.) The biggest customers for chronometers were the Royal Navy and Britain's merchant marine. A consequence of the success of the chronometer manufacturing sector was its undoubted contribution to the role of the Royal Navy and the merchant marine in securing Britain's commercial and economic hegemony in the nineteenth century. Britain's global influence had begun during earlier centuries, long before the invention of chronometers. But, after Waterloo, the chronometer sector helped Britain's merchant marine to dominate the world's transoceanic commerce. Raw materials (cotton, timber, and silk) were imported to the 'workshop of the world', and manufactured goods were exported. Among the exports were many English-made chronometers but, alas for its parent industry, few English watches were sold abroad (Chapter 16).

Old and new customers for chronometers

The post-war growth in overseas trade boosted the demand for chronometers, and the instrument's earlier customers reappeared. They were headed by the Board of Longitude, whose need for chronometers for expeditions had been suspended during the war (apart from Mathew Flinders' expedition to Australia).[46] After Waterloo, the Board determined to resume its surveys and continue mapping hitherto uncharted coastlines, including plotting Britain's transoceanic trade routes.[47] Eventually, their wide-ranging maps, unmatched by any other country, gave invaluable navigational data to Britain's merchant ships. The Board's acquisition of even relatively modest numbers of new instruments was important to chronometer makers because it helped instil confidence in establishing longitude by chronometer. As the stock of instruments increased, so did the numbers taken on later surveys and expeditions. On his first great voyage of exploration fifty years earlier, Captain Cook had navigated by rule of thumb. On his second, he took an observatory regulator to check the going rates of K1 (Larcum Kendall's first copy of H4) and three Arnold chronometers. On his third, he took K3 (Kendall's third copy), one of the five chronometers also taken by Vancouver for his expedition between 1791 and 1794.[48] Flinders, too, had taken five: the use of chronometers combined with lunar observations helped him to achieve scientific accuracy in his charting of coastal Australia.[49]

The published records of these expeditions revealed the convenience and reliability of establishing longitude by chronometer. The advantage of carrying several came if some broke down or performed erratically, as had happened with Vancouver's Earnshaw's chronometer No. 1514.[50] Erratic readings from one instrument out of several were easy to identify and discount.[51] Some instruments could be assigned to the inshore survey boats if they were 'not being used for navigation and determining meridian distances'. Thus, John Ross took thirteen to the Arctic in 1818. One was his own, three belonged to his astronomer, five came from the Admiralty and three more were lent by Parkinson & Frodsham, keen for publicity.[52] Captain Sabine, astronomer on Parry's expedition to search for the Northwest Passage in 1819, carried fourteen; in 1821 Captain W.H. Smyth, mapping the Mediterranean, took five by Arnold and three by Parkinson & Frodsham. Like makers of other navigational instruments, leading chronometer manufacturers advertised on trade cards about where they might be cleaned, adjusted, or rated.[53] Firms that were willing to lend several instruments for long expeditions competed to promote their products in advertising pamphlets or in articles for naval journals.[54] To aid Dr John Tiarks' survey to establish Madeira's longitude, the Board instructed Pond to 'send to the island ten or twelve (as you may judge proper) of the best going chronometers now under your charge, in the care of a proper person'. Pond allocated fifteen instruments in 1822.[55] Between 1821 and 1826, Captain Richard Owen used fifteen chronometers to survey and record positions of hundreds of coastal promontories along several thousand miles of African coasts. Owen compiled nearly 300 'accurate charts and a table of latitudes and longitudes that were used for many decades afterwards' and filled in some of the 'most significant gaps in the navy's charts of the world'.[56] Clearly, the more chronometers carried on a survey or expedition, the better. Robert Fitzroy took twenty-two on the *Beagle*. They included seventeen box and five pocket chronometers; eleven were government-owned, and six were FitzRoy's own.[57] By 1832, the authors of *A Very Brief Account of the Chronometer*, wrote that 'the very general adoption of the Chronometer, particularly in long voyages, is the best proof of its value; and it is more than probable, that, in a very few years, no vessel will sail without one'.[58] In the late 1830s, batches of Dent's chronometers, set to Greenwich time, were sent by the Astronomer Royal to check the longitudes of major observatories in the British Isles (Edinburgh, Dublin, Armagh, Oxford, Cambridge, Portsmouth) and abroad (Paris, Hamburg, and New York).[59] The stock of the Admiralty's instruments grew steadily. The longitude of Valencia – Ireland's most westerly point – was determined in 1844 with the loan of thirty chronometers: five were from Dent, two each from both Parkinson & Frodsham and Charles Frodsham, and four were from Molyneux. Ten others, also by Molyneux, were loaned from the collection of the wealthy amateur astronomer, the Rev. Richard Sheepshanks.[60] The other half-dozen were government-owned.[61] Thirty years later, Lord Lindsay took fifty with him to determine the longitude of Mauritius.[62] Their extensive use on expeditions was made possible by the Admiralty's large stock of instruments, in turn a consequence of the increase in their manufacture.

The steadily growing reputation of the reliability of chronometers for navigation owed much to the benign influence of an individual not directly connected with their production. Lieutenant Henry Raper (1799–1859) helped to expound their practical utility by publishing the accumulated longitudinal findings of navigators. His life's work was to coordinate the publication of longitudes determined by the expeditions of the 1820s and 1830s. He cumulated the results of over 200 maritime 'secondary meridians' that were believed to be reliably established on five continents. Eighteen places had longitudes accepted as 'thoroughly determined'. He also listed where 'rates' of chronometers might be confidently checked.[63] Raper published his results in instalments from 1839 in *The Nautical Magazine and Naval Chronicle*. Eventually, they were consolidated in his *magnum opus*, tables of maritime positions published as *The Practice of Navigation and Nautical Astronomy*. After 1840 copies were issued to all ships of the Royal Navy and the East India Company. This lent authority to its wider use by the rest of the merchant marine.[64]

Along with the coastline surveys led by the Board of Longitude, an old client, the market was widened by some new customers. Compared with the demand from ships, that from land surveys was much smaller. Nevertheless, they were important for the favourable publicity they created about the merits of the instruments. Box chronometers with large movements in gymbals were as easily carried on land as at sea and obviated the need for cumbersome tent observatories (like those used by Cook and Vancouver) in which longcase regulators might take several days to be set up and 'settle'. Chronometers were used in surveys of two of the world's then largest unmapped territories and, no doubt, in others. The Great Trigonometrical Survey of India started in 1802 and lasted over seventy years. As part of Britain's Empire, India was regarded as a portion of her 'home market'. The theodolites and box chronometers used to establish longitudes were English-made – an understandable continuation of the EIC's use of English-made chronometers on its ships.[65] The scientific consequences of the survey of India were impressive: permanent observatories were established for the chronometers to be serviced and rated. Later, the building of India's railways created a need for master clocks, to which ordinary clocks and watches were synchronised.

Of the 'known' ninety-odd chronometers bought by the EIC and the Indian government before 1860, sixty were by English firms; Dent led with twelve, Parkinson & Frodsham supplied ten and Cummins and McCabe eight each. Earnshaw, Barraud, and Arnold were not far behind. Individual sales in ones and twos came from Margetts, Brockbank, Harris, Tobias, Fletcher and Charles Frodsham. English chronometer makers enjoyed favoured access to these customers. Of the 1500 box chronometers supplied to the EIC and the government of India over a century, nearly all were probably English made.

President Jefferson's purchase from France of the Louisiana territory in 1803 nearly doubled the area of the new United States. In the great land survey that the President subsequently commissioned, only one chronometer was used in the mapping expedition commanded by Merewether Lewis and William Clarke. Initially, the surveyors intended to determine longitude by the lunar method, using an equatorial telescope (one that compensated for the Earth's rotation). Instead, perhaps knowing of the use of chronometers on the contemporary survey of India, Captain Lewis carried an Arnold chronometer for which he was specially trained in its use.[66] Although demand for land surveys amounted to a small portion of the market for chronometers, knowledge of their use in India and America reinforced favourable publicity of their merits.

Foreign competition

Most of the demand for chronometers came from shipping engaged in transoceanic trade; as that trade increased, it motivated the firms able to supply them. Because Britain commanded so much of the world's trade, it greatly favoured England's chronometer makers, especially those who had pioneered during the early stages of the instrument's development. Unlike watchmaking, its parent industry, chronometer makers faced relatively weak foreign competition. Switzerland's watches may have conquered Britain's home and export markets in the nineteenth century, but the landlocked Swiss had no navy to initiate demand for Swiss chronometers. (Later in the century its best makers excelled in pocket chronometers. Chapter 16.) Elsewhere in Europe, excellent chronometers were made by Le Roy in Paris, Urban Jurgensen in Copenhagen, and Andreas Hohwu in Amsterdam. After Waterloo, their national markets for chronometers were limited: the transoceanic trade of their national merchant marines was small compared with that of Britain. So, too, with most other European countries that had horological industries. Germany's north coastal trade was mainly confined to the Baltic and North Sea, where its merchant ships had less need of instruments for transoceanic navigation. By 1860, fewer than 200 Prussian ships had chronometers, and most of those were English. Until German horology became self-sufficient in the early twentieth century, firms that made or serviced its chronometers depended on English instruments.[67] Similarly, the United States' leading chronometer specialists – Bliss, and Negus, of New York City – sold and serviced English instruments. Bond of Boston was supplied by Morris Tobias's nephew in Liverpool, who handled exports of new and used instruments.[68] British ships dominated transoceanic trade and English makers consequently enjoyed the largest share of the world's limited demand for box chronometers.

Supply in the 1840s and 1850s

When Airy resumed the Greenwich Trials in 1840 new, more rigorous, stipulations were applied. Henceforth, trials would be carried out at room temperature to enable a daily rate and, from them, weekly averages were calculated.[69] The reforms stimulated energetic competition amongst leading makers, notably Arnold & Dent, Parkinson & Frodsham, Barraud & Lund, Brockbank, Atkins, and McCabe. They were followed by a dozen smaller firms that included Clement Harris, John Carter, John French, Hunter & Edwards, Cummins & McCabe, Margetts, Harris, Tobias, Fletcher, and James Murray.[70] Stricter requirements at the Trials were reinforced in 1849 when a six-week oven test was introduced, at temperatures between 75 and 100 degrees Fahrenheit (21–37 degrees Celsius). A cold box test was added later.[71] The trials still allowed – and rewarded – 'any important improvement' in either principle or construction which might advance performance or reduce cost.[72] But no prizes were guaranteed, only the distinction of winning and the likelihood – not a promise – that the Admiralty would buy the best instruments. Airy's new policy cleverly retained the prestige and incentive of the Trials whilst cutting their cost. It directly stimulated output and led to lower prices and better-quality instruments.

Static technology and longevity

The easy access to the market enjoyed by England's leading firms was helped by the longevity of box chronometers. Chronometers were not rendered obsolete by dramatic technical innovations. After about 1820 the instrument's technology was stabilised and the market for new instruments was limited. Incremental improvements might be added to basic models when instruments were serviced or refurbished. Early efforts to achieve the chimera of mechanical perfection failed, notably those that attempted to solve the problem of 'middle-temperature errors' (temperature fluctuations that affected a chronometer's performance). John Gottlieb Ulrich's efforts to eliminate such variations were judged by Astronomer Royal George Airy as 'perhaps the most remarkable instance of misapplied ingenuity which was ever seen. It is utterly useless'. [A century later Rupert Gould described Ulrich's escapement as 'the most complicated escapement ... ever devised ... very expensive to make and very difficult to adjust'.[73]] More effective than Ulrich was James Sweetman Eiffe, whose efforts earned an Admiralty award of £300 in 1842.[74] Probably the most successful improvement was Airy's own. It later enabled Victor Kullberg to include it for an extra £2 5s and engrave on the dial the words 'with Airy's Supplementary Compensation'.[75] Minor refurbishments were important because they extended the life of old instruments without rendering them obsolete. Improvements that helped performance included better oil, instead of the 'vastly inferior vegetable oils' used at first, that made pivots glutinous. [Napoleon is alleged to have asked Breguet to 'give me the perfect watch'; Breguet is said to have replied 'Give me the perfect oil, and I will give you the perfect watch'.] Better knowledge of preparing oil came in 1810 with the explanation that the best olive oil should be 'washed with water five or six times, then left undisturbed for three or four months'.[76] But problems with oil persisted, and in the 1820s the Society of Arts offered a 'Gold Medal or Fifty Guineas' for those who invented or discovered 'the best oil for chronometers or watches'.[77]

The mostly static technology of chronometers meant their working lives could be extended. As the numbers of navy and merchant ships increased in size, weight, and number, new chronometers were not needed to keep pace. Old chronometers were renovated and transferred to new ships. Vaudrey Mercer's survey of the Chronometer Ledgers at Greenwich revealed that some individual instruments worked for between fifty to eighty years, longer than the lifetimes of most of the ships on which they served.[78] Like many other products made in Victorian Britain, the best box chronometers were exceptionally well-made. Their longevity limited new demand. A 'replacement demand' could not be created by changing colour or style as, for example, with modern automobiles.

Business successes and failures

Making mechanisms capable of accuracy to within a few seconds a month under variable sea conditions was an uncertain and difficult business. Chronometers were the most complex of all 'high-technology' pre-industrial mechanisms. It is not known how many firms between 1820 and 1860 started and finished chronometers from scratch with Prescot's rough movements. As the Molyneux-Webster episode showed, independent firms could buy-in instruments and 'finish' them. In 1861 Collinson's *Directory* identified nearly 1,300 small 'watchmaking' firms in London.[79] Over ninety claimed 'chronometer-making' as an occupation, but almost certainly most of those either made parts or offered specialist skills. Another twenty-eight firms in Liverpool seemed mostly to be agents who offered sales and servicing. The ability to make and finish chronometers from Prescot's rough movements was concentrated in perhaps a dozen or so firms. For those that were successful, profits were high (as they had been for great makers during English horology's golden era). But by the late nineteenth century, there was no guarantee of success for every firm that tried. Some pioneer companies continued profitability after the death of their founders because they were succeeded by able descendants and new partners. The great John Arnold died in 1799 and the firm was then led by his proficient son John Roger, who, in 1830 entered a partnership with Edward John Dent that lasted until 1840. When John Roger died in 1843, Dent secured the whole of the old Arnold business and the House of Arnold (as 'Arnold & Dent') continued to be the Admiralty's largest supplier.[80] Between 1821 and 1835 the Royal Navy bought forty new Arnold instruments. The firm's annual output increased from about a dozen in the 1820s (mostly box chronometers), to sixty in the 1830s. Arnold & Dent lived on, resurrected under the name 'Frodsham'. John Arnold's eminent contemporary pioneer and rival, Thomas Earnshaw, Senior, died in 1829, but the direction of his firm had in 1815 already passed to his son Thomas Junior. He ran it successfully until 1854. Earnshaw's sales to the Admiralty were not as many as Arnold's: before 1821 his workshop supplied fifteen instruments but thereafter provided only six more. Leadership of other pioneer firms also passed smoothly to new generations. The brothers John and Myles Brockbank were succeeded by relatives, John Edward, and William, who successfully joined with George Atkins. Other Admiralty's customers in these years included Barraud, French, Parkinson & Frodsham, and Pennington. Collectively, these firms and a few others formed the most prosperous sector of England's horological industries.

Nevertheless, not all who made or tried to make chronometers ran successful businesses. Several firms – including some who were once successful – eventually failed, perhaps from commercial incompetence or because of the mechanical shortcomings of their instruments. Dr Bryden has identified eleven firms described as 'chronometer makers' that became bankrupt between 1799 and 1849; they included Eiffe, Cole, and Moncas. Fourteen insolvent debtors included several well-known names: Massey, Penlington, Ulrich, Webster, and even Earnshaw. Among thirty-one whose partnerships at one time or another went out of business were the French Brothers, Parkinson & Frodsham, Brockbank, Molyneux, Tobias, and Ulrich.[81] Chronometer manufacturing could be profitable, but it carried risks, and some of those who were once successful were liable to fail.

Demand, supply, and price

What is clear is that because of its relatively static technology and the success of its leading firms, chronometer manufacturing had become systematised by mid-century. In his 1837 lecture to the Royal Institution,

Edward J. Dent explained how the division of labour for watch-and chronometer-making was even more rigorously organised than described earlier by Petty and Campbell (Chapter 4). Dent's firm used forty-three different 'artificers' (workshop or outworker specialists) to make a watch's twenty-five main parts from 165 pieces (one of which, the fusee chain, might contain up to 826 pieces).[82] Consequently, the price of a reliable Arnold & Dent chronometer had settled at £40, about a twelfth of the cost of Kendall's famous copy (K1) of Harrison's prize-winning instrument seventy years earlier. [The fall in prices in some ways compares with those since 1950 of the cost of televisions and computers, but the exponential growth in demand for those was quite different from the slow growth in demand for chronometers.] By 1842, Dent thought

> The chronometer may now be considered as an instrument of comparatively general manufacture. It is no longer dependent upon government patronage: the universal conviction of its importance and utility has so increased the demand, as to secure vigorous competition on the part of the artist and render it an article of commerce.[83]

The phrase 'vigorous competition' was Dent's way of saying that supply had caught up with demand. Indeed, the potential capacity of firms to supply chronometers was greater than the effective demand for them. The longevity of old box chronometers became an annoying problem for those firms, like Dent, that made new ones. Worried about the slow growth of replacement demand for his firm's instruments, Dent suggested to Airy that Arnold chronometers older than forty years, but still in service, should be withdrawn and new Dent instruments substituted. Frodsham echoed the same grumble in the 1850s.[84]

The balance between demand and supply explains the steadiness of prices by mid-century. Dent's 'systematised production' and procedures were followed by other makers, and chronometer manufacturing had indeed become 'thoroughly stabilised'.[85] Over fifty years, prices had fallen from the 150 guineas charged by Mudge and others; Arnold's and Earnshaw's box chronometers cost sixty-five to eighty guineas; Earnshaw's pocket chronometers were thirty guineas. But by 1855 the cost of making a basic top quality two-day instrument with a brass-bound mahogany or rosewood box, 'ivory-engraved tablets, winder and all appurtenances, and with a plain Earnshaw balance' was, Professor Torrens estimated, 'within a few shillings of £14'. An auxiliary balance cost another couple of pounds. Springing, timing, and examining were also extra, done either by the 'maker' himself or by an outside specialist at between £2 and £4. The total manufacturing cost was about £17. The selling price within the trade (i.e. from the 'real' maker to a retailer) was between £21 and £25. These, Torrens continued, were 'London prices for the very highest class of work'. Liverpool-made instruments were a couple of pounds less. On top of this was the retailer's profit, resulting in a selling price to the customer of 'up to £50' for the best chronometers that had achieved high places in the Greenwich Trials. These prices, Torrens concluded, remained 'practically without change for about [another] fifty years, as did the prices paid to the workmen in the various branches'.

A mature and successful sector

By1859, the Royal Navy had 750 chronometers for its approximately 1,000 different vessels, of which 610 were at sea, eighty were with various makers for repair and refurbishment and sixty were either at Greenwich or at naval stores in Portsmouth or Devonport.[86] The estimated annual replacement demand for worn-out instruments was only five or six. It was an ample stock for sixty warships at home, including seven flagships, and 130 abroad, including twelve flagships. Flagships were issued with three chronometers, but others had one. For the next half-century, despite the further huge growth in numbers of ships and their tonnage in the Royal Navy and merchant marine, a comfortable balance continued between demand for and supply of the instruments. Chronometer firms and their workshops were kept busy and profitable, not only by making *new* instruments, but by servicing and refurbishing old ones.

****

England's chronometer manufacturing sector had grown during the French wars and matured in peacetime. It had successfully surmounted challenges during war and of peace. Theoretically, its few leading firms by 1860 could comfortably supply Britain's – and the world's – demand for new instruments and service its old ones. In 1858, England's chronometer makers were joined by two new enterprises, when the firms of Thomas Mercer and Victor Kullberg broke into and then dominated Britain and the world's chronometer markets. After 1860, whilst the parent watchmaking industry declined, English chronometer makers maintained their ascendancy and led the world (Chapter 16).

Notes

1 F. von Osterhausen, 'The Brockbanks: Chronometers Makers of London', *Antiquarian Horology*, Part 1, 26/3 (Sept. 2001), 244–56; Part 2, 26/4 (Dec. 2001), 355–71; also A.D. Stewart, 'Pennington of London: A Brief History of the Family, the Firm and Their Chronometers', *Antiquarian Horology*, 34/3 (September 2013), 367–84; id., 'John and Miles Brockbanks: Their Life and Work', *Antiquarian Horology*, 36/4 (Dec. 2015), 519 notes that Barraud became a major supplier to the East India Company.

2 Simon C. Davidson, 'Marine Chronometers: The Rapid Adoption of New Technology by East India Captains in the Period 1770–92 on Over 500 Voyages', *Antiquarian Horology*, 40/1 (March 2019), 76–91; see graph on

p. 80; for a review see Phillip Arnott, 'Chronometers on East India Company Ships 1800 to 1833', *Antiquarian Horology*, 30/4 (Dec. 2007), 481–500, and Appendix, for a list of chronometers belonging to the Company and its officers.

3 J.H. Leopold, 'The Third Seafaring Nation: The Introduction of the Marine Chronometer in the Netherlands', *Antiquarian Horology*, 22/6 (Summer 1998), 486–500.

4 Anthony G. Randall, 'Thomas Earnshaw's Numbering Sequence', *Antiquarian Horology*, 17/4 (summer 1988), 367–71 notes that ten supplied by Earnshaw are listed in the war years as 'government issue' (perhaps for training?).

5 For Barraud see Enid Mary Barraud, *Barraud: The Story of a Family* (London: Research Publishing, 1967); Cedric Jagger, *Paul Philip Barraud: A Study of a Fine Chronometer Maker, and of His Associates and Successors in the Family Business, 1750–1929* (Ticehurst: Antiquarian Horological Society, 1968); id., *The Supplement to Paul Philip Barraud* (Ticehurst: Antiquarian Horological Society, 1979); id., [lecture] 'Paul Philip Barraud', *Antiquarian Horology*, 6 (Dec. 1968), 28–31.

6 Stewart, 'John and Miles Brockbank: Their Life and Works', 218 (Table 2).

7 Rupert T. Gould, *The Marine Chronometer* (1923: London: Holland Press, 1960), 20, 112–13; Vaudrey Mercer, *John Arnold and Son, Chronometer Makers, 1767–1843* (Ticehurst, Antiquarian Horological Society, 1972), 148–150; E.M. Barraud, *Barraud: The Story of a Family*, 76; and Jagger, *Paul Philip Barraud*. About half of English chronometers were made by Arnold, Earnshaw, and Barraud: David Landes, *Revolution in Time: Clocks and the Making of the Modern World* (Cambridge, MA: Harvard UP), 184. Tony Proctor, 'Pocket Chronometer 912 by John Adam Mangar', *Antiquar ian Horology*, 32/2 (June 2010), 220, suggests that most pocket chronometers were made after1800.

8 Nicholas Blake and Richard Lawrence, *The Illustrated Companion to Nelson's Navy* (London: Chatham, 2005), 48–51; and Rif Winfield, *British Warships in the Age of Sail 1793 – 1817: Design, Construction, Careers and Fates* (London: Chatham, 2005), 213, 'Analysis of War Losses'; approximately 400,000 were in the armed forces. The population in 1811 was about 18 million.

9 Richard Sorrenson, 'The State's Demand for Accurate Astronomical and Navigational Instruments in Eighteenth-century Britain', in Bermingham and Brewer (eds.), *Consumption of Culture* (1985). Britain's Hydrographic Office had been established in 1795 with Alexander Dalrymple (formerly with the EIC) as its hydrographer.

10 *Horological Journal*, 9/2 (Oct. 1866), 23.

11 Leonard Weiss, *Watchmaking in England, 1760–1820* (London: Robert Hale, 1982), ch.6, 'Fusee Chains', 95–100, names Frederick Shick of Clerkenwell (established in 1780) as a maker. Trade *Directories* classify 'chain makers' as makers of chains for clock weights, or 'fob' chains for waistcoats.

12 Allen White, *The Chain Makers: A History of the Watch Fusee Chain Industry* (Christchurch: privately published, 1967; 2nd ed., Christchurch, Christchurch Historical Society, 2000), 4–5. Sue Newman, *The Christchurch Fusee Chain Gang: Who They Were, What they Did, How they Lived* (Stroud: Amberley, 2010), 129–31.

13 White, *Chain Makers*, 4–5.

14 LMA/CLC/L/CD/E/002/MS03951/39: Printed pamphlet: 'Regarding the Decay of the Watch Trade, and Suggestions for its Improvement'. Also Isaac Rogers' evidence to the 1817 Commons inquiry: *1817 Minutes*, 42–46.

15 Jane Humphries, 'Childhood and Child Labour in the British Industrial Revolution,' *The Economic History Review*, 66/2 (May 2013), 395–418, at www.jstor.org/stable/42921562
16 Newman, *Christchurch Fusee Chain Gang*, 129ff. By the late nineteenth century the chronometer-manufacturing firm of Mercer made its own chains. During the Great War it coordinated the production of all chronometer chains at its St Albans establishment (Chapter 17).
17 For an illustrated account of the expedition see Robin Fisher, *Vancouver's Voyage: Chartering the Northwest Coast, 1791–95*. (Seattle: University of Washington Press, 1992).
18 Alun C. Davies, 'Vancouver's Chronometers', in Robin Fisher and Hugh Johnston (eds.), *From Maps to Metaphors: The Pacific World of George Vancouver* (Vancouver: British Columbia UP, 1993), 70–84, 305–11; and id., 'Testing a New Technology: Captain George Vancouver's Survey and Navigation in Alaskan Waters, 1794,'in Haycox, Barnett, and Liburd (eds.), *Exploration in the North Pacific* (Seattle and London: Washington UP, 1997); and id., 'Horology and Navigation: The Chronometers on Vancouver's Expedition, 1791–95', *Antiquarian Horology*, 21/3 (Spring 1994), 244–55.
19 William Wales, *The Method of Finding Longitude At Sea, by Timekeepers: To Which Are Added, Tables of Equations to Equal Altitudes* (London: Wingrave & Hansard printers, 2nd ed. 1800); Joseph Whidbey, 'Remarks on Timekeepers, the Compass, &c,' *The Naval Chronicle*, 2 (1799), 505–12; J. F. Cole, 'Chronometers and the Royal Navy,' *Horological Journal*, 58 (1915), 715–19.
20 For example, Thomas Earnshaw, *Longitude: An Appeal to the Public* (London: Printed for the Author,1808; reprinted with an introduction by R. John Griffiths (St Helens: British Horological Institute, 1986), has numerous laudatory references to the performance of Earnshaw's chronometer no. 1514 on Vancouver's expedition.
21 Cited by Phillip Arnott, 'Chronometers on East India Company Ships 1800to 1833', *Antiquarian Horology*, 30/4 (Dec. 2007), 487–88.
22 Winfield, *British Warships in the Age of Sail,* xiv, for tables of annual expenditure on the Navy, and number of vessels in commission (and tables of other categories of vessels and ships) between 1793 and 1817. For a general survey see Clive Emsley, *British Society, and the French Wars, 1793–1815* (London: Macmillan, 1979).
23 J.E.D. Williams, *From Sails to Satellites: The Origin and Development of Navigational Science* (Oxford: Oxford UP, 1992), 103.
24 The *Nelson Mass* (Hoboken XX: 11) was the third of the six High Masses Haydn wrote between 1796 and 1802.
25 Rory McEvoy, 'Admiral Lord Nelson and the Commemorative Domestic Clock', *Antiquarian Horology*, 32/5 (March 2011), 665–88; the watch is illustrated on p. 687.
26 Catherine Cardinal (ed.), *Ferdinand Berthoud 1727–1807, Horloger Mécanicien du Roi et de la Marine* (La Chaux-de-Fonds, Musée international d'Horlogerie, 1984), 30, 43–44. I owe this reference to Anthony J. Turner.
27 Daryl M. Hafter, 'The Business of Invention in the Paris Industrial Exposition of 1806', *Business History Review*, 58/3 (Autumn, 1984), 317–35, at http://www.jstor.com/stable/3114551. The event attempted to encourage contemporary French industry, including watchmaking.
28 Rupert T. Gould, *Early Marine Chronometers* (illustrated lecture delivered at the British Horological Institute, 21 November 1923; published as a pamphlet, 1923).17–23; also Hilary King, 'Surviving Marine Chronometers by Louis Berthoud', *Antiquarian Horology*, 24/2 (Summer 1998), 119–21, who

notes that some of Berthoud's instruments intended for war use were assigned to Captain Nicholas Baudin's expedition to Australia, 1800–04.

29 Tony Mercer, *Chronometer Makers of the World: With [an] Extensive List of Makers and Craftsmen* (Colchester: N.A.G Press, 1991), 28, and especially Ch.6, 'The British Admiralty Plan of 1805', 41–45.

30 *Explanations of Timekeepers, Constructed by Mr Thomas Earnshaw and the Late Mr John Arnold*, published By Order of the Commissioners of Longitude, 1806); see facsimile reprint by the British Horological Institute in *Principles and Explanations of Timekeepers by Harrison, Arnold, and Earnshaw* (Upton: British Horological Institute, 1984)

31 Barry E. O'Meara, *Napoleon in Exile, or A Voice from St. Helena* (London 1882; reprint Cambridge: Cambridge UP, 2015). Extract in *Antiquarian Horology*, 24/3 (Autumn 1998), 269

32 David Syrett, 'The Role of the Royal Navy in the Napoleonic Wars after Trafalgar, 1805–14', *Naval War College Review*, 32/5 (Sept.–Oct. 1979), 71–84, at https://www.jstor.org/stable/44641939.

33 This topic offers scope for future research.

34 LMA/CLC/L/CD/E/033/MS03962: 'List of Names and Addresses of Clock and Watchmakers in London, Arranged Topographically'; LMA/CLC/L/CD/E/032/MS03977: 'A directory of clock and watchmakers, and of workmen and shopkeepers, carrying on any part of the trade in any respect', by Henry Clarke (1811).

35 David Penney and Valerie Finch, 'William Howells, Watchmaker: Part 1', *Antiquarian Horology*, 16/6 (June 1987), 585–91 (quote, 588).

36 David J. Raymond, 'The Royal Navy in the Baltic from 1807–1812' (unpublished PhD thesis, Florida State University, Tallahassee, FL., 2010), 205–10; A.N. Ryan, 'The Melancholy Fate of the Baltic Ships in 1811', *The Mariner's Mirror*, 50/2 (1964), 123–34, DOI: 10.1080/00253359.1964.10657766; and Michael Durey, '"A Perfect Hurricane": Naval Disaster Off Jutland, 1811', *Northern Studies: The Journal of the Scottish Society for Northern Studies*, 40 (2008), 71–81 at http://researchrepository.murdoch.edu.au/id/eprint/13805.

37 'A Naval Captain', Letter on Chronometers, *The Naval Chronicle*, vol. XXVII (1812), 121–22.

38 A.D. Stewart, 'A Comparison of Early Timekeepers, from Harrison to Earnshaw', *Antiquarian Horology*, 38/1 (March 2017), 90–100.

39 Yuto Ishibashi, '"A Place for Managing Government Chronometers": Early Chronometer Service at the Royal Observatory Greenwich', *Mariners Mirror*, 99:1 (February 2013), 52–66. John Pond (1767–1836) was Astronomer Royal from 1811 to 1835; C. Andrew Murray, 'John Pond (*bap.* 1767, *d.* 1836)', *ODNB*.

40 Trevor H. Levere, 'Chronometers on the Arctic Expeditions of John Ross and William Edward Parry: With Notes on a Letter from Messrs. William Parkinson & William James Frodsham', *Annals of Science*, 51 (1994), 165–75, 171, at https://doi.org/10.1080/00033799400200181

41 David Evans, letter in *Antiquarian Horology*, 9/8 (Sept. 1976), 939. Webster apparently made chronometers sold by Litherland, Davis & Co., who 'in all probability did not manufacture all their chronometers, if indeed they made any of them.'

42 Vaudrey Mercer, *John Arnold and Son*, 172.

43 Gould, *The Marine chronometer*, 262.

44 Cambridge University Library, Royal Greenwich Observatory MSS 5/229, Pond to Admiralty, undated letter, c. August 1828.

45 J.A. Bennett, 'George Biddell Airy and Horology', *Annals of Science*, 37 (1980), 269–85; Robert W. Smith, 'A National Observatory Transformed:

Greenwich in the Nineteenth Century', *Journal for the History of Astronomy*, 22/1 (Feb. 1991), 21–30, at doi:10.1177/002182869102200104; m R. Vaudrey Mercer, *Dent*, 118–49.

46 Matthew Flinders, *A Voyage to Terra Australis ... in the Years 1801, 1802, and 1803 in His Majesty's ship the Investigator* (London: 1814, 2 vols plus Atlas: Facsimile reprint, London: Nicol, 1966). In April 1802 Flinders met with Captain Nicholas Baudin and compared their longitudinal findings. Baudin had four chronometers by Louis Berthoud: see Hilary King, 'The Marine Chronometers of the Baudin Expedition to Australis, 1800–1804', *Antiquarian Horology*, 23/6 Winter 1997), 509–21.

47 Adrian Webb, 'The Expansion of British Naval Hydrographic Administration, 1808–1829' (unpublished PhD thesis, Exeter University, 2010), online at http://hdl.handle.net/10036/116990; 300–08 discusses the chronometers issued by the Admiralty (Table, p. 304).

48 Johnathan Betts, 'The Eighteenth-Century Transits of Venus, the Voyages of Captain James Cook, and the Early Development of the Marine Chronometer', *Antiquarian Horology*, 21/1 (Autumn 1993), 60–69.

49 Kenneth Morgan, 'Finding Longitude: The *Investigator* Expedition, 1801–1803', *International Journal of Maritime History*, 29/4 (Nov. 2017, 771–87, at https://doi.org/10.1177/0843871417725688

50 Alun C. Davies, 'Vancouver's Chronometers', in *From Maps to Metaphors: The Pacific World of George Vancouver,* ed. R. Fisher and H. Johnston (Vancouver: British Columbia UP, 1993), 70–84, 305–311.

51 Ishibashi, '"A Place for Managing Government Chronometers": 52–66: see Figure 1, showing the increase in the number of voyages using chronometers. at http://dx.doi.org/10.1080/00253359.2013.766998

52 Vaudrey Mercer, *The Frodshams: The Story of a Family of Chronometer Makers*, Antiquarian Horological Society Monograph No. 21 (Ticehurst: Antiquarian Horological Society, 1981), 23–31.

53 M.A. Crawforth, 'Trade Cards for the Scientific Instrument Industry', *Annals of Science*, 42 (1985), 465; https://doi.org/10.1080/00033798500200331; also Silvio A. Bedini, *Thinkers and Tinkers: Early American Men of Science* (New York: Scribners, 1975), 224–25; David Penney, 'Evidence from the Transient: The Importance of Ephemera for a Proper Understanding of the Clock and Watch Trades: Part 1', *Antiquarian Horology*, 29/6 (Dec. 2006), 792–95, esp. figs. 6 and 7.

54 Christopher Wood, 'Extracts from a Parkinson and Frodsham Pamphlet', *Antiquarian Horology*, 9 (Dec.1974), 46–50, notes that the purpose of advertisers' booklets was 'unashamedly commercial'.

55 Cambridge University Library, RGO MS113: letter, 6 July 1822, Admiralty to Pond, authorising 'an expedition to ascertain ... the longitude of Funchal'.

56 Stuart Jennings, 'Chronometers on the 1821–26 Royal Navy African Survey', *Antiquarian Horology*, 40/2 (June 2019), 200–14 (quote, 202). Richard Owen, *Tables of Latitudes and Longitudes by Chronometer of Places in the Atlantic and Indian Oceans; Principally on the West and East Coast of Africa; to Which Is Prefixed An Essay of the Management and Use of Chronometers* (London: 30 pp. pamphlet, 1827). Also David Harries, 'The Chronometer Pioneer (Commander Richard Owen),' *Horological Journal*, 122 (1979), 37–43.

57 Simon C. Davidson and Peter Linstead-Smith, 'W.E. Frodsham No.1. Another Chronometer Identified from HMS Beagle's Second Voyage', *Antiquarian Horology*, 37/3 (Sept. 2016), 366–76 (372).

58 [Parkinson & Frodsham], *A Brief Account of the Chronometer with Remarks upon those Furnished by Parkinson to the Expeditions of Captains*

Ross, Parry, Sabine, King, Lyn, Foster and Other Distinguished Navigators (London: pamphlet, probably 1832), 1–2. Also Ishibashi, 'Managing Chronometers', 52–66.

59 Anon., 'Chronometer Accuracy: Verification of the Longitude of Paris', *The Nautical Magazine and Naval Chronicle* (1838), 402; and Christopher Wood, 'The Determination of the Difference in Meridians of the Paris and Greenwich Observatories', *Antiquarian Horology*, 24/3 (Autumn 1998), 234–36, who describes the firing of multiple rockets at predetermined times in 1826. Also Thomas R. Robinson, 'On the Longitude of the Armagh Observatory, Given by Fifteen Chronometers of Arnold and Dent, &c.', *The Transactions of the Royal Irish Academy*, 19 (1843), 110–20, at https://www.jstor.org/stable/30079128. For Dent's role in determining foreign longitudes, see Vaudrey Mercer, *Dent*, 66–70.

60 A.M. Clerke, rev. Michael Hoskin, 'Richard Sheepshanks (1794–1855)', *ODNB*.

61 Christopher Wood, 'Robert Molyneux's Astronomic Clocks and Chronometers', *Antiquarian Horology*, 9/4 (Sept. 1975), 413–25.

62 LMA/CLC/B/141/MS14537/001-002/1: Kullberg Order Book, noting the recovery of one of Lindsay's instruments, Kullberg No. 1232, after twenty four years immersion in the Nile.

63 Henry Raper, 'On the Necessity of Adopting Secondary Meridians', *The Nautical Magazine and Naval Chronicle* (1839), 461. Raper was sometime Secretary of the Royal Astronomical Society.

64 Henry Raper, *The Practice of Navigation and Nautical Astronomy* (1840: London: Potter, 10th ed., 1880, 20th and last ed., 1920), viii–ix; J. K. Laughton, rev. Derek Howse, 'Henry Raper (1799–1859)', *ODNB*; Charles H. Cotter, 'A Brief Historical Survey of British Navigation Manuals,' *Journal of Navigation*, 36 (1983), 245, at doi:10.1017/S0373463300024954

65 Simon C. Davidson, 'Box Chronometers for India, 1800–1936', *Antiquarian Horology*, 35/4 (Dec. 2014), 1107–24; see Appendix; also Andrew S. Cook, 'Alexander Dalrymple and John Arnold: Chronometers and the Representation of Longitude on East India Company Charts', *Vistas in Astronomy*, 26 (1983), 189–95.

66 Silvio A. Bedini, 'The Scientific Instruments of the Lewis and Clark Expedition', *Great Plains Quarterly*, IV (1984), 54–69 (especially 60–61), at https://www.jstor.org/stable/24467603: the 'Arnold' cost $250 (plus 75 cents for the key) and had a balance wheel and escapement of 'the most improved construction'. Also id., *Thinkers and Tinkers: Early men of Science* (New York: Scribners, 1975), 330–31; also Richard S. Preston, 'The Accuracy of the Astronomical Observations of Lewis and Clark', *Proceedings of the American Philosophical Society*, 144/2 (June 2000), 168–91, at www.jstor.org/stable/1515630

67 Günther Oestmann, abstract of '*En route* to the "German Chronometer": The introduction of precision timekeeping in the German Mercantile Marine and Imperial Navy in the Nineteenth Century', Paper for the Twenty-third *Congress of History of Science and Technology: Ideas and Instruments in Social Context, Budapest,* Session T35 (Scientific Instruments), {August 1st, 2009), 1–8; also id., '"Towards the "German chronometer"; The Introduction of Precision Timekeeping in the German Mercantile Marine and Imperial Navy in the Nineteenth Century', *Antiquarian Horology,* 35/3 (Sept. 2014), 949–63.

68 Michael Edidin, *English Watches for the American Market: A History of Watchmaking by the Tobias Families of London and Liverpool* (NAWCC *Bulletin*, Part 1: Oct. 1992), 515–44 (esp. 526–28); (Part 2: Dec. 1992), 659–93 (esp. 681–93).

69 For a description of the chronometer room in 1850 see 'The Planet Watchers of Greenwich', extract from Charles Dickens's *Household Words*, 25 May 1850, and 'Commentary' by Jonathan Betts, *Antiquarian Horology*, 21/4 (Summer 1994), 350–51.
70 LMA/CLC/L/CD/E/006/MS03943/8: newspaper clipping citing *Morning Herald*, 4 Nov 1842 and *The Times*, 5 November 1842.
71 Marvin Whitney, *The Ship's Chronometer* (Cincinnati, OH, American Watchmakers Institute, 1985), 41.
72 Ishibashi, 'Managing Chronometers', 52–66.
73 Dee Helmore, *A Quest for Perfection: The Life of John Gottlieb Ulrich: Chronometer Maker* (High Wycombe, privately published, 2012), Also, Vaudrey Mercer, *Dent*, 250–74.
74 George Foster, 'James Sweetman Eiffe, 1800–1880', *Antiquarian Horology*, 5/8 (Sept. 1967), 284–86.
75 LMA/CLC/B/141/MS14538/1: Kullberg Order Book vol. 1, 224, 24 April 1878; also Vaudrey Mercer, *Dent*, 483–84.
76 E. Walker, 'On Purifying Olive Oil for the Pivots of Chronometers', *The Philosophical Journal*, 36 (1810), 372–74, citing P.P. Barraud's endorsement of Walker's method. For a later proposal, see L. Hebert, 'Plumbago for Chronometers', *Transactions of the Society, for the Encouragement of Arts, Manufactures, and Commerce*, 46 (1827), 48–54, at www.jstor.org/stable/41327070
77 [Society of Arts], 'Premiums Offered in Session 1822–23', *Transactions of the Society, for the Encouragement of Arts, Manufactures, and Commerce*, 40 (1822), xiv, at www.jstor.org/stable/41325963.
78 R. Vaudrey Mercer, *Arnold*, 223–76: 'Appendix XVI: Chronometer Records at Greenwich'; id., The Life and Letters of E.J. Dent, Chronometer Maker, and Some Account of His Successors (Ticehurst: Antiquarian Horological Society, 1977),737, records that Arnold's chronometer number 114, 'purchased before 1829', saw service on nine ships before being 'exchanged for hack watches' in 1909. Also the Greenwich Index of Chronometers at the National Maritime Museum, Greenwich for the long service of individual chronometers. Records were kept from 1822 to 1917. See *Mariners' Mirror*, 58 (Nov. 1972), 104–05.
79 Collinson's *Directory*, 1861, Part 5, the '*Watch, Chronometer, and Clock Trades' Directory*' (London: Collinson & Co., 1861).
80 Ishibashi, 'Managing Government ', 52–66, Figure 2 shows the dominance of Arnold (and Dent) as suppliers to the Admiralty, 1822–35.
81 Extrapolated from D.J. Bryden, 'The London Gazette as a Source for the History of the English Horological Trade, 1720–1849', *Antiquarian Horology*, 37/4 (Dec. 2016), 477–95.
82 Note in *Journal of the Franklin Institute*, 20 (1839), 139–40; also Vaudrey Mercer, *Dent*, 208.
83 Edward J. Dent, *An Abstract from Two Lectures on the Construction and Management of Chronometers, Watches and Clocks* (London: Adams Brown, 1842), 5.
84 R. Vaudrey Mercer, Dent, 329–33 for Dent's complaint and for Frodsham's, 427–28.
85 David S. Torrens, 'Carriage Clocks and Chronometers', *Horological Journal*, 88/11 (Aug. 1946), 320–22; (quotes that follow are from 322).
86 Charles K. Aked, 'Longitude and the Marine Chronometer', *Antiquarian Horology*, 8/8 (1974), 873; W.E. May, 'How the Chronometer Went to Sea', *Antiquarian Horology*, 9/6 (March 1976), 654.

Part 3

Decline

11 Revolution in America

Evolution in Switzerland

The 'American system' revolutionises watchmaking

The remarkable changes in methods of watchmaking that developed in the United States in the 1860s derived partly from the earlier example in the making of clocks. At the beginning of the century, large scale production of clock parts was achieved by a few firms in New England. Their parts were as interchangeable as was then possible and assembled in factories.[1] The first examples were small mantle or wall clocks, made of wood. Later, brass was used. But watches and their movements were still mostly imported from Europe, and of the nearly 3,000 described as 'watchmakers' in the thirty-six states in the 1850 census, most were repairers.[2] Making miniscule parts of watches was deemed impossible because their parts required tolerances beyond the competence of contemporary machine tools. For watches, precision to 1:1,000 inch was needed and, for excellent ones, even finer accuracy. Early attempts had been unsuccessful, for a mixture of technical and financial reasons. The aborted Ingold episode in London had probably come closest (Chapter 9). Just over a decade after Ingold's failure, a new attempt was made (unconnected with Ingold) at Roxbury near Boston. It showed promise. The firm then relocated to Waltham, a dozen miles away, also in the state of Massachusetts. Between 1850 and 1854 its ninety employees made about 1,000 watches, at a rate of about thirty watches a week.[3] Quality was not especially good, and the quantity was hardly different from the output of a couple of Clerkenwell firms using their traditional labour-intensive methods using outworkers. Although during the financial crisis of 1857 demand fell and forced a 50 per cent wage cut, Waltham reorganised, re-financed, and survived. Annual output grew to about 14,000 watches. It succeeded because its managers believed in the beneficial evolutionary practice of 'learning by doing': a second generation of machine tools would be better than the first, and a third, better still. This assumption was borne out. The Company's success initiated a major shift in the method and location of production in many of the world's watchmaking economies. The successful transformation in production methods merits the phrase 'revolution in watchmaking'.

DOI: 10.4324/9781003227823-14

Waltham's watches were based on the simplest form of lever movement and, like those made in Switzerland, needed fewer parts than Clerkenwell's conventional creations. Initially, they were guaranteed for ten years and available in only three styles and qualities. They became archetypal products of the 'American system' of manufacturing, like the revolvers of Colonel Samuel Colt and the sewing machines of Isaac Singer. By the 1890s, as William Sellers observed, the 'system' was extended to make other products:

> for more than half a century this country has been [possessed of] a system of manufacturing peculiar to itself, developed first in the manufacture of firearms, and subsequently to a great variety of products, such as the sewing machine, the typewriter, the bicycle and the watch, in all of which we stand today unrivalled.[4]

A few years later, Sellers could have added 'automobiles' to his list. Eventually, watches, like small arms and other products of the system, were marketed in the regular stock of country merchants and sold by mail order through the catalogues of Montgomery Ward and Sears Roebuck (which, by 1887, had a fifty-page mail-order list devoted entirely to watches).[5] By 1900, Waltham employed 2,500 workers who made about 1,200 watches a day. Amy Glasmeier concluded that between them Waltham and Elgin 'transformed the world's watch industry' (Figure 11.1).

The Civil War gave Waltham a great boost and the firm had a good war.[6] After a Bible, what better farewell present could a family give a

WALTHAM WATCH FACTORY, SOUTH SIDE, WALTHAM, MASS.

Figure 11.1 Waltham Factory Building, south side. Copyright: David Penney. http://www.antiquewatchstore.com/.

young soldier than a watch? Waltham stepped in with the '*Ellery*', popularly named 'The Soldier's Watch'. Watches helped officers' co-ordinate troop movements, artillery fire and, especially, railroad supply trains. The *Ellery* helped make 'Time-awareness' more widespread.[7] During the war, Waltham's annual production increased to about 80,000 or 90,000. It fed a growing market that attracted into existence competing companies, and at least eighteen more watch factories were born in a few decades. Entrance into the industry was easy ... but so was exit. As frequently happens in new industries (like televisions, computers, motor cars, radios, pianos), at first few firms grow, dominate, and survive; some are taken over, or fail. In American watchmaking, the first dominant firm was Waltham. The next most important and successful was at Elgin, Illinois, some thirty-five miles from Chicago. Elgin at first made fewer models than Waltham but encouraged buyers to select a watch case they could afford to fit the movement they had chosen.[8]

The ninth census 1870 and the Centennial exhibition, 1876

The magnitude of the watchmaking revolution was revealed to the world in 1870 in the publication of the United States' Ninth Census. It identified a dozen large watchmaking firms that used machine tools to make parts that were assembled in factories. Only three had fewer than a hundred workers, seven had between a hundred and a thousand, and two employed over a thousand.[9] The statistics disclosed an American industry with a structure in great contrast to watch industries in Europe, notably those in Switzerland and England. Europe's watch industries comprised outworkers in hundreds of small, independent workshops, each employing a few workers using handcraft methods of production. Apart from Rotherham in Coventry and Longines in Switzerland, no watchmaking firms employed large workforces. The sheer size of American companies and their revolutionary method of production enabled comparatively vast outputs. Elgin alone made about 300 watches a day (about 100,000 a year) and even small new American companies reputedly made about 8,000–15,000 watches annually. By 1876, America's watch factories collectively made about 250,000 watches a year, comfortably exceeding the British watch industry's annual output. Their array of qualities, too, was impressive: the best American watches were claimed to be as reliable and as precise as good Swiss products.

In the 1860s, their first decade, American watch firms were understandably preoccupied with their home market. A few infiltrated Britain's markets on a modest scale, but most American watch firms had little interest in Europe or in the great international industrial exhibitions in London (1862), Paris (1867), and Vienna (1873).[10] But the Centennial Exhibition in Philadelphia in 1876 offered an ideal opportunity on home territory to demonstrate their watches to the rest of the world.[11] They did so. At the Centennial, the most remarkable horological contribution was from Waltham. Observers were stunned by the extent of its display and the innovating flair of its advertising and marketing.[12] Waltham mounted a colossal exhibit of 2,200 gold and silver watches and their movements, the product of 'six working days at 10 hours per day'.[13] Waltham's intention to compete seriously in the world's markets was subsequently revealed when its exhibit was improved and reused in other international exhibitions – in Paris (1878 and 1889), Melbourne and Sydney (1879 and 1880), Vienna (1873), and the Inventions Exhibition in London (1885; see Figure 13.1).[14]

The revolution's effect on Switzerland's watch industry

Waltham's display of watches, and the revolutionary methods by which they were made, had an immediate and profound impact in Switzerland, home of the world's leading and largest watchmaking industry. Swiss watchmakers had triumphed at London's Great Exhibition in 1851, and over the next two decades had captured much of Britain's market. They emulated their success at London in New York's own Crystal Palace exhibition in 1853, when twenty-six Swiss firms offered a 'magnificent' display.[15] Sales of Swiss watches subsequently spread across the United States and agencies were set up, in New York, Boston, Philadelphia, New Orleans, even in distant San Francisco. At later international exhibitions in London, Paris, and Vienna, dozens of Swiss firms showed watches that were 'calculated to suit the taste and means of all classes of purchasers', especially at 'the cheap end [where] the Swiss cannot be beaten'.[16] Switzerland's grip on the world's watch markets tightened during the 1860s. Their watch exports to the United States doubled between 1864 and 1872, when Americans bought an average of about a quarter of a million Swiss watches a year. Then, over three years, Swiss watch exports collapsed. The Centennial Exhibition in 1876 offered an opportunity for the Swiss to find out why (Table 11.1).

There were several reasons for the breakdown. Three lay beyond the control of Swiss watchmakers. First, the collapse of New York's stock market in 1873 triggered a fall in demand for all goods, not just watches. Next, American tariffs were increased. The Morrill tariff of 1861 was initially intended to raise revenue to pay for the Civil War but, by the 1870s, tariffs had become intentionally protectionist, explicitly to shield America's infant industries like watchmaking. Third, by the early 1870s the watchmaking revolution, led by Waltham and Elgin, had made good progress in its home market. A fourth reason lay entirely with the Swiss themselves. Swiss watchmakers had taken the American market for granted, just as had exporters from Coventry and Liverpool a decade earlier (Chapter 13).

Table 11.1 Swiss watch exports to the United States, 1864–76

Year	*Numbers in thousands*
1864	169
1865	226
1866	262
1867	207
1868	209
1869	206
1870	330
1871	342
1872	366
1873	204
1874	187
1875	134
1876	75

Source: *Horological Journal*, 19/6 (Feb. 1877), 80–81.

Jacques David, Eduard Favre-Perret, and Swiss recovery

Longines, Switzerland's largest watchmaking firm, sent its technical director, Jacques David, to the Exhibition to enquire why its exports had collapsed. When he arrived in New York he found abundant evidence of Swiss complacency: one of their main dealers had at least 4,000 Longines watches in his stores that he could not sell. 'Customers quite simply did not want Swiss watches any more', he reported, 'and the retailers did not hesitate to liquidate them at a loss'.[17] At the Exhibition, the good quality and value for money of American machine-made watches also triggered a report by Eduard Favre-Perret, Switzerland's representative on the international jury. Jacques David's report to Longines and Favre-Perret's account to the Federal High Council of Swiss Watchmakers, together helped change Switzerland's watchmaking industry.[18] Favre-Perret was especially impressed by the successful application of the 'American system' to watchmaking. Although complete interchangeability of parts had not yet been achieved, he realised that machine-made watches were good enough to command the gap in the market between the two kinds of watches in which Switzerland hitherto excelled, namely

> the good simple cheap watch [and the excellent] very complicated watches at a great price ...This gap is all the more regrettable as the mass of products of our main competitors, the North Americans, are placed precisely between these two categories.[19]

Favre-Perret stressed the new system's impact on productivity. In America, the average annual output for each employee was 150 watches, whereas the productivity of the average individual among the 40,000 workmen in Switzerland was forty watches. David's report and Favre-Perret's warnings were unambiguous, prescient, widely publicised, and aroused much interest – even in America.[20] Although the American system of manufacturing watches could not be transplanted overnight to Geneva, nevertheless the collective message behind both reports was that Swiss firms ought to adopt American machine tools when and as best they could. They should and could adapt appropriate aspects of the American system to their own idiosyncratic *établissage* method of production. Only if they did so, the message ran, could output per worker then increase.

And, slowly, it did. The Swiss began to change ... not overnight, but gradually and effectively. Annual output of watches per Swiss worker rose from sixty-five in 1876, to 170 in 1900, to 330 by 1913.[21] An essential feature of the American system was that it enabled as much interchangeability of parts as was then possible. For watches, it led to greater uniformity that simplified their making and repair. David's recommendations included the need to establish a School of Mechanics 'like our excellent schools of horology'. Above all, Swiss watch firms must co-operate, 'not work separately any more, as we have done up to now, but join our efforts together'.[22] Favre-Perret's strictures were also successful. Consequently, over the next twenty years, appropriate aspects of the American system were progressively adapted to the idiosyncratic Swiss watch industry. The changes were evolutionary and unhurried, not revolutionary and sudden. Production gradually became transferred from small manual workshops to larger mechanised factories, in which parts were made to specified dimensions and tolerances. The Swiss system shifted from reliance on its *établissage* system of small-scale production in cottages, to an intermediate form that included machine tools which made large numbers of standard parts in centralised factories. Longines introduced machines to make and finish watches in a factory and remained Switzerland's largest company. For most of Swiss watchmaking there was only partial vertical integration, but enough to achieve sufficient economies of scale and lower costs. Small enterprises continued to make cases, escapements, dials, and wheels, increasingly with machine tools. The old Swiss craft system had been, in economists' terminology, 'a vertically specialised system of horizontal fragmentation organised around a highly skilled and malleable labour force'.[23] When it adapted parts of the American system it created 'an intermediate form of organisation that combined mechanization and partial vertical integration'. The Swiss industry's recovery was achieved not by transplanting a full-blown 'American system' overnight, but by progressively importing American machine tools that modified and modernised its *établissage* system. Standard parts were made on a large scale in centralised factories, and overall flexibility 'maintained through dispersed design and assembly activities'.[24]

That the responses of the Swiss industry were successful became evident in later international exhibitions. Leading Swiss firms consolidated their efforts and collaborated with smaller watch companies. The institutional response of the Swiss watchmaking industry to the challenge of Waltham was in marked contrast to that of the British Horological Institute (as we will see in Chapter 13.) In 1878 at Paris, 146 Swiss watch firms sent exhibits. Nine won gold medals. Collectively, they re-asserted the Swiss industry's importance and reaffirmed its determination to catch up.[25] A year later in Sydney, they mounted another cooperative effort. As 'The International Watch Company' they showed watches 'of the third order of merit' (that is, those explicitly aimed at the bottom of the market).[26] When the Australian exhibition moved to Melbourne in 1880, differences among individual firms were further subsumed under the aegis of 'The Swiss Manufacturing Association', organised and coordinated by a Commissioner who selected watches that best suited time-tests for juries to inspect. The outcome was more praise, prestige, and another gold medal.[27] Indications of the measure of their success gradually became clear. In 1870, some 35,000 watchmakers had been employed in the Swiss Jura, mostly in home workshops. By 1900, watches were predominantly made in factory units to which homeworkers were subcontracted. Their factories were much smaller than their giant American competitors, but nevertheless they produced standardised parts made to specified dimensions and tolerances. In 1901, the average number of workers per firm was 37.5. Only seven firms employed over 500 workers, and just one had over a thousand.[28] Nevertheless, by the turn of the century the lessons learned at Philadelphia and the subsequent changes enabled their successful reassertion in international marketplaces. Jacques David's and Favre-Perret's exhortations in 1876 about the merits of the 'American system' had been listened to and acted upon with good effect.

Technical, organisational, and marketing advances after 1876

In America, Waltham and its competitors further enhanced the 'American system' as watchmaking technology continued to evolve. Over several decades Waltham and other watch-making firms designed and built 'pneumatically controlled, self-feeding, self-acting, self-gauging, automatic machine tools to produce interchangeable watch parts'.[29] They reduced hand-finishing for watches at the top end of the range to a minimum but did not eliminate it.[30] The accuracy of a watch depended on the precision with which each part was made before being assembled, and 'finished' or 'tuned' to achieve accuracy. Total interchangeability was not quite yet within grasp, as David Penney makes clear, because

> fitting was always likely to be needed. Thus, a repairer could not just order up a replacement for, say, a Model '72 balance staff. They had to supply Waltham with the serial number. Waltham would then check their records and take note of the working tolerances

> allowed on that particular batch, perhaps even on that particular day. They could then supply a balance staff from a batch with the same tolerances.[31]

Improvements to the first screw-making machines by Charles Vander Woerd and Edward A. Marsh greatly increased productivity and enabled one man to make 1,200 fine screws a day. Their measurements were gauged to 1/2500 of an inch. They were so small, Donald Hoke explained, 'that more than 100,000 are required to weigh a pound. The balance wheel, after being machined, weighs only seven grains, and when fitted with sixteen gold screws weighs 7.2 grains'. Successive generations of screw-making machines at Waltham increased productivity so that daily output of screws increased from 500 before 1859 to between 50,000 and 60,000 after 1885. In the three decades between 1854 and 1885 labour costs fell by 99 per cent. 'In 1854 it took twenty-four work days to produce a watch', Hoke continued, 'by 1907 it was down to 1.37 work days'.[32] New automatic or semi-automatic machines cut escape wheels, balance wheels, and hair springs and, by 1884, sophisticated steel machine cutters with sapphire teeth handled ninety blanks at a time. Other engineering advancements included the use of heavy presses and better-quality steel.

Not all changes were to do with advances in machine technology. A feature of the American system included the efficient organisation of an assembly line. Waltham watches had about 150 parts and the different grades were made and assembled in 3,750 different operations. The co-ordination of all of this was a formidable task. It included the notable innovation of installing miniature railroad tracks in front of some benches that allowed workers to slide wheeled chairs 'past a row of automatic machines, inserting wire into one end of each machine and collecting finished, fully interchangeable parts from the other end'.[33] Waltham demonstrated the vertical integration typical of industries in the United States, where firms expanded by reaching backward into the supply chain and forward into the distribution system. A sophisticated marketing system supported retailers supplied with a full catalogue of spare parts for each grade of watch. Innovative advertising reinforced customer satisfaction, loyalty, and demand. The outcome was a remarkable variety of watches of different qualities, reflected in prices from $3.00 to $75.00 and upwards, depending upon the case. Waltham's lowest grade watches required the retailer to do the final adjusting, but the finest qualities took up to five months between starting and finishing. The highest grades had more jewels, a temperature compensation balance, and a 'micrometre regulator'.[34]

Among other reasons for Waltham's success were that its watchmakers combined the requirements of product design and production technology, just as wooden-movement clockmakers had done earlier. Waltham's technicians had borrowed some features from England but otherwise there was little connection with earlier watchmaking production methods. Like the Swiss in the Jura, they had adopted the simpler 'going barrel' and discarded the fusee and its chain, the power transmission system that was the quintessence of Clerkenwell's watches. This eliminated hundreds of parts and simplified a difficult manufacturing process. Waltham also abandoned the English duodecimal system (arranged around measurements of 1/30th inch in watchmaking) for centimetres and the metric scale and redesigned their gauges to accommodate the new standardised measurements. Waltham's system involved the '*go/no go*' gauges (pioneered by New England's wooden clockmakers). It developed them further, for a much more demanding application. First, a basic model of the part was made; then a set of master '*go/no go*' gauges were constructed to fit the model; finally, sets of inspectors' or working gauges were made for use on the shop floor.

In the scramble to enter the market, other companies pioneered their own strategies. Between 1860 and 1880 twenty-five firms joined Waltham. Elgin led the way. In 1880, Elgin's annual output of 700,000 amounted to just over a half of Waltham's 1.2 million.[35] By 1900, the two giants each employed 2,500 workers who made about 1,200 watches a day. As Amy Glasmeier concluded, between them Elgin and Waltham 'transformed the world's watch industry'. They supplied an international market of a size beyond the comprehension of any in Coventry's biggest firms, let alone any of Clerkenwell's masters, outworkers, or dealers. But in the United States, the road was not always smooth. Cutthroat competition led to overproduction and drastic price-cutting. Sometimes only a few firms survived before another round of expansion led to further intense competition. August Bolino concludes that for every successful watch company, like Waltham or Elgin, 'there were at least ten failures'.[36] Knowledge of this uncertainty may well explain why Clerkenwell's companies were circumspect about their own putative expansion; they were content to concentrate on a small but profitable domestic luxury market, and leave the mass market to Coventry, the Swiss, and the Americans.

Niche markets: railroad watches

Between 1860 and 1920 the United States was transformed from a predominantly agricultural economy to one with a large and growing urban-industrial sector. The population tripled from about 30 million to over 90 million. Despite a recession in the 1880s, personal incomes increased. Much of the home market was effectively protected from foreign competition by successive tariffs. Morrill in 1861, McKinley in 1890, and Dingley in 1897 affected not only English watch and clockmakers, for a range of other British manufacturers struggled to compete with the domestically-produced products of the United States. Steep exclusionary tariffs had initially been enforced during the Civil War, and they remained in response to the economic crisis of the 1870s. Transatlantic trade to the United States' eastern ports was more easily monitored and tariffs enforced than had been possible for the British when they tried to prevent smuggling across a narrow English Channel.

Market categories: 'railroad' and 'dollar' watches

As demand grew and the supply of watches increased, distinct market categories emerged. Michael Harrold has identified three broad groups.[37] One was for conventional jewelled watches, built for a long life and, like Waltham's best grades, amenable to repair. A second group comprised inexpensive jewelled watches of lower quality materials that gave a poorer performance but still kept 'adequate' time – especially if routinely synchronised to reliable public clocks (like in those towns with railroad stations that received time signals by telegraph).[38] Harrold's third category comprised firms that made especially cheap watches, eventually even watches without the jewel bearings that reduced friction between metal parts. These were the 'dollar watches', the first-time buys afforded by many working people.

Included in the top-quality spectrum were 'railroad watches', bought by well-off customers who wanted good quality and reliability. Initially, they were aimed at persons who worked on or used railroads. Waltham's early advertising explicitly claimed that they were 'eminently suitable' for railroad engineers and conductors for whom 'accurate timekeeping was important and robustness essential'. Station managers, conductors, drivers, ticket salesmen, porters, and passengers wanted to know if the 11.25 was on time. Greater demand for 'railroad watches' was an indirect consequence of the five transcontinental railroads that linked Atlantic and Pacific oceans after 1869. Railroad mileage reached a quarter of a million by 1914; about 40,000 locomotives carried millions of tons of freight and accounted for millions of passenger journeys. The demand for accurate, reliable, 'railroad' watches had increased in 1891, following a catastrophic train crash that occurred because an engineer's watch was a few minutes slow. It lent impetus to the need for a specified measure of accuracy and reliability for watches used by railroad employees. By the turn of the century, the lobbying influence of the annual conventions of American watch inspectors successfully imposed minimum measurable standards for 'approved' railroad watches. They had to be 'easy to read, easy to repair, and easy to keep in time'.[39] They were subjected to trials, during which they were adjusted in five positions over a temperature variation of fifty degrees to achieve a minimum accuracy of plus or minus 30 seconds a week.[40] These regulations created a special market for some American firms, like the Hamilton Watch Company (founded in 1892).[41] Foreign competition was stymied because although best quality Swiss and English watches might have satisfied the desirable criteria, they had to surmount high tariff barriers that made them too expensive. As Glasmeier observed, 'the [American] railroad watch standard ... effectively locked out foreign competition'.[42] The American Watch Trust influenced its government's policy more successfully than its British equivalents – the Clockmakers' Company and the British Horological Institute – were ever able to do with theirs.

'Dollar' watches and falling prices

At the other end of the quality spectrum were extremely cheap watches. Ironically, a notable early contribution to this category had originated not in the United States but in Switzerland. Watches designed by George Roskopf (1813–89), German born but a naturalised Swiss, were endorsed by Belgian railways for their employees as 'railway watches'. They were not of the same high quality as the later American railroad watches, but Roskopf initiated a breakthrough in the 'cheap watch' market aimed at working-class pockets. Indeed, Roskopf's watches were commonly known as the 'people's watches'. Their low cost was because they included an escapement (of the pin pallet type, later widely used in cheap wristwatches) and their movements were cased in base metals.[43] The original patent was filed in 1867 and Roskopf's watches won a bronze medal in the Paris exhibition of that year.[44] About 100,000 were made during his lifetime and, in the long run about 20 million, under patents to makers in other countries. His watches gave an impetus in the United States to the demand for cheap watches.

Among several pioneer American firms that rose to the challenge was the Auburndale Watch Company (1876–83). It made about 1,000 inexpensive watches ($10 to retailers) with some jewelled bearings and a movement which rotated in the barrel. The latter caused problems because 'they did not run well and many were returned to the makers ... it was an inadequate timepiece, even for an inexpensive watch'. [45] The company turned to making stop-watches instead. More successful was the Waterbury Company. Their products were essentially miniature clocks set in large watch cases three inches wide by one inch deep. Their first watches had a 'long wind' because they were powered by an elongated spring of nine feet. Some were given away 'free' with a man's suit; others were offered as competition prizes by newspapers.[46] It is estimated that Waterbury in 1880 accounted for about 3 or 4 per cent of American output, about 100,000 units out of a total of 2.7 million. Waterbury's agents were the brothers Robert and Charles Ingersoll, middlemen who sold watches to other dealers and, later, to the public through mail order catalogues.[47] They subsequently became celebrated in their own right in the horological history of Britain as well as the United States (Chapter 12).

Robert Ingersoll was an archetypal Yankee inventor who had patented small novelties, including a rubber stamp printing outfit, a toy typewriter, a propelling pencil, a dollar sewing machine and a key ring. When he ordered 1,000 miniaturised clocks, initially for $1.50 each from a machinist in New York City and followed it with an order for another 10,000 more, he transformed American watchmaking. The clock movements were assembled from mass-produced parts, without jewelled bearings. Eventually, he decided to 'make them a little smaller, sell them for a dollar, and [they] will be in everyone's pocket'. To sell the watches he launched a brilliant advertising campaign. Just as in 1861 Waltham used the Civil War and in 1876 the Centennial exhibition as springboards, so in 1893 Robert Ingersoll took advantage of the Columbian Exposition in Chicago.[48] When the price *did* fall to a dollar in 1896 with a model called the *Yankee,* it gave rise to the immortal advertising copy 'The Watch that Made the Dollar Famous'. By 1899 Waterbury made 8,000 a day for Ingersoll and by 1910 some 3½ million a year. Technically the watches were 'robust to the point of crudity'. They had, George Daniels commented, 'a vigorous action induced by a very fierce mainspring [to] ensure their going, although the rate could not always be relied on'.[49] They were easier and cheaper to replace than to repair.

Half a century after Waltham's successful application of the American system, its success could be seen in the vast output of watches of different qualities and in the dramatic fall in the cost of buying one. Over time the price of watches had steadily fallen in the United States. Good quality English levers that cost about $50 in the 1820s were down to $30 in the 1850s. Swiss equivalents cost perhaps half, at $15. Then Waltham's watchmaking revolution dramatically reduced prices further. The first Waltham watches at $40 had been relatively expensive for ordinary workers earning a dollar a day: it amounted to about one-tenth of their annual income. Prices fell to about $10 in the 1880s.[50] Until the turn of the century traditional watches, set with 'jewelled' bearings, dominated even the cheap end of the market. As the annual output of all watch factories increased, the 'dollar watch' companies caught up, offering extremely cheap, machine-made non-jewelled watches. By 1910, they were comfortably in the lead, making 58 million movements compared to 41 million jewelled watches. The selling price of an unjewelled watch, at about $3.50 in the 1870s, fell to a dollar by the end of the century. And at the bottom end, the choice widened. The New York store, Bloomingdales, offered a range of ten different quality watches 'for men, women, boys, and girls' in 1910 costing from less than two dollars up to one at $7.50 that was guaranteed for twenty years.[51]

Prices did not necessarily equate with quality or value for money. The lifetimes of even good quality watches depended on how often they were cleaned. Annual or eighteen-month cleaning and re-oiling was recommended. For cheap models, the high replacement demand was reflected

Table 11.2 Harrold's estimated output, in millions, of Jewelled and Dollar watches, 1880–1930

	1880	*1890*	*1900*	*1910*	*1920*	*1930*
Jewelled	3	11	23	41	63	80
Dollar	1	5	18	58	115	186

Source: Harrold, *American Watchmaking*, 49–50

in their enormous output.[52] Table 11.2 reveals how much they tapped into the colossal world market that low prices had created.

Assembly lines gathered speed and, by 1930, Harrold estimated that the aggregate output of American watch factories amounted to 266 million. They included about 86 million jewelled watches, led by Elgin at 33 million and Waltham at 27 million. Dollar watches amounted to about 186 million (Ingersoll 74 million, Westclox 50 million, New Haven 20 million, Waterbury 12 million; Ansonia and Ingraham 10 million each). In terms of quantity, the dollar watch had triumphed in the marketplace.[53] It had 'challenged the fundamental economic basis of the American watch industry', Glasmeier concluded, because it was 'a watch that working people could afford'.[54]

Unforeseen developments: overproduction and 'dumping'

Making watches in the vast numbers indicated in Harrold's table had unforeseen consequences. The fall in prices led to cut-throat competition and shrinking profits. Inevitably, some firms failed. Of twenty-five new watchmaking companies formed after 1860, only a few survived beyond 1880. Of the twenty new companies launched after 1880 only half lasted beyond 1900. Overproduction contributed to another unforeseen consequence, when supply sometimes outstripped effective demand. Some firms made more watches than America's internal market could comfortably absorb: 'Years of expansion had created more companies than the market could easily support', Harrold explained, 'the average American watch was thus produced in huge numbers, at an ever-decreasing price, with a correspondingly decreasing profit margin'.[55] When supply outstripped effective demand it created in a kind of 'reverse Malthusian crisis': that is, more watches were made than were being bought – at least, in their home market. Consequently, rather than letting watches accumulate in inventories, firms 'dumped' their surplus output abroad at prices lower than they charged at home – occasionally at prices even below the cost of production. Unlike Britain and Europe, the United States had no ancient guilds that had attempted to control their industries. But the 'Trusts' that emerged in the late nineteenth century, as noted, succeeded in imposing standards for railroad watches. In so doing they followed roughly the same mercantilist objectives as once had London's Clockmakers' Company. Both institutions aimed to control prices in a tariff-protected home market. The American watch industry's Trust was organised in 1885 by the country's largest watch and case manufacturers – the National Association of Jobbers. It later discarded the name, dissolved in 1886, and simply carried on without a title. The practice aroused much hostility in the United States because it violated the spirit of the Sherman anti-trust law of 1890, intended to outlaw such practices in American industries.[56] As Vincent Carosso commented, 'trade associations in the watch industry were not successful'.[57] And, as we shall see, 'dumping' also provoked resentment in Britain (Chapter 12).

The Swiss industry fights back: wristwatches

The successful implementation of the 'American system' by United States watch companies revolutionised watch production in the United States and forced changes in Switzerland. Americans remained dominant in their tariff-protected home market and did especially well in tariff-free Britain (Chapter 12). But in the rest of the world's watch markets, the Swiss fought back. Their successes at international exhibitions in Australia (1879–80), London (1885), Chicago (1893), and Paris (1889 and 1900) opened new markets. A measure of the Swiss recovery was that by 1882 their exports to the United States returned to their pre-crisis level, although they never regained their earlier dominance. In the rest of the world, the Swiss surged ahead. Between 1890 and 1914 their annual watch exports to all countries grew from 3 million units in 1885 to 8 million by 1900 and to 14 million by 1914. Over about three decades the Swiss watch industry achieved a remarkable, sustained, annual growth rate of 5.6 per cent.[58]

One reason for Switzerland's resurgence was its dominance in the early years of the rapidly growing niche market for wristwatches. When the Swiss watchmaking industry recovered after 1876, its transformation had been gradual but steady. They did not set up large factories like those in the United States. In an unforeseen way this gentler evolution worked to its benefit when, at the turn of the century, a new demand emerged for a further miniaturisation of pocket watches in the form of wristwatches. It represented the single greatest shift in the style of wearing a watch for three and a half centuries. For Swiss watch firms, demand for them came by chance at a time when capital investments in their own industry were relatively low. As they were in any event renewing capital equipment, coincidentally, they were enabled to move more easily into making standardised wristwatch parts. They were better placed than big American firms, whose existing heavy investment in machines 'locked' them into continuing to make 'conventional' pocket watches.

For American factories to re-tool with new machines dedicated to make wristwatches would be expensive. So the Swiss were able to leap-frog American watchmaking companies.[59] The Swiss had made watches for hundreds of years but, in the new wristwatch market, they luckily enjoyed the benefits of a late start. Between 1889 and 1900 wristwatches formed a growing portion of the over 50 million watches of all kinds made in Switzerland. By 1920, wristwatches amounted to a quarter of all the Swiss watch industry's production.[60] Switzerland had recovered its leadership in the world's markets and, fortuitously, its industry was also able to adapt to making wristwatches.[61] By the time of the Great War Swiss watches again dominated the world's watch markets (Chapter 17). Switzerland had learned the lessons of the American system and regained the lead it had established by the mid-nineteenth century as the world's largest supplier of watches. In contrast, Clerkenwell's watchmakers and the new British Horological lInstitute rejected the American system, and their industry's decline continued (Chapters 12–14).

Notes

1 J. J. Murphy, 'Entrepreneurship in the Establishment of the American Clock Industry', *Journal of Economic History*, 26 (1966), 169–80, at https://www.jstor.org/stable/2116226; Henry Terry, *American Clock Making: Its Early History and Present Extent of the Business* (Waterbury, CT: Giles & Son, 1870).

2 Mary L. Booth, *New and Complete Clock and Watchmakers' Manual ... With an Appendix Containing a History of Clock and Watchmaking in America* (New York: Wiley, 1877), 280.

3 Charles W. Moore, *Timing a Century: History of the Waltham Watch Company*, Harvard Studies in Business History, XI (Cambridge, MA: Harvard UP, 1945), Ch. 3 'The Waltham Pocket Watch'; also Vincent P. Carosso, 'The Waltham Watch Company: A Case History', *Bulletin of the Business History Society*, 23/4 (Dec. 1949), Doi:10.2307/3110545, JSTOR 3110545

4 William Sellers, in Chauncey Depew, *One Hundred Years of American Commerce* (New York: Haynes, 1895; 1895: reprinted Montana: Whitefish, 2010): within a few years of writing this, Sellers could have added automobiles; also John E. Sawyer, 'The Social Basis of the American System of Manufacturing', *The Journal of Economic History*, 14 (1954), 361–79, at https://www.jstor.org/stable/2114247

5 Online at http://www.pocketwatchrepair.com/histories/sears-roebuck.php.

6 H.M. Gitelman, 'The Labor Force at Waltham Watch during the Civil War Era', *The Journal of Economic History*, 25/2 (June 1965), 214–43, at https://www.jstor.org/stable/2116148, notes the 'sharply rising demand for watches generated during the Civil War' (p. 228).

7 Carlene Stevens, '"The Most Reliable Time": William Bond, the New England Railroads, and Time Awareness in 19th-Century America', *Technology and Culture*, 30 (Jan. 1989), 1–24, at https://doi.org/10.2307/3105429 and https://www.jstor.org/stable/3105429

8 Carosso, 'The Waltham Watch Company', 171ff.

9 *Twelfth Census of the United States* (Census Bulletin 173, May 21, 1902): William A. Countryman, 'Report on the 'Growth of the US Watch Industry, 1870–1900: Table 1', 'Watches and Watch Cases', 485–98.

10 John Allwood, *The Great Exhibitions* (London: Studio Vista, 1977), passim.
11 Dee Brown, *The Year of the Century: 1876* (New York, Charles Scribners, 1966); J.S. Ingram, *The Centennial Exposition: Described and Illustrated: Being a Concise and Graphic Description of This Grand Enterprise Commemorative of the First Centenary of American Independence* (Philadelphia, PA: Hubbard Bros., 1876), at http://archive.org/details/centennialexposi00ingr
12 For the Swiss reaction, see Pierre-Yves Donzé, *History of the Swiss Watch Industry: From Jacques David to Nicolas Hayek* (Pieterlen Switzerland: Peter Lang AG, 2012: 3rd ed. 2014), 30ff, 56: 'The Shock of Philadelphia'.
13 *BPP* (1877), vol. 6: James C. Watson, 'Horological Instruments ... Philadelphia Exhibition', 823–24.
14 Richard C. McCormick, 'Our Success in Paris in 1878', *The North American Review*, 129, no.272 (1879), 1–22, at https://www.jstor.org/stable/25100773; Alun C. Davies, 'Horology at International Exhibitions, 1851–1900', *Antiquarian Horology*, 33/5 (Sept. 2013), esp. 598–99.
15 Ivan D. Steen, 'America's First World's Fair: The Exhibition of the Industry of All Nations at New York's First Crystal Palace, 1853–1854', *The New York Historical Society Quarterly*, 47 (1963), 256–87; also Robert C. Post, 'Reflections of American Science and Technology at the New York Crystal Palace Exhibition of 1853', *Journal of American Studies*, 17/3 (Dec. 1983), 337–56, at www.jstor.org/stable/27554357; and William C. Richards, *A Day in the New York Crystal Palace and How to Make the Most of It* (New York: Putnam, 1853), 147. Visitors were intrigued by the smallest of Patek Philippe's watches, with an outside diameter of less than a third of an inch.
16 Edward Young, *Labor in Europe and America: A Special Report on the Condition of the Working Classes in Great Britain ... Also in the United States and British America* (Washington, DC: Government Printing Office, 1876), see 'Watchmakers wages in Britain'.
17 Andre Francillon, *History of Longines. Translation of Histoire de la Fabrique des Longines Précédée d'un Essai sur le Comptoir Agassiz*, published by Companie des Montres Longines, Translated and published online by Richard Watkins at https://www.watkinsr.id.au/Francillon.pdf; also Richard Watkins, 'Jacques David – and a Summary of "American and Swiss Watchmaking in 1876"', *NAWCC Bulletin*, No. 250 (June 2004), 294–302, at http://www.watkinsr.id.au/Art1876.pdf
18 Jacques David, *American and Swiss Watchmaking in 1876. (Rapport a la Société Intercantonale des Industries du Jura sur la Fabrication de L'horlogerie aux Etats-Unis* (Saint-Imier: Compagnie des Montres, 1876; translated by Richard Watkins, online at http://www.watkinsr.id.au/david.html
19 Eduard Favre-Perret, 'Watchmaking in the United States', *Watchmaker, Jeweller and Silversmith* (5, Feb. 1877), 200–01; 'Report' by [US] Consul Mason of Basle (1880) in *US Consular Reports* (Washington, DC), vol. 1 (1881), 574; also *Horological Journal*, 19/6 (Feb. 1877), 81, and Fortunat F. Mueller-Maerki's review of the proceedings of a colloquium on 'The American Challenge in Watchmaking', *Antiquarian Horology*, 33/3 (March 2012), 365–66.
20 See the *New York Jewellers' Circular and Horological Review*, 'Report on Paris Exhibition', 9/2 (March 1878), xviii–xix and 21, and letters in the subsequent July issue.
21 Donzé, *Swiss Watch Industry*, 33; A brief account of progress made between 1876 and 1890 is in William Simpson, 'Swiss Watchmaking Industry'. *The Journal of the Society of Arts*, 39/2028 (Oct. 1891), 850–51, at www.jstor.org/stable/41328292
22 Donzé, *Swiss Watch Industry*, 40.

23 Amy K. Glasmeier. *Manufacturing Time: Global Competition in the Watch Industry, 1795–2000*, Perspectives on Economic Change (New York: Guilford Press, 2000), 130 and for subsequent quotations.
24 August C. Bolino, 'British and American Horology: A Comment on Hoke', *Journal of Economic History*, 48/3 (Sept. 1988), 667, at https://www.jstor.org/stable/2121544 noted that 'the Swiss machinery emphasised single operations: whereas American factories tended to use complex machines performing many operations in sequence'.
25 *BPP* 1880 32: Paris Universal Exhibition (1878): *Reports of the Commissioners on Horology.*
26 [Sydney International Exhibition, 1879] *Official Record: Horology, Class 310* (Sydney, International Exhibition, 1881), 401–21.
27 'Reports and Letters on the Melbourne Exhibition', *Horological Journal*, 23 (May 1880), 116–19; (July 1880), 150–52; (Aug. 1880), 162–63.
28 Donzé, *Swiss Watch Industry*, 35.
29 Donald J. Hoke, *Ingenious Yankees: The Rise of the American System of Manufacture in the Private Sector* (New York: Columbia UP, 1990), 181, 203ff; also id., 'Ingenious Yankees: The Rise of the American System of Manufactures in the Private Sector', *Journal of Economic History*, 46/2 (June 1986), 489, at https://www.jstor.org/stable/2122179; also Alun C. Davies, 'Horology, Technology, and Ingenious Yankees', *Antiquarian Horology*, 22/1 (Spring 1995), 69–73.
30 W.F. Durfee, 'The History and Modern Development of the Art of Interchangeable Mechanisms', *Transactions of the American Society of Mechanical Engineers*, 22 (1895), 1225–57; and Joseph Wickham Roe, *Interchangeable Manufactures in American Industry* (Birmingham, AL: Newcomen Society of North America, 1939).
31 David Penney, email, 11 January 2009.
32 Donald J. Hoke, 'British and American Horology', *Journal of Economic History*, 47/2 (June 1987), 322, at https://www.jstor.org/stable/2122231.
33 Henry Ford and Frederick Winslow Taylor would have approved this ergonomically satisfying concept. Ford got the idea of applying the American system after visiting Waltham: H.M. Gitelman, 'The Labor Force at Waltham Watch during the Civil War Era', *The Journal of Economic History*, 25/2 (June 1965), 230, fn. 33, at https://www.jstor.org/stable/2116148
34 Hoke, *Ingenious Yankees*, 183–84.
35 Glasmeier, *Manufacturing Time*, 118–20.
36 August C. Bolino, 'British and American Horology: A Comment on Hoke', *Journal of Economic History*, 48/3 (Sept. 1988), 667, at https://www.jstor.org/stable/2121544: 'Most companies failed, or were absorbed by others that later failed', citing the examples of Auburndale, Tremont, Keystone, Aurora, Cornell, Manhattan, Marion 'and many others'.
37 Michael C. Harrold, *American Watchmaking: A Technical History of the American Watch Industry, 1850–1930* (Columbia PA: NAWCC, 1981).
38 Alexis McCrossen, *Marking Modern Times: A History of Clocks, Watches, and Other Timekeepers in American Life* (Chicago: Chicago UP, 2013), 47–49.
39 Glasmeier, *Manufacturing Time*, 126.
40 Harrold, *American Watchmaking*, 79.
41 Glasmeier, *Manufacturing Time*, 127–28.
42 Glasmeier, *Manufacturing Time*, 131.
43 F.J. Britten, *Britten's Old Clocks and Watches and their Makers* (London: Batsford, 1899; 9th revised edition, Woodbridge: Antique Collector's Club, 1982), 146–47; Maxwell Cutmore, *Watches, 1850–1980* (Newton Abbot: David & Charles, 1989), 54–56 Eugene Jacquet and Alfred Chapuis,

Technique and History of the Swiss Watch (1953; London: Hamlyn, 1970 ed.), 167–69; David Thompson, 'Roskopf', *Watches* (London, British Museum, 2008), 132–33; also report of a lecture by Jim Wastell on 'The History of the Dollar Watch', *Antiquarian Horology*, 24/5 (Spring 1999), 467–68. For a journalist's account, see Robert Froman, 'The Watch that made the Dollar Famous', *Challenge*, 1/5 (1953), 28–31, at www.jstor.org/stable/40716575.

44 BPP 1867–68, vol. 30: *Report from the Commissioners: Paris Exhibition, 1867*: 'Report on horological instruments', by C.R. Weld.

45 David Thompson, 'Auburndale Watch Company', *Watches* (London: British Museum, 2008), 130–31; Harrold, *American Watchmaking*, 55–56; Edwin A. Battison, *The Auburndale Watch Company: The First American Attempt Toward the Dollar Watch* (Project Gutenberg online 2009: eBook #29934, at https://www.gutenberg.org/files/29934/29934-h/29934-h.htm).

46 Joseph Anderson (ed.), *The Town and City of Waterbury, Conn., from the Aboriginal Period to the Year 1895* (New Haven: Price, Lee & Co., 1896), vol. 3, 377–81, 399–402; quote 400; David Thompson, 'New England Watch Company: Waterbury', *Watches* (London: British Museum, 2008), 138–39.

47 Harrold, *American Watchmaking*, 56; Cutmore, *Watches*, 153–54.

48 A comprehensive survey is Reid Badger, *The Great American Fair: The World's Columbian Exposition and American Culture* (Chicago, IL: Nelson Hall, 1979).

49 George Daniels, *English and American Watches* (London: Abelard-Schuman, 1967), 51.

50 Glasmeier, *Manufacturing Time*, 115, 121ff.

51 Bloomingdales' (New York) *Diary and Catalogue for 1910*, at https://libmma.contentdm.oclc.org/digital/collection/p16028coll13/id/2844).

52 McCrossen, *Marking Modern Times* (2013), 81.

53 Harrold, *American Watchmaking*, 52.

54 Glasmeier, *Manufacturing Time*, 125.

55 Harrold, *American Watchmaking*, 51.

56 Randle Edwin Dahl, 'The American Watch Movement Manufacturing Industry: A Survey Based on the Journals of the Trade' (unpublished Ph.D. thesis, Clark University, Worcester, MA, 1941), especially Chapters 6 and 7, which trace the origins and development of watch trusts from the 1880s; also McCrossen, *Marking Modern Times*, Ch. 3.

57 Carosso, 'The Waltham Watch Company', 173.

58 David S. Landes, *Revolution in Time: Clocks and the Making of the Modern World* (Cambridge MA: Belknap, Harvard University Press, 1983). Table 7, 384; For contemporary notes on the transition from small workshops to watch factories by 1891 see Simpson, 'Swiss Watchmaking Industry', 850–51, at https://www.jstor.org/stable/41328292

59 Glasmeier, *Marketing Time*, 128.

60 Donzé. *Swiss Watch Industry*, 58.

61 Harrold, *American Watchmaking*, 37.

12 Consequences for Britain

Reaction to the Centennial: the productivity gap

A relevant indication of the effect that Waltham's 'revolution in watchmaking' had on the English watch industry could be seen in its reaction to the Centennial Exhibition in Philadelphia in 1876. It was another in the series of major international industrial exhibitions – in Dublin, New York, Paris, Vienna – that followed London's Great Exhibition at the Crystal Palace in 1851.[1] Subsequently, annual statistics published in the *Horological Journal* had revealed British horology's steadily worsening balance of horological trade with other countries. Exports, especially those to the United States, had declined. The protective Morrill tariff, initially imposed during the Civil War, was blamed. For English watch firms the prospect of participating in the Centennial exhibition was viewed with a mixture of indifference and hostility: it was seen as an opportunity to make their displeasure at the tariff known by their near absence.[2] Apart from the Anglo-Swiss firm of Nicole Nielsen (always alert to the opportunity of international exhibitions) most English watch firms recoiled from competition in a distant arena. Only fourteen representatives from scores of English firms bothered to visit Philadelphia. American reaction to the snub was disdain, best summed up by James Watson, the American juror on the 'Horological Instruments' panel. He dismissed 'the old-fashioned, clumsy English lever watch, with fusee and chain still made and sold in considerable quantities for home demand. They have long since ceased to be sent abroad as in olden times'. Among those delegates who did attend were, notably, several chronometer manufacturers. Reaction to the display of English chronometers was different. Frodsham sent examples, as did Joseph Sewill of Liverpool. Dent's display included instruments by Mercer, Kullberg, and James Poole. All were greeted with approval. Watson's glowing verdict on English chronometers that, yet again, they were 'the very best possible specimens' was proudly reprinted in the British Commission's report to Parliament.[3]

The exhibition's horological section revealed the differences between the structures of the watch industries in New and old England. An initial productivity gap had become enormous, and continued to widen.

DOI: 10.4324/9781003227823-15

Clerkenwell's traditional methods still prevailed; even wheels were hand finished. But in Waltham, as a report in *The Times* newspaper commented, and *The Spectator* reprinted,

> ...there are nearly 1,200 different machines, besides duplicates, in use there, and more than 120 different machines are used to form and perfect the escapement. There are seven automatic screw-making machines, all tended by one man. Each of the machines produces 3,000 minute screws of various sizes, per day, from the pin of wire; and each screw is complete, with thread, head, and slot. It will take 200,000 of the smaller screws to make 1 lb., and the factory now supplies nearly all the screws required for watch repairs through-out the country. The factory also completes 375 watch movements daily, and the market for these is extending so rapidly, even in this country, that the London agency alone sold 23,040 watch movements last year, i.e., the fruits of ten weeks' production...[4]

Over the next decade, the productivity gap opened further. By about 1880 an American worker with a twenty-ton punch 'blanked out' about 10,000 wheels a day. Traditional methods may have been tolerable for Clerkenwell's firms that made small numbers of excellent watches for the top end of the trade. But for the future of England's watchmaking industry, the productivity differences were ominous. As the *Horological Journal's* annual 'balance of trade' tables revealed, England's watchmakers were losing their home market and their once-healthy export markets, not only to the Swiss as before, but also to American firms.

Impact of American watches on Britain's home market

The world's watch market was inexorably growing. The United States' population increased from 38 million in 1870 to 92 million by 1910. It constituted a vast home market that stimulated the emergence of new watch companies which attempted to emulate Waltham and Elgin. All had factories. One consequence was that a larger production of watches was made that could sometimes be sold at home (Chapter 11). Watch firms then looked for other markets. An obvious target was Britain: its population of 31 million in 1871 rose to 42 million by 1911.[5] It offered American firms an enticing extension of their home market. Britain's legal and commercial milieu was especially favourable. 'Time-awareness' was almost ubiquitous and many in employment had, or wanted to have, watches. Public transport and the working day in factories, businesses, and shops were organised around Greenwich Mean Time, to which railway timetables were synchronised.[6] Britain was the hub for much of the world's trade. Britain's empire was run by English speakers. Above all, in Britain itself there were neither tariff nor language barriers. It was an open market, especially tempting to American watch firms. Clerkenwell's watchmakers simply assumed that the technical superiority of the best English compared with American watches was self-evident, and did not need publicity: 'good wine needed no bush'. This over-confident – even arrogant – approach contrasted with the robust sales strategies of American firms, whose export achievements by 1875 shocked observers: 'The success of American watches in England has been utterly surprising to the old fogies on both sides of the water'.[7]

In 1878, all of Waltham's watches sent to the Paris international exhibition were sold within a week. In the same year, Waltham sold 400 watches to the British-India State Railway, and the *Horological Journal* commented that 'we could only wonder what our British makers were doing, that such an order should have been given'.[8] In the following year, the Great Northern Railway Company bought twenty watches from Waltham for the use of guards on the Scottish express. This initial dribble of American exports of railroad watches to Britain eventually became a flood. Waltham was not the only American company to taste success abroad. Another enterprising pioneer firm, the Illinois Watch Company, mounted a sales campaign that explicitly stressed the merits of non-magnetic railway watches. It prompted the *Horological Journal* to wonder 'Are there no non-magnetic watches of home production to be had?'[9] The issue became even more urgent in 1890 with the opening of London's underground railway network, when the magnetic effect of electric trains on the time-keeping of ordinary watches was alleged to be malign. Eventually, Smith & Son of the Strand devoted several pages of their *Guide to the Purchase of a Watch* in 1900 to advertise their 'Non-Magnetizable Watches'. Most of the watches that Smith's offered were 'magnetic', but for an extra cost they could be de-magnetised.[10] Eventually, the doomed Lancashire Watch Company, just before its demise (Chapter 15), offered the *Vigilant*, a 'railway watch' in a nickel case at three guineas, made non-magnetic for an extra 10s.[11] Ironically, in the country that had pioneered railways, the cream of the market for 'railroad watches' was lost to American firms.

The modest initial trickle of American railway watches was joined by cheap watches from a new generation of American watch companies. The *Horological Journal* lamented that inexpensive watches like 'the despised Waterbury [were] steadily creeping into recognition' in Britain's shops: this was perhaps because one of Waterbury's two newest models had a 'seconds' hand.[12] For first-time buyers, machine-made jewelled and non-jewelled 'dollar' watches seemed to offer better value for money than even Coventry's cheapest. The British market, hitherto dominated by the Swiss, now became the target for large export drives by American watch firms. In this, they were overtly urged by the United States' energetic Consular service.

America's consular service

In the Republic's early years the United States' consuls had merely reported local conditions in the country to which they'd been assigned, not specific export opportunities.[13] For horological firms, this has changed in the 1840s with the advent of New England's factory-produced clocks. The United States' consuls corresponded directly with Chauncey Jerome's and other 'Yankee' clock firms and helped them to establish direct connections with foreign import agencies.[14] The same strategy was extended to Hong Kong in 1844, enabling inroads into Britain's former Far Eastern markets (Chapter 5). Jerome's example was followed forty years later by America's new watch firms. The monthly *US Consular Reports* reveal that some consuls acted as unofficial trade agents for several industries when they sent specific market information to the State Department. It was much to the benefit of potential exporters among America's rapidly growing industries, like watches, bicycles, sewing machines, and even canned tomatoes. Such information was invaluable especially, as we shall see, when the output of watch factories sometimes exceeded the effective demand from America's domestic market.[15]

Watch exports to Britain were explicitly encouraged by Claude Meeker, the American consul in Bradford. He reported opportunities for the sale of American watches and clocks (and a variety of other American products) in the Midlands and north of England.[16] His well-informed despatches alerted potential exporters of likely difficulties and warned against using 'very respectable but conservative English middlemen as agents'. Opportunities for American firms were great, he enthused: 'the general run of customers *asks* for watches with the Waltham works'. The Bradford jewellers, Fattorini & Sons, had a stock of some 20,000 watches from Waltham as well as 'great numbers' from Elgin and other firms.[17] American clocks and watches, once despised for their alleged shoddiness, were building up reputations for being 'good value for money'.[18] The intrinsic qualities of alarm and mantel clocks made by the Seth Thomas Company were held in especially high repute, Meeker reported, not merely because they were cheap.[19]

Similar advice from the United States consulate service helped exports from American watch companies in European markets, hitherto dominated by the Swiss. Advice from their consul in Trieste, Frederick W. Hossfield, in the *Consular Reports of* June 1902 was reprinted for other consuls in a pamphlet *How to Find a Market*. Like Meeker, Hossfield advised American horological firms to employ American not foreign agents, who were 'rarely as efficient as American salesmen'. Above all, in Europe they should correspond in the relevant foreign language:[20]

> American watches will not sell themselves, like American wheat or cotton. Their excellence and their comparatively moderate prices

should be brought to the notice of foreign importers and dealers, and for this purpose letters and circulars in English are of little avail, as they usually go to the wastepaper basket ... Satisfactory and permanent markets for our manufactured goods can... be best established abroad by our own salesmen who are familiar with the customs and languages of people among whom trade is sought ... It will surprise the Swiss watch and the German clock manufacturers when their American rivals decide to dispatch a few wide-awake drummers across the Atlantic to work up a trade for the American timepiece.

The Ingersoll brothers

The greatest American influence on the British watch market came from the Ingersoll brothers, Charles and Robert – the latter was the man behind the memorable slogan 'The watch that made the dollar famous' (Figure 12.1). After they reorganised their Connecticut factory in 1898 as the *New England Watch Company,* its output reached a million a

Figure 12.1 Robert Ingersoll (1859–1928) Portrait. Copyright: David Penney. http://www.antiquewatchstore.com/.

year. By 1901, the company was sending from 6,000 to 8,000 watches weekly to England and discussing an order from a London wholesaler for 1 million. That consignment eventually included a Boer War souvenir model with a coloured dial that showed Victoria and some of her generals.[21] Britain's open market was seduced by the marketing strategies that Robert Ingersoll innovated in 1905. At first, he had personally called on London's horological wholesalers, but found their responses disappointing. He then mounted a campaign of full-page and half-page advertisements in national newspapers and magazines and mailed 15,000 copies of a promotional leaflet ('*Our Silent Salesman*') to retail jewellers across the country whose names and addresses were extracted from Kelly's *Directories*. Their window displays showed five-shilling ['dollar'] watches, guaranteed for a year. Some more expensive new models were introduced, including the *Ingersoll-Trenton* which sold for a guinea, and the *Traveller*, a watch with a porcelain dial mounted in a metal frame covered with Morocco leather. The *Auto* had a special case for mounting on a motor car dashboard, ostensibly to enable the user to tell lighting-up time.[22] Gradually, then briskly, Ingersoll's business flourished.

Other American companies followed Ingersoll's lead into the British market. The New Haven Company started in 1880 (like Waterbury) was one of several that eventually rivalled Ingersoll's successes. Others included the Western Clock Company (later Westclox) in 1899, Ansonia in 1904 and Ingraham in 1912. Ingersoll itself expanded when it absorbed rival watch companies (Trenton in 1908, New England in 1914).[23] The Company eventually failed in 1922 but by then it had produced over 60 million watches. The least one can say of Ingersoll's watches is that, like Henry Ford's Model T, it created a demand for a better product.

Dumping and tariff reform re-emerge

Managers of American watch companies openly regarded Britain as an extension of their own domestic market and frequently remarked on the absence of language problems and Britain's free trade policy.[24] In 1885, the *Horological Journal* commented that, but for the existence of the British market, American watch factories 'would this summer have had two months' additional vacation'. [25] 'Over-production' occurred when some watch factories accumulated large inventories, exceeding the number saleable in the home market, especially if they had agreed to a fixed price with retailers. It is unclear how many of those watches were explicitly 'dumped' in British and other markets following 'overproduction', for the two markets were seen as one. In the 1880s, Waltham alone sold about 60,000 watches a year in Britain. High tariffs in the United States' protected its own watch industry and caused managers of European watch firms (like T.P. Hewitt of the Lancashire Watch Company) to see this as simply 'unfair' (below, and Chapter 15). American firms took a different view. They claimed such exports were legitimate: they fed gaps in Britain's market that English watchmakers were unable or unwilling to satisfy. Either way, British firms simply could not compete at their prices.

One reaction to the invasion of foreign watches was that English watch firms yearned for the return of tariff protection. They supported Joseph Chamberlin's attempt to reintroduce protection into English politics through the Tariff Reform League, even though tariffs had been utterly ineffective in excluding Swiss watches in the decades before free trade. Their champion was T.P. Hewitt, manager in the 1890s of the struggling Lancashire Watch Company in Prescot (Chapter 16). In September 1904, he complained to a joint meeting of the Tariff Reform Commission and the British Horological Institute about the unfairness of the United States' high protective tariffs. It had, he claimed, 'thrust English and Continental makers out of their [own] country'.[26] A retaliatory tariff of 20 per cent, he thought, would protect Britain's home and imperial markets. But most working-class voters remained hostile to protection, and the hopes of Hewitt and his fellow tariff reformers were resoundingly crushed in 1905 when David Lloyd George became President of the Board of Trade. Lloyd George was a leading protagonist of free trade in a Liberal government that believed that cheap imported watches were among the economic advantages it brought to British consumers.

The Liberal Party's overwhelming landslide victory in the election of 1906 ended the forlorn hope that Britain's watchmaking industry might be revived through a protective tariff. Free traders advocated the Social Darwinist view that weak industries would – should – go to the wall. One of Lloyd George's protégés, Sir Leo George Chiozza, pointedly drew unfavourable comparisons between watchmaking, an old industry, and bicycle manufacture, a new one:

> as to a watch or a cycle, the obvious comment is that the enormous importation of cheap watches seems to show that we do not shine in their manufacture; while the small and decreasing importation of cycles as clearly indicates that we are more than able to hold our own in another direction.[27]

By the early 1900s, imported watches exceeded a million a year. An episode then occurred that illustrated – and revived – the issue of the alleged dumping of American watches.

Excellent, top-class watches – made in the United States in 1907 at a cost price of $42.50 – had been sold to American retailers. They were obliged to sign an agreement not to sell them in the United States for less than $60 each. Then, to enable the company to clear its stocks, several thousand of its 'surplus output' (probably from a 'production overrun') was sold for $30 a movement to a New York dealer, Charles A. Keane, for export to Britain. Keane, through an agent, then shipped them back to the United States. No tariff needed to be paid for they were, after all, American made! They were then offered for sale in the United States at $42.50, thus simultaneously making a profit above their cost price, whilst also undercutting those watches that earlier were agreed to be sold in the United States at the fixed price of $60. When the American Watch Trust attempted to cut off Mr Keene's supply, Keene asked Lloyd George, at the Board of Trade, to rule that such attempts (to interfere in Britain's trading arrangements) amounted to 'coercion and an operation in restraint of trade' and were, consequently, illegal.[28] That good quality watches were being off-loaded abroad, by American watch companies at attractive prices was much to the benefit of British customers. It was a policy opposed, unsuccessfully, both by the American Watch Trust and by the English watchmaking industry.

Britain's wristwatch market

American dominance in the niche markets for 'railroad' and 'dollar' watches were the main features of the American penetration of Britain's market in the 1880s and 1890s. By the early twentieth century, Britain's most distinctive new niche market was that for wristwatches. Wristwatches had first appeared in Britain in their modern form in the 1880s when ladies who rode to hounds wore watches in specially made leather bracelets strapped to their wrists. They became popular and for social occasions were set in gold bracelets.[29] But by the mid-1890s most ladies watches were hung from *chatelaines*. In the first decade of the century, demand grew for watches strapped to wrists, encouraged by the bicycle boom: it was obviously easier to glance at a wristwatch than to take out and return a pocket watch.[30] By 1910, the *Horological Journal* regularly carried advertisements for wristwatches.[31] The lead in supplying them came from Swiss companies (Chapter11). Longines first captured the new market in Britain when they made 'wrists' for leading London retailers (who, in time-honoured practice, put their own names on the dials).[32] As the British market for wristwatches grew, American firms caught up, and Waltham and Ingersoll supplied movements for cases made in Aaron Dennison's Birmingham factory (Chapter 15). Ingersoll imported parts of wristwatch movements to be assembled in London in 1911.[33] They included a slim ladies' version of a standard wristwatch, fitted with lugs and a strap, sold as the *Midget* for 8s 6d. Their output of all types of watches, including wristwatches, eventually amounted to about 4,000 a day, or over a million a year.[34] Nevertheless, the American watch industry, hampered by its massive fixed-machine investment in pocket watch production, left Britain's wristwatch market, as Glasmeier concluded, 'almost completely to the Swiss industry' (Chapter 11). [35]

In the emerging market for wristwatches, British firms once again trailed both Swiss and Americans. Some well-established London retailers like J.W. Benson and makers like Nicole Nielsen entered the wristwatch market in a small way.[36] Eventually, the three largest British firms made wristwatches, though their output is unknown. Williamson of Coventry aimed at the cheaper end of the market but, because it owned the Buren Watch Company in Switzerland, it is unclear what portions of their watches were English or Swiss. Coventry's other large firm, Rotherham, made small wristwatch movements and matching cases, dials and hands. During the Great War, it stopped making watches and converted to making war *materiel* (Chapter 17), but after 1918 it returned to wristwatch production. The third English firm to make wristwatches was the Lancashire Watch Company in Prescot, just before it became bankrupt in 1910 (Chapter 15). Marketing wristwatches in Britain was a triumph for the Swiss, well ahead of substantial but late American involvement, and the much smaller British contribution. The shrinking share of its own home market for wristwatches was another illustration of the decline of England's watch industry. So, too, was the loss of its once secure export markets.

Loss of export markets

Well before the impact of Waltham's watchmaking revolution was felt, Britain's export markets were being lost. During the peak years of Britain's watchmaking pre-eminence in the late eighteenth century, Carlo Cipolla estimated that more than half of Clerkenwell's output was exported – a reflection of the excellence of English watchmaking and Britain's standing in world trade.[37] Clocks and watches were exported to India, the Ottoman Empire, China, and to the newly independent United States. Not so many were exported to those European countries that had their own watch firms or to where Swiss watches were already dominant. Even after the long interruption of the French and Napoleonic wars, some horological export markets survived. But although Britain had become the 'workshop of the world' these old horological markets were fading, inexorably. For the rest of the century, English watchmaking's share in the world's output fell further. Between 1862 and 1902, the aggregate annual production of watches in the world more than tripled, but England's share fell from about 6 per cent to 2½ per cent.[38] By 1914 it had fallen even further, to about 1 per cent or less. Why? What were the main stages in and reasons for this decline?

Liverpool's and Coventry's exports decline

Liverpool's and Coventry's watch exports to the United States had begun their decline in the 1850s, well before the effects of Waltham's watchmaking revolution were felt. Until then, Liverpool's small watch finishing hub had been relatively healthy. In 1834, some 143 firms belonged to one or other of horology's many branches in the city; twenty-eight made ancillary products such as cases and glasses or provided services such as engraving and gilding.[39] In 1841, Liverpool's watch output was reported to be about 8,000 a year, consisting of modestly priced watches, mostly exported to the United States, thanks to M.I. Tobias and his network of relatives and agents.[40] They had included 'large full plate movements without cases, packed in tin-lined boxes ... to "The States" at £100 a dozen!... one firm here alone sending about 200 of such watches a week and paying the men proportionate prices for the work'.[41] Then exports suddenly declined. Why? As William Rodgers later explained in his memoir, he thought blame lay with both masters and workmen: their poor sales strategies had fouled their own nests.

> Watches were exported without cases in what were called 'block movements ... with poor mainsprings, and fusee chains so thin that they frequently broke before they were shipped out ... everyone was content with the old method of production, old models of construction, and old ways of distribution... and what afterwards seemed a temporary slackness developed into a permanent stagnation.[42]

The subsequent successes of Waltham and Elgin took the matter out of the hands of Liverpool's firms. The American civil war and the introduction of the Morrill tariff saw duty on imported watches increase from 12 to 20 per cent, then to 25 per cent (and even higher with the Dingley tariff of 1897). Rodgers thought that American tariffs, combined with the success of Waltham's revolution in watchmaking, explained the demise of Liverpool's small watch finishing industry. Although in 1871, the United States still imported from Britain 'watches, and parts of, and watch materials and movements' to the value of $3.1 million; by 1890 the value of that trade had fallen to $25,000, less than 1 per cent of what it had been twenty years earlier.[43] Liverpool's once-important American export market had virtually disappeared. By the end of the century, only John Kellie's Liverpool firm was left, lone survivor of Thomas Russell & Son, a once-great exporting firm. Rodgers explained that 'most of the Liverpool manufacturers wisely closed up and the few who went on, hoping for a revival, mostly failed... the time has gone for ever'. Thereafter, the United States' rigorously enforced protective tariffs hindered even Clerkenwell's expensive, top-class watches, from competing in America.[44]

Coventry's watch exports suffered a similar decline, and for much the same reason. Before 1850 their flourishing export market to the United States included about half of Rotherham's output. When exports plummeted, the young John Rotherham (1838–1905), heir to and later proprietor of the family's watchmaking firm went to America in 1856 to investigate. In a memoir written almost half a century afterwards he explained that when he

> called on the large merchants in New York, and they shewed me drawer after drawer of Coventry watches, not one of which would go. They had been sent out with insufficient care, and the cost of repairing them out there was so great that they simply lay there, and the people who bought them were disgusted, and so was I.[45]

Chastened, young Rotherham visited the Waltham watch factory, then on the eve of its success. He returned and warned the English industry of the potential threat posed by the application of the 'American system' to watchmaking. He recalled that his warnings went unheeded, partly because the slump in Rotherham's American exports was temporarily offset by a surge in demand following the Australian gold rush. When John Rotherham eventually assumed control of his family's firm he was influenced by his early experiences. He welcomed some new ideas and initiatives and attempted to adopt features of the American system. We shall see (Chapter 15) that, in 1880, after further examining Swiss machines and seeing the consequences of the 'American system', he installed machine tools in his Coventry factory.[46] In the meantime, Coventry's export market to the United States, like Liverpool's, was lost. Two decades later the Swiss firm Longines experienced a similar decline in its exports (Chapter 11). Unlike watch firms in Coventry and Liverpool, the Swiss learned from their trauma.

Lost imperial and foreign markets

As Britain's share of the United States' watch market shrank, so did its remaining transatlantic watch markets. In 1869, Henry Ganney bemoaned the loss of markets that were 'once peculiarly English' – in Canada, Cuba, and the West Indies. English clocks lost out to the popular factory-made models from New England because 'Yankee' clocks were easily set up, adjusted, reliable and – above all – cheap.[47] The watch market followed suit in the 1880s, with the notable shrinking of former well-established imperial markets in South Africa, Singapore, Australia, and New Zealand. As their populations and economies grew, so their markets fell to American exporters of a variety of products such as sewing machines, canned goods, and what were called 'Yankee notions' miscellaneous novelties (like Birmingham's 'toys') including pins, needles, hooks, scissors, combs, buttons, and other trinkets. Those commodities included clocks and watches. In South Africa, for example, British goods had once received automatic preference. In 1882, the American consul in Cape Town reported that American timepieces 'command ready sales and good prices. This trade is worth looking after'.[48] Singapore became another market under threat. There, American clocks again led the way, because they were cheap and within the reach of 'even poor natives'. They were 'very reliable timekeepers, besides being small and of neat appearance and finish, well made, [and] they recommended themselves'.[49] In Singapore, it cost about $5 to get a watch cleaned. As a reliable Yankee clock cost only about $3, the American consul reported that the owner of a watch in need of cleaning 'can afford to lock his watch up until he gets to a place where it can be attended to for less money. The clock trade is not only getting on nicely but looking up'. American watches followed. By the early 1880s, only American companies regularly exported watches to Singapore and its hinterland.[50] British watches companies were nowhere to be seen, even in English-speaking countries like New Zealand and Australia. The once-exclusively British imperial markets there also slipped away: between 1870 and 1914 the size of their combined population grew from about 2 to 5 million. The United States' *Consular Reports* recorded that in the 1870s sales of American watches and clocks in New Zealand at $912,000 a year, were a 'small but growing' market. Then sales accelerated. Mr Bartlett, a leading jeweller in Queen Street, Auckland, explained that

> it is difficult to sell an English Watch... everyone seems to want an American watch...There is not a boy or a servant girl in the country who can raise five pounds who does not want to invest it in an American watch.[51]

Encouragement by America's energetic consular officials was a notable feature of the successful invasion of Britain's former export markets. Government employees such as consuls were supposedly not permitted to function as commercial travellers and there is no firm evidence to support the suspicion that some strayed beyond the legal boundaries. Nevertheless, American consuls in the antipodes enthusiastically pointed out opportunities and potential pitfalls in detailed reports that found their way to watch exporters. The consul in Auckland, New Zealand, performed his duties so enthusiastically that his reports read as if he was a proselytising sales agent for Waltham watches. Consul G.W. Griffin's reports on the international exhibitions held in Sydney in 1879 and Melbourne in 1880 were unqualified paeans of praise for Waltham watches that might have come straight from that company's advertising department.[52] In the Exhibitions, Waltham's stunning displays (further developed from those in the 1876 Centennial, 1878 Paris, and 1885 London 'Inventions' exhibitions) impressed juries and won prize medals.[53] Waltham's simple and effective marketing strategies subsequently swept up the Australian market. Its agents and branch offices appeared in principal towns. Its head office in Sydney occupied 'a large and magnificent quarters, known as the Waltham buildings'.[54] There was nothing like it from any Clerkenwell or Coventry firm. The market for English watches in the antipodes, as elsewhere, was lost.

Conclusion

By the early twentieth century, most of Britain's once healthy watch exports had all but vanished. Their demise was a consequence of the revolution in watchmaking that had spread from America to Switzerland. The Great War finished the job (Chapter 17). It dealt a mortal blow to the last remnants of English watchmaking's export trade, even in the furthest redoubts of the Empire. Low-priced but poor-quality Coventry and Liverpool watches could not compete on Waltham and Elgin's tariff-protected home ground, and certainly not elsewhere. The maximum combined annual production of England's four biggest companies – Ehrhardt's in Birmingham, Rotherham and Williamson in Coventry, and the LWC in Prescot – was under 200,000, not more than Clerkenwell's had been at its peak over a century earlier. It was tiny compared with the output of American watch firms: Waltham alone made over 20 million watches between 1880 and 1914, Elgin another 14 million. The Swiss watch industry had recovered so well after the trauma of 1876 that its exports exceeded 60 million watches between 1885 and 1900, and between 1900 and 1913, another 137 million.[55]

In Britain, there was grudging acceptance of the loss of its watch industry's old export markets. A comment in *The Times* newspaper (reprinted in the *Clerkenwell News* in 1856) explained that 'The world is a very large market, in which every man above a savage desire to have a watch' (sic).[56] That market was vast and growing inexorably. Why had English watchmaking been unable to retain its initial dominance, even in its home market? Charles Frodsham, like so many others, blamed the loss of Britain's markets on lack of enterprise, poor marketing skills, and American tariffs.[57] Watchmakers in Liverpool and Coventry had long struggled to compete with Swiss watches, either those imported legally or smuggled. But for many, the key explanation for the decline of England's watch industry lay in Clerkenwell's complacency with its quintessential best-quality watch – the traditional bulky key-wound watch with a fusee. By 1900, the *Horological Journal* grieved that 'our export trade has gone astray [and] we have only ourselves to thank'.[58] The last few horological exports to the United States were few, but high in individual value. They consisted of some top-grade watches, and chronometers from Kullberg or Mercer for Bond of Boston, or Bliss and Negus of New York (Chapter 16). By 1900, even the aggregate value of that trade was low. Britain's Consul-General at San Francisco reported in 1903 that British clocks and watches were 'hardly on the market at all' in the United States.[59] By 1910, exports of 'English' watches could be counted only in hundreds in a world market of many millions. The best of Clerkenwell's customised watches were the horological equivalents of hand-built Rolls Royce cars, but they competed in a world market where first-time buyers wanted watches analogous to Henry Ford's Model T (or later, the Volkswagen Beetle). The decline of Britain's home and foreign markets was a consequence of Waltham's successful adoption of the 'American system' followed by Switzerland's gradual modification of their *établissage* 'system'. We shall see that the British Horological Institute, the new voice of English watchmaking, refused to recognise the merit of training apprentices in the use of machine tools until it was too late to revive the industry (Chapter 13). Clerkenwell chose to ignore the new technology, with terminal consequences (Chapter 14). In Britain's other watchmaking hubs attempts to adapt elements of the American system met with mixed success (Chapter 15).

Notes

1 John Allwood, *The Great Exhibitions* (London: Studio Vista, 1977), 51–57. After London, 1851, there followed exhibitions in New York, Dublin, Paris, and Vienna. It was generally believed that exhibitions stimulated economic growth.
2 Alun C. Davies, 'Britain and the American Centennial Exhibition, 1976', *Journal of the Royal Society of Arts*, 132 (Dec. 1976), 28–31, at https://www.jstor.org/stable/41372433
3 James C. Watson, 'Horological Instruments ... Philadelphia Exhibition', *BPP*, 1877, vol. 6, 823–24, 851, and for following quote.
4 Comment in *The Spectator*, 28 Dec. 1878 on Thomas Connolly's recent report to *The Times* newspaper.
5 Phyllis Deane & W.A. Cole, *British Economic Growth 1688–1959* (Cambridge: Cambridge UP, 1962), 8 and 328–29.
6 Ian R. Bartky, 'The Adoption of Standard Time', *Technology and Culture*, 30/1 (Jan.1989), 25–56, at https://doi.org/10.2307/3105430
7 *American Horological Journal*, 6/6 (July 1875), 132.
8 *Horological Journal*, 21/4 (Dec. 1878), 43–46; Richard C. McCormick, 'Our Success at Paris in 1878', *The North American Review*, 129/272 (July 1879), 7, at https://www.jstor.org/stable/25100773.
9 *Horological Journal*, 31/11 (July 1889), 169.
10 James Nye, *A Long Time in Making: The History of Smiths* (Oxford: Oxford UP, 2014), 13.
11 Alan Smith, *Lancashire Watch Company, 1889–1910* (Fitzwilliam, NH: Roberts, 1972), Part 2: 61.
12 *Horological Journal*, 31/7 (Feb. 1889), 89; also, see the reproduction of the 1885 advertisement 'Watchmaking on the Naugatuck', in *Antiquarian Horology*, 17/3 (Spring 1988), 281.
13 Emory R. Johnson et al., *History of the Domestic and Foreign Commerce of the United States* (Washington DC: Carnegie Institute, 1915) II, 190–91, 276.
14 John Joseph Murphy, 'The Establishment of the American Clock Industry: A Study in Entrepreneurial History' (unpublished PhD thesis, Yale University, 1961), 212–17; and id., 'Entrepreneurship in the Establishment of the American Clock Industry', *Journal of Economic History*, 26 (1966), 169–80, at https://www.jstor.org/stable/2116226; also Chauncey Jerome, *History of the American Clock Business for the Past Sixty Years, and a Life*

... *Written by ... Himself* (New Haven, CT: Dayton, 1860), 60; also Alun C. Davies, 'An Invasion in Time: American Horology and the British Market', *Antiquarian Horology*, 30/6 (June 2008), 829–44; and 'Comment on Invasion', *Antiquarian Horology*, 31/5 (Sept. 2009), 706–10.

15 On the US consular service, see Thomas G. Paterson, 'American Businessmen and Consular Service Reform, 1890s to 1906', *Business History Review*, 15 (1966), 77–97, esp. 85–87, at https://doi.org/10.2307/3112303 and https://www.jstor.org/stable/3112303; and Richard Hume Werking, 'Selling the Foreign Service: Bureaucratic Rivalry and Foreign Trade Promotion, 1903–12', *Pacific Historical Review*, XLV (1976), 185–207, esp. 185–88, at https://doi.org/10.2307/3638494. The several series of consular reports can be traced in the British Library; see *General Catalogue of Printed Books* (London: British Museum, 1966), vol. 244, 445–46.

16 They included 'brass valves, files, shears, razors, shaving soap, turbine water wheels, furniture, printing presses and materials, boots and shoes, and a great variety of food products, especially tinned'.

17 *U.S. Consular Reports*: no. 195 (Dec. 1896), 597–98. The report was dated 10 October 1896). Fattorini later became famous for making the first chess clock.

18 *Horological Journal*, 31/ 11 (July 1889), 165.

19 *ASP*: 126: 57 Congress, 1st sess., House of Representatives, Doc. No.708, part 2: *Special Consular Reports: Silver and Plated Ware in Foreign Countries*: vol. XXXIII (Part 2) (Washington, DC, 1902).

20 *U.S. Consular Reports*, 70/264 (Sept. 1902), 33ff.

21 *Horological Journal*, 42 (1901), 145–46.

22 Enforced by the 'Lights on Vehicles Act' of 1907.

23 Obituary notice of Robert H. Ingersoll in *Horological Journal*, 71/1 (Oct. 1929), 44–45.

24 *Horological Journal*, 28/2 (October 1885), 28).).

25 *Horological Journal*, 27/12 (Aug. 1885), 163–66.

26 T.P. Hewitt, *English Watchmaking under Free Trade* (np: pamphlet, 1903), 8; *Horological Journal*, 46/10 (June 1904), 137–39, for Hewitt's' address and the debate at the BHI.

27 Leo G. Chiozza (ed.), *Free Trade versus Protectionism* (np: pamphlet, 1902), 'Introduction'. Sir Leo George Chiozza (1870–1944), was a supporter and *protégé* of Lloyd George, and author of *The Triumph of Nationalization* (London: Cassell, 1920).

28 *Horological Journal*, 49/11 (July 1907), 182–83, 'American Watches: Vigorous Campaign against the Watch Trust'; and *Horological Journal*, 50/11 (July 1908), 80–81.

29 *Horological Journal*, 30/4 (Dec. 1887), 50.

30 Gary Allan Tobin, 'The Bicycle Boom of the 1890s: The Development of Private Transportation and the Birth of the Modern Tourist', *Journal of Popular Culture*, 7/4 (May 2004), 838–49, at https://doi.org/10.1111/j.0022-3840.1974.0704_838.x

31 Dennis Harris, 'Wristwatches 1810–1920: An Introductory Study', *Antiquarian Horology*, 17/4 (Summer 1988), 357–66.

32 Samuel Smith & Son, Charles Frodsham, Harrods, J.W. Benson, Dent, Sir John Bennett, and the Army & Navy Stores: see David Penney, 'English Wristwatches', *Antique Collecting*, 35 (April 2000); and id., 'Wristwatches', at http://www.antiquewatchstore.com/ (2011), on which following paragraphs draw heavily.

33 See advertisements in *Horological Journal*, 53, passim, for Waltham and Swiss lever bracelet watches. C.K. Aked, in a review of E.J. Tyler's *Craft of*

the Clockmaker, in *Antiquarian Horology*, 8 (June 1974), 763–64, notes the existence of a 'Thommen's Watch Company Catalogue', dated 1 January 1910, which shows "wrists", i.e. wristwatches. Also, Davies, 'An Invasion in Time', 844.

34 David Thompson, 'Robert Ingersoll & Bro.', *Watches* (London: British Museum, 2008), 140–41, illustrates a 1915 American wristwatch.

35 Glasmeier, *Marketing Time*, 140–41.

36 Penney, 'Watchmaking', at http://www.antiquewatchstore.com/, sub 'Nielsen'.

37 Carlo Cipolla, *Clocks and Culture* (London: Collins, 1967), 75 (drawing evidence from Atkins and Overall, *Company of Clockmakers*, 263).

38 T.P. Hewitt, *English Watchmaking under Free Trade* (np: pamphlet, 1903).

39 Geoffrey Timmins, *Made in Lancashire: A History of Regional Industrialisation* (Manchester: Manchester UP: 1998).

40 On the earlier colonial trade see W.D. Hoyt, 'A London Shopkeeper's Struggle to Recover a Colonial Debt', *Maryland Historical Magazine*, 45 (June 1950), 126–33; Edwin Butterworth, *A Statistical Sketch of the County Palatine of Lancaster* (1841: Manchester: Lancashire and Cheshire Antiquarian Society, 1965), 57.

41 William Rodgers, 'The Decline of English Watchmaking: Reminiscences of the Latter Half of the Nineteenth Century', *Watchmaker, Jeweller and Silversmith* (Special Home and Colonial Number), 25 (Aug. 1899), 939–41 and for subsequent quote.

42 Rodgers, 'Decline of English Watchmaking', 939.

43 *Statistical Tables Exhibiting the Commerce of the United States with European Countries from 1790 to 1890* (Washington, DC: Bureau of Statistics, Treasury Department, 1893); also *ASP*: 154/11; 52nd Congress, 2nd Session House of Representatives, *Miscellaneous Document* 117 (Washington, DC, 1893). The 1871 figure for exports included chronometers.

44 *BPP*, 1878, 13 (Cmnd.328), 'Report from the Select Committee on Gold and Silver (Hall Marking) Together with Proceedings of Committee, Minutes of Evidence, and Appendix', qq. 2,462 to 2,467.

45 *Horological Journal*, 45/7 (March 1903), 85–86.

46 [Wembley Exhibition pamphlet], *English Clocks and Watches and Their Makers* (London: Alexander Stuart, 1924), 45–47.

47 *Horological Journal*, 11/8 (April 1869), 90; his diagnosis and complaints were echoed by James M. Poole, 'The Future of the English Watch Trade', *Watchmaker, Jeweller and Silversmith* 7 (June 1887), 171–73, and Adam Galbraith, 'The Decline of the British Watchmaking Industry', *Watchmaker, Jeweller and Silversmith,* 34 (June 1908), 727–35.

48 *ASP*, 125: *Consular Reports*, no.18 (April 1882), 574.

49 *ASP, 125: Consular Reports*, no. 23 (Sept. 1887), 635.

50 *ASP, 125: Consular Reports*, no. 19 (May 1882), 40.

51 *ASP, 125: Consular Reports,* no. 19 (May 1882), 530–55.

52 ASP, 125 *Consular Reports*, no. 18 (April 1882), 534–35.

53 Alun C. Davies, 'Horology at International Exhibitions, 1851–1900', *Antiquarian Horology*, 33/5 (Sept. 2012), 602–05.

54 *ASP, 125: Consular Reports*, no. 35 (Nov. 1883), 4.

55 David S. Landes, *Revolution in Time: Clocks and the Making of the Modern World* (Cambridge, MA: Belknap, Harvard UP, 1983), 381–84, Appendix B.

56 *The Times*, 28 March 1856, reprinted in Supplement to *Clerkenwell News*, 6 Dec. 1856.

57 *Horological Journal*, 4/8 (April 1862), 91.

58 *Horological Journal*, 42/11 (July 1900), 150.

59 *Board of Trade Journal*, 41 (June 1903), 536.

13 The British Horological Institute

Ignoring the Elephant

Passing the baton: from guild to institute

Since 1631 the institutional home of English watchmaking had been its guild, the Clockmakers' Company. It was the industry's voice during and after the French wars, when the challenge of Swiss competition grew. The guild's mercantilist policy was straightforward: it wanted the government to protect the industry by enforcing tariffs. By the middle of the nineteenth century, it was clear the policy had failed: watches were products that were small in bulk, light in weight, high in value, and not too difficult to smuggle. For a small force of customs officers it was hard to enforce tariffs on a long coastline. By the time free trade triumphed, the energies of the Company's leaders were deflated by their long and unsuccessful struggle. In 1858, the guild bowed out of day-to-day involvement with its industry and stood aside for the British Horological Institute (BHI) that became the new voice of English horology. The old guild survived, continued to elect Aldermen to the Guildhall and, like London's other ancient guilds, held annual dinners to aid their charities.[1] In the late 1870s, it again became involved, in a small way, in the issue of training apprentices. In the meantime, the focus of English watchmaking switched to the new Institute, and especially to its opinions about the plight of the industry as expressed through correspondence and debates, reported in its monthly *Horological Journal*.

****

The establishment of the BHI coincided with the single event that, in retrospect, can be seen as important to watchmaking as had been the innovation of the balance spring two centuries earlier. In Waltham, Massachusetts, also in 1858, there occurred a revolution in the making of watches when the 'American system' of manufacturing was successfully applied to make watch parts, with machine tools, in a factory. The inaugural issue of the new Institute's monthly *Journal* included two articles that explicitly addressed this event. Thereafter the consequences of Waltham's 'revolution' for English watchmakers' became a *leitmotif* in

DOI: 10.4324/9781003227823-16

the Institute's debates. The central issue – sometimes addressed directly, but more often obliquely – was the continued viability of Clerkenwell's traditional methods of production. Waltham's revolution became the 'elephant in the room', denied, rejected – even derided – by many members, but always visible to a few. It was not until the 1880s, when the success of the Waltham's revolution was incontrovertible, that the Institute discussed whether the training in the use of machine tools should – or should not – be included in the syllabus that instructed its School's apprentices.

Of the two articles about Waltham in the *Journal*'s first issue, one was enthusiastic, the other hostile.[2] The first was a reprint of a benign article in a New York journal, *Leslie's Illustrated News,* that favourably described Waltham's factory. It intimated that the factory might emulate the paternalistic practices of new textile factories, in which women were employed at lower wages and lived in dormitories. Some textile factories held bible classes and sewing bees at the end of the work day.[3] The successful application in factories that made six-shooting revolvers for Colonel Samuel Colt and small arms for Eli Whitney was especially attributed to the 'American system'. If applied to watchmaking, the article continued, 'it must be obvious to anyone ... that such a system directed by Yankee skill and ingenuity, must very nearly approach perfection, and greatly excel handicraft production'. Moreover, the new production procedures obviated the need for seven-year apprenticeships: 'ordinary' workers with a little training could supervise the machines and 'not one... need be a watchmaker'.[4] The article explained that Waltham's watches were based on the simplest form of lever movement, with fewer parts than conventional watches. Like Swiss watches they had going barrels, not complicated fusees. Broken parts might more easily be replaced, and repairs made more quickly. Waltham's watches were initially finished in just three styles and qualities and were guaranteed for ten years. They were sold by country merchants and, eventually, could be bought through the mail order catalogues of Montgomery Ward and Sears Roebuck (Chapter 11). The most ominous note for British watchmakers was that the new watches were 'already furnished at half the price of the English lever watch and can be manufactured at the rate of 20,000 per annum with present means'.

The second item about Waltham in the *Journal*'s first issue was a letter from 'ONE WHO ADMIRES GOOD WORK'. It relentlessly criticised machine-made watches. It claimed that American watches in general – including Waltham's – were 'nothing very alarming ... a rough and tasteless agglomeration of parts'. It was a foretaste of innumerable later articles, letters and editorials that stressed the inferiority of machine-made watches compared with those made by Clerkenwell's traditional methods. One contributor concluded later that 'the [American] product was inferior ... the going barrel was quite rudimentary ... the wheels and pinions were of the roughest make'. Valentine Knight, the BHI's first president, concluded that the Yankee watches were 'mere toys, trumpery trash'.[5] Thirty years later James Poole (brother of the chronometer maker John) reluctantly conceded the fatal underestimations in the initial British responses to American watches:

> The Briton despised them all, and perhaps with reason, as at first the best quality American watch was not to be compared in finish with the everyday English lever; but in two points it won out, first in price, and secondly timekeeping for the price.[6]

It must be remembered that the *Journal* reflected the views and values of the BHI's members, who were craftsmen in a declining handcraft industry. Not until 1875 did a prescient warning alert the trade of the full implications of machine-made American watches for Britain's domestic watch market. It came not from the BHI's *Horological Journal* (directed at outworkers and masters) but in an editorial in the *Watchmaker Jeweller & Silversmith* (a trade journal, intended mostly for retailers):

> The New Invasion is upon us; of that there can be no mistake.... It is no use in scolding at the invading tide, it is here; the resistless wave is silently rising all over England ... we will endeavour to give such facts and details of this invasion as we have been able to ascertain ... At the western end of the Viaduct, on the south side of Holborn Circus, facing the Prince Consort's equestrian statue, the rambler in the metropolis will find himself before one of those newly-built palaces – monuments of commerce in elaborate stonework – which are the glory of trade and the pride of the modern Londoner. Upon its dark, enamelled, facial band, deeply indented in letters of gold, are the ominous words **AMERICAN WATCH COMPANY**. *These* are the invaders. [7]

The new Institute's difficulties

The new Institute got off to an unsteady start. For two decades after its foundation, it was more pre-occupied with its own survival than with addressing the threat posed by American machine-made watches. Its founders seemed more conscious of England's glorious horological past than of present and future commercial considerations, but they were also ambitious. They wanted their Institute to have a library, reading room, museum, classes for apprentices and a forum for lectures. They intended to support charities, especially one for an horological Asylum – 'a comfortable home for the declining years of those who, by age or infirmities, are reduced to the necessity of becoming recipients of other men's bounty'.[8] But first there were more urgent problems. Its headquarters in Clerkenwell meant meetings were remote from putative members in Prescot, Liverpool, and Coventry. The latter city was home to English watchmaking's two largest firms, Rotherham and Williamson, whose collective annual output was probably approaching – and would soon exceed? – that of Clerkenwell's small firms. Coventry's workers, like hundreds of horological jobbers and retailers across the country, were far distant from the BHI. Yet even in Clerkenwell only a few outworkers joined, despite their relatively easy access to meetings. Those who did join faced problems because Council meetings started at 9.00 p.m. If they attended, they would not get home before midnight.[9]

By 1869 membership had fallen from 370 to 315 and, of those, forty were amateurs, non-professional gentlemen whose hobby was a scientific interest in horology. Only 275 members were 'in the trade' and some among them failed to keep up subscriptions.[10] According to *Kelly's Directory* by 1872, out of the 1,400 who still worked in the horological industry in London, barely 300 were members. Low membership inevitably resulted in financial problems and after a dozen years, the BHI was in debt. The initial formula for clearing debt – through subscriptions at an annual dinner – ended in 1871. The *Journal* appeared only because of the editor's goodwill; he declined payment but, when the secretary left in June 1872 he, too, threatened to resign. Only two or three members regularly contributed to the *Journal,* prompting complaints about its lack of 'original, interesting and useful matter'.[11] Neither president nor vice-president attended the annual meeting in that August; the chair was taken by the Treasurer (who was owed £19 8s 7d). A founding member, David Glasgow, concluded that 'The Institute had never been in a worse financial position than now'.[12] When the Council tried to increase the subscription, ninety-six members agreed but forty-four dissented. The others did not reply. The Institute seemed near to collapse. In the wider national economy, growth was decelerating. Despite free trade in Britain, tariffs were rising in Europe, and leading nations were beginning to catch up with Britain industrially. After 1873 businesses in many industries, not only watchmaking, suffered from low – and falling – profit rates and price deflation: during the prolonged depression of the late 1870s, prices on commodities in Britain fell by as much as 40 per cent with a consequent effect on wages. As in earlier cyclical depressions, watches were a deferrable purchase. Like other handcraft industries that made consumer goods, watchmaking entered a difficult period.

The BHI survived only because of donations from a few well-off individuals, notably Miss Angela Burdett-Coutts, the millionaire philanthropist persuaded to help the BHI by John Jones, watchmaker of the Strand.[13] Her support transformed the BHI's financial problems. At almost a blink of an eye, the nearly moribund Institute was resuscitated. Debt was cleared, subscriptions, membership, journal sales and advertisements all increased, and by 1875 a surplus of about £60 was invested in a Building Fund. In December 1878, the BHI had accumulated an 'eminently satisfactory' balance of £77 and by August 1879 a new building was nearly completed on land donated by the Marquis of Northampton in Northampton Square.[14]

Better times: the Horological Club and its excursions

The Institute's new home did not – could not – reverse English watchmaking's decline. But for a few years, its Clerkenwell members' morale blossomed when social activities at the new headquarters offered a lighter side to a watchmaker's life.[15] Seventy members attended the first meeting of a 'Horological Club' in December 1879, in a spacious room with comfortable furniture, tables, chessboards, and playing cards. Ten members lent £2 each and a £25 piano was bought, enabling musical evenings.[16] Annual dinners resumed, and were well supported. The Club became a sanctuary during the industry's hard times in the 1880s, and its excursions were pleasant and interesting. Some were to popular attractions like the Crown Jewels, the Royal Mint, and rambles through beauty spots in Epping Forest, Sussex Downs and the Surrey Hills.[17] Insights into the rich legacy of British horology came from trips to Kew and Greenwich Observatories and the great clock in Westminster.[18] Gillett's and Thwaites & Reed's factories both demonstrated the scope and success of Britain's turret clock sector. Visits to Nicole Nielsen's firm in London and John Wycherley's in Prescot revealed the co-existence of quite different watchmaking technologies: Nielsen made small numbers of exquisite watches for the top end of the market (Chapter 14), whilst Wycherley tried to 'modernise' the industry by introducing standardised measurements, a prelude to his partner T.P. Hewitt's drive to mass produce watches (Chapter 15). The Club met weekly until 1892. Then it folded, partly a consequence of Clerkenwell's continued decline, partly because a new secretary could not be found.

The *leitmotif* of the 'American system' was the almost hidden theme of several excursions: it afforded members the opportunity to discuss 'the elephant in the room'. The moving spirit behind these visits was Henry Ganney, a leading 'reformer' at the Institute. After a trip to the Enfield Rifle Factory he explicitly drew benign analogies between gun-making and horology when he hinted in the *Journal* that 'most know there are similarities between the manufacture of small arms and ordinary watches and clocks in the United States'.[19] Seventy members who visited Woolwich Arsenal in October 1874 were exposed to the machine technology that had revolutionised small engineering in the United States and was now transforming some of watchmaking's sister industries in Britain.[20] Visits to Messrs Hobbs, Hart & Company's factory revealed other new machine tools and innovative production methods that had transformed lock-making after 1851.[21] Other successful adaptions of the 'American system' were exposed in visits to firms within easy reach of Clerkenwell – Woolwich Arsenal, British Telegraph, Siemens Electric, The Emery Wheel

Factory. Even if few could afford a trip to the United States, exposure to new ideas, new tools, and new technology were all around them.

Ignoring the elephant: defending the fusee

The Institute's debates were well attended and fully reported in the *Journal*. The consequences for traditional English watchmaking of Waltham's revolution were always in the background, but rarely directly addressed. On occasions when they were talked about, the debates revealed the continued strong resistance to technological innovation by those in a manufacturing system whose hand-craft technology had enjoyed ascendancy for two centuries. Change was antithetical in traditional watchmakers' culture. Clerkenwell's watchmakers and the BHI felt that their craft, which exemplified patient methodical actions, was threatened by new techniques. Successful technological change depended, as Mokyr has pointed out, on 'an encouraging social environment'. It was conspicuously absent in the BHI's debates. Without a supportive environment, technological conservatism persisted.[22]

That Clerkenwell's milieu opposed innovation was revealed in numerous articles and accounts of debates in the *Journal* about the merits or disadvantages of new *versus* old methods of production. One discussion in 1859 compared the current robust revival of the silk and lace industries with the lethargic economic health of the jewellery trades (that, in this context, included watchmaking). All were craft industries that made luxury products. But silk and lace had successfully introduced machine production, enabling the creation, and exploitation, of the growing middle-class market. Only a small portion of that market had so far been tapped by English watchmaking, and the new Institute's members were urged to follow the example of the silk and lace industries. If watchmaking, members were told, 'set itself the task of showing that cheapness and ability are compatible [then] it will find an enormous market amongst the 30,000,000 people on these islands, the greater part of whom have never yet been the patrons of horology'.[23]

In the face of such arguments most of the Institute's members resolutely defended Clerkenwell's old methods. In another debate, concerning a recent surge in Swiss imports, the supposed threat of Waltham's watches was also alluded to (even before many had reached the British market). In a discussion about the technical superiority of the fusee (which Clerkenwell retained) compared with the going barrel that Swiss, Coventry, and now American watchmakers had accepted, it was argued that the best quality watches, clocks, and – incontrovertibly – chronometers, *needed* a fusee. Speakers objected to

> abandoning a principle that has brought much honour to the horologists of this country [merely for] the dreary idea of competing with

> [the Swiss] in price... if then we must make low-priced watches, let them possess these distinctive English features, the fusee and lever escapement. But is it desirable to do so? What has Coventry gained by making low-priced watches but sunk their name [to] the lowest in the Kingdom. Had they made good watches, the name of Coventry would have been a credit... instead of the disgrace it is.[24]

Counter arguments stressed the complications of fusees: their chains accounted for over 800 separate pieces. Swiss movements were simpler because going barrels had only eighty to a hundred pieces. Henry Ganney argued that Clerkenwell could only compete commercially if the fusee was abandoned for the going barrel – and also, he wryly observed, used the uncomplicated but accurate cylinder escapement that had been invented by England's great George Graham in the eighteenth century. But custom and entrenched opinion died hard. Even non-experts accepted the fusee's superior technical efficiency but ignored or minimised its extra cost. And so its virtues continued to triumph, as did the relative merits of lever and duplex escapements and the superiority of jewelled watch movements. At the end of the debate, members arrived at the anodyne conclusion that 'those who wished for superior timepieces' would prefer the superior equalising power of the fusee, 'while those who followed the fashion, and made flat watches, would employ a going barrel and low numbered pinions' – a token nod to watchmakers in distant Coventry. Thus, Clerkenwell's small firms continued to make watches with fusees for the minor but still-profitable luxury market. Not all ignored the fusee, for Nicole Nielsen, Golay, and the Guyes (Chapter 14) made going barrel watches, at prices as high or even higher than watches with fusees. Nevertheless, Clerkenwell's share of Britain's market continued downwards.[25] Most of Britain's market was left to the Swiss and Coventry, later to be joined by Waltham, Elgin, and other American firms.

With hindsight, Clerkenwell's reactions can be seen as ill-judged. Yet at the time, from the perspective of small firms, they were understandable. In the short term, their response to the challenge of new technology was not irrational. Small firms that relied on a myriad of outworkers were wary about the large capital investment needed to compete in the world markets that the Swiss and Americans already commanded. Later, this caution was reinforced when small firms became aware of the tribulations arising from the cut-throat competition of new watchmaking companies in America (Chapter 11). While some companies – like Waltham and Elgin – succeeded, many went under. Safer than shouldering uncertain prospects, they thought, it was better to continue supplying a small luxury market at home.[26]

The same theme resurfaced twenty years later in debates on the merits and drawbacks of Clerkenwell's traditional technology. They were reported in the *Horological Journal* under the title of 'The Fusee and

Farewell to it'.[27] By then BHI members were acutely aware of the devastating consequences of Waltham's revolution for British watch markets. B.P. Johnson, a founder member who had become one of the Institute's few 'reformers', directly attributed the continued plight of English watchmakers to Clerkenwell's reliance on fusees. He claimed it 'stamped out the growth of intelligence in the maker, quadrupled the expenditure of time and raised an effective barrier against the improvement of tools'.[28] David Glasgow, an expert on traditional horological technology and author of a standard watchmakers' bench book, sprang to defend the fusee. He thought the fusee was essential if only to prevent the establishment of the 'abominable' factory system: 'I must acknowledge to a perfect hatred of [factories. They are] an oligopoly of trade, seeking in the nineteenth century to fill the place of the feudal aristocrat in the Middle Ages, and ends in nothing but stolid communism'.[29] Glasgow reflected a widespread hostility to the Marxist surge in the 1880s that contributed to the establishment of the Social Democratic Federation (1881), the Labour Emancipation League, and the Fabian Society (both in 1884).[30] Another founding member of the Institute, John Jones, endorsed Glasgow's view of the undesirable technical consequences:

> It would be suicidal to the whole purpose of the Institute if it were to abandon one of the highest forms of intellectual contrivances which the mechanical world has ever seen... it would introduce error where now is perfection and diminish the command England exercises at present only by producing the finest timekeepers in the world.[31]

And so the technical superiority of fusees was yet again reasserted. It was supported by allusions to the superiority that Clerkenwell's chronometers, all with fusees, had repeatedly demonstrated at international industrial exhibitions. English makers dominated the world's chronometer market (Chapter 16).[32] E.D. Johnson, initiator of the debate, stressed that if ordinary clocks and watches with fusees went wrong, repairs were expensive. Nevertheless, in 1880 most Clerkenwell makers retained the fusee, kept their traditional production methods and supplied the small – but still profitable – top end of the market. Coventry's firms sold what they could to the market's middle and bottom end that was increasingly falling to ever-growing imports of American and Swiss watches. The 'workshop of the world' was losing its home and former export markets.

The most indefatigable reformer was Henry Ganney. His perceptive but pessimistic analyses featured regularly in letters to the *Journal* as well as in contributions to the Institute's debates. 'The position of the horological trades is a national reproach', he expounded. But most in the Institute ignored his views.[33] Outside the industry others did not. The British Association for the Advancement of Science asked him to report on village industries in general – and horology in particular – when it met in Birmingham in 1886. Ganney hoped that a newly founded British Clock Company (BUCC) in Birmingham itself might in time make cheap watches as well as cheap clocks. Perhaps with these, and with the continued superiority of English marine chronometers, Britain might then be able to flourish at 'both ends of the trade'? If so, he added,

> we only need to fill up the space in between, which is great. The attempt to create, in Clerkenwell, a horological aristocracy during the past twenty-five years [has] failed... It may be worthwhile to turn our attention to a large trade in English work, remembering that to secure cream we must have a large supply of milk.[34]

Machine tools and the Institute's school

The superiority of fusees and traditional horological technology was at the heart of debates in the Institute's first two decades. Later discussions focussed more explicitly on machine tools and their role in training apprentices. The Institute's apprenticeship classes had got off to a faltering start in the 1860s. The classes had no formal syllabus, were not popular, and by 1869 only one survived.[35] Even the inducement of prizes in 1873 (£5 'for good work') failed to encourage sufficient prospective watchmakers to enrol.[36] What eventually motivated the BHI reformers to introduce changes were the exhibits by Swiss and French schools of watchmaking at the 1878 Paris exhibition. Compared with the English equivalents they were impressive.[37] Henry Ganney memorably reported how 'he was struck with the melancholy fact that watchmaking was the only English industry that showed an absolute decline'.[38]

The Institute's new school opened in 1880. It was a division of the recently established 'City and Guilds' Institute, founded by sixteen of the City of London's livery companies to deflect criticism that the resources of the ancient Guilds were being neglected. It hoped that the training of crafts would promote 'the Education of the working classes'.[39] Even with the City and Guilds' involvement, the school for apprentice watchmakers failed to flourish. Poor attendance at the classes resulted in more financial problems for the Institute. This prompted the Clockmakers' Company's officials to emerge from their charity dinners and once more become active in their industry's affairs. A committee was appointed to inquire 'into to the merit of our teaching and to see how far we were worthy of their assistance'.[40] After two inspections the committee found 'a good many faults': discipline was poor because instructors had 'not sufficient control over pupils to keep them until they are efficient workmen'. More importantly, it found 'no machinery for watchmaking' in the curriculum. The 'elephant' was at last coming into view. But then the Institute's members indignantly repudiated their own committee's report on the grounds that because the school was an educational and not a manufacturing establishment, any attempt to *make* watches 'would give us the ill-will of our supporters'.[41] Those 'supporters' were of course the conservative majority of the BHI's members, who wanted instruction to continue in Clerkenwell's traditional hand-craft methods. Like their forefathers during the Ingold episode, they emphatically did not welcome the idea of parts made by new machine tools. This was despite Leonard Waldo's much publicised explanation to the Society of Arts in 1885 (and to the wider watchmaking community) of the success of the 'American system' in Waltham and Elgin.[42]

Notwithstanding opposition to machine tools, the School wanted better premises. A benevolent Goldsmiths' Company came to horology's aid and gave £500 to help extend the Institute's building by adding another storey.[43] The Clockmakers' Company, too, contributed towards completing the Institute's workshops.[44] Better premises and tutors resulted in a modest improvement in the School's presentation at the 1885 Inventions Exhibition, although it – and everything else horological – was outshone by another of Waltham's remarkable displays. At the 1876 Centennial and again at Paris in 1878, Waltham's stunning displays impressed juries and won prize medals. At London's 'Inventions' exhibitions, Waltham repeated its triumphs (Figure 13.1).

Despite routine revelations in the monthly *Journal of Statistics* of annual output, imports, and exports, the contentious issue about the use of

Figure 13.1 Waltham at London's Inventions Exhibition, 1885. Copyright: David Penney. http://www.antiquewatchstore.com/.

machine tools in instructing apprentices remained unresolved. English horology's growing trade imbalances lent support to arguments that the School's instruction syllabus should abandon teaching hand-craft skills. Instead, it should expose apprentices to the advantages of the 'American system'. Six horological schools in France and Switzerland already taught their apprentices how to use machine tools, and 'it behoved the Institute to keep to the front'.[45] There was also a growing awareness of the need to address the wider horological constituency beyond Clerkenwell. This led, in 1889, to what became a much-acclaimed Correspondence Class run by T.D. Wright. He had established the 'Watch and Clock Repairers' Examinations' – a belated acknowledgement of the prescience of Henry Ganney's warning that British horology would soon be 'dominated by jobbers, not makers'.[46]

Training apprentices: Northampton Polytechnic, Prescot and Coventry

The establishment of the Northampton Polytechnic Institute in Northampton Square in 1906 finally enabled the instruction of apprentices in machine-tool technology. The 'Poly' offered classes for jewellers, silversmiths, metalworkers, civil, and mechanical engineers (Figure 13.2).

Clerkenwell's horological needs received special attention when T.D. Wright was co-opted as Director of its Horological Department, in

Figure 13.2 Northampton Institute, 1912. Copyright: James Nye.

effect subsuming the Institute's old School into the new Polytechnic. A fresh syllabus included a class on 'the principles of the design of automatic machinery'. It was a grudging and belated formal concession to the need for instruction in the use machine tools, several decades after Waltham's revolution. Some classes were well attended, but those in horological drawing and theory were not. Enrolment for courses on the principles and design of automatic machinery was disappointing because they 'failed to attract [horological] students to any adequate extent'.[47] Classes in the use of machine tools arrived too late to reverse Clerkenwell's decline. They could only postpone the demise of its traditional watchmaking. The reasons were clear. In classes for the Polytechnic's other engineering trades

> students were counted by hundreds... in goldsmiths' and silversmiths' work, in engraving and in jewellery, the work of the [Northampton Polytechnic] Institute has been remarkably successful... the optical school... has been firmly established... with a far larger number of students than have ever attended the horological classes.

It was twilight in Clerkenwell. The Polytechnic's horological classes failed to attract students, not because of administrative failings, or poor teaching, but because employment in watchmaking's declining industry was unattractive.

Clerkenwell's belated but unsuccessful attempt to accept machine tools was repeated in the other watchmaking communities in Prescot and Coventry. Prescot's Technical School, established in 1892, was supported by a local rate and by funds from the County Council. Its horological classes included a three-year course of instruction, with compulsory attendance for recruits to the recently established (but to be short-lived) Lancashire Watch Company's factory.[48] A similar attempt in Coventry was made to stimulate interest in watchmaking amongst potentially bright students. The city's Watch Trade Protection Association offered competitive scholarships at the local Technical Institute. Those responsible for organising the courses did their best. But it was not possible to *force* students to take up watchmaking as a career. By 1902, it was deemed to have failed.[49] Again, the reasons were clear: alternative employment offered better pay. Coventry's automobile and bicycle industries presented better opportunities. London's flourishing economy promised even more prospects.

The BHI's problems prompt reforms

In every year after 1900 more than a million Swiss and American watches poured into Britain, despite the availability of factory-made 'English' watches from the Lancashire Watch Company in Prescot and from Rotherham and Williamson in Coventry (Chapter 15). As demand for old-fashioned English fusee watches gradually faded, so did Clerkenwell. Once again the BHI fell into financial difficulties. By August 1902, its income was barely sufficient to meet the cost of maintaining its premises.[50] Discontent with the Institute was expressed in a letter to the *Journal* in 1903:

> The methods of the Institute were those of a past and somewhat effete generation; ... the Institute was a small, exclusive club rather jealous of its own respectability, and somewhat indifferent to many of the vital interests of the various crafts it made pretence of patronising. A club into which admission was regulated not so much by merits and talents as by the friendly offices of someone on the Council.[51]

The decline of watchmaking in Clerkenwell contrasted with the robustness of its American counterpart. The Institute's *Journal* and New York's *Jewellers Circular and Horological Review* accurately reflected the differences: in February 1891, the New York publication became weekly rather than monthly. Its circulation was over 10,000 copies per issue.[52] By contrast, the BHI's membership, at 461 in 1884, fell back to only 245 by August 1904.

Fortunately for the Institute, a new generation of 'reformers' emerged, under the influence of the Institute's energetic young secretary, F.J. Britten.[53] They saved the Institute but were unable to halt the decline of Clerkenwell (Chapter 14). Nevertheless, they addressed several basic issues that their predecessors had ignored. A sub-committee was set up to consider how better to market 'English watches', and to supervise British horology's impending display for the St Louis exhibition in Missouri in 1904. It met with the Tariff Reform Commission to discuss a protective tariff, though with no success (Chapters 12 and 15) and convened a committee on education and training with the Educational Committee of the Northampton Institute.[54] The new reforming brooms swept sufficiently briskly to ensure the survival of the BHI beyond the Edwardian era and the turmoil of the Great War. The Institute survived the terminal throes of Clerkenwell's traditional watchmaking industry after three centuries, and actively participated in the temporary resurrection of British watchmaking in the 1930's (Postscript). It still represents British horology today.

Why earlier reformers failed

Why did reformers fail to persuade the BHI's members to modernise during the half-century before the Great War? These were the crucial decades that preceded English watchmaking's terminal decline. Might

Clerkenwell's handcraft industry have been persuaded to adapt to new methods of production, as the Swiss had done successfully following their trauma at Philadelphia in 1876? The Institute's debates had revealed the struggle between most members' conservative attitudes against arguments to 'change or otherwise perish'. Other old craft industries had similar struggles about the persistence of traditional pre-industrial methods of production. In the leather industry, old oak-bark tanning eventually succumbed to new chemical methods and London-based guilds (leather sellers, curriers, and tanners) lost out. Similar resistance to the introduction of modernisation was also experienced in other well-established labour-intensive industries like shipbuilding, cotton spinning, printing, and shoemaking (although the latter eventually succumbed and used sewing machines). But Clerkenwell resisted change. Its watchmakers, in a culture steeped in tradition, were victims of an anti-technical ideology.[55]

Resistance by members of the BHI was partly a conservative reaction to the formidable personalities of the Institute's three leading 'reformers'. Perhaps if those reformers had coordinated efforts, might they have succeeded? Perhaps not. Their personalities and careers were quite different. The first protagonist, Sir John Bennett, had been active in the Institute's founding. But he was a retailer, not a manufacturer. His interests and motives were commercial, not technical, or scientific. He imported watches from Switzerland and exported them to India and Japan. Despite his warnings to Clerkenwell about the dangers of Swiss competition, he happily sold Swiss watches in his Cheapside emporium. Clerkenwell workmen regarded him as a hypocrite because he included 'hybrids' or 'half-breeds' (Swiss movements in English cases) in his displays at exhibitions – notably at Paris in 1878.[56] He was unpopular, and his advocacy of change and reform was counterproductive.[57]

The second leading reformer was Sir Edmund Beckett Denison (later Lord Grimthorpe), a successful barrister, gifted amateur horologist, famous for designing Big Ben's 'double three-legged gravity escapement'. Its success as an accurate timekeeper made it a national icon and helped inspire the spread of public turret clocks across the nation's towns. For forty years after 1867, he was the BHI's second President, an office he accepted only on condition that he would not be expected to attend any meetings, especially the fund-raising annual dinners, which he abhorred. He was notoriously cantankerous and quarrelsome and his frequent letters to *The Times* newspaper on all manner of things were marked by their acerbity. Those who disagreed with him were dismissed as fools and knaves and, as a barrister, he frequently resorted to litigation. He, too, aroused resentment among the Institute's ordinary members.[58]

The third prominent moderniser was Henry Ganney, self-described as 'an humble artisan'. He was a prodigious correspondent, a tireless debater in favour of reform, and the inspiration behind the Horological Club's excursions to see the 'American system' applied in other industries.

Whilst Bennett reflected the interests of London's retailers, and Denison's lofty scepticism – and sarcasm – was aimed at Clerkenwell's antiquated methods, it was Henry Ganney's critical views that best illuminated the industry's technical and commercial plight. His frequently rehearsed solution for revitalising English watchmaking was 'mechanisation'. But his route to it was unpopular. Watchmakers, he thought, should 'cooperate' through a joint-stock company with £1 shares, like Coventry's Watch and Tool Society (Chapter 15). The idea was disliked by Clerkenwell's fiercely independent outworkers in small workshops with rarely more than four or five workers. Ganney's resilience in defeat in debates (no matter how overwhelming) became legendary. For thirty years the *Horological Journal* reported his arguments and the indignant responses of his opponents.[59] In despair, he migrated to New York in 1898 to edit an American horological journal and did not return until 1901. By then Bennett was dead, and Grimthorpe long past his prime. Ganney's absence – and age when he returned – removed crucial reforming energy.[60]

The three reformers moved in different social circles in an era of sharp class awareness. In their own ways, each clashed with the conservative majority in the Institute, sometimes bitterly but rarely successfully. Each spoke for their distinct but narrow interests. Although their diagnoses of the industry's problems were broadly similar because of their dissimilar personalities and social status they never coordinated efforts. If they had united, might they have succeeded? Probably not, for resistance to change amongst Clerkenwell's watchmakers was too strong. With the best will in the world, the BHI was unlikely to have led Clerkenwell's watchmaking industry to respond positively to the watchmaking revolution. New methods and technologies were successful in America because there were no substantial traditional industries to oppose change. They were successfully adopted in Switzerland because watchmaking there was of much greater importance to its national economy than it was in Britain. To survive, Swiss watchmaking had either to change or perish. In Britain, even at its distinguished peak in the late eighteenth century, watchmaking was never more than a minor industry. Thus Clerkenwell drifted on (Chapter 14). Temporarily successful adjustments to elements of the 'American system' came from a firm in Birmingham and two firms in Coventry. But the most comprehensive attempt in Prescott to modernise English watchmaking unequivocally failed (Chapter 15).

Notes

1 LMA/CLC/L/CD/F/007/MS03988 is a 'Scrap book of papers'. It includes menus for the Company's dinners. They were not for those with fainthearted appetites: sample menus show ten courses plus coffee, and an impressive choice of hock, champagne, port, claret, and liqueurs. For an account of one such dinner, see *Horological Journal*, 27/5 (Jan. 1885), 62–63.

2 *Horological Journal,* 1/1 (Sept. 1858), 22–24, 32.
3 See Charles W. Moore, 'Some Thoughts on the Early Labor Policy of the Waltham Watch Co.', *Business History Review,* 13/2 (April 1939), 25–29. Labour relations there were exemplary: there were no disturbances for a period of nearly seventy-five years.
4 *Horological Journal,* 1/1 (Sept. 1858), 13ff, for this and subsequent quotations; Alun C. Davies, 'An Invasion in Time: American Horology and the British Market', *Antiquarian Horology,* 30/6 (June 2008), 838ff.
5 *Horological Journal,* 7/9 (May 1865), 102–04.
6 James M. Poole, letter on 'The Future of the English Watch Trade', *Watchmaker, Jeweller, and Silversmith,* 7 (June 1887).
7 *Watchmaker, Jeweller, and Silversmith,* 1/2 (July 1875), 28–9.
8 *Horological Journal,* 1 (Sept. 1858), 16. The asylum eventually consisted of thirteen red-bricked houses, built for £3,500. They gave free residence and fuel to eleven males and four widows. Males had annuities of £20; females, of £13. See LMA/CLC/125/MS21339/001-006, 'Watch and Clock Makers' Benevolent Institution: Annual Report and Accounts: 6 Volumes Covering 1849–1910; and. W. Pinks, *The History of Clerkenwell,* (London: Charles Herbert, 2nd. ed., 1881), 317–18.
9 *Horological Journal,* 13/6 (Feb. 1871), 1–2.
10 *Horological Journal,* 12/6 (Feb. 1870), 68–69.
11 *Horological Journal,* 14/10 (June 1872), 116.
12 *Horological Journal,* 14/12 (Aug. 1872), 138.
13 Alan Midleton, 'The History of the BHI: Part 7: The Early Years, The Crisis Years, 1858–72', *Horological Journal,* 151 (January 2008), 26–27; also Edna Healey, 'Angela Georgina Burdett-Coutts, *Suo jure* Baroness Burdett-Coutts (1814–1906)', *ODNB.*
14 *Horological Journal,* 18/6 (Feb. 1879), 71–74, and 18/12 (Aug. 1879), 1545–158, for accounts of half-yearly General Meetings at which the trade depression and the new building were discussed. See also F.J. Britten, 'Reminiscences of Early Workers at the British Horological Institute. No. 1, Mr John Jones', *Horological Journal,* 46/3 (Nov. 1903), 32–35; and Anon., drawing from F.J. Britten's 1903 account, 'Forgotten Benefactor: Jno Jones–Watchmaker', *Horological Journal,* 99/12 (Aug. 1957), 472–73.
15 Alun C. Davies, 'On Excursion and On Song: The BHI views New Technology in the 1870s and 1880s', *Antiquarian Horology,* 33/2 (Dec. 2011), 207–20.
16 For the availability of pianos at around this price, see Cyril Ehrlich, *The Piano: A History* (1976; Oxford: Clarendon, rev. ed., 1990), 9–10.
17 Midleton, 'History of the BHI', *Horological Journal,* Part 9 (March 2008), 114–15.
18 Davies, 'On Excursion and On Song', 207–20.
19 *Horological Journal,* 11/8 (April 1869), 90–91.
20 *Horological Journal,* 14/6 (Feb. 1875), 81.
21 Charles Hobbs 'picked' Bramah and Chubb locks, previously thought impregnable, at the Great Exhibition in 1851; see Ian McNeil, *Joseph Bramah: A Century of Invention, 1749–1851* (Newton Abbott: David & Charles, 1972), Ch. 14, 'The Great Lock Controversy: A Postscript', 190–201.
22 Joel Mokyr, 'Technological Inertia in Economic History', *Journal of Economic History.* 52/2 (June 1992), 325–38, at https://www.jstor.org/stable/2123111.
23 *Horological Journal,* 1/1 (1859), 19.
24 *Horological Journal,* 4/5 (Jan. 1862), 55
25 *Horological Journal,* 1 (1858–59), 132–33; 2 (1859–60), 31, 47–50, 63–65.

26 Donald Hoke, 'Ingenious Yankees, The Rise of the American System of Manufactures in the Private Sector', *Journal of Economic History*, 46/2 (June 1986), 489–91, at https://www.jstor.org/stable/2122179; id., 'British and American Horology: Time to Test Factor-Substitution Models, *Journal of Economic History*, 47/2 (June 1987), 321–27, at https://www.jstor.org/stable/2122231; August C. Bolino, 'British and American Horology: A Comment on Hoke', *Journal of Economic History*, 48/3 (Sept. 1988), 665–68, at https://www.jstor.org/stable/2121544; and Donald Hoke's response, 'British and American Horology: A Reply to Bolino', *Journal of Economic History*, 49/3 (Sept 1989), 715–19 at https://www.jstor.org/stable/2122514.

27 The series was reported in the *Horological Journal* in three parts; 22/4 (Dec. 1879), 43–44; 22/5 (Jan. 1880), 60–61 and 22/6 (Feb. 1880), 78.

28 Also for subsequent quotes, *Horological Journal,* 22/4 (Dec. 1879), 43–44.

29 David Glasgow, *Watch and Clockmaking* (London: Cassell, 1885, 2nd ed. 1891), in the series *Manuals of Technology*, edited by Professor Ayrton and R. Wormwell; *Horological Journal,* 22/5 (Jan. 1880), 57–61; also Alan Midleton, 'History of the BHI', *Horological Journal*, 151/7 (March 2008), 114ff.

30 For background, see Mark Bevir, 'Republicanism, Socialism, and Democracy in Britain: The Origins of the Radical Left', *Journal of Social History*, 34/2 (Winter, 2000), 351–68, at https://www.jstor.org/stable/3789988; also Richard Wood, 'The Hall-Marking Agitation, with a Glance at Former Periods of Depression in the Watch Trades', *Horological Journal*, 29/7 (March 1887), 98–101.

31 *Horological Journal,* 22 (Feb. 1880), 78; Alan Midleton, 'History of the BHI', *Horological Journal* (Jan. 2008), 24, and (Sept 1958), 563.

32 Alun C. Davies, 'Horology at International Exhibitions, 1851–1900', *Antiquarian Horology*, 33/5 (Sept. 2013), 591–608.

33 See, especially. his assessment of the consequences of the revolution in watchmaking: Henry Ganney, 'Machine Watchmaking', *Horological Journal*, 26/9 (May 1884), 115–20.

34 *Horological Journal,* 29/2 (Oct. 1886), 31–32.

35 *Horological Journal,* 11/12 (Aug. 1869), 134.

36 *Horological Journal,* 16/1 (Sept 1873), 1.

37 Davies, 'Exhibitions', esp. 600–02; also Thomas R. Wotruba, 'The Horological World of Francois Arsene Margaine', *Antiquarian Horology*, 35/2 (June 2014), 807–21, esp. 814–15; *Horological Journal,* 30/2 (Oct 1887), 29.

38 Ganney's *Report on the Paris Exhibition of 1878* appeared as 'The Practical Value of Horological Schools, and their Work at the Paris Exhibition of 1878', *Horological Journal*, 22/11 (July 1880), 142–47.

39 Roderick Floud, 'Technical Education and Economic Performance: Britain, 1850–1914', *Albion: Journal of British Studies*, 14/2 (Summer 1982), 153–71.; Michael Argles, *South Kensington to Robbins: An Account of English Technical and Scientific Education since 1851* (London: Longman, 1964), Chapters 2 and 3; Stephen F. Cotgrove, *Technical Education and Social Change* (London: Ruskin House, 1958), Chapters 3 and 4; and Gordon W. Roderick and Michael D. Stephens, *Education and Industry in the Nineteenth Century: The English Disease?* (London: Longman, 1978), 156–60.

40 *Horological Journal,* 27/12 (Aug. 1885), 162–64.

41 *Horological Journal,* 26/12 (Aug. 1884), 163–64.

42 Leonard Waldo, 'The Mechanical Art of American Watchmaking', *Journal of the Society of Arts*, 34 (1885–86), 740–51, at http://www.jstor.org/stable/23852799. Waldo's lecture was reprinted in *The Jewellers' Circular and Horological Review* (New York), XVII (July 1886), 186–90; there is an

abstract in *Horological Journal,* 28/8 (April 1886), 117–22. On the American system and horology, see Alun C. Davies, 'British Watchmaking and the American System', *Business History,* 35/1 (January 1993), 40–54.

43 *Horological Journal,* 26 /6 (Feb. 1884), 71–72.

44 *Horological Journal,* 26/12 (Aug. 1884),157; *Horological Journal,* 30/2 (Oct. 1887), 29–30

45 *Horological Journal,* 28/5 (Feb. 1886), 83–84. For Swiss schools and the modernisation of their teaching methods, see Pierre-Yves Donzé, *History of the Swiss Watch Industry: From Jacques David to Nicolas Hayek* (2012: Pieterlen Switzerland: Peter Lang AG, 3rd ed., 2014), 16, 44.

46 Julien J.S. Tripplin, *Watch and Clock Making in 1889: The French Industrial Exhibition: Being an Account and Comparison of the Exhibits in the Horological Section of the French International Exhibition … With a View of the British Watch and Clock Making Sections* (London: Crosby Lockwood, 1890), 11; id., 'Recent Progress in British Watch and Clockmaking', *Horological Journal,* 32/8 (April 1890), 120–24.

47 R. Mullineux Walmsley, 'Horological Education in Clerkenwell', *Horological Journal,* 47/1 (Sept. 1904), 2–4, and for the subsequent quotation.

48 *Horological Journal,* 35/2 (Oct 1892), 31.

49 *Horological Journal,* 45/1 (Sept. 1902), 10–11.

50 *Horological Journal,* 44/12 (Aug. 1902), 152.

51 *Horological Journal,* 46/1 (Sept. 1903), 14–15.

52 The New York *Jewellers Circular and Horological Review,* 21/12 (Jan. 1891), 21: 'It will become in the fullest sense a trade newspaper, handy in form, typographically neat and editorially substantial'.

53 Jonathan Betts, 'Notes from the Librarian: Britten had Talent', *Antiquarian Horology,* 41/4 (Dec. 2020), 508–09, on the multiple editions of Britten's *Handbook* and his monumental *Old Clocks and Watches and Their Makers.*

54 *Horological Journal,* 46/12 (Aug. 1904), 169–76. See also the brief account by 'J. McL', 'Looking Back Sixty Years: A Reminiscent Christmas Feature', *Horological Journal,* 105/4 (Dec. 1963), 386–87.

55 For more on this theme, see Mokyr, 'Technological Inertia in Economic History', 325–38, at: https://www.jstor.org/stable/2123111

56 Richard Good, 'An Enamelled Gold Minute Repeating Striking Watch with Arms, Crest, and Cypher of Sir John Bennett', *Horological Journal* (Jan. 1984), 12–22; for illustrations of the watch at the Paris exhibition, 1878 see Davies, 'Horology at International Exhibitions'; also [Royal Society of Arts], *Artisan Reports on the Paris Universal Exhibition of 1878* (London: Low, Marston, Searle, & Rivington, 1879), 437–64; Cuss, *Country Life Watches,* 10.

57 Report of a lecture on Sir John Bennet by Richard Harvey in *Antiquarian Horology,* 24/6 (Summer 1999), 574–75; David Thompson, 'Sir John Bennett', *Watches* (London: British Museum, 2008), 128–29.

58 Lord Grimthorpe (Edmund Beckett Denison), *A Rudimentary Treatise on Clocks and Watches and Bells* (London: Weale, 1860); Peter Ferriday, *Lord Grimthorpe, 1816–1905* (London: Murray, 1957).

59 *Horological Journal,* 2/11 (July 1860), 145.

60 *Horological Journal,* 44/1 (Sept. 1901), 9, notes that 'Mr Henry Ganney, the horological Will-o'-the-Wisp, located at New York for three years past, has lately re-appeared to his old Clerkenwell friends'.

14 Twilight in Clerkenwell

Ignoring the Market

Measuring Clerkenwell's decline

Measuring the extent of Clerkenwell's decline can be done in several ways. One is in the steady fall in output of what had once been their staple product – movements in silver cases. In 1796, the Goldsmith's Hall assayed 191,000 precious metal cases for Clerkenwell's movements – the largest amount produced by any watchmaking centre in Europe. They included 6,500 in gold cases and 185,000 in silver. By 1840, its annual output of movements was under 100,000, about half of its former peak.[1] By 1850, it had shrunk further. In the 1860s the Swiss sold more watches in Britain than were made in Clerkenwell. In the 1870s Clerkenwell's share in Britain's watch markets shrank again, when factory-made American watches joined Swiss. By the late 1880s, Clerkenwell's share of watches sold in the world's markets was miniscule. By 1900, the luxury market for gold-cased watches had grown slightly, to just over 7,000. But only 5,146 silver cases were assayed for movements.[2] Ninety-seven per cent of Clerkenwell's once-staple product had vanished.

Another indication of decline that can be seen is in the contraction of Clerkenwell's workforce. Even at its peak, in the late eighteenth century 'horology' was always a minor industry in London. By the 1850s amongst the city's industries, 'horology' ranked only fourteenth, after tobacconists, commercial clerks, lawyers, messengers and porters, civil servants, domestic servants, plumbers, painters, glaziers, bakers, confectioners, and medical workers. It employed about the same number of workers as glue and tallow makers, greengrocers, stationers, bookbinders, carriage makers, and coal heavers. The industry's structure still reflected the specialisms outlined earlier by Petty, Campbell, and Pearson. In 1851, horology's several branches in the city employed 4,847 persons (mostly males), not quite 2 per cent of London's workers.[3] The 1860s and 1870s saw further decline. *Collinson's Trade Directory* in 1861 identified twenty broad categories, with just over 4,000 horological craftsmen in nearly 1,300 small units.[4] Most supplied clockmakers, but 312 firms provided the crucial supporting technologies that made and assembled watches and chronometers.[5] Ominously, another forty units

DOI: 10.4324/9781003227823-17

were described, as 'importers' – agencies for Swiss and, later, American watches. *Kelly's* 1872 *Directory* used a different analytical taxonomy which revealed that fifty-two firms supplied parts and services to 124 'watch manufacturers' (that is, those shops or firms that commissioned Clerkenwell's watches). They numbered only about a third of those listed a decade earlier by Collinson.[6] The essential structure of the industry remained but, indisputably, it had shrunk.

The contraction of watchmaking in Clerkenwell contrasted with that of other contemporary industries that flourished in Britain. It was also markedly different from contemporaneous watchmaking in the United States. There, two of its twelve firms employed more than 1,000 workers. Compared with Clerkenwell's tiny workshops, they enjoyed massive economies of scale and huge productivity advantages (Chapter 11). Yet all competed to sell watches in the world's markets. Clerkenwell's horological workforce continued to shrink. In 1907, the *Census of Production* identified 5,567 horological workers still 'employed in [Britain's] watch and clock factories and workshops, male and female'. Only 288 were described as 'outworkers'.[7] By 1911, even that number of outworkers had fallen to 236.[8] The rest, 'employed in factories', were in Coventry and Birmingham [The LWC in Liverpool had failed in 1910 (Chapter 15)]. Those few hundred outworkers, 'in workshops', were the remnants in Clerkenwell of the estimated 7,000 outworkers the horological industry had employed in 1801.

As we saw in Part 1 the industry's decline had started during the French wars, when cheap, smuggled Swiss watches first entered Britain in substantial numbers. In the early 1840s, the failure of the Ingold's attempt to modernise Clerkenwell's industry, left it locked into its pre-industrial production methods. Other watchmaking hubs in Britain tried, with limited success, to modernise (Chapter 15). After 1860, Clerkenwell rejected the revolutionary production methods pioneered by Waltham. Swiss watch firms didn't: after 1876 they gradually adapted their *etablissage* system of production and by1900 had re-established their lead in the world's watch markets. But Clerkenwell remained 'locked-in' to its old handcraft technology, despite the favourable huge domestic and foreign markets that unfolded all around them. Given the right incentives and leadership, Clerkenwell's outworkers, like the Swiss, had transferrable skills that they might have adapted to accommodate the new technology. But they didn't.

Clerkenwell's lost markets

Let us look more closely at those 'lost' markets. Clerkenwell, in London, was at the centre of one of the world's most lucrative markets. Distribution costs for watches, as the Swiss had shown, were a relatively trivial portion of the final selling price of a watch. For Clerkenwell's makers, they were lower than those of any rivals, whether in Britain or not. On

Clerkenwell's own doorstep London's population boomed. In three successive decades after 1850 the metropolis grew by about half a million (2.3m in 1851 to 2.8m in 1861, then to 3.2m). By 1900 London's population exceeded 6 million and rose to 7 million in 1911. Londoners enjoyed ample distribution facilities: in 1861 about 600 'Goldsmiths, Silversmiths and Jewellers' shops sold watches, clocks, jewellery, and silverware. By 1911, those shops employed over 27,000 assistants (a quarter of them women). The metropolitan market was served by a plethora of specialist horological shops, like Sir John Bennett's (from 1846 at 65 Cheapside, with its figures of Gog and Magog), Samuel Smith's (founded in 1851, after 1872 at 85 The Strand), and Asprey of Bond Street (founded 1781). Other horological specialists included Barraud & Lund, Frodsham, Dent, Hamilton & Inches, and Usher & Cole. The city's emporia matched the *Bon Marche* in Paris, or Macy and Wanamaker in New York and Philadelphia. All the great departmental stores – Harrods (1849), Liberty (1875), Gamages (1878), and Selfridges (1909) – sold watches.

If the range of outlets to sell watches was ideal, so was the importance of the need to know the time. The acceptance of Greenwich Mean Time (GMT) was widespread. In the centre of London, Big Ben's quarters and hours could be heard up to twenty seconds later within a radius of about five miles: it enabled watches of even mediocre accuracy to be checked regularly.[9] Outside the city, Britain's market for watches also expanded, as population nearly doubled from just over 27 million in 1851 to about 45 million in 1911.[10] The railway network hastened the abandonment of local times when GMT was conveyed by telegraph to station clocks.[11] Public transport, factories, businesses, and shops were organised around GMT.[12] As living standards and disposable incomes improved, so did the desire to own watches and the ability to pay for them. David Landes reminds us that the demand for watches accompanied the adoption of 'modern living [including] a whole bundle of new work and life requirements... Use of timepieces [grows] fastest in those countries on the steepest part of the development curve'.[13] Many adult males and some women in employment already owned watches. If they did not, they wanted one. Through the Victorian and Edwardian eras Britain was well advanced on its own development curve: it was a major industrial power, and the world's leading trader with unequalled access to foreign and imperial markets.

The question remains: why did Clerkenwell fail to exploit these opportunities? Other English watch firms, in Birmingham, Coventry, and Liverpool, *did* attempt to adjust to the new technology, with mixed success (Chapter 15). With hindsight, the opportunity cost of Clerkenwell's inability to supply this vast market was, ultimately, the death of its industry. The domestic market that Clerkenwell failed to exploit enabled approximately 40–50 million watches to be imported between 1850 and 1914. Perhaps a million watches were made in Britain by firms in Birmingham,

Coventry and Liverpool. Between 1899 and 1914, the largest aggregate output of Britain's most successful firm, Williamson of Coventry, was about half a million (Chapter 15). But only a tiny number of watches bought in Britain, counted in thousands, were made in Clerkenwell.

Why did Clerkenwell fail?

Explanations of Clerkenwell's failure lie in the interaction of three characteristics. First, Clerkenwell made the 'wrong kind of watches' for a mass market. Second, the luxury market it did cater for, was small and shrinking, although (paradoxically) profitable for its remaining suppliers. Third, the system of commissioning and making its watches was ponderous and labour-intensive. The rest of this chapter explores these explanations, summarises what is known about commissioning firms, and concludes with the consequences for Clerkenwell's outworkers and its physical environment.

The 'wrong kind of watch'

Clerkenwell's makers persisted with the fusee and key winding long after going barrels and stem winding had proved their worth. Consequently, their watches were expensive, unfashionable, and inappropriate for the newly unfolding mass market. Even when its leading firms, like Nicole Nielsen (see below), made watches with going barrels they were still exceedingly expensive. From the beginning Clerkenwell's traditional watches had fusees, not going barrels. They were thick, looked old-fashioned, and wound by opening the back to fit and turn a key. Although a pioneer of keyless work had been the Englishman, Thomas Prest, his winding device would not work in watches with a fusee. Britain's watch owners, Landes observed, 'had been taught to look on [the fusee] as the hallmark of a well-made timepiece'.[14] When Adrien Philippe (of the Patek Philippe Company) patented a stem winding device in 1844 for use with going barrels, it was quickly adopted by Swiss (and Anglo-Swiss) makers. It proved successful, everywhere, except with Clerkenwell's traditional firms, who were slow to adopt 'stem winding'. Clerkenwell's makers clung on to the fusee for decades before they began using the going barrel; and 'even when they did', Landes noted, 'they clung on to key winding'.[15] Furthermore, the internal parts of Clerkenwell's best movements were engraved, sometimes lavishly. Even steel pinions inside movements were polished for decorations that could not be seen by their owners. In 1876, James Watson, a juror at the 1876 Centennial Exhibition, scathingly commented that the English lever watch was the 'wrong kind, clumsy, with fusee and chain ... [still] made and sold in considerable quantities for home demand [but which had] long since ceased to be sent abroad as in olden times'.[16] Even in Clerkenwell some voices grudgingly conceded that it was 'the fusee which had lost us the American market'.[17] E.D. Johnson concluded that

> The Swiss, the French, the Germans, the Americans, leapt in to the ring, brandishing a watch, but never a fusee amongst the lot; and each lays claim to victory by virtue of four things. Firstly, I am very good looking; secondly, I go very nicely; thirdly, I am very cheap; fourthly, I have no chain to break. And against all these four, poor old England has nothing to offer but the memory of what she was in her youth, and that she still retains her dear old barrel, fusee, and chain![18]

Lord Grimthorpe, on one of his rare Olympian appearances, at a BHI debate in 1880 about the merits of fusees, pointed out that 'All the world did not want very superior watches ... a watch that will go correctly within a minute a week is quite sufficient for most people'.[19] Grimthorpe's assertion was supported by ample contemporary testimony that pointed to the retention of the fusee as the reason why Clerkenwell's watches failed to appeal to a mass market. First-time buyers in Britain and elsewhere instead chose less expensive Swiss and American machine-made watches with going barrels because they 'look well, go well, and wear well'.[20] The *Horological Journal* reported in 1891 that going barrels were preferred to traditional Clerkenwell models 'with spring and plates as soft as lead, and as pretty as a saucepan'.[21] The technical superiority of movements with fusees was not much more expensive than movements with going barrels: it was the additional complications in movements for either kind that added to their cost, as can be seen in Nicole Nielsen's pricelist (below). Yet some watches with fusees continued to be made by firms filling special orders, even after the turn of the century.

Clerkenwell's small watch market

The second reason for Clerkenwell's decline was the limitations of the market for which it catered. Concentration on making expensive watches for a luxury market was an outcome of Britain's distinct class system. Survival of the luxury market through the Edwardian era poses a paradox: it explains why Clerkenwell's industry declined (because it ignored opportunities to supply other markets), yet the few firms that supplied expensive watches were profitable. The luxury watch market was small. At its top end, it comprised some extremely rich individuals and their families, large landowners, and industrial and business tycoons. They enjoyed big, sometimes vast, incomes and assets. They could afford, if they wished, some remarkable creations. One example was the watch made for John Jacob Astor IV: it was a 'clock watch, minute repeater, split second, perpetual calendar, 18-carat gold case, 5oz, ... costing £1,000'. It was reputed to be with Lord Astor when he drowned in the *Titanic*.[22] There were sufficient well-off gentry who also could afford to buy Clerkenwell's expensive watches, made with either fusees or going barrels. Highly-paid professionals could also afford expensive watches, as might lesser gentry with assets not exclusively dependent on earned incomes. Before 1914, barristers annually earned between £450 and £500 and some, much more. Medical doctors earned about £400 annually and could afford to buy Clerkenwell's watches that cost between £20 and £50 or more. It was the continuation of this market into the 'Indian summer' of the Edwardian era that helped to prolong the survival of Clerkenwell's last firms. But it was at the cost of ignoring the much larger markets for the middle and working classes. By concentrating almost exclusively on supplying the demand from the small luxury market, David Landes concluded that Clerkenwell's watchmakers 'simply missed their chance, and the more they lost ground the more they consoled themselves with the thought that they were right, and their customers were wrong'.[23]

The middle class market that Clerkenwell ignored was larger than that of their precursors, the 'emerging middling classes' that had stimulated the eighteenth century's 'consumer revolution' (Chapter 5). It included army officers, clergy, and those with incomes of about £200 annually, who might afford from £10 or so for a Clerkenwell-made watch and would perhaps buy one for anniversary, coming-of-age, wedding, or retirement gifts. At the bottom of this category were those with incomes up to £150 annually, who were slightly better off than skilled craftsmen or clerks, for whom Clerkenwell's watches were just too expensive.[24] This group included many of the potential customers advised by J.B. Thomas in his 1863 pamphlet *Watches: what to buy and how to use them*. Thomas helpfully explained differences in price and quality between English watches and imported Swiss watches:

> All low-priced watches are Swiss made, such as are sold in silver cases at from 20 shillings to 70 shillings each; and in Gold Cases from £3 10s to £8 10s. ... If you cannot afford an English Lever, buy a plain, strong Swiss, or more commonly called, Geneva Watch.[25]

The largest market in Britain was 'working class'. In the Edwardian era, it comprised about three-quarters of the population. Although many wanted watches (and if employed in transport perhaps needed them), for those prospective purchasers Clerkenwell's watches were impossibly expensive. Instead, they bought the cheaper watches made in Coventry or imported from Switzerland or America. Even in the early nineteenth century, as E.P. Thompson explained, some manual workers bought watches from militia or harvest bounties, because it was a useful way of saving; watches could be pawned in emergencies. By the end of the century advertisements for inexpensive watches emphasised their low cost and widespread availability: the status of watches had changed from 'luxury items' to 'affordable necessities'. The importation of American 'dollar' watches hastened this transformation, encouraged by advertisers who often featured instalment payment plans to help widen demand.[26] By the late nineteenth century watch owners who earned between £80 and £100 per year even included some building workers and others engaged in dirty working environments, as advertisements offered inexpensive watches with India-rubber coverings for protection.[27] Low-paid outdoor workmen like agricultural labourers, with earnings of between £40 and £52 a year, might buy a £1 watch and a 5s chain. Second-hand watches, costing a few pounds or less, were also within reach. The extent and nature of this large domestic market for watches were never addressed by the firms that commissioned and the outworkers that made Clerkenwell's watches. In the era of free trade there was an almost unlimited availability of a range of alternative watches imported from Switzerland and America, at every price.

Commissioning watches

The third explanation for Clerkenwell's decline is related to the first two. Expensive watches for a small market sustained an archaic commissioning system that made watches by labour-intensive methods. The impetus – the initiative – for the creation of Clerkenwell's hand-made watches lay mostly on the demand side – with individual customers, via an intermediary retailer. The commissioning shop might, at most, order some watches in advance of demand to show to customers. This sharply contrasted with the initiative for the creation of machine-made watches, which lay on the supply side, with manufacturers (like Rotherham or Williamson in Coventry). Clerkenwell's outworkers thus depended on shops that were *not* exclusively reliant on selling their watches. They were only a small part of the retailer's overall business. Shops happily stocked and sold a wide range of machine-made watches made elsewhere in Britain, Switzerland, or America. They were cheaper and were simply better value for money. If or when the Clerkenwell link became uneconomic, retailers could drop it. And they did, especially when machine-made watches of equal or even better quality became available. Glimpses into how Clerkenwell's watches were traditionally commissioned can be seen in the following case studies.

Birch, Connell, and others

In 1840, William Birch took over William Turner's Fenchurch Street horological shop established in 1825. Thereafter, as well as selling and repairing watches made in Coventry and Switzerland, Birch extended his business for the next few decades by ordering 1,615 special watches made in Clerkenwell. Birch, of course, was just one of several similar commissioners of the outworkers. The volume of his orders declined in the 1880s because, one must assume, of the growing availability of cheaper, machine-made, imported watches of good quality. Subsequently, if an occasional customer still wanted a traditional 'Clerkenwell' watch, Birch simply bought-in already 'finished' watches from one of the few remaining commissioning firms. The name 'Birch' was then engraved on their dials.[28] A similar pattern emerged in William George Connell's horological shop at 83 Cheapside. Connell, too, offered customers watches that were to be made in Clerkenwell to agreed specifications at prices between £10 and £25.[29] Over four decades of his business lifetime he contracted for 1,264 of those watches, an average of about thirty a year.[30] His Order Books, like Birch's, give details of each watch, names of outworkers who made them, and what they charged. The watches were empiricisms, made individually, not even in small batches, for the Order Books reveal few identical specifications. Entries give the costs of different parts and sizes (levers at sizes 18¾ and 16¾ for £1; sizes 6¾ to 14¾ for 16s). Various qualities of 'finishing' incurred different charges. Silver cases typically cost 15s 6d and those in gold upwards from £3 4s. Buying a watch from Connell or Birch was like buying a 'bespoken' suit from a good tailor. The cost of a Savile Row suit depended on the cloth's quality, the buyer's height and size, the style of lapel, and number of pockets and buttons. Similarly, Clerkenwell's 'bespoken watches' were composed to the customer's requirements (no doubt with Connell's or Birch's recommendations). After 1860 Connell's commissions for Clerkenwell's watches declined, in consecutive decades from 526, to 318, to 174 and finally to 133, or from about one a week to one a month. The records of Birch and Connell show a clear fall in demand for Clerkenwell watches from the late 1880s, notably when excellent quality machine-made American and Swiss watches became available (below).

Some of the large department stores and specialist horological shops acted as intermediary commissioners for other independent retailers, For example, Frodsham's records show they 'made' (i.e., instigated the commission of) Clerkenwell's watches on behalf of more than forty other shops.[31] Usher & Cole commissioned watches and chronometers, explicitly with 'the top plates and barrel bars stoned grey' [left blank], so that when they were sold on to another retailer 'they could be finished off by engraving the name of the purchasing firm'.[32] The firm was less known for their own 'named' watches than for the watches they contracted on behalf of Asprey, or Hamilton & Inches, and other shops whose names comprised 'a litany of the famous retailers of the day'.[33] Eventually, their 'middleman' role became more important, and they ceased commissioning themselves. Instead they bought-in 'finished' watches from the few remaining commissioning specialists, like Nielsen or, for chronometers, Kullberg or Mercer (Chapter 16).

Clerkenwell's last surviving makers: Golay, Nicole Nielsen, and Guye

By the turn of the century, fewer retailers still commissioned Clerkenwell's watches. The overall picture is not clear. The names on dials are of the retailers who sold them, not the cohort of small firms – aptly described by Landes as 'semi-anonymous' – that still commissioned outworkers. Among them was Hector Golay, who came to Clerkenwell from the Vallée de Joux in about 1870; he was an agent for Audemars Piguet in Switzerland, maker of luxury watches, complicated chronographs, repeaters, and clock watches.[34]

More is known about Nicole Nielsen's firm, reputed to have commissioned the best watches in Clerkenwell.[35] Adolph Nicole become renowned when awarded the patent for a 'keyless' mechanism (stem winding) for going-barrel watches. They were displayed in 1851 in London's Crystal Palace and then at exhibitions in New York, Paris, Philadelphia, Vienna, Sydney, and Melbourne.[36] Nielsen supplied fine watches for over half a century to about thirty select retailers like Dent and Frodsham, others to retailers in Sydney, Shanghai, and Tiffany in New York.[37] The firm specialised in complicated pieces – chronographs with split seconds, repeating quarters and minutes, calendars, and phases of the moon: if some special refinements were needed, they were sent to Switzerland.[38] It was the extra complications that increased their prices (Figure 14.1).

Nicole Nielsen's enterprise was small. Census returns indicate its workshop employed ten men in 1871 and eighteen by 1881. They occasionally sent watches to Switzerland for extras (thus 'part Swiss') but it is not known if the firm sometimes drew on Clerkenwell's outworkers. Their exact output is uncertain. Pierantonio Maragna has estimated, from serial numbers over the firm's lifetime of ninety-three years, that Nielsen made about 23,000 watches. This amounted to an annual average of 250 watches, or about four or five a week.[39] Output was probably higher in the firm's peak years of activity in the late Victorian and Edwardian eras, but it was miniscule compared with the millions of watches made each year in Switzerland's cantons and in America's giant factories (Chapter 11). When Henry Ganney visited the workshop in 1884 its organisation still exemplified Clerkenwell's traditional technology: 'all the power required', he reported, 'depended on a foot-lathe'. His description stressed that 'the timekeepers turned out here were made for different shopkeepers, each of whom, far from appreciating uniformity with his fellow tradesmen, wanted watches as 'distinct in size and style as possible. In some cases, it is a *sine qua non* that a particular type of watch designed for one customer shall be reserved especially for him'.[40] Five years later, when a BHI excursion visited the firm, its *Journal* explained that the workshop had expanded in an *ad hoc* fashion, and an

Figure 14.1 Nicole Nielsen watch for Dent. Courtesy: Tony Maragna.

element of modern technology had at last appeared: its basement now had an engine made by Nicolaus Otto of Deutz, Germany. It was an internal combustion device (a precursor of automobile engines) that drove shafting at 500 rpm: gearing accelerated speeds of some polishing lathes up to 3,000 rpm. Various tools were connected by friction clutches that engaged or disengaged transmission from the driving shaft to the driven shaft.[41] The most complicated watches were finished individually. Nicole Nielsen's workshop had become a small factory, but the *Horological Journal* reported it was quite unlike any other in size and organisation.

> The various workshops ... do not follow on in any regular order, but are rather straggled about in somewhat inconvenient situations, a not unusual occurrence where an old business has been gradually enlarged and added to as occasion demanded. [The gold and silver cases] were 'designed to be as fashionably slim as possible ... achieved by doing away with the dome, hinges, and having a Snap-on bezel and back.[42]

Nielsen and other Clerkenwell and Prescot firms still operated from workshops that even at their largest, were in another world compared with giant American factories (Compare Pybus's workshop in Figure 2.2, Chapter 2, with Waltham's factory in Figure 11.1, Chapter 11). Despite the *ad hoc* nature of its premises, Nielsen's *1910 Catalogue* illustrates an extraordinary variety of expensive watches. Its pricelist reveals fifty-four different classes or 'types', ranged from some modestly priced 'grade 2, ladies' at £10, through a variety of ladies and gentlemen's repeaters different sizes, escapements, and jewelling options at prices up to £92.[43] Further up the range were watches with a perpetual calendar, minute repeater and a minute recording clock, costing from £180 to £240 and above (£240 would then have been a comfortable annual income for a middle-class family). The menu for their most expensive watches ('Prices on Application') offered a dazzling array of options; a perpetual calendar, windows for moon, morning and evening stars, times for sunrise and sunset, split seconds minute recording chronograph for timing the first and second in a race, minute recorder, minute repeater, and even a barometer. As well as telling the time, such watches enabled their owners to display their wealth. But the occasional exotic and expensive commissions, like that from Lord Astor, could not preserve Clerkenwell's old industry forever. Although Emil Nielsen had worked for the Waltham Company for some years and 'had some American tools or tools modelled on American ideas', he did not fully embrace the 'American System' that was currently enabling American companies to achieve prodigious levels of output.[44] Nicole Nielsen used machine tools to make some components but, as Henry Ganney explained, 'did not desire any notice of the merits of their tools and machinery be given to the world, as they did not wish their watches to be known as machine-made, their business being of a select and aristocratic character'.[45]

The firm of P & A Guye is of special interest because it seems to have explicitly attempted self-sufficiency in their own factory. August Guye and his brothers had been brought up as watchmakers in St. Olivier, Switzerland. They arrived in London in 1856, first to a small workshop in Northampton Square, then in 1875 to St Bride's Street and finally to a 'large and well-lit building' in Farringdon Road. Compared with Clerkenwell's traditional workshops the Guyes' most distinctive feature was that, apart from bought-in dials, they used machine tools to make all the other watch parts in their own 'factory'.[46] It must be stressed that the Guyes did not adopt the 'American system' on the lines of Waltham and Elgin, although, in an indirect way, they came nearer to the concept than other Clerkenwell firms. August Guye was an autodidact who developed his machine tools from first principles, without external influences. He claimed he had never visited another watch factory that used machine tools, either in Coventry or the United States. The *Watchmaker, Jeweller, and Silversmith* explained that Guye had developed 'a most comprehensive plant for advanced watch manufacture'. The Farrington Road site was much larger than the typical workshops of most Clerkenwell outworkers, with a floor space of 3,500 square feet for over a hundred employees. It made them the largest firm in Clerkenwell. They operated eighty or ninety machine tools, driven (like Nicole Nielsen's) by overhead shafting powered by one of Otto's new engines. Machine tools made various parts of the movements and their cases, but 'finishing', springing, timing, and examining, was still done by hand (just as at first had been the practice in Waltham). Guyes' watches were limited to just three different-sized movements with standard calibres (a contrast with Nielsen's innumerable choices). This allowed the same size wheels, pinions, and escapements in each movement. Because there was a constant checking of gauges, the 'interchangeability' of parts was impressive for English watches of these grades:

> Messrs Guye particularly pride themselves upon ... interchangeability and finish ... Of the quality of interchangeability of these escapements we have had ocular demonstration, having seen one taken out of one finished watch and put into another without any alteration being required, this ... being a triumph of mechanical art.[47]

The Guyes made watches 'for the trade only'. Their advertisement insisted they were 'strictly wholesale manufacturers, and wanting to protect our customers, WE NEVER EXHIBIT'. [48] Only the retailer's name appeared on the dial. They made a small number of watches at prices which, although expensive, were still a little cheaper than other Clerkenwell watches of roughly comparable quality.

The Guyes' watch parts, made with machine tools, gave a hint of what might have evolved if only they had been tried half a century earlier. Perhaps an indigenous 'British system of manufacture' might have developed? The market was there, but a crucial element – entrepreneurial innovation – was absent. By the 1890s, it was far, far, too late. It was a tentative step in the direction of larger-scale production, but a very long way behind what Americans had achieved a generation earlier. The Guyes' machine tools made standardised parts with tolerances that allowed some interchangeability. They did not attempt to make large numbers of watches at low prices for the bottom end of the market. They made what they hoped was a better watch, not necessarily a cheaper one. Output was modest. In the 1890s, it amounted to about 200 watches a week – fewer than 10,000 a year.[49] Henry Ganney compared them with a contemporary American factory that turned out 1,100 watches in a day: 'Messrs. Guye will take two or three months' to make a similar number.[50]

Other indications of Clerkenwell's decline

Another facet of Clerkenwell's decline can be glimpsed in the affairs of Frodsham of Bond Street. The firm had especially prospered under Charles Frodsham (1810–1871), and between 1858 and 1866 its annual profits averaged a healthy £5,000.[51] In 1871, the firm passed to Charles's youngest son, Harrison Mill Frodsham, and difficulties arose. Like Birch and Connell, Frodsham's business with Clerkenwell's outworkers also tailed off. Of the 255 expensive watches, Frodsham sold between

1877 and 1880 only ninety-seven were 'bespoken', made in Clerkenwell. Then Frodsham, too, bought-in finished watches and had the firm's name inscribed on the dials. Maintaining a fully-equipped workshop had become uneconomic: to start a Prescot rough movement in their workshop and commission Clerkenwell's outworkers was for them no longer profitable.[52] So unfinished stock was sold, and the workshop became smaller. Peculiar consequences followed, because of the firm's contract for maintaining hundreds of clocks and watches of Buckingham Palace and other residences. The royal deal had become an expensive white elephant because, to fulfil it, Clerkenwell's outworkers would be needed. Harrison Frodsham worried that if knowledge of that 'came to H.M.'s ears (and we have our enemies) ... we should be dismissed with great loss of prestige'.[53] Harrison Frodsham complained that the cost of the arrangement was much underestimated:

> It is a great expense ... I have always found it so even [during] the quiet times of Her late majesty; what it will be with the King [Edward VII], who will be often there, and is a most awful stickler for time!

This was an oblique reference to Edward VII's imposition of 'Sandringham Time', with clocks set thirty minutes in advance of GMT in royal households at Sandringham, Windsor, and Balmoral to allow more 'evening' daylight for winter hunting. Thereafter, the firm concentrated on selling clocks and watches ready-made elsewhere, not commissioned from Clerkenwell. Frodsham visited the Army and Navy Stores, with its 'magnificent stock ... to my dismay... marked at prices we cannot even buy at [from Clerkenwell]'.[54] Like many other firms with their roots in Clerkenwell's illustrious past, Frodsham's formula for survival was to reorganise, diversify, and sell watches made in Coventry, Switzerland, or the United States.[55] Thereafter if there were occasional subsequent special orders for Clerkenwell's watches, they could be bought in, completed, from the few remaining specialists.[56] Whilst Clerkenwell's best products were excellent, by the turn of the century, so were many factory-made ones.

Competition from imported quality machine-made watches

After 1870 the annual tables in the *Horological Journal* relentlessly recorded the growth of Swiss and American watch imports.[57] In the 1880s Switzerland, recovering from the trauma it had suffered in 1876, still accounted for about two-thirds of the world's approximately two and a half million watches then being made annually.[58] In the same decade, American watch firms accelerated their export drive to Britain.

Under this two-pronged foreign invasion, the few hundred Clerkenwell watches ordered annually by Birch, Connell, and others, amounted to only a miniscule portion to Britain's domestic market. After 1900 imports of watches rose to over a million a year; between 1900 and 1914 they amounted in aggregate to nearly 29 million. Clerkenwell could not compete in quantity; it had succeeded in supplying quality products to a small luxury market. But before the end of the century, competition in quality – especially in value for money – was being challenged. Imported machine-made watches were becoming available, described as almost equal in quality, but much cheaper.[59] An early entry was the 'Riverside Maximus', one of Waltham's high-quality grades developed after 1875. By 1883 the American Association for the Advancement of Science pointed out that machine-made watches now offered excellent value for money:

> [The] practical question is not how good a watch it is possible to make, as how cheaply can you make a watch of the first class. One has long been able to get as good a watch as can be made from Frodsham or Jurgensen by paying from $300 to $500 for it. What the world has gained from [Waltham's watchmaking] revolution is the ability to command a watch equal, or but little inferior, to the best, but at less than half the old price.[60]

The differences in prices for high-quality watches widened, as it had when dollar watches entered the bottom of the market. In the 1890s challenges to Clerkenwell's quality watches came firstly from Bahn Bonniksen (1859–1935), a Danish instructor at Coventry's Technical Institute.[61] Bonniksen's workshop employed twenty men making 'Karrusel' watches (movements with revolving escapements) aimed at the top end of the market. Other Coventry firms made them by license. They put the small market for Clerkenwell's watches under pressure when, between 1895 and 1904, Karrusels scored highly in the Kew Observatory Trials (seven of the best forty-six in 1895, sixty rated 'specially good' out of the best ninety-six in 1896, and twenty-one of the best fifty-one in 1897).[62] In 1903, George Duckworth observed that

> when a machine-made watch, which will last some years and keep very fair time, can be produced for 10s or less, and is sold retail at 15s or 20s, there is no chance for a large sale of even a decidedly superior hand-made article, which costs five times as much.[63]

After 1904, Swiss watches of excellent quality also pulled ahead of Clerkenwell's best watches at the Kew Trials, thanks to the application of Dr Charles Guillaume's *anibal* (a nickel-steel alloy applied to bimetallic balances, it eliminated 'middle-temperature error').[64] In 1907, Swiss watches by Ditisheim (by 1913 using Guillaume's *invar* and *elinvar*) took first prize at Kew in the pocket watch category, every year. 'Thus was British watchmaking robbed of its final consolation', David Landes commented, 'stripped of its last illusion'.[65] The rationale of Clerkenwell's speciality – the precision and quality of its best hand-built watches – was being matched and beaten.[66]

The decline

Not all of Britain's excellent watches were made in Clerkenwell. Some, like Bonniksen's, originated in Coventry. Even before Clerkenwell's luxury watch market was cut short by the Great War, a Coventry firm that catered for expensive demands had failed. The most famous watchmaking bankruptcy occurred in Coventry in 1909. Joseph William Player made perhaps the most exclusive single watch ever assembled, more expensive even than that for Lord Astor. It was specially created for the American financier J.P. Morgan (wealthier than Astor). Professor Torrens described it as 'an English lever one-minute tourbillon, clock, watch, and repeater, perpetual calendar, with equation of time, sunrise and sunset, tides, phases and age of the moon, sidereal time, and GMT, and other astronomical indications'. Its construction took four years, drained Player's creative and commercial energies, and his firm became insolvent.[67] Player went under. By contrast, Nicole Nielsen's firm in Clerkenwell survived because, in 1904, it diversified and made motor accessories as well as watches. During the Great War Nielsen also made speedometers, taxi meters and magnetos – all a far cry from its earlier consummate creations. The Great War changed the world and the Great Depression in the 1930s terminated Clerkenwell's lingering, traditional watchmaking industry. It sank from dusk to twilight, then to night.

Clerkenwell's deteriorating environment

As Clerkenwell's watchmaking industry ebbed, so its environment deteriorated. The main topographical features of its streets and squares, established in the late eighteenth century, had become shoddy by the late nineteenth century (Figure 14.2).[68]

Its physical decline by 1861 was described by the investigating journalist, John Hollingshead, who painted a depressing picture of the district in his *Ragged London*. Some homes, he noted, 'were not fit for human habitation', whilst others were the 'worst nests of overcrowding ...[in] close, ill-ventilated dwellings'.[69] Clerkenwell Road was opened in 1878 as a direct route from New Oxford Street to the London Docks, after some of London's worst slums were demolished to clear the way.[70] In his bleak novel *The Nether World*, set in 1880, George Gissing described the 'cleaner end' of a Clerkenwell which 'consists of decently

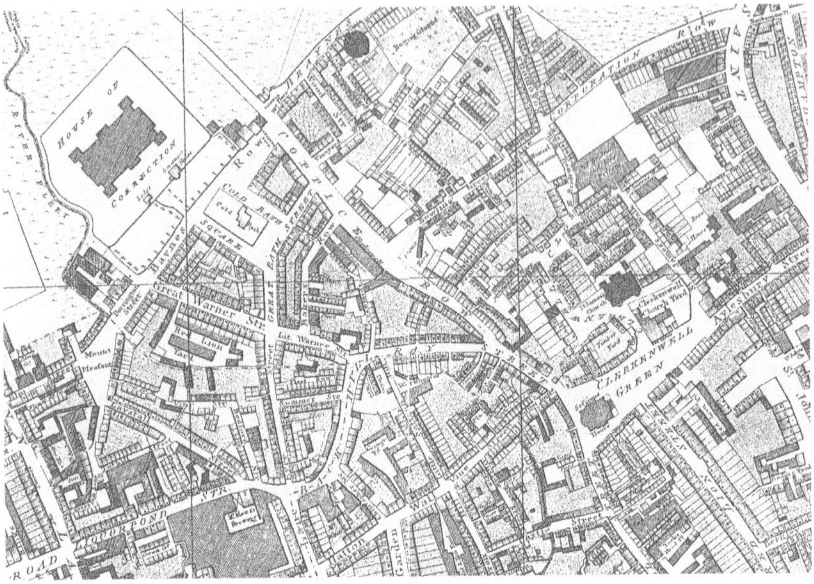

Figure 14.2 'Richard Horwood's early nineteenth-century map, showing the extent of Clerkenwell', from Richard Tames, *Clerkenwell and Finsbury Past* (Historical Publications, 1999).

depressing houses occupied, in the main, as the lower windows and front doors indicate, by watchmakers, working jewellers, and craftsmen of allied pursuits'.[71] Its houses had become 'decently depressed' because of the stagnant or falling incomes of those watchmakers who owned them. George Herbert Duckworth, in his survey for Charles Booth's *Life and Labour in London*, commented that the locality was 'a very rough district; [it] seems worse now than ten years ago'. He thought that incomes had declined by 30 per cent over the previous twenty years.[72] Workmen with nimble fingers and an understanding of basic mechanics found they could do much better elsewhere:

> The wages paid and the prices obtained for the work of our trade, do not bear comparison with those of any other whatsoever. Here you have a really skilled man doing, in many cases, beautiful work for prices that a bicycle repairer would have a good laugh at.[73]

The long-established expertise of Clerkenwell's outworkers was obsolete, and by becoming bicycle-makers they were de-skilling themselves. But making bicycles did have a special attraction: 'To watchmakers it was like working with giant tools', Adam Galbraith explained, 'the result was watchmakers left the trade they had served, or were serving their time to, and went to the easier and, in many cases, better paid one of making cycles'.[74] By the early twentieth century, Clerkenwell's remaining outworkers were old men, many of whom 'gradually became nothing else than repairers [even though initially] ... they were [once] highly specialist men under an intricate system of labour and unfamiliar with the watch mechanism as a whole'.[75] Duckworth noted that their earnings had declined:

> The number of old men is very noticeable ... as in all dwindling trades ... some of them, as their own trade shrinks, may sacrifice their special skill and take to general repairs ... Earnings are less than they used to be. Highly skilled men receive £2 to £3 for a full week's work, where they used to make £3 or £4 for perhaps four days only... their wages have fallen 30 per cent in the last twenty years ...'[76]

Clerkenwell's primary occupations had shifted from horology to general engineering trades. Even within watchmaking's many narrow specialisms some – but not all – outworkers had transferable skills that enabled them to gain alternative employment in the new industries which made motor accessories, gas meters, printing machinery, and even machines for making aerated water.[77]

Clerkenwell's watchmaking industry was once preeminent in Europe. It had decayed during the era when Britain led the world in international trade, finance, shipping, textiles, heavy engineering, and much else. During the twentieth century many of Britain's other industries that made consumer goods – pianos, cars, motorbikes, cycles, radios, computers, and television sets – also experienced a similar absolute and relative decline. Like watchmaking, most had once enjoyed ascendancy, at least in their home market. Watchmaking was the first to wither. Clerkenwell ignored Waltham's successful application of the 'American system', and Switzerland's adaption to it. Instead, it persisted with labour-intensive methods to made expensive models for a shrinking luxury market in which it faced formidable competition from machine-made watches that cost less. But, elsewhere in Britain's watchmaking industry, a different story unfolded. In Birmingham, Coventry, and Liverpool belated efforts were made to modernise their watchmaking hubs by adapting certain features of the American system. The temporary but limited success of some of those firms, and the resounding failure of another, is examined in Chapter 15.

Notes

1 *The Times*, 13 April 1843.
2 Preface to Kelly's *Directory*, 1901, vi–vii.

3 Leonard D. Schwarz, *London in the Age of Industrialization: Entrepreneurs, Labour Force and Living Conditions, 1750–1850* (Cambridge: Cambridge UP, 1992), 40.
4 Collinson's *Directory*, 1861, Part 5, the 'Watch, Chronometer, and Clock Trades' Directory' (London: Collinson & Co., 1861).
5 Specialists made 'springs, wheels, hands, motions, pallets, pendants, pinions, protectors, liners, balances, barrels, caps, cases, escapements, fusees and keys'. Others who provided services were 'polishers, gilders, jewelers, and finishers'.
6 Kelly's *1872 Directory* counted 124 'watch manufacturers' among Clerkenwell's approximately 1,250 'Watch and Clock Makers'. It was an unhelpfully broad description that included craftsmen, retailers and jobbers all sheltering under the label 'watchmaker or clockmaker'. They were served by 534 'firms' (independent workshops) that belonged to thirty-eight categories; fifteen had fewer than ten firms, twelve had between ten and twenty, and nine more than twenty firms.
7 *BPP*, 1911, vol.101, *Census of Production, taken in 1907*, 160–61.
8 M.I. Michaels, 'Fine Metals and Instrument Trades', Part II of London Industries III', of Herbert Llewellyn Smith (director), *The New Survey of London Life and Labour*, Vol VIII (London: King and Co., 1934), 194, Table 1: entry for 'Jewelry, silverware, clocks and watches' reporting 130 'on an Occupational Basis', and 106 'on an Industrial Basis'.
9 Alun C Davies, 'Greenwich and Standard Time', *History Today,* 28 (1978), 194–99; David Rooney and James Nye, 'Greenwich Observatory Time for the Public Benefit': Standard Time and Victorian Networks of Regulation', *The British Journal for the History of Science*, 42/1 (March 2009), 5–30, at https://www.jstor.org/stable/25592207.
10 Phyllis Deane and W.A. Cole, *British Economic Growth 1688–1959* (Cambridge: Cambridge UP, 1962), 8 and 328–29; *BPP* 1917, 35: 483 (Cd.8491): *Census of England and Wales, 1911: General report with Appendices*; and *BPP* 1917, 80, 45; (Cd.6896), *Census for Scotland*, 1911.
11 For the telegraph and railways, see Iwan Rhys Morus, '"The Nervous System of Britain": Space Time and the Electric Telegraph in the Victorian Age', *The British Journal for the History of Science*, 33/4 (Dec. 2000), 455–75, at www.jstor.org/stable/4028030
12 The Washington 'meridian conference' in 1884 was accepted as the basis for international time zones. Wide-ranging surveys are in Vanessa Ogle, 'Whose Time Is It? The Pluralization of Time and the Global Condition, 1870s–1940s', *The American Historical Review*, 118/5 (Dec. 2013), 1376–402, at www.jstor.org/stable/23784581; and Eviatar Zerubavel, 'The Standardization of Time: A Sociohistorical Perspective', *American Journal of Sociology*, 88/1 (July 1982), 1–23, at www.jstor.org/stable/2779401. For the telling of time in Berlin, see Michael J. Sauter, 'Clockwatchers and Stargazers: Time Discipline in Early Modern Berlin', *The American Historical Review*, 112/3 (June 2007), 685–709, at https://www.jstor.org/stable/40006666
13 David S. Landes, *Revolution in Time: Clocks and the making of the Modern World* (Cambridge, MA: Harvard UP, 1983), 325.
14 Landes, *Revolution in Time,* 296.
15 Landes, *Revolution in Time*, 297. But John Griffiths comments that 'Admiralty deck watches were usually going barrel by 1890, many using Preston frames'.
16 James C. Watson: 'Horological Instruments ... Philadelphia Exhibition', *BPP,* 1877/6, 823–24 Juror's report on 'Horological Instruments' at the 1876 Centennial Exhibition in Philadelphia, reprinted as part of the British Commission's own report to parliament,

17 *Horological Journal,* 22/5 (Jan. 1880), 57–61, and for subsequent quotations. The debate was reported as 'The Wisdom of Substituting the Going Barrel for the Fusee in English Watch Manufacture'.
18 *Horological Journal,* 22/11 (July 1880), 153–54; letter from E.D. Johnson; also, Alan Midleton, *Horological Journal,* 150/10 (Nov. 2008), 444ff, and 150/12 (Dec. 2007), 486ff.
19 *Horological Journal,* 22/11 (July 1880), 153–54.
20 ['S.N.'], 'The Watchmaking Industry in Switzerland', *Science: The American Association for the Advancement of Science,* 1/11 (April 1883), 296–97, at https://doi.org/10.1126/science.ns-1.11.296.
21 *Horological Journal,* 33/11 (Aug. 1891), 165–66.
22 *Horological Journal,* 112 (Sept 1969), 24; also *New York Times,* 28 Nov. 2013, at https://www.nytimes.com/2013/11/29/fashion/tracing-a-precious-relic-of-the-titanic.html. For watches recovered from the *Titanic,* see Rory McEvoy, 'A Time to Remember', *Antiquarian Horology,* 37/4 (Dec. 2016), 522–29.
23 David S. Landes, 'Watchmaking: A Case-Study in Enterprise and Change,' *Business History Review,* 53 (1979), 20, at https://doi.org/10.2307/3114685.
24 John D. Burnett, *A History of the Cost of Living* (Harmondsworth: Penguin, 1969), passim.
25 Andrew James, 'Watches – A Pamphlet by J.B. Thomas', *Antiquarian Horology,* 31/2 (Dec. 2008), 223–28 includes a transcription of the booklet. Similar advice was offered by Albert Holland, 'How to Take Care of a Watch', *The Decorator and Furnisher,* 15/2 (Nov. 1889), 42, at www.jstor.org/stable/25585930
26 Roy Church, 'Advertising Consumer Goods in Nineteenth-Century Britain: Reinterpretations', *Economic History Review,* 53/4 (Nov. 2000), 638, 642, at https://www.jstor.org/stable/2598598. Instalment payments were a later version of the 'clock clubs' that had helped spread demand for clocks in the eighteenth century: see William Linnard, 'A Clock Club in Milford Haven in 1805', *Antiquarian Horology,* 37/1 (March 2016), 101–04.
27 *Horological Journal,* 31/10 (June 1889), 145–46.
28 Alun C. Davies, 'The Repair and Manufacture of Watches in London in the Nineteenth Century: The Business Records of Turner & Birch, 1835–1920', *Antiquarian Horology,* 17/5 (1988), 478–82. See Turner's Stock book: LMA/CLC/521/MS14469, William Turner, watch repairer of Fenchurch Street (fl.1825–40): Jobbing or Workday Book, with names of customers, owners, make and numbers of watches, nature of repairs required, and cost; and LMA/CLC/521/MS18446. Watch books of William Birch (1815–1903), of 173 Fenchurch Street are in LMA/CLC/B/024/MS14470/001 to 005: (5 vols 1840–1920), recording Birch's rough movements, finished by outworkers, and the amounts they were paid. The Watch books run from 1840 to 1920, in five volumes.
29 Connell's father was the cautious watchmaker who sat on the fence during the Ingold episode (Chapter 9). See LMA/CLC/B/057/MS14,373/001 and 002: Connell's Stock books, 1847–1902 (2 vols.), and LMA/CLC/B/057/MS14,374: Account Book, 1862–99. Connell's records are now at the London Metropolitan Archives (LMA). They were originally listed as 'Stock books of an unidentified clock and watch maker'. Internal evidence indicates they were from Connell, 83 Cheapside. They record manufacturing costs of watches numbered from 6,502 to 7,660 and show retail prices and sales of individual clocks, watches, and chains. Another account book recorded the costs of components and prices charged by outworkers.
30 LMA/CLC/B/057/MS14,374: Account Book, 1862–99. Records manufacturing costs of watches numbered from 6,502 to 7,660 and shows retail

prices, sales of individual clocks, watches and chains, and the costs of components and prices charged by outworkers.

31 R. Vaudrey Mercer, *The Frodshams: The Story of a Family of Chronometer Makers* (Ticehurst: Antiquarian Horology Society Monograph No. 21, 1981), Appendices IX and X for watches, and XI for Kullberg's supply of chronometers and XII for Mercer's supply of chronometer clocks. For names of makers who supplied the various firms trading under the name of Dent, see id., *The Life and Letters of E.J. Dent, Chronometer Maker, and Some Account of His Successors* (Ticehurst, Antiquarian Horological Society, 1977). 727: Appendices IX for chronometers and X for [watch and clock] 'manufacturers.

32 For this and the following information see John Francis Cole & T.P. Camerer Cuss, *A Watchmaking Centenary: Usher and Cole, 1861–1961* (20 page pamphlet published by the firm in 1961), at http://freepages.genealogy.rootsweb.ancestry.com/~usher/usheruk/docs/UsherCole150dpi.pdf

33 Cole & Cuss, *Centenary*, 8.

34 David S. Landes, *Revolution in Time: Clocks and the Making of the Modern World* (Cambridge, MA: Harvard UP, 1983), 297. When he retired in 1910 the business passed to his son, E.H. Golay.

35 Richard Good, 'Two Masterpieces by Nicole Nielsen', *Horological Journal*, 112/11 (July 1969), 10–13.

36 Dent's winning displays of watches included some supplied by Nicole & Capt; Alun C. Davies, 'Horology at International Industrial Exhibitions, 1851–1900', *Antiquarian Horology*, 33/5 (Sept. 2012), 591–608.

37 David S. Torrens, 'Some Notes on the History of Machine Watchmaking', *Horological Journal*, 89/8 (April 1947), 184; R. Vaudrey Mercer, *Frodshams*, Ch. 11 'Nicole Nielsen & Co.', 198–205; the range of Frodsham's customers can be seen in LMA/CLC/B/176/MS19910: Record of retail sales; and LMA/CLC/B/176/MS19914/001-005: Customers and manufacturers, 1900–41.

38 Usher & Cole's supplier for repeating work was 'Robert of Geneva'; Cole & Cuss, *Centenary*, 14.

39 See reports of lectures by Tony Maragna on Nicole Nielsen & Co., in *Antiquarian Horology*, 28/4 (Dec. 2004), 507–08; and 28/6 (June 2005), 796–97. I am grateful to him for the subsequent quotes and other information, in emails in 2017, 2018, and 2021.

40 Henry Ganney, 'Machine Watchmaking', *Horological Journal*, 26/9 (May 1884), 115–20. Ganney gives a detailed technical account of watchmaking in Guye's factory, with reference also to Nicole Nielsen's methods.

41 David Penney thinks that the company 'used machines and manufacturing systems based on those of Pierre-Frederic Ingold': see David Thompson's report of David Penney's lecture on Ingold, *Antiquarian Horology*, 29/1 (Sept. 2005), 99.

42 Visit of BHI members to Nicole, Nielsen's watch factory, *Horological Journal*, 31/10 (June 1889), 145–46, for the following quotations.

43 David Penney (ed.), *High-class English Watches: Manufactured by Nicole, Nielsen and Co. Ltd.* (London: 2002: Facsimile reprint of Trade Catalogue, circa 1910 (London: David Penney, 2010); also https://www.antiquewatchstore.com/content/13-nicole-nielsen-co

44 Ingold's earlier machines possibly 'inspired' Nicole: see David Thompson's report of a lecture by David Penney, *Antiquarian Horology*, 29/1 (Sept. 2005), 98–99.

45 Henry Ganney, 'Machine Watchmaking', *Horological Journal*, 26/9 (May 1884), 115–20.

46 *Watchmaker, Jeweler and Silversmith*, 15/12 (June1890), 11; *Horological Journal*, 35/6 (Feb. 1893), 85–86.
47 *Watchmaker, Jeweler and Silversmith*, 15/12 (June 1890), 10–11.
48 *Watchmaker, Jeweler and Silversmith*, 16/4 (July 1890), back cover advertisement.
49 Maxwell Cutmore, *Watches: 1850–1980* (Newton Abbott: David & Charles, 1989), 108–09 estimates 500 a month from 1880 to 1900, and probably a total of 120,000 in various models and sizes.
50 Henry Ganney, 'Machine Watchmaking', *Horological Journal*, 26/9 (May 1884), 117.
51 They included 139 chronometers for Bond & Son of Boston, between1834 and 1865; also R. Vaudrey Mercer, 'Charles Frodsham; Maker of Marine Chronometers', *Clocks*, 6 (Oct. 1983), 17–19; and Mercer, *Frodshams*, 37–38.
52 LMA/CLC/B/043/MS19904/001: Charles Frodsham's Watches Manufacturing Book (1876–89).
53 LMA/CLC/B/043/MS19904: Minutes of the Board of Directors 1893–1939 and of Annual General Meetings 1894–1939. (Managing Director's Report, 23 May 1894).
54 LMA/CLC/B/043/MS19904: 'Directors' Meeting, 24 December 1917', 350 ff.
55 Mercer, *Frodshams*, 263–64.
56 In 1911 its new owners, Devon Instruments Ltd., shifted production to make speedometers and motor accessories. They eventually sold Frodsham's stock and goodwill to Messrs North & Son, makers of Watford Speedometers and magnetos. See LMA/CLC/B/043/MS19904: Charles Frodsham Minute Book, 1893–1939 (Managing Director's Report, 24 Dec. 1917).
57 BPP, 1870, vol. 63: Trade and Navigation: Export and Import tables. Between 1880 and 1913 the influx of imports became a flood. Annual returns for those years are in the *Annual Accounts, Trade and Navigation (U.K.)* in the Parliamentary Papers, under the heading *Annual Statement of the Trade of the United Kingdom with Foreign Countries and British Possessions*. See the Bibliography for full references.
58 Edward Young, *Labor in Europe and America: A Special Report on the Condition of the Working Classes* (Washington, DC, Government Printing Office, 1875), 608.
59 *Horological Journal*, 33/11 (Aug. 1891), 165–66.
60 ['S.N.'], 'The Watchmaking Industry in Switzerland', *Science: The American Association for the Advancement of Science*, 1/11 (April 1883), 296–97.
61 Bahne Bonniksen, *The Karrusel Watch: By Its Inventor* (Plymouth: Latimer Rend, 1905); Obituary, 'The late Mr Bahne Bonniksen', *Horological Journal*, 77/8 (April 1935), 242.
62 Clare Woodward, 'Bahne Bonniksen, Inventor and Manufacturer of the Karrusel Watch. A Biography of a Famous Coventry Watchmaker: Part 1: 'The Early Years', *Antiquarian Horology*, 41/1 (March 2020), 44–56; Part 2, 41/2 (June 2020); 'The Success of the Karrusel Watch', 235–46 (esp. 240ff, 'Success in the Kew trials'); 41/3 (Sept. 2020); Part 3, 'The Success of the Karrusel Watch, Continued', 319–40, surveys manufacturers and retailers of the watches; and Part 4 'The Great Inventor', 41/4 (Dec. 2020), 531–38.
63 G.H. Duckworth, 'Watches and Clocks' in Charles Booth (ed.), *Life and Labour of the People in London: Second Series,* Vol 2*: Industry* (London: Macmillan, 1903), 27.
64 T.E. White, 'The Testing and Certification of Watches at the Kew Observatory and National Physical Laboratory, 1884–1978', *Horological Journal*, 127/12 (Aug. 1984), 15–17.

65 Landes, *Revolution in Time*, 299–300.
66 Greenwich Trials had served as a stimulus for chronometer makers since 1822. Perhaps if Kew-style watch trials had existed before the mid-1880s, the best English watches would have scored highly. But the performance of foreign firms might have sounded alarm bells for other English watch firms.
67 David S. Torrens, 'Joseph William Player, 1865–1956: An Appreciation', *Horological Journal*, 98/2 (Oct. 1956), 628, 632; the watch is illustrated and described in 'An Astronomical Watch', *Horological Journal*, 51 (April 1909), 118–19.
68 J. Eric Haswell, 'Fifty Years in Clerkenwell: Some Personal Reminiscences', *Horological Journal*, 100 (1958), 580–81; and Rita Shenton, 'Clerkenwell: A Nostalgic Walk-About', *Clocks*, 1 (Feb. 1979), 12–16.
69 John Hollingshead, *Ragged London in 1861* (London: Everyman, 1986); 'Clerkenwell and the City Borders', 9–35 (quotes, 15, 21).
70 T.E. White, 'A Clerkenwell Tour of Fifty Years Ago', *Antiquarian Horology*, 10/3 (Summer 1977), 340–46.
71 George Gissing, *The Nether World* (1889: London: Smith Elder; reprinted London: Dent, 1973), 11; Hollingshead, *Ragged London in 1861*, 13ff.
72 Duckworth, 'Watches and Clocks' in Booth, *Life and Labour*, 28.
73 *Horological Journal*, 24/2 (Oct. 1891), 23. Watchmakers in Clerkenwell were not the only outworkers to suffer lower earnings: unsurprisingly, the status and incomes of southwest Lancashire's watchmakers and toolmakers also declined: see Neil Cummins and Cormac Ó Gráda, 'Artisanal Skills, Watchmaking, and the Industrial Revolution: Prescot and Beyond', *UCD Centre for Economic Research: Working Paper Series*, WP19/24, October 2019, pp.41. Online at https://econpapers.repec.org/paper/ucnwpaper/201924.htm, 4–5.
74 Adam Galbraith, 'The Decline of the British Watchmaking Industry', *Watchmaker, Jeweler and Silversmith*, 34 (June 1908), 733.
75 M.I. Michaels, 'Fine Metals and Instrument Trades', Part II of London Industries III', of Herbert Llewellyn Smith (director). *The New Survey of London Life and Labour*, Vol VIII (London: King and Co., 1934), 160–61.
76 Duckworth, 'Watches and Clocks', in Booth, *Life and Labour*, 25, 29.
77 J.E. Martin, *Greater London: An Industrial Geography* (London: Bell, 1966), 13–15; Peter Geoffrey Hall, *The Industries of London since 1861* (London: Hutchinson. 2006), 153.

15 Attempting the 'American System'

Birmingham, Coventry, and Liverpool

Attempts to modernise

Clerkenwell's watchmaking continued to decline after 1850 because it was 'locked-in' by its obsolete pre-industrial production methods. The retention of the fusee and key winding by many firms meant its market was limited. But elsewhere in Britain half-a-dozen watchmaking firms attempted to adopt elements of the new production methods in the hope that they, too, might successfully compete with Swiss and American imports. Coventry's two biggest companies – Rotherham and Williamson – adopted some parts of machine-tool production, but with mixed success. They made a modest impact in their home market, but there is no evidence that they developed large export markets to challenge the Swiss and, later, the Americans. A new hub of English watchmaking appeared in Birmingham, and two attempts to modernise the production system were made; one was moderately successful, the other, failed. So did the most ambitious attempt to replicate American production methods in Prescot/Liverpool. This chapter surveys these episodes and assesses reasons for their respective failures or achievements and concludes with an account of the successful establishment of a watch case making firm.

Birmingham: the Time Works

In the mid-nineteenth century, Birmingham was the location of many small horological and industrial manufacturers. Collinson's *Directory* in 1861 listed sixty-six entries for 'watchmakers'; they were either retailers who sold watches or jobbers who repaired them. None 'finished' watches. Yet the city became the first location in Britain where a firm attempted to make watches in a factory rather than in small workshops. It occurred after William Ehrhardt, a German watchmaker who in 1851 visited London's Great Exhibition, and stayed on (like Victor Kullberg, the Swedish chronometer maker) to start a watchmaking business.[1] Ehrhardt hoped that his enterprise would emulate the Birmingham Small Arms (BSA) Company that had successfully pioneered the application in Britain of the 'American system of manufacturing'. That development

DOI: 10.4324/9781003227823-18

had followed the Report to Parliament about the successful application of the 'American system' to make small arms – and small mantel clocks – in the United States.[2] In the context of Britain's national security, small arms were important. The government was the largest single customer by far of companies that made small arms; the report successfully induced the reorganisation of its production by bringing sixteen small firms into a factory and start using, in 1861, the 'American system of manufacture' to make small arms.[3] Ehrhardt was aware of this precedent. He, too, wanted to 'break through the old methods of making watches and start on entirely new principles ... because traditional methods would need to be overcome'.[4] He knew of Clerkenwell's opposition to Ingold's attempt, and that Coventry already had in Rotherham a large (by British standards) well-established watchmaking firm, and a variety of smaller firms. He was unwilling to set up his project in Clerkenwell or Coventry, where traditional methods prevailed. He chose Birmingham and hoped to follow the example of BSA.

At first, he found it difficult to get 'good and able men', until the outbreak in 1861 of civil war in the United States' slowed up watchmakers' migration. Information about the initial phase of his company's existence is obscure, except that rough movements from Prescot were apparently finished in his outworkers' homes in the traditional manner. Yet Ehrhardt's enterprise evidently prospered to the extent that in 1874 he built *the Time Works*, a factory in suburban Hockley, Birmingham's centre of the jewellery and 'toy' trades. He introduced machine tool production in stages, first to drill 'the frames to ensure good depth', and then to other branches 'until in the present factory every part of the watch is made'. Later, even an electric machine for winding watches was introduced, 'to save time'.[5]

Ehrhardt's adoption of features of the American system was cautious and piecemeal. Machine tools were gradually introduced to replace traditional ways of making watch parts: they included 'up to date American lathes' and pinion cutting machines. In 1889 the editor of the *Watchmaker, Silversmith and Jeweller* thought Ehrhardt's enterprise was 'an excellent example of labour-saving machines in the watch industry, since one person is able to attend to four machines'. But productivity per employee remained low because, crucially, some traditional labour-intensive methods were retained. Whereas American and Swiss watch firms introduced machine-made parts straight into the watch, in the *Time Works* parts were still polished by hand in a polishing shop and finishing room.[6] When Ehrhardt died in 1897 his obituary noted that 500 watches were made in a week by 400 workers (an approximate output of 25,000 a year) at a rate of just over a watch a week for each employee. By comparison, Elgin's output in Illinois exceeded 300 watches a day. Productivity improved when Ehrhardt's sons, William and Gustav Victor, inherited the firm. By 1900, there were more machines and fewer workers: 250 employees (including girls) made 600–700 watches per week, an annual output of around 30,000 watches. At its peak, the *Time Works* became one of England's largest watch companies, yet it made only a fraction of the output of leading contemporary American firms.[7] The *Time Works* survived through the Great War but folded in 1924. By then, D.H. Bacon estimated, it had produced an aggregate of 775,000 watches over almost fifty years at an annual average of about 15,000.[8]

The English Watch Company

A second Birmingham watchmaking company in the 1870s also adopted aspects of the 'American system'. The origins of this enterprise lay in Tremont, Massachusetts, in a firm established out of the debris of a failed Swiss-American enterprise (intended to make watch parts in Switzerland, then to be assembled and 'finished' in America). The company later relocated to nearby Melrose and, when that failed in 1868, new investors were found. They established *The Anglo-American Watch Company* in Birmingham, England, in 1871 with Aaron Lufkin Dennison, a pioneer in Waltham's earlier success, as manager. Then it, too, failed. Apparently 'neither the machinery, nor the work that it produced, was at all up to the standard... deemed necessary for a good, enduring, sound, English watch'.[9] As we shall see later, Dennison set up his own successful watchcase factory in Birmingham.

In the meantime machine tools from the failed Tremont/Melrose/Anglo-American enterprise were sold for £5,500 in 1874 to William Bragge, a railway entrepreneur and a former surveyor in South America.[10] Bragge renamed it as *The English Watch Company*, reconfigured the factory's layout, and added some machine tools. But, like Ehrhardt, his adoption of rudiments of the 'American system' was also tentative. When Bragge's restructuring began in 1877, the *Watchmaker, Jeweller, and Silversmith* described the firm's premises and production methods and noted that interchangeability, a quintessential element of the American system, was indeed present in the

> admirable system of gauging in use. Every wheel, pinion, pivot and screw is (sic) gauged, and beyond the very narrow margin of variation within which interchange of parts can be ensured all are rejected.[11]

Despite the company's American pedigree, it still made English-type watches, 'devised to meet the liking of the English trade and to give them a watch in all respects English in style and in all respects machine made'. Although Bragge's watches had going barrels, not fusees, they still *looked* traditionally English.[12]

The *English Watch Company* enjoyed modest success for a time. Stockholders in 1885 had a dividend of 5 per cent, despite the general economic slump of the 1880s.[13] Buildings were enlarged and £950 was spent on a new steam engine – intended to increase production by 50 per cent. It was hoped it would be 'ready for when a future revival of trade calls for it'.[14] But that revival never came, at least in time to save the *English Watch Company*. The tide of imported cheap Swiss and American watches kept rising. Bragge's enterprise suffered the same fate as did a myriad of contemporary new American watch firms that tried to catch up with Waltham and Elgin.[15] It limped on for another ten years until it was liquidated in 1894. Over its lifespan of twenty-three years, its aggregate production is estimated to be 200,000–250,000 watches, an average production of around 10,000 a year.[16] The company itself survived until it abandoned watchmaking in 1898 and the enterprise metamorphosed into the Claremont Cycle Company. Some of its watchmaking machine tools were bought by Williamson of Coventry (see below).

Coventry: Rotherham

Elements of the 'American system' were also tried by three Coventry firms, with varying degrees of success. During peak periods of production between the 1850s and the 1860s Coventry's annual production (extrapolated from statistics of assays of precious metal cases) overtook Clerkenwell's declining output, and the city became the largest British centre for watchmaking.[17] Watchmaking never dominated the city's industries but, for a time, it became the next biggest, after ribbon weaving.[18] Its watches were cheaper than Clerkenwell's, mainly because most were 'finished' in proto-factories by poorly paid apprentices. Coventry's oldest and then foremost firm, Rotherham & Sons of 27 Spon Street, had origins believed to date from 1747. In the 1850s Rotherham combined factory and outworker production and made up to 9,000 watches annually and was then the largest single watchmaking enterprise in Britain (Chapter 3).

When John Rotherham (1838–1905) inherited his family's firm in the 1870s he attempted to modernise it on American lines. It arose from his experience as a young man when he had visited the United States and, to his shame, saw the poor quality of Rotherham's exports (Chapter 12). He was aware that Waltham's methods had revolutionised watchmaking in the United States and after 1876 were being successfully adapted by the Swiss. He, too, hoped to modernise his family firm. He sent his manager to Waltham to buy a complete range of machine tools that were installed in 1880; some were afterwards 'copied and duplicated and, no doubt, modified and improved'.[19] One of the new machines was 'for cutting a stack of escape wheels at a time' (like that in Waltham's display at the 1885 Inventions Exhibition).[20] Production increased. By 1888 the firm employed 400–500 workers including a hundred women. Output reached 100 watches a day (about 30,000 a year).[21] It was a substantial increase over the 150 a week (7,500 a year) reported by Harriet Martineau in 1852 (Chapter 3). But, like Ehrhardt in Birmingham, productivity was still small compared with those of contemporary American watch factories that, like Switzerland, exported to Britain many tens of thousands of watches each year.

Why? One reason it never matched the output of its American rivals was that despite John Rotherham's progressive views, some traditional production methods persisted. Rotherham was a benevolent, paternalistic owner-manager, but lacked the ruthlessness needed to implement the complete 'American system'. John Rotherham was not as 'locked-in' to old technology as were his Clerkenwell counterparts: new machines were adopted tentatively, but they resulted in an uneasy coexistence of old with new production methods. A special department was retained for assembling and finishing by hand a mixture of parts, some made by machine tools and some still hand-crafted. Old workmen were employed, with their tools, methods, and customs. John's son, Hugh, later recollected that, after the introduction of a sophisticated machine that enabled parts to be measured to within 1/1,000 inch, an old employee insisted that it was quite impossible that there would be a thousandth part of an inch. 'When I tried to explain it to him, although I took a hair out of his head, put it in a gauge, and showed him it measured 3/1,000 thick, he was still incredulous'.[22] Perhaps the firm (like the Lancashire Watch Company (LWC) a few years later) tried to satisfy too large a range of demands for different qualities and models of watches. Its display at the Paris exhibition in 1889 included quite ordinary grades, up to those with Kew Observatory 'A' certificates.[23] In 1907, a description of production methods at the firm's factory showed how much of the old craft-based technology persisted. Even dials were still hand painted

> by a very skilled workman ... He uses his tools...with amazing dexterity. He rules the minute divisions...by the aid of a mechanical divider...the maker's name, formed...in capitals less than one fortieth of an inch high...are painted in 'freehand' between faint parallel lines.[24]

Rotherham survived the Great War by making war materiel but stopped making watches in the 1920s. Then, like other former watchmaking companies, it diversified and made assorted engineering products.

The cooperative movement company

A second attempt in Coventry to introduce watchmakers to the American system occurred in the late 1880s. It arose from the despairing reaction of the rump of the city's small independent outworkers to knowledge of Rotherham's modernisation plans, and of the more geographically distant but equally threatening advent of the LWC in Prescot (below). The proposed LWC threatened to absorb and replace Prescot's traditional rough movement making; it offered Coventry's remaining small workshops an opportunity to supply an alternative source of frames. Up to 2,000 outworkers in Coventry's small watchmaking units still used traditional handcraft methods of production: the 1851 census recorded 1,679 'watchmakers' in the city; by 1861 had risen to 2,037.[25] Charles Bray reported to the British Association for the Advancement of Science in 1857 that these small workshops employed two-thirds of the city's 'outdoors' workforce; the rest were 'indoors' (in proto-factories like Rotherham's).[26] *Kelly's Post Office Directory* reported in 1868 that 192 of these small watchmaking 'firms' still endured; they comprised about 10 per cent of the nearly 2,000 different commercial businesses in the city.[27] Watchmaking's workforce peaked in the early 1880s, busy supplying a flurry of exports to the last imperial markets in India and Australasia before American companies moved in (Chapter 12).[28] Despite the rising number of cheap imported watches, Coventry's small watchmaking firms had somehow hung on, in cut-throat competition with each other, museum-like relics of a bygone era. Then they made a last stand in the form of a cooperative. The intention was that in their collective future, they would adopt more machine tools.

On evidence of the dismal fate of earlier efforts at cooperation by small firms, their likelihood of success was not good. In the early 1840s, independent outworkers had tried to agree on standard prices for piecework through an Association of Watchmakers. Only seventy joined – too few to force better terms on employers. The Association was stillborn. Fifteen years later, inspired by the apparent success of similar attempts by Coventry's ribbon-weavers to collaborate, another group organised an association of over 600 watchmakers. It lasted for a few months but then was pulled apart by the separate interests of case makers, dial makers, and engravers. It, too, was abandoned. A similar fate befell a Coventry Watch and Tool Society that briefly flitted in and out of existence in 1862.[29]

Consequently, the Coventry Watch Movement Company, established in 1889, was a last-ditch attempt by the city's independent workmen to come to terms with hard economic and commercial realities.[30] Temporary factory premises were found, and some machines were bought.[31] It may be an overstatement to claim that Coventry's small craftsmen subsequently tried to apply the 'American system' to make watches, but they certainly adopted machine tools, the crucial first rung on that ladder. Thereafter, progress was too little and far too late for the industry. The downward spiral in the fortunes of small watchmakers could not be reversed by a cooperative. By 1894 a stream of bankruptcies was reported in Coventry newspapers; the depression in watchmaking districts became so acute that (as in 1797 and 1817) soup kitchens were opened. In 1896, the number of 'watch manufacturers' had fallen to 103, and 'parts makers' to 214. By 1912 only thirty-five 'manufacturers' and 121 parts makers survived, but they no longer made watches.[32]

The watchmaking co-operative had failed because it had no coherent production or marketing strategies. Members were split on the question of whether to meet every requirement of the trade or to concentrate on making fewer models. They failed to agree. When an order for a small number of movements came, a large production run was started and surpluses to immediate requirements were then put in stock. Attempts to market the surpluses were unsuccessful. An annual general meeting in 1902 revealed a turnover of £5,084, wages of £3,066, and that (unsold) goods in stock were valued at £5,357.[33] The *Watch Movement Company* limped on, half-heartedly; 'there were never enough potential investors', D.H. Bacon concluded, 'and the company was destined for failure from the start'.[34] It made a loss in 1904–05, but managed small profits of a few hundred pounds between 1906 and 1909.[35] It then turned the corner, not by making more or better or cheaper watches, but when it realised survival lay with making other things with their machine tools. The Company's constituents – a cooperative of small firms – were willing to serve the growing demands of Coventry's new engineering industries, supplying parts for makers of bicycles, sewing machines, motorcycles and motor cars. By 1912, its profits were £1,178 and the annual meeting noted that 'the Company's business is now so largely outside the watch trade [that] the Directors have decided to alter its name to *The Coventry Movement Company, Ltd'*.[36] The price of survival was a metamorphosis.

Williamson

The most successful adoption in Coventry – and of any watch firm in Britain – of the rudiments of the American system was by the firm 'H. Williamson'. Henry Williamson was a London wholesale jewellery and watch retailer who created a successful multi-national enterprise, with watch factories in Buren and La Chaux-de-Fonds in Switzerland. The firm's other interests included a busy and lucrative optical repair workshop in London and a diamond department in Amsterdam. In 1895, it bought Charles Huton Errington's small watch business in Coventry. Errington's workshops could well have been in Clerkenwell, for it had made only bespoke watches: 'not a single watch on hand ...was not ordered' (sic). When the Williamson firm took over, new ideas were introduced such as 'worker-ownership' for those 'in the lower ranks' who could subscribe a shilling or two at a time. The new approach was successful and the subsequent growth of Williamson, in the context of the continued decline of English watchmaking, was remarkable. At its sixth annual general meeting, gross profits of £80,787 were announced and further expansion was planned. Williamson was showing the way that Clerkenwell's firms might have followed.

The adoption of Errington's old factory gave the company the opportunity to introduce essential elements of the 'American system'. Following the failure in 1894 of Bragge's *English Watchmaking Company* in Birmingham, Williamson bought their machines for its new factory. It employed 270 workers, and, from evidence of surviving photographs, some were women.[37] It used several automatic lathes and presses and, like Rotherham's factory, had its own machine-tool room. Heating and ventilation were good: 'the general cleanliness, healthiness, and good order prevailing were the subject of much appreciative comment' (sic). A principal feature of the 'American system' – interchangeability – was purposefully attempted. If possible, English watchmaking's traditional hand fitting was to be eliminated:

> All the old systems of fitting and finishing by hand labour are with us methods of the past, instead of which we have delicate machines of the latest type, many of which are working automatically, and with skilled labour, making and finishing the component parts with an accuracy hitherto unknown in the trade in this country.[38]

Williamson's multi-national character encouraged the firm to introduce a level of marketing and advertising expertise not achieved by any other English watchmaking company. By 1904, it had a national network of 764 retailers that offered sufficient channels to allow robust competition with Swiss and American imports in the home market. Its production and marketing strategies sensibly limited its main offerings to a basic seven jewel model in 1907, followed by others in 1909 and 1910. The advertising campaign for its leading model, the *Astral,* was very persuasive. It sold at the fixed price of 19s 6d with a certificate claiming that the watch was timed in two positions to be within 'ten seconds mean daily rate'.[39] The intended impression was that this was somehow comparable to watches with a Certificate from Kew Observatory. By 1911, the model was advertised as accurate to within eight seconds per twenty-four hours, 'the only cheap watch with such a certificate', though again it was not made clear that its certificate was self-awarded.[40] More expensive hand-finished versions of its best watches with sixteen and twenty-one jewels were also available. Williamson's relative success gave a sense of security to its workers and demonstrated that an English firm could successfully and profitably make watches, with machine tools, in a factory. In 1913 record profits of £87,413 were announced, largely ascribed to the success of the *Astral*; 'at its price', the *Horological Journal* thought, 'it is the world's best watch and the world's best value'.[41]

Between 1899 and 1913 Williamson's output was about half a million watches, at perhaps 30,000 a year. Rotherham's firm also averaged about

30,000. The annual output of Ehrhardt's *Time Works* is estimated to have been about 15,000 a year, that of the *English Watch Company* about 10,000. The short-lived LWC (below) made about 50,000 in its best years. But the world's market for watches was vast. Free trade left Britain's watch market open to brutal competition, and between 1899 and 1913 Britain imported over 28 million watches, overwhelmingly from Swiss and American firms. Sheltered by McKenna's emergency tariff protection Williamson survived the turmoil of the Great War (Chapter 17). But when it became bankrupt, nearly twenty years after the war, its aggregate output is estimated to have been only 600,000 watches, more than any other British company until then. Together, all the British watch companies accounted for only a small fraction of the millions of jewelled and unjewelled watches estimated to have been made in the world.[42] Nevertheless, Williamson was more successful in introducing elements of the 'American system' than its Prescot rival, the *Lancashire Watch Company*.

Liverpool's small watch finishing hub had reached the peak of its production by the middle of the nineteenth century. Thereafter, exports to its once-important American market declined because the Morrill tariff, after the 1860s, shielded America's domestic watch market and facilitated the success of Waltham, Elgin, and other companies. Liverpool's small watchmaking firms declined because they, too, had become complacent, like Rotherham of Coventry (above) and Longines of Switzerland (Chapter 11).[43] William Rodgers, the Liverpool watchmaker in a memoir (written in 1899) explained that the city's firms had lost their export market because the watches they had exported were of poor quality. 'When Americans began to make watches for themselves', Rodgers continued, 'repairers in that country condemned English watches as "rotten" and refused to have anything to do with them' (Chapter 12).[44] As Liverpool's export market declined, so did its domestic market. That was easily filled by watches made in Coventry, or by imports. Professor Torrens had 'little doubt' that Liverpool's decline left customers in their former markets able to buy 'finished watches cheaper in Coventry than they could make them up for themselves, and they did'.[45] A few miles away, Prescot's labour-intensive movement-making cottage industry was also shrinking, especially after 1877, for the reasons T.P. Hewitt vividly described (Chapter 2). Until then Prescot's annual output was still about 120,000 rough movements. Thereafter, as John Griffiths explained, its 'confined and decayed little watch factories [became] almost deserted'.[46]

Wycherley and Hewitt

A last-minute attempt to avert the Prescot industry's complete disappearance came from John Wycherley, a maker of various watch parts (Figure 15.1). He realised that salvation lay in reforming traditional methods of production. He moved his workshop into a three-floor

Figure 15.1 John Wycherley (1817–1891). Copyright: David Penney. http://www.antiquewatchstore.com/.

factory building that became the largest watchmaking unit in Prescot. It employed about 120 workers, including thirty to forty girls.[47] Wycherley was convinced the main reason for the decline of English watchmaking was not just American tariffs but the traditional, inefficient, production methods of the English industry. They were exemplified by the lack of an agreed standard gauge. [48] His firm made eight types of movements, the differences between each being 7/100 inch. Other firms had similar idiosyncratic characteristics that resulted in what David Landes accurately termed the 'Achilles heel of English watchmaking'.[49] Wycherley's argument in favour of an accepted 'standard gauge' represented the first crucial step on the road to standardisation and (eventually) interchangeability – the essential feature of the American system. But opposition to uniform standards and the use of machine tools was then as deeply embedded in Prescot as it was in Clerkenwell. Notably, some screws were still made by hand at a rate of four a minute; this prompted David Glasgow, a dogged defender of traditional methods (Chapter 13), to express his low opinion of the American system: 'If then a man can make by hand in this way 1,800 good screws in a day of ten hours, watchmaking can gain little by having them made by a machine'.[50] Yet in Waltham by 1885, screw-making machines made between 50,000 and 60,000 a day, equivalent to the daily output of about thirty of English watchmaking's outworkers using traditional methods.

Figure 15.2 Thomas Peter Hewitt (1848–1933). Copyright: David Penney. http://www.antiquewatchstore.com/.

Wycherley realised that one reason why so many old production methods survived in Prescot was the relatively small size of Clerkenwell's luxury market. It enabled small firms, like Nicole Nielsen and Guye, to stress the uniqueness of their own products (Chapter 14). Wycherley saw the need to address those other, much larger, parts of Britain's watch market that, he thought, needed innovations: they included advertising, marketing and other features of the American system.[51] Although Wycherley was fully aware of the limitations of traditional English watchmaking, he was unable to do much about it in his working life, other than point to its deficiencies. In 1882, his business passed to his partner, T.P. Hewitt (Figure 15.2), who took several further steps. Hewitt resolved to rescue Prescot's ancient declining watch-component industry by setting up an American-style factory to make entire watches, with the 'American system' as a template. [52]

Hewitt and the LWC

Hewitt's intentions were initially met with hostility by Prescot's community of movement-making outworkers. But then he gained crucial support from a few civic leaders; they included the vicar and, most importantly, the sixteenth Earl of Derby (Frederick Arthur Stanley, second son of the fourteenth Earl who had been three times Prime Minister). The

Earl's country seat, Knowsley Hall with its 2,500-acre estate, was in the parish. The Earl's support lent the project an aura of respectability. A public meeting in May 1887 agreed to try to raise £100,000 to form *The British Watch Company*. The sum was subsequently amended to a more modest £50,000 (but reverted to £100,000 in 1895) and the name changed to the LWC.[53]

The LWC's problems started when over £20,000 of its seed capital was spent buying out Prescot's independent outworkers. It was a benign, paternalistic, gesture that was intended to overcome opposition from displaced local small-parts craftsmen. But it proved to be a mistake because the former outworkers brought their tools and methods into the factory.[54] Like Ehrhardt's attempt in Birmingham and Rotherham's in Coventry, this contributed to the very inefficiencies that the new enterprise was intended to eradicate. Hewitt had visited the Elgin Watch Company's factory in Illinois where he had seen the 'American system' successfully applied to make watches. He wanted explicitly to model his Prescot factory on it and sent his manager to America to buy machine tools. In the time-lag, before they were delivered and installed 'much of the early work... was probably a continuation of making older Lancashire models until new designs could be introduced'.[55] Custom died hard. In this instance, it was encouraged to continue with the predictable consequence that, Professor Alan Smith concluded, 'the old craftsmen did not like to change their ideas'. By clinging to some of the old workmen and their methods Hewitt's intention to adopt the American system stumbled at this first phase.

Hewitt's determination to revive England's watchmaking industry was indicated by the size of its eleven-and-a-half-acre site. Its main building, the largest watch factory in England, was a three-story workshop 300 feet by twenty-eight feet (in all 25,000 square feet of working space). Two other workshops enabled the new firm to employ about 1,000 workers (the maximum reached, in 1903).[56] Machines included an 80-horsepower engine and a variety of lathes, grinding and milling machines, and presses. Special machine tools were bought from half a dozen American and at least sixteen English firms; the factory's own tool room made others.[57] Originally, the firm hoped for an annual production of about 60,000 watches. Annual output reached about 50,000 between 1893 and 1900 and then steadily declined. By 1903, both output and employment had fallen: the former to 500 watches a day, the work force to 750. The company started to make losses in 1904. At that time watches imported into Britain exceeded a million a year. Not surprisingly, the firm became bankrupt in 1910. Employees were notified of its impending closure in January 1911 and production stopped in March after an auction disposed of tools and fittings.[58] A small engineering firm acquired its assets and survived for another twenty years.

The reasons for the LWC's collapse were like those of English watchmaking's other contemporary failures. As with Rotherham, the LWC's production strategies were poor. It offered an exceptionally wide range of models in a vain effort to compete with imported Swiss and American watches that already offered watches in every conceivable size, style, and price. The LWC also tried to match too many categories: it made over fifty models in eleven calibres, but still offered some key-wound models![59] Several came with different numbers of jewels, in a variety of finishes. The company also made English wall clocks with seven different dial sizes, each in five different qualities, at prices from just over a pound to eight guineas.[60] It made itself a prisoner of unquantifiable demands for too many idiosyncratic consumer requirements. It 'kept in stock until the very end a range of watches and their parts which', Alan Smith wrote, 'were going out of fashion fifteen years before'. Its marketing strategies were also inadequate. Prices ranged from a pound or two in nickel cases up to £10, £15, or £25 in silver and gold cases.[61] Demand at the bottom end of the market was already amply provided for by cheap Swiss and American models. The *John Bull* pocket watch, LWC's cheapest, was a direct challenge to Ingersoll's *Yankee*, 'the watch that made the dollar famous'. The *John Bull* sold to the trade at 3s 9d each, with a recommended retail price of five shillings. Its production line could make 2,000 watches a week but, despite a desperate last effort to capture the market for cheap watches, it sold only about 5,000 of the models in its last two years. It failed because it could not recover what it cost to set up in overheads, materials, and wages. The LWC's production runs, like those of the Coventry *Watch Movement Company*, made more than they could sell. Professor Smith concluded that 'had the company concentrated on a few basic designs and sizes and lowered manufacturing costs to a minimum, they might have succeeded'. But as well as clocks and watches, the LWC also made 'electric meters, counters, workmen's time registers, cycle gears, dies, lathes and every description of small mechanism'. Just a year or two before the LWC's demise, Hewitt's American contemporary, Henry Ford, adopted in Detroit exactly the opposite marketing strategy for his automobiles (another exemplary product of the American system). Customers were famously told they 'could buy his Model T in any colour you like, so long as it's black': in all, over 15 million Model T's were made and sold.

Other reasons for the LWC's failure must include poor managerial judgement. The Earl of Derby, prominent during the launch of the company, was uninvolved in its vital early years because he became Governor General of Canada, from 1888 to 1893. Hewitt's involvement was more crucial. He can be judged culpable on two counts. First, over several months in 1899 and 1900, when the LWC was running at an annual loss of £12,000, Hewitt was distracted by lengthy litigation against his leading English rival, Henry Williamson of Coventry. He had sued Williamson because they included a tiny percentage of their Swiss factory's parts in watches stamped 'Made in England': the litigation merged with a long-standing dispute about hallmarks.[62] This was at a time when over a million entirely foreign-made watches were legally imported, annually. Hewitt won the case on a technicality but was awarded risibly low damages of £20 and token costs of £10. His attention should have been on his factory, not flailing about looking for peripheral excuses for his firm's problems. The other episode that absorbed his time and energy was the chimera of the Tariff Reform Movement. Hewitt wrote a pamphlet, made speeches and attended hearings, all to no effect in support of an unsuccessful campaign in favour of the return of tariff protection.[63] The Liberal government's landslide victory in the 1906 general election ended the prospect that tariffs would be introduced. But by then it was too late for the LWC. It carried on for a few more years as the tide of imported watches surged higher, and then the LWC closed. What it had needed was to make and sell a small range of standardised, mass-produced watches. It was in a hopeless position, unable to compete with outputs of the well organised Swiss and giant American watch firms. So ended in failure the most advanced attempt to adopt the 'American system' to British watchmaking.

Birmingham: Dennison's success

We noted earlier that some small Clerkenwell firms like Nielsen and Golay prolonged their survival by concentrating on a narrow luxury market (Chapter 14). Other firms, like Ritchie in Edinburgh, Donovan in Dublin, and Hughes in Llangollen, made small numbers of watches to supply mostly local or regional demands (Chapter 3). The only British firm that successfully applied relevant features of the 'American system' was that created by one of Waltham's pioneers, Aaron Lufkin Dennison (Figure 15.3). After the failure of the Anglo-American company in the 1870s, Dennison abandoned his life-long attempts to make complete watches and instead focussed his attention on filling an opening in the supply chain. He designed new machinery, patented a screwed bezel, and established a company which made watch cases that could be supplied to any company making watch movements, and especially those companies, like Waltham, that exported bare movements.[64] Making watch cases involved fewer complications than manufacturing and assembling scores of miniscule parts to make movements. Most small watchmaking firms once had either made their own cases or bought them from specialist workshops. When in the 1850s Harriet Martineau visited Rotherham's firm in Coventry she described such a traditional case-making shop, where an old man and a boy used an engine-turning machine to engrave various circular and ornamental patterns on gold cases.[65] Later, larger companies like Ehrhardt's *Time Works,* included a department

Figure 15.3 Aaron Lufkin Dennison (1812–1895). Copyright: David Penney. http://www.antiquewatchstore.com/.

with a gas furnace 'capable of melting 120 ounces of silver in 20 minutes'. Separate units then engraved and gilded the cases.

Making watch cases in the traditional way was labour-intensive and inefficient. It was ripe for the application of a production system able to supply ready-made cases to any firms that made movements. Dennison's company was successful because it offered good quality cases at attractive prices. He supplied several of the surviving English watchmaking firms and, more importantly, through his old American contacts, he cornered the market for nearly all the silver cases needed for Waltham's extensive British trade. By 1886, his factory employed a hundred workers: they made 60,000–80,000 cases annually. Dennison himself stayed in active control of the firm until about a month before his death in January 1895. Famous as a pioneer in Waltham, but who had failed as an entrepreneur with the Tremont/Melrose, and Anglo-American Companies, the expatriate American limited his ambitions and made watchcases only. He succeeded.

Conclusion

Why did most attempts to introduce the American system to English watchmaking achieve either only temporary limited success, or fail? First, when the 'American system' was applied to make watches in Waltham in 1858, the system had already been launched in the United States about a half-century earlier. It had succeeded on several engineering fronts, notably to make wooden clocks, axes, and small arms, before it was applied to make watches. Donald Hoke has traced the interaction between technological change in these commodities and the marketplace.[66] Axes and wooden clocks required broader tolerances than watch parts. But the concept and principles were successfully established. Also, American watchmaking had never experienced a long and deep-rooted labour-intensive craft production system characteristic of English and European watchmaking. Resistance to change in the United States was never strong. The balance of its factors of production (ample raw materials but relatively scarce hand-craft skills) favoured labour-saving innovations.[67] In Britain, resistance to change in hand-crafted products was deeply engrained. Whereas start-up costs for small craft production units were relatively low, by the 1880s for a full-blown watch factory, they were large, especially if they wished to compete with American giants. The Swiss gradually bridged the gap and successfully adapted their *établissage* system. The LWC's attempt failed: it was simply too late to catch up. After the Ingold episode, the impetus for radical change in English watchmaking was rejected, and the momentum passed elsewhere. Later attempts to introduce the 'American system' were mostly piecemeal. It was difficult to enforce it on a long-established craft industry with many small independent firms and a workforce steeped in traditional methods. Britain's small arms industry in Birmingham was an exception; it was unable to resist modernisation because its largest customer was the government, able to enforce modernised production methods impelled by reasons of national security. Unlike its contemporary British industries – textiles, shipbuilding, heavy engineering, and small arms – an already weak industry like watchmaking was further enfeebled by free trade. It became a small, relatively unimportant industry whose product could be made more cheaply elsewhere.

Notes

1 Obituary to William Ehrhardt in *Horological Journal*, 40/5 (Jan. 1898), 63.
2 Nathan Rosenberg (ed.), *The American System of Manufactures* (Edinburgh: Edinburgh UP, 1969), reprints 'Report of the Committee on the Machinery of the United States, 1854–55', in *BPP*, 1854–55, Vol. 50.
3 Alun C. Davies, 'British Watchmaking and the American System', *Business History*, 35/1 (1993), 40–54. BSA later applied the 'American system' to make motorbikes and bicycles.
4 *Horological Journal*, 40/5 (Jan. 1898), 64.
5 *Watchmaker, Jeweller and Silversmith*, 25/8 (Aug. 1889). 942.
6 *Watchmaker, Jeweller and Silversmith*, 25/8 (Aug. 1889), 942–45.

7 Employment and output statistics from *Horological Journal*, 33/5 (Jan. 1891); 40/5 (Jan. 1898), 64; and 42/5 (Jan. 1900), 59–60.

8 Bacon, 'Watch Production', 117–33; Maxwell Cutmore, *Watches, 1850–1980* (Newton Abbot: David and Charles, 1989), 89, suggests 500,000 over the fifty years spanning 1874 and 1924.

9 Roy Church, 'Nineteenth Century Clock Technology in Britain, the United States, and Switzerland', *Economic History Review*, 2nd ser., 28/4 (Nov 1975), 616–30, at https://doi.org/10.2307/2599615; Henry Abbott, *The Watch Factories of America* (Chicago, IL: Hazlitt, 1888), reprinted in Alan Smith, *Lancashire Watch* Company, 69–70; David Glasgow, 'Watchmaking by Machinery', in *The New Technical Educator* (London: Cassell, 1890), at http://www.watkinsr.id.au/glasgow.pdf

10 G.B. Smith rev. Carl Chinn, 'William Bragge (1823–84)', *(ODNB)*.

11 *Watchmaker, Jeweller and Silversmith*, 5 (Sept. 1877), 54–56.

12 Anon., 'Obituary: William Bragge', *Watchmaker, Jeweller and Silversmith*, 10 (July 1884), 1–4.

13 David Greasley, 'British Economic Growth: The Paradox of the 1880s and the Timing of the Climacteric', *Explorations in Economic History*, 23/4 (Oct. 1986), 416–44.

14 *Horological Journal*, 27/11 (August 1885), 171.

15 August C. Bolino, 'British and American Horology: A Comment on Hoke', *Journal of Economic History*, 48/3 (Sept. 1988), 667, at https://www.jstor.org/stable/2121544: The American companies that failed, 'or were absorbed by others that later failed' included Auburndale, Tremont, Keystone, Aurora, Cornell, Manhattan, Marion 'and many others'.

16 Bacon, 'Watch Production', 120; Cutmore, *Watches, 1850–1980*, 83, estimated 200 men made 300 watches a week for fifteen years, indicating an aggregate output of about 250,000.

17 BPP, 1887, vol. 66, 'Return, Relating to Gold and Silver Plate ... and Gold and Silver Watch Cases Which Have Been Hall-marked in Each Year from 1878–79 to 1886–67'.

18 Alun C. Davies, 'Old and New Technology in Watchmaking in Coventry, 1850–1920', *Antiquarian Horology*, 18/4 (Winter 1989), 397–410.

19 David S. Torrens, 'Some Notes on the History of Machine Watchmaking', *Horological Journal*, 89/8 (April 1947), 184.

20 'Inventions Exhibition' in *Horological Journal*, 27/10 (June 1885) 135–37; C.J. Hewitt, 'The Horological Exhibits in the Inventions Exhibition', *Horological Journal*, 30/10 (June 1888), 117–22, 129–38; id., 'Machine Watchmaking as Carried on by Messrs Rotherham and Sons', *Horological Journal*, 30/10 (June 1888), 144–45; also Anon., *English Clocks and Watches and Their Makers* (Wembley Exhibition pamphlet, published by *Horological Journal*, 1924), 45–47.

21 Cutmore, *Watches, 1850–1980*, 91.

22 Hugh Rotherham, 'The Watch Trade Past and Present', *Horological Journal*, 70/9 and 10 (May and June 1928), 162–64, 180–82. Other relevant references are in *Horological Journal*, 45/4 (December 1902), 49, and 45/7 (March 1903), 85–88. Also John Woodward, 'Rotherham and Sons, Ltd., the Firm, and the Family' (Typescript MS, Coventry Public Library, 1975). This contains transcriptions of taped conversations. I am grateful to Mr A.J. Mealey, sometime principal librarian at CPL, for photocopies.

23 J.J.S. Tripplin, *Watch and Clock Making in 1889: Being an Account and Comparison of the Exhibits in the Horological Section of the French International Exhibition* (London: Crosby Lockwood, 1890), 51–54.

24 Archibald Williams, *How It Is Made: Describing in Simple Language How Various Machines and Many Articles in Common Use Are Manufactured from Raw Materials* (London: Nelson, 1907), quotation 299–301.
25 *BPP, Census Returns,* 1863, 53 (Part 11), 475 et seq., and 510 et seq.)
26 Charles Bray, *The Industrial Employment of Women: Being a Comparison between the Conditions of the People in the Watch Trade in Coventry in Which Women Are Not Employed; and the People in the Ribbon Trade, in Which They Are Employed:* Paper read to the British Association for the Advancement of Social Sciences: October 1857 (London: Longman, 1857); also, sources cited in Searby, 'Weavers and Freemen' indicate that Bray made his survey in 1851.
27 E.R. Kelly (ed.), *The Post Office Directory of Warwickshire* (London: 1868): 'Coventry: Commercial', 1026–38; White's *Directory*, 560, cited by Searby, 'Weavers and Freemen', 12; [Lascelles and Co.] *Directory and Gazetteer. City of Coventry and Neighbourhood* (Coventry, Lascelles, 1850), cited by Prosser, 'Coventry Urban Community', 62. Also, Ian Greaves, 'A Study of English Watch Jewelling', *Antiquarian Horology,* 35/4 (Dec. 2014), 1085–106 for watch jewelling firms in Coventry, esp. 1102–06.
28 Bailey, 'Coventry Ribbon and Watch Trades', 143–45.
29 *Horological Journal*, 4/5 (Jan. 1862), 52–53; 5/1 (Sept. 1862), 9–10.
30 D.H. Bacon, 'The Coventry Watch Movement Manufacturing Company Limited', *Antiquarian Horology*, 20/6 (Summer 1993), 502–17 examines its creation and troubled existence.
31 *Horological Journal*, 31/9 (June 1889), 149.
32 Bailey, 'Coventry Ribbon and Watch Trades', 144.
33 *Horological Journal*, 44/10 (July 1902), 147–48.
34 Bacon, 'Coventry Watch Movement Company', 517.
35 Davies, 'Old and New Technology in Coventry, 1950–1920', *Antiquarian Horology*, 18/4 (Winter 1989), 397–410.
36 *Horological Journal*, 50/10 (July 1908), 195; 51/10 (July 1909), 178–79; 53/4 (Dec. (1910), 59; 55/4 (Dec. 1912), 56; Church, 'Clock Technology'; A.E. Harrison, 'The Origins and Growth of the United Kingdom Cycle Industry to 1900', *Journal of Transport History* (3rd Ser.), 6 (March 1985), 41–70.
37 Cutmore, *Watches, 1850–1980*, 81; also 'The Errington-Williamson Combination', *Watchmaker, Jeweller and Silversmith*, 21/11 (Nov. 1895), 689–90.
38 *Horological Journal*, 45/7 (March 1903), 97–98; also see *Horological Journal*, 46/7 (March 1904), 102–03; 47/3 (Nov. 1904), 33–35.
39 *Horological Journal*, 49/7 (March 1907), 113–14; 50/7 (March 1908), 126; 51/4 (Dec. 1908), 61.
40 *Horological Journal*, 53/2 (Oct. 1910), 31; 52/7 (March 1911), 109–10.
41 *Horological Journal*, 55/7 (March 1913), 108–09.
42 Bacon, 'Watch Production', 131; Michael C. Harrold, *American Watchmaking: A Technical History of the American Watch Industry, 1850–1930* (Columbia PA, NAWCC, 1981), 49–50.
43 Geoffrey Timmins, *Made in Lancashire: A History of Regional Industrialisation* (Manchester: Manchester UP, 1998), 199; Census returns reveal Lancashire's watch and clock workers fell from 3,117 in 1881 to 1,885 in 1911.
44 William Rodgers, 'The Decline of English Watchmaking: Reminiscences of the Latter Half of the Nineteenth Century', *Watchmaker, Jeweller and Silversmith (Special Home and Colonial Number)*, 25 (Aug. 1899), 939–41.

45 Prescot Museum MS archives: letter from David S. Torrens to T.C. Barker, 1952; also Robert Kemp, 'The Coventry watch trade', *Horological Journal*, 126/9 (March 1984), 17–20.
46 John Griffiths, 'The Rise and Fall of Toolmaking in Lancashire', *Journal of the North West Society for Industrial Archaeology and History*, (1994), 6, citing the *Prescot Reporter*.
47 *Horological Journal*, 19/11 (Aug. 1877), 158–60; also obituary, *Horological Journal*, 9/2 (Oct. 1891), 17–19.
48 See lecture by Wycherley to the BHI Council on 12 Sept. 1867, in *Horological Journal*, 10/2 (Oct. 1867), 18–21; also Wycherley's evidence in 'Report of the Commissioners Appointed to Inquire the Truck Commission in 1870' and its Minutes of Evidence: *BPP*, 1871, vol. 36, 657–59.
49 David S. Landes, *Revolution in Time: Clocks and the Making of the Modern World* (Cambridge, MA: Harvard UP, 1983), 232.
50 David Glasgow, *Watch and Clockmaking* (London: Cassell, 1885).
51 Anon, 'Obituary: Death of Mr John Wycherley', *Horological Journal*, 34 (Oct. 1891), 17–19.
52 Alun C. Davies, 'Thomas Peter Hewitt, 1848–1933) Watch Manufacturer', in D. J. Jeremy (ed.) *Dictionary of Business Biography*, vol. 3 (London: Butterworths, 1985), 186–88; also *Horological Journal*, 32 (Feb. 1890), 85 – 89.
53 Alan Smith, *The Lancashire Watch Company, 1889–1910* (Fitzwilliam, NH: Roberts, 1973), 11–12; Smith's analysis is in Part 1. Part 2 is a reprint of the *LWC Trade Catalogue*, circa 1905; Part 3 reprints articles by Henry G. Abbott (a pseudonym for George H. Hazlitt), publisher of *The American Jeweller*, 1893, vol. XIII). Thanks to Professor Smith, more is known about the LWC than of any other English watchmaking company of this era. See also John G. Platt, *Lancashire Watch Company: History and Watches* (Chester: Inbeat Publications, 2016). This transcribes a comprehensive collection of items about the LWC from journals, newspapers, and pamphlets.
54 Most was taken in shares, and £5,000 was paid in cash. Smith, *Lancashire Watch Company*, 18–19 for descriptions and 20–28 for illustrations.
55 Smith, *Lancashire Watch Company*, 17, 31–32 for quotes.
56 James U. Pool's account of his visit, in *Horological Journal*, 30/4 (Dec. 1887), 62–63.
57 Smith, *Lancashire Watch Company*, 29.
58 Smith, *Lancashire Watch Company*, 40–43 for following quotes.
59 Landes, *Revolution in Time*, 298.
60 Smith, *Lancashire Watch Company*: Part 2, *Catalogue*, 61.
61 Smith, *Lancashire Watch Company*, 39.
62 The hall-mark dispute was because English-made cases were hall-marked, exported empty, filled with foreign movements, and then reimported and sold – on the strength of the hall-mark – as English-made watches. The issue limped along from the late 1870s and came to a head in 1900; see *Horological Journal* 42/5 (Jan. 1900), 58–62; 42/7 (Feb. 1900), 76–77; and especially 42/8 (April 1900) 105–06,*'Regina v H. Williamson, Ltd.'*
63 *Horological Journal*, 45/12 (Aug. 1903), 164–65; 46/4 (Dec. 1903), 57–58; 46/10 (June 1904), 137–39; 47/1 (Sept. 1904), 5–6; for a survey, see Andrew S. Thompson, 'Tariff Reform: An Imperial Strategy, 1903–1913', *The Historical Journal*, 40/4 (1997), 1033–54, at https://doi.oeh./10.1017/S0018246X97007565
64 Philip T. Priestley, *Aaron Lufkin Dennison: An Industrial Pioneer and His Legacy* (Columbia PA: NAWCC, 2009) has much information about

technical inventions, patents, watch movement sizes, and an illustrated price guide to Waltham movements in Dennison's cases.

65 Harriet Martineau, 'Time and the Hour', *Household Words,* 6th March 1852.

66 Donald R. Hoke, *Ingenious Yankees: The Rise of the American System of Manufactures in the Private Sector* (New York and Oxford: Columbia UP, 1990); and Alun C. Davies, 'Horology, Technology, and Ingenious Yankees', *Antiquarian Horology*, 22/1 (Spring 1995), 69–73.

67 Hrothgar J. Habakkuk, *American and British Technology in the Nineteenth Century: the search for labour-saving inventions* (Cambridge: Cambridge UP, 1962); Peter Temin, 'Labor Scarcity and the Problem of American Industrial Efficiency in the 1850s', *Journal of Economic History*, 26/3 (Sep. 1966), 277–98, at https://www.jstor.org/stable/2115648

16 English Chronometers Defy Decline

The market for chronometers, c.1860

A common feature of many industries is that when their markets grow rapidly, small firms fall away and leave production dominated by a few large firms that then apply economies of scale. As they get bigger, they usually benefit from technological advances. Automobiles and computers are contemporary examples. The watchmaking industry in the United States in the nineteenth century was another: a score or more firms came into existence, but only a handful successfully continued. In Coventry, too, watchmaking once comprised scores of small firms but, by the end of the century, was dominated by the two large firms of Williamson and Rotherham. This evolution did not happen in Clerkenwell, where small firms persisted until the Great War. The consequence was that English watchmaking lost most of its home and foreign markets to Swiss and American watches. But one sector of the English industry had a quite different experience. English firms dominated the world's chronometer market.

The world's markets for watches had grown rapidly. In Tudor times, Britain's market for watches could first be measured in dozens or scores, a century later, in hundreds and, after another century, in thousands. By the twentieth century Britain's annual watch market exceeded hundreds of thousands, and then millions. Similar exponential growth can be seen later in the production of other consumer durables, for example, motor cars, radios, televisions, computers, and smartphones. But the market for chronometers was quite different. After 1860 demand *did* grow, and supply increased to meet it. But the rate of growth of both was gradual, unlike that for watches. At almost any time between 1860 and 1914, a few English chronometer firms could have, if required, probably comfortably supplied most of the world's effective demand. Among those English firms, two stood out. This chapter surveys why and how the new firms of Victor Kullberg and Thomas Mercer pulled away from their English competitors – and led the rest of the world – in chronometer manufacturing.

In 1860, the chronometer market was supplied by a handful of well-established firms, led by Parkinson & Frodsham, Barraud & Lund, Brockbank, Dent, and Charles Frodsham. Perhaps a dozen other independent

DOI: 10.4324/9781003227823-19

craftsmen or small firms may have bought-in basic models, 'finished' them, and put their own names on the dials. Only a few leading firms acquired rough movements from Prescot and then engaged in the elaborate process of commissioning their completion, drawing on their own workshop and the specialist skills of a score of Clerkenwell's outworkers. Among the few 'makers' who bought basic models to be 'finished' included, among others, Carter, French, Hunter & Edwards, Cummins & McCabe, Margetts, Harris, Tobias, Fletcher, and James Murray. Their individual share in making the instrument is not known, for names and serial numbers on dials do not tell the whole story. In 1858 chronometer manufacturers in England were joined by two new firms, Victor Kullberg and Thomas Mercer. Between them, they almost became a duopoly, but never an oligopoly. Neither Mercer nor Kullberg nearly monopolised production, nor did a cartel emerge. Other firms retained a share of the market.

Kullberg's and Mercer's precise share of the world market between 1860 and 1914 is not known. Evidence from its *Manufacturing Books* indicates that the House of Kullberg 'made' about 8,000 instruments, mostly before 1920. During the firm's lifetime (1858 to the 1930s) about two-thirds were box chronometers; most of the rest were pocket (or deck) watches with chronometer escapements.[1] Thomas Mercer's serial numbers indicate his firm made about 11,000 instruments before the end of the Great War and, over the firm's lifetime, about 30,500 movements.[2] Some were for carriage clocks, but most were for marine chronometers. All had a reputation for outstanding quality. No other chronometer makers came close to their combined outputs during the six decades before the Great War. How, then, did Kullberg and Mercer pull away from the rest of the pack?

The rise of Kullberg and Mercer

Victor Kullberg and Thomas Mercer had similar backgrounds (Figures 16.1 and 16.2). Each had trained in chronometer-making during their apprenticeships. Both gravitated to London in the 1850s. Mercer, born in 1822 in Liverpool, had been apprenticed to his grandfather William Walker, a watch movement maker in St. Helens, Lancashire. He started work in 1843 for Thomas Russell, a Liverpool nautical optician who supplied the port with navigational equipment.[3] The young Mercer learned the 'top end of the [chronometer] trade' (finishing, springing and adjusting) and 'made' his own watches – that is, he acquired rough movements from Prescot, subcontracted for some work, and 'finished' the watches himself. In 1854, Thomas went to London intending to emigrate. According to his grandson's colourful memoir

> [Thomas]... packed all his worldly possessions into two bags and took the stagecoach to London, where he purchased a one-way

> ticket to America. Whilst awaiting his passage, he took a last stroll around London, and a benevolent fate led his steps to Leadenhall Street. There, displayed in the window of John Fletcher, an illustrious maker of the period, Thomas saw a fine chronometer. His intense interest immediately aroused, he entered the shop and on sudden impulse asked for employment. Happily, John Fletcher did employ him and thus, by his sudden impulse, Thomas altered, at the age of 32, the whole planned pattern of his life.[4]

After four years with Fletcher, he set up on his own as a chronometer maker. He moved three times before settling in 50 Spencer Street, Clerkenwell. Then in 1874, he moved his entire workshop to St Albans, a small town about twenty miles away because, as we shall see below, he hoped to become less dependent on Clerkenwell's outworkers.

Details of Victor Kullberg's early life are scantier.[5] He was born in 1824 in Wisby on the island of Gotland, Sweden. At the age of sixteen he, too, became apprenticed to a watch and chronometer manufacturer and in 1843 moved to Copenhagen where he worked for the eminent horologist, Louis Urban Jurgensen. Kullberg went to London to see the Great Exhibition in 1851, perhaps also drawn by the pull of Clerkenwell. He stayed on as an independent outworker making chronometer escapements and, in 1856, set up on his own account in Islington. After another move or two, he settled in 1858 at 105 Liverpool Road, where the firm remained until it folded in the 1930s.

For sixty years Kullberg and Mercer led the world in making high-quality chronometers. Their successes were earned in two arenas: at home, in the annual Greenwich Trials, and abroad, at the great international industrial exhibitions. Trials and exhibitions were shop windows for makers and marketplaces for buyers. Mercer's successes are often obscured, because many of his winning chronometers had on their dials the names and numbers of retailers or independent craftsmen. For example, his biggest customer was Joseph Sewill, Liverpool's leading 'nautical optician' (one of over 150 different chandlers to whom Mercer supplied chronometers by the 1890s). Between 1858 and 1918 Sewill bought more than 850 instruments from the House of Mercer.[6] Sewill won prize medals at international exhibitions in 1862, 1864, and 1867 and topped the Greenwich Trials in 1874 – all with Mercer's instruments, but with his own name on the dials. At Philadelphia, in 1876 Mercer made prize-winning chronometers, entered with Frodsham's and Dent's names on dials. Only once, in 1911, did Mercer's firm head the lists at Greenwich under its own name. The firm's instruments – as Sewill's example illustrates – much-benefited retailers and independent 'makers'.[7]

Kullberg's record was outstanding. In 1864 in only his second attempt at the Greenwich Trials, his instruments were placed first and second out of eighty submitted by his Clerkenwell rivals. In 1872, he won again.

Figure 16.1 Thomas Mercer (1822–1900). Copyright: David Penney. http://www.antiquewatchstore.com/.

This cemented his reputation, which he reinforced with another six victories in the 1880s. In the other great showground – international industrial exhibitions – he won a gold medal in 1862 at London's second Great Exhibition. The following year at the Vienna exhibition his chronometers were described as 'in a state of all but absolute perfection, both as regards workmanship and timekeeping ... anything superior to his work could scarcely be imagined'. The mean rate over five months for two of his instruments was within a fifth of a second a month (although in observatories, not on a moving ship).[8] In the United States Centennial Exhibition in Philadelphia in 1876 Kullberg's instruments so deeply impressed James Watson, the American adjudicator, that he concluded they were 'the very best possible specimens'.[9] Kullberg collected medals in Paris in 1878, and Melbourne and Sydney in 1879 and 1880. At Paris in 1889 once more 'the finest exhibits were from Mr Kullberg'. After his death in 1890, Victor's successors in the House of Kullberg continued their triumphs at the Paris exhibition in 1900.[10] Charles Allix observed that, after he died 'his name, like that of the great Breguet, lost no impact whatsoever'.[11] Awards, medals, and prizes were proudly recorded on the firm's business correspondence.[12]

Demand and supply: static technology

Explanations for the sustained reputations for the excellence of the two firms lie partly in understanding the differences in the demand for and supply of chronometers and watches. A watch was a desirable purchase,

Figure 16.2 Victor Kullberg (1824–1890). Copyright: David Penney. http://www.antiquewatchstore.com/.

among the first thing people wanted when they could afford one. A cheap watch, accurate to a few minutes (or less) a week was satisfactory; it could easily be synchronised to mean time by public clocks in towns or railway stations through telegraphs (eventually, by radio time signals). But cheap watches had a short lifespan that led to a replacement demand, frequently for a better-quality watch. Demand for chronometers was different. They were complex scientific mechanisms, with hand-made parts, assembled and fine-tuned by experts. With regular servicing, their lifetimes, especially those made after about 1820, usually outstripped those of the ships on which they served. There was a steady demand for servicing and refurbishment, but a small one for replacements. Stocks of chronometers accumulated faster than the annual increase in the numbers of the new ships. This relatively small demand and the delicate skills needed in their construction meant that trying to mass-produce them – like Waltham's watches – was uneconomic.[13] Their longevity was almost comparable to a good longcase clock than to most watches. Annual demand for new instruments from navies and merchant marines amounted at most to a few scores. This tended to favour British firms because Britain's navy and marine were by far the biggest customers. By 1880 almost a quarter of world trade was British-owned, as was more than a half of world shipping. For almost a century, between about 1830 and 1914, Britain was the world's leading trading nation; its ships accounted for about a third of the world's merchant shipping tonnage and dominated transoceanic trade routes.

As the number and tonnage of ships in Britain's and the world's merchant and national navies increased after 1860, wooden sailing vessels were replaced by bigger and faster steam ships with iron or steel hulls. Britain's merchant marine increased from 20,000 ships in 1840 to 27,000 by 1910 – by about a third; but the tonnage they displaced quadrupled, from 2.8 to 11.6 million tons.[14] The Royal Navy enjoyed similar impressive growth. In 1859 it had about 1,000 vessels of different categories. Thirty years later a Naval Defence Act directed that its battleships should be equal to the combined strength of the next two largest navies (then France and Russia). In the 1890s British shipyards built about four-fifths of the world's new vessels. Another expansion between 1904 and 1909 led to ten new battleships, thirty-eight cruisers and other vessels. By 1914, the Royal Navy had sixty dreadnaught battleships (displacing over a million tons) and almost 600 cruisers, submarines, and patrol boats (displacing 2 1/3 million tons). Its navy was roughly four times larger than that of her single biggest rival, Germany.[15]

As the numbers of British ships grew, their aggregate tonnage greatly increased. But when old ships were decommissioned, their navigation instruments were not. Chronometers were serviced, refurbished if necessary, then reallocated. Some chronometers made by Arnold in the early nineteenth century served consecutively on ten or more ships. Dozens of instruments made in the 1820s were in service for over eighty years before being de-commissioned.[16] Between 1860 and 1914 annual demand for new chronometers from the British Admiralty rarely exceeded three or four dozen (about 5 per cent of existing stock) and, in most years, fewer. Between 1897 and 1920 some 1,497 chronometers were submitted for trial at Greenwich, an annual average of eighty-three.[17] Only just over half, 801, were bought by the Admiralty. Annual purchases exceeded fifty at most in the 1890s but then fell to only twelve or fewer, even during the boom in building *Dreadnaughts* between 1906 and 1911. In 1910, for example, sixty-six box chronometers and 173 chronometer watches were submitted for trial. The Admiralty took just eight box chronomters and thirty-five chronometer (deck) watches.[18] The need for regular servicing of old chronometers was large, whilst demand for new ones was small. Similar characteristics applied to the demand for chronometers by navies and merchant marines in the rest of the world. Well before the end of the century additions to the Royal Navy's ships, irrespective of tonnage, could comfortably be supplied from the Admiralty's accumulated stocks, topped up by the small output of a few firms. Instruments allocated to the score or so of new *Dreadnaughts* could have been comfortably furnished from existing stock. The market for new chronometers was small and, crucially, it favoured British makers.

Demand for chronometers came mostly but not exclusively from the maritime world, from ships needing to determine or confirm longitudes. A minor demand came from land surveyors, notably from the Great Trigonometrical Survey of India, on-going between 1800 and 1936. Simon Davidson has shown that aggregate demand from their surveyors over more than a century and a quarter amounted to about 1,500 instruments.[19] Private demand for chronometers was miniscule. A few were bought by wealthy yachtsmen, or amateur astronomers (like the rural clergymen, the Rev. Richard Sheepshanks, who had the time, interest and money to indulge in leisurely scientific pastimes).[20] One wealthy man bought a Kullberg two-day chronometer for the dashboard of his Rolls Royce in 1912.[21] But the cumulative effect of such private sales was small, though they eventually proved important, when 'parsonage chronometers' were called in during the Great War (Chapter 17).

Kullberg no. 4070 and Mercer no. 2001

At first Kullberg's and Mercer's newly established firms, like the others, used Clerkenwell's traditional system of production. It proved comfortably adequate for the slow growth of new demand. The system of production, well described in the 1840s by Edward J. Dent (Chapter 10), had essentially derived from that developed by Tompion and others for watches, and by Arnold and Earnshaw for chronometers.[22] Kullberg, Mercer, and other firms may themselves have made only one small part of the instrument, but crucially they oversaw its assembly and adjustment. They were accountable for its existence, like spiders at the centre of a web. At first, both firms made chronometers using Clerkenwell's independent outworkers to supplement their own workshops. The House of Kullberg relied on their traditional methods of production and the skills of Clerkenwell's outworkers: in 1881 only seven men and a boy were employed in his workshop.[23] Mercer, as we will see, moved to St Albans in 1874 and attempted to be more self-sufficient. He employed 16 men in 1870, falling to 12 in 1900 (presumably because machine tools increased productivity).[24]

Fortunately, we have outlines of the sequences of production followed by each of their Houses. Their methods were basically the same and they must often have used the same outworkers – 'Abbott for detents, Travers for fusees'. Kullberg's No. 4070 was an Admiralty order for a two-day chronometer. Started in February 1880 from a Prescot rough movement in Kullberg's workshop, it left for fourteen separate journeys through the hands of at least nine outworkers for jewelling, escapements, springing, casing, and boxing, before it was returned to the workshop. Its cost of production was £17 5s. By January 1882, it remained in stock for a year whilst its timing was regulated – a procedure that could not be hurried. Finally, on 9 August 1883, it was cleaned, oiled, and boxed, with an ivory number plate attached, ready for service about forty-two months after it had been started in 105 Liverpool Street.[25] This method of production remained essentially unchanged, although after Victor's death his successors may have speeded up some stages.

The production sequence of Mercer's No. 2001 was similar to that of Kullberg's No. 4070. Mercer's 2001 was started in 1872, before his move to St Albans. Its construction has been graphically described by his son, Frank. First, the rough movements, comprising

> fusee, barrel, and arbor, frame, wheels and pinions, all made up in the little workshops in Prescot, packed in sets of a dozen, were distributed by Thomas Foster whose job it was to allocate the various parts of the movement, to be 'stripped and numbered before starting on their various journeys to specialists in jewelling, pinions, balances. Eventually, after passing through many hands they were returned to Thomas, who made the steel spring and 'after getting the movement to time, he would rate and adjust; and when ready would take it down to spot and polish, when it would be reassembled and despatched to the waiting customer'.[26]

In 1961, after a century that included two world wars and journeys of millions of miles, chronometer No. 2001 was returned to Mercer's repair shop. A rusted hairspring was replaced with one made of palladium and then it was 'to all intents and purposes good for another hundred years'. The methods of production used by Kullberg and Mercer revealed a seeming paradox: chronometers were assembled from hand-crafted components made in different places. Yet the best were among the finest and most complex examples of contemporary precision technology, accurate up to fractions of a second a week.

Reform in St Albans

Although Clerkenwell's labour-intensive system worked adequately to make a steady supply of top-quality watches and chronometers, Thomas Mercer was dissatisfied. He wondered if productivity might be increased with better organisation. By the 1870s, many formerly handcraft British industries (led by textiles) had concentrated production in factories. For watches, Waltham's success had already revolutionised watchmaking in the United States. But Clerkenwell's independent outworkers were still as hostile to change as they had been to Ingold thirty years earlier. They were specialists, jealous to preserve their narrow skills in small branches of an otherwise declining hand-craft industry.[27] Nevertheless in the 1870s, Mercer hoped to improve production by keeping closer control over some processes. His views of the current inadequacies of Clerkenwell's methods had been aired in November 1861 at the new Horological Institute in a debate in which he outlined the merits of a technology that used standardised and interchangeable parts.[28]

> A great many of these evils [that afflict British watchmaking] I believe are of easy remedy, without, to a great extent, destroying our present trade arrangements, if our manufacturers would ... map out a plan, and arrange every detail to given sizes, in no case letting men work by judgement, always to scale; making the decimal sizing and the duplicate system the base to work from... [This] 'system', and production in great quantities, constituted the secret of Swiss success; and by this system, America hopes to supersede our trade; but if we can get in the wedge, in whole or part, towards improvement, we may count on future success. [29]

In 1874 his business in Spencer Street, Clerkenwell, was relocated to St Albans, about twenty-five miles away. He alleged that the reason to move was ill health, as he was affected by Clerkenwell's polluted atmosphere. So he transplanted his company to Hertfordshire's countryside. Ostensibly it was healthier than London for Mercer's bad chest. But Clerkenwell did *not* have Merthyr's iron furnaces, or the polluting chimneys of Lancashire's textile factories. Mercer still returned there weekly to see dealers, outworkers, and 'carry' Greenwich Time back to St Albans.[30] His move to St Albans was an attempt at self-sufficiency, to obviate reliance on Clerkenwell's specialist outworkers. He was partially successful. In a two-storied garden workshop at his new house in Prospect Road, St Albans, his grandson has described how Mercer stood at a high bench alongside his key workers.[31] But it went only part of the way towards the new 'system' he desired, for rough movements from Prescot were still needed.[32] In St Albans hand work still prevailed, although more machines helped. They included 'a miller, treadle lathe, spotting machines, twin lap and a hand press', operated by the eighteen or twenty workmen who lived nearby. By arranging for their work to be done in proximity to each other Mercer had eliminated some – but not all – of the inadequacies of the old system. He was perhaps halfway towards centralised production in his mini factory. Nevertheless, the reorganisation was moderately successful, for annual output increased from about 150 instruments in the 1880s to about 170 by the time he died in 1900. His chronometers cost £2 or £3 less than Kullberg's. Output remained at about three instruments a week – a reflection of the limited demand and the slow, careful, construction, and assembly essential for such complex and intricate mechanisms.

Able successors

Success at Greenwich Trials and international exhibitions only partly explains the continued ascendancy of the two firms. After their founders died both firms, fortunately, had able successors (as had Arnold and Earnshaw, half a century earlier). Following Victor Kullberg's death in 1890 an obituary in the *Horological Journal* celebrated his 'brilliant career' and his 'commanding genius'.[33] The House he established continued its success for another thirty years. Kullberg had not married, but two of his natural sons and a nephew, Peter John Wennerstrom, inherited.[34] Wennerstrom bought out their interests and, with his own sons George and Paul, carried on the business. With Sanfrid Lundqvist at first in the firm's employment and then in ownership, the House of Kullberg triumphed time and again at Greenwich. It led the lists sixteen times between 1890 and 1914, with eight chronometers in the first ten in 1913.[35] Just as a century earlier, John Arnold and his son had headed the Admiralty's leading suppliers and repairers so the House of Kullberg, thanks to Victor's talented successors, commanded an equivalent reputation in the late nineteenth and early twentieth century.

Thomas Mercer's firm, too, was blessed with able successors. Thomas died suddenly, during a visit to Paris for the 1900 International Industrial Exhibition, where he was to have been a juror.[36] The business passed to his two young sons, Tom and Frank. The former had four years' experience in the firm, the latter only two. Nevertheless, they were determined to pursue their father's intention to make the business less dependent on Clerkenwell's outworkers. Indeed, some of those outworkers, on hearing of the sudden accession of the two youngsters, tried to block supplies to drive the firm out of business. They had guessed, correctly, that following more self-sufficiency in St Albans, employment in Clerkenwell would shrink further.[37] Their attempts were unsuccessful, and the Mercer brothers continued to reorganise production. First, with the aid of a local mechanic who designed and made a fusee cutting machine, St Albans became less reliant on Clerkenwell's outworkers. Eventually, other innovations were made that also lessened ties with their old suppliers in Prescot. And when Frank Mercer returned from the international exposition in St Louis in 1904 and 1905, further progress was made towards realising Thomas's vision of self-sufficiency. Frank had travelled extensively through the eastern United States and visited watch factories and machine tool shops. On his return he bought, on the expert advice of the managing director of Rotherham in Coventry (also busy modernising), not American but Swiss semi-automatic machine tools. They included a Petermann automatic lathe and gear cutter specially designed for watchmaking. It was another illustration of the lessons successfully learned by the Swiss three decades earlier at the Centennial Exhibition. Not only had the Swiss watch industry caught up with American watchmaking, but their machine tool industry, too, was taking the lead.

Domestic competition: leading firms and independents

Another way by which the Houses of Mercer and Kullberg comfortably led the chronometer market and sustained their pre-eminence was by attracting rival firms as customers. The competition was never eliminated but, by 1900, the two firms were clearly ascendant. In the early twentieth century, other firms were still 'making very small quantities ... Dents, Johannsen, and Usher and Cole, with 'Gardner, Webb, Hewitt, Isaac and Parkinson & Frodsham'.[38] Mercer and Kullberg saw off domestic and foreign rivals because both concentrated primarily on chronometers and only incidentally made top quality carriage clocks and watches. As time passed, some former competitors bought from Kullberg and Mercer. It was no longer economic for them to make up every kind of horological order from scratch. Commissioning, assembling, and finishing a chronometer was complex, and Kullberg and Mercer were specialists who did little else (just as Nicole Nielsen made watches exclusively for leading retailers). Charles Frodsham (1810–1871), for example, had initially commissioned his own marine chronometers and watches with chronometer escapements. All were top quality. Eventually, it became more cost-effective to buy them already finished and Kullberg's *Order Books* reveal that they made Frodsham twenty-two chronometers before 1866. Over the next decade, Kullberg supplied Frodsham with about twenty instruments a year at prices of between £22 and £30 for two and eight-day models. [39] Mercer's firm, too, supplied others who were once rivals. For example, Brockbanks & Atkins bought 159 chronometers from Mercer between 1865 and 1918, and Frodsham & Keen, Liverpool, acquired 139 of Mercer's instruments between 1899 and 1918. Mercer supplied instruments to over 370 different 'makers', who were mostly retailers. During the Great War, because Usher & Cole's retail and repair commitments were their most important priority they, too, bought completed chronometers from Mercer and had their own name engraved on the dials (Chapter 17).

Independent craftsmen often 'finished' basic models bought-in from major firms. Their incentive was to do well at the annual Greenwich Observatory Trials. Their importance both to suppliers and buyers had been recognised when Airy resumed them in 1844. Good performances at the Trials lent prestige, and this encouraged participation from smaller firms, like Gardner, Webb, Hewitt, Isaac, and J.U. Poole. They specialised in springing and 'finishing' basic instruments that most likely were made by Kullberg or Mercer, but now with their own names and numbers on the dials. After 1888 rigorous new tests were instigated for deck watches (pocket chronometers) and records of their performances were published in appendices to the annual volumes of *Greenwich Observations*.[40] Their performances were measured against a long-case regulator, revealing their losing or gaining rates over different lengths of time, positions and temperatures. After the Trials, the Admiralty, the single largest customer for box chronometers and deck watches, undertook to buy those that headed the list. Aware of the danger of unnecessarily bloating their already large stock, they cautioned that purchases would be 'according to ... annual requirements'.

Perhaps the most successful of the independent makers was Johan Ernest Adolph Uhrig, of Quadrant Road off Essex Road, London. Between 1886 and 1892, he successively broke the House of Kullberg's long winning streak. Trial winners understandably scooped most publicity but, for independents, taking part and simply doing well – without necessarily topping the list – was an achievement. Regional 'makers' also participated, including two from Glasgow (Edward & Sons and Whyte & Co.), and one each from Bristol (Blair), Liverpool (Penlington), and Ireland (Moore of Belfast). It is not known how many basic Mercer and Kullberg models – or those from other firms – performed at the Trials under the names and numbers of retailers or independent craftsmen.[41] Those who sold to the Admiralty were henceforth allowed to engrave on their dials 'Maker to the Royal Navy' (the style chosen by Shepherd & Co., and Barraud) or 'Maker to the Admiralty' (preferred by John Fletcher and Victor Kullberg). The prestige of those titles was also claimed by retailers like 'John Forrest, Maker to the Admiralty', who sold many but did not make any. Although his name was on the dial he, like many others, never 'made' a chronometer. [42] Webster of Cornhill, London, 'made' chronometers for the Liverpool firm of Litherland, Davis & Company. They were another firm that 'in all probability did not manufacture all their chronometers, if indeed they made any of them'.[43] Kullberg's *Order Books* reveal several examples of old instruments (not necessarily originally by Kullberg) that were renamed and renumbered.[44] Kullberg left his own name and number on chronometers supplied to the Admiralty for the Royal Navy but put the retailer's name and number on instruments supplied to foreign admiralties. Hence Kullberg No. 8888 became Lilly No. 1929 when bought by the Imperial Japanese Navy. If a retailer did not want his name engraved, the entry in the *Order Book* simply stated, 'Kullberg as usual; 1429'. After an old chronometer came in for repair it became difficult to identify the original maker from the retailer. An entry of 9 June 1871 specified that chronometer 'Campbell 466' was to be 'thoroughly cleaned and repaired and lacquered as new. Dial to have name taken out and H. Hughes engra. [ved] as under: H. Hughes 59 Fenchurch St. London no. to be inser[te]d 1022'.[45] Similarly, 'Kullberg No. 1,378' became 'M. del Rego, 45 South Castle St., Liverpool, No. 2,386'; and 'Kullberg No. 1,363' became 'Webster, Cornhill, London, 14,688'. The impact and importance of Kullberg and Mercer were greater than seemed evident by their names on chronometer dials.

Foreign competition

Foreign chronometer 'makers', too, could buy basic Kullberg models on which they paid a little extra to have their own names and numbers engraved on the dials. Unlike their parent industry, watchmaking, Britain's chronometer makers comfortably met and surmounted foreign competition. London's firms had always enjoyed an easy, almost privileged, access to the Royal Navy and Britain's merchant marine. But as their reputations rose, Kullberg and Mercer also supplied an impressive range of international customers. This was partly because after 1815 rival chronometer manufacturers in other maritime nations – France, Holland, and Spain – had smaller marines and navies to motivate their own chronometer makers. Unlike Britain, foreign nations did not have such extensive world-wide empires with which to trade. France's illustrious chronometer-manufacturing sector struggled to survive after 1815. Her leading maker, LeRoy of Paris, still made complete instruments from scratch, but the French navy's demand was small. To encourage chronometer manufacturing sea trials were organised and the best-performing instruments were bought at a fixed price of 2,000 francs. France had a fixed budget of 50,000 francs a year for replacements and repairs. In 1850 it had 300 box and hundred pocket chronometers.[46] By 1889, its navy's annual purchase of new chronometers had fallen to about forty.[47] As the French navy's demands continued to diminish, Louis LeRoy complained in 1899 about the low replacement demand: 'the French Admiralty buys very few chronometers, perhaps five or six a year, having more than 600 of them in stock'.[48]

Similar features of demand and supply applied in other formerly leading maritime countries, like Holland. By the end of the century '*Dupont en Zoon, Horologemakers, Rotterdam*' bought Kullberg instruments for which they supplied tabs in advance: 'Please make for the firm Dupont en Zoon the following number, when not to [too much?] trouble make it with our medaile' (sic). Accordingly, Kullberg 4205 became Dupont 119, and Kullberg's 4341 became Dupont 120.[49] Mercer, too, supplied foreign makers with completed instruments when they no longer finished their own. Andreas Hohwu in Amsterdam bought seventy Mercer chronometers between 1899 and 1916.[50] Among the handful of outstanding European chronometer manufacturers who survived from the pioneering era was Urban Jurgensen of Copenhagen. The reputation of that great maker's firm was further enhanced by his talented son and successor, but it is not clear how many instruments Louis Urban Jurgensen made from scratch. Eventually, he, too, finished-off basic models made by Kullberg. For example, Kullberg No. 1571 had a two-day movement fitted by Kullberg himself, with escapement, balancing, finishing, springing, chain, and jewelling done by his outworkers. It then had 'Urban Jurgensen No. 111' engraved on it and was sent from Kullberg to Copenhagen to be rated and fine-tuned by Jurgensen.[51]

At first, navies of emerging nations with growing economies depended heavily on English chronometers. When Prussia under Bismarck expanded its industrial, military, and naval ambitions, Germany's horological sector gradually moved into chronometer manufacturing. Before 1890 its navy and merchant marine still relied on imported instruments and one supplier, Eppner of Berlin, bought his from Kullberg.[52] Facilities for rating and servicing were gradually added and a naval observatory was built. Not until 1910–11 at Hamburg's annual Trials were 98 per cent of chronometers German in origin. Rapid development followed and, by the Great War, Germany's chronometer manufacturing sector was essentially self-sufficient.[53] Other European chronometer makers also bought and 'finished' British models. In land-locked Switzerland, without a marine but with its best watches renowned in world markets, its horology was led at the end of the century by Paul Ditisheim. He, too, had his name and number engraved on basic Kullberg models that he then sprung and finished.[54] Switzerland's other illustrious contemporary horologist, Ulysse Nardin, avoided the market for box chronometers and specialised instead in complicated watches and pocket chronometers. His great reputation (like Kullberg's) was based on prizes at international exhibitions. His firm's status was enhanced when it used balances of the nickel-steel alloy (*Invar* and *Elinvar*) developed by the son and grandson of watchmakers, Dr Charles Guillaume (for which he was awarded the Nobel Prize in physics in 1920).[55]

Similarly, across the Atlantic: chronometer 'makers' initially depended heavily on English completed instruments or their parts. The United States' navy – like its merchant marine – bought chronometers from England. By 1835, its navy owned fifty-four instruments. Twelve were reported to be of the 'very best' quality, eight were 'second rate', and thirty-four were 'indifferent and unreliable'. Over the next decade, the navy bought more until it had about 120 instruments, with 'eighty on shore and on trial'.[56] No American firm completed instruments from scratch; at first, each also depended on assorted English firms for chains, fusees, glass, and on Prescot for rough movements.[57] During the War of 1812, an embargo prevented the export of required horological parts from England, and William C. Bond, later director of the Harvard College Observatory, made the first United States' chronometer. Randall Brooks concluded that 'after the war he probably once again reverted to the purchase of chronometer parts which he then assembled'.[58] Bond of Boston's reported lifetime 'output' of chronometers was 1,200, but it is impossible to know for what portion of each instrument was the firm responsible, or how many were bought-in.[59] Similarly, John Bliss, New York, started in 1824 as a repairer in the watch, clock, and jewellery business, and specialised in servicing chronometers. He, too, imported parts from England and then assembled and finished them. Whitman & Creighton began their own line in the 1840s when they bought English rough movements to which they added jewels and dials, before springing and adjusting. By 1852, they had accounted for nearly 200 instruments. Throughout that firm's existence – until about 1940 – they are credited with making around 3,500 instruments, mostly made for merchant shipping after the Great War.[60] Negus & Company, another leading firm established in 1848 in Wall Street, New York, also acted as one of Kullberg's agents. Thomas Negus had trained in England and his repair and servicing business took off when he lent a good chronometer to a sea captain as a temporary replacement for one being repaired. He, too, bought-in basic models before springing and finishing them. Like Bliss, Negus also reputedly finished 3,500 instruments. About a dozen or so lesser American 'makers' were dealers – 'nautical chandlers' – who sold and serviced chronometers.[61]

Kullberg's and Mercer's agents

Two reasons help to explain why foreign chronometer makers relied on, rather than challenged, Kullberg and Mercer. First, many foreign ships bought chronometers when in an English port and subsequently had them serviced there or with their agents elsewhere. Second, Kullberg and Mercer each built up a worldwide network of representatives.[62] Their global presence was nurtured in major ports by chandlers who, as well as selling nautical instruments and charts could, crucially, arrange for chronometers to be cleaned, refurbished, and rated.[63] Over time, the number of such outlets shrank, as did the number of makers. In 1880, there were 237 'nautical opticians' in British ports, including 112 in London. Eventually, these competing outlets rationalised and decreased in number. By 1913 only thirty-six were left in London and eighty-eight in British provincial cities and ports. This contraction reflected the growing concentration of production by a few firms, led by Kullberg and Mercer, and a rationalisation of their agents.[64] They were in every major British port and city: in Aberdeen, Glasgow, Edinburgh, Dublin, Belfast, and Southampton. Liverpool had forty-one retailers of scientific instruments that included chronometers.[65] Kullberg's *Order Books* had addresses for 484 agents: the firm's reach extended to Bombay, Cairo and other imperial and colonial outposts. In northern Europe Kullberg had strong connections in the Baltic, with whom Victor and his successors conducted correspondence in Swedish and German.[66] Mercer had agencies in Arendel, Oslo, Copenhagen, Amsterdam, Antwerp, Hamburg, Bremerhaven, Rotterdam, Genoa, Nantes, and Marseilles, as well as in Boston, New York, Philadelphia, and Tokyo.[67] Major trading companies in Austria, Italy, Japan, and China were also customers, as were several foreign observatories. Kullberg and Mercer sold and serviced chronometers for other national navies as well as for the Royal Navy.[68] By the eve of the Great War England's watchmaking industry was frail but its offspring, chronometer-manufacturing, was robust. During the Great War (Chapter 17), makers of mechanical chronometers enjoyed a brief, final, golden era before they, too, became victims of new technologies.

Notes

1 LMA/CLC/B/141/MS14537/001-002: Kullberg's Manufacturing Books.
2 Letter from F.A. (Tony) Mercer to author, 18 August 1977: 'The annual figures vary between 20 in the early days and 600 during the boom periods (the wars) ... Mercer made at least three times as any other chronometer maker in the world'.
3 For Mercer's firm the starting point is by his grandson: F.A. (Tony) Mercer, *Mercer Chronometers: Radical Tom Mercer and the House He Founded* (Ashford: Brant Wright, 1978). The Mercer archives were originally deposited in the Prescot Horological Museum and are now in the Liverpool World Museum. They include notes by Frank ('Punch') Mercer (son of Thomas, father of Tony). I am grateful to John Griffiths (then Curator) for help when I consulted them. Other information is in Eric M. Bruton 'Revolution at Mercers', *Horological Journal,* 96/6 (Feb. 1954), 88–91; Anon. (probably Eric M. Bruton?), 'Thomas Mercer Ltd., Chronometer Makers for a Hundred Years', *Horological Journal,* 100/11 (July 1958), 426–28; F.A. Mercer, 'A Company as Old as the Institute', *Horological Journal,* 126/10 (June 1983), 31–33; id., 'Thomas Mercer: Maker of Chronometers Since 1858', *Port of London: Magazine of the Port of London Authority* (Summer 1976), 50–51; id., 'A Dynasty Dedicated to the Sea and Time-keeping', *Clocks*, 1 (Sept. 1978), 22–25, is a reprint of the former. Also Alun C. Davies, 'Thomas Mercer, 1822–1900: Chronometer Manufacturer', in *Dictionary of Business Biography*, ed. D.J. Jeremy (London: Butterfield, 1986), 4, 218–20.
4 Mercer, 'A Company as Old as the Institute', 32.
5 Anon., 'Our Portrait Gallery: Mr. Victor Kullberg', *Invention and Inventors' Mart* (October 17, 1885), 1083; Paul M. Chamberlain, *It's about Time*, 435–37; Charles Allix, *Carriage Clocks: Their Historical Development* (Woodbridge, Antique Collectors Club, 1974), 282–86. In 1962 the Swedish Academy of Engineering Sciences dedicated its commemorative medal for 1962 in celebration of the centenary of a turning point in Kullberg's career: see *Horological Journal,* 104 (1962), 708. Also Alun C Davies, 'Victor Kullberg, 1824–1890: Chronometer Manufacturer', in Jeremy, D.J. (ed.), *Dictionary of Business Biography*, 3 (1985), 628–29.
6 Tony Mercer, *Chronometer Makers,* 163–65, 178–79, 229.
7 Tony Mercer, letter, 18 August 1977: 'Mercer supplied chronometers to 370 outlets with the retailer's name on the dial: Frodsham, Dent, Breguet, Leroy were some of the few'.
8 Aldred M. Rogers, and J.S. Turnbull, 'Timekeepers, Clocks, Watches and Chronometers', *Artisans' Reports on Vienna, 1873* (London: Society for the Promotion of Scientific Knowledge, 1874), 30, 36.
9 James C. Watson, 'Horological Instruments ... Philadelphia Exhibition', *BPP* (1877), vol. 6, 823–24.
10 *BPP,* 1901, vol. 31: *Reports from Commissioners: Paris International Exhibition, 1900*; Report by J.J.S. Tripplin, 543–49.
11 For the demise of the firm, see David S. Torrens, 'Sanfrid Lundquist: The Death of the Last Surviving Partner Closes the Famous Firm of Victor Kullberg', *Horological Journal,* 89 (1947), 246–47; and Alun C. Davies, 'David Smyth Torrens, 1897–1967, an Horological Memoir', *Antiquarian Horology,* 6 (1984), 564–84, esp. 576. Allix, *Carriage Clocks*, 286, describes some of Kullberg's workmen towards the end of the firm's life.
12 David Penney, 'Evidence from the Transient: The Importance of Ephemera for a Proper Understanding of the Clock and Watch Trades, Part II', *Antiquarian Horology*, 30/1 (March 2007), 45–50.

13 Not until the exigencies of the Second World War and the need for radio silence was sufficient demand for new instruments to induce the Hamilton Watch Company in America to mass produce excellent instruments.

14 Sarah Palmer, 'The British Shipping Industry 1950–1914', in Lewis R. Fischer and Gerald E. Ponting, *Change and Adaptation in Maritime History: the North Atlantic Trade in the Nineteenth Century* (St. John's NL: Maritime History Group, Memorial University of Newfoundland, 1985), especially 'National Merchant Shipping Tonnages and their Share of the World Fleet, 1850–1911', Tables 1 and 2, 90–93; Alun C. Davies, 'The Life and Death of a Scientific Instrument: The Marine Chronometer, 1770–1920', *Annals of Science,* 35 (1978), 509–25, Table IV: https://doi.org/10.1080/00033797800200391

15 P.N. Davies, 'British Shipping and World Trade: Rise and Decline 1820–1939', in Tsunehiko Yui and Keiichiro Nakagawa (eds.), *Business History of Shipping: Strategy and Structure* (Tokyo: Tokyo UP, 1985), 68–69; other background is in B.R. Mitchell, *European Historical Statistics, 1750–1970* (London: Palgrave Macmillan, 1975), table G4; H.J. Dyos and D.H. Aldcroft, *British Transport: An Economic History from the Seventeenth Century to the Twentieth* (Leicester: Leicester UP, 1974), 248.

16 R. Vaudrey Mercer, *John Arnold & Son, Chronometer Makers, 1767–1843* (Ticehurst, *Antiquarian Horological Society*, 1972), 223–76: Appendix XVI, 'Chronometer Records at Greenwich'.

17 Compiled from 'Astronomer Royal's Reports to the Board of Visitors', from which abstracts appeared in most years from 1890 to 1920 in the *Horological Journal.*

18 *Nature,* 84 (18 August 1910), 210.

19 Simon C. Davidson, 'Box Chronometers for India, 1800–1936', *Antiquarian Horology*, 35/4 (Dec. 2014), 1107–24. Table on 1112 lists 1563 chronometers sold to India and concludes it is reasonable to assume that the total number of box chronometers supplied for use there from 1800 to 1936 was in the region of 1,8free 00 to 2,000.

20 For example, the Rev. Richard Sheepshanks loaned ten of his instruments to help in the survey of Valencia in 1844. See A.M. Clerke, rev. Michael Hoskin, 'Richard Sheepshanks (1794–1855)', *ODNB* (2004).

21 LMA/CLC/B/141/14,285: Ledger 10, 15 January 1912; Alun C. Davies, 'The House of Kullberg', *Antiquarian Horology*, 35/1(March 2014), 645. This draws on the range of Kullberg's archives at LMA/CLC/B/141/Ms14537-46, and 14546-54.

22 For technical descriptions of chronometers by the pioneer firms see Abraham Rees, *Rees's Clocks, Watches and Chronometers (1819–20): A Selection from the Cyclopaedia; or Universal Dictionary of Arts, Sciences and Literature* (Newton Abbot: David & Charles reprint, 1970), 24–47. For an expert explanation of 'How the Marine Chronometer Was Made', see Chapter 2 of Jonathan Betts, *Marine Chronometers at Greenwich: A Catalogue of Marine Chronometers at the National Maritime Museum, Greenwich* (Oxford: Oxford UP and National Maritime Museum, 2017), 73–96.

23 Darlah Thomas, 'A Snapshot of the Watchmaking Industry in England through the Lens of the 1881 Census', *Antiquarian Horology*, 40/1 (March 2019), 47.

24 Tony Mercer, letter 18 August 1977 (and for subsequent quote).

25 LMA/CLC/B/141/MS14537/2: Kullberg Manufacturing Books, 452; and LMA/CLC/B/141/MS14538, Kullberg Order Books, 395, 398c; Kullberg's no. 4070 is discussed and illustrated in Alun C. Davies, 'The Life and Death of a Scientific Instrument: The Marine Chronometer, 1770–1920', *Annals of*

Science, 35 (1978), 509–25, at https://doi.org/10.1080/00033797800200391; Betts, *Marine Chronometers at Greenwich*, 486–88.

26 Frank Mercer, 'The Story of Chronometer 2001 ... and After', *Horological Journal*, 103/9 (May 1961), 281–82, for quotations.

27 *Horological Journal*, 34 (1891), 23.

28 See Mercer's contribution in the debate 'On the Best Means of Improving the Watch Trade', *Horological Journal*, 4/5 (Jan 1862), 51–56; also *Clerkenwell News*, 4 Dec. 1861. His views were as prescient as those of John Wycherley, in the latter's lecture to the BHI in Sept. 1867: *Horological Journal*, 10/2 (Oct. 1867), 18–21; also evidence to the Truck Commission in 1870: *BPP*, 1871, vol.36, 657–59.

29 See *Clerkenwell News*, 4 Dec. 1861, and the debate 'On the Best Means of Improving the Watch Trade', *Horological Journal*, 4/5 (Jan 1862), 51–56.

30 It was transmitted to horologists via 'Arnold', a precision watch made in 1794, certified correct to within one-tenth of a second of Observatory time: see David Rooney, *Ruth Belville: the Greenwich Time Story* (London: NMM, 2008); and Hannah Gay, 'Clock Synchrony, Time Distribution and Electrical Timekeeping in Britain 1880–1925', *Past and Present*, No. 181 (Nov. 2003), 107–40, at https://www.jstor.org/stable/3600787

31 The firm moved again, in 1912, to Eywood Street, St Albans

32 Tony Mercer, *Mercer Chronometers,* 28 et seq., and 43.

33 Obituary, 'Victor Kullberg', *Horological Journal,* 33 (1890), 185–87; he died of pleurisy on 7 July 1890 and is buried in Highgate cemetery:

34 Obituary, 'Peter John Wennerstrom', *Horological Journal,* 77 (1935), 175.

35 Rupert T. Gould, *The Marine Chronometer: Its History and Development* (1923: London: Holland Press, 1960), 266 for the winners' table; Alun C. Davies, 'Horology at International Industrial Exhibitions, 1851–1900', *Antiquarian Horology*, 33/5 (Sept. 2012, 591–608.

36 Mercer, *Mercer Chronometers*, 54. Thomas Mercer died a wealthy man. With equivalent assets in the present century he would have been a millionaire. His gross personal estate was valued at nearly £15,000, and his gross real estate (22 houses and shops in St Albans, London, and the Isle of Man) at nearly £11,000, and his stock, plant, machinery, fixtures and fittings at £2,500.

37 Mercer, *Mercer Chronometers*, 54–55.

38 Tony Mercer, Letter, 18 August 1977.

39 Vaudrey Mercer, 'Charles Frodsham; Maker of Marine Chronometers', *Clocks*, 6 (Oct. 1983), 17–19. The Frodsham archives are in the Guildhall Library at LMA/CLC/B/043/MS19904; also LMA/CLC/B/141/MS14538/1-8: Kullberg Ledgers, 1857–92, Vol. 1, 63; also LMA/CLC/B/141/MS14539. Numbers on chronometers do not necessarily indicate output: Frodsham's chronometer numbers started at No. 1,000, or perhaps 1,400: Vaudrey Mercer, *Frodsham*, 78.

40 Published annually by HMSO. Trials lasted 16 weeks for deck watches and 29 weeks for box chronometers

41 F.A. (Tony) Mercer in letter to *Antiquarian Horology*, 9/6 (March 1976), 708, commented that names on dials of chronometers ascribed to ten companies, most connected with Lord Kelvin, were all made by other firms.

42 *Horological Journal,* 36/7 (Mar 1894), 112.

43 David Evans, letter in *Antiquarian Horology*, 9/8 (Sept. 1976), 939.

44 LMA/CLC/B/141/14,538: Order Books, vols. 1 – 8. Entries specified orders for watches, chronometers, and repair work, and were from individuals and retailers from all over the world.

45 LMA/CLC/B/141/14,538/:, p.63.

46 Marvin E. Whitney, *The Ship's Chronometer* (Cincinnati, OH, Watchmakers Institute Press, 1985), 57–58, 324, 370, 393–94.

47 J.J.S. Tripplin, *Watch and Clock Making in 1889; Being an Account and Comparison of the Exhibits in the Horological Section of the French International Exhibition ... With a View of the British Watch and Clock Making Section* (London: Crosby Lockwood, 1890), 40.

48 Letter from 'L. Leroy, Chronometer Maker to the [French] Navy', *Horological Journal*, 42 (1899), 56. Leroy did consistently well in the French trials between 1895 and 1904, winning in eight of those years.

49 LMA/CLC/B/141/MS14538/001-008: p.393 (25 May 1881).

50 Tony Mercer, *Mercer Chronometers: History, Maintenance and Repair* (Ashbourne: Mayfield Books, 2003), Appendix 6, 'Index of all known Mercer Chronometers', 187, 216.

51 LMA/CLC/B/141/MS14537/001-002: 17 August 1869; also Derek Pratt and Peter Baumberger, 'Urban Jurgensen & Sonner, Copenhagen', *Horological Journal*, 133/6 (Dec. 1990), 196–201.

52 Kullberg's box chronometer, No. 3715 supplied to Eppner in 1877, reappeared forty years later in England, to be re-dialled for use by Joseph Sewill of Liverpool. David Penney suggests it might have been returned as part of post-war reparations agreements.

53 Günther Oestmann, *Auf dem weg zum 'Deutschen Chronometer'* (Bremen: Deutsche Maritime Studien 21, 2012), 497–500. For a summary in English see id., 'En Route to the German Chronometer: The Introduction of Precision Timekeeping in the German Mercantile Marine and Imperial Navy in the 19th Century', [Paper for the 23rd Congress of History of Science and Technology: Ideas and Instruments in Social Context (Budapest: Session T35 (Scientific Instruments), August 1st, 2009]; also id. *Antiquarian Horology*, 35/3 (Sept 2014), 949–63. I am grateful to Günther Oestmann for much helpful correspondence.

54 See Figure 11 in Alun C. Davies, 'Rise and Decline of Chronometer Manufacturing', *Antiquarian Horology*, 12 (Autumn 1980), 293; also David S. Torrens, 'Paul Ditisheim: A Tribute to a Great Horologist', *Horological Journal*, 87/4 (Dec. 1945), 410ff; also id., 'Notes on Elinvar', *Horological Journal*, 81/5 (Jan. 1939), 26–28.

55 Robert W. Cahn, 'An Unusual Nobel Prize', *Notes and Records of the Royal Society of London* (2005) 59/145–153: DOI:10.1098/rsnr.2004.0082.

56 Steven J. Dick, 'Centralizing Navigational Technology in America: The U.S. Navy's Depot of Charts and Instruments, 1830–1842', *Technology and Culture* , 33/3 (July 1992), 467–509, especially 'The Rise of the Chronometer in America', 485–96, at https://www.jstor.org/stable/3106634

57 Whitney, *Ship's Chronometer*, 82–85, 95–96.

58 Randall C. Brooks, 'Nautical Instrument Makers in Atlantic Canada', *Nova Scotia Historical Review*, 6 (Jan.1986), 36–54 (47), at https://www.researchgate.net/publication/275155416_Nautical_Instrument_Makers_in_Atlantic_Canada; id., 'Richard Upham Marsters: The First Chronometer Maker in North America', at https://www.researchgate.net/publication/266277872

59 Whitney, *Ship's Chronometer*, 345.

60 Whitney, *Ship's Chronometer*, 336–37.

61 Whitney, *Ship's Chronometer*, 342, 351; also Michael C. Harrold, *American Watchmaking: A Technical History of the American Watch Industry, 1850–1930* (Columbia, PA. NAWCC, 1981), 116–17.

62 *Horological Journal*, 23/8 (April 1881), 102–07: Official 'exports' of British chronometers amounted to only about 4 per cent of the value of British

horological products exported between 1867 and 1870. The annual average number of chronometers exported was 91, valued at £27 each.

63 Gloria Clifton, 'New Light on Chronometer-Makers and the Scientific Instrument Trades in the Nineteenth Century', *Antiquarian Horology*, 37/3 (Sept. 2016), 327–48: quote, 327.

64 'Kelly's Directories': *The Post Office Directory of the Watch and Clock ... and General Fancy Trades Throughout England, Scotland and Wales* (London: Kelly, 1880 and 1913). By 1937 retailers who offered chronometer services had fallen to 16 in London and 22 in the rest of the UK: Davies, 'Marine Chronometer', 522, Table VI.

65 Clifton, 'New light on Chronometer-makers', 335 and Table 2.

66 Kullberg had agents in Liverpool, Glasgow, Dundee, Greenwich, Newcastle, Manchester, Edinburgh, Belfast, Sunderland, Coventry, Plymouth, Swansea, Hull, Newport, Bristol, Dublin, and Cardiff. See his Order Books, LMA/CLC/B/141/MS14538/1-8 (also for footnote 67, below).

67 Mercer, *Chronometer Makers*, 155–236, for lists of customers and places; Gould, *Marine Chronometer*, 131–34. 262.

68 In the 1870s Kullberg's foreign agents included Bond & Son, Boston; Buhre, St Petersburg; Cash & Murray, Calcutta; De Kemel, Antwerp; Hoglund, Stockholm; Howhu, Amsterdam; Iverson, Bergen; Jurgensen, Copenhagen; Lindroth, Stockholm; Muller, Shanghai; Schiebach & Muller, Trieste; Wirren, St Petersburg.

17 The Great War and After

Outbreak of chauvinism

The declaration of war prompted optimism in the Watchmaker, Jeweller, and Silversmith, whose editors viewed the onset of hostilities with relish. After September 1914, its issues carried the following straps or sub-headings:

War!
Keep Cool.
Our Opportunity
Your motto: business as usual
Help your country by pushing trade
To keep the flag of commerce flying: the Duty of all
To the Manufacturer: Overseas trade calls you.[1]

These slogans at the foot of the trade journal's pages revealed reactions in the horological and jewellery industries to the onset of war. It was viewed as an 'opportunity' because horological firms in Clerkenwell and Coventry with blurred memories of their former golden age hoped the war might revive protectionism. They expected imports of watches would be stopped or disrupted, so that English manufacturers would be given an opportunity to regain their domestic market and, perhaps, enable them even to re-capture some former export markets ('Overseas trade calls you'). War meant a demand for watches from all branches of military services. Events bore this out, especially for the industry's elite chronometer sector: navigation instruments were essential for Britain's merchant marine and Royal Navy.

As enthusiasm for the war grew, patriotism quickly gave way to jingoism and anti-German hysteria. Horological trade journals presented a popular face to their readers. They found it expedient to advise caution, given the prominent part played in British horology by French Huguenots and their descendants, followed by German and Swiss immigrants (the latter often with German-sounding names) especially in the retail and repair trade. There was a danger that, in the wave of bellicose war fever and

DOI: 10.4324/9781003227823-20

anti-German frenzy that swept the country, 'grave injury may be done to our greatest friends by a careless generalisation over foreign terms'.[2]

The warning was apposite. Within a few months, flag-waving slogans coloured trade advertisements. Elaborate protestations of loyalty were announced. This was especially true of Anglo-Swiss multi-national firms with Germanic-sounding names. Thus Messrs Stauffer, Son, & Company decorated their advertisements with Swiss and English flags and reminded their customers 'that all the watch bracelets supplied by them are British made, as Messrs Stauffer, Son & Co. have never stocked German bracelets'. In September 1915, their advertisements proclaimed, 'The Watch officially presented to Sergt. Michael O'Leary, VC, in the City of Cork in July 1915 was one of their 'Peerless' movements, with luminous face and hands'. Another example was Borgzinners Limited, which promised that they were 'keeping warm the places of those of our staff who are serving their Country at the Front'. The long-established London firm of Kammerer Kuss continued to soften its spelling to Cammerer Cuss. Coventry's companies brandished their loyalty: Rotherham advertised 'reliable service watches' and 'English military wrist watches'; Williamson began a series of full-page advertisements that led with the words 'ENGLISH CLOCKS' in giant type. Usher & Cole simply stated: 'We supply the British Navy!' and, indeed, they were especially busy during the war servicing and rating chronometers.[3]

Unexpected reintroduction of tariffs

War revived demands for tariff protection by the leaders of the British Horological Institute – demands that had last been heard during the abortive Fair Trade movement at the turn of the century, although there was not much expectation in horological circles that the Liberal government would move in the direction of Protection. Nevertheless, to help pay for the war effort the new Chancellor of the Exchequer (who succeeded Lloyd George) Reginald McKenna introduced a War Budget in September 1915 which imposed import duties to fund the ever-increasing cost of the war.[4] They included the heavy duty of 33 1/3 per cent on imported watches, classified as a 'luxury good'. The *Horological Journal* admitted with astonishment that it was as if

> a bombshell was dropped into the Horological world... The Trade was taken completely by surprise, and no adequate reason has been discovered why this particular industry should have been selected for what looks like experimental purposes. However, no serious complaints have been heard in the trade at the imposition of the duty, but a little inconvenience has been caused by the unexpectedness of it, and it will take some time for that part of the trade which is principally affected to settle down to the new conditions.[5]

On the morning after the McKenna tariff was announced, 'the telephone bells were set ringing by those concerned' and a meeting of the London Wholesale Jewellers' and Allied Trades' Association was convened to discuss the implications. They unanimously resolved to increase the current selling price of imported clocks and watches by one third. After over half a century of free trade the English watchmaking industry believed that at last it had been granted the tariff protection for which it long yearned. In the first great war, with Napoleon a century earlier, smuggled watches had easily evaded tariffs. In the 'total war' after 1914, this would not be so easy. Questions that occupied the minds of the British Horological Institute (BHI's) executive committee were about the nature of the new protective tariff. Should it be temporary or permanent?... applied to all countries? ... or just to enemies?... how high should it be? Unsurprisingly, the committee favoured the continuation of the emergency tariff even after the end of hostilities, so that 'never again will our German enemies be allowed to use our markets as they did before the war'.[6] London's Chamber of Commerce, too, favoured a prolonged war and hoped that a protective tariff would be retained 'permanently, if possible, but in any event [for] not less than ten years'.[7]

War or peace, tariff protection or free trade, neither solution could resurrect overnight the former Golden Age of English horology. The eagerness with which the BHI welcomed the reintroduction of tariffs can be easily understood in the light of the huge trade imbalance between horological imports and exports during the last five pre-war years, when English clock and watchmaking firms had struggled to survive. Between 1909 and 1913, Britain imported 17 million watches and 13 million clocks. As both Switzerland and the United States were then still neutral, the BHI hoped that English firms would replace the German clocks that had been so successful in world markets. In 1912–13 German firms had exported 750,000 clocks, compared with a mere 30,000 from Britain. The *Horological Journal* echoed the Board of Trade's hope that this market, hitherto German, might somehow be captured.[8] But even a massive *ad valorem* tariff could not suddenly enable British makers to compete with German alarm clocks, imported in 1913 at only 1s 1d each.[9] There was no realistic possibility that, instantaneously, British clock factories could step up production and somehow supply such numbers.

Attempts to develop new trade

Throughout the war the Board of Trade's Commercial Intelligence Department urged the desirability of replacing enemy trade and published several memoranda to this effect.[10] It is unclear how helpful these pleas to increase exports were for England's watch and clock making firms, hitherto unable to hold more than a small share of their home market. and whose former export markets had all but vanished. The *Board of*

Trade Journal optimistically reported that there were openings for British goods in a variety of places where hitherto 'enemy-made' clocks and watches had been sold.[11] Other commercial intelligence reports, too, hoped that the war opened up possible targets for the exports of alarm clocks.[12] Reality asserted itself when the British Industries Fairs urged that English clock firms should 'walk before they ran': first, they ought to promote import substitution, by encouraging production for the home market to replace German imports.[13]

Competition between the watchmaking industries of the two leading protagonists was less intense than that for clockmakers. Germany's watch trade was tiny, amounting to only about 6 per cent of the value of its clock trade. Rivalry between English and German watchmaking firms in export markets had been minor. In 1913, the annual value of German watch exports to Britain was £27,550 and to other countries £69,750, making a total of £97,300. Exports of all British horological goods to Germany were only £11,300 and for English watches, a mere £600. Table 17.1 shows sources of watch imports in 1913.

The presence of American watches in Britain was understated by these figures; the value and thus quantity of parts imported from the United States indicated the extent to which American-made watch movements were now cased in England, mostly by Dennison's company in Birmingham. They took no account of watches made in Britain by American firms. Exports of English watches in 1913 numbered 6,458 at a value of £5,531 (about 17s a piece). They showed that a small foreign watch trade was still supplied by English firms (mostly, a residual portion of the imperial market), but that it amounted to a minuscule share of the world's market for watches. The few exports of medium priced and

Table 17.1 Watches and parts imported into Britain in 1913 from the USA, Germany and Switzerland

Origin	*Product*	*Number*	*Value (£)*
USA	Watches (cased)	278,274	28,911
	Movements and parts		120,388
	Total		149,299
Germany	Watches (cased)	218,050	21,980
	Movements and parts		5,570
	Total		27,550
Switzerland	Watches (cased)	3,306,864	1,028,318
	Movements and parts		31,573
	Total		1,059,891

Source: *Horological Journal*, 60/12 (Aug. 1918), 129, citing Report of the Departmental Committee appointed by the Board of Trade to consider the position of the engineering trades after the war: Report on Watches and clocks.

cheap English watches had long been slipping away, the victim of American dollar watches. The Great War finished the job. Before the war, Britain had supplied about 40 per cent of the value of clocks and watches exported to South Africa (Switzerland supplied 27 per cent, Germany 16 per cent, and the United States 14 per cent). After the war, the United States' share soared to 51 per cent, Switzerland's to 39 per cent, whilst Britain's share fell to a 9 per cent. The effect of the war was to end English watchmaking's presence, even in its imperial markets.[14] The tiny size to which England's watchmaking industry had shrunk can be seen when compared to that of Switzerland. The Swiss benefitted from the war because they supplied both sides. In 1914, they made just over 12 million movements (down from an annual average between 1911 and 1913 of nearly 16 million). Between 1915 and 1918 Swiss watchmaking enjoyed a massive boom, making annually over 18 million watches.[15]

Coventry and the war

The Great War delivered an almost merciful deathblow to Coventry's few remaining small watchmaking units. By 1914 of the city's 156 surviving 'outworker' firms, almost half were listed as 'workshops without power', museum relics from the Victorian era. But for Coventry's two large watchmaking firms, Rotherham and Williamson, the war had quite different impacts. During the war, Rotherham made no watches at all because its resources were entirely turned over to supply war material. It made 'the more complicated forms of fuses' using clockwork mechanisms: [At gunnery trials their fuses 'would explode a shell seven miles to a fiftieth part of a second' (sic.)]. Several firms had tried to make them, but only Rotherham succeeded, and it became the army's sole supplier. It also made 100,000 'friction tubes' a week. ['Friction tubes' had a lanyard attached, with length proportional to the size of the gun, which when fired caused friction inside the tube which ignited a powder charge, 'much like striking a match'.] This, Hugh Rotherham ruefully observed, was good for the war effort, but 'very bad for the tools, bad for the workmen... and bad for watchmaking generally'.[16] War contracts enabled Rotherham to survive as a firm but, like the earlier Coventry Movement Company, the price was metamorphosis. By the late 1920s, it had diversified into making assorted engineering items that required complicated mechanisms, such as meters with slot machines, totalizers for betting, speedometers, petrol gauges, indicators for optical instruments, and carburettors – 'tubes of all sizes for mixing the gas in motors'.[17]

Coventry's other large watchmaking firm, Williamson, had a better war-time experience. At first, complications arose from the company's multi-national composition. The war's impact was first felt at their Buren factory when its workmen were called up to join the Swiss army (then in a state of armed neutrality) on the French border with the Jura. Production was interrupted, orders were cancelled, and its trade ceased. Thus the initial impact of the 'deplorable war' reduced the firm's profits and 'completely arrest[ed] our progress; indeed a portion of our business [has been] brought to a complete standstill'. Williamson had not been doing well before the war. Annual profits had fallen from a comfortable £27,000 in 1912 and £23,000 in 1913 to only £12,000 in the year ending 31 December 1914.[18] Such a trend pointed to a fate like that of the recently expired Lancashire Watch Company. Nevertheless, the clouds of war brought silver linings for, as the firm's chairman noted, the end of clock imports from Germany 'presented an opportunity'. Unfortunately, the government refused to allow any partly foreign-made clocks to be imported; this hindered an intended extension to Williamson's Buren factory in Switzerland. Although Williamson somehow managed to obtain licenses to import small numbers, for a time it was unable to take full advantage of Buren's putative capacity.[19]

As the war continued things improved and Williamson prospered. The firm came to enjoy unprecedented levels of profitability. Government contracts to make watches led to net profits of £47,000 in March 1916. Following McKenna's protectionist budget, the company's annual report enthused that

> the present state of the country is almost comparable to that of a highly protected country. Imports are reduced to the minimum, our greatest [domestic] competitor [Rotherham] is out of the market, and we and our Allies are consuming the products of our workshops. The consequence is that labour is well-paid.[20]

Net profits grew from £67,000 in 1917 to £105,000 in 1918, when dividends of 5 per cent on Ordinary shares were announced. The financial position of the company was declared 'excellent, the cash and debts being twice the amount due to creditors' and the 'reserves and contingencies fund' was added to by substantial amounts.[21] Government contracts kept Williamson busy, making 'large quantities of watches [which] are being used by both Army and Navy'. Their optical workshop in London worked flat out to fill 500 ophthalmic orders a day. A new factory was opened at Chezard, Switzerland, 'for the production of a special type of cheap watch... for which there will unquestionably be a big demand'.[22] Williamson's Buren factory eventually resumed full production and it, too, flourished.

Chronometers: an Indian summer

In Britain, the two sectors of the watch industry most affected by the war – and which most benefited from it – were firms that made chronometers and wristwatches. Suppliers of chronometers experienced a surge in demand brought about by a massive increase in the size of the Royal Navy between 1914 and 1918. Manpower in shipping nearly doubled, from 250,000 to about 450,000. As in earlier wars, most sailors, especially officers, wanted watches if they did not already have one. The number of warships doubled, from 648 to 1,354. When ships were lost in action, so were their instruments. Some 223 major ships were casualties of the sea war, including forty-one battleships and cruisers.[23] A massive ship rebuilding programme resulted. A side-effect was an unprecedented demand for navigation instruments. It upset the previous near-equilibrium between the supply of and demand for chronometers. Hitherto the potential capacity of makers to supply instruments had enabled them comfortably to meet effective demand. According to Thomas Russell & Son, one of Liverpool's leading retailers, the level of new demand was unmatched 'since the days of 1870- at which date we... recall the difficulties of supply'.[24] After 1914, the increase in demand for new chronometers was extraordinary; every ship loss and new commission pumped up requirements. New chronometers could not be made overnight by traditional labour-intensive methods; it took time for Kullberg and Mercer to increase supply in Clerkenwell and St Albans. A sudden acceleration of output was difficult for a small, and aging workforce.

To enlarge its stocks the government adopted two approaches. First, it appealed to the public to sell, loan or donate chronometers. This was legally enforced in 1917 by the Defence of the Realm Regulations that authorised the Hydrographer of the Navy to acquire the 'name, number, date of manufacture, description and present purpose' for which every chronometer in the country was used. Those that were thus recruited were called 'parsonage' chronometers (because some wealthy clerics owned superior timekeepers to which they synchronised other house clocks and, perhaps, indulged in the hobby of astronomy).[25] To bring them up to Admiralty standard they were sent for overhaul and repair to the remaining makers. Usher & Cole, for example, undertook to service and refurbish chronometers; in all 'about 140 were converted before the end of hostilities in November 1918'.[26]

The second strategy was to try to increase the supply of new instruments. Thus Frank Mercer, scion of his family's great chronometer-making firm, was called out of the Army after two years and ordered by the Admiralty to return to St Albans to direct his firm's workshops.[27] First, he tried to secure the supply of fusee chains and found that their construction had almost stopped in Christchurch, the only British location where this essential component was made (Chapter 10). Just one firm survived there. 'The tools were intact, primitive but usable', Mercer commented, 'and the one craftsman who was left had... finished but was alive and very helpful'. Mercer arranged for the tools to be bought and shipped to St Albans, where he intended to centralise production. He then went to Prescot to look for movements 'in a form that would cut out the waste of effort of doing things twice, and which had gone on for a century'. Mercer's graphic description illustrated the debilitated condition of one facet of English chronometer manufacturing:

> It was an afternoon in early winter that I arrived in uniform, and I explained to them what was required, there was no question of price – they could ask what they liked, but it was to be done our way... That night we were full of the task ahead and we always retired to the Kings Arms to cement the matter, and I went to bed a satisfied man. Alas in the morning all was changed. They refused to cooperate in the slightest degree, and I went back a depressed man. The Admiralty [agent] said I had sergeant-majored them and went himself and got a worse reception than I did. All these things at the time seemed so sad and unnecessary, but one must not forget they were all old and had been years in the craft. They had to all [intents] and purposes slept for many years, and the rousing up was too much for them...'

Mercer nevertheless pressed ahead and eventually succeeded in concentrating most chronometer production at his St Albans factory. The Admiralty hoped that he would increase chronometer output five-fold. By the end of the war, he had expanded it seven-fold. During the war years, the firm's employees increased from 24 in 1914 to 68 in 1918 (40 men and 28 women).[28] An indication of how output increased can be seen in Table17.2.

Despite the loss of over 5,000 ships of all sizes, the Admiralty's reserve stock of instruments remained adequate, aided by the retrieval of parsonage chronometers and boosted by Mercer's efforts in St Albans.[29] Consequently, by the end of the war, stocks of chronometers were vast. Mercer's war-time efforts left the Admiralty with a supply of instruments

Table 17.2 Average annual issues of chronometers from Admiralty stock and numbers sent for repair, in selected years between 1890 and 1915–19

Years	*Average annually issued*	*Average annually repaired*
1890	703	368
1897–99	1115	403
1901–05	1326	599
1907–10	1516	644
1911–14	1679	841
1915–19	5316	2074

Source: Compiled from annual abstracts of the 'Astronomer Royal's Reports to the Board of Visitors', in the *Horological Journal* from 1890 to 1920.

that proved to be greater in the post-war years than was the effective demand for them. Thereafter these surplus stocks, with the increased use of the new technology of radio time-signals, hastened the decline in the manufacturing of new chronometers.

Wristwatches

Just as the American civil war boosted demand for Waltham's pocket watches, so the Great War stimulated demand for wristwatches, mainly to the benefit of the American and Swiss firms that already led in their production (Chapter 12). They became popular among the military, perhaps because pocket watches were deemed unsuitable for warfare: wrist watches performed a functional need by freeing up the hand needed to take a watch out of a pocket. At first, wire lugs were soldered on to pocket watches, and a leather strap was attached. Then watch companies, led by Ingersoll, copied and made 'military trench watches'. They offered a 'serviceman's watch' that included a face with a black dial and yellow luminous painted numbers.[30] They were advertised as being legible on night duty in the trenches 'where the slightest glimmer of light, even the striking of a match, may lead to serious disaster'. A specially designed watch was made for submarine personnel. It was watertight, non-magnetic, and less susceptible to expansion and contraction in temperature fluctuations. Some manufacturers even converted ladies watches into military timepieces to keep up with demand. By 1918, about 85 per cent of Ingersoll's watches had luminous dials. In the armed forces of both protagonists, the wearing of wristwatches became popular, particularly among telephone and signal units.[31] Early in 1916 Williamson's annual report noted that 'one soldier in every four wears a wristlet watch, and the other three mean to get one as soon as they can. Wristlet watches are not luxuries...'[32]

Wristwatches became popular firstly with officers and then they became attractive to the public. 'Until comparatively recently', the *Horological Journal* commented, 'the bracelet watch has been looked upon in this country as more or less a joke. Vaudeville artists and moving picture actors have utilized it as a fun maker. Now... the status of the watch is changing'.[33] A spurt in domestic demand was attributed to the blackout caused by the need to take precautions against Zeppelin bombing raids.

> People used formerly not to bother much about their watches, because there are so many clocks about. But now after dark these are both invisible and silent. Consequently many people... found the need for a reliable timekeeper of their own.[34]

When the demand for wristwatches accelerated it resulted in the greatest shift in the style of wearing a watch since the introduction of men's waistcoats about a century and a half earlier. In December 1917 the

Horological Journal, perhaps with some exaggeration, observed 'The wristlet watch was little used by the sterner sex before the war, but now is seen on the wrist of nearly every man in uniform and of many men in civilian attire'.[35] By the end of the war 'it could be said that age of the pocket watch was over. Never again, Sunday best apart, was the pocket watch to have the importance it once held in male attire'.[36] Wristwatches, with or without luminous dials, were henceforth well established in the British market.

The horological workforce

The war radically changed the nature and prospect of the horological labour force. Employees prospered in the busy chronometer sector and in Williamson's watch factory. So did those in other watchmaking firms that diversified and made war materiel, like Rotherham, the Coventry Cooperative, and even the local engineering firm that rose out of the ashes of the LWC.[37] All became busy with war orders. The war particularly affected the employment of younger workers in the industry because of the military's almost insatiable demand for recruits. Grimshaw, Baxter & Elliott, the leading clockmaking firm, reported that 'a large number of employees have joined the Army, Navy, and various branches of the service... it has been found impossible to replace the men'. It is likely that watchmaking firms were similarly affected. When Grimshaw re-tooled a new factory, put up to replace German imports, he employed women.[38] Frodsham also lost some of their skilled men to war service and munitions work. Because of difficulties in obtaining supplies, the firm closed its speedometer and motor accessories department and sold the stock and goodwill to Messrs Robert Benson North & Son.[39]

One problem was partly solved by recruiting women into factories where they were converted into semi-skilled machine-tool operators. Replacing watch repairers was more difficult. At first, German prisoners of war who had themselves been watchmakers or repairers were kept in camps on the Isle of Man and did repairs for some British firms. But the practice aroused complaints, on the grounds that they were undercutting prices charged by the native jobbers who had not joined the army.[40] The shortage of watch repairers persisted and, by the end of the war. it had become a 'great scarcity... new blood was needed: the repairer of the future must be among the elite of craftsmen both in capability and pay'.[41]

This touched the heart of the problem. Low rates of pay in the industry had been noted in Booth's survey of Clerkenwell in the 1890s. Watchmaking was simply unable to compete with wages offered by newer, competing, sister industries. In Coventry and elsewhere, those responsible for organizing repair courses did their best, but it was not possible to force students to take up watchmaking as a career and then to keep them. In 1916, in the middle of the Great War, the *Horological Journal* observed:

> Coventry failures in the watch trade [subsequently] started in the engineering trade and made Coventry a success... The most successful men in the engineering trade were those who had at first had an horological training... Boys who had gone through the technical classes and learned their business and had a year's training in the workshops were able to earn twice as much at making taximeters and instruments of that sort.[42]

The difficulty of recruiting skilled craftsmen for repair work, and the uncertain structure of the post-war industry worried the BHI's officials.[43] One solution was to train disabled ex-servicemen. Wounded soldiers were therefore encouraged to enrol for special repairing classes at the BHI and in technical schools in Willesden, Barnsley, Manchester, Worthing, Wrexham, Swansea, and elsewhere if needed. Starting wages of 27s 6d a week were promised, with the incentive of 5s weekly bonuses at the end of the year. There was also mention of a 'clock factory for disabled men'.[44] Although it was conceded that 'scientific and technical training is a matter of several years, and the industry has suffered neglect for a generation or so...' even one year's instruction would be beneficial. Appeals were made to the trade to 'help these men'.[45] At first, it seemed to work. Under the auspices of the Trade Advisory Committee only six months after the end of the war about 400 disabled ex-servicemen were being trained in London and another 200 elsewhere.[46] But by 1921 there were complaints that the training of disabled ex-servicemen was overdone; 'all that was happening was that an oversupplied trade was being further crowded with inefficient workers, who expected £4 a week after twelve to eighteen months' training'.[47] The intentions had been well-meaning, but the consequences were unacceptable to those already in the industry. Well before the end of the war the BHI debated the future of the industry. Frank Mercer, currently immersed in manufacturing chronometers for the war effort, argued that

> The time was ripe for a new start, and the old methods should be swept away. He had formed an opinion that it was doubtful whether the watchmaking industry could be revived, but he felt confident that the future of clockmaking was bright, especially if we recognised that the electric clock was the clock of the future.[48]

Mercer's remarks prompted W.E. Tucker, managing director of Williamson, to read a paper at the BHI on 'The future of British Horology'. This inaugurated another of the incessant self-examinations to which the Institute had always been prone, with its familiar variations about the woes of British watchmaking.[49] The debate started with the admission that the rump of England's traditional watchmaking industry, with its remaining outworkers in Clerkenwell, Coventry and Prescot was, to all intents and purposes, dead. Although his prediction about electric clocks proved inexact and optimistic, Mercer was correct in his conclusion that England's old watchmaking industry could not be revived. Even firms like Williamson that had enjoyed war-induced prosperity, now faced a cold post-war era in which they would again be exposed to massive competition from Switzerland and the United States. The 1914–18 War administered the coup de grace to the English watch industry, despite the fine quality of the work by Clerkenwell's remaining makers.

Armistice and afterwards

The armistice delivered a mortal blow to the demand for new chronometers, although it took some time for production to die. Overnight the bottom dropped out of the market for the instruments. Outstanding orders for the Royal Navy were abruptly cancelled. Even the Greenwich Trials, which had run almost annually for nearly a century, were abandoned, and Henry Raper's *The Practice of Navigation and Nautical Astronomy*, routinely in print since 1840, published its twentieth and last edition in 1920.[50] In 1923, the Astronomer Royal received letters from impoverished craftsmen pleading for more orders for chronometers. The problem was that the old instruments were so good they did not wear out.[51] By the late 1920s, it was increasingly difficult to find skilled workmen able to service and maintain the Admiralty's own large stock of instruments. Firms that had once made chronometers, like Usher & Cole, were absorbed by Camerer Cuss & Company in New Oxford Street; they moved into the retailing and repair end of the antiquarian horological market.[52] The two great chronometer firms, Mercer and Kullberg, experienced different destinies. The House of Mercer survived because it successfully diversified into specialist instrument making. In the nineteen twenties it made 'cat's whiskers for the first radios, electricity meters, cigarette-lighters, fly-traps, cine-cameras, x-ray switches, cigarette lighters, and 'anything that kept the staff busy'.[53]

The House of Kullberg's fate was different. The firm's business records reveal its protracted terminal decline. During war years Kullberg had constructed an average of nearly 150 new instruments a year; annual receipts for manufacturing and repairs had amounted to over £4,200. Kullberg had been busy and profitable. After the Armistice, only a handful of chronometers were finished. Through the 1920s as demand for new instruments virtually ceased, even repair work fell to a third of its former level. The House of Kullberg's annual revenue shrank to a few hundred pounds in the 1930s and the great firm withered away.[54] The effect of what was to be crucial nail in the mechanical chronometer's coffin had been anticipated as early as 1912 when the Astronomer Royal wondered 'if the chronometer was not already a thing of the past, superseded by wireless telegraphy?' The noted inventor Frank Hope-Jones forecast that 'chronometer manufacturing would be ousted by wireless telegraphy, as the art of steel engraving [was] killed by the photographic process'.[55] The emerging technology of radio time-signals obviated reliance on mechanical timepieces and enabled ordinary timepieces to help determine longitude. The end of chronometer manufacturing by the House of Kullberg effectively marked the demise of England's traditional watchmaking. The last generation of craftsmen grew old, died, and was not replaced.[56] Clerkenwell had been at the heart of the English watchmaking industry since the seventeenth century. Traditional watchmaking and chronometer manufacturing died, to borrow T.S. Eliot's phrase, 'not with a bang but a whimper'.

Acknowledgments

The evidence and analysis of this chapter draw heavily on my 'English Horology and the Great War', *Antiquarian Horology*, 32/5 (March 2011), 535–50. © Antiquarian Horological Society.

Notes

1 *Watchmaker, Jeweller and Silversmith*, 40/9 (Sept. 1914), passim.
2 *Watchmaker, Jeweller and Silversmith*, 40/10 (Oct 1914), 1303.
3 See advertisements in *Horological Journal* (Nov.1914, et seq.), and in *Watchmaker, Jeweller and Silversmith* (Jan. 1915 et seq.)
4 McKenna resigned when Lloyd George eventually succeeded Asquith as Prime Minister.
5 *Horological Journal*, 58/2 (Oct. 1915), 20.
6 *Horological Journal*, 59/1 (Sept. 1916), 10–11.
7 *Horological Journal*, 59/1 (Sept. 1916), 12.
8 *Horological Journal*, 57/6 (Feb 1915), 69–72, reprinting information from the Board of Trade's Commercial Intelligence Pamphlet, number 102.
9 Indeed, after the war, trade in alarm clocks renewed, with prices firstly at 14s and then at 9s 6d, and 6s in 1920 as conditions stabilised and output increased: *Horological Journal*, 62/4 (Dec. 1920), 41.
10 *Horological Journal*, 57/6 (Feb. 1915), 6; 57/1 (Sept. 1914), 10–11.
11 *Board of Trade Journal* (Jan. 1915), 163; (June 1915), 805; and (Dec. 1916), 875.
12 *Board of Trade Journal* (Dec. 1915), 660; (Jan. 1916), 100–01; and (Sept. 1916), 755.
13 The Fairs were held annually until 1939, except in 1925, the second year of Wembley's British Empire Exhibition.
14 *ASP*: 128/3: United States Department of Commerce, Supplement to Commerce Reports (May 1922): Trade information Bulletin No 24: *South African Trade in Watches and Clocks*, by Peter J. Stevenson.
15 Many watches and instruments were made for the American Expeditionary Forces. See *ASP*: 130: U.S. Bureau of Foreign and Domestic Commerce:

Special Agents' Series: No. 210, *Switzerland: A Commercial and Industrial Handbook*, by H. Lawrence Groves (1921), 54–57. For the boom in the Swiss horological industry caused by the war – and the stagnation which followed it, with details of the output of various categories of timepieces, see Groves; also *ASP* 132, U.S. Bureau of Foreign and Domestic Commerce: Miscellaneous Series. No. 90, *The Economic Position of Switzerland during the War*, by Louis A. Rufeuer (1919), 36–37. For British reports on Swiss horology see *Board of Trade Journal*, 105/1239 (Aug. 1920), 246; and *Board of Trade Journal*, 106/1279 (June 1921), 606.

16 Hugh Rotherham, 'The Watch Trade Past and Present', *Horological Journal*, 70/10 (June 1928), 182.

17 Henry Cooke, 'Visit of BHI Members to Coventry', *Horological Journal*, 71/12 (Aug. 1929), 282–84.

18 *Horological Journal*, 57/7 (March 1915), 101–02: Report of the 17th Ordinary Share Meeting of H. Williamson, Ltd.

19 *Horological Journal*, 60/7 (March 1918), 68–70.

20 *Horological Journal*, 58/7 (March 1916), 97.

21 *Horological Journal*, 59/7 (March 1917), 79; 60/7 (March 1918), 68; 61/7 (March 1919), 82.

22 *Horological Journal*, 59/7 (March 1917), 79–81.

23 For war statistics, see http://www.navalhistory.net/WW1NavyBritishAdmiraltyEstimates1919.htm Table 1, 'Numbers of H.M. Ships at the Outbreak of War and at Date of the Armistice'; Table 2, 'H.M. Ships and Auxiliary Vessels completed ... 1914–1918'; Table 3, 'Losses of H.M. Ships from all causes between 1914 and 1918'.

24 Advertisement in Kelly's *Directory, 1917*, 21.

25 *Horological Journal*, 60/4 (Dec. 1917), 14, sets out Regulation 15C; also *Horological Journal*, 61/6 (Feb. 1919), 65.

26 J.F. Cole, and T.P. Camerer Cuss, *A Watchmaking Centenary: Usher and Cole, 1861–1961* (np probably London: pamphlet, 1961): online at http://freepages.genealogy.rootsweb.ancestry.com/~usher/usheruk/docs/UsherCole150dpi.pdf], 20; and Terence Camerer Cuss, 'Usher & Cole Workbooks', *Antiquarian Horology*, 39/3 (Sept. 2018), 368–74 (quote, 369).

27 *Horological Journal*, 59/1 (Sept. 1917), 1–2. See also typescript memoir by Frank Mercer in Mercer Archives, Prescot Museum, [now in Liverpool] entitled 'Christchurch 1916'. The following paragraph draws from this source.

28 Tony Mercer, letter, 18 August 1977.

29 Calculated from annual abstracts of 'Astronomer Royal's Reports to the Board of Visitors', *Horological Journal.*

30 The girls who painted them regularly twirled the paint brushes between their lips to get a good point', not knowing then of the toxicity of radium: Eric Street, 'The Hazards of an Early Luminous Watch', *Antiquarian Horology*, 13/4 (June 1982), 383–84.

31 *Horological Journal*, 59/2 (Oct. 1916), 18–19; also Lawrence Wright, *Clockwork Man: The Story of Time* (London: Elek, 1968), 206–07.

32 *Horological Journal*, 58/7 (March 1916), 98.

33 *Horological Journal*, 59/2 (Oct. 1916), 18–19.

34 *Horological Journal*, 57/3 (Nov. 1914), 11 and 36.

35 *Horological Journal*, 60/4 (Dec 1917), 41.

36 David Penney, 'Wristwatches', in davidpenney@antiquewatchstore.com

37 The Great War generated demand in the former Lancashire Watch Company for specialised work on ships' clocks and compasses and other military requirements. In the 1920s it made ticket punching machines for tram cars;

during the Second World War it dropped 'clock' from its title and made small parts. It closed in 1969.

38 *Horological Journal*, 57/9 (May 1915), 123.
39 LMA/CLC/B/043/MS19904: 350ff, Frodsham Directors Meeting, 24 Dec. 1917.
40 *Horological Journal*, 58/10 (June 1916), 133.
41 *Horological Journal*, 60/4 (Dec. 1917), 37.
42 *Horological Journal*, 59/1 (Sept. 1916), 11.
43 *Horological Journal*, 60/5 (Jan. 1918), 46 and id., 60/10 (June 1918), 104.
44 *Horological Journal*, 60/12 (Aug. 1918), 138; and 61/2 (Oct. 1918), 14–16.
45 *Horological Journal*, 61/6 (Feb. 1919), 68.
46 *Horological Journal*, 61/7 (March 1919), 74.
47 *Horological Journal*, 63/5 (Jan. 1921), 63.
48 *Horological Journal*, 60/1 (Sept. 1917), 2.
49 The debate can be followed in the *Horological Journal*.
50 *Horological Journal*, 62/10 (1920), 150–51; and Henry Raper, *The Practice of Navigation and Nautical Astronomy* (1840: London: J.D. Potter, 20th and last ed. 1920),
51 Jonathan Betts, *Time Restored: The Harrison Timekeepers and R.T. Gould, the Man Who Knew (Almost) Everything* (Oxford: Oxford UP and National Maritime Museum, 2006), 121.
52 Usher & Cole, *A Watchmaking Centenary*, passim; Terence Camerer Cuss, 'Usher & Cole Workbooks', *Antiquarian Horology*, 39/3 (Sept 2018), 368–74.
53 F.A. (Tony) Mercer, Radical Tom Mercer and the House He Founded (Ashford, Brant Wright, 1978), 97; also letter, 18 August 1977.
54 For more details see Alun C. Davies, 'The Life and Death of a Scientific Instrument: The Marine Chronometer', *Annals of Science*, 35 (1978), at https://doi.org/10.1080/00033797800200391
55 *Horological Journal*, 55/5 (Jan. 1913), 73
56 A.J. Meadows, *Greenwich Observatory: II: Recent History, 1836–1975* (London: Taylor and Francis 1975), 59ff.

Postscript
The Third Horological Era

Britain's watch industry's temporary resurrection

Britain's domestic watchmaking industry was reborn in 1932, resurrected like a phoenix from the ashes, and it flourished for a decade or two. Its reincarnation was led by Samuel Smith's company, founded in 1851. Initially, the firm had retailed clocks, watches, and jewellery before expanding its manufacturing interests to include motor accessories. Expansion into other fields transformed a family firm into a professionally-run managerial multinational enterprise. Then, in the 1930s, Smiths reinvented itself and built an entirely new business in clocks and watches. It took advantage of innovations in electrical equipment to make alarms and electric clocks by circumventing traditional mechanical clock technology, thus lending some merit to Frank Mercer's prognosis (Chapter 17). A moribund sector of British manufacturing was temporarily reincarnated. Recognising the great shift in the nature of demand, Smiths made wristwatches in Cheltenham, Enfield and, in partnership with Ingersoll, at Ystradgynlais, an old iron town near Swansea. By 1948, Smiths had become 'probably the largest single manufacturer of clocks and watches in the world'.[1] But, like its Clerkenwell forbears in the first and second eras of traditional mechanical watchmaking it, too, became a victim of new technologies. The sources of power in the technology of the first horological era were falling weights and unwinding springs. The second horological era, dating from the middle seventeenth century, greatly refined precision, with pendulums for clocks, main springs for watches, better raw materials, and improved organisation of production. The third horological era was based on new technologies in the form of batteries, quartz crystals, and an electronics revolution. Smith's horological division limped on until 1982. Then, after 132 years, time ran out for the firm's connection with timekeeping. With it any went serious attempt by British firms at competition in the world's watch markets.

The third horological era

The Second World War had temporarily revived mechanical chronometers because of the need to keep radio silence, and when radio reception was sometimes at the mercy of weather conditions. Once again in Britain, old instruments were called in for refurbishing. But the centre of their manufacture moved to the United States. A sufficiently large war-induced demand for new instruments resulted in the Hamilton Watch Company successfully applying the 'American system' to mass produce chronometers of exceptionally high quality.[2] After the war, new technologies evolved at a dizzying pace and time-keeping devices entered its third era. Many hundreds of years had spanned the two earlier eras of mechanical clockwork. As important as the impact of the pendulum, balance spring, and wheel-cutting engines, and as dramatic as was Waltham's revolution had been, so too was the impact of the new electronic technologies on precision, output, and prices. The long dominance of mechanical timepieces came to an end. Spring-powered watches gave way to electric ones, facilitated by miniaturised motors and batteries. Quartz crystal watches enabled phenomenal precision to be achieved.[3] Their versatility permitted multiple complex functions. As well as telling the time and date, even relatively cheap watches could perform several functions: they could track sleep, monitor fitness (count steps) and health (record heartbeats and count calories), and much else. Mechanical chronometers almost disappeared, except as collectables. Quartz movements rendered checking radio updates unnecessary. Fairly inexpensive Global Positioning System (GPS) receivers gave the position of a yacht, ship, or car to within a few feet anywhere on the earth.[4]

In the world's watch markets, competition in the third era was at first led by Switzerland, Japan, and Russia – the latter's annual output in the 1950s alone reached 24 million watches. By 1970, the output of Switzerland's watch firms exceeded 70 million: it was almost matched by Japan in the 1980s. In the 1990s, the world's watch firms made about 500 million watches annually. But in Britain, there were only a handful of small firms and a few individual watchmakers who still made small numbers of very expensive watches. Britain's once-great mechanical watch industry had disappeared.

Notes

1 James Nye, *A Long Time in Making: The History of Smiths* (Oxford: Oxford UP, 2014); Richard Good, 'Smiths at Cheltenham: The Rise and Fall of 20th Century English Watchmaking', *Horological Journal*, 141/10 (Oct. 1999), part 1; 340–42; part 2, *Horological Journal*, 141/11 (Nov. 1999), 372–74.

2 A.G. Randall, 'Hamilton Marine Chronometer No. 503', *Antiquarian Horology*, 19/3 (Spring 1991), 261–70. The exceptional war demand resulted in Hamilton making over 13,000 instruments, at a monthly average of 430.

3 Amy Glasmeier, 'Technological Discontinuities and Flexible Production Networks: The Case of Switzerland and the World Watch Industry', *Research Policy*, 20 (1991), 469–85. https://doi.org/10.1016/0048-7333(91)90070-7

4 J.E.D. Williams, *From Sails to Satellites. The Origin and Development of Navigational Science* (Oxford: Oxford UP, 1992), 104.

Bibliography

Abbreviations

ASP American State Papers
BPP British Parliamentary Papers
BWCC British Watch and Clock Company
LMA London Metropolitan Archives
LWC Liverpool Watch Company
NAWCC National Association of Watch and Clock Collectors (USA: 'Bulletin of the')
ODNB Oxford Dictionary of National Biography (2004: online from major libraries)
UP University Press

Primary Sources

A: Manuscripts

London Metropolitan Archives **(Formerly catalogued as Guildhall Archives)**
1. The Worshipful Company of Clockmakers.

See John Bromley, *The Clockmakers' Library: The Catalogue of the Books and Manuscripts of the Worshipful Company of Clockmakers* (London: Sotheby, 1977); and S.E. Atkins and W.H. Overall, *Some Account of the Worshipful Company of Clockmakers* (London: Privately printed, 1881)

LMA/CLC/L/CD/B/001/MS02710/001/1–14: Clockmakers' Company, Court Minute Books, 14 vols from 1632–1933.

LMA/CLC/L/CD/C/015/MS02722: Register of turnover of Apprentices.

LMA/CLC/L/CD/E/001/MS02727/001–002: Committee for … the more effectual suppression of malpractices in the trade, 1808–1815' (2 vols: vol. 1, 1808–13. vol. 2, 1813–15).

LMA/CLC/L/CD/E/029/MS02728: Committee appointed to examine illicit introduction of foreign clocks and watches; 1814 to 1819.

LMA/CLC/L/CD/E/006/MS03943: Papers on various subjects, 1671–1860

LMA/CLC/L/CD/C/001/MS03939/1 Apprentices, 1632–96.

LMA/CLC/L/CD/E/008/MS03940/001 and LMA/CLC/L/CD/E/008/MS03940/002: patents, hallmarks, and imports.

LMA/CLC/L/CD/G/003/MS03941/41 person not having served apprenticeship, 1654.

LMA/CLC/L/CD/G/003/MS03941/54: Petition on Apprenticeships.

LMA/CLC/L/CD/G/003/MS03941: January 1832 (Sixth) Memorial to the Treasury.
LMA/CLC/L/CD/A/013/MS03942/17: Charter and Byelaws of the Company, 1795.
LMA/CLC/L/CD/E/006/MS03943/10: Ingold prospectus, 28 October 1842.
LMA/CLC/L/CD/E/006/MS03943/11: intended agents for the BWCC.
LMA/CLC/L/CD/E/006/MS03943/12, 13, 14, concerning the BWCC
LMA/CLC/L/CD/E/006/MS03943/88: newspaper clippings, 1842.
LMA/CLC/L/CD/E/028/MS03944/15, 16, 17, 24. Assorted resolutions.
LMA/CLC/L/CD/E/028/MS03944/22/28/35–43/45/46–55/56/59/60/63/64/65/92/93: Memorials, newspaper clippings (dated 1823, 1828, and 1839).
LMA/CLC/L/CD/E/002/MS03951/ 43–45, 53a, 60, 61, 62, 63, 65, 66. Correspondence.
LMA/CLC/L/CD/E/002/MS03951/27–33/49, 56, 58 and 59. Correspondence with the Treasury.
LMA/CLC/L/CD/E/002/MS03951/68: Resolutions of meeting, 2 June 1814.
LMA/CLC/L/CD/E/002/MS03951/69: Copy of a circular letter 6 June 1814.
LMA/CLC/L/CD/E/002/MS03951/73, newspaper advertisements on 1817
LMA/CLC/L/CD/E/002/MS03951/74. Clockmakers' Company Circular
LMA/CLC/L/CD/E/002/MS03951/74a: Report, and List of Donations Received.'
LMA/CLC/L/CD/E/002/MS03951/81: Letter on the distress of the trade.
LMA/CLC/L/CD/E/031/MS03961: Vulliamy's 'census', 1782,
LMA/CLC/L/CD/E/033/MS03962: names and addresses, arranged topographically.
LMA/CLC/L/CD/E/032/MS03977: Henry Clarke's Census 1813
LMA/CLC/L/CD/B/005/MS03975: Abstracts, and index to journals of the Clockmakers' Company (1632–1816).
2. **William Birch of Fenchurch Street,**
LMA/ CLC/B/024/MS14,470: (Watch books, 1840–1920: 5 vols)
3. **William Connell: of 22 Myddleton Street, and 83 Cheapside.**
LMA/CLC/B/057/MS14373/1 and 2. Stock books, 1847–1902.
LMA/CLC/B/057/MS14,374: Account Book, 1862–1899.
4. **Daniel Desbois and Sons, of High Holborn**
LMA/CLC/B/064/MS14284: Daybooks, 1855–1916 (11 vols.)
LMA/CLC/B/064/MS14285/010, ledger, 15 January 1912.
5. **Charles Frodsham: of Bond Street (later of New Bond Street).**
LMA/CLC/B/043/MS19904: Minute Book, 1893–1939.
LMA/CLC/B/043/MS19906/001: Watch Manufacturing Book (1876–89).
LMA/CLC/B/176/MS19910: Record of retail sales.
LMA/CLC/B/176/MS19914/001–005: Customers and manufacturers, 1900–41.
6. **Victor Kullberg, 105 Liverpool Road**
For a note on the Kullberg archives see Bromley, *Clockmakers' Library*, 117–18. Also A.C. Davies. 'House of Kullberg', *Antiquarian Horology*, 35/11 (March 2014), 635ff. The main divisions are:
LMA/CLC/B/141/MS14537/001–002: Manufacturing Books.
LMA/CLC/B/141/MS14538/001–008: Indexed by Customer, private and retail.
LMA/CLC/B/141/MS14539/001–004: Ledgers of business with Retailers, 1857–92.

LMA/CLC/B/141/MS14537-46 and LMA/CLC/B/141/MS14546-54. Shop Day Books, Workshop Repair Books, Letter Books (Out and In), Journals, Stock-lists, and Account books with various outside repairers and suppliers.

7. **Preston and Sons of Prescot, Lancs. movement makers**

LMA/CLC/B/141/MS14545/7–8: Cash Books for Parr's Bank, 1893–1904.

LMA/CLC/B/MS138: two volumes describing parts c1890–95 and 1892–1914.

8. **William Turner of Fenchurch Street**

LMA/CLC/B/176/MS19914/001–005; Customers and manufacturers, 1900–41.

LMA/ CLC/B/024/MS14469: Workday book, 1834–39: 1 vol.

9. **Thwaites and Reed: Clockmakers of Bowling Green.**

LMA/CLC/B/215/MS6788/002 and 003: (vol. 2, 1788–98; vol. 3, 1798–1804.

LONDON, Patent Office

No. 9,511 (8 Nov. 1842) and No. 9,752 (1 Jan. 1843) relating to the Ingold episode.

LONDON, Public Record Office: Board of Trade Papers.

BT: 334/2531; BT:1/407/44; BT:5/51/595, 8 and BT:1/545/2050/57: Ingold episode

LONDON: London University, Senate House Library (UofL/MSS)

MS755 (1784–1818), Isaac Rogers papers (1788–1818) and manuscript (1784–1814) material, including letters, petitions and historical articles (W.A.S. Hewins, rev. George White, 'Rogers, Isaac (1754? –1839?), watch and clock-maker', *ODNB* (2004)).

MS 755, Material Relating to the Clockmakers' Company: Folios 1–11, Folios 39–40, 44, 46–47 (1790), Folios 88–89, 91, 93–101: Folios 106–07: *The Case of the Distressed Watch and Clockmakers* (1798: Pamphlet); Folios 129, 147, 149 and 159–74.

CAMBRIDGE, University Library: Greenwich Observatory's Longitude papers.

RGO MSS 5/229 (1–120); Admiralty's Letters on Chronometers to Pond, 1820s.

CARDIFF St Fagans Folk Museum

'Samuel Roberts, *Register of Clock, 1755–74*': photographic facsimiles made in the 1930s and the 1970s.

EDINBURGH: See National Register of Archives (Scotland),

No. 0248: Records of James Ritchie and Son (Clockmakers) Ltd., formerly of 12 South St James Street, Edinburgh; Head Office, at 54 Broughton Street, EH1 3SA

MSS vol. 1: Repairs Book, 1809–1812; (cited as *Shop Book*); vol. 2: Watch Book.

MANCHESTER Central Library

The Stubs Archives; Boxes 24 and 25: catalogues, price lists, pattern books, orders, invoices, correspondence between Stubs and outworkers in the Prescot area.

Local History Collection: index listing horological entries in newspaper clippings.

PRESCOT: Horological Museum (Now in LIVERPOOL National Museum)

Typescript memoir by Frank Mercer, entitled "Christchurch 1916".

Typescript "Interim Report," on "Prescot Horological Workshops," Jan. 1983.

Miscellaneous: Letter from Theo Barker to Professor David S. Torrens, 1952.

B. Primary Published

Newspapers and Journals

The Times

Clerkenwell News (at Kew)

Horological Journal, The (Monthly since Sept. 1858).

Watchmaker, Jeweller, and Silversmith, The (Monthly since August 1875).

***American Horological Journal* (1869–73)** *(at New York Public Library)*
***Jewellers' Circular and Horological Review* (1874 on)** (at NYPL)

British Parliamentary Papers (BPP)

Year: Vol. no: Description

1797: Act of Parliament: 'Duties on Clocks and Watches Act 1797 (38 Geo. III, c. 108).
1797–98: Vol. 53: Petitions, 27 February 1798, concerning Pitt's Tax.
1799–1800: Vol. 109: Accounts and Papers, 51, 1009 (2) and 1,013 (2), Relating to Pitt's tax.
1813–14: Vol. 69; *and* 1817–18: Vol. 72; *and* 1818: Vol. 73; *and* 1819: Vol. 74: 'Petitions of Grievances.'
1817: Vol. 6: 'Statement of Inconveniences', with subsequent correspondence.
1817: Vol. 6: Minutes of Evidence and Report on Petitions of Watchmakers of Coventry' (hereafter *1817 Minutes).*
1818: Vol. 1: 'Bill for the Relief of Watchmakers and for Preventing Frauds in their Trade'.
1818: Vol. 9: Report from the Select Committee 'On the Petitions of Watchmakers of Coventry': Appendix 2, Gold and Silver Watch Cases Assayed, 1796–1817. (hereafter *1818 Report*).
1819: Vol. I-B: A Bill to Regulate the Manufacture of Clocks and Watches.
1824: Vol. 3: Act for Regulating Duties on Imports and Exports of Clocks and Watches ... in Warehouses, ... Without Payment of Duty on the First Entry Thereof. [4 George IV, Ch. 24, sec. 81].
1825: Vol. 3: An Act for the Regulation of the *Customs* Duty Paid on Importation of Foreign Clocks and Watches; Reduced from 50% to 25%). [6 George IV, Ch.107]:
1828: Vol. 1: An Act to Amend Laws Relating to Customs: [9 George IV. Ch 76: 1828.]
1830: Vol. 25: Gold and Silver Watch Cases Annually Stamped at Goldsmith's Hall, London, 1814 to 1829,
1832–33: Act of Parliament, 'Regulating Importation of Clocks and Watches': [3 and 4 William IV, Ch. 52, section 58].
1833: Vol. 33: 'Clocks and Watches Exported since 1825 Showing the Ports of Exportation; also the Number of Clocks and Watches Imported since 1825'.
1836: Vol. 14: 'Report on Commerce and Manufactures of Switzerland by Sir John Bowring.'
1840: Vol. 5: Report on Import Duties, Together with Minutes of Evidence.
1840: Vol. 24: 'Report from Assistant Commissioners, Hand-loom Weavers, ... on Watchmakers' Wages in Coventry, 1838.'
1843: Vol. 1: 'A Bill to Amend Customs Laws... [Concerning] Foreign Makers' Names on the Frame and Face'.
1824 Vol. 17: Excise Licences: Dealers in Watches.

1846–47 [8 and 9 Victoria: cap 86, section 68]: 'Foreign Clocks and Watches, Made in Imitation of the British, Forbidden to be Imported. Warehoused and Reexported.'

1852 Vol. 1: Second Report for the Commissioners for the Exhibition of 1851.

1854 Vol. 36: New York Industrial Exhibition (1853). Reports (i) of British Commissioners; (ii) of Wallis on manufacturing; (iii) of Whitworth on machinery.

1854–55 Vol. 50: 'Report of the Committee on the Machinery of the United States.'

1863 Vol. 53 (part 11): Census Returns for 1861.

1863 Vol. 66: Returns for Imports and Exports: Clocks and Watches, 1840, 1852, 1860–1862. Import Duties Levied ... by Foreign Tariffs on Horological Items).

1864 Vol. 58: Number and Value of Watch Cases (Gold and Silver) Assayed from 1850–63.

1867 Vol. 64: Return of Gold and Silver Watch Cases Number of Watches (1864–66).

1867–68 Vol. 30: Report from the Commissioners: Paris Exhibition, 1867: 'Report on Horological Instruments', by C.R. Weld.

1870 Vol. 63: Trade and Navigation: Export and Import Tables. 1880–1913.

1871 Vol. 36: 'Report of the Commissioners into the Truck System (in 1870)', and Minutes.

1877 Vol. 66: Report on Gold and Silver (Hall Marking), with Minutes, and Appendix.

1877 Vol. 36: Report on the Philadelphia Exhibition, by James C. Watson. 'Horological Instruments'.

1878 Vol. 13: Report on Gold and Silver (Hall Marking), with Minutes, and Appendix.

1880 Vol. 32: Paris Universal Exhibition, 1878: Reports of the Commissioners: Horology.

1880–1913: Imports and Exports.

The annual returns for the years 1880–1913 are from the *Annual Accounts, Trade and Navigation (U.K.)* in the Parliamentary Papers, under the heading *Annual Statement of the Trade of the United Kingdom with Foreign Countries and British Possessions*. The date of the Volume contains returns for the previous year. Hence BPP 1880 (vol. number 71) covers the year 1879. Subsequently, 1881 (87); 1882 (68); 1883 (70); 1884 (78); 1884–85 (75); 1886 (64–1); 1887 (80); 1888 (97); 1889 (75–1); 1890 (72); 1890–91 (82); 1892 (77); 1893–94 (88); 1894 (84); 1895 (95–1); 1896 (83); 1897 (87–1); 1898 (99–1); 1899 (95); 1900 (86–1); 1901 (76–1); 1902 (98); 1903 (69, 70); 1904 (90, 91); 1905 (79, 80); Suppl. 1905 (78–1); 1906 (116, 117); Suppl. 1906 (114); 1907 (82, 830); 1908 (103); 1909 (82, 83); 1910 (87, 88–1); 1911 (79, 80); 1912–13 (85); 1914 (83); 1914–16 (64); 1916 (25).

1893–94 Vol. 91: Chicago Exhibition: Miscellaneous Reports.

1901 Vol. 31: Paris International Exhibition, 1900. 'Clocks, Watches and Timepieces', by J.J.S. Tripplin.

1911 Vol. 101: Census of Production, 1907: Watch and Clock Factories and Workshops.

1917 Vol. 35: Census of England and Wales, 1911: General Report with Appendices.
1917 Vol. 80: 45 (Cd.6896), Census for Scotland, 1911.

British Government Publications

Commons Journal

Vols 34 (1773); 53 (1797–98); 69 (1813–14); and 72 (1817).

Hansard,

1st series, Vol. 27 (for French war crisis, 1814).
3rd series, Vol. 47 (for the Ingold episode, 1842–44).

American State Papers:

i) Consular reports and government papers

American State Papers, [Hereafter ASP]. (Available in the State Paper Room, British Library; Publication is always by the US Department of State, Washington, DC). The several series of consular reports can be traced in [British Museum], *General Catalogue of Printed Books* (London: British Museum, 1966), vol. 244, 445–46. The series start in 1880 and contain occasional reports from consuls on horological trading opportunities. Vols. 1 to 22 are entitled 'Consular Reports.' In Sept 1882 they become 'Monthly Consular Reports', and the series ends with no 357 in June 1910. It resumes with *ASP* 128, US Bureau of Manufactures: *Daily Consular and Trade Reports, New Series, 1910–14.* (54 vols), and continues with *ASP* 128 (2), *Ditto: 1915–21* (65 vols).

ASP, 125: vol. 1 (1881), 'Report' by [US] Consul Mason of Basle (1880).

ASP, 125: Consular Reports, no.18 (April 1882), 534–35, 574.

ASP, 125: Consular Reports, no. 19 (May 1882), 40, 530–55

ASP, 125: Consular Reports, no. 23 (Sept. 1887), 635.

ASP, 125: Consular Reports, no. 35 (Nov. 1883), 4.

ASP, 126: 57 Congress, 1st sess., House of Representatives, [HR] Doc. No.708, part 2: *Special Consular Reports: Silver and Plated Ware in Foreign Countries*: vol. 33 (1902).

ASP, 128/3: *Trade Information Bulletin* No 24: United States Department of Commerce, *Supplement to Commerce Reports* (1922): *South African Trade in Watches and Clocks*, by Peter J. Stevenson.

ASP, 130: U.S. Bureau of Foreign and Domestic Commerce: *Special Agents' Series*: No. 210, *Switzerland: A Commercial and Industrial Handbook*, by H. Lawrence Groves (1921), 54–57.

ASP, 132, U.S. Bureau of Foreign and Domestic Commerce: Miscellaneous Series. No. 90, *The Economic Position of Switzerland during the War*, by Louis A. Rufeuer (1919), 36–37.

ASP, 154/11; 52nd Congress, 2nd Session HR, *Miscellaneous Document*, 117 (1893): *Watches and Clocks*, Statistical Tables Showing US Trade with European Countries from 1790 to 1890.

ASP, 158 Dept. of Commerce and Labour: Analysis of the Foreign Commerce of the US, showing the principal articles forming trade, 1895–1905 (1906)

ASP, 158/5 Ditto: Exports of Manufactures from the US and their Distribution by Articles and Countries, 1800–1906 (In detail, 1895–1905). (1907)

(ii) United States Patents and Census Offices

32 Congress: 1st Session: House Doc no. 102: Edward Riddle. 'Report of the World's Exposition', in *Report of the Commissioner of Patents, 1851.*

Tenth Census, 1880: Manufactures, 183/2: Charles H. Fitch. 'Report on the Manufacture of Interchangeable Mechanisms'.

Twelfth Census, 1900; William Countryman. 'Report on the Growth of the US Watch Industry, 1870–1900.'

Secondary Sources

A. Unpublished Theses and Typescripts

Bailey, F.A. 'MS on Lancashire Watchmaking', Prescot Museum Archive (now in Liverpool World Museum).

Cookson, Gillian. 'The West Yorkshire Textile and Engineering Industry, 1780–18950' (unpublished D. Phil. thesis, York University, 1994), at ID uk.bl.ethos.387169

Dahl, Randle Edwin. 'The American Watch Movement Manufacturing Industry: A Survey Based on the Journals of the Trade' (PhD thesis, Clark University, Worcester, MA, 1941),

Fairclough, Oliver. 'Joseph Finney and the Clock and Watchmakers of Eighteenth Century Liverpool.' (MA thesis, Keele University, 1975).

Mercer, Frank. 'Christchurch 1916' (Typescript Memoir in Mercer Archives, Prescot Museum (now Liverpool World Museum), courtesy of John Griffiths, Former Curator.

Murphy, John Joseph. 'The Establishment of the American Clock Industry: A Study in Entrepreneurial History' (PhD thesis, Yale University, 1961).

Prosser, Robert F. 'Coventry: A Study in Urban Continuity' (MA thesis, Birmingham University, 1955).

Raymond, David J. 'The Royal Navy in the Baltic from 1807–1812' (PhD thesis, Florida State University, Tallahassee, FL, 2010), at https://fsu.digital.flvc.org/islandora/object/fsu:176354/datastream/PDF/view

Searby, Peter. 'Weavers and Freemen in Coventry, 1820–1861: Social and Political Traditionalism in an Early Victorian Town' (PhD thesis, Warwick University, 1972), at http://webcat.warwick.ac.uk/record=b1735976~S15

Tang, Jeffrey D. 'Timely Success: The Role of Locational Lock-in and Path-dependence in the Rise of the South-west Lancashire Watchmaking Industry' (MPhil thesis, Oxford University 1996).

Wang, Tsai-Yeh. 'British Women's Travel Writings in the Era of the French Revolution' (Unpublished PhD thesis, University of Birmingham, 2010), at https://etheses.bham.ac.uk/id/eprint/1029/1/Wang10PhD.pdf.

Ward, R.A.H. 'Watchmaking in the Liverpool Area Before 1730' (BPhil. thesis, Liverpool University, 1970).

Webb, Adrian. 'The Expansion of British Naval Hydrographic Administration, 1808–1829' (unpublished PhD thesis, Exeter University, 2010), at http://hdl.handle.net/10036/116990

Woodward, John. 'Rotherham and Sons, Ltd., the Firm and the Family' (Coventry Public Library, 1975: Typescript MS, Courtesy of Mr A.J. Mealey, sometime principal librarian at CPL).

Wright, Michelle. 'Time, Consciousness, and Narrative Play in Late Medieval Secular Dream Poetry' (PhD thesis, University of Glamorgan, 2007), at https://core.ac.uk/download/pdf/388411.pdf

B. Primary and Secondary Printed Articles and Books

Note: Past numbers of the *Horological Journal* (from 1858) and *Antiquarian Horology* (from 1956) can now be accessed online by members of the British Horological Institute and the Antiquarian Horological Society).

Allen, Aaron M. *The Locksmith Craft in Early Modern Edinburgh* (Edinburgh: Society of Antiquaries of Scotland, 2007).

Allen, G. C. *The Industrial Development of Birmingham and the Black Country, 1860–1927* (London: Routledge, 1929).

Allen, R.C. 'Why the Industrial Revolution Was British: Commerce, Induced Invention, and the Scientific Revolution,' *The Economic History Review*, 64/2 (May 2011), 357–84, at www.jstor.org/stable/41262428

Allix, Charles. Carriage Clocks: *Their Historical Development* (Woodbridge: Antique Collectors Club, 1974).

Allix, Charles. 'Mudge Milestones, Watch Dates,' *Antiquarian Horology*, 13 (Summer 1981). 627–34.

Allwood, John. *The Great Exhibitions* (London: Studio Vista, 1977).

Anderson, Joseph (ed.). *The Town and City of Waterbury, Conn., from the Aboriginal Period to the Year 1895*, vol. 3 (New Haven, CT: Price, Lee and Co., 1896).

Andrewes, William J.H. 'Even Newton Could Be Wrong,' in Andrewes (ed.), *Quest* (1996).

Andrewes, William J.H. 'Finding Local Time at Sea, and the Instruments Employed,' in Andrewes (ed.), *Quest* (1996).

Andrewes, William J.H. (ed.). *The Quest for Longitude: Proceedings of the Longitude Symposium, Harvard University, 1993* (Cambridge, MA: Harvard UP, 1996). [Hereafter Andrewes (ed.), *Quest*.]

Anon. ['A Naval Captain']. 'Letter on Chronometers,' *The Naval Chronicle*, XXVII (1812), 121–22.

Anon. 'Chronometer Accuracy: Verification of the Longitude of Paris,' *The Nautical Magazine and Naval Chronicle* (1838), 402.

Anon. 'Reports and Letters on the Melbourne Exhibition,' *Horological Journal*, 23/9 (May 1880), 23/11 (July 1880), 150–52; 23/12 (Aug. 1880), 162–63.

Anon. 'Obituary: William Bragge,' *Watchmaker, Jeweller and Silversmith*, 10 (July 1884), 1–4.

Anon. 'Our Portrait Gallery: Mr. Victor Kullberg,' *Invention and Inventors' Mart* (17 October 1885), 1083.

Anon: 'Obituary: Victor Kullberg,' *Horological Journal*, 33 (1890), 186–87.

Anon. 'Obituary: Death of Mr John Wycherley,' *Horological Journal*, 34 (Oct. 1891), 17–19.

Anon. 'Obituary: William Ehrhardt,' *Horological Journal*, 40/5 (Jan. 1898), 63.

Anon. 'Obituary: Robert H. Ingersoll,' *Horological Journal*, 71/1 (Oct. 1929), 44–45.

Anon. 'Obituary: Peter John Wennerstrom,' *Horological Journal*, 77 (1935), 175.

Anon. 'Obituary: The Late Mr Bahne Bonniksen,' *Horological Journal*, 77/8 (April 1935), 242.

Anon. (drawing from F.J. Britten's 1903 account). 'Forgotten Benefactor: Jno Jones—Watchmaker,' *Horological Journal*, 99/12 (Aug. 1957), 472–73.

Anon. (probably Eric M. Bruton). 'Thomas Mercer Ltd., Chronometer Makers for a Hundred Years,' *Horological Journal*, 100/11 (July 1958).

Anon. 'London Makers Who Opened up China,' *Clocks*, 3 (July 1980), 39–40.

Argles, Michael. South Kensington to Robbins: *An Account of English Technical and Scientific Education since 1851* (London: Longmans, 1964).

Arnott, Phillip. 'Chronometers on East India Company Ships 1800 to 1833,' *Antiquarian Horology*, 30/4 (Dec. 2007), 487–88.

Ashton, T.S. 'The Domestic System in the Early Lancashire Tool Trade,' *The Economic Journal*, 36, Issue Supplement_1 (Jan. 1926), 131–40, at https://doi-org.eres.qnl.qa/10.1093/ej/36.Supplement_1.131

Ashton, T.S. *An Eighteenth Century Industrialist: Peter Stubs of Warrington, 1756–1806* (Manchester: Manchester UP, 1939).

Ashton, T.S. *The Industrial Revolution 1760–1830* (London: Oxford U.P., 1948).

Atkins, S.E. and W.H. Overall. *Some Account of the Worshipful Company of Clockmakers* (London: Privately printed, 1881), 289–90.

Audetat, E. *Pierre-Frédéric Ingold, 1787–1878* (Biele: Annales Biennoises, VIII (1934), 60–80.

Aveni, Anthony. *Empires of Time: Calendars, Clocks, and Cultures* (New York: Basic Books/Harper Collins, 1989).

Aveni, Anthony. 'Time's Empire,' *The Wilson Quarterly*, 22/3 (Summer 1998), 44–57, at www.jstor.org/stable/40259774

Backinsell, William G.C. *The Medieval Clock in Salisbury Cathedral* (South Wiltshire Industrial Archaeology Society: Historical Monograph 2, 1977).

Bacon, D.H. 'The Coventry Watch Movement Manufacturing Company Lim ited,' *Antiquarian Horology*, 20/6 (Summer 1993), 502–17.

Bacon, D.H. 'Watch Production in English Factories, 1870–1930,' *Antiquarian Horology*, 23/2 (Winter 1996), 117–33.

Bacon, D.H. *Watchmaking in Llangollen by Robert Hughes: A Genuine Late Nineteenth Century Welsh Watch Manufacturer*, Antiquarian Horology New Series, no. 5 (Ticehurst: Antiquarian Horological Society, 2000).

Badger, Reid. *The Great American Fair: The World's Columbian Exposition and American Culture* (Chicago, IL: Nelson Hall, 1979).

Bailey, F.A. 'An Old Watchmaker's Workshop,' *Transactions of the Ancient Monuments Society*, 1 (1953), 3–8.

Bailey, F.A. and T.C. Barker, 'The Seventeenth-Century Origins of Watchmaking in South-west Lancashire', in Harris (ed.), *Liverpool and Merseyside* (1969), 1–15.

Bailey, J.R. 'The Struggle for Survival in the Coventry Ribbon and Watch Trades, 1865–1914,' *Midland History*, 7 (1982), 132–52.

Baillie, Granville H. Watches: *Their History, Decoration and Mechanism* (1929); (London: NAG Press, 1979).

Baines, Edward. *The History of the County Palatine and Duchy of Lancaster* (rev. ed. by John Harland, continued and completed by Brooke Harford, 2 vols. (London: John Heywood, 1868–70).

Baker, P.H.J. 'Early Lancashire Watch Fusee Engines,' *Antiquarian Horology*, Part 1, 21/3 (Spring 1994). 215–28; and Part 2, 21/4 (Summer1994), 315–21.
Barder, Richard C.R. *English Country Grandfather Clocks* (Newton Abbott: David & Charles, 1983).
Barder, Richard C.R. *The Georgian Bracket Clock, 1714–1830* (Woodbridge: Antique Collectors Club, 1993).
Barfoot, Peter and John Wilkes. *The Universal British Directory of Trade and Commerce*, 5 volumes (London: Published by and printed for the patentees, 1790).
Barker, Theodore C. *Three Hundred Years of Red Lion Square, 1684–1984* (London: Borough of Camden, 12pp pamphlet, 1987).
Barker, Theodore C. and Dorian Gerhold. *The Rise and Rise of Road Transport, 1700–1900* (Cambridge: Cambridge UP, 1993, new ed., 1995).
Barker, Theodore C. and John R. Harris. *A Merseyside Town in the Industrial Revolution: St Helens, 1750–1900* (London: Routledge, 1954).
Barnet, Jo Ellen. 'Clock Making and Time Measurement,' in Mokyr (ed.), *Oxford Encyclopaedia of Economic History*, vol. 1 (Oxford: Oxford UP, 2001)
Barraud, E.M. *Barraud, The Story of a Family* (London: Research Publishing, 1967).
Bartky, Ian R. 'The Adoption of Standard Time,' *Technology and Culture*, 30/1 (Jan.1989), 25–56, at https://doi.org/10.2307/3105430
Bates, Alan (compiler). *Directory of Stage Coach Services* (Newton Abbott: David and Charles, 1969).
Battison, Edwin A. *The Auburndale Watch Company: The First American Attempt toward the Dollar Watch* (Project Gutenberg online 2009: eBook #29934, at https://www.gutenberg.org/files/29934/29934-h/29934-h.htm).
Bauer, Martin (ed.), *Resistance to New Technology: Nuclear Power, Information Technology, and Biotechnology* (Cambridge: Cambridge UP, 1995).
Baugh, Daniel A. 'The Sea-Trial of John Harrison's Chronometer, 1736,' *Mariners' Mirror*, 64 (1978), 235–40.
Bedini, Silvio A. *Thinkers and Tinkers: Early American Men of Science* (New York: Scribners, 1975).
Bedini, Silvio A. 'The Mechanical Clock and the Scientific Revolution,' in Maurice, Klaus and Otto Mayr (eds.), *The Clockwork Universe: German Clocks and Automata* (Washington, DC: Smithsonian, 1980).
Bedini, Silvio A. 'The Scientific Instruments of the Lewis and Clark Expedition,' *Great Plains Quarterly*, 4/1 (Winter 1984), 54–69, at https://www.jstor.org/stable/24467603
Bedini, Silvio A. and Francis R. Maddison. 'Mechanical Universe: The Astrarium of Giovanni de'Dondi,' *Transactions of the American Philosophical Society* (1966: New Series, vol. 56, part 5), 1–69, at https://doi.org/10.2307/1006002.
Beeson, C.F.C. 'Knibb and the Anchor Escapement,' *Antiquarian Horology*, 3/10 (June 1961), 208–09.
Beeson, C.F.C., T.O. Robinson, and F.A.B. Ward. 'The Invention of the Anchor Escapement: Debate,' *Antiquarian Horology*, 7/10 (June 1971), 225–28.
Bektas, M. Yakup, and Maurice Crosland. 'The Copley Medal: The Establishment of a Reward System in the Royal Society, 1731–1839,' *Notes and Records of the Royal Society of London*, 46/1 (1992), 43–76, at www.jstor.org/stable/531440

Bennett, James A. *Church, State and Astronomy in Ireland: 200 Years of Armagh Observatory* (Belfast: Queen's University Institute of Irish Studies, 1990).

Bennett, James A. 'George Biddell Airy and Horology,' *Annals of Science*, 37 (1980), 269–85, at https://doi.org/10.1080/00033798000200241

Benson-Beevers, S. 'Benjamin Gray: Short Biography,' *Antiquarian Horology*, 1/1 (March 1955), 76–77.

Berg, Maxine. *The Age of Manufactures, 1700–1820: Industry, Innovation and Work in Britain* (London: Routledge, 1994).

Berg, Maxine 'New Commodities, Luxuries and their Consumers in Eighteenth Century England,' in Berg (ed.), *Consumers and Luxury* (1999).

Berg, Maxine (ed.), *Luxury and Pleasure in Eighteenth Century Britain* (Oxford: Oxford UP, 2007).

Berg, Maxine and Helen Clifford (eds.). *Consumers and Luxury: Consumer Culture in Europe, 1650–1850* (Manchester: Manchester UP, 1999).

Berg, Maxine, and Elizabeth Egar (eds.). *Luxury in the 18th Century: Debates, Desires and Delectable Goods* (London: Macmillan, 2003).

Bermingham, Ann and John Brewer (eds.). *The Consumption of Culture, 1600–1800: Image, Object, Text* (London: Routledge, 1985).

Berner, G.A., and E. Audétat (trans. Richard Watkins, 2008). 'Pierre Frédéric Ingold 1787–1878,' *Schweizer Pioniere der Wirtschaft und Technik*, 13, 1962, at http://www.watkinsr.id.au/Ingold2.pdf

Betts, Jonathan. 'The Eighteenth Century Transits of Venus, the Voyages of Captain James Cook, and the Early Development of the Marine Chronometer,' *Antiquarian Horology*, 21/1 (Autumn 1993), 60–69.

Betts, Jonathan. Commentary on extract 'The Planet Watchers of Greenwich,' from Charles Dickens's *Household Words*, 25 May 1850, *Antiquarian Horology*, 21/4 (Summer 1994), 350–51.

Betts, Jonathan. 'Arnold and Earnshaw: The Practicable Solution,' in Andrewes (ed.), *Quest* (1996).

Betts, Jonathan. 'Josiah Emery: Watchmaker of Charing Cross: Part 1,' *Antiquarian Horology*, 22/5 (Spring 1996), 394–401; Part 2, Precision Pioneer, 22/6 (Summer 1996), 510–23; Part 3, *The Lever Escapement*, 23/1 (Autumn 1996), 26–44.

Betts, Jonathan. 'The Growth of Modern Timekeeping,' in Kristin Lippincott (ed.), *The Story of Time* (London: Merrell Holberton and National Maritime Museum, 1999).

Betts, Jonathan. *Time Restored: The Harrison Timekeepers and R.T. Gould the Man Who Knew (Almost) Everything* (Oxford: Oxford UP and the National Maritime Museum, 2006).

Betts, Jonathan. 'John Hyacinth de Magellan, 1722–1790,' Part 1, 'Horological and Scientific Agent,' *Antiquarian Horology*, 27/5 (Sept. 2003), 509–17; Part 2, 'The Early Clocks,' 28/2 (June 2004), 173–83; Part 3, 'The Later Clocks and Watches,' 30/1 (March 2007), 25–44.

Betts, Jonathan. *Marine Chronometers at Greenwich: A Catalogue of Marine Chronometers at the National Maritime Museum, Greenwich* (Oxford: Oxford UP and the National Maritime Museum, 2017).

Betts, Jonathan. 'Notes from the Librarian: Britten had Talent,' *Antiquarian Horology*, 41/4 (Dec. 2020), 508–09.

Bevir, Mark. 'Republicanism, Socialism, and Democracy in Britain: The Origins of the Radical Left,' *Journal of Social History*, 34/2 (Winter, 2000), 351–68; online at https://www.jstor.org/stable/3789988
Biagioli, Mario. 'From Prints to Patents: Living on Instruments in Early Modern Europe,' *History of Science*, 44 (2006). https://doi.org/10.1177%-2F007327530604400202
Bird, Joanna, Hugh Chapman, and John Clark (eds.). *Collecteana Londoniensia: Studies in London Archaeology and History Presented to Ralph Merrifield* (London: London and Middlesex Archaeological Society, 1978).
Biucchi, B.M. 'The Industrial Revolution in Switzerland,' (1969), in Carlo M. Cipolla (ed.), *The Fontana Economic History of Europe, vol. 4, book 2, The Emergence of Industrial Societies* (London: Collins, 1973).
Blake, Nicholas and Richard Lawrence. *The Illustrated Companion to Nelson's Navy* (London: Chatham, 2005).
Bloomingdales: *Bloomingdales' (New York) Diary and Catalogue for 1910*, at https://libmma.contentdm.oclc.org/digital/collection/p16028coll13/id/2844).
Bodley-Scott, David. 'Watch Jewelling,' *Horological Journal*, 132/12 (Aug 1990),
Bolino, August C. 'British and American Horology: A Comment on Hoke,' *Journal of Economic History*, 48/3 (Sept. 1988), 667, at https://www.jstor.org/stable/2121544
Bonnant, Georges. 'The Introduction of Western Horology in China,' *La Suisse Horlogère* (International Edition) 1 (1960), 28–38.
Bonniksen, Bahne. *The Karrusel Watch: By Its Inventor* (Plymouth: Latimer Rend, 1905).
Booth, Mary L. *New and Complete Clock and Watchmakers' Manual ... With an Appendix Containing a History of Clock and Watchmaking in America* (New York: Wiley, 1877).
Bopp, William C. 'Some Early English Table Clocks,' *Antiquarian Horology*, 8/8 (September 1974), 838–53.
Bos, H.J.M. et al. (eds.). *Studies on Christiaan Huygens* (London: Routledge, 1980).
Boullin, David J. 'The Art of Scientific Instruments,' *Clocks*, 8 (July 1985).
Boullin, David J. 'Historical Clerkenwell,' *Horological Journal*, 130/1 (July 1987).
Bray, Charles. *The Industrial Employment of Women: Being a Comparison between the Conditions of the People in the Watch Trade in Coventry in Which Women Are Not Employed; and the People in the Ribbon Trade, in Which They Are Employed*, A paper read to the British Association for the Advancement of Social Sciences: October 1857 (London: Longman, 1857).
Breen T.H. '"Baubles of Britain": The American and Consumer Revolutions of the Eighteenth Century,' *Past and Present*, no. 119 (May 1988). https://doi.org/10.1093/past/119.1.73
Britten, F.J. *Former Clock and Watchmakers and their Work* (London: Spon, 1894), new edition, *Old Clocks and Watches and their Makers* (London: Spon, 1956; reprinted Woodbridge: Antique Collectors' Club, 1978).
Britten, F.J. 'Reminiscences of Early Workers at the British Horological Institute. No. 1, Mr John Jones,' *Horological Journal*, 46/3 (Nov. 1903), 32–35.
Bromley, John. *The Clockmakers' Library: The Catalogue of the Books and Manuscripts of the Worshipful Company of Clockmakers* (London: Sotheby, 1977).

Brooks, Randall C. 'Nautical Instrument Makers in Atlantic Canada,' *Nova Scotia Historical Review*, 6 (Jan. 1986), 36–54, https://www.researchgate.net/publication/275155416_Nautical_Instrument_Makers_in_Atlantic_Canada.

Brooks, Randall C. 'Richard Upham Marsters: The First Chronometer Maker in North America,' (Jan. 2014), online at https://www.researchgate.net/publication/266277872

Brown, Dee. *The Year of the Century: 1876* (New York: Charles Scribners, 1966).

Brown, Joyce. 'Guild Organization and the Instrument-Making Trade, 1655–1830: The Grocers' and Clockmakers' Companies,' *Annals of Science*, 36 (1979), 1–34, at https://doi.org/10.1080/00033798700200261.

Brown, Joyce. *Mathematical Instrument Makers in the Grocer's Company, 1688–1800: With Notes on Some Earlier Makers* (London: Science Museum, 1979).

Brown, Lucy. *The Board of Trade and the Free Trade Movement, 1830–42* (Oxford: Oxford UP, 1958).

Bruegel, Martin. "'Time That Can Be Relied upon." The Evolution of Time Consciousness in the Mid-Hudson Valley, 1790–1860,' *Journal of Social History*, 28/3 (Spring1995), 547–64, at www.jstor.org/stable/3788464

Bruland, Kristine. 'Patterns of Resistance to New Technologies in Scandinavia: An Historical Perspective,' in Bauer (ed.), *Resistance to New Technology*.

Brusa, Guiseppe and Charles Allix. 'Julien and Pierre Le Roy; Their Business, Their Relatives, and Their Namesakes,' *Antiquarian Horology*, 7/7 (June 1972), 588–606.

Bruton. Eric M. 'Revolution at Mercers,' *Horological Journal*, 96/6 (Feb. 1954), 88–91.

Bruton, Eric. *Dictionary of Clocks and Watches* (London: Archer House. 1962).

Bruton, Eric. *The Illustrated History of Clocks and Watches* (New York: Little, Brown, 2000).

Bryden, D.J. 'Evidence From Advertising for Mathematical Instrument Making in London, 1556–1714,' *Annals of Science*, 49/4 (1982), 301–36, at https://doi.org/10.1080/00033799200200281

Bryden, D.J. 'Bankrupt and Insolvent Scientific Instrument Makers: The *London Gazette* as a Source for the History of the English Instrument Trade: 1720–1849,' *Bulletin of the Scientific Instrument Society*, no.123 (2014), 28–44 and no.124 (2014), 31–38.

Bryden, D.J. 'The London Gazette as a Source for the History of the English Horological Trade, 1720–1849,' *Antiquarian Horology*, 37/4 (Dec. 2016), 477–95.

Buck, Paul. 'Black Forest Clockmakers, Carriers and Retailers with United Kingdom Connections,' *Antiquarian Horology*, 26/4 (Dec. 2001), 389–406.

Buggins G.T.E. and Anthony J. Turner. 'The Context of Production, Identification, and Dating of Clocks by A. and J. Thwaites,' *Antiquarian Horology*, 8 (1973), 372–81.

Buggins, Geoffrey T.E. and F.B.M. Devereux. 'John Thwaites,' *Antiquarian Horology*, 1/11 (June 1956), 161–63.

Bunt, E.F. 'An Eighteenth Century Watchmaker and his Day-book,' *Antiquarian Horology*, 8 (1973), 175–82.

Burchall, Adrian. 'Pitt's Clock and Watch Tax: A Reassessment,' *Antiquarian Horology*, 13/5 (Sept. 1982), 454–61.

Burn, D.L. 'The Genesis of American Engineering Competition, 1850–70,' *Economic History*, II (Jan. 1931), 292–311.

Burnett, John D. *A History of the Cost of Living* (Harmondsworth: Penguin, 1969).

Burnett, John D. and A.D. Morrison-Low. 'Vulgar and Mechanick': *The Scientific Instrument Trade in Ireland, 1650–1921* (Dublin: National Museums of Scotland and Royal Dublin Society, 1989).

Burton, M. Diane and Tom Nickols. 'Prizes, Patents and the Search for Longitude,' *Explorations in Economic History*, 64 (April 2017), 21–36. https://doi.org/10.1016/j.eeh.2016.09.001

Butterworth, Edwin. *A Statistical Sketch of the County Palatine of Lancaster (1841)* (Manchester: Lancashire and Cheshire Antiquarian Society, 1965).

Cahn, Robert W. 'An Unusual Nobel Prize,' *Notes and Records of the Royal Society of London, 59* (2005), 145–53, at doi:10.1098/rsnr.2004.0082

Cain, Peter J. *Economic Foundations of British Overseas Expansion, 1815–1914* (London: Palgrave Macmillan, 1980).

Cain, Peter J. 'British Free Trade: Economics and Policy, 1850–1914,' *Refresh: Recent Findings of Research in Economic & Social History* (1999), Online.

Camerer-Cuss, T.P. *The Story of Watches* (London: MacGibbon and Kee, 1952).

Camerer-Cuss, Terence P. 'John Moore and Sons,' *Antiquarian Horology*, 6/1 (Dec. 1968), 32ff.

Camerer-Cuss, Terence. *Early Watches* (Littlehampton: Country Life, 1971).

Camerer-Cuss, Terence P. *The Camerer Cuss Book of Antique Watches* (1976: revised ed., by T.A. Camerer Cuss (Woodbridge: Antique Collectors Club, 1994).

Camerer-Cuss, Terence. *The English Watch, 1585–1970: A Unique Alliance of Art, Design, and Inventive Genius* (Woodbridge: Antique Collectors' Club, 2009).

Campbell, Robert. *The London Tradesman, Being a Compendious View of All the Trades, Professions, Arts* (London: Gardner, 1747).

Cardinal, Catherine (ed.). *Ferdinand Berthoud 1727–1807, Horloger Mécanicien du Roi et de la Marine* (La Chaux-de-Fonds: Musée international d'Horlogerie, 1984).

Cardinal, Catherine (trans. Jacques Pages), *The Watch, from Its Origins to the Nineteenth Century* (Secaucus, NJ: Wellfleet Press, 1988).

Cardinal, Catherine. 'Ferdinand Berthoud and Pierre le Roy: Judgement in the Twentieth Century of a Quarrel Dating from the Eighteenth Century,' in Andrewes (ed.), *Quest* (1996).

Cardwell, Donald S.L. *Turning Points in Western Technology: A Study in Technology, Science and History* (Cambridge: Science History Publications, 1972).

Carosso, Vincent P. 'The Waltham Watch Company: A Case History,' *Bulletin of the Business History Society*, 23/4 (Dec. 1949), 165–87, at doi:10.2307/3110545, JSTOR 3110545

Carrington, R.F. and R.W. 'Pierre Frederic Ingold and the British Watch and Clockmaking Company,' *Antiquarian Horology*, 10/6 (Spring 1978), 698–714.

Carrington, Roger F. 'The British Watch and Clock Making Company: Some Further Notes,' *Antiquarian Horology*, 19/1 (Sept. 1990), 44–46.

Chamberlain, Paul. *It's About Time* (1941; London: Holland Press, 1978).
Chambers, Jill. *Buckinghamshire Machine Breakers—The Story of the 1830 Riots* (Letchworth: Chambers, 1991).
Chapiro, Adolph. 'Jean-Antoine Lépine, 1720–1814: An 'Unknown' Maker,' *Antiquarian Horology*, 9/4 (Sept. 1975), 443–54.
Chapiro, Adolphe. 'Lépine, Breguet, and the Origins of the Lever Escapement in France,' *Antiquarian Horology*, 14/4 (Dec. 1983), 369–96; and 'Addendum,' *Antiquarian Horology*, 14/6 (Jan. 1984), 616–17.
Checkland, Sydney. *The Rise of Industrial Society in England* (London: Longmans, 1966).
Cheetham, F. H. 'Notes on Some Ormskirk Watch and Clock Makers,' *Transactions of the Antiquarian Society of Lancashire and Cheshire*, 51 (1936), 1–10.
Chiozza, Sir Leo George (ed.). *Free Trade versus Protectionism* (np, pamphlet, 1902).
Church, Roy. 'Nineteenth Century Clock Technology in Britain, the United States, and Switzerland,' *Economic History Review,* 2nd ser. 28/4 (Nov. 1975), 616–30, at https://doi.org/10.2307/2599615 and https://www.jstor.org/stable/2599615
Church, Roy. 'Advertising Consumer Goods in Nineteenth-Century Britain: Reinterpretations,' *Economic History Review*, 53/4 (Nov. 2000), 621–45, at https://www.jstor.org/stable/2598598
Cipolla, Carlo M. *Clocks and Culture* (Norton: London, 1967; part of *European Culture and Overseas Expansion* (Harmondsworth: Penguin, 1970), at doi:10.1086/ahr/73.5.1473
Cipolla, Carlo (ed.). *The Fontana Economic History of Europe: vol. 2, The Sixteenth and Seventeenth Centuries* (Glasgow: Collins, 1974).
Cipolla, Carlo M. *Before the Industrial Revolution: European Society and Economy, 1000–1700* (London: Routledge, 3rd ed. 1976).
Clapham, Sir John Harold. 'Europe After the Great Wars, 1816 and 1920,' *Economic Journal*, 30 (Dec. 1920), 423–35, at https://doi.org/10.2307/2222868
Clapham, Sir John Harold, *An Economic History of Modern Britain* (3 vols, Cambridge: Cambridge UP, 1926–38).
Clapham, Sir John Harold. *The Bank of England: A History* (2 vols., 1944; Cambridge: Cambridge UP, 1970).
Clark, G. Kitson. 'Hunger and Politics in 1842,' *Journal of Modern History*, 25 (1953), 355–74. https://www.jstor.org/stable/i332166
Clark, Peter. (ed.). *The Cambridge Urban History of Britain, vol. 2, 1540–1840* (Cambridge: Cambridge UP, 2000).
Clark, Peter and R.A. Houston. 'Culture and Leisure: 1700–1840,' in Peter Clark, ed., *The Cambridge Urban History of Britain, vol. 2, 1540–840* (Cambridge: Cambridge UP, 2000).
Clark, Victor S. *A History of Manufactures in the United States* (3 vols., Washington, DC: Carnegie Institute, 1929).
Clarkson, Leslie A. *The Pre-industrial Economy in England, 1500–1700* (London: Batsford, 1971).
Clarkson, Leslie A. *Proto-Industrialization: The First Phase of Industrialization?* (London: Studies in Economic and Social History, Macmillan, 1985).
Clay, C.G.A. *Economic Expansion and Social Change: England 1500–1700: Vol. 1, People, Land and Towns* (Cambridge: Cambridge UP, 1984).

Clercq, Peter R. de. (ed.). *Nineteenth Century Scientific Instruments and Their Makers* (Amsterdam: Fourth Scientific Instrument Symposium 23–26 October 1984, 1985).

Clifton, Gloria. *Directory of British Scientific Instrument Makers, 1550–1851* (London: National Maritime Museum, 1995).

Clifton, Gloria. 'New Light on Chronometer-makers and the Scientific Instrument Trades in the Nineteenth Century,' *Antiquarian Horology*, 37/3 (Sept. 2016), 327–48.

Cline, Duane A. *Navigation in the Age of Discovery: An Introduction* (Little Rock, AK: Heritage Press, 1990).

Clutton, Cecil. Review of Ferdinand Berthoud, *Histoire de la mesure du temps par les horloges* (1802: reprinted 1976), *Antiquarian Horology*, 10/2 (Spring 1977), 218–20.

Clutton, Cecil, G.H. Baillie, and Courtney Ilbert. *Britten's Old Clocks and Watches and their Makers* (London: Spon, 1956; London: Methuen, 9th rev. ed., 1982).

Clutton, Cecil and George Daniels. *Watches* (London: Batsford, 1971).

Cole, John Francis. 'Chronometers and the Royal Navy,' *Horological Journal*, 58 (1915), 715–19.

Cole, John Francis and T.P. Camerer Cuss. *A Watchmaking Centenary: Usher and Cole, 1861–1961* (20-page pamphlet published by the firm in 1961: online at http://freepages.rootsweb.com/~usher/genealogy/usheruk/docs/UsherCole150dpi.pdf)

Collinson's *Directory. The London Wholesale, Manufacturing, and Retail Goldsmiths, Silversmiths, Jewellers, Watchmakers, Opticians, and Cutlers. 1861: Part 5, the 'Watch, Chronometer, and Clock Trades' Directory,'* (London: Collinson, 1861).

Cook, Andrew S. 'Alexander Dalrymple and John Arnold: Chronometers and the Representation of Longitude on East India Company Charts,' *Vistas in Astronomy*, 26 (1983), 189–95.

Cook, Sir Alan. 'Time and the Royal Society,' *Notes and Records of the Royal Society of London*, 55/1 (Jan. 2001), 9–27, at www.jstor.org/stable/532142

Cooke, Henry. 'Visit of BHI Members to Coventry,' *Horological Journal*, 71/12 (Aug. 1929), 282–84.

Cookson, Gillian. 'Millwrights, Clockmakers, and the Origin of Textile Machines,' *Textile History*, 27/1 (1966), 43–59, at https://doi.org/10.1179/004049696793711680

Cookson, Gillian. 'Innovation, Diffusion, and Mechanical Engineers in Britain, 1780–1850,' *Economic History Review*, 47/4 (1994), 749–53, at https://doi.org/10.2307/2597715

Cooper, Carolyn C. 'The Portsmouth System of Manufacture,' *Technology and Culture*, 25/2 (April 1984), 182–225, at https://doi.org/10.2307/3104712

Corbeiller, Clare Le. 'James Cox and His Curious Toys,' *The Metropolitan Museum of Art Bulletin*, New Series, 18/10 (June 1960), 318–24, at https://www.metmuseum.org/toah/hd/jcox/hd_jcox.htm.

Cotgrove, Stephen F. *Technical Education and Social Change* (London: Allen and Unwin, 1958).

Cotter, Charles H. 'A Brief Historical Survey of British Navigation Manuals,' *Journal of Navigation*, 36 (1983), 237–40, at doi:10.1017/S0373463300024954

Cowham, Mike. 'Portable Sundial Making in Nuremberg,' *Antiquarian Horology*, 29/1 (Sept. 2005), 45–50.

Cox, Nancy. *The Complete Tradesman: A Study of Retailing*, 1550–1820 (Aldershot: Ashgate, 2000).

Crawforth, M.A. 'Trade Cards for the Scientific Instrument Industry,' *Annals of Science*, 42/5 (1985), 453–542, at https://doi.org/10.1080/00033798500200331

Crawforth, M.A. 'Instrument Makers in the London Guilds,' *Annals of Science*, 44 (1987), 319–77, at https://doi.org/10.1080/00033798700200261

Crisford, Andrew. 'Thomas Wright in the Poultry, London, No. 2228,' *Antiquarian Horology*, 9/7 (June 1976), 785–88.

Crisford, Andrew. *Masterpieces from the Asprey Collection*: Vol. 1, *Abraham-Louis Breguet* (London: Quartet Books, 1994).

Crom, Theodore. *Horological Wheel Cutting Engines, 1700 to 1900* (Gainesville, FL: Crom, 1970).

Crom, Theodore. 'A Few Eighteenth Century Liverpool/Prescot Area Toolmakers,' *Antiquarian Horology*, 19/4 (Summer 1991). 419–30.

Crommelin, C.A. 'Planetaria: A[n] Historical Survey,' *Antiquarian Horology*, 1 (March 1955), 70–75.

Cromwell, T. *History and Description of the Parish of Clerkenwell* (1828; London: British Library Historical Print Editions, 2011).

Crouzet, François. 'Wars, Blockade, and Economic Change in Europe, 1792–1815,' *The Journal of Economic History*, 24/4 (Dec. 1964), 567–88, at https://EconPapers.repec.org/RePEc:cup:jechis:v:24:y:1964:i:04:p:567-588_06

Cummings, Genevieve. *How the Watch Was Worn: A Fashion for 500 Years* (Woodbridge: Antique Collectors Club, 2010).

Cummins, Neil and Cormac Ó Gráda. 'Artisanal Skills, Watchmaking, and the Industrial Revolution: Prescot and Beyond,' *UCD Centre for Economic Research: Working Paper Series*, WP19/24, October 2019, pp.41, at https://econpapers.repec.org/paper/ucnwpaper/201924.htm

Cunliffe, Marcus. 'America at the Great Exhibition of 1851,' *American Quarterly*, 3 (1951), 115–26, at http://www.jstor.org/stable/27557689

Curti, Merle. 'America at the World's Fairs, 1851–1893,' *American Historical Review*, 55 (1950), 833–56, at http://dx.doi.org/10.2307/1841163

Cutmore, Maxwell (pseudonym for D.H. Bacon). *Watches: 1850–1980* (Newton Abbott: David and Charles, 1989).

Daly, Gavin. 'English Smugglers, the Channel, and the Napoleonic Wars, 1800–1814,' *Journal of British Studies*, 46/1 (Jan.2007), 30–46, at https://www.jstor.org/stable/10.1086/508397

Daly, Gavin. 'Napoleon and the "City of Smugglers,' 1810–1814,' *The Historical Journal*, 50/2 (2007), 333–52, at https://doi.org/10.1017/S0018246X07006097

Dane, E. Surrey. *Peter Stubs and the Lancashire Hand Tool Industry* (Altrincham: John Sherratt, [1975).

Daniels, George. *English and American Watches* (London: Abelard-Schuman, 1967).

Daniels, George. *The Art of Breguet* (London: Sotheby's, 1975).

Daniels, George. *All in Good Time: Reflections of a Watchmaker* (London: Premier Print, 2000).

Darken, Jeff and John Hooper. *English Thirty Hour Clocks: Origin and Development, 1600–1800* (Yateley, Hants: Penita Press, 1997).

Darvall, Frank O. *Popular Disturbances and Public Order in Regency England: Being an Account of the Luddite and Other Disorders in England during the Years 1811–17* (Oxford: Oxford UP, 1970).

Daumas, Maurice 'Precision Mechanics,' in Singer, *History of Technology*: Vol. IV, *The Industrial Revolution* (Oxford: Oxford UP, 1958).

Daumas, Maurice (ed.). *A History of Technology and Invention: Progress through the Ages: Volume 2, The First Stages of Mechanisation, 1450–1725* (3 Vols., New York: Crown Publishers, 1969; London: John Murray, reprinted 1980).

Daunton, Martin. *Progress and Poverty: An Economic and Social History of Britain, 1700–1850* (Oxford: Oxford UP, 1995).

David, Jacques, (trans. Richard Watkins). *American and Swiss Watchmaking in 1876 (Rapport a la Société Intercantonale des Industries du Jura sur la Fabrication de L'horlogerie aux Etats-Unis* (Saint-Imier: Compagnie des Montres, 1876), at http://www.watkinsr.id.au/david.html

Davidson, Simon C. 'Box Chronometers for India, 1800–1936,' *Antiquarian Horology*, 35/4 (Dec. 2014), 1107–24.

Davidson, Simon C. 'The Use of Chronometers to Determine Longitude on East India Company Voyages,' *Mariner's Mirror*, 102/3 (July 2016), 344–48. https://doi.org/10.1080/00253359.2016.1210326

Davidson, Simon C. 'Marine Chronometers: The Rapid Adoption of New Technology by East India Captains in the Period 1770–92 on Over 500 Voyages,' *Antiquarian Horology*, 40/1 (March 2019), 76–91.

Davidson, Simon C. and Peter Linstead-Smith. 'W.E. Frodsham No.1. Another Chronometer Identified from HMS Beagle's Second Voyage,' *Antiquarian Horology*, 37/3 (Sept. 2016), 366–76.

Davies, Alun C. 'The First Irish Industrial Exhibition: Cork 1852', *Irish Social and Economic History*, 2 (1975), 46–59, at https://www.jstor.org/stable/24337058

Davies, Alun C. 'The Society of Arts and the Dublin Exhibition of 1853,' *Journal of the Royal Society of Arts* (June 1975), 433–36, at https://www.jstor.org/stable/41372165

Davies, Alun C. 'Britain and the American Centennial Exhibition, 1976,' *Journal of the Royal Society of Arts*, 132 (Dec. 1976), 28–31, at https://www.jstor.org/stable/41372433

Davies, Alun C. 'Greenwich and Standard Time,' *History Today*, 38/3 (March 1978).

Davies, Alun C. 'The Life and Death of a Scientific Instrument: The Marine Chronometer, 1770–1920,' *Annals of Science*, 35 (1978), 509–25, at https://doi.org/10.1080/00033797800200391

Davies, Alun C. 'Ireland's Crystal Palace, 1853,' in J.M. Goldstrom and L.A. Clarkson (eds.), *Irish Population, Economy and Society: Essays in Honour of the Late K.H. Connell* (Oxford: Clarendon, 1981), 149–70.

Davies, Alun C. 'Rise and Decline of Chronometer Manufacturing,' *Antiquarian Horology*, 12 (Autumn 1980), 293: [translated as 'Aufstieg und Niedergang der Chronometerherstellung in Grossbritannien,' *Alte Uhren*, 3 (1981), 165–76; and reprinted in *Bulletin of the National Association of Watch and Clock Collectors* (USA), 24 (1982), 617–33.]

Davies, Alun C. 'Aaron Lufkin Dennison, 1812–1895' in D.J. Jeremy (ed.), *The Dictionary of Business Biography*, 2 (1984), 64–65.

Davies, Alun C. 'David Smyth Torrens, 1897–1967, An Horological Memoir,' *Antiquarian Horology*, 6 (1984), 564–84.

Davies, Alun C. 'Thomas Peter Hewitt, 1848–1933: Watch Manufacturer,' in D. J. Jeremy (ed.), *Dictionary of Business Biography*, vol. 3 (London: Butterworths, 1985), 186–88.

Davies, Alun C. 'Rural Clockmaking in Eighteenth Century Wales: Samuel Roberts of Llanfair Caereinion, 1755–1774,' *Business History Review*, 59 (1985), 49–75. https://doi.org/10.2307/3114855

Davies, Alun C. 'Victor Kullberg, 1824–1890: Chronometer Manufacturer,' in D.J. Jeremy (ed.), *Dictionary of Business Biography*, vol. 3 (London: Butterworths, 1985), 628–29.

Davies, Alun C. 'Thomas Mercer, 1822–1900: Chronometer Manufacturer,' in D.J. Jeremy (ed.), *Dictionary of Business Biography*, vol. 4 (London: Butterworths, 1986), 218–20.

Davies, Alun C. 'The Repair and Manufacture of Watches in London in the Nineteenth Century: The Business Records of Turner and Birch, 1835–1920,' *Antiquarian Horology*, 17/5 (1988), 478–82.

Davies, Alun C. 'Old and New Technology in Watchmaking in Coventry, 1850–1920,' *Antiquarian Horology*, 18/4 (Winter 1989), 397–410.

Davies, Alun C. 'Starting up a Watchmaking Business: James Ritchie of Edinburgh, 1809–1812,' *Antiquarian Horology*, 20/3 (Autumn 1992), 260–72.

Davies, Alun C. 'Time for a Change? Technological Persistence in the British Watchmaking Industry,' *Material History Review: Revue d'histoire de la culture materielle*, 36 (1992), 57–64, at https://journals.lib.unb.ca/index.php/MCR/article/view/17529

Davies, Alun C. 'British Watchmaking and the American System,' *Business History*, 35/1 (1993), 40–54, at https://doi.org/10.1080/00076799300000003

Davies, Alun C. 'Vancouver's Chronometers,' in Robin Fisher and Hugh Johnston (eds.), *From Maps to Metaphors: The Pacific World of George Vancouver*, (Vancouver: British Columbia UP, 1993), 70–84, 305–11.

Davies, Alun C. 'Horology and Navigation: The Chronometers on Vancouver's Expedition, 1791–95,' *Antiquarian Horology*, 21 (Spring 1994), 244–55.

Davies, Alun C. 'Horology, Technology, and Ingenious Yankees: Review Essay,' *Antiquarian Horology*, 22/1 (Spring 1995), 69–73.

Davies, Alun C. 'British Watchmaking, 1842–43: Technical Expertise and Public Decisions,' *Proceedings of the International Symposium on Technology and Society* (Princeton, NJ: Princeton University, 1996), 438–47.

Davies, Alun C. 'Testing a New Technology: Captain George Vancouver's Survey and Navigation in Alaskan Waters, 1794,' in Stephen Haycox, James Barnett, and Caedmon Liburd (eds.), *Exploration in the North Pacific, 1741–1805* (Seattle and London: Washington UP, 1997), 103–15.

Davies, Alun C. 'An Invasion in Time: American Horology and the British Market,' *Antiquarian Horology*, 30/6 (June 2008), 829–44; also 'Comment on Invasion,' *Antiquarian Horology*, 31/5 (Sept. 2009), 706–10.

Davies, Alun C. 'The Ingold Episode Revisited: English Watchmaking's Pyrrhic Victory,' *Antiquarian Horology*, 31/5 (Sept. 2009), 637–54.

Davies, Alun C. 'On Excursion and On Song: The BHI Views New Technology in the 1870s and 1880s,' *Antiquarian Horology*, 33/2 (Dec. 2011), 207–20.

Davies, Alun C. 'Horology at International Exhibitions, 1851–1900,' *Antiquarian Horology*, 33/5 (Sept. 2013), 591–608.

Davies, Alun C. 'Time-consciousness in the Aran Isles,' *Antiquarian Horology*, 34/3 (Dec. 2013), 539–40.

Davies, Alun C. 'The House of Kullberg,' *Antiquarian Horology*, 35/1 (March 2014), 635–648.

Davies, Alun C. 'Keeping time at Shalstone: The Horological Tribulations of the Purefoys, 1735 to 1752,' *Antiquarian Horology*, 36/1 (March 2015), 61–83.

Davies, Alun C. 'Horological patents, 1662–c.1800: Restraining Trade, Stifling Innovation or Rewarding Invention?,' *Antiquarian Horology*, 37/1 (March 2016), 82–100.

Davies, Alun C. 'Swiss Watches, Tariffs and Smuggling with Dogs,' *Antiquarian Horology*, 37/3 (Sept. 2016) 377–83.

Davies, Alun C. and Sir Peter Froggatt. 'David Smyth Torrens: Physiologist and Horologist, 1897–1967,' *Hermathena, Journal of Trinity College, Dublin*, 140 (1986), 11–31, at https://www.jstor.org/stable/23042039; also 'DST, a Biographical Note,' *Hermathena*, 146 (1989), 49–52.

Davies, P.N. 'British Shipping and World Trade: Rise and Decline, 1820–1939,' in Yui and Nakagawa (eds.), *Business History of Shipping: Strategy and Structure* (Tokyo: Tokyo UP, 1985), 68–69.

Davis, Ralph. *The Industrial Revolution and British Overseas Trade* (Leicester: Leicester UP, 1979).

Deane, Phyllis. *The First Industrial Revolution* (Cambridge: Cambridge UP, 1965).

Deane, Phyllis and W.A. Cole. *British Economic Growth 1688–1959* (Cambridge: Cambridge UP, 1962).

Dent, Edward J. *An Abstract from Two Lectures on the Construction and Management of Chronometers, Watches and Clocks* (London: Adams Brown, 1842).

Depew, Chauncey (ed.). *One Hundred Years of American Commerce: A History of American Commerce by 100 Americans* (1895; New York: Haynes; Kessinger Publishing Reprint, 2010).

Dexter, J.T. (ed.). *Modern Industries: A Series of Reports on Industry and Manufactures as Represented in the Paris Exhibition in 1867 by Twelve British Workmen* (London: Macmillan, 1868).

Dick, Steven J. 'Centralizing Navigational Technology in America: The U.S. Navy's Depot of Charts and Instruments, 1830–1842,' *Technology and Culture*, 33/3 (July 1992), 467–509, at https://www.jstor.org/stable/3106634

Ditisheim, Paul. 'Pierre le Roy, 1717–1785,' *Horological Journal*, 83/5 (Jan. 1940), 20–23 (reprinted from *Revue Chronometrique*).

Dohrn Van Rossum, Gerhard. 'Regulating Working Hours and Time-Keeping Devices in the Middle Ages: An Addendum to Gian Carlo del Vecchio's Contribution,' *Antiquarian Horology*, 16/2 (June 1986), 145–47.

Dohrn Van Rossum, Gerhard. 'The Diffusion of the Public Clock in the Cities of Late Medieval Europe, 1300–1500,' in B. Lepetit and J. Hoock (eds.), *La Ville est l'innovation en Europe* (Paris: Ecole des Hautes Etudes en Sciences Sociales, 1987).

Donzé, Pierre-Yves. *History of the Swiss Watch industry: From Jacques David to Nicolas Hayek* (2012: Pieterlen, Switzerland: Peter Lang AG, 3rd ed., 2014).

Duckworth, G.H. 'Watches and Clocks' in Charles Booth (ed.), *Life and Labour of the People in London*: Second Series, Vol 2: *Industry* (London: Macmillan, 1903), 24–34.

Dunn, Richard, and Rebekah Higgitt. *Finding Longitude* (London: Collins, 2014).

Dunn, Richard and Rebekah Higgitt. *Ships, Clocks and Stars: The Quest for Longitude* (London: Collins and Royal Museums Greenwich, 2014).

Durey, Michael. '"A Perfect Hurricane": Naval Disaster Off Jutland, 1811,' *Northern Studies: The Journal of the Scottish Society for Northern Studies*, 40 (2008), 71–81 at http://researchrepository.murdoch.edu.au/id/eprint/13805.

Durfee, W.F. 'The History and Modern Development of the Art of Interchangeable Mechanisms,' *Transactions of the American Society of Mechanical Engineers*, 22 (1895), 1225–57.

Dyos, H.J. and D.H. Aldcroft. British Transport: *An Economic History from the Seventeenth Century to the Twentieth* (Leicester: Leicester UP, 1974).

Earle, Peter. *The Making of the English Middle Class: Business, Society, and Family Life in London, 1660–1730* (London: Methuen, 1989).

Earle, Peter. *A City Full of People: Men and Women of London, 1650–1750* (London: Methuen, 1994).

Earnshaw, Thomas. *Longitude: An Appeal to the Public* (London: Printed for the Author, 1808; reprinted with an introduction by R. John Griffiths (St Helens: British Horological Institute, 1986).

Edidin, Michael. *English Watches for the American Market: A History of Watchmaking by the Tobias Families of London and Liverpool* (*NAWCC Bulletin* in two parts: Part 1 (Oct. 1992), 515–44; Part 2 (Dec. 1992), 659–91.

Education Committee. 'Report on Clerkenwell in 1843,' *Journal of the Statistical Society of London*, 6 (1843), at https://www.jstor.org/stable/2338010

Ehrlich, Cyril. *The Piano: A History* (1976; Oxford: Clarendon, rev. ed., 1990).

Ehrman, John. *The Younger Pitt:* vol. 3, *The Consuming Struggle* (Stanford, CA: Stanford UP, 1996).

Eland, George E. (ed.). *Purefoy Letters, 1735–1753* (London: Sidgwick and Jackson, Ltd, 1931; reprinted, ed., L.G. Mitchell, 1973).

Elmers, Chris. 'The Impact of the 1797 Tax on Clocks and Watches on the London trade,' in Joanna Bird, Joanna, Hugh Chapman, and John Clark (eds.), *Collecteana Londoniensia: Studies in London Archaeology and History Presented to Ralph Merrifield* (London: London and Middlesex Archaeological Society, 1978), 388–400.

Elmers, Chris. Report of 'a Lecture on Clerkenwell,' *Antiquarian Horology*, 12 (Spring 1981), 549–50.

Elmers, Chris ['C.E,']. 'Watch and Clockmaking,' in Celina Fox (ed.), *London: World City, 1800–1840* (London: Yale UP and the Museum of London, 1992).

Emsley, Clive. *British Society and the French Wars, 1793–1815* (London: Macmillan, 1979).

Epstein, Stephen A. *Wills and Wealth in Medieval Genoa*, 1150–1250 (Cambridge, MA: Harvard UP, 1984).

Epstein, Stephen A. 'Business Cycles and the Sense of Time in Medieval Genoa,' *Business History Review*, 62 (Summer 1988), 238–60, at https://doi.org/10.2307/3116000
Eser, Thomas. 'The Henlein Exhibition at the Germanisches Nationalmuseum: A Look Back, a Look Forward and New Discoveries,' *Antiquarian Horology*, 37/2 (June 2016), 199–212.
Evans, Chris, and Alun Withey. "An Enlightenment in Steel? Innovation in the Steel Trades of Eighteenth-Century Britain." *Technology and Culture*, 53/3 (July 2012), 533–60, at www.jstor.org/stable/41682700.
Evans, David M.W. 'Liverpool Watchmakers,' *Antiquarian Horology*, 9/6 (March 1976), 705.
Evans, David M.W. 'Peter Litherland, Liverpool, and the Rack Lever,' *Antiquarian Horology*, 32/1 (March 2010), 93–96.
Evans, Jeremy. 'The Numbering of Tompion's Watches: Series and System,' *Antiquarian Horology*, 14 (June 1984), 585–97.
Evans, Jeremy. 'Horological Wheel-Cutting by Mechanical Means: An Early Reference and Some Further Notes,' *Antiquarian Horology*, 24/6 (Summer 1999), 551–55.
Evans, Jeremy L. *Thomas Tompion at the Dial and Three Crowns* (Ticehurst: Antiquarian Horological Society, 2006).
Eversley, D.E.C. 'The Home Market and Economic Growth in England, 1750–80,' in E.L. Jones and G.E. Mingay (eds.), *Land, Labour and Population in the Industrial Revolution: Essays Presented to J.D. Chambers* (London: Edward Arnold, 1967).
Fairclough, Oliver. 'Louis Recordon, King George III and Richard Simmons: An Account of a Royal Presentation Watch,' *Antiquarian Horology*, 9/5 (Dec. 1975), 551–55.
Faraday, Christina Juliet. 'Tudor Time Machines: Clocks and Watches in English Portraits c.1530–c.1630,' *Renaissance Studies*, 33/2 (April 2019), 239–66, at doi: 10.1111/rest.12517
Farrer, William and J. Brownbill, eds. *Victoria History of the County of Lancashire, Vol. 3, Sub Prescot Township* (London: Archibald Constable, 1907).
Favre-Perret, Eduard. 'Watchmaking in the United States,' *Watchmaker, Jeweller and Silversmith* (Feb. 5, 1877), 200–01.
Fernandez, Maria P. and C. Pedro. 'David Mells, Musician and Clockmaker and an Analysis of the Clockmaking Trade in 17th Century London,' *Antiquarian Horology*, 16/6 (June 1987), 602–17.
Fernandez, Maria P. and Pedro C. Fernandez. 'Precision Timekeepers of Tokugawa Japan and the Evolution of the Japanese Domestic Clock,' *Technology and Culture*, 37/2 (April 1996), 221–48, at www.jstor.org/stable/3106815
Ferriday, Peter. *Lord Grimthorpe, 1816–1905* (London: Murray, 1957).
Fischer, Lewis R. and Gerald E. Ponting (eds.). Change and Adaptation in Maritime History: *The North Atlantic Trade in the Nineteenth Century* (St. John's, NF: Maritime History Group, Memorial University of Newfoundland, 1985).
Fisher, F.J. 'The Development of London as a Centre of Conspicuous Consumption in the Sixteenth and Seventeenth Centuries,' *Transactions of the Royal Historical Society*, 4th ser., 30 (1948), 37–50, at https://doi.org/19.2307/3678697

Fisher, F.J. 'London as an 'Engine of Economic Growth,' in J.S. Bromley and E.H. Kossmann (eds.), *Britain and the Netherlands:* Vol. 4, *Metropolis, Dominion and Province* (The Hague: Martinus Nijhoff, 1971).

Fisher, Robin. *Vancouver's Voyage: Chartering the Northwest Coast, 1791–95* (Seattle: University of Washington Press, 1992).

Fisher, Robin and Hugh Johnston (eds.). *From Maps to Metaphors: The Pacific World of George Vancouver* (Vancouver: British Columbia UP, 1993).

Flinders, Matthew. *A Voyage to Terra Australis ... in the* Years *1801, 1802, and 1803 in His Majesty's ship the Investigator* (London: 1814, 2 vols., plus Atlas: Facsimile reprint, London: Nicol, 1966).

Floud, Roderick C. *The British Machine Tool Industry, 1850–1914* (Cambridge: Cambridge UP, 1967).

Floud, Roderick C. 'Technical Education and Economic Performance, 1850–1914,' *Albion*, 14/2 (Summer 1982), 153–81, at https://doi.org/10.2307/4049189

Floud, Roderick and Donald McCloskey. *The Economic History of Britain since 1700* (Vol. 1, 1700–1860) (2nd ed., Cambridge: Cambridge UP, 1994).

Foot, M.R.D. and H.C.G Mathew (eds.). *The Gladstone Diaries with Cabinet Minutes and Prime Ministerial Correspondence* (14 vols; Oxford: Clarendon, 1968–94), vol. 3, *1840–47* (1974).

Forbes, Eric G. 'The Foundation and Early Development of the Nautical Almanac,' *Journal of the Institute of Navigation*, 18/4 (Oct. 1965), 301–401, at https://doi.org/10.1017/S0373463300046324

Forbes, Eric G. 'The Origin and Development of the Marine Chronometer,' *Annals of Science*, 22 (March 1966), 1–25, at https://doi.org/10.1080/00033796600203005

Forbes, Eric G. 'Index to the Board of Longitude Papers at the Royal Greenwich Observatory,' *Journal of the History of Astronomy*, Part 1 (1970), and Part 2 (1971), at https://doi.org/10.1177%2F002182867000100215

Forbes, John. 'Search, Immigration. and the Goldsmiths' Company: A Study in the Decline of its Powers,' Ch. 8 in Ian Anders Gadd and Patrick Wallis (eds.), *Guilds, Society and Economy in London, 1450–1800* (London: Centre for Metropolitan History, Institute for Historical Research, 2002), 115–25.

Foster, George. 'James Sweetman Eiffe, 1800–1880,' *Antiquarian Horology*, 5/8 (Sept. 1967), 284–86.

Fox, Celina (ed.). *London: World City, 1800–1840* (London: Yale UP and the Museum of London, 1992).

Fox-Bourne, H.R. *England's Merchants: Memoirs in Illustration of the Progress of British Commerce* (2 vols., London: Chatto and Windus, 1886).

Fraiture, Eddy, and Paul Van Rompay. 'Clock and Watchmaking in Belgium, 1300–1830,' *Antiquarian Horology*, 33/1 (Sept. 2011), 27–45.

Francillon, Andre. *History of Longines*. Translation of *Histoire de la Fabrique des Longines Précédée d'un Essai sur le Comptoir Agassiz*, published by Companie des Montres Longines, 2004; translated and published online by Richard Watkins. https://www.watkinsr.id.au/Francillon.pdf

Frankel, Jeffrey A. 'The 1807–1809 Embargo against Great Britain,' *Journal of Economic History*, 42/2 (June 1982), 291–308. https://doi.org/10.1017/S0022050700027443

Fraser, J.T. and N. Lawrence (eds.). *The Study of Time: Proceedings of the Second Conference of the International Society for the Study of Time* (New York: Springer-Verlag, 1975).
Fritzsche, Bruno. 'Switzerland,' in Mokyr (ed.), *Oxford Encyclopaedia of Economic History*, vol. 5 (Oxford: Oxford UP, 2003).
Froman, Robert. 'The Watch That Made the Dollar famous,' *Challenge*, 1/5 (1953), 28–31, at www.jstor.org/stable/40716575.
Fry, Howard T. *Alexander Dalrymple (1727–1808) and the Expansion of British Trade* (London: Cass for the Royal Commonwealth Society, 1970; reprinted, Routledge, 2006).
Gadd, Ian Anders, and Patrick Wallis (eds.). *Guilds, Society and Economy in London, 1450–1800* (London: Centre for Metropolitan History, Institute for Historical Research, 2002).
Galbraith, Adam. 'The Decline of the British Watchmaking Industry,' *Watchmaker, Jeweller and Silversmith*, 34 (June 1908), 727–35.
Ganney, Henry. 'Report of Watch and Clock Making,' *Artisan Reports on the Paris Universal Exhibition of 1878* (London: Society of Arts, 1879).
Ganney, Henry. 'The Practical Value of Horological Schools, and their Work at the Paris Exhibition of 1878,' *Horological Journal*, 22/11 (July 1880), 142–47.
Ganney, Henry. 'Machine Watchmaking,' *Horological Journal*, 26/9 (May 1884), 115–20.
Gay, Hannah. 'Clock Synchrony, Time Distribution and Electrical Timekeeping in Britain 1880–1925,' *Past and Present*, No. 181 (Nov. 2003), 107–40, at https://www.jstor.org/stable/3600787
Gayer, A.D., W.W. Rostow, and A.J. Schwartz. *The Growth and Fluctuation of the British Economy, 1790–1850* (2 vols. 1953, Oxford: Clarendon, reprinted 1975).
George, M. Dorothy. *London Life in the Eighteenth Century* (London: Kegan Paul, 1925)
Gies, Frances and Cathedral Joseph. *Forge and Waterwheel: Technology and Invention in the Middle Ages* (New York: Harper Collins, 1994).
Gissing, George. *The Nether World* (London: Smith Elder, 1889; reprinted London, Dent, 1973).
Gitelman, H.M. 'The Labor Force at Waltham Watch during the Civil War Era,' *The Journal of Economic History*, 25/2 (June 1965), 214–43, at https://www.jstor.org/stable/2116148
Glasgow, David. *Watch and Clockmaking,* in the series *Manuals of Technology*, edited by Professor Ayrton and R. Wormwell (London: Cassell, 1885).
Glasgow, David. 'Watchmaking by Machinery,' *The New Technical Educator* (London: Cassell, 1890), at http://www.watkinsr.id.au/glasgow.pdf.
Glasmeier, Amy. 'Technological Discontinuities and Flexible Production Networks: The Case of Switzerland and the World Watch Industry,' *Research Policy*, 20 (1991), 469–85. https://doi.org/10.1016/0048-7333(91)90070-7
Glasmeier, Amy K. *Manufacturing Time: Global Competition in the Watch Industry, 1795–2000* (Perspectives on Economic Change) (New York: Guilford Press, 2000).
Glennie, Paul and Nigel Thrift. *Shaping the Day, A History of Timekeeping in England and Wales, 1300–1800* (Oxford: Oxford UP, 2009).

Goaman, Muriel. *English Clocks* (London: Michael Joseph, 1967).
Gockerell, Nina. 'Telling Time without a Clock,' in Maurice and Mayr (eds.), *Clockwork Universe.*
Good, Richard. 'Two Masterpieces by Nicole Nielsen,' *Horological Journal*, 112/10 (July 1969), 10–13.
Good, Richard. 'An Enameled Gold Minute Repeating Striking Watch with Arms, Crest, and Cypher of Sir John Bennett,' *Horological Journal*, 126/5 (Jan. 1984), 12–22.
Good, Richard. 'Smiths at Cheltenham: The Rise and Fall of 20th Century English Watchmaking,' *Horological Journal*, 141/10 (Oct 1999), part 1; 340–42; part 2,141/11 (Nov. 1999), 372–74.
Goodman, David and Colin A. Russell. *The Rise of Scientific Europe, 1500–1800* (Sevenoaks: Open University and Hodder and Stoughton, 1991).
Gould, Rupert T. 'The History of the Chronometer,' *The Geographical Journal*, 57/4 (April 1921), 253–68, at www.jstor.org/stable/1780557
Gould, Rupert T. *Early Marine Chronometers* (illustrated lecture delivered at the British Horological Institute, 21 November 1923; published as a pamphlet, 1923).
Gould, Rupert T. *The Marine Chronometer: Its History and Development* (1923; London: Holland Press, 1960).
Gould, Rupert T. 'John Harrison and his Timekeepers,' *Mariner's Mirror*, 21 (1935), 115–39.
[Great Exhibition, 1851]. *First Report of the Commissioner for the Exhibition of 1851* (London: Spicer, 1852).
[Great Exhibition, 1851]. *Reports of the Juries* (3 vols, London: Spicer, 1852), vol. 2, Class Xb, 'Report on Horological Instruments'.
Greasley, David. 'British Economic Growth: The Paradox of the 1880s and the Timing of the Climacteric,' *Explorations in Economic History*, 23/4 (Oct. 1986), 416–44.
Greaves, Ian. 'A Study of English Watch Jewelling,' *Antiquarian Horology*, 35/4 (Dec. 2014), 1085–106.
Griffiths, R. John (editor, with introductory comment). *Thomas Earnshaw, Longitude: An Appeal to the Public, 1808* (St Helens: British Horological Institute, 1986).
Griffiths, R. John. 'Methods of Cutting Wheels and Pinions in Horology: An Historical Review: Part 1,' *Horological Journal*, 136/7 (March 1992). 296–99; Part 2, 136/8 (April 1992), 344–49.
Griffiths, R. John. 'The Rise and Fall of Toolmaking in Lancashire,' *Journal of the North West Society for Industrial Archaeology and History* (1994), 3–8.
Griffiths, R. John 'The Early Watchmakers of Toxteth Park Near Liverpool, and the Origins of the Industry, the Aspinwalls, with Some Notes on their Successors,' *Antiquarian Horology*, 27/2 (December 2002), 163–78.
Grimthorpe, Lord (Edmund Beckett Denison), *A Rudimentary Treatise on Clocks and Watches and Bells* (London: Weale, 1860).
Grimthorpe, Lord (Edmund Beckett Denison). 'Minerva of Science,' speech reported in *Horological Journal*, 22/3 (Nov. 1879), 29ff.
Gurman, S.J. and S.R. Harratt. 'Revd Dr William Pearson (1767–1847): A Founder of the Royal Astronomical Society,' *Quarterly Journal of the Royal*

Astronomical Society, 35/3 (1994), 271–92, at http://adsabs.harvard.edu/full/1994QJRAS.35.271G

Gwynn, Robin D. Huguenot Heritage: *The History and Contribution of the Huguenots in Britain* (London: Routledge, 1985).

Habakkuk, Hrothgar John. *American and British Technology in the Nineteenth Century: The Search for Labour-Saving Inventions* (Cambridge: Cambridge UP, 1962).

Hackmann, W.D. 'The Nineteenth Century Trade in Natural Philosophy Instruments in Britain,' in de Clercq (ed.), *Nineteenth Century Scientific Instruments* (Amsterdam: Boerhaave Museum, Leiden, and Rodopi, Amsterdam, 1985).

Hafter, Daryl M. 'The Business of Invention in the Paris Industrial Exposition of 1806,' *Business History Review*, 58/3 (Autumn, 1984), 317–35, at http://www.jstor.com/stable/3114551

Hall, A. Rupert. 'Robert Hooke and Horology,' *Notes and Records of the Royal Society of London*, 8/2 (1951), 131–48, at https://www.jstor.org/stable/i355395

Hall, A. Rupert. *The Revolution in Science, 1500–1750* (London: Longman, 1983).

Hall, Peter Geoffrey. *The Industries of London since 1861* (London: Hutchinson. 2006).

Hana, W.F.J. (trans. E.J. Tyler), *English Lantern Clocks* (Poole: Blandford Press, 1977).

Harries, David. 'The Chronometer Pioneer (Commander Richard Owen),' *Horological Journal*, 122 (1979), 37–43.

Harris, Dennis. 'The Early Wrist Watch in Times of War, 1899–1920,' *Horological Journal*, 140/12 (Aug. 1998), 275–78.

Harris, John R. (ed.). *Liverpool and Merseyside: Essays in the Economic and Social History of the Port and its Hinterland* (London: Cass, 1969).

Harris, John R. *The British Iron Industry, 1700–1850* (London: Macmillan and Economic History Society, 1988).

Harris, J. R. 'French Industrial Espionage in Britain in the Late Eighteenth Century,' *Journal of the Royal Society of Arts*, 137/5398 (Sept. 1989), 629–34, at www.jstor.org/stable/41375003

Harris, John R. *Essays in Industry and Technology in the Eighteenth Century: England and France* (Aldershot: Variorum, 1992).

Harris, John R. 'French Industrial Policy under the Ancien Regime and the Pursuit of the British Example,' *Histoire, Économie et Société*, 12/1 (1993), 93–100, at https://www.jstor.org/stable/23611290.

Harris, John R. *Industrial Espionage and Technology Transfer: Britain and France in the Eighteenth Century* (Aldershot: Ashgate, 1998),

Harrison, A.E. 'The Origins and Growth of the United Kingdom Cycle Industry to 1900,' *Journal of Transport History* (3rd Ser.), 6 (March 1985), 41–70.

Harrold, Michael C. *American Watchmaking: A Technical History of the American Watch Industry, 1850–1930* (Columbia, PA: NAWCC, 1981).

Harte, Negley B. 'Rees's Clocks Watches Chronometers and Naval Architecture: A Note,' *Maritime History*, 3 (1973), 92–95.

Harvey, Charles, Edmund M. Green, and Penelope J. Corfield. 'Continuity, Change, and Specialization within Metropolitan London: The Economy of

Westminster, 1750–1820,' *The Economic History Review*, 52/3 (Aug. 1999), 469–93, at www.jstor.org/stable/2599141

Haswell, J. Eric. 'Fifty Years in Clerkenwell: Some Personal Reminiscences,' *Horological Journal*, 100 (1958), 580–81.

Haycox, Stephen, James Barnett, and Caedmon Liburd (eds.). *Enlightenment and Exploration in the North Pacific, 1741–1805* (Seattle: Cook Inlet Historical Society and the Anchorage Museum of History and Art, Washington UP, 1997).

Hayter, Carol. 'Instruments for Measuring Time' [extracts from *The Pictorial Gallery of Arts*, 1847], *Antiquarian Horology*, 8/2 (March 1973), 187.

Hazlitt, William C. *The Livery Companies of the City of London: Their Origin, Character, Development and Social and Economic Importance* (London: Sonnenschein, and New York: Macmillan, 1892).

Hebert, L. 'Plumbago for Chronometers,' *Transactions of the Society, for the Encouragement of Arts, Manufactures, and Commerce*, 46 (1827), 48–54, at www.jstor.org/stable/41327070

Helmore, Dee. *A Quest for Perfection: The Life of John Gottlieb Ulrich: Chronometer Maker* (High Wycombe: Privately published, 2012).

Henderson, W. O. 'J. C. Fischer: A Swiss Industrial Pioneer,' *Zeitschrift Für Die Gesamte Staatswissenschaft/Journal of Institutional and Theoretical Economics*, 119/2 (April 1963), 361–76, at www.jstor.org/stable/40748679

Henderson, W.O. 'Introduction: Industrial Switzerland,' in W.O. Henderson (ed.), *J.C. Fischer and His Diary of Industrial England, 1814–51* (London: Cass, 1966).

Herring, David Webster. *The Lure of Clocks: An Account of the James Arthur Collection of Clocks and Watches at New York University* (New York: New York UP, 1932).

Hewitt, C.J. 'Machine Watchmaking as Carried on by Messrs Rotherham and Sons,' *Horological Journal*, 30/10 (June 1888), 144–45.

Hewitt, C.J. 'The Horological Exhibits in the Inventions Exhibition,' *Horological Journal*, 30/10 (June 1888), 117–22, 129–38.

Hewitt, T.P. *English Watchmaking under Free Trade* (np: pamphlet, 1903).

Higgitt, Rebekah. 'Challenging Tropes: Genius, Heroic Invention, and the Longitude Problem in the Museum,' *Isis*, 108/2 (June 2017), 371–80, at https://doi.org/10.1086/692691

Hindle, Brooke and Steven Lubar. *Engines of Change: The American Industrial Revolution, 1790–1860* (Washington, DC: Smithsonian, 1986).

Hirschfeld, C. 'America on Exhibition: The New York Crystal Palace,' *American Quarterly*, 9/2 (Summer 1957), 101–16, at https://www.jstor.org/stable/i327337

Hobden, Heather. 'The Sing-Song Trade,' *Antique Clocks*, 11/7 (December 1988).

Hobhouse, Christopher. *1851 and the Crystal Palace* (London: John Murray, 1851).

Hohenberg, Paul M. and Lynn Hollen Lees. *The Making of Urban Europe, 1000–1950*, Harvard Studies in Urban History (Cambridge, MA: Harvard UP, 1985).

Hoke, Donald R. 'Ingenious Yankees: The Rise of the American System of Manufactures in the Private Sector,' *Journal of Economic History*, 46/2 (June 1986), 489, at https://www.jstor.org/stable/2122179.

Hoke, Donald R. 'British and American Horology: Time to Test Factor-Substitution Models, *Journal of Economic History*, 47/2 (June 1987), 321–27, at https://www.jstor.org/stable/2122231.

Hoke, Donald R. 'British and American Horology: A Reply to Bolino,' *Journal of Economic History*, 49/3 (Sept. 1989), 718, at https://www.jstor.org/stable/2122514.

Hoke, Donald R. *Ingenious Yankees: The Rise of the American System of Manufacture in the Private Sector* (New York: Columbia UP, 1990).

Holland, Albert. 'How to Take Care of a Watch,' *The Decorator and Furnisher*, 15/2 (Nov. 1889), 42, at www.jstor.org/stable/25585930

Holland, Julian. 'From Archimedes to Newton: James Mann the Younger in Fleet Street and Ludgate Street,' *Bulletin of the Scientific Instrument Society*, No. 137 (June 2018), 10–17.

Hollingshead, John. *Ragged London in 1861*, with 'Introduction and Notes' by Anthony S. Wohl (London: Everyman, 1986),

Honig, Peter. 'History and Mathematical Analyses of the Fusee,' in Maurice and Mayr (eds.), *Clockwork Universe*).

Horrell, Sara, Jane Humphries and Ken Sneath. 'Consumption Conundrums Unravelled,' *The Economic History Review*, 68/3 (August 2015), 830–57, at www.jstor.org/stable/43910109

Hoult, James. 'Prescot Watchmaking in the Eighteenth Century,' *Transactions of the Historical Society of Lancashire and Cheshire* (New ser.), 61 (1925), 39–53.

Hoult, James. 'Old Prescot Chronometer Makers,' *Horological Journal*, 68/5 (Jan. 1926), 100–04.

Hounshell, David A. *From the American System to Mass Production: The Development of Manufacturing Technology in the United States* (Baltimore, MD: Johns Hopkins UP, 1984).

Howse, Derek. 'The Principal Scientific Instruments taken on Captain Cook's voyages of exploration, 1768–80,' *Mariners' Mirror*, 65 (1979), 119–35.

Howse, Derek and Beresford Hutchinson. *The Clocks and Watches of Captain James Cook, 1769–1969* (London: Antiquarian Horological Society, 1969).

Hoyt, W.D. 'A London Shopkeeper's Struggle to Recover a Colonial Debt,' *Maryland Historical Magazine*, 45 (June 1950), 126–33.

Hudson, Pat. *The Industrial Revolution* (London: Edward Arnold, 1992).

Humphries, Jane. 'Childhood and Child Labour in the British Industrial Revolution,' *The Economic History Review*, 66/2 (May 2013), 395–418, at www.jstor.org/stable/42921562

Hunt, Bishop C. *The Development of the Business Corporation in England, 1800–1867* (1936; Cambridge, MA: Harvard UP, reprinted 1969).

Hunt, Robert (ed.). *Hunt's Handbook to the Official Catalogues* (London: Clowes and Sons, 1851).

Hutchinson, Beresford. 'Some Observations on the Timekeepers of Thomas Mudge,' *Antiquarian Horology*, 10/6 (Spring 1978), 714–19.

Hyde, Francis E. *Mr Gladstone and the Board of Trade* (London: Cobden-Sanderson, 1934).

Ilbert, C.A. 'A Tompion Broadsheet in French,' *Antiquarian Horology*, 1/5 (March 1955), 78–79.

Imlah, Ann G. *Britain and Switzerland 1845–60: A Study of Anglo-Swiss Relations During Some Critical Years for Swiss Neutrality* (London: Longmans, 1966).

Ingram, J. S. *The Centennial Exposition: Described and Illustrated: Being a Concise and Graphic Description of This Grand Enterprise Commemorative of the First Centenary of American Independence* (Philadelphia, PA: Hubbard Bros., 1876), at http://archive.org/details/centennialexposi00ingr

[Inventions Exhibition, 1885]. *Horological Catalogue* (London: Simpson & Sons, 1885).

Ishibashi, Yuto. '"A Place for Managing Government Chronometers": Early Chronometer Service at the Royal Observatory Greenwich,' *Mariner's Mirror*, 99/1 (Feb. 2013), 52–66, at http://dx.doi.org/10.1080/00253359.2013.766998.

[J. McL.] 'Looking back Sixty Years: A Reminiscent Christmas Feature,' *Horological Journal*, 105/4 (Dec. 1963), 386–87.

Jacquet, Eugene and Alfred Chapuis (trans. David S. Torrens), *Technique and History of the Swiss Watch* (1953; London, Spring Books/Hamlyn; reprint, Littlehampton, 1970).

Jagger, Cedric. *Paul Philip Barraud: A Study of a Fine Chronometer Maker, and of His Associates and Successors in the Family Business, 1750–1929* (London: Antiquarian Horological Society, 1968), and id., *The Supplement to Paul Philip Barraud* (id. 1979).

Jagger, Cedric. 'Paul Philip Barraud,' *Antiquarian Horology*, 6 (Dec. 1968), 28–31.

Jagger, Cedric. *Royal Clocks: The British Monarchy and Its Timekeepers 1300–1900* (London: Robert Hale, 1983).

Jagger, Cedric. *The Artistry of the English Watch* (Newton Abbott: David and Charles, 1988).

James, Andrew. 'Watches – A Pamphlet by J.B. Thomas,' *Antiquarian Horology*, 31/2 (Dec. 2008), 223–28; includes a transcription.

Jardine, Lisa. *The Curious Life of Robert Hooke: The Man Who Measured London* (London: Harper Collins, 2003).

Jefferys, James B. *Retail Trading in Britain, 1850–1950* (Cambridge: The National Institute of Economic and Social Research: Economic and Social Studies, vol. 13, 1954).

Jennings, Stuart. 'Chronometers on the 1821–26 Royal Navy African Survey,' *Antiquarian Horology*, 40/2 (June 2019), 200–14.

Jeremy, David J. 'Damming the Flood: British Government Efforts to Check the Outflow of Technicians and Machinery, 1780–1843,' *Business History Review*, 51 (1977), 1–34. https://doi.org/10.2307/3112919

Jerome, Chauncey. *History of the American Clock Business for the Past Sixty Years, and a Life... Written by... Himself* (New Haven, CT: Dayton, 1860).

Johnson, Emory R. et al. *History of the Domestic and Foreign Commerce of the United States* (Washington, DC: Carnegie Institution, 1915), vol. II.

Jones, E.L. and G.E. Mingay (eds.). *Land, Labour and Population in the Industrial Revolution: Essays Presented to J.D. Chambers* (London: Edward Arnold, 1967).

Kellett, J.R. 'The Breakdown of Guild and Corporate Control over the Handicraft and Retail Trade in London,' *Economic History Review* (2nd Ser.), 10 (1958), 381ff. https://doi.org/10.1111/j.1468-0289.1958.tb00013.x.

Kelly, Morgan and Cormac Ó Gráda. 'Adam Smith, Watch Prices, and the Industrial Revolution,' *Quarterly Journal of Economics*, 131[4] (2016), 1727–52, at https://doi.org/10.1093/qje/qjw026

Kelly's *Directory*, [for London, Coventry, Liverpool, etc: At Guildhall Library, London]. *The Post Office Directory of the Watch and Clock ... Trades Throughout England, Scotland and Wales* for 1862 and 1868, 1872, 1875, 1880, 1887, 1892, 1897, 1901, 1905, 1913 and 1917.
Kemp, Robert. 'Watch Movement making in Prescot,' *Antiquarian Horology*, 13/1 (Sept. 1981). 77–81.
Kemp, Robert. 'The Coventry Watch Trade,' *Horological Journal,* 126/7 (March 1984), 17–20.
Khan, B. Zorina. 'Inventing Prizes: A Historical Perspective on Innovation Awards and Technology Policy,' *The Business History Review*, 89/4 (Winter 2015), 631–60, at www.jstor.org/stable/43896955
King, Andrew. 'John Harrison, Copley Medalist,' in Vaughan (ed.), *Royal Society and the Fourth Dimension* (1993).
King, Andrew. 'John Harrison, Clockmaker at Barrow, Near Barton upon Humber, Lincolnshire'; in Andrewes (ed.), *Quest* (1996).
King, Andrew. 'Winner or Loser: Did John Harrison Win the Longitude Prize?,' *Antiquarian Horology*, 37/1 (March 2016), 73–81.
King, Hilary. 'The Marine Chronometers of the Baudin Expedition to Australia, 1800–1804,' *Antiquarian Horology*, 23/6 (Winter 1997), 509–21.
King, Hilary. 'Surviving Marine Chronometers by Louis Berthoud,' *Antiquarian Horology*, 24/2 (Summer 1998), 119–21.
Kitto, Tony. 'John Flamstead, Richard Towneley and the Equation of Time,' *Antiquarian Horology*, 25/2 (Dec. 1999), 180–84.
Koberer, Wolfgang. 'On the First Use of the Term "Chronometer," *Mariner's Mirror*. 102/2 (2016), 203–05.
Kraminer, Jan. 'Swedish Forgeries,' *Antiquarian Horology*, 29/3 (March 2006), 330–34.
Kurz, Otto. *European Clocks and Watches in the Near East* (London: Studies of the Warburg Institute, vol. 34, 1975).
Landes, David S. *The Unbound Prometheus: Technological Change and Industrial Development in Western Europe from 1750 to the Present* (Cambridge: Cambridge UP, 1969).
Landes, David S. 'Watchmaking: A Case-study in Enterprise and Change,' *Business History Review*, 53/1 (Spring 1979), 1–39, at https://doi.org/10.2307/3114685
Landes, David. 'The Creation of Knowledge and Technique: Today's Task and Yesterday's Experience,' *Daedalus*, 109/1 (Winter 1980), 111–20, at www.jstor.org/stable/20024651
Landes, David S. *Revolution in Time: Clocks and the Making of the Modern World* (Cambridge, MA: Belknap, Harvard UP, 1983).
Landes, David S. 'Hand and Mind in Time Measurement: The Contributions of Art and Science,' The Royal Society's Wilkins Lecture, London 1988, *Notes and Records of the Royal Society of London*, 43/1 (January 1989), 57–69, at http://www.jstor.org/stable/531718
Landes, David S. 'What Room for Accident in History? Explaining Big Changes by Small Events,' *Economic History Review* (New Series) 47/4 (Nov. 1994), 637–56. www.jstor.org/stable/2597710
Landes, David S. *The Wealth and Poverty of Nations: Why Some Are So Rich, and Some Are So Poor* (London: Little Brown, 1998).

Landes, David S. 'Clocks and the Wealth of Nations,' *Daedalus*, 132/2 (Spring 2003), 20–26, at https://www.jstor.org/stable/20027836

Lane, Joan. *Apprenticeship in England, 1600–1914* (London: University College Press, 1996).

Launtink-Ferguson, Annie. 'The Origin of the Clockwork-escapement,' *Nature*, 330 (17 December 1987), 615.

Law, Rodney J. 'Review of Laycock. *John Harrison* (1976),' *Antiquarian Horology,* 10 (Spring 1977), 220–21.

Laycock, W.S. *The Lost Science of John 'Longitude' Harrison* (Ashford: Brant Wright, 1976).

Le Goff, Jacques. 'Le temps du travail dans la 'crise' du XIVe siècle: du temps médiéval au temps moderne,' included and translated in *Time, Work and Culture in the Middle Ages* (Chicago, IL: Chicago UP, 1980).

Legg, Marie-Louise (ed.). *The Synge Letters: Bishop Edward Synge to His Daughter Alicia, Roscommon to Dublin, 1746–1752* (Dublin: Lilliput Press, 1996), 52–53.

Leopold, J.H. 'Clockmaking in Britain and the Netherlands,' *Notes and Records of the Royal Society of London*, 43 (1989), at https://doi.org/10.1098/rsnr.1989.0012

Leopold, J.H. 'Christiaan Huygens, The Royal Society and Horology,' in Denys Vaughan (ed.), *The Royal Society and the Fourth Dimension: The History of Timekeeping*, Antiquarian Horological Society Monograph No. 27 (Ticehurst: Antiquarian Horological Society, 1993).

Leopold, J.H. 'The Third Seafaring Nation: The Introduction of the Marine Chronometer in the Netherlands,' *Antiquarian Horology*, 22/6 (Summer 1998), 486–500.

Leopold, J.H. and Clare Vincent. 'An Extravagant Jewel: The George Watch,' *Metropolitan Museum Journal*, 35 (2000), 7 + 137–49, at https://doi.org/10.2307/1513030 https://doi.org/10.2307/1513030 and https://www.jstor.org/stable/1513030

Leopold, J.H. and M.L. Wayman. 'General introduction and Analytical Methods,' in Wayman (ed.), *Ferrous Metallurgy of Early Clocks and Watches: Studies in Post medieval Steel* (London: British Museum, 2000).

Leppington, C. H. d'E. 'The Evolution of an Industrial Town,' *The Economic Journal*, 17/67 (Sept. 1907), 345–57, at www.jstor.org/stable/2220473

Levere, Trevor H. 'Chronometers on the Arctic Expeditions of John Ross and William Edward Parry: With Notes on a Letter from Messrs. William Parkinson and William James Frodsham,' *Annals of Science*, 51 (1994), 165–75, at https://doi.org/10.1080/00033799400200181

Liebowitz, S.J. and Stephen E. Margolis. 'Path Dependence, Lock-in, and History,' *Journal of Law, Economics, & Organization*, 11/1 (April 1995), 205–26, at https://doi.org/10.1093/oxfordjournals.jleo.a036867

Linnard, William. 'Shaping the Day in Wales: Indications of Awareness of Clock Time in Wales before 1800,' *Antiquarian Horology*, 34/3 (December 2013), 526–38.

Linnard, William. 'A Clock Club in Milford Haven in 1805,' *Antiquarian Horology*, 37/1 (March 2016), 101–04.

Lloyd, H. Alan. 'George Graham: Horologist and Astronomer,' *Horological Journal* (Nov. 1951), 707–17.

Lloyd, H. Alan, 'George Graham, Horologist and Astronomer,' *Journal of the Royal Society of Arts*, 100/4861 (May 1951), 30–49, at www.jstor.org/stable/41365289
Lloyd, H. Alan. 'The Origin of the Fusee,' *The Antiquaries Journal*, 31 (July–Oct. 1951), at. https://doi.org/10.1017/S000358150007637X
Lloyd, H. Alan. 'Mechanical Timepieces,' in Singer (et al., eds.) *History of Technology: Vol. III* (1957).
Lloyd, H. Alan. *The Collector's Dictionary of Clocks* (London: Country Life, 1964).
Loomes, Brian. 'The Fromanteel Story,' *Antiquarian Horology*, 9/2 (March 1975), 179–85.
Loomes, Brian. *Country Clockmakers and their London Origins* (Newton Abbot: David and Charles, 1976).
Luckhurst, K. *The Story of Exhibitions* (London: Studio Publications, 1951).
Luu, Lien Bich. *Immigrants and the Industries of London, 1500–1700* (Aldershot: Ashgate, 2005).
MacLeod, Christine. 'The Peculiarities of Yorkshire inventors: A Reply,' *Journal of Economic History*, 47/4 (1994), 754–59, at https://doi.org/10.1111/j.1468-0289.1994.tb01401.x
Maguire, J.F. *The Industrial Movement in Ireland, as illustrated by the National Exhibition of 1852* (Cork: John O'Brien, 1852). Online at http://www.corkpastandpresent.ie/history/corktradeexhibitions/uploadexhibition/croppedpdfs/1852_exhibition.pdf
Mahoney, Michael S. 'Christiaan Huygens: The Measurement of Time and of Longitude at Sea,' in H.J.M. Bos et al. (eds.), *Studies on Huygens*, Bos, H.J.M. et al. (eds.), *Studies on Christiaan Huygens* (London: Routledge, 1980).
Marshall, Alfred, *Principles of Economics* (1890; London: Macmillan, reprinted 1964), at doi: 10.1007/978-1-137–37526-1
Martin, J.E. *Greater London: An Industrial Geography* (London: Bell, 1966).
Martineau, Harriet. 'Time and the Hour,' *Household Words*, 6 March 1852.
Mathews, Godfrey W. 'Some Notes on the Liverpool Election of 1806,' *Transactions of the Historical Society of Lancashire and Cheshire*, 79 (1927), 74–85.
Mathias, Peter. *The First Industrial Revolution: The Economic History of Britain, 1700–1914* (London: Routledge, 1969), at https://doi.org/10.4324/9780203820865.
Matthew, H.G.C. 'Disraeli, Gladstone, and the Politics of Mid-Victorian Budgets,' *The Historical Journal*, 22/3 (Sep. 1979), 615–43, at https://www.jstor.org/stable/i324990
Matthew, H.G.C. (ed.). *The Oxford Dictionary of National Biography (ODNB)* (Oxford: Oxford UP, 2004, and online via major libraries).
Maurice, Klaus, and Otto Mayr (eds., trans. H. Bartlett Wells), *Clockwork Universe: German Clocks and Automata, 1550–1650* (Washington, DC: Smithsonian, 1981).
Maurice, Sigrid and Klaus. 'Counting the Hours in Community Life of the 16th and 17th Centuries,' in Maurice and Mayr, *Clockwork Universe* (1981).
May, W.E. *A History of Marine Navigation* (New York: Norton, 1973).
May, W.E. 'The Logbooks Used By the Ships of the East India Company,' *Journal of Navigation*, 77 (1974), 120–22.
May, W.E. 'How the Chronometer Went to Sea,' *Antiquarian Horology, 9/6* (March 1976), 638–63.

McCloskey, Donald. '1780–1860: A Survey,' in Roderick Floud and Donald McCloskey (eds.), *The Economic History of Britain since 1700, Vol 1, 1700–1860* (Cambridge: Cambridge UP, 1994).

McConnell, Anita. 'From Craft Workshop to Big Business – The London Scientific Instrument Trade's Response to Increasing Demand, 1750–1820,' *London Journal*, 19/1 (May 1994), 36–53, at https://doi.org/10.1179/ldn.1994.19.1.36

McCormick, Richard C. 'Our Success in Paris in 1878,' *The North American Review*, 129/272 (1879), 1–22. https://www.jstor.org/stable/25100773

McCrossen, Alexis. 'The "Very Delicate Construction" of Pocket Watches and Time Consciousness in the Nineteenth-Century United States,' *Winterthur Portfolio*, 44/1 (Spring 2010), 1–30, at https://doi.org/10.1086/651538

McCrossen, Alexis. *Marking Modern Times: A History of Clocks, Watches and Other Timekeepers in American Life* (Chicago, IL: Chicago UP, 2013).

McCulloch, John R. *A Dictionary, Practical, Theoretical and Historical of Commerce and Commercial Navigation* (London: Longmans, 2nd ed., 1859).

McEvoy, Rory. 'Admiral Lord Nelson and the Commemorative Domestic Clock,' *Antiquarian Horology*, 32/5 (March 2011), 665–88.

McEvoy, Rory. 'A Time to Remember,' *Antiquarian Horology*, 37/4 (Dec. 2016), 522–29.

McInnes, Angus. 'The Emergence of a Leisure Town: Shrewsbury, 1660–1760,' *Past and Present*, No. 120 (August 1988), 53–67, at https://doi.org/10.1093/past/120.1.53

McKendrick, Neil, John Brewer, and J. H. Plumb. The Birth of a Consumer Society: *The Commercialization of Eighteenth-century England* (Bloomington: Indiana UP, 1982).

McNeil, Ian. *Joseph Bramah: A Century of Invention, 1749–1851* (1968; Newton Abbott: David and Charles, 1972).

McNutt, Jenifer P, and Richard Whatmore. 'The Attempts to Transfer the Genevan Academy to Ireland and to America, 1782–1795,' *The Historical Journal*, 56/2 (June 2013), 345–68 (esp. 353–55), at www.jstor.org/stable/24528840

Meadows, A.J. *Greenwich Observatory: II: Recent History, 1836–1975* (London: Taylor and Francis, 1975).

Mercer, F.A. (Tony). 'Thomas Mercer: Maker of Chronometers since 1858,' *Magazine of the Port of London Authority* (Summer 1976), 50–51.

Mercer, F.A. (Tony). 'A Dynasty Dedicated to the Sea and Time-keeping,' *Clocks*, 1 (Sept. 1978), 22–25.

Mercer, F.A. (Tony) *Mercer Chronometers: Radical Tom Mercer and the House He Founded* (Ashford: Brant Wright, 1978).

Mercer, F.A. (Tony). 'A Company as Old as the Institute,' *Horological Journal*, 126/10 (June 1983), 31–33.

Mercer, F.A. (Tony). *Chronometer Makers of the World: With [an] Extensive List of Makers and Craftsmen* (Colchester: N.A.G Press, 1991).

Mercer, F.A. (Tony). *Mercer Chronometers: History, Maintenance and Repair* (Ashbourne: Mayfield, 2003).

Mercer, Frank 'The Manufacture of Files, 1773–1935,' *Horological Journal*, 77/5 (Jan. 1935), 136–41.

Mercer, R. Vaudrey. 'Peter Litherland and Co.,' *Antiquarian Horology*, 3 (June 1962), 316–23.

Mercer, R. Vaudrey. *John Arnold and Son, Chronometer Makers, 1762–1843* (London: Antiquarian Horological Society, 1972).
Mercer, R. Vaudrey. *The Life and Letters of E.J. Dent, Chronometer Maker, and Some Account of his Successors* (Ticehurst: Antiquarian Horological Society, 1977).
Mercer, R. Vaudrey. *The Frodshams: The Story of a Family of Chronometer Makers*, Antiquarian Horological Society Monograph No. 21 (Ticehurst: Antiquarian Horological Society, 1981).
Mercer, R. Vaudrey. 'Benjamin Gray and the Vulliamys: An Attempt to Decipher the Cryptic Code Which they Used on their Watches,' *Antiquarian Horology*, 14/3 (Sept. 1983), 266–71.
Mercer, R. Vaudrey. 'Charles Frodsham; Maker of Marine Chronometers,' *Clocks*, 6 (Oct. 1983), 17–19.
Mesnage, Pierre (trans. Eileen B. Hennessy), Chapter 13: 'The Building of Clocks,' in Daumas, *History of Technology*, Vol, II, *The First Stages of Mechanisation, 1450–1725* (London: John Murray, 1980).
Michaels, M.I. 'Fine Metals and Instrument Trades,' Part II of *London Industries III*,' of Herbert Llewellyn Smith (director). *The New Survey of London Life and Labour*, Vol VIII (London: King and Co., 1934).
Midleton, Alan. 'The History of the BHI,' *Horological Journal* (in 18 parts, monthly from July 2007 to January 2009).
Millburn, John R. 'The Fleet Street Address of Graham and his Successors,' *Antiquarian Horology*, 8/3 (June 1973), 299–301.
Minchington, Walter. 'Patterns and Structure of Demand, 1500–1750,' in vol. 2 of Carlo Cipolla (ed.), *The Fontana Economic History of Europe: The Sixteenth and Seventeenth Centuries* (New York: Barnes and Noble, 1977).
Mitchell, B.R. *European Historical Statistics, 1750–1970* (London: Palgrave Macmillan, 1975).
Mokyr, Joel. *The Lever of Riches: Technological Creativity and Economic Progress* (Oxford: Oxford UP, 1990).
Mokyr, Joel. 'Technological Inertia in Economic History,' *Journal of Economic History*, 52/2 (June 1992), 325–38, at: https://www.jstor.org/stable/2123111
Mokyr, Joel (ed.). *Oxford Encyclopaedia of Economic History*, 5 vols. (Oxford: Oxford UP, 2003)
Montes, Mary. *Brown Boots in Earlsdon: A Study of a Watchmaking Community, Its Rise and Fall* (Coventry: Historical Association Pamphlet no.15, 1989).
Moore, Charles W. *Timing a Century: History of the Waltham Watch Company* (Cambridge, MA: Harvard Studies in Business History, Harvard UP, 1945).
Moore, Dennis S. and Philip T. Priestley. 'Some Account of Liverpool Watch Case Makers, 1785–1798,' *Antiquarian Horology*, 23/4 (Summer 1997), 341–53.
Morgan, Kenneth. 'Finding Longitude: The *Investigator* Expedition, 1801–1803,' *International Journal of Maritime History*, 29/4 (Nov. 2017, 771–87, at https://doi.org/10.1177/0843871417725688
Morpurgo, Enrico. 'The Clock and the Pendulum,' *Antiquarian Horology*, 2 (1958), 138–43.
Morrison, Kathryn. *English Shops and Shopping: An Architectural History* (New Haven, CT and London: Yale University Press, 2003).

Morrison-Low, Alison. *Making Scientific Instruments during the Industrial Revolution: Science, Technology and Culture, 1700–1945* (Aldershot: Ashgate, 2007).

Morus, Iwan Rhys. "The Nervous System of Britain': Space, Time and the Electric Telegraph in the Victorian Age,' *The British Journal for the History of Science*, 33/4 (Dec. 2000), 455–75, at www.jstor.org/stable/4028030

Mraz, Gottfried. 'The Role of Clocks in the Imperial Hororaria for the Turks,' in Maurice and Mayr, *The Clockwork Universe* (1980).

Mueller-Maerki, Fortunat F. Review of the Proceedings of a Colloquium on 'The American Challenge in Watchmaking,' *Antiquarian Horology*, 33/3 (March 2012), 365–66.

Mui, Hoh-Cheung and Lorna H. Mui. 'Trends in Eighteenth Century Smuggling Reconsidered,' *Economic History Review*, 28/1 (Feb. 1975), 28–42, at https://www.jstor.org/stable/2594370

Mui, Hoh-Cheung and Lorna H. Mui. *Shops and Shopkeeping in the Eighteenth Century* (Kingston, and London: McGill UP, 1989).

Muir, Ramsay. *A History of Liverpool* (1907: Liverpool: William and Norgate for Liverpool UP, reprinted 1970).

Mumford, Lewis. *Technics and Civilization* (New York: Harcourt, Brace, 1934).

Mumford, Lewis. *Art and Technics* (New York: Columbia UP, 1952).

Murphy, John Joseph. 'Entrepreneurship in the Establishment of the American Clock Industry,' *Journal of Economic History*, 26 (June 1966), 169–86, at https://www.jstor.org/stable/2116226

Musson, A.E. and Eric Robinson. 'The Origins of Engineering in Lancashire,' *The Journal of Economic History*, 20/2 (June 1960), 209–33, at https://doi.org/10.1017/S0022050700110435

Musson, A. E. and Eric Robinson. *Science and Technology in the Industrial Revolution* (Manchester: Manchester University Press, 1969).

[National Maritime Museum], *The Old Royal Observatory: The Story of Astronomy and Time* (London: National Maritime Museum, Greenwich, 1991).

Neale, J.A. 'Joseph and Thomas Windmills,' *Antiquarian Horology*, 16/6 (June 1987), 573–82.

Neale, J.A. 'Report of a Lecture by John Leopold on "The Wholesale Trade in Watches in the Eighteenth Century,"' *Antiquarian Horology*, 19/4 (Summer 1991), 392.

Neale, J.A. *Joseph and Thomas Windmills: Clock and Watchmakers, 1671–1737*, Antiquarian Horological Society New Series No. 3 (Ticehurst: Antiquarian Horological Society, 1999).

Needham, Joseph et al., *Heavenly Clockwork: The Great Astronomical Clocks of Medieval China*, Monograph No. 1 (1960; Cambridge: Antiquarian Horological Society and Cambridge UP, 2nd ed. with a supplement by John H. Combridge, 1986).

Nelthropp, Harry L. *A Treatise on Watchwork, Past and Present* (London: Spon, 1863).

Nicholas, S.J. 'The American Export Invasion of Britain: The Case of the Engineering Industry, 1870–1914,' *Technology and Culture*, 21/4 (Oct. 1980), 578–88, at https://doi.org/10.2307/3104081 and https://www.jstor.org/stable/3104081

Nockolds, Mrs G.W. 'Early Timekeepers at Sea,' *Antiquarian Horology*, 4/4 (Sept. 1967), 110–13.
North, Douglass C. 'Sources of Productivity Change in Ocean Shipping, 1600–1850,' *Journal of Political Economy*, 76/5 (Sept/Oct. 1968), 953–70, at https://doi.org/10.1086/259462
Nye, James. *A Long Time in Making: The History of Smiths* (Oxford: Oxford UP, 2014).
Oddy, J. Jepson. European Commerce: *Shewing New and Several Channels of Trade with the Continent of Europe* (London: Richardson, 1805).
Oestmann, Günther. 'Abstract of "En route to the "German Chronometer": The Introduction of Precision Timekeeping in the German Mercantile Marine and Imperial Navy in the Nineteenth Century,' *23rd Congress of History of Science and Technology: Ideas and Instruments in Social Context*, Session T35 (Budapest: Scientific Instruments Conference, 2009), 1–8.
Oestmann, Günther. *Auf dem weg zum 'Deutschen Chronometer'*, (Bremen: Deutsche Maritime Studien 21, 2012).
Oestmann, Günther. '"Towards the "German chronometer". The Introduction of Precision Timekeeping in the German Mercantile Marine and Imperial Navy in the Nineteenth Century,' *Antiquarian Horology*, 35/3 (Sept. 2014), 949–63.
Oestmann, Günther. 'Early Watches: The Argument Over Priority in Italy and Germany,' *Antiquarian Horology*, 39/1 (March 2018), 92–97.
Ogilvie, Sheelagh. 'The Economics of Guilds,' *Journal of Economic Perspectives*, 28/4 (2014) 169–92, at doi:10.1257/jep.28.4.169.
Ogilvie, Sheelagh. *The European Guilds: An Economic Analysis* (Princeton, NJ: Princeton UP, 2019).
Ogle, Vanessa. 'Whose Time Is It? The Pluralization of Time and the Global Condition, 1870s–1940s,' *The American Historical Review*, 118/5 (Dec. 2013), 1376–402, at www.jstor.org/stable/23784581
Ó Gráda, Cormac 'Did Science Cause the Industrial Revolution?,' *Journal of Economic Literature*, 54/1 (2016), 224–39, at www.jstor.org/stable/43932447
Osterhausen, F. von. 'The Brockbanks: Chronometers Makers of London,' *Antiquarian Horology*, Part 1, 26/3 (Sept. 2001), 244–56; Part 2, 26/4 (Dec. 2001), 355–71.
Otto, Heinrich. 'Obituary, T.D. Wright,' *Horological Journal*, 76/4 (Dec. 1933), 417–20.
Owen, Richard. *Tables of Latitudes and Longitudes by Chronometer of Places in the Atlantic and Indian Oceans; Principally on the West and East Coast of Africa; to Which Is Prefixed An Essay of the Management and Use of Chronometers* (30 pp. pamphlet, London: Hydrographic Office, 1827).
Pagani, Catherine. 'Clockmaking in China under the Kangxi and Qianlong Emperors,' *Arts Asiatiques*, 50 (1995), 76–84, at https://www.jstor.org/stable/i4013820
Palliser, D.M. (ed.). *The Cambridge Urban History of Britain*: Vol. 1, *c.600–c1540* (Cambridge: Cambridge UP, 2000).
Palmer, Sarah. 'The British Shipping Industry, 1850–1914,' in Lewis R. Fischer and Gerald E. Ponting (eds.), *Change and Adaptation in Maritime History: The North Atlantic Trade in the Nineteenth Century* (St John's: Maritime History Group, Memorial University of Newfoundland, 1985), 89–115.

Parker, Jon. 'Was there High-Quality, Wholesale Movement Manufacture in Seventeenth-century London?', *Antiquarian Horology*, 40/4 (Dec. 2019), 469–86.

Parkinson and Frodsham. *A Brief Account of the Chronometer with Remarks upon those Furnished by Parkinson to the Expeditions of Captains Ross, Parry, Sabine, King, Lyn, Foster and other Distinguished Navigators* (London: pamphlet, probably 1832)

Parry, J. H. *Trade and Dominion: The European Overseas Empires in the Eighteenth Century* (New York: Praeger, 1971).

Paterson, Thomas G. 'American Businessmen and Consular Service Reform, 1890s to 1906,' *Business History Review*, 15/1 (1966), 77–97, at https://doi.org/10.2307/3112303 and https://www.jstor.org/stable/3112303.

Paton, Leslie. 'The Iron and Steel Available to the Horological Masters of the Past,' *Antiquarian Horology*, 15/1 (Sept. 1984), 47–52.

Payne, P.L. *British Entrepreneurship in the Nineteenth Century* (London: Macmillan Studies in Economic History, 1974).

Penney, David. 'Review of Adolphe Chapiro,' *Jean-Antoine Lépine, horloger (1720–1814)* (Paris, 1988), in *Antiquarian Horology*, 18/4 (Winter 1989), 427–28.

Penney, David. 'Thomas Mudge and the Longitude: A Reason to Excel,' in Andrewes (ed.), *Quest* (1996).

Penney, David. 'English Wristwatches,' *Antique Collecting*, 35 (April 2000).

Penney, David. 'Pierre Frederick Ingold (1787–1878): His Impact on Watchmaking both in Europe and America,' in *Boston: Cradle of Industrial Watchmaking, NAWCC Supplement* No. 5 (Columbia, PA: NAWCC Bulletin, 2005).

Penney, David. 'Evidence from the Transient: The Importance of Ephemera for a Proper Understanding of the Clock and Watch Trades: Part 1,' *Antiquarian Horology*, 29/6 (Dec. 2006), 792–95; Part II,' *Antiquarian Horology*, 30/1 (March 2007), 45–50.

Penney, David (ed.). *High-class English Watches: Manufactured by Nicole, Nielsen and Co. Ltd., Facsimile Reprint of Trade Catalogue, circa 1910* (London: David Penney, 2010).

Penney, David. 'Watchmaking' online at http://www.antiquewatchstore.com/

Penney, David and Valerie Finch. 'William Howells, Watchmaker: Part 1,' *Antiquarian Horology*, 16/6 (June 1987), 585–91.

Pinks, W. *The History of Clerkenwell* (London: Charles Herbert, 2nd. ed., 1881).

Platt, John G. *Lancashire Watch Company: History and Watches* (Chester: Inbeat Publications, 2016).

Pollard, Sidney. *Britain's Prime and Britain's Decline: The British Economy 1870–1914* (London: Edward Arnold, 1989).

Poole, James M. 'The Future of the English Watch Trade,' *Watchmaker, Jeweller and Silversmith*, 7 (June 1887), 171–73.

Portman, Derek. 'Henry Marc Brunel: Civil Engineer,' *Construction History*, 20 (2004), 71–83, at www.jstor.org/stable/41613878

Poskett, James. 'Sounding in Silence: Men, Machines and the Changing Environment of Naval Discipline, 1796–1815,' *The British Journal for the History of Science*, 48/2 (no. 177) (June 2015), 213–32, at https://www.jstor.org/stable/26898183

Post, Robert C. 'Reflections of American Science and Technology at the New York Crystal Palace Exhibition of 1853,' *Journal of American Studies*, 17/3 (Dec. 1983), 337–56, at www.jstor.org/stable/27554357

Pratt, Derek and Peter Baumberger. 'Urban Jurgensen and Sonner, Copenhagen,' *Horological Journal*, 133/6 (1990), 196–201.
Prest, John. *The Industrial Revolution in Coventry* (Oxford: Oxford UP, 1960).
Preston, Richard S. 'The Accuracy of the Astronomical Observations of Lewis and Clark,' *Proceedings of the American Philosophical Society*, 144/2 (June 2000), 168–91, at www.jstor.org/stable/1515630
Price, Derek J. de Solla. 'On the Origin of Clockwork, Perpetual Motion Devices, and the Compass,' (*United States National Museum Bulletin*, No. 218. 1959), 81–112; at https://doi.org/10.2307/3101119 and https://www.jstor.org/stable/3101119
Priestley, Philip T. *Aaron Lufkin Dennison: An Industrial Pioneer and His Legacy* (Columbia PA, NAWCC, 2009).
Proctor, Tony. 'Pocket Chronometer 912 by John Adam Mangar,' *Antiquarian Horology*, 32/2 (June 2010), 220–24.
Prouty, Roger. *The Transformation of the Board of Trade, 1830–1855: A Study of Administrative Reorganisation in the Hey-day of Laissez-Faire* (London: Heinemann, 1957).
Pryce, W.R.T. and T.A. Davies. *Samuel Roberts, Clockmaker: An Eighteenth Century Craftsman in a Welsh Rural Community* (Cardiff: National Museum of Wales, 1985).
Quill, Humphrey. *John Harrison: The Man Who Found Longitude* (London: John Baker, 1966).
Quill, Humphrey. 'John Harrison, His Rivals and Imitators,' *Antiquarian Horology*, 5/10 (March 1978), 362–67.
Randall, Adrian J. 'Reinterpreting "Luddism": Resistance to New Technology in the British Industrial Revolution,' in Martin Bauer (ed.), *Resistance to New Technology: Nuclear Power, Information Technology, and Biotechnology* (Cambridge: Cambridge UP, 1995).
Randall, Adrian J. 'The "Lessons" of Luddism,' *Endeavour*, 22/4 (1998), 152–55.
Randall, Anthony G. 'Thomas Earnshaw's Numbering Sequence,' *Antiquarian Horology*, 17/4 (Summer 1988), 368–71.
Randall, Anthony G. 'Hamilton Marine Chronometer No. 503,' *Antiquarian Horology*, 19/3 (Spring 1991), 261–70.
Randall, Anthony G. 'The Timekeeper that Won the Longitude Prize,' in Andrewes (ed.), *Quest*, 1996).
Randall, Anthony G. and Richard Good. *Catalogue of Watches in the British Museum, VI, Pocket Chronometers, Marine Chronometers, and other Portable Precision Timekeepers* (London: British Museum, 1990).
Randall, Elizabeth. 'A Special Case? London's French Protestants,' in Debra Kelly and Martyn Cornick (eds.), *A History of the French in London: Liberty, Equality, Opportunity* (London: University of London Press (2013), at www.jstor.org/stable/j.ctv512xmz.2
Raper, Henry. 'On the Necessity of Adopting Secondary Meridians,' *The Nautical Magazine and Naval Chronicle* (1839).
Raper, Henry. *The Practice of Navigation and Nautical Astronomy* (1840; London: J.D. Potter, 10th ed. 1880; 20th and last ed. 1920).
Rees, Abraham. *Rees's Clocks, Watches and Chronometers (1819–20): A Selection from The Cyclopaedia; or Universal Dictionary of Arts, Sciences and Literature* (Newton Abbot: David & Charles reprint, 1970).

Reid, Douglas A. 'The Decline of St Monday, 1766–1876,' *Past and Present*, no. 71 (May 1976), 70–101, at https://www.jstor.org/stable/650355.

Reid, Thomas. *A Treatise of Clock and Watch Making, Theoretical and Practical* (Edinburgh: John Fairbairn, 1826; 2nd ed. 1844).

Richards, William C. *A Day in the New York Crystal Palace and How to Make the Most of it* (New York: Putnam, 1853).

Riello, Giorgio. 'Strategies and Boundaries: Subcontracting and the London Trades in the Long Eighteenth Century,' *Enterprise and Society*, 9/2 (June 2008), 243–80. https://doi.org/10.1017/S1467222700006959

Roberts, Andrew. *Napoleon the Great* (London: Allen Lane, 2014).

Robey, John A. *The Longcase Clock Reference Book* (2 vols. Ashbourne: Mayfield, 2001).

Robey, John A. 'Eardley Norton's 1771 Patent for Striking Clocks and Repeating Watches,' *Antiquarian Horology*, 30/1 (March 2007), 88–95.

Robey, John A. 'Moorfields and Clock-Brass Founders: Part 1: The London Horological Trades in Moorfields,' *Antiquarian Horology*, 33/4 (June 2012), 479–86.

Robinson, Howard. *Britain's Post Office: A History of Its Development from the Beginning to the Present Day* (Princeton, NJ: Princeton UP, 1953).

Robinson, Thomas R. 'On the Longitude of the Armagh Observatory, Given by Fifteen Chronometers of Arnold and Dent,' *The Transactions of the Royal Irish Academy*, 19 (1843), 110–20, at https://www.jstor.org/stable/30079128

Roderick, Gordon W. and Michael D. Stephens. *Education and Industry in the Nineteenth Century: the English Disease?* (London: Longman, 1978).

Rodgers, William. 'The Decline of English Watchmaking: Reminiscences of the Latter Half of the Nineteenth Century,' *Watchmaker, Jeweller and Silversmith* (Special Home and Colonial Number), 25 (Aug. 1899), 939–41.

Roe, Joseph Wickham. *Interchangeable Manufactures in American Industry* (Birmingham, AL: Newcomen Society of North America, 1939).

Rogers, Aldred M. and J.S. Turnbull. 'Timekeepers, Clocks, Watches and Chronometers,' *Artisans' Reports on Vienna, 1873* (London: Society for the Promotion of Scientific Knowledge, 1874), 30–36.

Rooney, David. *Ruth Belville: The Greenwich Time Story* (London: National Maritime Museum, 2008).

Rooney, David, and James Nye. 'Greenwich Observatory Time for the Public Benefit': Standard Time and Victorian Networks of Regulation,' *The British Journal for the History of Science*, 42/1 (March 2009), 5–30, at https://www.jstor.org/stable/25592207

Rose, Ronald E. *English Dial Clocks* (Woodbridge: Antique Collector's Club, 1978).

Rosenberg, Nathan (ed.). *The American System of Manufactures* (Edinburgh: Edinburgh UP, 1969), reprints the 'Reports of the [British Parliamentary] Committee on the Machinery of the United States, 1854–55,'

Rosser, Gervase. 'Urban Culture and the Church, 1300–1540,' in D.M. Palliser (ed.), *The Cambridge Urban History of Britain*: Vol. 1, c.600–*c1540* (Cambridge: Cambridge UP, 2000).

Rotherham, Hugh. 'The Rise and Wane of English Watchmaking,' *The Practical Watch and Clock Maker* (15 May 1928), 170–72.

Rotherham, Hugh. 'The Watch Trade Past and Present,' *Horological Journal*, 70/9 (May 1928), 162–64, and 70/10 (June 1928), 180–82.

Rotherham, Kevit. 'Watches and Clocks,' *Horological Journal* (Jan. 1924), 86–88.

[Royal Society of Arts]. *Artisan Reports on the Paris Universal Exhibition of 1878* (London: Low, Marston, Searle, and Rivington, 1879), 437–64.

Rule, John. *The Labouring Classes in Early Industrial England, 1750–1850* (London: Longmans, 1986).

Ryan, A.N. 'The Melancholy Fate of the Baltic Ships in 1811,' *The Mariner's Mirror*, 50/2 (1964), 123–34, doi: 10.1080/00253359.1964.10657766

Ryan, Isadore. 'Republicans Seeking Asylum,' *History Ireland*, 26/2 (2018), 22–25, at www.jstor.org/stable/90019384

Sadler, D.H. *Man Is Not Lost: A Record of 200 Years of Astronomical Navigation With the Nautical Almanac, 1767–1967* (London: National Maritime lMuseum, l968).

Salomons, Sir David Lionel. *Breguet, 1747–1823* (London: Privately printed, 1923: Isha Books, reprint 2013).

Samuel, Raphael. 'Workshop of the World: Steam Power and Hand Technology in Mid-Victorian Britain,' *History Workshop*, 3/1 (Spring 1977), 6–72, at https://www.jstor.org/stable/4288092

Saul, S.B. *The Myth of the Great Depression 1873–96* (London: Macmillan Studies in Economic History, 2nd ed. 1985).

Saunier, Claudius, (trans. Julius Tripplin and Edward Rigg). *Treatise on Modern Horology in Theory and Practice* (London: Foyle, 1881).

Saunier, Claudius. *The Watchmaker's Handbook: Intended as a Workshop Companion for those Who Are Engaged in Watchmaking and the Allied Mechanical Arts* (translated, revised, and augmented by Julius Tripplin and Edward Rigg (1882; London: Hazlitt Walker, 1903).

Sauter, Michael J. 'Clockwatchers and Stargazers: Time Discipline in Early Modern Berlin,' *The American Historical Review*, 112/3 (June 2007), 685–709, at https://www.jstor.org/stable/40006666

Sayers, R.S. *A History of Economic Change -in England 1880–1939* (Oxford: Oxford UP, 1967).

Schwarz, Leonard D. 'London Apprentices in the Seventeenth Century: Some Problems,' *Local Population Studies*, 38 (1987), 18–22, at https://www.jstor.org/stable/40056439

Schwarz, Leonard D. *London in the Age of Industrialisation: Entrepreneurs, Labour Force and Living Conditions, 1750–1850* (Cambridge: Cambridge UP, 1992).

Scoville, Warren. 'The Huguenots and the Diffusion of Technology,' *Journal of Political Economy*, 60/4 (Aug. 1952), 294–311, at https://www.jstor.org/stable/1828923

Searby, Peter. 'Watchmaking in Coventry,' *Warwickshire History*, 3 (1976), 106–04; reprinted in *Antiquarian Horology*, 10/4 (Sept. 1977), 465–68.

Searby, Peter. Also id., 'Chartists and Freemen in Coventry, 1838–1860,' *Social History*, 2/6 (Oct. 1977), 761–84, at www.jstor.org/stable/4284734

Sellers, William. 'American Watches and Clocks' in Chauncey M. Depew (ed.), *One Hundred Years of American Commerce* (1895; New York: Haynes; Kessinger, reprint 2010).

Shears, P.J. 'Huguenot Connections with the Clock-Making Trade in England,' *Proceedings of the Huguenot Society of London*, 20 (1966), 158–76.

Shenton, Rita. 'Clerkenwell: A nostalgic Walk-About,' *Clocks*, 1 (Feb. 1979), 12–16.

Shenton, Rita. 'The Coventry Watch Trade,' *Clocks*, 7 (Nov. 1984), 17–21.

Simons, Eric N. 'Benjamin Huntsman: Clockmaker Pioneer in Casting Steel,' *Metallurgica*, 51 (1955), 181–84.

Simpson, William. 'Swiss Watchmaking Industry,' *The Journal of the Society of Arts*, 39/2028 (Oct. 1891), 850–51, at https://www.jstor.org/stable/41328292.

Singer, Charles, et al. (eds.). *A History of Technology*: Vol. III, *From the Renaissance to the Industrial Revolution, c.1500–1750*, Volume IV, *The Industrial Revolution, c.1750–1850* (Oxford: Clarendon, 1957).

Smart, William. *Economic Annals of the Nineteenth Century* (2 vols., London, MacMillan, 1917).

Smiles, Samuel. *Industrial biography: Iron Workers and Tool Makers* (1863; reprint Newton Abbott: David and Charles, 1967).

Smiles, Samuel. *The Huguenots: Their Settlements, Churches and Industries in England and Ireland* (1867; London: Routledge, reprinted 1997).

Smiles, Samuel. 'John Harrison: Inventor of the Marine Chronometer,' *Longman's Magazine*, 1/2 (December 1882), 156ff.

Smiles, Samuel. 'John Harrison: Inventor of the Marine Chronometer,' Vol. 2, Ch. 3, in Smiles (ed.), *Men of Invention and Industry* (London: Clowes and Sons, 1884).

Smith, Adam, *The Wealth of Nations*, ed., Andrew Skinner, (1776; Harmondsworth, Penguin; 1976).

Smith, Alan. *The Lancashire Watch Company, Prescot, Lancashire, England, 1889–1910* (Fitzwilliam, NH: Roberts, 1973).

Smith, Alan. *Clocks and Watches* (London: Ebury, 1975).

Smith, Alan. 'Introduction and Technical Commentary: The Lancashire Watch and Watch Tool trade,' *A Catalogue of Tools for Watch and Clock Makers by John Wyke of Liverpool* (Charlottesville, VA: Virginia UP, 1978).

Smith, Alan. 'Summary of a Lecture on Wyke,' *Antiquarian Horology*, 10/4 (1978), 736.

Smith, Alan (ed.). *A Catalogue of Tools for Watch and Clock Makers by John Wyke of Liverpool* (Charlottesville, VA: Henry Francis du Pont Winterthur Museum, and Virginia UP, 1978).

Smith, Alan (ed.). *The Country Life International Dictionary of Clocks* (New York: Putnam, 1979).

Smith, Alan. 'An Eighteenth Century Watchmaker's Notebook: the Lancaster-London Connection,' *Antique Collecting* (March 1985). The notebook is also reprinted, with an expanded commentary, in *Antiquarian Horology*, 15 (Dec. 1985), 605–25.

Smith, Herbert Llewellyn (director). *The New Survey of London Life and Labour*, Vol VIII (London: King and Co., 1934).

Smith, Robert W. 'A National Observatory Transformed: Greenwich in the Nineteenth Century,' *Journal for the History of Astronomy*, 22/1 (Feb. 1991), 21–30, at 10.1177/002182869102200104

Smith, Roger. 'The Devil Tavern Group: An Eighteenth Century Horological Trade Association,' *Antiquarian Horology*, 24/5 (Spring 1999), 427–31.

Smith, Roger. 'Benjamin Vulliamy's Library: A Collection of Neo-Classical Design Sources,' *The Burlington Magazine*, 141/1155 (June 1999), 328 – 37, at www.jstor.org/stable/888303

Smith, Roger. 'James Cox (c. 1723–1800); A Revised Biography,' *The Burlington Magazine, CXLII* (No. 1167) (June 2000), 353–61, at https://www.jstor.org/stable/888937.
Smith, Roger. 'The Swiss Connection: International Networks in Some Eighteenth-Century Luxury Trades,' *Journal of Design History*, 17/2 (2004), 123–39. https://www.jstor.org/stable/3527171
Smith, Roger. 'Some mid-Eighteenth Century Craftsmen: Gray and Vulliamy Outworkers and Suppliers, c.1760,' *Antiquarian Horology*, 29/3 (March 2006), 348–58.
Smith, Roger. 'The Sing Song Trade: Exporting Clocks to China in the Eighteenth Century,' *Antiquarian Horology*, 30/5 (March 2008), 629–58.
Smith, Roger. 'Justin Vulliamy (1712–97) and the Protestant Swiss Community: Networks, Institutions and National Identity in Eighteenth-Century London,' *Huguenot Society Journal*, 30/3 (2015), 327–45.
Smith, Roger. 'Penduliers neuchâtelois et connexions londoniennes,' *La neuchâteloise: Histoire et technique de la pendula neuchâteloise, XVIIIe-XXIe siècle* (Musee international de l'horologerie, Le Locle, 2017).
['SN']. 'The Watchmaking Industry in Switzerland,' *Science: The American Association for the Advancement of Science*, 1/11 (April 1883), 296–97, at https://doi.org/10.1126/science.ns-1.11.296
Sobel, Dava. *Longitude: The True Story of a Lone Genius Who Solved the Greatest Scientific Problem of His Time* (London: Fourth Estate, 1995).
Sobel, Dava and William J.H. Andrewes, *The Illustrated Longitude* (London: Fourth Estate, 1998).
[Society of Arts]. 'Premiums Offered in Session 1822–23,' *Transactions of the Society, for the Encouragement of Arts, Manufactures, and Commerce*, 40 (1822), xiv, at www.jstor.org/stable/41325963.
Society of Arts. *Artisan Reports on the Paris Universal Exhibition of 1878* (London: Sampson Low, Marston, Searle and Rivington, 1879).
Sorbom, Per (ed.). *Transport Technology and Social Change, Conference Symposium no.2, 1979* (Stockholm: Tekniska Museet, 1980).
Sorrenson, Richard. 'The State's Demand for Accurate Astronomical and Navigational Instruments in Eighteenth-century Britain,' in Bermingham and Brewer (eds.), *Consumption of Culture* (1985).
Sorrenson, Richard. 'George Graham, Visible Technician,' *The British Journal for the History of Science*, 32/2 (June 1999), 203–21, at https://www.jstor.org/stable/4028084
Spence, Craig. *London in the 1690s: A Social Atlas* (London: Institute of Historical Studies, 2000).
Sproule, J. *The Irish Industrial Exhibition of 1853* (Dublin: McGlashan, 1854).
Steen, Ivan D. 'America's First World's Fair: The Exhibition of the Industry of all Nations at New York's first Crystal Palace, 1853–1854,' *The New York Historical Society Quarterly*, 47 (1963), 256–87.
Stephens, Carlene. "'The Most Reliable Time": William Bond, the New England Railroads, and Time Awareness in 19th-Century America,' *Technology and Culture,* 30 (Jan. 1989), 1–24, at https://www.jstor.org/stable/3105429
Stewart, Alexander D. 'Pennington of London: A Brief History of the Family, the Firm and their Chronometers,' *Antiquarian Horology*, 34/3 (Sept. 2013), 367–84.

Stewart, Alexander D. 'Barwise and Sons: Watchmakers to the King. A Brief History of Family and Firm,' *Antiquarian Horology*, 35/1 (March 2014), 621–34.

Stewart, Alexander D. 'John and Miles Brockbank, their Life and Work,' *Antiquarian Horology*, 36/4 (Dec. 2015), 502–20.

Stewart, Alexander D. 'The British Naval Chronometers of 1821,' *Antiquarian Horology*, 37/2 (June 2016), 247–52.

Stewart, Alexander D. 'A Comparison of Early Timekeepers, from Harrison to Earnshaw,' *Antiquarian Horology*, 38/1 (March 2017), 90–100.

Stigler, George J. 'The Division of Labor Is Limited by the Extent of the Market,' *Journal of Political Economy*, 59/3 (June 1951), 185–93

Strassmann, W. Paul. Risk and Technological Innovation: American Manufacturing Methods *during the Nineteenth Century* (Ithaca, NY: Cornell UP, 1959).

Street, Eric. 'The Hazards of an Early Luminous Watch,' *Antiquarian Horology,* 13/4 (June 1982), 383–84.

Sutton, Paul. 'Soup and Supervision: The Metropolitan Watch and Clock Making Trade 1797–1817,' *Journal of Historical Sociology*, 9/3 (Sept. 1996), 315–34.

[Sydney International Exhibition, 1879], *Official Record: Horology, Class 310* (Sydney: Government Printing Office, 1881).

Symonds, R.W. Thomas Tompion: *His Life and Work* (London: Batsford, 1951).

Symonds, R.W. 'Medieval Clocks and the English Lantern Clock,' *Antiquarian Horology* (Supplement no. 1, March 1953).

Syrett, David. 'The Role of the Royal Navy in the Napoleonic Wars After Trafalgar, 1805–14,' *Naval War College Review*, 32/5 (Sept.–Oct. 1979), 71–84, at https://www.jstor.org/stable/44641939

Taylor, Eva G.R. *Navigation in the Days of Captain Cook* (London: National Maritime Museum, 1974).

Taylor, J.C. and A.W. Wolfendale. 'John Harrison: Clockmaker and Copley Medallist: A Public Memorial At Last,' *Royal Society Journal of the History of Science: Notes and Records*, 61/1 (January 2007), at https://doi.org/10.1098/rsnr.2006.0164

Temin, Peter. 'Labor Scarcity and the Problem of American Industrial Efficiency in the 1850's,' *Journal of Economic History*, 26/3 (Sep. 1966), 277–98, at https://www.jstor.org/stable/2115648

Temin, Peter. 'Two Views of the British Industrial Revolution,' *The Journal of Economic History*, 57/1 (March 1997), 63–82, at www.jstor.org/stable/2951107

Terry, Henry. *American Clock Making: Its Early History and Present Extent of the Business* (Waterbury, CT: Giles and Son, 1870).

Thirsk, Joan. *Economic Policy and Projects: The Development of a Consumer Society in Early Modern England.* Ford Lectures (Oxford: Oxford UP, 1978).

Thomas, Darlah. 'A Snapshot of the Watchmaking Industry in England through the Lens of the 1881 Census,' *Antiquarian Horology*, 40/1 (March 2019), 36–58.

Thompson, Andrew S. 'Tariff Reform: An Imperial Strategy, 1903–1913,' *The Historical Journal*, 40/4 (1997), 1033–54, at https://doi.oeh./10.1017/S0018246X97007565

Thompson, David. 'The Watches of Ellicotts of London: Part 1,' *Antiquarian Horology*, 23/4 (Summer 1997), 306–21; Part II, 23/5 (Autumn 1997), 429–42.
Thompson, David. *Clocks* (London: British Museum, 2004).
Thompson, David. *Watches in the Ashmolean Museum* (Oxford: Ashmolean Museum Handbook, 2007)
Thompson, David. *Watches* (London: British Museum, 2008)
Thompson, Edward P. 'Time, Work-Discipline, and Industrial Capitalism,' *Past and Present*, 38 (1967), 56–97, at http://www.jstor.org/page/info/about/policies/terms.jsp
Thorndike, Lynn. 'Invention of the Mechanical Clock about 1271 AD,' *Speculum*, 16/2 (April 1941), 242–43, at https://doi.org/10.2307/2853618
Timmins, Geoffrey. *Made in Lancashire: A History of Regional Industrialization* (Manchester: Manchester UP, 1998).
Tobin, Gary Allan. 'The Bicycle Boom of the 1890s: The Development of Private Transportation and the Birth of the Modern Tourist,' *Journal of Popular Culture*, 7/4 (May 2004), 838–49. https://doi.org/10.1111/j.0022-3840.1974.0704_838.x
Tomalin, Marcus. 'The Intriguing Complications of Pocket Watches in the Literature of the Long Eighteenth Century,' *The Review of English Studies*, New Series, Vol. 66, No. 274 (April 2015), 300–21, at https://www.jstor.org/stable/24541234
Toot, Peter. 'Should Breguet's Box Chronometer No 2741 Be Run? The Potential Decision-making Protocols in Horological Conservation,' *Antiquarian Horology*, 41/3 (Sept. 2020), 373–82.
Torrens, David S. 'Rule of Thumb,' *Horological Journal*, 80/11 (July 1938), 29–30.
Torrens, David S. 'Nail and Cork,' *Horological Journal*, 80 (Feb. 1938), 22, 24; reprinted in Allix, *Carriage Clocks* (1974), 409–12.
Torrens, David S. 'Notes on Elinvar,' *Horological Journal*, 81/5 (Jan. 1939), 26–28.
Torrens, David S. 'Obituary: Edwin Turner Cottingham, 1869–1940,' *Horological Journal*, 82/9 (May 1940), 170–71.
Torrens, David S. 'The Chronometer Clock,' *Horological Journal*, 85/9 (May 1943), 112 [Also 'Correction,' *Horological Journal*, 85/11 (July 1943), 162.
Torrens, David S. 'Early Jewel Bearings,' *Horological Journal*, 87/5 (Jan. 1945), 21.
Torrens, David S. 'Five Hundred Years,' *Horological Journal*, 87/7 (March 1945), 82–85.
Torrens, David S. 'Paul Ditisheim: A Tribute to a Great Horologist,' *Horological Journal*, 87/4 (Dec. 1945), 410ff.
Torrens, David S. 'Carriage Clocks and Chronometers,' *Horological Journal*, 88/11 (Aug. 1946), 320–22.
Torrens, David S. 'Of Many Things,' *Horological Journal*, 89/4 (Dec. 1946), 557–59.
Torrens, David S. 'Obituary: Sanfrid Lundquist: The Death of the Last Surviving Partner Closes the Famous Firm of Victor Kullberg,' *Horological Journal*, 89 (1947), 246–47.
Torrens, David S. 'Some Notes on the History of Machine Watchmaking,' *Horological Journal*, 89/8 (April 1947), 177–78, 183–84.

Torrens, David S. 'Obituary, Harry Pybus: Last of the Prescot Watchmakers,' *Horological Journal* (Aug.1952), 515–16.

Torrens, David S. 'Joseph William Player, 1865–1956: An Appreciation,' *Horological Journal*, 98/2 (Oct. 1956), 628, 632.

Torrens, David S. 'Heinrich Otto: An Appreciation,' *Horological Journal*, 108/8 (July 1966), 13.

Treherne, Alan. *The Massey Family: Clock, Watch, Chronometer and Nautical Instrument Makers* (Newcastle under Lyme: Newcastle Borough Museum, 1977).

Treherne, Alan. 'Unfinished or Raw Movements "In the Grey,"' *Your Time* (Ticehurst: Antiquarian Horological Society, Northern Section, 2008).

Treherne, Alan. 'The Contribution of South-west Lancashire to Horology: Part 1: Watch and Chronometer Movement Making and Finishing,' *Antiquarian Horology*, 31/4 (June 2009), 457–76.

Treherne, Alan. Report of a lecture on 'Litherland Lever Watches,' *Antiquarian Horology*, 33/3 (March 2012).

Tripplin, Julien J.S. 'Recent Progress in British Watch and Clockmaking,' *Horological Journal*, 32/8 (April 1890), 120–24.

Tripplin, Julien J.S. *Watch and Clock Making in 1889: The French Industrial Exhibition: Being an Account and Comparison of the Exhibits in the Horological Section of the French International Exhibition ... With a View of the British Watch and Clock Making Sections* (London: Crosby Lockwood, 1890).

Tupling, G.H. 'The Early Metal Trades and the Beginnings of Engineering in Lancashire,' *Transactions of the Historical Society of Lancashire and Cheshire*, 61 (1949), 11–25.

Turner, Anthony J. 'Anglo-Saxon Sundials and the 'Tidal' or 'Octaval' System of Time-measurement,' *Antiquarian Horology*, 15 (1) (Sept. 1984).

Turner, Anthony J. *Early Scientific Instruments: Europe, 1400–1800* (London: Sotheby, 1987).

Turner, Anthony J. 'Berthoud in England, Harrison in France: The Transmission of Horological Knowledge in Eighteenth Century Europe,' *Antiquarian Horology*, 20/3 (Autumn 1992), 219–39.

Turner, Anthony J. 'In the Wake of the Act, but Mainly Before,' in Andrewes (ed.), *Quest* (1996).

Turner, Anthony J., Herve Chayette, and Jean-Claude Sabrier, *Mr. Breguet chez Cheyette* (London and Paris, Rogers Turner Books, 2010).

Turner, Anthony J. 'The Tribulations of Jean Helot,' *Antiquarian Horology*, 32/6 (June 2011).

Turner, Anthony J. 'From Sun and Water to Weights: Public Time Devices from Late Antiquity to the Mid-Seventeenth Century,' *Antiquarian Horology*, 35/1 (March 2014), 649–62.

Turner, Anthony J. (ed.). *John Carte on Horology and Cosmology: A Transcription, with Introduction and Notes, of Bodleian Library Ms Carte 264ff. 18r–57r*, Turner and Devereux Occasional Paper No.5 (Ticehurst and Le Mesnil-le-Roi: Antiquarian Horological Society and Rogers Turner Books, 2014).

Turner, Gerard L'E. 'The Auction Sale of Larcum Kendall's Workshop, 1790,' *Antiquarian Horology,* 5 (1967), 269–75.

Turner, Gerard L'E. 'The London Trade in Scientific Instrument-Making in the 18th Century,' *Vistas in Astronomy*, 20 (1976). 173–82, at https://doi.org/10.1016/0083-6656(76)90029-5

Turner, Gerard L'Estrange. 'The Portuguese Agent: J.H. de Magellan,' *Antiquarian Horology*, 9/1 (Dec. 1974), 74–77,

Tyler, E. J. 'Horology in Soho,' *Clocks*, 8 (April 1986), 13.

Uchida, Hoshimi. 'The Spread of Timepieces in the Meiji Period,' *Japan Review*, 14 (2002), 173–92, at www.jstor.org/stable/25791261

Unwin, George. *The Guilds and Companies of London* (London: Methuen, 1908).

Urešová, Libuše, *European Clocks: An Illustrated History of Clocks and Watches* (London: Perrage Books, 1986).

Van Dulken, Steven. *British Patents of Invention, 1617–1977: A Guide for Researchers* (London: British Library, 1999).

Vaughan, Denys (ed.). *The Royal Society and the Fourth Dimension: The History of Timekeeping*, Monograph No. 27 (Ticehurst: Antiquarian Horological Society, 1993).

[Victoria and Albert Museum], *The International Exhibition of 1862* (London: Victoria and Albert Museum, 1962).

Voth, Hans-Joachim. 'Time and Work in Eighteenth-Century London,' *The Journal of Economic History*, 58/1 (March 1998), 29–58, at www.jstor.org/stable/2566252

Voth, Hans-Joachim. *Time and Work in England, 1750–1830* (Oxford: Clarendon, 2000).

Vries, Jan de. 'Luxury in the Dutch Golden Age in Theory and Practice,' in H.J.M. Bos et al. (eds.), *Studies on Christiaan Huygens* (London: Routledge, 1980).

Vulliamy, David G. *The Vulliamy Clockmakers* (London: Antiquarian Horological Society, 2002).

Waddington, Trevor. 'Archibald Miller: Clockmaker and the Hammermen of Glasgow,' *Horological Journal*, 24/3 (Autumn 1998), 229–33.

Wadsworth, Francis. 'A History of Repeating Watches,' *Antiquarian Horology*, 4/12 (1965), 364–67, and 5/2 (March1966), 48–52.

Wadsworth, Francis. 'Some early 19th Century Workmen,' *Antiquarian Horology*, 19/4 (Summer 1991), 401–12.

Waldo, Leonard. 'The Mechanical Art of American Watchmaking,' 34/1 (21 May 1886), 740–75, at http://www.jstor.org/stable/23852799; reprinted in *The Jewelers Circular and Horological Review* (New York), XVII (July 1886), 186–90; also an abstract in *Horological Journal*, 28/8 (April 1886), 117–22.

Walker, E. 'On Purifying Olive Oil for the Pivots of Chronometers,' *The Philosophical Journal*, 36 (1810), 372–74.

Wallace, Irving. *The Fabulous Showman: A Biography of P.T. Barnum* (New York: Knopf, 1959).

Walmsley, R. Mullineux. 'Horological Education in Clerkenwell,' *Horological Journal*, 47/1 (Sept. 1904), 2–4.

Ward, R.A.H. 'A watchmaker's Pocket Book,' *Transactions of the Lancashire and Cheshire Historic Society*, 122 (1971), 153–57, at https://www.hslc.org.uk/wp-content/uploads/2017/05/122-9-Ward.pdf

Ward, W.R. 'The Administration of the Window and Assessed Taxes, 1696–1798,' *English Historical Review*, 67 (Oct 1952), 522–42, at https://www.jstor.org/stable/556134

Warner, Deborah Jean. 'Astronomers, Artisans, and Longitude,' in Sorbom (ed.), *Transport Technology and Social Change* (Stockholm: Tekniska Museet, 1980), 131–40.

[Watch and Clock Makers' Benevolent Institution]. *Watch and Clock Makers' Benevolent Institution, for the Relief of Aged Necessitous Workmen of Good Character Belonging to the Several Branches in the Manufacture of Clocks and Watches, and of the Widows of Such Workmen: Instituted March 6th, 1815* (Clerkenwell: Berry, 1825), at jstor.org/stable/10.2307/60212945

Waters, D.W. 'Time, Ships and Civilization,' *Antiquarian Horology,* 4/3 (June 1963), 81–84.

Waters, D.W. 'The Instrumental and Astronomical Solutions to the Problem of Longitude at Sea in the Eighteenth Century,' in Sorbom (ed.), *Transport Technology and Social Change* (1980).

Watkins, Richard. 'Jacques David – and a Summary of 'American and Swiss Watchmaking in 1876,'' *NAWCC Bulletin*, No. 250 (June 2004), 294–302, at http://www.watkinsr.id.au/Art1876.pdf

Watson, Hugh F. *Keeping Time: A History of Clocks, Watches and Barometers in a Provincial Town from 1700 until 1900* (Grantham: Privately published, 2008).

Wayman, M.L. (ed.). *The Ferrous Metallurgy of Early Clocks and Watches: Studies in Post Medieval Steel* (London: British Museum Occasional Paper, no. 136, 2000),

Weaving, Allen H. 'Clocks for the Emperor,' *Antiquarian Horology*, 19/4 (Summer 1991), 367–89.

Weiss, Leonard. *Watchmaking in England, 1760–1820* (London: Robert Hale, 1982).

Wells, Roger A.E. *Wretched Faces: Famine in wartime England, 1793–1801* (Gloucester: Sutton, 1988).

[Wembley Exhibition*]. English clocks and Watches and their Makers* (London: Alexander Stuart and *Horological Journal*, 1924).

Werking, Richard Hume. 'Selling the Foreign Service: Bureaucratic Rivalry and Foreign Trade Promotion, 1903–12,' *Pacific Historical Review*, 45 (1976), 185–207. https://doi.org/10.2307/3638494

Wetherill, Lorna. *Consumer Behaviour and Material Culture in Britain, 1660–1760* (1988: London, Routledge, 2nd ed., 1996),

Whidbey, Joseph. 'Remarks on Timekeepers, the Compass,' *The Naval Chronicle*, 2 (1799), 505–12.

White Jr. Lynn. *Medieval Technology and Social Change* (Oxford: Clarendon, 1962).

White Jr. Lynn. 'The Act of Invention: Causes, Contexts, Continuities and Consequences,' [Proceedings of the *Encyclopaedia Britannica* Conference on the Technological Order], *Technology and Culture*, 3/4 (Autumn, 1962), 486–500, at https://www.jstor.org/stable/i355984

White, Allen. *The Fusee Chain Makers: A History of the Watch Fusee Chain Industry* (Christchurch: Privately published, 1967; 2nd Edition, Christchurch Historical Society and Red House Museum, 2010).

White, Ian. *English Clocks for the Eastern Markets: English Clockmakers Trading in China and the Ottoman Empire, 1580–1815* (London: Antiquarian Horological Society, 2012).

White, Sir George. *Clockmakers of London* (London: Worshipful Company of Clockmakers, 1998).
White, Sir George. '"Not a Bad Timekeeper": The English Lantern Clock in the Seventeenth Century,' *Antiquarian Horology*, 31/5 (Sept 2009), 621–36.
White, Sir George. 'Don't Mention the War! The Checkered Early Years of the Worshipful Company of Clockmakers,' *Horological Journal*, 38/2 (June 2017), 175–90.
White, T.E. 'A Clerkenwell Tour of Fifty Years Ago,' *Antiquarian Horology*, 10/3 (Summer 1977), 340–46.
White, T.E. 'The Testing and Certification of Watches at the Kew Observatory and National Physical Laboratory, 1884–1978,' *Horological Journal*, 127/12 (Aug. 1984), 15–17.
Whitney, Marvin E. *The Ship's Chronometer* (Cincinnati, OH: Watchmakers Institute Press, 1985),
Whitrow, G.J. Time in History: *The Evolution of Our General Awareness of Time and Temporal Perspective* (Oxford: Oxford UP, 1988).
Whyte, Donald. 'Petition of Edinburgh Watchmakers to Parliament, 1797–98,' *Antiquarian Horology*, 18/4 (Winter 1989), 417–22.
Williams, Archibald. *How it Is Made: Describing in Simple Language How Various Machines and Many Articles in Common Use are Manufactured from Raw Materials* (London: Nelson, 1907).
Williams, Chris H.K. 'Seventeenth and Eighteenth Century Clock Demand, Production and Survival: An Economic and Statistical Analysis,' *Antiquarian Horology*, 28/5 (March 2005).
Williams, Chris H.K. 'Sir Edward Dering's "Booke of Expences,' 1617–28: His Horological Purchases, William Barrett of Ashford and Jacques of London,' *Antiquarian Horology*, 31/2 (Dec. 2008), 194–200.
Williams, David. John Frost: A *Study in Chartism* (Cardiff: Wales UP, 1939).
Williams, David. *The Rebecca Riots, A Study in Agrarian Discontent* (Cardiff: Wales UP, 1955).
Williams, David J. 'The Birmingham Gun Trade and the American System of Manufactures,' *Transactions of the Newcomen Society*, 75 (2005), 85–106. https://doi.org/10.1179/tns.2005.004
Williams, David J. *The Birmingham Gun Trade* (Stroud: History Press, 2009).
Williams, J.E.D. *From Sails to Satellites: The Origin and Development of Navigational Science* (Oxford: Oxford UP, 1992).
Williams, Judith Blow. *British Commercial Policy and Trade Expansion, 1750–1850* (Oxford: Clarendon, 1972).
Winfield, Rif. *British Warships in the Age of Sail, 1793–1817; Design, Construction, Careers, and Fates* (London: Chatham, 2005).
Wood, Christopher. 'Extracts from a Parkinson and Frodsham Pamphlet,' *Antiquarian Horology*, 9 (Dec.1974), 46–50,
Wood, Christopher. 'Robert Molyneux's Astronomic Clocks and Chronometers,' *Antiquarian Horology*, 9/4 (Sept. 1975), 413–25.
Wood, Richard. 'The Hall-Marking Agitation, with a Glance at Former Periods of Depression in the Watch Trades,' *Horological Journal*, 29/7 (March 1887), 98–101.
Woodcroft, Bennett (ed.). *Alphabetical Index of Patentees of Inventions* (1854; London: Evelyn, Adams and Mackay, 1969 edn.)

Woodward, E. L. *The Age of Reform, 1815–70* (1939; Oxford: Clarendon, 1962).

Wotruba, Thomas R. 'The Horological World of Francois Arsene Margaine,' *Antiquarian Horology*, 35/2 (June 2014), 807–21.

Wright, Lawrence. *Clockwork Man: The Story of Time* (London: Elek, 1968).

Wright, Michael T. 'Robert Hook: The Curator's Experiments in Horology' in Denys Vaughan (ed.), *The Royal Society and the Fourth Dimension: the History of Timekeeping* (Ticehurst: Antiquarian Horological Society Monograph No. 27, 1993).

Wright, T.D. 'Lessons from the Paris Exhibition 1889' *Horological Journal*, 32/6 (Feb 1890), 89–91.

Wright, T.D. 'Watch and Clock Making: A Paper Read to the International Congress on Technical Education,' *Horological Journal*, 39/10 (July 1897), 145–49; and to the Society of Arts, at *The Journal of the Society of Arts*, 45, No. 2331 (July 1897), 843–47, at https://www.jstor.org/stable/41334302.

Wrigley, E.A. 'A Simple Model of London's Importance in Changing English Society and Economy, 1650–1750,' in Philip Abrams and E.A. Wrigley (eds.), *Towns in Societies: Essays in Economic History and Historical Sociology* (Cambridge: Cambridge UP, 1978).

Wylie, Neville. 'British Smuggling Operations from Switzerland, 1940–1944,' *The Historical Journal*, 48/4 (Dec. 2005), 1077–102 at www.jstor.org/stable/4091649

Young, Allyn. 'Increasing Returns and Economic Progress,' *The Economic Journal*, 38 (Dec. 1928), 527–42, at https://www.jstor.org/stable/2224097

Young, Edward. *Labor in Europe and America: A Special Report on the Condition of the Working Classes in Great Britain...* Also in *The United States and British America* (Washington, DC: Government Printing Office, 1875). http://name.umdl.umich.edu/AGC2750.0001.001

Yui, Tsunehiko and Keiichiro Nakagawa (eds.). *Business History of Shipping: Strategy and Structure* (Tokyo: Tokyo University Press, 1985).

Zerubavel, Eviatar. 'The Standardization of Time: A Sociohistorical Perspective,' *American Journal of Sociology*, 88/1 (July 1982), 1–23, at www.jstor.org/stable/2779401

Index

Note: **Bold** page numbers refer to tables; *italic* page numbers refer to figures and page numbers followed by "n" denote endnotes.

For Product Safety Concerns and Information please contact our EU
representative GPSR@taylorandfrancis.com
Taylor & Francis Verlag GmbH, Kaufingerstraße 24, 80331 München, Germany

www.ingramcontent.com/pod-product-compliance
Ingram Content Group UK Ltd.
Pitfield, Milton Keynes, MK11 3LW, UK
UKHW022347190926
475702UK00015B/2142
9781032131351